MW00911154

MCITP Guide to Microsoft Windows Server 2008, Enterprise Administration (Exam #70-647)

Darril Gibson

COURSE TECHNOLOGY
CENGAGE Learning™

Australia • Brazil • Japan • Korea • Mexico • Singapore • Spain • United Kingdom • United States

MCITP Guide to Microsoft Windows Server 2008, Enterprise Administration (Exam #70-647)
Darril Gibson

Vice President, Career and Professional Editorial: Dave Garza

Director of Learning Solutions: Matthew Kane

Acquisitions Editor: Nick Lombardi

Managing Editor: Marah Bellegarde

Product Manager: Natalie Pashoukos

Developmental Editor: Dan Seiter

Editorial Assistant: Sarah Pickering

Vice President, Career and Professional Marketing: Jennifer Ann Baker

Marketing Director: Deborah S. Yarnell

Senior Marketing Manager: Erin Coffin

Marketing Coordinator: Shanna Gibbs

Production Director:Carolyn Miller

Production Manager: Andrew Crouth

Senior Content Project Manager: Andrea Majot

Senior Art Director: Jack Pendleton

Manufacturing Buyer: Amy Rogers

Technical Editor: John Bosco

Compositor: PrePress PMG

Library of Congress Control Number: 2010923219

ISBN-13: 978-1-4239-0239-3

ISBN-10: 1-4239-0239-4

Course Technology
20 Channel Center
Boston, MA 02210
USA

Cengage Learning products are represented in Canada by Nelson Education, Ltd.

For your lifelong learning solutions, visit **course.cengage.com**

Visit our corporate website at **cengage.com**

Printed in the United States of America
1 2 3 4 5 XX 12 11 10

Brief Table of Contents

INTRODUCTION xi

CHAPTER 1
Designing Active Directory Domain Services **1**

CHAPTER 2
Designing Physical Topology **45**

CHAPTER 3
Designing and Implementing DNS **97**

CHAPTER 4
Designing and Implementing Group Policy **141**

CHAPTER 5
Designing Remote Access and Terminal Services Strategies **193**

CHAPTER 6
Designing and Implementing a PKI **243**

CHAPTER 7
Securing Windows Server 2008 Servers **291**

CHAPTER 8
Designing High Availability and Business Continuity **339**

CHAPTER 9
Designing Supporting Services **379**

CHAPTER 10
Designing Virtualization Strategies **415**

APPENDIX A
MCITP 70-647 Exam Objectives **441**

APPENDIX B
A Step-by-Step Guide to Using Server Virtualization Software **443**

GLOSSARY 477

INDEX 487

Table of Contents

INTRODUCTION xi

CHAPTER 1
Designing Active Directory Domain Services 1

Basic Review of Active Directory Domain Services 2
Active Directory Tree 2
Active Directory Forest 3
Schema 3
Trusts 3
Global Catalog 3
Organizational Units 4
Group Policy 4
Site 4

Creating a Learning Environment 4

Understanding Domain and Forest Functional Levels 9
Domain Functional Level 9
Forest Functional Level Capabilities 11

Designing Active Directory Domains and Forests 13
Autonomy vs. Isolation 13
Autonomy 14
Isolation 14
Creating a Separate Forest for a Separate Schema 14
Identifying Bandwidth Requirements for a Forest 14
Identifying Domain Requirements 15

Understanding Trusts 16
One-way and Two-way Trusts 16
Transitive and Non-Transitive Trusts 16
Creating Trusts Between Forests 17
Choosing the Authentication Method 18
Granting Access to Users in Another Forest 22
Implementing Selective Authentication 23

Using ADPrep 24
Preparing the Forest 25
Preparing a Domain 25
Preparing for RODCs 26

Migration Strategies 26
Active Directory Migration Tool (ADMT) 26
ADMT Versions Needed for Different Functional Levels 26
Interforest and Intraforest Migration 27
Understanding and Using SID History 27
Using SID Filtering 28
Using Alternative UPN Suffixes 30
Installing the ADMT 32
Enabling SID History for ADMT 33
Running ADMT 33

Chapter Summary 36

Key Terms 37

Review Questions 38

Case Projects 44

CHAPTER 2
Designing Physical Topology 45

Implementing Sites 46
Site and Site Link Benefits 46
Logon Optimization 47
Replication Optimization 47
Using Sites for Site-aware Applications 49
Creating Sites and Subnets 51

Creating Site Links 52
Understanding Bridgehead Servers 54
Full Mesh Replication Topology 56
Optimizing Replication with Hub and Spoke Sites 57

Designing the Branch Office 59
Deciding to Place a DC in a Remote Office 60
Deciding on a Writable DC or an RODC 61
Including DNS with the DC 61
Adding the Global Catalog or Enabling Universal Group Membership Caching 62

Understanding Operations Master Roles 64
The Infrastructure Master and the Global Catalog 66
Operations Masters and the ADPrep Tool 67
Transferring Operations Master Roles 67
Seizing Operations Master Roles 68

Using RODCs 73
Requirements for Adding RODCs 74
Installing RODCs from Media 74
Server Core and RODCs 76
Prestaging an RODC 80
RODC Passwords 81
RODC Filtered Attribute Set 83
Local Administrators Role on an RODC 85

Chapter Summary 87

Key Terms 88

Review Questions 90

Case Projects 95

CHAPTER 3
Designing and Implementing DNS **97**

Improvements in Windows Server 2008 DNS 98

Name Resolution in a Domain 99
Computer Names 99
Name Resolution Methods 99

DNS Zones, Zone Files, and Zone Resource Records 100
DNS Zones 101
DNS Files 102
DNS Resource Records 102
Understanding Dynamic Update and Secure Dynamic Update 105
DNS and Active Directory 107
Using Non-Site-Specific SRV Records 110

Designing DNS Zones 114
Primary Zones 114
Configuring Zone Transfers 116
Secondary Zones 119
ADI Primary Zones 123
GlobalNames Zones 124
Stub Zones 127
Delegated Subdomain 130

Designing Zone Replication Scope 131

Chapter Summary 132

Key Terms 133

Review Questions 134

Case Projects 139

CHAPTER 4
Designing and Implementing Group Policy **141**

Designing Organizational Units 142
Using OUs for Group Policy 142
Using OUs to Delegate Control 143

Designing Organizational Units 147
Designing Group Strategies 148
Redirecting Placement of New Accounts 150

Reviewing Group Policy Basics 151
Group Policy Scope 151
GPO Inheritance and Order of Precedence 153
Group Policy Setting Categories 154
Default Group Policies 155
Group Policy Management Console 156
Starter GPOs 156

Group Policy Settings 158
Device Installation Restrictions 159
Restrict Group Membership 161
Deploying Applications 164
Internet Explorer Proxy Settings 166
Printer Location Policies 169
IPSec 170

Manipulating GPO Deployments with Advanced Options 171
Blocking Inheritance 171
Enforcing GPOs 172
Filtering GPOs 173
WMI Filtering 176
Loopback Processing 177

Fine-Grained Account Policies 177
Requirements for Fine-Grained Policies 179
Creating Fine-Grained Policies 179

Chapter Summary 182

Key Terms 183

Review Questions 184

Case Projects 190

CHAPTER 5
Designing Remote Access and Terminal Services Strategies 193

Designing Remote Access 194
Tunneling Protocols 195
Choosing a Tunneling Protocol 195
Adding the Remote Access Service on Windows Server 2008 196
Network Access Policies 198
Using a RADIUS Server 202
Using a RADIUS Proxy 203

Network Access Protection 204
Components of NAP 205
Adding the NPS Service 207
System Health Agents, Validators, and NAP Agents 207
Creating a Health Policy 211
Creating a Remediation Server Group 212
Configuring Network Policy Settings 213
Other NAP Enforcement Methods 217
DHCP Enforcement 217
802.1x Enforcement 217
IPSec Enforcement 218

Planning for Terminal Services 218
Adding the Terminal Services Role 219
Configuring the Terminal Services Server 223
Terminal Services Licensing 226
TS RemoteApp 228
TS Web Access 230
TS Gateway 230
Terminal Services Authorization Policies for TS Gateway 230
TS Session Broker 232

Chapter Summary 234

Key Terms 235
Review Questions 237
Case Projects 241

CHAPTER 6
Designing and Implementing a PKI **243**
An Overview of PKI and Certificates 244
Trusted Certification Authorities 245
Public Key and Private Key 246
Encrypting Data 246
Digital Signatures 247
Certificates and EFS 249
Certificates and Smart Cards 249
Certificates and WinRM 250
Certificate Life Cycle Management 250
Certificate Enrollment 250
Certificate Revocation Lists 251
Validating the Certificate 252
Types of Certification Authorities 253
Root vs. Subordinate CA (CA Hierarchy) 253
Public CA vs. Private CA 253
Enterprise CA vs. Stand-Alone CA 255
Active Directory Certificate Services (AD CS) 256
Implementing AD CS 257
Certificate Templates 258
Installing Certificate Services 259
Certificate Services Administrative Separation 262
Online Responder Service 264
Issuing and Revoking Certificates 269
Deploying Trusted Root Certificates via Group Policy 275
Automatic Certificate Enrollment 277
Network Device Enrollment Service 279
Restricted Enrollment Agents 281
Chapter Summary 284
Key Terms 285
Review Questions 286
Case Projects 290

CHAPTER 7
Securing Windows Server 2008 Servers **291**
Hardening a System 292
Reducing the Attack Surface 293
Secure Computing Strategy 293
Server Core 293
Server Manager 294
Security Configuration Wizard 294
Creating GPOs from Security Policies 300
Compliance Auditing 302
Using MBSA 302
Using Scwcmd for Compliance Policies 308
Enabling Auditing 309
Keeping Systems Up to Date 313
Windows Update, Microsoft Update, and Automatic Updates 314
Windows Server Update Services 315
WSUS Capabilities 317
Reviewing WSUS Server Terminology 318
Using WSUS with Branch Offices 319
Using WSUS with Disconnected Networks 321

WSUS Requirements 322
Installing WSUS 323
Configuring Clients to Use WSUS with Group Policy 326
Perimeter Networks 328
Firewall Rules 329
Microsoft Firewall Products 330
Chapter Summary 330
Key Terms 331
Review Questions 332
Case Projects 336

CHAPTER 8
Designing High Availability and Business Continuity 339
Load Balancing and Fault Tolerance 340
Scalability 340
High Availability 341
Network Load Balancing vs. Failover Clusters 342
Network Load Balancing 343
Network Load Balancing Manager 343
Adding Network Load Balancing 344
Creating an NLB Cluster 345
Adding Hosts to an NLB Cluster 349
Web Servers in an NLB Cluster 349
Removing the NLB Cluster Service 350
Failover Clusters 351
Failover Cluster Requirements 352
Quorums 352
Cluster Storage and Storage Solutions 355
Logical Unit Numbers in Storage Arrays 355
Cluster Connectivity to Storage Solutions 356
Cluster-Aware Services and Applications 358
Failover Clusters for Multiple Sites 359
Adding the Failover Cluster Feature 359
Running the Validate a Configuration Wizard 360
Creating a Failover Cluster 362
Pausing, Stopping, and Removing Nodes in a Cluster 364
Removing a Failover Cluster 365
Active Directory Backup and Restores 366
Adding the Windows Server Backup Feature 366
Backing Up Active Directory 367
Restoring Active Directory 369
Performing an Authoritative Restore 371
Chapter Summary 371
Key Terms 373
Review Questions 374
Case Projects 377

CHAPTER 9
Designing Supporting Services 379
Understanding the System Center Suite 380
System Center Operations Manager 2007 381
System Center Configuration Manager 2007 381
Designing for Data Security 383
Using BitLocker Drive Encryption for Data Security 383
BitLocker Drive Encryption Requirements 384
BitLocker Drive Encryption Recovery 386
Designing for Data Accessibility and Redundancy with DFS 388
DFS Namespace 388

DFS Replication 394
SYSVOL Replication 395
Designing for Data Collaboration 396
Microsoft Windows SharePoint Services (WSS) 396
Microsoft Office SharePoint Server (MOSS) 402
Services for Network File System 403
Designing for Additional Active Directory Services 405
Active Directory Rights Management Services (AD RMS) 406
Active Directory Federation Services (AD FS) 406
Active Directory Lightweight Directory Services (AD LDS) 407
Chapter Summary 407
Key Terms 408
Review Questions 410
Case Projects 413

CHAPTER 10
Designing Virtualization Strategies **415**
Application Virtualization 416
Microsoft Application Virtualization 417
Microsoft Application Virtualization 4.5 Environment 417
SoftGrid Sequencer 419
Interacting with Terminal Services 419
Using Virtual PCs for Applications 420
Microsoft Virtual PC 420
Windows Virtual PC 421
Installing and Using Windows XP Mode 423
Server Virtualization 426
Server Consolidation 427
Hyper-V Prerequisites 428
Hyper-V and Server Licenses 428
Hyper-V Virtual Networks 429
Hyper-V Manager 430
Virtualization Management 434
System Center Virtual Machine Manager 434
Chapter Summary 435
Key Terms 436
Review Questions 437
Case Projects 440

APPENDIX A
MCITP 70-647 Exam Objectives **441**

APPENDIX B
A Step-by-Step Guide to Using Server Virtualization Software **443**

GLOSSARY **477**

INDEX **487**

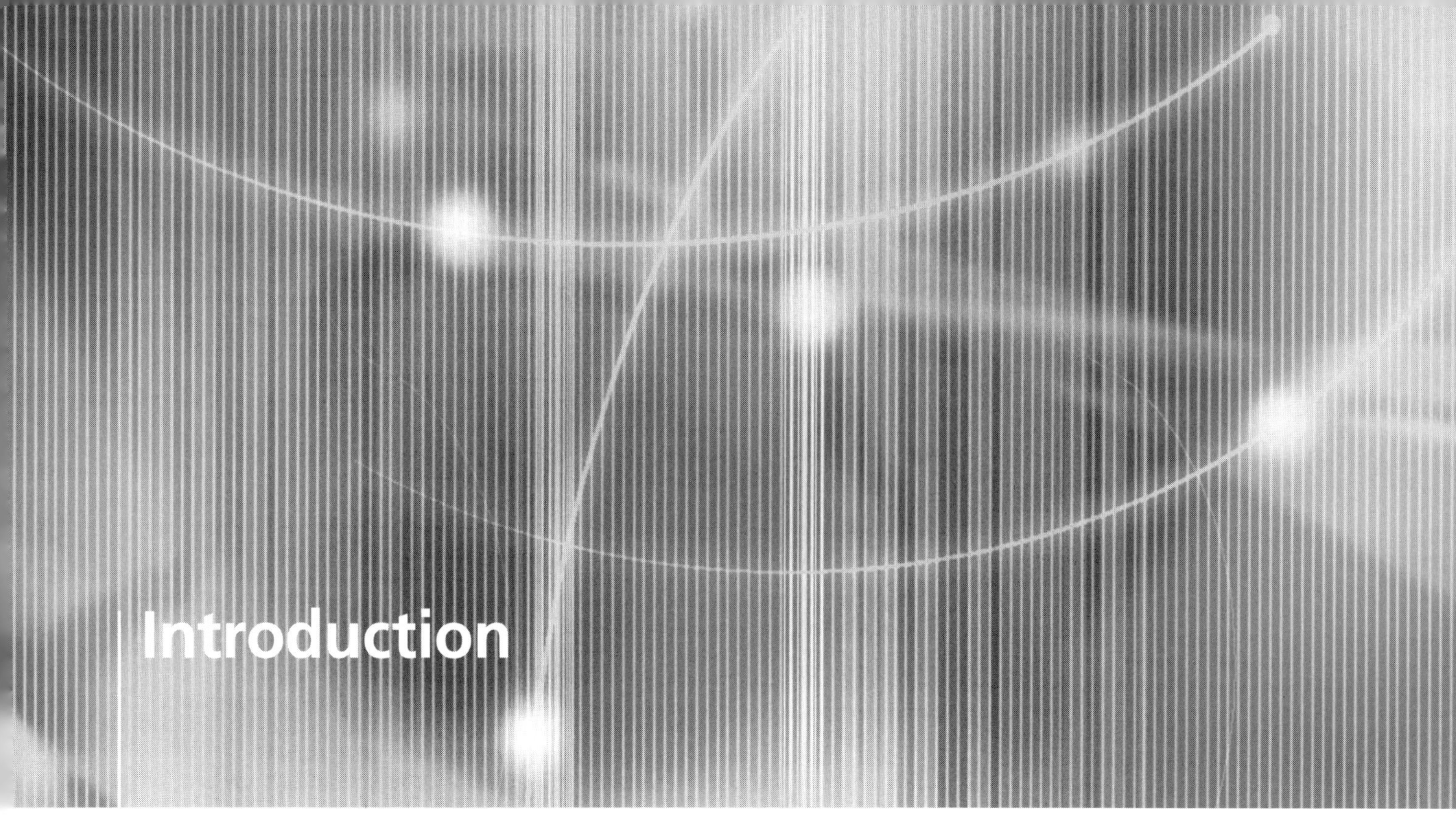

Introduction

MCITP Guide to Windows Server 2008, Enterprise Administrator (Exam 70-647) provides in-depth coverage of the 70-647 certification exam objectives and focuses on the skills needed to manage a Windows Server 2008 enterprise. The book contains approximately 85 hands-on activities and 40 skill-reinforcing case projects, so you'll be well prepared for the certification exam and will learn valuable skills to help you on the job.

After you finish this book, you'll have in-depth knowledge that will help you design several critical elements used in large enterprises, including Active Directory Domain Services, physical topology designs, DNS, Group Policy, remote access, Terminal Services, PKI, securing servers, network load balancing, failover clusters, and virtualization strategies.

Microsoft's MCSE certification program was one of the most popular certifications in the IT field. With Windows Server 2008, the MCSE was changed to Microsoft Certified Information Technology Professional (MCITP). The MCITP Enterprise Administrator certification is quickly becoming popular with employers and job-seekers alike.

Intended Audience

This book is intended for people who need to pass the 70-647 exam and earn the MCITP Enterprise Administrator certification. This valuable certification shows that you have expertise in planning and deploying Windows Server 2008 servers within an enterprise. The certification requires that you pass a total of five exams. The following four Windows Server 2008 exams are required:

- 70-640: Windows Server 2008 Active Directory, Configuring
- 70-642: Windows Server 2008 Network Infrastructure, Configuring
- 70-643: Windows Server 2008 Applications Infrastructure, Configuring
- 70-647: Windows Server 2008, Enterprise Administrator

An additional desktop operating system exam is also required. Any one of the following three exams counts as credit for the MCITP Enterprise Administrator certification:

- 70-620: Configuring Microsoft Windows Vista Client
- 70-640: Deploying and Maintaining Vista Client and 2007 Microsoft Office System Desktops
- 70-680: Windows 7, Configuring

It's expected that students will take the 70-647 exam after learning the concepts in the 70-640, 70-642, and 70-643 exams. Many of the concepts from these first three exams are covered in this book, but from a design and planning perspective rather than a configuration and management perspective. In other words, this book helps readers elevate their skills beyond day-to-day maintenance to plan and design networks and meet the changing needs of an enterprise.

When appropriate, this book reviews key concepts to help ensure that readers can connect planning and design objectives with learning how to configure and implement Windows Server 2008.

This book includes:

- A Windows Server 2008 Enterprise Edition evaluation DVD. It can be installed on a computer or a virtual machine that uses Microsoft Hyper-V, Microsoft Virtual Server, VMware Workstation, VMware Player, or VMware Server.
- Step-by-step hands-on activities that walk you through critical tasks. All activities have been tested by a technical editor, reviewers, and validation experts.
- Extensive review and end-of-chapter materials that reinforce your learning.
- Challenging, thought-provoking case projects that help you apply the concepts and technologies to real-world scenarios.
- Abundant screen captures and diagrams that visually reinforce the text and hands-on activities.
- A list of 70-647 exam objectives in Appendix A, which is cross-referenced with the chapters and sections that cover each objective.

Chapter Descriptions

This book is organized to help you understand the capabilities of Windows Server 2008 in an enterprise environment as they relate to the 70-647 exam objectives. Because most of these objectives are related to designing and planning, the book focuses on how to design Windows Server 2008 for different scenarios. The chapters often review topics that students are expected to have learned before, and then explain how to apply this information to the planning and design phases of IT projects in an enterprise. Each chapter covers objectives from the 70-647 exam; Appendix A provides a map of the objectives and the chapter where they're covered.

- **Chapter 1, "Designing Active Directory Domain Services,"** covers the details of designing domains and forests. It reviews the basic concepts of Active Directory Domain Services, including trusts, forest functional levels, domain functional levels, and modification of the schema using ADPrep. Chapter 1 also covers the Active Directory Migration Tool, which is used to migrate objects from one domain or forest to another.
- **Chapter 2, "Designing Physical Topology,"** starts with a review of how sites are used in large organizations that have multiple locations. The chapter describes how Active Directory can be configured with sites, subnets, site links, and site link bridges to use the physical infrastructure properly. It covers how to determine where servers must be placed to make the best use of the physical topology while maintaining security. Read-only domain controllers (RODCs) are also discussed, including their use in branch offices that lack physical security.
- **Chapter 3, "Designing and Implementing DNS,"** provides an overview and review of DNS, an integral component for the successful operation of any enterprise that runs Active Directory. Topics include DNS and Active Directory, DNS zones (primary, secondary, standard, ADI, GlobalNames, and stub zones), DNS records (A, PTR, SRV, and so on), DNS partitions (ForestDNSZones and DomainDNSZones), and zone transfers.
- **Chapter 4, "Designing and Implementing Group Policy,"** covers the design of an administrative model by configuring OUs and creating groups for delegation. You'll learn how

Group Policy is used to manage users and computers in a domain; the discussion includes the use of default group policy objects (GPOs), strategies for creating GPOs, and using the order of precedence to design and implement conflicting GPOS.

- **Chapter 5, "Designing Remote Access and Terminal Services Strategies,"** covers Terminal Services and network access strategies. Terminal Services allows clients to access a network from a remote location. Network Access Protection (NAP) includes many capabilities for improving security with remote and local clients.
- **Chapter 6, "Designing and Implementing a PKI,"** describes the Public Key Infrastructure (PKI), including the elements used to support a Certificate Authority (CA) to issue and manage certificates. To help identify the best solution for various design needs, the chapter describes the differences between enterprise, root, private, and public CAs. Microsoft's Certificate Services and certificate life cycle management are described in depth.
- **Chapter 7, "Securing Windows Server 2008 Servers,"** covers many of the methods used to harden a Windows Server 2008 server and keep it secure. For example, the Security Configuration Wizard (SCW) is used to create secure baselines, and the Microsoft Baseline Security Analyzer is used for compliance auditing. The chapter describes how to use Microsoft Update, Windows Update, and Windows Server Update Services to keep systems secure. It also provides basic details for designing firewalls to create perimeter networks and protect internal networks.
- **Chapter 8, "Designing High Availability and Business Continuity,"** describes load balancing and failover clusters, which ensure that services and data are available to users when needed. The design of failover clusters requires in-depth understanding of different server versions, quorums, storage capabilities, and the use of iSCSI and Fibre Channel connections. Active Directory backup and restore methods are also reviewed.
- **Chapter 9, "Designing Supporting Services,"** covers many of the support services that can enhance data accessibility, data redundancy, and data collaboration in a large enterprise: System Center Operations Manager (SCOM), System Center Configuration Manager (SCCM), Windows SharePoint Services (WSS), Microsoft Office SharePoint Server (MOSS), Distributed File System (DFS), Network File System (NFS), Active Directory Lightweight Directory Services (AD LDS), Active Directory Federation Services (AD FS), Active Directory Rights Management Services (AD RMS), and BitLocker Drive Encryption.
- **Chapter 10, "Designing Virtualization Strategies,"** describes the capabilities and uses of application virtualization, desktop virtualization, and server virtualization, which are key concepts to consider when designing a virtualization strategy. The chapter describes Microsoft's Application Virtualization 4.5, Microsoft Virtual PC, Windows Virtual PC, and Hyper-V.
- **Appendix A, "MCITP 70-647 Exam Objectives,"** maps each exam objective to the chapter and section where you can find information on that objective.
- **Appendix B, "A Step-by-Step Guide to Using Server Virtualization Software,"** provides instructions for performing selected activities in VMware Workstation or Microsoft Virtual PC.

Features

This book includes the following learning features to help you master the 70-647 exam objectives:

- **Chapter objectives.** Each chapter begins with a list of the concepts to be mastered. This list is a quick reference to the chapter's contents and a useful study aid.
- **Hands-on activities.** Hands-on activities are included in every chapter. These activities give you practice in setting up, managing, and troubleshooting a Windows Server 2008 server, with emphasis on Active Directory configuration. The activities give you a strong foundation for performing server administration in the real world.

- **Screen captures, illustrations, and tables.** Numerous screen captures and illustrations help you visualize theories and concepts and see how to use tools and software features. Tables provide details and comparisons of practical and theoretical information, and can be used for quick reviews.
- **Chapter summary.** Summaries at the end of each chapter provide a helpful way to recap and revisit the material covered.
- **Key terms.** All terms introduced with bold text appear in the Key Terms list at the end of the chapter. This list allows you to check your understanding of all terms introduced.
- **Review questions.** The end-of-chapter assessment begins with review questions that reinforce the concepts and techniques covered in each chapter. Answering these questions helps ensure that you have mastered important topics.
- **Case projects.** Each chapter closes with four case projects. These projects help you apply the chapter concepts to a real-world scenario.
- **DVD.** The DVD includes a free 120-day evaluation copy of Windows Server 2008 Enterprise Edition.

Text and Graphics Conventions

Additional information and exercises in this book help you understand the chapter discussions. Icons throughout the text alert you to these additional materials:

Tips offer extra information on resources, how to solve problems, and time-saving shortcuts.

Notes present helpful material related to the subject being discussed.

The Caution icon identifies important information about potential mistakes or hazards.

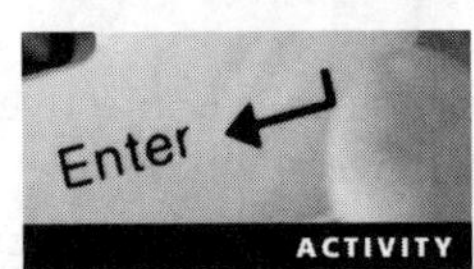

Each Hands-on activity in this book is preceded by the Activity icon.

Case Project icons mark the end-of-chapter case projects. These scenario-based assignments ask you to apply what you have learned in the chapter.

Test Preparation Software

The *MCITP Guide to Windows Server 2008, Enterprise Administrator (Exam 70-647)* includes an exam objectives coverage map in Appendix A. The guide also includes CertBlaster test preparation questions that mirror the look and feel of the MCITP exam. For additional information on the CertBlaster test preparation questions go to http://cengage.com/coursetechnology/ and follow these steps:

1. Enter ISBN 1423902394 in the Search box at the top, right side of the screen. This will bring you to this textbook on the Search Results page.
2. Click the "About this product" link under the Student section on the right side of the page.
3. Click the "Student Downloads" link on the right side of the page. A drop-down menu will appear.
4. Click the "CertBlaster for Exam #70-647" link to access the test preparation software.

For more information about dti test prep products, visit the Web site at *www.dtipublishing.com*.

Additional Downloads CD

Activities in Chapter 7 require several files that aren't included in Windows Server 2008. These files have been included on the CD in the back of the book for your convenience, in a folder named "Chapter 7 downloads."

Instructor's Resources

The following supplemental materials are available when this book is used in a classroom setting. These materials are provided to instructors on the Instructors Resource CD (ISBN 1-4239-0285-8).

- **Electronic Instructor's Manual.** The Instructor's Manual includes additional material to assist in class preparation, including suggestions for classroom activities, discussion topics, and additional activities.
- **Solutions.** The instructor's resources include solutions to all end-of-chapter material, including review questions and case projects.
- **ExamView®.** The textbook is accompanied by ExamView®, a powerful testing software package that allows instructors to create and administer printed, computer (LAN-based), and Internet exams. ExamView® includes hundreds of questions that correspond to the topics covered in this book, enabling students to generate detailed study guides that include page references for further review. The computer-based and Internet testing components allow students to take exams at their computers and save the instructor time by grading each exam automatically.
- **PowerPoint® presentations.** This book comes with Microsoft PowerPoint® slides for each chapter. They are included as a teaching aid for classroom presentation, to make available to students on the network for chapter review, or to be printed for classroom distribution. Instructors, feel free to add your own slides for additional topics you introduce to the class.
- **Figure files.** All the figures in the book are reproduced on the Instructor's Resource CD in bitmap format. Like the PowerPoint slides, they are included as a teaching aid for classroom presentation, to make available to students for review, or to be printed for classroom distribution.

Companion Lab Manual

A companion lab manual is available with this book. It includes additional exercises for every chapter to complement the exercises in this book. The ISBN of the lab manual is 1-4239-0286-6.

System Requirements

Activities in this book use two servers: DC1 and DC2. Both servers will run Windows Server 2008, which is installed by the students. DC1 is promoted to a domain controller of the Cengage.com domain early in the book, and it remains as a domain controller throughout the book. DC2 is modified in different activities to host Active Directory in a separate forest, in a child domain, and as a replica domain controller.

Most of the activities can be used in virtual environments, with the exception of the Hyper-V labs in Chapter 10, "Designing Virtualization Strategies." The Hyper-V role cannot be added to a virtual server.

Appendix B includes more details on different virtual environments, including Microsoft's Virtual PC, Microsoft Virtual Server, and VMware. You can use any virtual environment you want, but we recommend that you use Microsoft virtualization technologies because they are tested on the 70-647 exam. If the virtual environment gives you a choice, you should *always save your changes for all the exercises in this book*.

Hardware (Without Using Virtualization)

A minimum of two computers per student meeting the following requirements:

- 2 GHz or faster CPU
- 512 MB or more RAM (preferably more for better performance)
- 15 GB or more disk space
- DVD-ROM drive
- Super VGA or higher resolution monitor
- Mouse or pointing device
- Keyboard
- Network interface card connected to the classroom, lab, or school network

Hardware (Using Virtualization)

One computer is needed to act as the host machine and host the virtual environment. Three optional activities in Chapter 10, "Designing Virtualization Strategies," use Windows 7 as a host for a virtual environment, but for the rest of the book you can use any host machine and operating system that will host the virtual environment. The host machine should meet the following minimum requirements:

- 2.4 GHz or faster CPU
- 2 GB or more RAM (more is always better with virtualization)
- 40 GB or more disk space
- DVD-ROM drive
- Super VGA or higher resolution monitor
- Mouse or pointing device
- Keyboard
- Network interface card connected to the classroom, lab, or school network

Software

Windows Server 2008 Standard or Enterprise Edition (included with DVD in the book).

Virtualization

Windows Server 2008 can be loaded into a virtual server environment such as VMware Workstation, VMware Server, Microsoft Virtual PC, or Microsoft Hyper-V. The use of virtualization is highly recommended.

Acknowledgements

A book of this size and depth can't be done alone. I'm grateful for all of the assistance and I'd like to acknowledge the following people. First, I'd like to thank Nick Lombardi for the opportunity to write this book. Dan Seiter was a superb developmental editor, did a great job keeping this book on track, and was a joy to work with. Richard Robb did a good job writing the companion lab manual that can be used with this book, and he provided excellent feedback and insight on topics that I was able to implement. Through it all, my wife provided steady support, patience, and encouragement; as this book goes to press we'll be celebrating our 18th wedding anniversary.

Reviewers

Tim Garvey, Program Director
Westwood College
Anaheim, CA

Marcia C. Thompson, MSITM
ECPI College of Technology
Virginia Beach, VA

Jared Spencer, Lead Faculty
Westwood College
Clinton, PA

Daniel Zeismer, Professor
San Juan College
Farmington, NM

About the Author

Darril Gibson is the CEO of Security Consulting and Training, LLC. He regularly writes, teaches, and consults on a wide array of IT topics. He has been a Microsoft Certified Trainer (MCT) since 1999 and holds several certifications, including Security+, CISSP, ITIL Foundations v3.0, MCSA (Windows 2000 Server, Windows Server 2003), MCSE (NT 4.0, Windows 2000 Server, Windows Server 2003), MCTS, MCITP (Enterprise Administrator, Server Administrator, Consumer Support Technician, Enterprise Support Technician, Database Administrator, Database Developer), MCDBA, MCSD, and more. He has authored and co-authored several books. To see a full listing of his current books, you can go to Amazon.com and search for **Darril Gibson**.

Contact the Author

Feel free to contact Darril with any compliments, questions, suggestions, or corrections. He always enjoys hearing from people who have passed a certification exam after using one of his books. Your comments and suggestions can help improve the next edition of this book. You can send your e-mail to darril@mcitpsuccess.com.

Acknowledgements

A book of this size and depth can't be done alone. I'm grateful for all of the assistance and I'd like to acknowledge the following people. First, I'd like to thank Nick Lombardi for the opportunity to write this book. Dan Seiter was a superb developmental editor, did a great job keeping this book on track, and was a joy to work with. Richard Robb did a good job writing the companion lab manual that can be used with this book, and he provided excellent feedback and insight on topics that I was able to implement. Through it all, my wife provided steady support, patience, and encouragement; as this book goes to press we'll be celebrating our 18th wedding anniversary.

Reviewers

Tim Garvey, Program Director
Westwood College
Anaheim, CA

Jared Spencer, Lead Faculty
Westwood College
Clinton, PA

Marcia C. Thompson, MSITM
ECPI College of Technology
Virginia Beach, VA

Daniel Zeismer, Professor
San Juan College
Farmington, NM

About the Author

Darril Gibson is the CEO of Security Consulting and Training, LLC. He regularly writes, teaches, and consults on a wide array of IT topics. He has been a Microsoft Certified Trainer (MCT) since 1999 and holds several certifications, including Security+, CISSP, ITIL Foundations v3.0, MCSA (Windows 2000 Server, Windows Server 2003), MCSE (NT 4.0, Windows 2000 Server, Windows Server 2003), MCTS, MCITP (Enterprise Administrator, Server Administrator, Consumer Support Technician, Enterprise Support Technician, Database Administrator, Database Developer), MCDBA, MCSD, and more. He has authored and co-authored several books. To see a full listing of his current books, you can go to Amazon.com and search for **Darril Gibson**.

Contact the Author

Feel free to contact Darril with any compliments, questions, suggestions, or corrections. He always enjoys hearing from people who have passed a certification exam after using one of his books. Your comments and suggestions can help improve the next edition of this book. You can send your e-mail to darril@mcitpsuccess.com.

chapter 1

Designing Active Directory Domain Services

After reading this chapter and completing the exercises, you will be able to:

- Create a virtual lab for testing different forest and domain designs
- Plan for different domain and forest functional levels
- Design Active Directory Domain Services domains and forests
- Design trusts and implement a forest trust
- Prepare forests and domains for Windows Server 2008
- Create and use an alternative UPN
- Understand different tools used to migrate Active Directory objects

The processes used to design and implement Active Directory Domain Services are varied and complex. You can't just decide to build or migrate a forest one day and start it the next day. It takes planning and an in-depth understanding of the different tools you can use. In this chapter you'll review the basics of Active Directory, create your own virtual lab, and then jump into the design process.

When designing forests and domains, you need to answer two primary questions: "How many forests do I need?" and "How many domains do I need in each forest?" For most applications, a single-domain, single-forest design will work. However, you'll need a modified design on some occasions.

Once you decide on the number of forests and domains, you may need to implement different trusts if you're using more than one forest. An important consideration when creating trusts between forests is the decision to use forest-wide authentication or selective authentication.

After a short review of the Active Directory Preparation tool (ADPrep), you'll learn about migrating objects from one domain or forest to another. When studying migration, it's important to understand how a security identifier (SID) can be migrated and stored as SID history, and how SID history can be thwarted if SID filtering is used.

Basic Review of Active Directory Domain Services

This chapter covers many advanced topics related to Active Directory Domain Services (AD DS). Although you have probably studied Active Directory, it's worthwhile to review the basics. Refer to Figure 1-1 when reviewing these concepts.

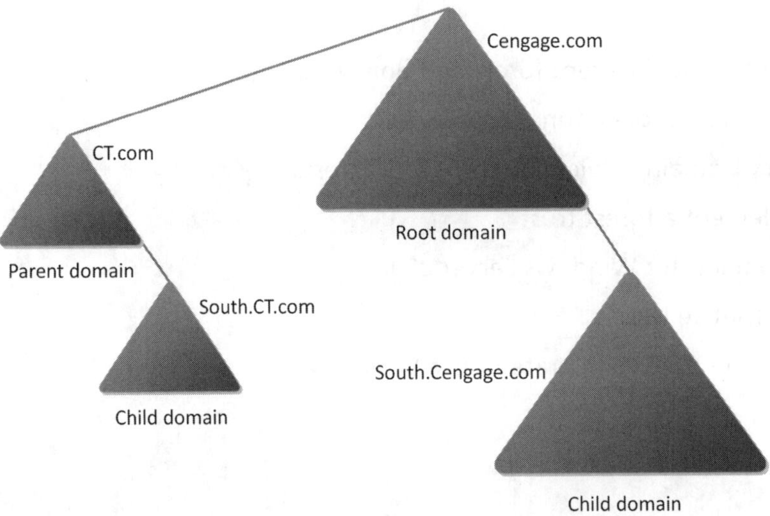

Figure 1-1 A two-tree, four-domain forest

Courtesy Course Technology/Cengage Learning

An **Active Directory domain** is an administrative boundary and holds a database of objects. Objects include users, computers, groups, and much more. An Active Directory domain is hosted on a server called a domain controller. The first domain created in a forest is referred to as the root domain. If additional domains are created using the same root namespace, they are called child domains.

Users in the Domain Admins group can do anything in their domain, but users in the Domain Admins group of one domain cannot administer another domain.

Active Directory Tree

An **Active Directory tree** includes one or more domains with a common namespace. As an example, a domain named Cengage.com could be created as the root domain in a forest. By itself, this domain is technically a tree (though it's not commonly called a tree). If a child domain were created and named South.Cengage.com, it would be part of the same tree as Cengage.com. Notice that the common namespace is Cengage.com. The common namespace must include a top-level name (such as .com) *and* a second-level name (such as Cengage). A top-level name by itself is not considered a common namespace.

You can create multiple trees within a forest. One tree could start with the root domain of Cengage.com and another tree could start with a domain name of CT.com. They have different namespaces, but notice that only the first domain in the forest (Cengage.com in this example) is referred to as the root domain.

All of the domains in a tree are in the same forest. All of these domains share the same schema and the same global catalog.

Active Directory Forest

An **Active Directory forest** includes one or more trees comprised of one or more domains. Technically, a single root domain is a forest, even if it doesn't have any child domains or other trees associated with it. A forest is considered a security boundary. Users in the Enterprise Admins group in a forest can administer any domain in the forest, but they cannot administer domains in other forests.

A forest has a common schema and a common global catalog shared by all domains in the forest. Additionally, each domain within the forest has built-in trust relationships with every other domain in the forest.

When depicted in figures (such as Figure 1-1), the root domain is drawn higher than the other domains. Additionally, a line is drawn from the root domain to the first domain in the other tree to indicate that both trees are in the same forest.

Schema

The **schema** for Active Directory defines the objects that can be created in Active Directory. You can create user, computer, and group objects in a domain because they are defined by the schema. Each of these objects has specific properties that are also defined by the schema. If an object isn't defined in the schema, it can't be added to Active Directory.

Occasionally, the schema needs to be modified. For example, before you can add a Windows Server 2008 domain controller to a Windows Server 2008 forest, you must run ADPrep /ForestPrep. **ADPrep** is an Active Directory preparation tool that can modify the schema by adding objects and properties needed to support Windows Server 2008 domain controllers. Modifying the schema is also called extending the schema.

Trusts

When a second or subsequent domain is added to a forest, **trust** relationships are automatically added to the parent domain. This allows users in the child domain to be granted access to resources in the parent domain. Additionally, users in the parent domain can be granted access to resources in the child domain.

Trusts within a forest are **transitive trusts**. Even though a domain may not have a direct trust relationship with every other domain in the forest, the transitive nature of trusts in a forest allows users within any domain to be granted access to resources to any other domain in a forest.

Global Catalog

The **global catalog** (GC) is a listing of all the objects in the entire forest. For a single-domain forest, the GC includes all the objects in the domain, which is all the objects in the forest. In a multi-domain forest, the GC includes all of the objects from each domain in the forest; however, the GC only includes a subset of the properties of these objects, which reduces its size in a multiple-domain forest.

As an example, a user object may have as many as 100 properties, such as the first name, last name, logon name, password, address, phone number, and more. The GC doesn't store all the properties, but only important ones such as logon name, password, and others designated in the schema.

The GC is hosted on a domain controller selected as a GC server. Each domain must have at least one GC server. Other servers and services on the network use Lightweight Directory Access

Protocol (LDAP) to query the GC for information on Active Directory. As an example, the logon process queries the GC for universal group membership each time a user logs on.

Organizational Units

An **Organizational Unit (OU)** is used within a domain to organize objects. From a technical perspective, there are two reasons to create an OU. First, if you want to use Group Policy to manage users and computers, you can place them in an OU and apply a Group Policy object (GPO) to the OU. Second, if you want to delegate permissions to administrators to manage a group of user and computer objects, you would create an OU, move the objects to the OU, and use the Delegation of Control Wizard.

OUs can also be used to organize objects to make it easier for administrators to manage them. As an example, it's common to place users, computers, and groups from a department or location into a single OU.

Group Policy

Group Policy is the tool used to automate the management and administration of users and computers in the domain. One or more settings can be created once in a GPO and then linked to a site, a domain, or an OU. The GPO settings apply to all users and computers in the scope of the GPO. It doesn't matter whether five users or computers are affected by the GPO, or five hundred, or five thousand or more. The single setting will be applied to all the users and computers affected by the GPO.

A GPO can be linked to a site, a domain, or an OU, which becomes the GPO's scope. For example, if a GPO is linked to an OU named Sales, it would have a scope of the Sales OU and would apply to all objects in that OU.

The primary tool used to manage Group Policy is the Group Policy Management Console (GPMC). Two default Group Policies are created in each domain: the Default Domain policy (which is linked to the domain) and the Default Domain Controllers policy (which is linked to the Domain Controllers OU).

Site

A **site** is a group of well-connected computers or well-connected subnets. For example, all of the rooms within a single building may be connected with a 1-Gb local area network (LAN). A second building could also be well connected with a 1-Gb LAN, but the two buildings may be linked together with a 256-Kb connection. In this example, each building could be considered a site because each is well connected within the building itself.

However, the two buildings are not well connected to each other. The 256-Kb link is significantly slower than the 1-Gb LAN links within each building. In this scenario, each building would be considered a separate site. Active Directory must be taught which sites exist within the forest. This is done with the Active Directory Sites and Services tool.

Creating a Learning Environment

Throughout this book, you'll explore Active Directory. You would benefit by having a domain controller and manipulating the settings yourself, but you probably don't have extra servers at home.

Instead, you can use Microsoft's Virtual PC to create your own test lab, either at home or in the classroom. The following activities will help you create a virtual lab that you can use throughout the book. These activities assume that you know how to install Windows Server 2008 and how to run DCpromo.

Microsoft Virtual PC will run on Windows XP, Windows Vista, and Windows 7. Windows 7 can be updated to install Windows Virtual PC (instead of Microsoft Virtual PC). The companion lab manual of this book includes a lab that leads you through the process of using Windows Virtual PC on Windows 7.

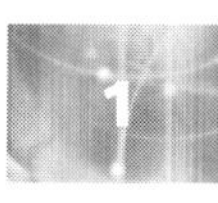

Microsoft Virtual PC is available as a free download from Microsoft. Go to *www.microsoft.com/downloads* and search for "Microsoft Virtual PC SP1." The current version is Microsoft Virtual PC 2007 SP1, and it supports Windows Vista and Windows Server 2008 virtual machines. After you download it, double-click its file icon, then use the installation wizard to install Microsoft Virtual PC on your system.

Activity 1-1: Creating a Virtual PC Environment

Time Required: 60 minutes
Objective: Create a virtual lab environment.

Description: You want to create a test lab of two domain controllers on your desktop PC. You must first install Windows Server 2008 on two separate Microsoft Virtual PC images on your system. These images will be promoted to domain controllers later. This lab assumes that you've installed Windows Server 2008 before, so detailed installation steps are not included.

Appendix B includes more details on different virtual environments, including Microsoft's Virtual PC, Microsoft Virtual Server, and VMware Server. You can use any virtual environment you want, but we recommend that you use Microsoft virtualization technologies because they are tested on the 70-647 exam. If the virtual environment gives you a choice, you should always save your changes for all the exercises in this book.

1. Log on to your desktop PC and start **Microsoft Virtual PC**. If the New Virtual Machine wizard appears, click **Next**. If the wizard does not appear, click **New**.
2. Review the information on the **Welcome** page and click **Next**.
3. On the **Options** page, accept the default option to **Create a Virtual Machine** and click **Next**.
4. Type **DC1** as the name and click **Browse**. Browse to a location on your system to store the virtual machine and click **Save**. Click **Next**.
5. Select **Windows Server 2008** as the operating system, which selects a default memory size of 512 MB and virtual disk size of 65,536 MB. Click **Next**.
6. If your system has enough RAM, select **Adjusting the RAM** and change the RAM size to **1024** (1 GB). Click **Next**. Click **Finish**. While your virtual machine is being created, it's blank. Next, you'll need to install the operating system.

A 32-bit host system with 4 GB of RAM installed will have about 3.3 GB of RAM available. You could dedicate 1 GB to one VPC machine, 1 GB to the second VPC, and leave the rest for the operating system. If you have only 2 GB of RAM in the system, you'll need to leave the memory at 512 MB for the VPC machines to be able to start them both at the same time, but the overall performance of the virtual machines will be much slower.

7. Insert the Windows Server 2008 DVD in the system's DVD reader. The DVD is available at the back of this book.
8. Select **DC1** in the **Virtual PC console** and click **Start**. In the **DC1 VPC**, click the **CD** menu, and select **Use Physical Drive D**, as shown in Figure 1-2. (If your installation DVD was assigned a different drive letter, select it instead.)
9. Select **Reset** from the **Action** menu on the **DC1 VPC** to restart the boot process. When asked if you're sure, click **Reset**. The virtual machine will restart and boot from the installation DVD. Complete the installation of Windows Server 2008 just as you would on a non-virtual server.

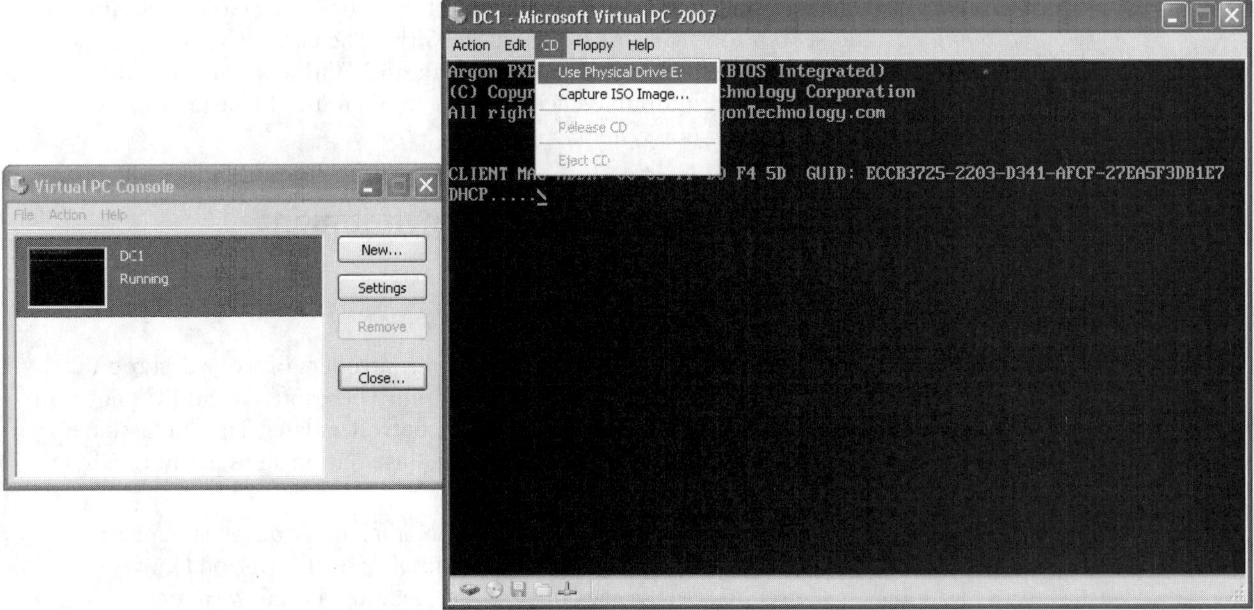

Figure 1-2 Starting the Virtual PC console

Courtesy Course Technology/Cengage Learning

10. Once you've made the basic choices and the installation reaches the **Installing Windows** page, return to the **Virtual PC console**. Select **DC1** and click **Settings**. This page can be used to adjust different settings for the virtual machine.
11. Select **Networking** and select **Adapter 1.** Change **Adapter 1** to **Local only**, as shown in Figure 1-3. If you have other network adapters available, select Not Connected for all of them except Adapter 1. The Local Only setting will allow the virtual machine to communicate with other virtual machines, but not with the host or the network. When configured this way, the virtual environment remains separate from the host system, but can communicate with other VPC machines.

When logging on to Virtual PC, use the right **ALT** key (the key to the right of the Spacebar) with the **Delete** key. The right ALT key mimics the CTRL+ALT keys.

12. When the installation is complete, perform the basic configuration of the server with the following settings:
    - Configure the password of the **Administrator** account to **P@ssw0rd.** Note that the sixth character is a zero (0).
    - Use the **Initial Configuration Tasks** window to change the time zone to your local time zone.
    - Select **Configure Networking** from the **Initial Configuration Tasks** window. Right-click **Local Area Connection** and select **Properties.** Disable **Internet Protocol Version 6** (TCP/IPv6) by unchecking the box. Select **Internet Protocol Version 4** (TCP/IPv4) and select **properties.** Configure a static IP address of **192.168.1.10,** subnet mask of **255.255.255.0,** and DNS server address of **192.168.1.10.** The default gateway can be left blank.
    - Use the **Initial Configuration Tasks** window to set the computer name to **DC1.** This will prompt you to restart the server; select **Restart Later.**

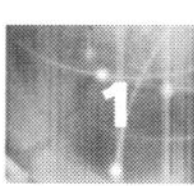

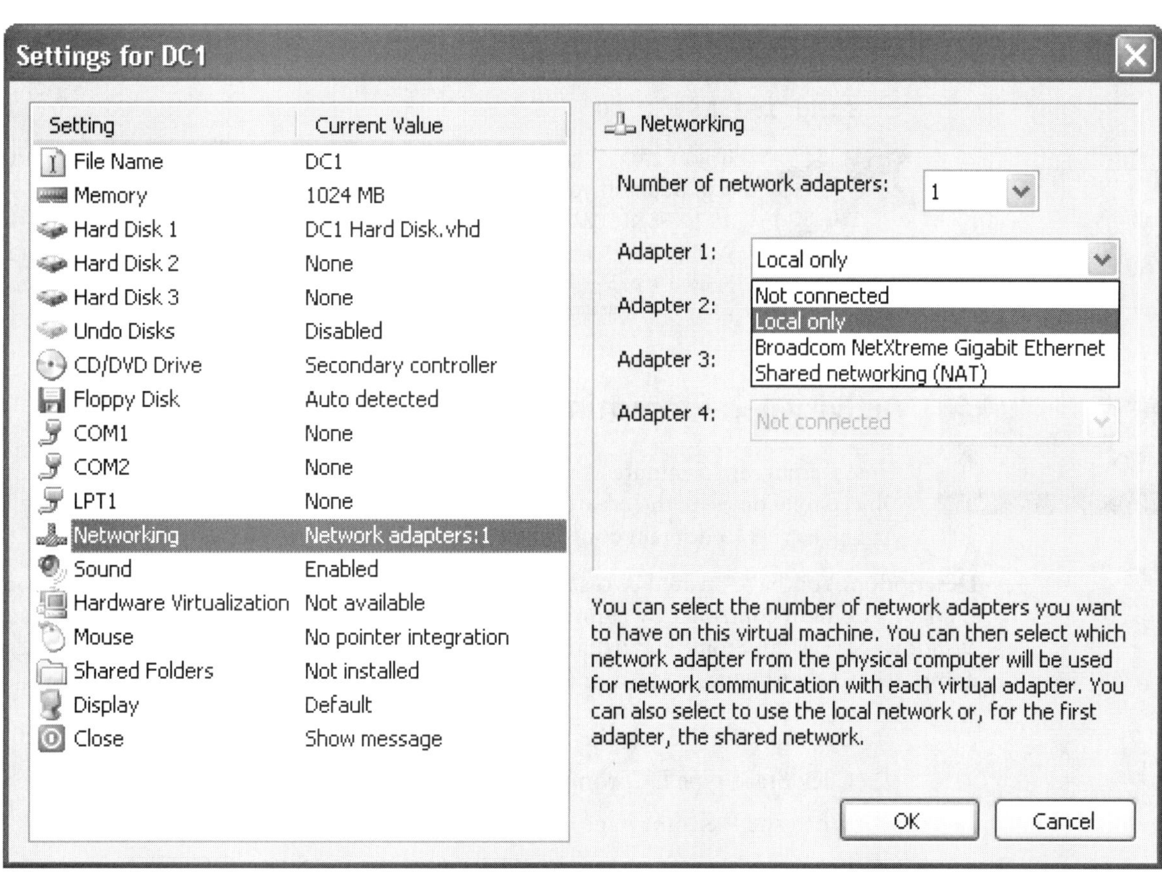

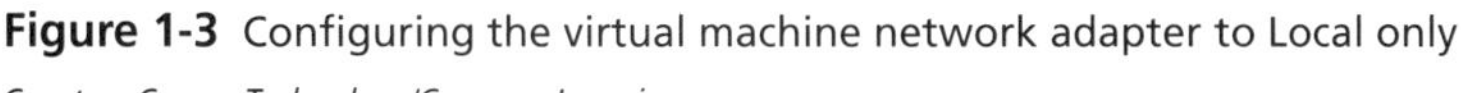

Figure 1-3 Configuring the virtual machine network adapter to Local only

Courtesy Course Technology/Cengage Learning

13. Press the right **ALT** key to allow your mouse to get out of the virtual PC window. Select **Install or Update Virtual Machine Additions** from the **Action** menu. If you aren't prompted to start the program from Auto Play, use Windows Explorer to browse to the D: drive, then right-click it and select **Install or Run Program**. Follow the wizard to complete the installation, and reboot when it is done. The Virtual Machine Additions will give you better control over the virtual environment.

14. Repeat the preceding procedures to create a second virtual machine named **DC2**, and use the following settings after the VPC machine has been created.

    - Configure the password of the **Administrator** account to **P@ssw0rd.**
    - Use the **Initial Configuration Tasks** window to change the time zone to your local time zone.
    - Select **Configure Networking** from the **Initial Configuration Tasks** window. Right-click **Local Area Connection** and select **Properties.** Disable **Internet Protocol Version 6** (TCP/IPv6) by unchecking the box. Select **Internet Protocol Version 4** (TCP/IPv4) and select **properties**. Configure a static IP address of **192.168.1.20**, subnet mask of **255.255.255.0**, and DNS server address of **192.168.1.10**. The default gateway can be left blank.
    - Use the **Initial Configuration Tasks** window to set the computer name to **DC2.**

15. Open a command prompt on **DC1** and verify that you can ping the IP address of DC2 (192.168.1.20). The following command should produce successful replies:

```
Ping 192.168.1.20
```

16. Open a command prompt on **DC2** and verify that you can ping the IP address of DC1 (192.168.1.10). The following command should produce successful replies:

```
Ping 192.168.1.10
```

If you cannot ping successfully, double-check the networking configuration on your virtual servers. Ensure that DC1 has an IP address of 192.168.1.10/24 and that DC2 has an IP address of 192.168.1.20/24. Additionally, confirm that you have configured the settings of the virtual Network Adapter to Local Only for both virtual machines. If you can't ping now, you will have problems with future activities.

Activity 1-2: Promoting DC1 to a Domain Controller

Time Required: 15 minutes
Objective: Complete the creation of your virtual lab environment by promoting both virtual servers to domain controllers.

Description: You have created two servers named DC1 and DC2. You will now promote DC1 to a domain controller by running DCpromo. This lab assumes that you have installed Windows Server 2008 on two virtual machines and completed the configuration of these computers so that they can communicate on the network.

1. Log on to **DC1** using the **Administrator** account and a password of **P@ssw0rd.**
2. Click **Start**, type **DCpromo** in the **Start Search** box, and press **Enter.**
3. When the **Welcome** page appears, click **Next.**
4. Review the information on the **Operating System Compatibility** page and click **Next.**
5. Select **Create a New Domain in a New Forest** and click **Next.**
6. Enter **Cengage.com** as the **FQDN of the Forest Root Domain.**
7. Accept the default **Forest Functional Level** of **Windows 2000** and click **Next.** You will change this setting later in this chapter.
8. Accept the default **Domain Functional Level** of **Windows 2000 Native** and click **Next.** You will also change this setting later in this chapter.
9. Select **DNS** on the **Additional Domain Controller Options** page. **Global Catalog** is also selected, but dimmed; the first DC must be a global catalog server. The Read-only Domain Controller (RODC) is not selectable because you can't have an RODC as the first DC in a domain.
10. A warning will appear, indicating that a delegation for the DNS server cannot be created. This is normal. Click **Yes** to continue.
11. Review the default selections on the **Location for Database, Log Files, and SYSVOL** page and click **Next.**
12. Enter **P@ssw0rd** in the **Password** and **Confirm Password** text boxes. Click **Next.**
13. Review the information on the **Summary** page and click **Next.** Select the check box for **Reboot on Completion.** DCpromo will run. When complete, DC1 will automatically reboot as a domain controller.

You can reconfigure DC2 to mimic different configurations if desired. For example, you can configure it to host a completely separate forest, a child domain, or a replica domain controller in the same domain. Activities later in this chapter and throughout the book will configure DC2 as a domain controller hosting a different forest, as a domain controller hosting a different domain in the same forest, and as a replica domain controller.

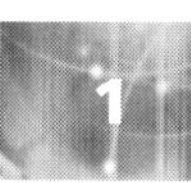

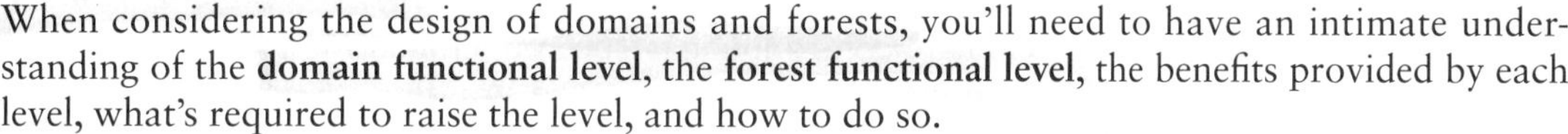

Understanding Domain and Forest Functional Levels

When considering the design of domains and forests, you'll need to have an intimate understanding of the **domain functional level**, the **forest functional level**, the benefits provided by each level, what's required to raise the level, and how to do so.

The functional level that is applied dictates the available capabilities within the domains and forest. As the functional levels are raised, more capabilities are added. When designing domains and forests, you'll often have a list of capabilities that you want. You must raise the domain and/or forest functional levels to gain these capabilities in the enterprise, but you can't raise the levels until all domain controllers in the enterprise are running specific versions of Windows Server.

As an example, imagine that the design calls for the use of different password policies in the same domain. Fine-grained password policies can be implemented if the domain functional level is set to at least Windows Server 2008. You can only raise the domain functional level to Windows Server 2008 when all domain controllers in the domain are running at least Windows Server 2008. Your design plans therefore must verify that all domain controllers are running at least Windows Server 2008 or include plans to upgrade them in order to support the different password policies.

Similarly, you may be designing a plan that will merge two companies, and you need to create a forest trust relationship between the two forests. Forest trusts are possible once the forest functional level has been raised to Windows Server 2003. You can only raise the forest functional level when all domains in the forest have reached the same level, and you can only raise the domain to a functional level when all the domain controllers are running the appropriate versions of Windows Server. Your design plans will need to include the following steps to support forest trusts:

- Verify that all domain controllers are running at least Windows Server 2003, and if not, include plans to upgrade them.
- Raise the domain functional levels of each domain in each forest to at least Windows Server 2003.
- Last, you'll need to raise the forest functional level of each forest to at least Windows Server 2003.

Once a domain functional level or forest functional level has been raised, it cannot be undone. Functional levels can't be lowered, only raised.

When preparing for the 70-647 exam, ensure that you have a solid understanding of the relationships between the operating system hosted on domain controllers, the domain functional levels, and the forest functional levels.

Domain Functional Level

A domain can be set to operate in different domain functional levels. Each of the levels provides different capabilities, and these capabilities increase as the functional level is raised to a higher level.

The different domain functional levels are:

- Windows Server 2000 Native
- Windows Server 2003
- Windows Server 2008
- Windows Server 2008 R2

A key to understanding the domain functional levels is knowing that they are directly related to the domain controllers in the domain. If you have any Windows 2000 domain controllers, you can't go beyond the Windows Server 2000 Native domain functional level. The default domain functional level is Windows Server 2000 Native. It will support domain controllers running on Windows Server 2000, Windows Server 2003, and Windows Server 2008. Windows NT 4.0 domain controllers are not supported in a domain that supports Windows Server 2008.

If all of your domain controllers have been upgraded to at least Windows Server 2003, you can then raise the domain functional level to Windows Server 2003. Similarly, if all of your domain controllers have been upgraded to Windows Server 2008, you can raise the domain functional level to Windows Server 2008.

An interesting phenomenon that often occurs when students encounter this topic is that they switch "domain controllers" in their minds to "servers." In other words, they think that all *servers* must run Windows Server 2008 to raise the level to Windows Server 2008. This is *not* true. Only the domain controllers must meet the required level. You can run Windows Server 2000 member servers in a domain at the domain functional level of Windows Server 2008.

Once a domain functional level has been raised, servers running older server operating systems cannot be promoted to domain controllers. For example, once you raise a domain functional level to Windows Server 2008, you will not be able to promote a server running Windows Server 2003 to a domain controller. You can still have older member servers (non-domain controllers) running in the domain because the domain and forest functional levels do not affect the requirements on member servers.

You gain different capabilities as you raise the domain functional level. Some of the more notable capabilities are shown in Table 1-1.

Table 1-1 Domain Functional Level Features

Domain Functional Level	Notable Features
Windows 2000 Native	Universal groups for security Group nesting SID history
Windows Server 2003	All features from Windows Server 2000 Native Selective authentication for users in trusted forest Redirection of new computers to something other than the default Computers container Redirection of new users to something other than the default Users container Renaming of domain controllers using Netdom
Windows Server 2008	All features from Windows Server 2003 Fine-grained password and account lockout policies Last interactive logon information AES 128 and 256 support for Kerberos DFS support for SYSVOL
Windows Server 2008 R2	All features from Windows Server 2008 Authentication mechanism assurance used with federated identity management Automatic service principle name (SPN) management

Fine-grained password and account lockout policies are a significant addition to Windows Server 2008. They allow you to have multiple policies in a single domain; in previous domain functional levels, you had to create a completely separate domain to have different policies. For example, if you had 25 users who required a more stringent password policy, you would have to create a completely separate domain to meet this need. However, if you raise the domain functional level to Windows Server 2008, you can now support multiple password policies (and multiple account lockout policies) in a single domain.

When using fine-grained password and account lockout policies, you can assign the policies to specific users or groups in the domain. Fine-grained policies will be explored further in Chapter 4.

To raise the domain functional level, use Active Directory Users and Computers. Right-click the domain and select Raise Domain Functional Level. Activity 1-3 leads you through this process.

Activity 1-3: Raising the Domain Functional Level

Time Required: 10 minutes
Objective: Understand how to raise the domain functional level to support fine-grained password policies.

Description: You are planning to implement fine-grained password policies in a domain and first want to raise the domain functional level to at least Windows Server 2008. Execute this lab on DC1.

1. Log on to **DC1** with the **Administrator** account and a password of **P@ssw0rd.**
2. Start **Active Directory Users and Computers** from the **Administrative Tools** menu.
3. Select the **Cengage.com** domain in **Active Directory Users and Computers**. Right-click the domain and select **Raise Domain Functional Level.**
4. Select **Windows Server 2008** as the **Domain Functional Level.** Your display will look similar to Figure 1-4. Click **Raise.**

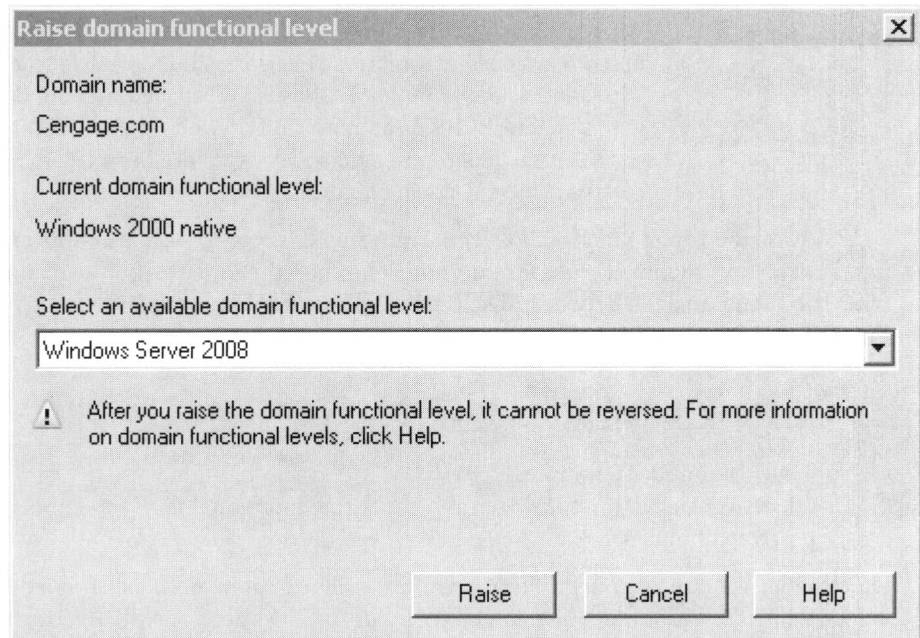

Figure 1-4 Raising the domain functional level in Active Directory Users and Computers
Courtesy Course Technology/Cengage Learning

5. Review the warning that the process can't be reversed and click **OK.**
6. A dialog box will appear, indicating that the process has been completed successfully. Click **OK.**

Forest Functional Level Capabilities

Forest functional levels apply to all domains in the forest and can be applied when all domains have been raised. For example, once all the domains have been raised to the Windows Server 2003 domain functional level, you can raise the forest functional level to Windows Server 2003. You cannot raise the forest functional level until all domains have been raised.

Knowing this, when you see the forest functional level is Windows Server 2008, you also know that every domain and domain controller in the forest must be running at least Windows Server 2008.

Table 1-2 shows the notable features of the different forest functional levels.

Table 1-2 Forest Functional Level Features

Forest Functional Level	Notable Features
Windows 2000	All default Active Directory features
Windows Server 2003	All features from Windows Server 2000 RODCs can be deployed (on Windows Server 2008 computers) Forest trusts can be enabled Selective authentication for users in trusted forest Domains can be renamed Linked-value replication
Windows Server 2008	All features from Windows Server 2003 No additional features are added
Windows Server 2008 R2	All features from Windows Server 2008 Active Directory Recycle bin (allows deleted objects to be easily restored)

When preparing for the 70-647, remember the features listed in Table 1-2 that are available at the Windows Server 2003 forest functional level. Trusts and selective authentication are explained in more detail later in this chapter. RODCs can only run on Windows Server 2008 domain controllers, and only after additional steps have been taken. RODCs are covered in more depth in Chapter 2.

You raise the forest functional level using Active Directory Domains and Trusts. Unlike raising the domain functional level, you do not right-click the domain, but instead right-click Active Directory Domains and Trusts and select Raise Forest Functional Level. Activity 1-4 leads you through this process.

Activity 1-4: Raising the Forest Functional Level

Time Required: 10 minutes

Objective: Understand how to raise the forest functional level to support fine-grained password policies.

Description: You are planning to implement fine-grained password policies in a domain and first want to raise the forest functional level to at least Windows Server 2008. Execute this lab on DC1.

1. Log on to **DC1** with the **Administrator** account and a password of **P@ssw0rd.**
2. Start **Active Directory Domains and Trusts** from the **Administrative Tools** menu.
3. Right-click **Active Directory Domains and Trusts** and select **Raise Forest Functional Level.** Notice that you do not right-click the domain name.
4. Select **Windows Server 2008** as the **Forest Functional Level.** Your display will look similar to Figure 1-5. Click **Raise.**
5. Review the warning that the process can't be reversed and click **OK.**
6. A dialog box will appear, indicating that the process has been completed successfully. Click **OK.**

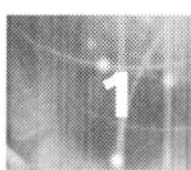

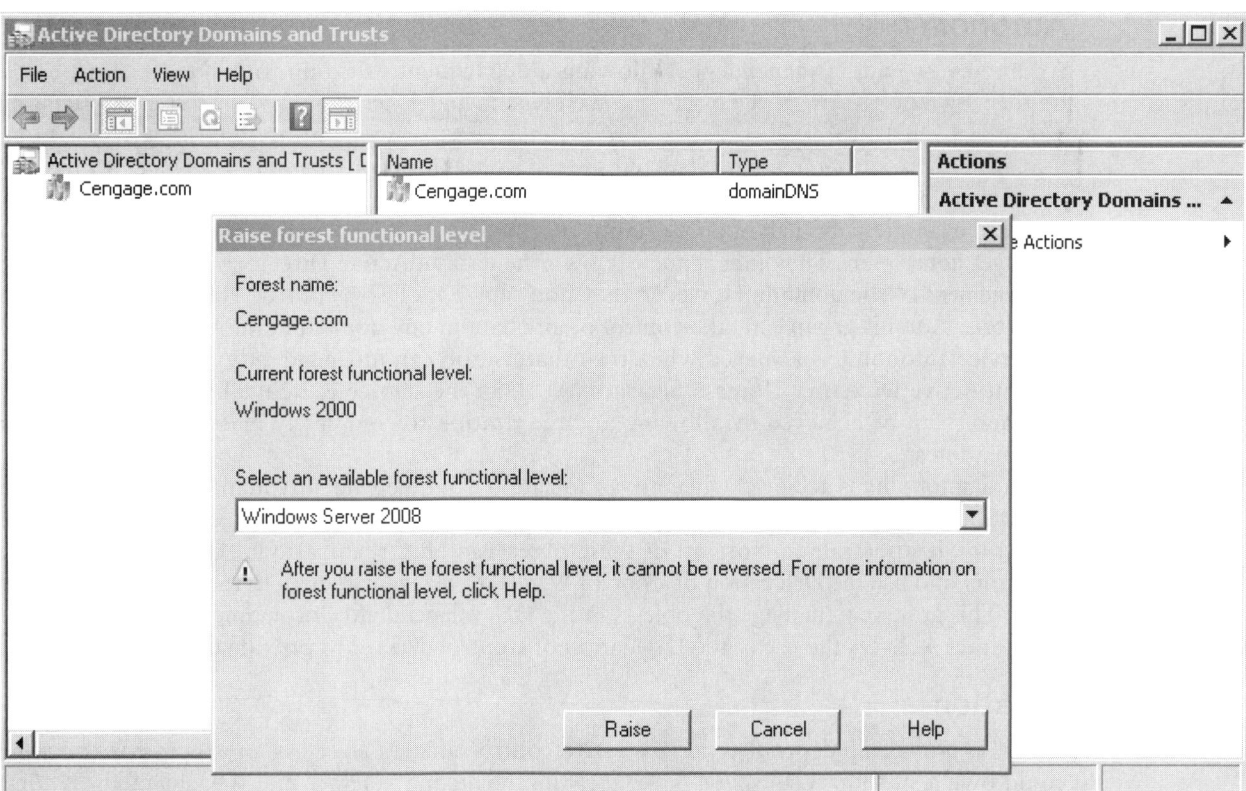

Figure 1-5 Raising the forest functional level in Active Directory Domains and Trusts

Courtesy Course Technology/Cengage Learning

Designing Active Directory Domains and Forests

Designing Active Directory involves determining the forest and domain structure. This is referred to as the logical structure of Active Directory. In Chapter 2, you will learn about the physical structure of Active Directory, which involves configuring sites and determining where specific domain controllers are located.

You need to answer the following primary questions when designing the local structure:

- How many forests are needed?
- How many domains are needed?

A single-domain forest will work for the majority of Active Directory designs. Whenever a single-domain forest meets your needs, that's exactly what you should use. It's easier to manage and maintain a single-domain forest, and it reduces the potential problems you may encounter with multiple domains and multiple forests.

Autonomy vs. Isolation

When deciding on the number of forests and domains you need, you often need to identify the **autonomy** and **isolation** requirements. These requirements are determined by the business needs, but are implemented by creating one or more forests. When considering autonomy and isolation, note two important points:

- Autonomy provides independent, but not exclusive, control of a resource.
- Isolation provides independent *and* exclusive control of a resource.

Autonomy

Autonomy provides independence, allowing a department or group to make decisions based on their own needs within the organization. This independence is achieved by creating separate domains within a forest if service autonomy is needed, or by creating separate OUs within a domain if data autonomy is needed. While autonomy does provide independence, it does not provide exclusive control over a resource.

As an example, a branch of an organization can have a child domain created that the branch manages completely. They independently own the data in Active Directory and provide all the management of the domain. However, they don't have exclusive control. Administrators in the Enterprise Admins group can take control of any data in any domain in the forest.

Service autonomy is achieved when the organization can independently manage the service. Within Active Directory Domain Services (AD DS), the service is Active Directory, so service autonomy can be achieved by allowing an organization to completely manage a child domain within a forest.

Data autonomy is achieved when an organization can independently manage the data. Within AD DS, the data comprises the users, computers, groups, and other objects stored in Active Directory. It's possible to store all of these objects in an Organizational Unit (OU) in Active Directory and use the Delegation of Control Wizard to delegate control to the OU for a group of users. This group can manage the objects in the OU independently, providing data autonomy.

Chapter 4 covers the use of the Delegation of Control Wizard to provide data autonomy.

Isolation

Isolation provides independent *and* exclusive control of a resource. As an example, a company could own a subsidiary. Business or legal requirements may dictate that the subsidiary is completely isolated from the parent. A separate forest can be created to provide this isolation. This approach is also referred to as using the separate forest as a security boundary.

Even when a company is isolated with a separate forest, it's still possible to share resources. For example, trust relationships can be created between the two organizations to enable sharing. The administrators in each forest have complete control over what resources are shared and who can access them.

To summarize the preceding discussion, if part of the organization needs autonomy, delegated control over an OU can provide data autonomy while a separate domain in the forest can provide service autonomy. If complete isolation is required, the design must include a separate forest.

Creating a Separate Forest for a Separate Schema

If a department or branch of the company needs to make extensive changes to the schema, but such changes are not needed elsewhere in the organization, you may choose to create a separate forest for this group. An example might be a development group that uses special applications. Remember, every forest has only one schema that is shared by all domains and stored on all domain controllers in the forest. If the schema is modified, this modification is replicated to all domain controllers in the forest.

Creating a separate forest provides isolation for the group and limits the complexities of the schema for most of the other users. Any changes to the schema used by the specific group will not be seen in the primary forest.

In this scenario, the development group will likely still need access to resources in the forest used by the majority of the users. A one-way forest trust can be created to grant them the access they need. This forest trust does not interfere with the isolation provided by the separate forest.

Identifying Bandwidth Requirements for a Forest

While the primary reason to create a separate forest is to provide isolation, you may also create a separate forest to limit or control replication. This can be especially valuable if the replication occurs between several different sites.

As a reminder, replication occurs between all domain controllers in a domain and all domain controllers in a forest. Every forest shares a single global catalog that holds a condensed copy

of every object in the forest. At a minimum, the contents of the global catalog are replicated to all domain controllers that are designated as global catalog servers in the forest, and at least one domain controller in every domain must be a global catalog server.

Replication within a well-connected site is rarely a problem. However, when replication occurs over a wide area network (WAN), the amount of bandwidth consumed is frequently a concern. Replication can be controlled using sites (which are covered in Chapter 2), but if the amount of replication will create an excessive burden on the available network bandwidth, you can create two separate forests to eliminate the replication traffic.

It's important to understand that replication within a domain and replication within a forest are different. Replication within a domain occurs between all its domain controllers and replicates all domain objects, including all of their attributes. Replication between domains in a forest is less extensive and doesn't include all domain controllers.

- Forest replication will replicate changes to the global catalog to all global catalog servers in the forest. The global catalog includes a copy of all objects in the forest, but only holds a subset of the properties of each object.
- Domain replication will replicate all additions, deletions, and modifications of any object in a domain to every domain controller in the domain. This includes all additions, deletions, and modifications of users, computers, groups, and more.

Identifying Domain Requirements

Just as you should start your design with a single forest, you should also start the design with a single domain. If you're operating in a single well-connected site, a single-domain forest can meet most needs. A single domain can handle more than 100,000 users, so the number of users is rarely a reason to create other domains.

The primary reason to create an additional domain is to provide service autonomy within a forest. If you create a child domain in an existing forest, a business entity can manage Active Directory in the domain. Users in the business entity can be added to the Domain Admins group granting full control over the domain.

Remember that autonomy does not provide complete isolation. Users in the Enterprise Admins group still have rights and permissions for any domain in the forest.

Beyond autonomy, there are two other reasons to create separate domains:

- To control replication traffic over WAN links
- To protect the root domain (and the Enterprise Admins group)

Each time a user is added, deleted, or modified in a domain, the change is replicated. Within a defined site, replication occurs within 15 seconds, but between sites, replication is compressed and sent on a schedule. By creating a separate domain for each site, the replication of these domain objects can be controlled. However, there will still be some replication of data to global catalog servers.

Microsoft has specific recommendations for when another domain should be added based on replication traffic and domains. Table 1-3 shows the maximum number of users in a domain based on the characteristics of the slowest link, and how much bandwidth is available for replication over this slowest link.

Table 1-3 Maximum Users in a Domain

Slowest Link Speed (Kbps)	Maximum Users if 5% bandwidth available	Maximum users if 10% bandwidth available
28.8	25,000	40,000
56	50,000	100,000
128	100,000	100,000
1,500	100,000	100,000

These figures are approximations, but they do give valid starting points. Note that even if you have an overworked slow link of 28.8 Kbps with only 5 percent bandwidth available for replication, your domain can still accommodate as many as 25,000 users. If your domain exceeds this number of users, you can consider updating the WAN links instead of creating a new domain.

The last reason to create a separate domain is to protect the root domain, and the accounts and groups in it. In some organizations a root domain is created, but very few accounts are added to it. Instead, the root domain stays empty and all the resources (users, computers, groups and so on) are added to the child domain. This provides an added layer of protection for the Enterprise Admins and Schema Admins groups and for the root domain Administrator account.

Understanding Trusts

Trust relationships are automatically created between domains in a forest, and can be created between individual domains in different forests or between forests. Trusts can be one-way or two-way, and transitive or non-transitive.

One-way and Two-way Trusts

Figure 1-6 shows how a typical one-way trust relationship is drawn. When this trust is created, users in Domain B can be granted access to resources in Domain A. (To be more precise, access isn't actually granted, but the trust relationship allows an administrator in Domain A to grant the access to users in Domain B. Because the arrow is pointing to Domain B, the trust is described as *Domain A Trusts Domain B*.)

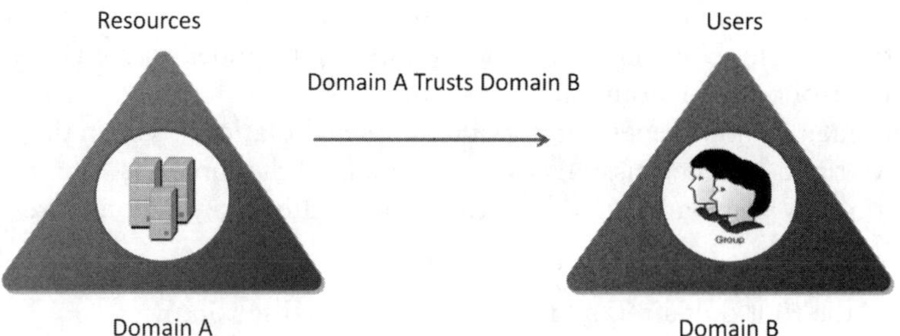

Figure 1-6 Typical one-way trust relationship

Courtesy Course Technology/Cengage Learning

When looking at trust relationship diagrams, you'll often see only the two domains and the arrow. The arrow always points to what is most important: people, not things. The arrow points to the domain that holds the users who can be granted access to the resources in the other domain.

In the figure, Domain A would be considered the trusting domain and Domain B would be considered the trusted domain. If the arrow was reversed to point to Domain A, the trust would be expressed as *Domain B trusts Domain A*.

When the arrow points both ways, or there are two one-way arrows, the trust is referred to as a two-way trust relationship. (Technically, a two-way trust is two separate one-way trusts.) In a two-way trust, users in each domain can be granted access to resources in both domains.

Transitive and Non-Transitive Trusts

Trusts can be transitive and non-transitive. A non-transitive trust creates an explicit trust relationship between two domains and is not transferred to any other domains. A transitive trust is

granted between several domains without creating explicit trust relationships between the different domains.

Figure 1-7 shows a single forest with four domains. Trusts within a forest are created between the domains as shown when DCpromo is executed. The figure shows a two-way trust between South.CT.com and CT.com, a two-way trust between CT.com and Cengage.com, and a two-way trust between Cengage.com and South.Cengage.com. However, because South.Cengage.com trusts Cengage.com, and Cengage.com trusts CT.com, the transitive trust allows South.Cengage.com to trust CT.com (and South.CT.com).

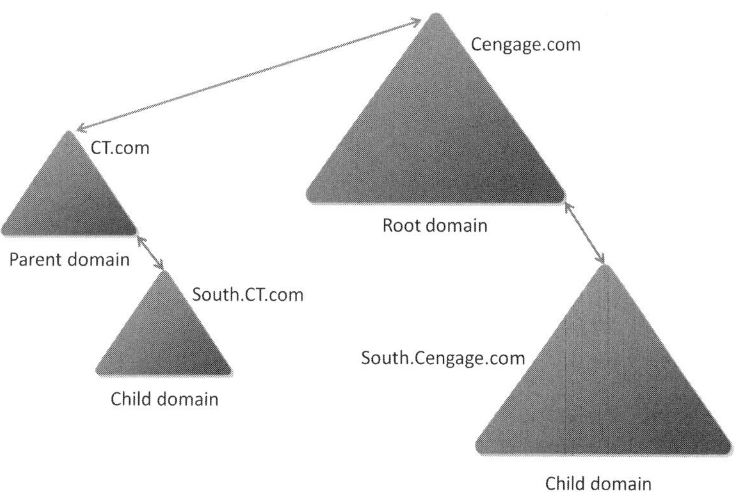

Figure 1-7 Transitive trusts in a forest
Courtesy Course Technology/Cengage Learning

Without transitive trusts, explicit trust relationships would have to be created between each domain. With three domains, you would need six two-way trusts to ensure that users in any domain in the forest can be granted access to resources in other domains. With four domains, you would need to add four more two-way trusts for a total of 10; five domains would require five more two-way trusts for a total of 15, and so on. This method was used before Windows 2000, when transitive trusts weren't available.

Trusts are managed in Active Directory Domains and Trusts, which is available in the Administrative Tools menu. You can right-click the domain, select Properties, and then click the Trusts tab. Figure 1-8 shows the Trusts tab selected, and the properties for the South.Cengage.com trust.

This trust is a parent-child trust between Cengage.com (the parent domain) and South. Cengage.com (the child domain). It's listed as a two-way trust, but you can see that two trusts actually are created in the Trusts tab. One trust is incoming and one trust is outgoing. If you looked at Active Directory Domains and Trusts on a domain controller in South.Cengage.com, you'd also see two one-way trusts created from that domain.

Creating Trusts Between Forests

When creating trust relationships between domains in two separate forests, you can create an **external trust** or a **forest trust.**

- **An external trust is non-transitive.** It only creates a trust relationship between two domains. If trusts are required between all domains in one forest and all domains in another forest (and you can't create a forest trust), you need to create a separate external trust between each of the domains.
- **A forest trust is transitive.** When a two-way forest trust is created, all users in any domain in either forest can be granted access to any resources in any domain in either forest. If desired,

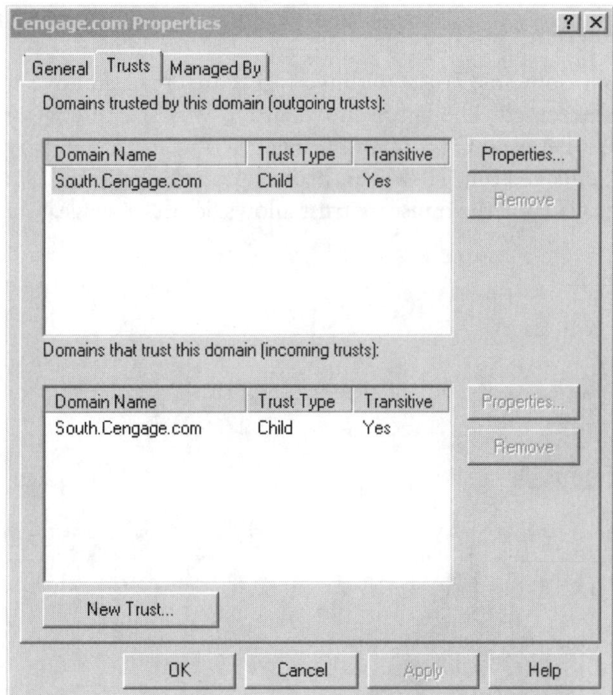

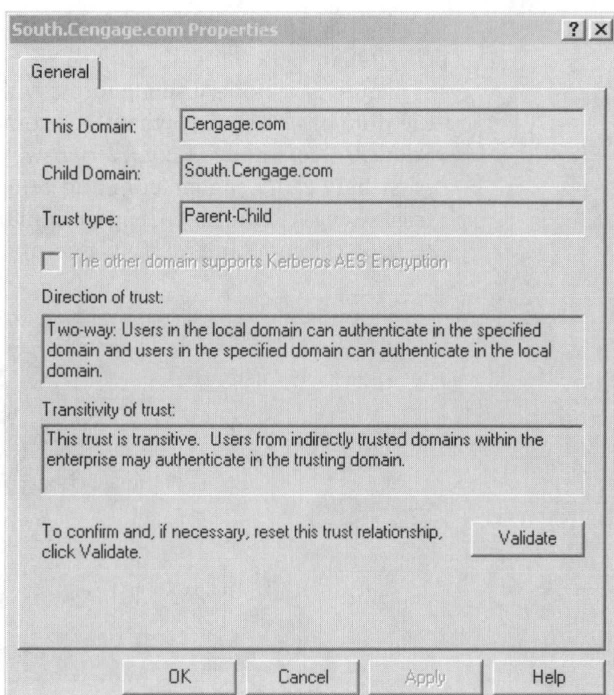

Figure 1-8 Viewing a trust in Active Directory Domains and Trusts

Courtesy Course Technology/Cengage Learning

you can restrict which users are granted access by using selective authentication instead of forest-wide authentication (which is explained in greater depth later in the next section).

Forest trusts became available in Windows Server 2003 and are important to understand. Before the availability of forest trusts, you were required to create separate external trusts from each domain in one forest with each domain in the other forest. However, a forest trust allows you to create one trust that is transitive between all domains.

A forest trust can only be created if the forest functional level has been raised to at least Windows Server 2003 in both domains.

Choosing the Authentication Method

When you create a forest trust between two forests, you will be prompted to choose either **forest-wide authentication** or **selective authentication**, as shown in Figure 1-9. If you need to change the authentication level between these two after the trust has been created, you can modify the properties of the trust.

- **Forest-wide authentication.** This option allows Windows to automatically authenticate any users in the other forest to access resources in the local forest. Users still need to be granted access to resources, but there is no restriction on which users can be granted access.
- **Selective authentication.** This option can be used to prevent users in the other forest from automatically being authenticated; if they aren't authenticated, they cannot access resources. You must grant the Allowed To Authenticate permission on individual servers or computers to specific users or groups. For example, if you want users in the G_PartnerProject group to be able to access resources on the FS1 server, you need to grant the Allowed To

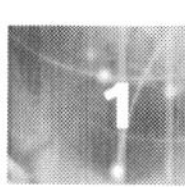

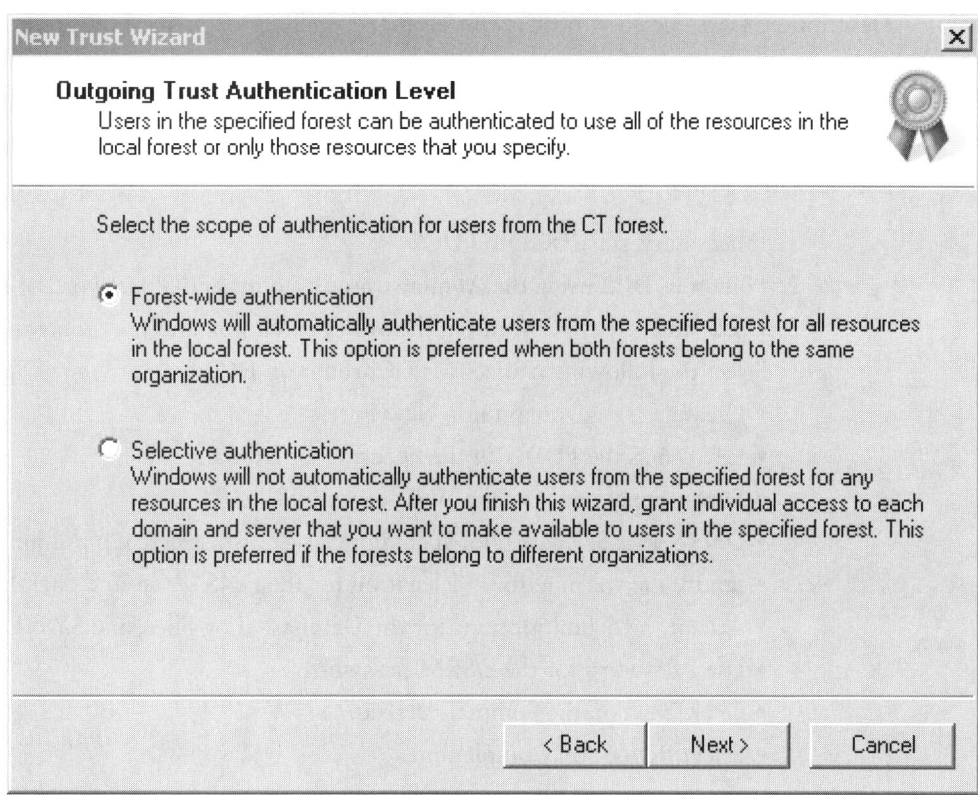

Figure 1-9 Choosing the trust authentication level

Courtesy Course Technology/Cengage Learning

Authenticate permission on FS1 to the G_PartnerProject group. Only members of this group will be allowed access, and they will only be allowed access to this server. If users are not granted the Allowed To Authenticate permission, they will not have access to the resource.

Forest-wide authentication is commonly selected when both forests are in the same organization. Selective authentication is commonly used when the two forests are in different organizations.

The difference between these two authentication methods is important. If you choose forest-wide authentication, any user can be authenticated, allowing access to be granted to any of these users. Forest-wide authentication should only be used if your organization implicitly trusts the other organization.

If the two forests are owned by different companies, you would almost always choose selective authentication. Activity 1-5 shows how a forest trust can be created with selective authentication. You'll also see how to grant the Allowed to Authenticate permission for selective authentication later in this chapter.

Activity 1-5: Creating a Forest Trust with Selective Authentication

Time Required: 30 minutes

Objective: Configure your virtual lab environment to mimic two forests. Create a forest trust between the two forests.

Description: DC1 currently hosts a forest named Cengage.com. You will promote DC2 as the first domain controller in a separate forest named CT.com. You will then use Active Directory Domains and Trusts to create a one-way forest trust with selective authentication. This will allow selected users in the CT forest to be granted access to resources in the Cengage forest. This lab assumes that you have completed the previous activities in the chapter.

1. If necessary, start **DC1** and **DC2.**
2. Log on to **DC2** using the **Administrator** account and a password of **P@ssw0rd.**
3. Click Start, type **DCpromo** in the **Start Search** box and press Enter.
4. Select the following choices for **DCpromo** on **DC2:**
   - Create a New Domain in a New Forest.
   - CT.com as the FQDN of the Forest Root Domain.
   - Forest Functional Level of Windows 2008.
   - DNS Server Selected (global catalog Server also selected, but dimmed).
   - Ignore the warning for a delegation for the DNS server and click Yes.
   - Accept the default options for the Database, Log Files, and SYSVOL locations.
   - Use P@ssw0rd for the DSRM password.
   - Click Next on the Summary screen.
   - Select Reboot on Completion.
5. After DC2 reboots, log on to **DC1** and start **Active Directory Domains and Trusts** from the **Administrative Tools** menu.
6. Right-click **Cengage.com** and select **Properties.** Select the **Trusts** tab.
7. Click **New Trust.** Review the information on the **Welcome** page and click **Next.**
8. Enter **CT** as the **Trust Name** (CT is the NetBIOS name of the forest you just created called CT.com). Click **Next.**
9. The **Trust Type** page will appear. Select **Forest trust** as shown in Figure 1-10. Click **Next.**

If Forest trust isn't shown as a choice, it indicates that one of the forests is not in the forest functional level of at least Windows Server 2003. Resolve this problem and try it again.

10. Select **Two-way** on the **Direction of Trust** page. Click **Next.**
11. Select **This Domain Only** to create the trust in your domain. Click **Next.**
12. On the **Outgoing Trust Authentication Level** page, select **Selective Authentication.**
13. Enter **P@ssw0rd** as the **Trust Password** twice. Click **Next.**
14. Review the information on the **Trust Selections** page and click **Next.** Review the information on the **Trust Creation Complete** page and click **Next.**
15. On the **Confirm Outgoing Trust** page, select **No, Do Not Confirm the Outgoing Trust** and click **Next.**
16. On the **Confirm Incoming Trust** page, select **No, Do Not Confirm the Incoming Trust** and click **Next.** Click **Finish.** Click **OK.**
17. Log on to **DC2** and repeat the preceding steps to create the same trust in that forest. Use the forest name **Cengage** as the Trust name instead of **CT.**

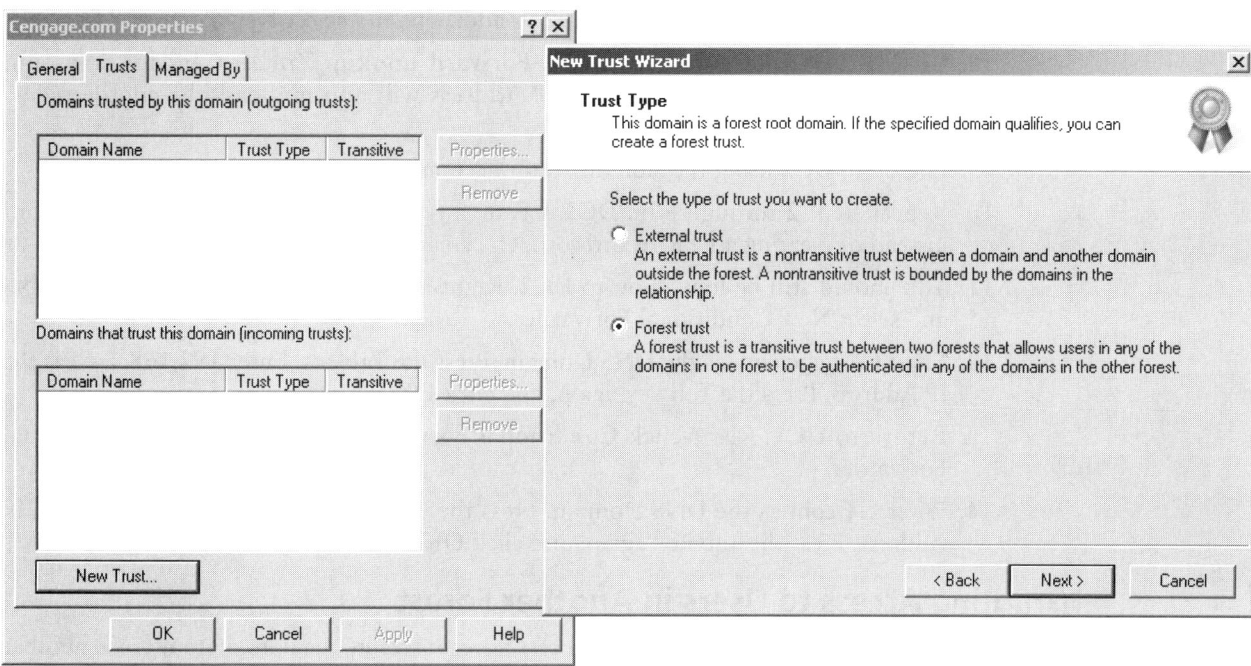

Figure 1-10 Creating a forest trust in Active Directory Domains and Trusts

Courtesy Course Technology/Cengage Learning

While this activity shows how to create the forest trusts, additional steps in DNS are required to ensure they work properly. A reverse lookup zone needs to be created on DC1 with a PTR record for DC1. A reverse lookup zone needs to be created on DC2 with a PTR record for DC2. A conditional forwarder needs to be created on DC1 for CT.com with an IP address of 192.168.1.20. A conditional forwarder needs to be created on DC2 for Cengage.com with an IP address of 192.168.1.10. DNS is covered in greater depth in Chapter 3.

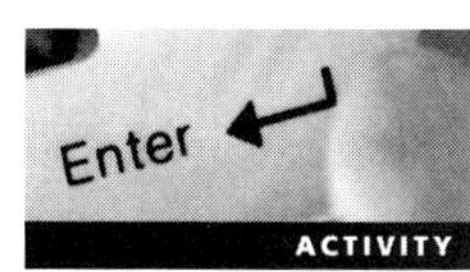

Activity 1-6: Configuring DNS to Support the Forest Trust

Time Required: 20 minutes
Objective: Configure DNS with a reverse lookup zone, pointer records, and a conditional forwarder.

Description: DNS is used when accessing resources in other domains that have a forest trust. While the trust can be created without the forest trust, you need to configure DNS to take adequate advantage of the trust.

1. Log on to **DC1** using the **Administrator** account and a password of **P@ssw0rd.**
2. Start **DNS** via the **Administrative Tools** menu.
3. Browse to the **Reverse Lookup Zones** node by expanding **DC1.** Right-click **Reverse Lookup Zones** and select **New Zone.**
4. Click **Next** to accept the default settings for all of the pages until you reach the **Reverse Lookup Zone Name** page.
5. Enter **192.168.1** as the **Network ID** on the **Reverse Lookup Zone Name** page.
6. Accept the default options for the remaining choices and click **Finish.**

7. Right-click the new zone (1.168.192.in-addr.arp) and select **New Pointer (PTR)**.
8. Click **Browse**. Double-click **DC1, Forward Lookup Zones, Cengage.com**, and select **DC1**. Click **OK**. The **Host IP Address** will automatically be configured as **192.168.1.10**. Click **OK** again.
9. Log on to **DC2** using the **Administrator** account and a password of **P@ssw0rd**.
10. Repeat steps 2 through 8 on **DC2**. Create a reverse lookup zone on that server, but instead of creating a PTR record for DC1, create a **PTR** record for **DC2**.
11. You should still be logged on to **DC2**. Right-click **Conditional Forwarders** in **DNS** and select **New Conditional Forwarder**.
12. Enter **Cengage.com** as the **DNS Domain**. Press the Tab key. Enter **192.168.1.10** as the **IP Address**. Press the Tab key again, and click **OK**.
13. Return to **DC1**. Right-click **Conditional Forwarders** and select **New Conditional Forwarder**.
14. Enter **CT.com** as the **DNS Domain**. Press the Tab key. Enter **192.168.1.20** as the **IP Address**. Press the Tab key again, and click **OK**.

Granting Access to Users in Another Forest

Once a forest trust is created, you can grant access to resources in one domain to users in another domain. As a simple example, you can grant access to a shared folder named Projects in the Cengage.com domain to users in the CT.com domain.

Figure 1-11 shows how a forest trust relationship is reflected when modifying permissions for a resource. A folder named Projects exists on DC1 (in the Cengage.com domain).

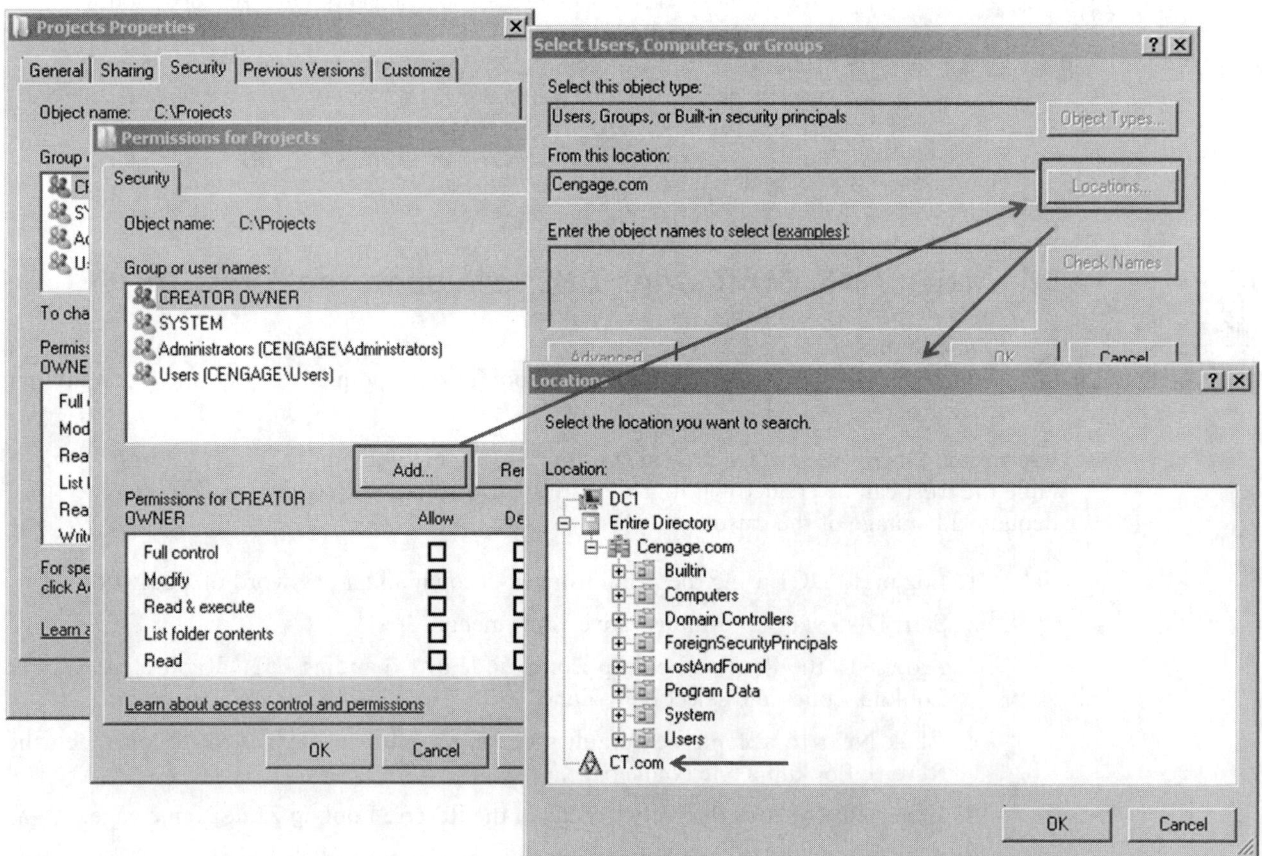

Figure 1-11 Selecting users from another forest

Courtesy Course Technology/Cengage Learning

You can take the following steps to reach this display:

- Right-click the folder and select Properties.
- Select Security to access the NTFS permissions.
- Click Edit and then click Add to add a user.
- Click Locations.
- Any location in the Cengage.com domain (the current selection) can be selected, or CT.com (at the bottom of the Locations dialog box) can be selected to access users in that domain.

Once the other domain is selected as the location, users in the other domain can be located and granted access to the resource. You can use this same procedure if forest-wide authentication or selective authentication is used. However, if selective authentication is used, you must take an additional step.

Implementing Selective Authentication

When selective authentication is implemented on a forest trust, you need to grant the Allowed to Authenticate permission on each server or computer where access is granted. This is done through Active Directory Users and Computers, as shown in the following activity.

Activity 1-7: Granting the Allowed to Authenticate Permission

Time Required: 15 minutes
Objective: Allow users in another forest to access resources on DC1 by enabling the Allowed to Authenticate permission.

Description: You have created a forest trust between your forest (Cengage.com) and another forest (CT.com) using selective authentication. You want to grant members of the Domain Admins group in the other forest access to DC1 in your forest. You must first enable the Allowed to Authenticate permission for DC1 from Active Directory Users and Computers.

1. Log on to **DC1** using the **Administrator** account and a password of **P@ssw0rd**.
2. Start **Active Directory Users and Computers** via the **Administrative Tools** menu.
3. Click the **View** menu and select **Advanced Features**. This selection enables you to view the **Security** tab when viewing the server properties page.
4. Double-click the **Domain Controllers** container. Right-click **DC1** and select **Properties**.
5. Select the **Security** tab. Click **Add**.
6. Select **Locations**. Select **CT.com** and click **OK**.
7. Click **Advanced**. Click **Find Now**.
8. When prompted, enter **CT\Administrator** as the user name and **P@ssw0rd** as the password. Click **OK**. You will see a listing of all user and computer accounts in the CT domain.
9. Double-click **Domain Admins** and click **OK**. With the **CT\Domain Admins** group selected, click the **Allowed to authenticate** check box in the Allowed column. The group will also be granted **Read** permissions. Your display will look similar to Figure 1-12.
10. Click **OK** to close the properties of **DC1**.
11. Close all open windows.

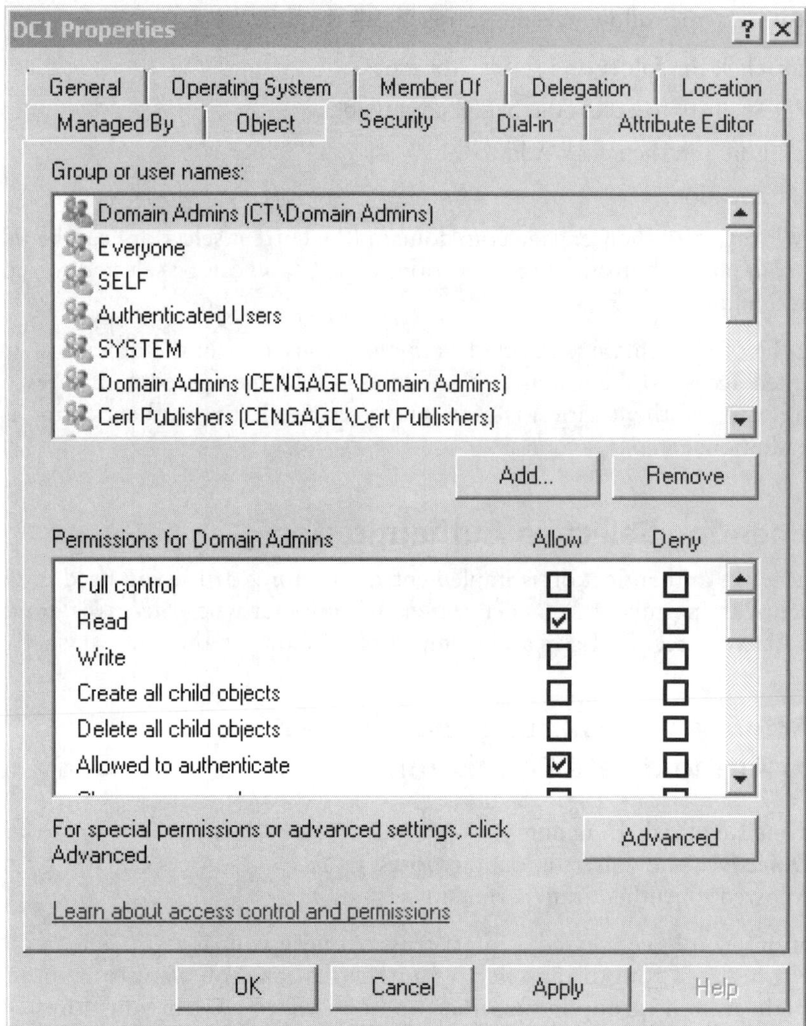

Figure 1-12 Granting Allowed to Authenticate permission to the Domain Admins group in a trusted domain

Courtesy Course Technology/Cengage Learning

Using ADPrep

When preparing your domain or forest, you will often need to run the Active Directory Preparation (ADPrep) tool. ADPrep is a command-line tool that is available in the Sources\ADPrep folder of the installation DVD. It must be run with elevated permissions by clicking Start, right-clicking Command Prompt, and selecting Run As Administrator.

ADPrep is needed if your forest started with servers other than Windows Server 2008. In other words, if the first domain controller in the forest was Windows Server 2000 or Windows Server 2003, you'll need to use ADPrep to prepare the forest to accommodate different Windows Server 2008 features before a Windows Server 2008 domain controller can be added.

ADPrep has three major switches that you should know about and understand:

- **/ForestPrep** to prepare the forest for Windows Server 2008 or Windows Server 2008 R2 domain controllers. ADPrep /ForestPrep is run on the schema master.
- **/DomainPrep** to prepare the domain for Windows Server 2008 or Windows Server 2008 R2 domain controllers (after the forest has been prepared). ADPrep /DomainPrep is run on the infrastructure master.
- **/RODCPrep** to prepare for read-only domain controllers. This only needs to be run once; it can be run on any domain controller in the forest.

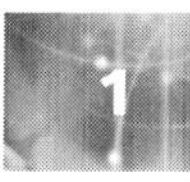

Operations master roles (such as schema master and infrastructure master) are covered in more depth in Chapter 2. These roles are hosted on individual domain controllers. Only one schema master exists in the entire forest. Only one infrastructure master exists in each domain.

Preparing the Forest

The ADPrep /ForestPrep command modifies the schema of the forest. It must be run on the server that is currently hosting the schema operations master role. Only one domain controller in the forest holds this role; normally, it's the first server promoted to a domain controller in the forest.

You can easily determine what servers hold all the roles by opening a command prompt and entering the following command:
netdom query fsmo

If the first domain controller in your forest was created on a Windows Server 2008 or Windows Server 2008 R2 server, you don't need to run ADPrep /ForestPrep. The schema was created using the extensions when the forest was created. If you're not sure, you can try to run it. If it's not needed, you will be informed by the system and no modifications will be made.

You need to be a member of each of the following groups to run the ADPrep /ForestPrep command:

- Enterprise Admins group
- Schema Admins Group

To run the ADPrep /ForestPrep command, insert the installation DVD in your system's DVD reader. Open a command prompt with administrative permissions and enter the following command.

```
D:\Sources\ADPrep\ADPrep /ForestPrep
```

This command assumes that your DVD reader has been assigned the letter D. If it is assigned a different letter, substitute that letter in the command.

The case you use for commands at the command prompt rarely matters, and doesn't matter with the ADPrep command. For example, you can type "ADPrep," "ADprep," or "adprep." The entire command could be entered as all lowercase, all uppercase, or a mixture of both.

ADPrep will perform updates to the schema that take some time, but it doesn't require any other user interaction.

Once ADPrep has finished, you need to give replication some time to ensure that the changes are replicated to all domain controllers in each domain in your forest before running the ADPrep /DomainPrep command. For a well-connected site, this will be done in minutes. If your enterprise includes sites connected via WAN links, the time needed for replication depends on your physical structure and how the site links are configured.

Preparing a Domain

After ADPrep /ForestPrep has been run and you are sure it has replicated to each domain controller in your forest, you can begin preparing the domains. If you try to run the ADPrep /DomainPrep command before ADPrep /ForestPrep, you will receive an error.

The ADPrep /DomainPrep command should be run on the server that holds the infrastructure operations master role. Every domain will have one domain controller that hosts this role. You must be a member of the Domain Admins group to run the command, and the command must be run from a command prompt with administrative permissions. After the command is run, you will be able to promote Windows Server 2008 and Windows Server 2008 R2 servers to domain controllers.

You can also run ADPrep /DomainPrep /GPPrep. This is similar to the /DomainPrep switch, but it also provides updates to enhance the Resultant Set of Policy (RSOP) tool when used in Planning Mode.

Preparing for RODCs

If you want to add RODCs to your environment, you must also run the ADPrep /RODCPrep command. You need to run this command to prepare for RODCs even if the first domain controller in your forest was created on a Windows Server 2008 or Windows Server 2008 R2 server.

The ADPrep /RODCPrep command can be run on any domain controller in the forest, and it only needs to be run once. You must be a member of the Enterprise Admins group to run this command.

Migration Strategies

Active Directory Domain Services (AD DS) domains and forests can often be redesigned for a variety of reasons: to accommodate a restructure of the organization, to reflect changes in the physical layout of the organization, or to reduce the complexity of the organization by reducing the number of domains or forests.

When performing any type of migration or upgrade to an existing forest, the time spent planning it will help prevent problems during the upgrade. Several factors can affect the upgrade or migration:

- **Time constraints**. An abbreviated schedule can affect the amount of time for planning and the ability to do a logical phased upgrade.
- **Resource availability**. Resources include hardware resources and manpower resources. Without adequate resources, planning and testing often suffer.
- **Funding**. Funding goes hand in hand with resource availability. A migration or upgrade costs money, including funds for new operating systems, new hardware, and the reallocation of manpower. If a budget isn't approved for a migration project, it may fail before it starts.
- **Application compatibility**. The upgrade of the operating system can affect the usability of different applications. While most server applications will work better on Windows Server 2008 than on Windows Server 2003, line of business applications may need to be patched or upgraded due to differences in .NET versions used in the different operating systems.

Active Directory Migration Tool (ADMT)

The **Active Directory Migration Tool** (ADMT) can be used to migrate objects from one domain to another within the same forest or between different forests. Objects that are commonly migrated include users, computers, and groups.

As of this writing, the current version of ADMT is version 3.1. You must use at least ADMT v3.1 to migrate resources to a Windows Server 2008 forest that is in a forest functional level of Windows Server 2008 or greater. You can obtain a free copy of ADMT from Microsoft's download site (*www.microsoft.com/downloads*) by searching for "ADMT."

When using ADMT to migrate accounts, you refer to the domain or forest from which accounts are migrating as the source, and refer to the domain or forest to which the accounts are migrating as the destination.

Microsoft has published an extensive migration guide titled *ADMT v3.1 Guide: Migrating and Restructuring Active Directory Domains*. You can download this guide for free by searching on "ADMT Migration Guide."

ADMT Versions Needed for Different Functional Levels

Target domains must be operating in one of the following domain functional levels when using ADMT v3.1:

- Windows Server 2000 Native
- Windows Server 2003
- Windows Server 2008

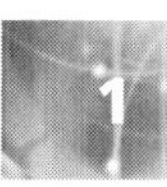

What's missing is the ability to migrate objects from a domain in a domain functional level of Windows 2000 mixed. This domain functional level supports running NT 4.0 domain controllers. You're probably not using NT 4.0 domain controllers today, but if you are, you must remove or upgrade them first and then raise the domain functional level. Alternatively, you can use ADMT v3.0 to migrate objects from NT 4.0 domains.

Windows Server 2008 domain controllers can't operate in the same domain as Windows NT 4.0 domain controllers.

When using ADMT v3.0, the target forest must be operating in a forest functional level of Windows Server 2003 or less. If it is running in a forest functional level of Windows Server 2008, ADMT v3.0 will not be able to migrate accounts from the target forest. Instead, you need to use ADMT v3.1.

Interforest and Intraforest Migration

- Migration of objects is handled a little differently depending on whether the objects are being migrated between domains in separate forests or migrated between domains in the same forest. These two types of migrations are referred to as interforest and intraforest migrations.
- **Interforest migration.** Objects are migrated between domains in separate forests.
- **Intraforest migration.** Objects are migrated between domains in the same forest.

Table 1-4 shows some of the important differences between interforest and intraforest migrations.

Table 1-4 Comparison of Interforest and Intraforest Migrations

Migration Consideration	Interforest	Intraforest
Object preservation	Objects are cloned or copied	Objects are deleted from the source
SID history	Optional	Required
Password retention	Optional	Always retained

Understanding and Using SID History

A **security identifier (SID)** is used to uniquely identify an object in a domain (and in a forest). When an object is created, the SID is created. This SID is used to grant access to any objects in the domain.

Account SIDs are created by combining unique relative identifiers (RIDs) used within the domain with a SID that uniquely identifies the domain. All SIDS within the domain will have the same domain SID component, and when combined with unique RIDs, each object will have a unique SID.

Access to any resource within the domain is controlled by a Discretionary Access Control List (DACL). Figure 1-13 shows the NTFS DACL for a folder named Study Notes. Each user is uniquely identified by a SID. However, when the screen is displayed, the system looks up the SID and displays the common name.

In the figure, Sally has been added and granted full control for the resource. Now imagine that Sally's account is migrated to another domain in the forest. When the account is migrated, a new SID is created and assigned for the new account and the original account is deleted.

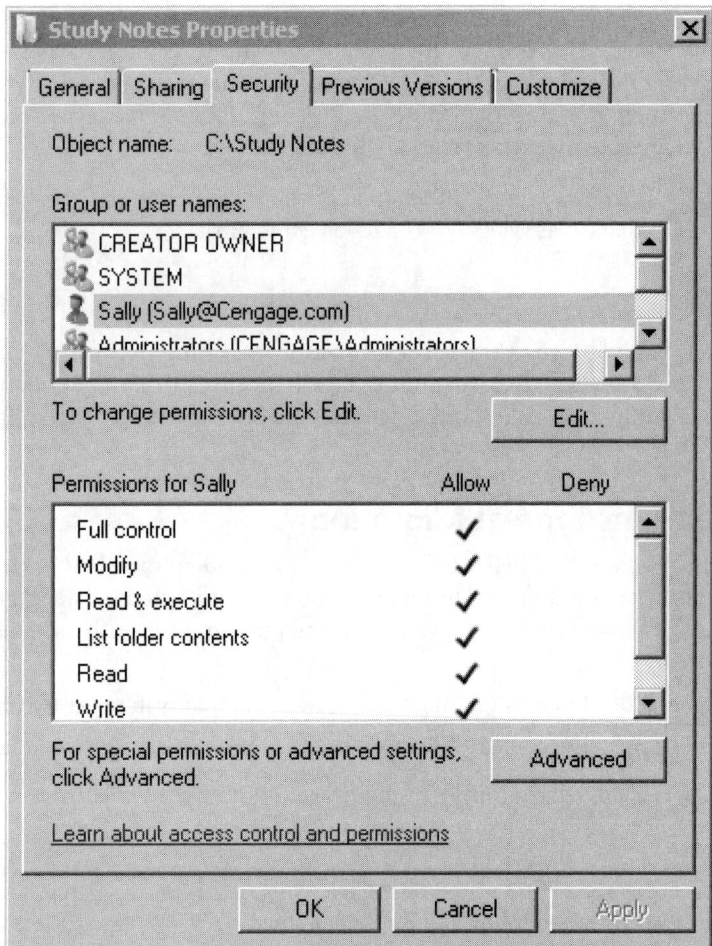

Figure 1-13 Viewing SIDs in a DACL

Courtesy Course Technology/Cengage Learning

Do you see the problem? Unless something is done, Sally would lose access to the resource. Her original SID has access, but her new account has a new SID. The solution is to implement **SID history**.

When SID history is implemented, you can import the original SID when importing the account. The new account still needs a new SID assigned by the new domain, but the original SID can be retained and used to access resources. Users will thus retain access to data and resources they had in the original domain.

ADMT supports the retention of SID history. Additionally, an account can support multiple SIDs included in SID history. For example, an employee who has worked for a company for the past 10 years and gone through several migrations can retain multiple SIDs in the SID history.

However, even when SID history is migrated, it can be prevented from being used if SID filtering is enabled.

Using SID Filtering

While SID history is a useful feature in a fully trusted environment, it can present a security risk if you are migrating accounts between forests that aren't completely trusted.

Here's the risk. If an attacker obtains SID history data, he can assign these SIDs to the SID history attributed to accounts he creates in his own domain. These new accounts will now have access to resources based on the SIDs listed in SID history.

SID filtering (also referred to as SID filter quarantining) prevents this risk by blocking the use of any SIDs that did not originate in the same domain. In other words, SID filtering prevents the use of SID history. SID filtering is automatically enabled when a forest trust is created with selective authentication, and when an external trust is created between two domains in different

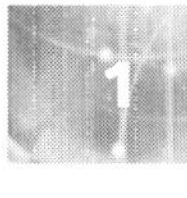

forests. If you want users or groups to be able to access a resource using SID history, you must disable SID filtering.

If users can't access resources in their original domain after their accounts have been migrated, check to see if the accounts include SID history. If SID history is included, verify that SID filtering is disabled.

You can disable SID filtering using the Netdom command on the trusting domain. For example, consider Figure 1-14, which depicts a one-way trust between Cengage.com and CT.com. Cengage.com is the trusting domain, so Netdom should be executed on a domain controller in the Cengage.com domain.

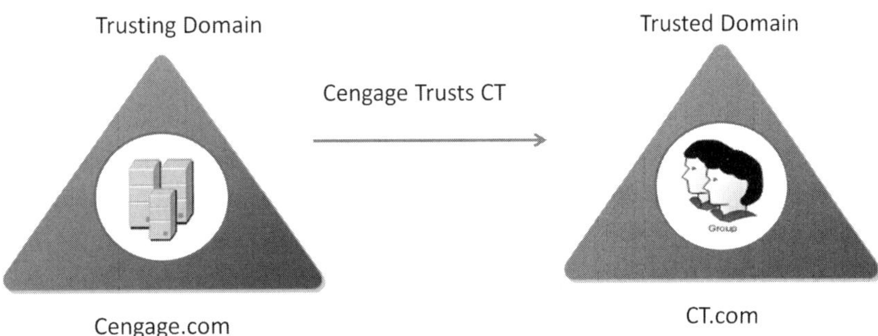

Figure 1-14 One-way trust between Cengage and CT

Courtesy Course Technology/Cengage Learning

Netdom needs to be executed from the command prompt with elevated permissions. Additionally, the command must be run using an account that is a member of either the Domain Admins or Enterprise Admins group. The format of the Netdom command is:

```
Netdom trust <TrustingDomainName> /domain:<TrustedDomainName>
/quarantine:No

/userD:<DomainAdministratorAcct> /passwordD:<DomainAdminPwd>
```

If you are logged on with an administrator account in either the Domain Admins or Enterprise Admins group and have started the command prompt using Run As Administrator, you can omit the administrator credentials. The following command shows how SID filtering is disabled for the trust shown in Figure 1-14.

```
Netdom trust cengage /domain ct /quarantine: No
```

If SID filtering was already disabled, the command will output the following text:

"SID filtering is not enabled for this trust."

You can toggle between disabled and enabled states by changing the /quarantine switch to Yes or No.

SID filtering should only be disabled after careful consideration. When SID filtering is disabled, it removes the security boundary between the forests and eliminates any isolation that previously existed. It should only be disabled if the administrators of the source domain fully trust the administrators of the target domain.

Activity 1-8: Verifying SID Filtering Status

Time Required: 15 minutes

Objective: Check to see if SID Filtering is on or off.

Description: You are migrating user accounts and including SID history. You want to verify that SID history can be used when users try to access resources in the source domain. This activity assumes that a forest trust has been created between two forests in previous activities.

1. Log on to DC1 using the **Administrator** account and a password of **P@ssw0rd**.
2. Open a command prompt with administrative permissions by clicking **Start**, right-clicking **Command Prompt**, and selecting **Run As Administrator**.
3. Enter the following command:

   ```
   netdom trust cengage /domain ct /quarantine: no
   ```

   The output should indicate that SID filtering is not enabled because the forest trust is set to forest-wide authentication.
4. Enter the following command to enable SID filtering:

   ```
   netdom trust cengage /domain ct /quarantine: yes
   ```
5. Enter the following command to disable SID filtering:

   ```
   netdom trust cengage /domain ct /quarantine: no
   ```

   Your display should look like Figure 1-15.

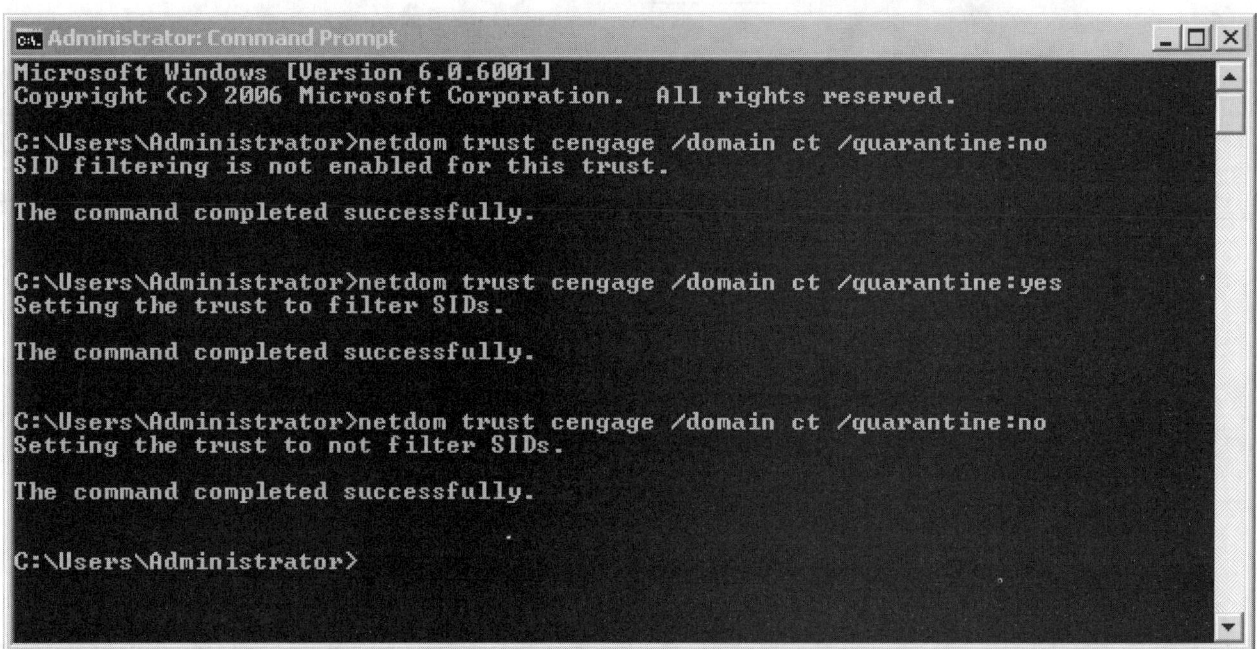

Figure 1-15 Disabling SID filtering

Courtesy Course Technology/Cengage Learning

6. Close the command prompt.

Using Alternative UPN Suffixes

A User Principal Name (UPN) allows a user to log on with an account that looks like an e-mail address. For example, a user named Sally in the CT.com domain would have a default UPN of Sally@CT.com.

It's also possible to create **alternative UPN suffixes** and assign these to users in the domain. For example, users in the CT.com domain may have been using a UPN of username@CT.com to log on. When they are migrated into another domain such as Cengage.com, the CT.com suffix won't be available by default, which may cause some confusion and problems for these users.

To avoid this confusion, you can add an alternative UPN suffix of CT.com in the Cengage.com domain. Alternative suffixes are added using Active Directory Domains and Trusts.

Activity 1-9: Creating an Alternative UPN Suffix

Time Required: 10 minutes
Objective: Create an alternative UPN suffix and assign it to a new user.

Description: You are planning to migrate accounts from the CT.com domain. These users use UPNs to log on, and you want to create a solution that allows them to use the same UPNs. This activity requires a single domain controller in a domain.

1. Log on to **DC1** using the **Administrator** account and a password of **P@ssw0rd.**
2. Start **Active Directory Domains and Trusts** via the **Administrative Tools** menu.
3. Right-click **Active Directory Domains and Trusts** and select **Properties.** Note that you need to right-click the top line in the console, not the domain name.
4. Enter **CT.com** as the name of the **Alternative UPN Suffix** and click **Add.** Your display will look similar to Figure 1-16. Click **OK.**

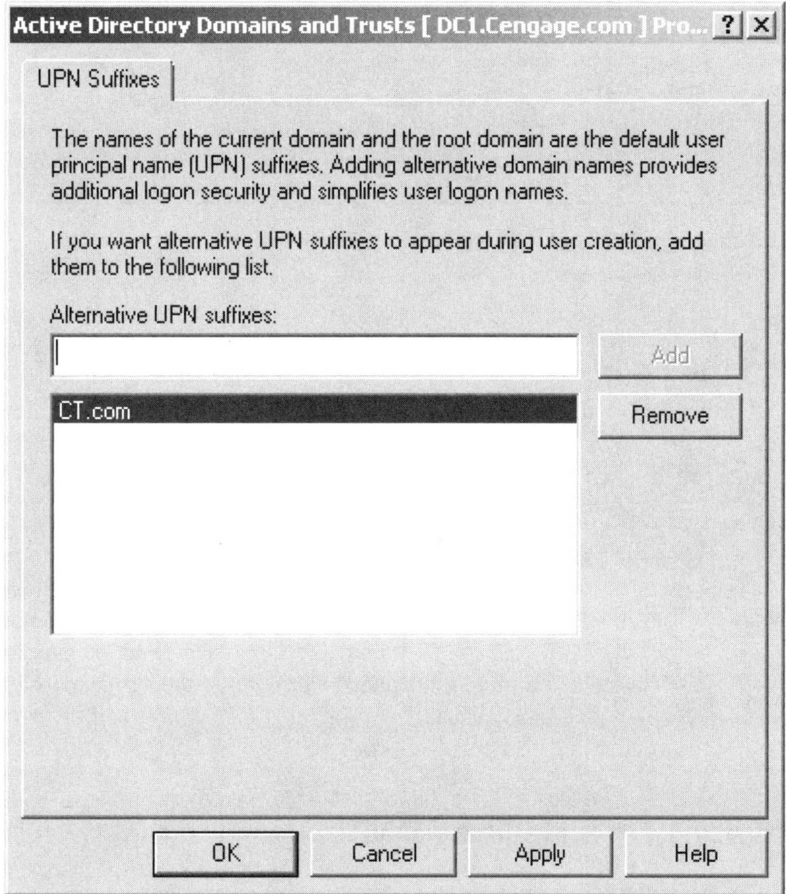

Figure 1-16 Creating an alternative UPN suffix
Courtesy Course Technology/Cengage Learning

5. Start **Active Users and Computers** from the **Administrative Tools** menu.
6. Right-click the **Users** container and select **New User.**
7. Enter **Sally** as the user's **First name,** and **Sally** as the **User logon name.** Select **@CT.com** from the drop-down box, as shown in Figure 1-17. Click **Next.**
8. Type **P@ssw0rd** in the **Password** and **Confirm Password** boxes. Click **Next.** Click **Finish.**
9. Close all open windows.

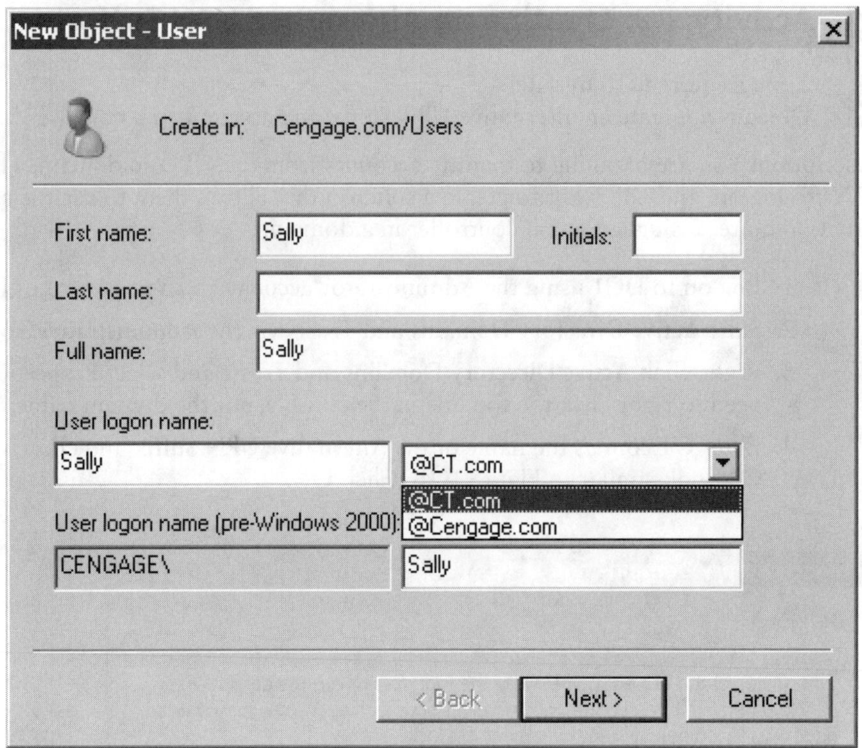

Figure 1-17 Assigning an alternative UPN suffix to a user account

Courtesy Course Technology/Cengage Learning

Installing the ADMT

ADMT v3.1 should be installed and run on a Windows Server 2008 domain controller in the target domain. If any previous versions of ADMT were installed on this domain controller, they should be uninstalled first.

The virtual machines running Windows Server 2008 do not have Internet access and should not be reconfigured to have Internet access. The ADMTsetup31.exe file should be downloaded from Microsoft's download site (*www.microsoft.com/downloads*) using the host system. The ADMT file can then be copied from Windows Explorer in the host system and pasted to Windows Explorer in the virtual machine, as long as the Virtual Machine Additions have been added as mentioned in Activity 1-1, step 14.

Activity 1-10: Installing ADMT

Time Required: 10 minutes

Objective: Install the Active Directory Migration Tool (ADMT).

Description: You are planning to use the ADMT to migrate objects from one forest to another. You first need to install the ADMT on a domain controller in the target domain.

1. Log on to **DC1** using the **Administrator** account and a password of **P@ssw0rd.**
2. Open **Windows Explorer** and browse to the location of the **ADMTsetup31.exe** installation file. Double-click this file to start the installation. Click **Run** when prompted.
3. Click **Next** on the **Welcome** screen. Review the **License Agreement,** select **I Agree,** and click **Next.**

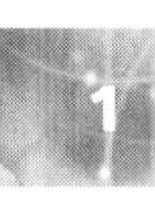

4. Accept the default setting for the **Customer Experience Improvement Program**, and click **Next.**
5. On the **Database Selection** page, use the default setting of **Use Local SQL Server 2005 Express Edition** and click **Next.**
6. Select **No, Do Not Import Data From an Existing Database (Default)** and click **Next.**
7. When the installation is complete, click **Finish.**

Enabling SID History for ADMT

As of this writing, you must take several extra steps to allow SID history to work between different forests. The ADMT v3.1 documentation indicates that ADMT will take care of these steps automatically when ADMT is run the first time, but the problem persists with an interforest migration. Perhaps v3.2 will resolve the problem.

This section is included only for people who need to perform this task at their jobs. Because the ADMT documentation does not describe the actual operation, you should not expect to see a test question on the concepts in this section. When preparing for the exam, it's more important to know what SID history is, know that it can be migrated, and know that it can be managed with SID filtering.

The extra steps are:

- Create a domain local group in the source domain named *netBiOSDomainName$$$*. For example, in CT.com, you'd create a group named CT$$$ because the NetBIOS name of CT.com is CT.
- Modify the registry of the PDC emulator on the source domain. Create a DWord value of TcpipClientSupport (or modify it if it already exists) in the HKEY_LOCAL_MACHINE\System\CurrentControlSet\Control\LSA subkey. Set the value to 1.
- Enable Success and Failure for Account Management in the Default Domain Controller Policy of both the source and target domains.
- Install and configure the Password Export Server (PES) service tool.

Running ADMT

After ADMT v3.1 is installed, you can start it and begin the migration process. You will need to have a trust relationship established between the target and forest domains. Any of the following trusts can be used:

- A trust between two domains in the same forest (which can be a direct parent-child trust or a transitive trust)
- An external trust between two domains in different forests
- A forest trust between two separate forests

The following activity shows that you can use ADMT to perform a test migration of a group account.

Activity 1-11: Running a Test Migration with ADMT

Time Required: 30 minutes
Objective: Run the Active Directory Migration Tool (ADMT).

Description: You are planning to use the ADMT to migrate objects from the CT forest to the Cengage forest. Before doing the migration, you want to run it on a test object. The following activity assumes that previous activities have been completed, creating two separate forests named Cengage.com (on DC1) and CT.com (on DC2), and that a forest trust has been established between the two forests.

1. Ensure that both DC1 and DC2 are started. Log on to **DC2** using the **Administrator** account and a password of **P@ssw0rd.**
2. Start **Active Directory Users and Computers** and expand the **CT.com** domain. Right-click the **Users** container and select **New Group**. Name the group **G_TestMig** and accept the default setting of **Global** as the **Group Scope** and **Security** as the **Group Type.** Click **OK.** You will migrate this group to the target domain.
3. Log on to **DC1** using the **Administrator** account and a password of **P@ssw0rd.**
4. Start **ADMT** by clicking **Start, Administrative Tools,** and **Active Directory Migration Tool.**
5. Right-click **Active Directory Migration Tool** and select **Group Account Migration Wizard,** as shown in Figure 1-18.

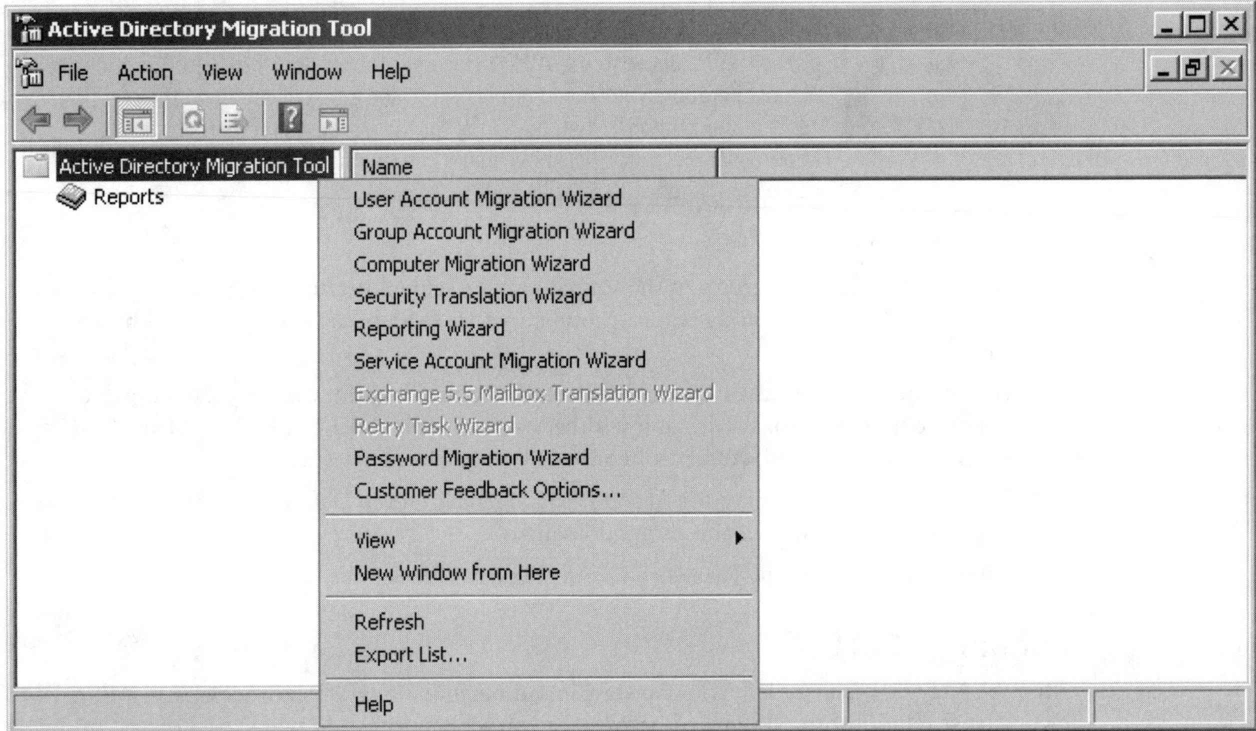

Figure 1-18 Selecting Group Account Migration
Courtesy Course Technology/Cengage Learning

6. Review the information on the **Welcome** page and click **Next.**
7. On the **Domain Selection** page, type **CT.com** as the **Source Domain** and select **\\DC2.CT.com** as the **Source Domain controller.** Type **Cengage.com** as the **Target Domain** and select **\\DC1.Cengage.com** as the **Target Domain controller.** Your display will look similar to Figure 1-19. Click **Next.**
8. On the **Group Selection Option** page, accept the default setting of **Select Groups from Domain** and click **Next.**
9. Click **Add** on the **Group Selection** page. Click **Advanced** and click **Find Now** to list all of the groups in the target domain. Select the **G_TestMig** group created earlier. Click **OK** twice to return to the **Group Selection** page. Click **Next.**
10. On the **Organizational Unit Selection** page, click **Browse.** Notice that you can browse to any OU or container in the target domain. Select the **Users** container and click **OK.** Click **Next.**
11. Accept the default settings on the **Group Options** page and click **Next.**

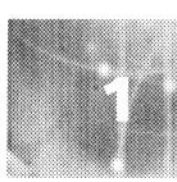

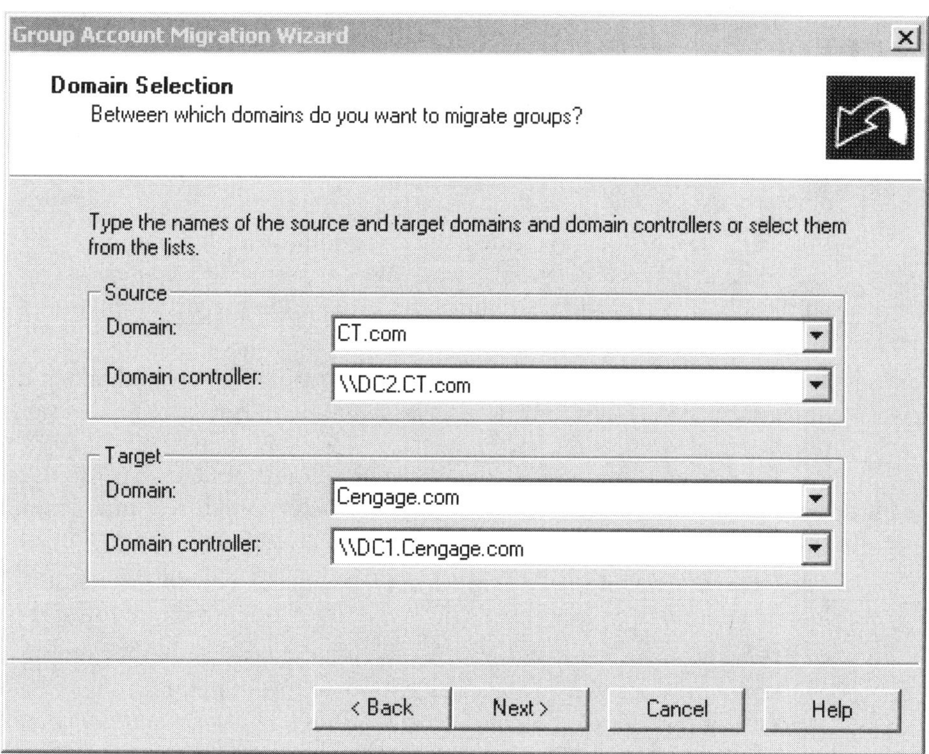

Figure 1-19 Completing the source and target domain selections

Courtesy Course Technology/Cengage Learning

12. Review the information on the **Object Property Exclusion** page and click **Next.**
13. Review the information on the **Conflict Management** page and click **Next.**
14. Review the information on the **Completion** page and click **Finish.** The migration of the group will finish. Your display should look similar to Figure 1-20. Click **Close** on the **Migration Progress** page.

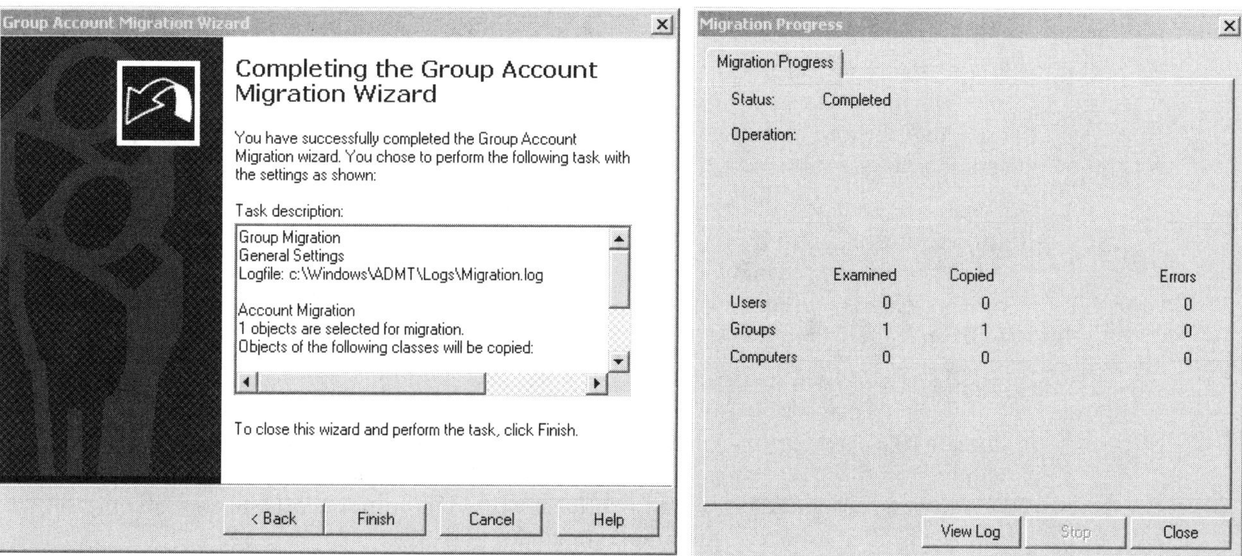

Figure 1-20 Successfully migrating a group

Courtesy Course Technology/Cengage Learning

15. Start **Active Users and Computers** on **DC1.** Browse to the **Users** container. You will see the **G_TestMig** group that you migrated.

Chapter Summary

- The logical structure of Active Directory includes domains, trees, and forests. All domains in a forest share a common schema and a common global catalog. A forest is a security boundary and provides isolation. A domain is an administrative boundary where domain objects are replicated.
- Virtual PC can be used to create a test environment for learning and testing design plans and strategies. This type of test environment is useful for students and for administrators on the job. Changes and procedures can be tested in the virtual environment without affecting the production environment.
- The domain functional level dictates what features are available in a domain. The domain functional level must be at least Windows Server 2003 to use selective authentication in a forest trust, and it must be at least Windows Server 2008 to create fine-grained password policies or fine-grained account policies. The domain functional level must be raised in all domains in the forest before the forest functional level can be raised.
- The forest functional level dictates what features are available in a forest. The forest functional level must be at least Windows Server 2003 to create forest trusts and to use RODCs.
- Most organizations will create a single-domain forest, but multiple domains and/or forests are sometimes required. Primary considerations include the autonomy and isolation desired. Separate domains in a single forest and separate OUs can provide autonomy, but not isolation. A separate domain provides service and data autonomy; an OU provides data autonomy only.
- A separate forest provides isolation. Common reasons to create a separate forest are to provide isolation for legal or business requirements, to create a separate schema, or to control replication of the global catalog.
- When entities in different forests need to share resources, trusts can be created. An external trust provides a domain-to-domain trust relationship, and a forest trust allows all domains in one forest to trust all domains in the other forest. Trusts can be one-way or two-way. When a one-way trust is drawn, it points to the users that are being trusted and is expressed as "Domain A trusts Domain B" (when users are located in Domain B).
- Forest trust authentication can be either forest-wide or selective. Selective authentication is used when users in the trusted domain are not all trusted. When selective authentication is used, the Allowed to Authenticate permission must be granted to users or groups on a per-server basis.
- The Active Directory Preparation (ADPrep) tool is used from the command line to prepare a forest or domain to host Windows Server 2008 domain controllers. ADPrep /ForestPrep is run first on the schema master, and then ADPrep /DomainPrep is run on the infrastructure master in the domain. If read-only domain controllers (RODCs) need to be added, ADPrep /RODCPrep is run on any domain controller in the forest.
- ADMT v3.1 is used to assist with migrations into Windows Server 2008 forests. It is a free download available from Microsoft, and can be used to migrate objects from a source domain to a target domain. The SIDs used in the source domain can also be migrated, and will be stored as SID history in the accounts in the target domain. If SID filtering is enabled on the trust, accounts will not authenticate with SIDs stored in SID history. SID filtering can be disabled using the Netdom command.

Key Terms

Active Directory domain An administrative boundary that contains users, computers, and other objects. At least one or more domains are contained in a forest. The first domain in the forest is referred to as the root domain.

Active Directory forest A group of one or more domains organized in one or more trees. All domains in a forest share a common schema and a common global catalog.

Active Directory Migration Tool (ADMT) A free download available from Microsoft that can be used to migrate objects from a source domain to a target domain. ADMT v3.1 should be used for migrations involving Windows Server 2008.

Active Directory tree A group of one or more domains with a common namespace. A forest can have one or more trees.

ADPrep The Active Directory Preparation tool, used to prepare a forest and domains for Windows Server 2008 servers. It is run with the /ForestPrep switch first, and then with the /DomainPrep switch. It can also be used with the /RODCPrep switch to allow the introduction of read-only domain controllers (RODCs).

Alternative UPN suffix A separate UPN suffix can be created using Active Directory Domains and Trusts. This alternative UPN suffix can then be used to assign different UPNs for users in the domain.

Autonomy Provides independent but not exclusive control of a resource. A separate domain in a forest can provide service and data autonomy. A separate OU within a domain can provide data autonomy.

Domain functional level The level of the domain that dictates what features are available within the domain. The domain functional level can be raised to a higher level after all domain controllers have been updated to that level. For example, if the domain functional level is Windows Server 2003, it can be raised to Windows Server 2008 after all domain controllers have been upgraded to Windows Server 2008.

External trust A non-transitive trust created with a domain in a separate forest. The trust can be one-way or two-way, but an external trust is not transitive.

Forest functional level The level of the forest that dictates what features are available in the forest. The forest functional level can be raised to a higher level after all domains in the forest have been raised. For example, if the forest functional level is Windows Server 2003, it can be raised to Windows Server 2008 after all domains in the forest have been raised to Windows Server 2008.

Forest trust A transitive trust created between two forests. Forest trusts are supported in Windows Server 2003 forest functional level.

Forest-wide authentication Used in a forest trust when the other forest is fully trusted. Forest-wide authentication allows all users in each forest to be granted access to any resources in the trusting forest.

Global catalog A database of all objects in the entire forest, but with only a subset of the attributes of those objects. The global catalog is hosted on domain controllers called global catalog servers, and the global catalog is replicated to all global catalog servers in the forest.

Group Policy An administrative management tool that allows administrators to configure a setting once in a Group Policy object (GPO) and apply the policy to all users in a domain, in an organizational unit, or in a site. GPOs can be linked to a site, domain, or OU using the Group Policy Management Console (GPMC).

Isolation Provides independent and exclusive control of a resource. A separate forest is needed to provide isolation.

Organizational Unit (OU) A special container within Active Directory that allows Active Directory objects (such as users, computers, and groups) to be organized. Group Policy objects can be linked to an OU and administrative control can be delegated to an OU.

Schema A definition of objects and attributes in a forest. Each forest has only one schema and objects created in the forest must be defined by the schema. The schema can be modified (commonly called extending the schema) using a tool such as ADPrep.

Selective authentication Used in a forest trust when the other forest is not fully trusted. Selective authentication requires that users or groups be granted the Allowed to Authenticate permission on each server they will access.

Security Identifier (SID) A security identifier used to uniquely identify objects in a domain and a forest.

SID filtering When enabled on a trust, prevents SID history from being used when a user accesses a resource. SID filtering is enabled by default when selective authentication is used and disabled by default when forest-wide authentication is used. SID filtering can be enabled and disabled with Netdom.

SID history An attribute in a user account that holds a listing of one or more SIDs assigned to a user. SID history allows users to access resources in the source domain without redoing the permissions in the source domain.

Site A group of well-connected hosts or subnets. Sites are typically connected to each other through slower wide area network (WAN) links.

Transitive trust A trust relationship that transits throughout a forest. If Domain A trusts Domain B, and Domain B trusts Domain C, then the transitive trust allows Domain A to trust Domain C.

Trust A relationship between two domains (or two forests) that allows users in one domain to access resources in the other domain. A trust can be one-way or two-way. A one-way trust allows users in a trusted domain to access resources in a trusting domain. Trusts are automatically created as transitive trusts within a forest, but can also be created between domains outside of the forest, or even other forests.

Review Questions

1. Your network currently consists of a single-domain forest. Domain controllers and member servers are running both Windows Server 2003 and Windows Server 2008. You want to implement a second lockout policy for personnel working in the R&D department. What should you do? (Choose all that apply.)
   a. Upgrade all domain controllers to Windows Server 2008.
   b. Raise the domain functional level to Windows Server 2008.
   c. Raise the forest functional level to Windows Server 2008.
   d. Upgrade all member servers to Windows Server 2008.
2. Your network is currently configured as a three-domain forest. The root domain is named Cengage.com and includes the majority of the users. The two child domains are named R&D and Scientists; both were created to support more stringent password policies for specific users in the organization. You want to restructure the forest to reduce the number of domains. What should you do?
   a. Upgrade the root domain to Windows Server 2008 and migrate all accounts to this domain. Delete the two child domains.
   b. Upgrade either of the child domains to Windows Server 2008. Migrate all accounts to this domain, leaving only two domains.
   c. Retain the three domains and create fine-grained password polices for each domain.
   d. Create a new forest and move the two child domains to the new forest. Create a forest trust between the forests.

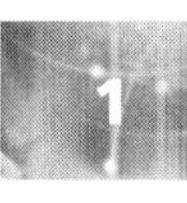

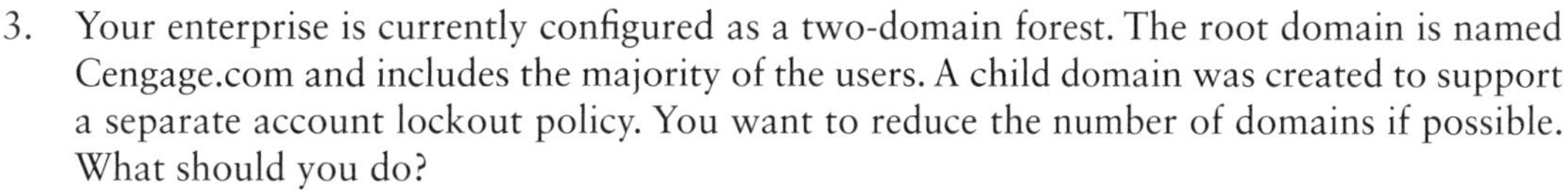

3. Your enterprise is currently configured as a two-domain forest. The root domain is named Cengage.com and includes the majority of the users. A child domain was created to support a separate account lockout policy. You want to reduce the number of domains if possible. What should you do?
    a. Create a new forest and move the two domains to the new forest.
    b. Upgrade the child domain to Windows Server 2008. Migrate all accounts to this domain and delete the root domain.
    c. Retain the two domains and create fine-grained account lockout polices for each domain.
    d. Upgrade the root domain to Windows Server 2008 and migrate all accounts to this domain. Delete the child domain.
4. You administer an enterprise that uses the Windows Server 2008 forest functional level. A junior administrator is trying to promote a Windows Server 2003 member server to a domain controller, but it fails. Why would this fail?
    a. A Windows Server 2003 member server cannot be promoted to a domain controller.
    b. A Windows Server 2003 server cannot be promoted to a domain controller if the forest functional level is set to Windows Server 2008.
    c. A Windows Server 2003 server cannot be promoted to a domain controller unless the domain functional level is set to Windows Server 2008.
    d. The forest functional level must be demoted to Windows Server 2003 first.
5. You are planning to deploy an RODC to a remote office. The forest functional level is Windows Server 2003 and the domain functional level is also Windows Server 2003. What, if anything, must be done to the functional levels to support the RODC?
    a. Nothing.
    b. Raise only the domain functional level to Windows Server 2008.
    c. Raise only the forest functional level to Windows Server 2008.
    d. Raise both the domain functional level and the forest functional level to Windows Server 2008.
6. Your company has recently purchased another company. The other company is running in the forest functional level of Windows Server 2000 and your forest is running in the forest functional level of Windows Server 2003. You want to configure the forests so that you can easily grant users in any domain in either forest access to resources in any domain in either forest. What should you do first?
    a. Enable a forest trust.
    b. Create a UPN.
    c. Raise the forest functional level of the other company's forest to Windows Server 2003.
    d. Raise the forest functional level of both forests to Windows Server 2008.
7. Figure 1-21 shows your current Active Directory Domain Services structure. It includes two forests. Cengage.com is located in the United States and CourseTech.com is located in England. The root domain in each forest is located in the headquarters office for that country. The child domains in both forests are located in remote offices in the same country. The forest functional level of each is currently Windows Server 2000. You need to redesign the structure to minimize the number of forests and domains.

    The resulting structure should minimize replication between the headquarters offices in the United States and England. Administrators should be able to grant users in any domain access to resources in any other domain. How many forests and domains should your design include?
    a. Create a single-domain forest.
    b. Create two single-domain forests and set both to at least forest functional level Windows Server 2003.

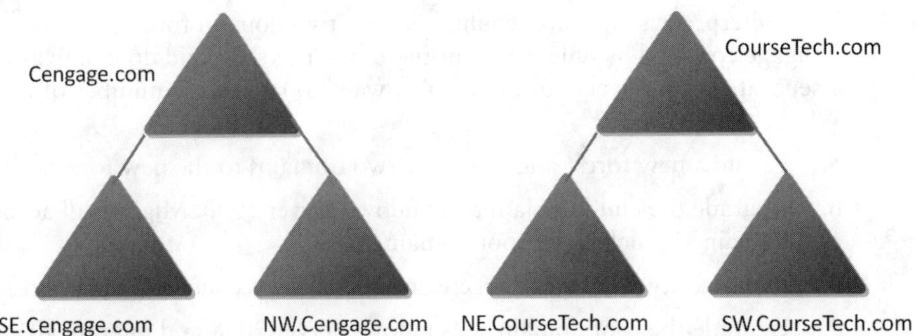

Figure 1-21 Current forest structure

Courtesy Course Technology/Cengage Learning

  c. Leave the forests and domains as shown, but ensure the forest functional level is at least Windows Server 2003.
  d. Leave the forests and domains as shown, but ensure the forest functional level is at least Windows Server 2008.

8. You are designing the logical structure for an organization and its subsidiary. The subsidiary needs to achieve service autonomy. What design should you create?
   a. A one-domain forest, with an OU for the subsidiary.
   b. A two-domain forest, with a child domain for the subsidiary.
   c. Two separate forests, with a forest trust relationship between the two.
   d. Two separate forests, without a forest trust.
9. Your enterprise is configured as shown in Figure 1-22.

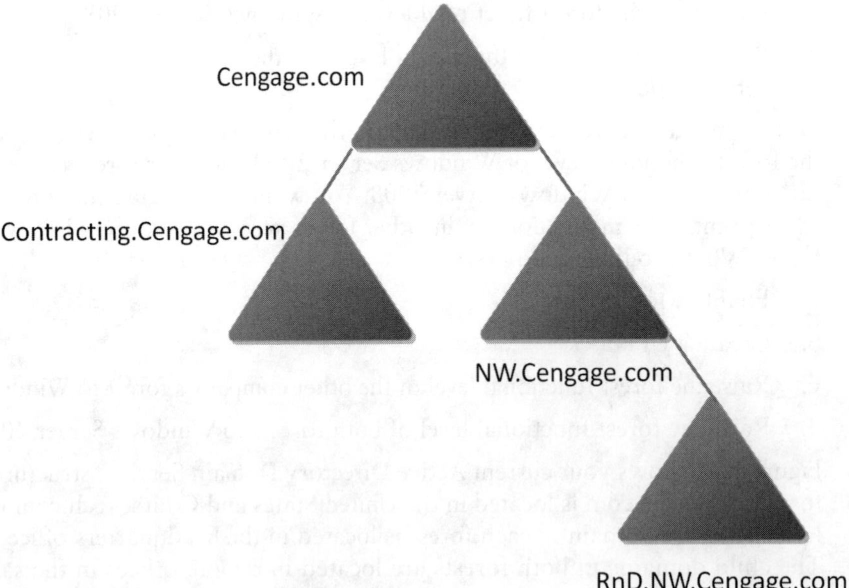

Figure 1-22 Cengage forest structure

Courtesy Course Technology/Cengage Learning

The Contracting.Cengage.com domain was created to provide service autonomy. RnD.Cengage.com was created to support separate password and account lockout policies. Data autonomy is needed in the NW.Cengage.com domain. You want to reduce the organization to the least number of domains. What should you do?

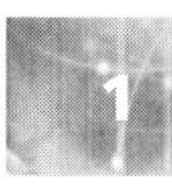

a. Reduce the forest to a single domain: Cengage.com.
b. Reduce the forest to two domains: Cengage.com and NW.Cengage.com.
c. Reduce the forest to two domains: Cengage.com and Contracting.Cengage.com.
d. Reduce the forest to two domains: Cengage.com and RnD.NW.Cengage.com.

10. You have users in both the root domain and a child domain in your forest. You have decided to consolidate the forest to a single domain. How can you move the users from the child domain to the root domain?
    a. Use Active Directory Users and Computers with the Move command.
    b. Use Active Directory Users and Computers with drag-and-drop mouse commands.
    c. Use ADMT.
    d. Use ADPrep.

11. You are creating a trust relationship between two forests. You want to ensure that the trusts are transitive and that only authorized users from each trusted forest can be granted access to resources in the other forest. What should you create?
    a. Forest trust with forest-wide authentication
    b. Forest trust with selective authentication
    c. External trust with forest-wide authentication
    d. External trust with selective authentication

12. You administer a domain named Cengage.com. Cengage.com has created a partnership with a company named Course Technology that has a forest named CourseTech.com. A specific set of users in the G_PartnerProject group has members from multiple domains in their forest and needs access to a server named FS1 in your domain. What should you create to accommodate this need?
    a. Create a one-way forest trust so that Cengage trusts CourseTech with selective authentication.
    b. Create a one-way forest trust so that CourseTech trusts Cengage with selective authentication.
    c. Create a one-way external trust from Cengage to CourseTech with forest-wide authentication.
    d. Create a one-way external trust from CourseTech to Cengage with forest-wide authentication.

13. You are called in as a consultant to assist a company in designing a logical structure for Active Directory. The company is currently a single entity, but is being divided into two separate business units. Each business unit needs to completely manage its own Active Directory infrastructure. What would you recommend?
    a. Create a single domain with different OUs for each business unit.
    b. Create a two-domain forest.
    c. Create a single forest with two separate trees.
    d. Create two separate forests.

14. Your organization has a partnership with another company and a two-way forest trust has been created between both companies using selective authentication. The other company has a group named G_JointProject that includes users from different domains in their forest. A server administrator has granted the group access to a share on a server named FS1. What, if anything, needs to be done to allow these users access to the share?
    a. Nothing. Once the server administrator granted access, they have access.
    b. Reconfigure the forest trust as an external trust.

c. Reconfigure the forest trust with forest-wide authentication.

d. Grant the Allowed to Authenticate permission for FS1 to the G_JointProject group.

15. You are preparing to promote the first Windows Server 2008 server to a domain controller in an established forest. The forest currently only includes Windows Server 2003 domain controllers. What must be done before the server can be promoted?

a. Run ADPrep /ForestPrep.

b. Run ADPrep /Domain Prep.

c. Run ADPrep /ForestPrep and then run ADPrep /Domain Prep.

d. Run ADPrep /Domain Prep and then run ADPrep /ForestPrep.

16. Your organization has a single forest running in the forest functional level of Windows Server 2003 and currently has only Windows Server 2003 domain controllers. You are preparing to add Windows Server 2008 domain controllers and plan on running the ADPrep /ForestPrep command. Where should this be run?

a. First DC in the root domain

b. Domain naming master

c. Schema master

d. PDC emulator

17. You are creating the Active Directory logical design for a large organization. A group of users in the R&D department will be using an application that requires extensive changes to the schema. These changes aren't needed by other users in the organization and the design should prevent the other users from seeing the changes. Users in the R&D department require access to resources in the organization. How should you design the logical structure? (Choose two.)

a. Create a two-domain forest.

b. Create two forests.

c. Create a forest trust with forest-wide authentication.

d. Create a forest trust with selective authentication.

e. Create a parent-child trust.

18. You are creating the logical structure design for a large organization to accommodate plans to restructure the organization. When the restructure is completed, the company will have three business units. The first two business units should share a global catalog so that applications can do searches of Active Directory. Legal requirements dictate that the third business unit must be completely separate from the other two. Replication within each business unit should be minimized. What design should you choose?

a. Create a single one-domain forest and use OUs for each business unit.

b. Create two one-domain forests. Place the first two business units in one forest, and one domain in the second forest.

c. Create two forests. Create separate domains for the first two business units in one forest. Place the third business unit in a single domain in the second forest.

d. Create three forests. Place each business unit in a separate forest.

19. Your company (named Cengage) has established a partnership with another company (named Course Technology). Both companies have Active Directory forests running in the forest functional level of Windows Server 2003. Users in the Course Technology forest need to access resources on several servers in your forest, but users in Cengage will not need to access resources in the other forest. You are asked to design a trust solution to accommodate this need. What would you recommend?

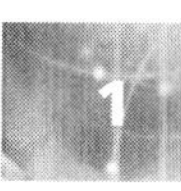

a. Create a one-way forest trust so that Course Technology trusts Cengage. Use forest-wide authentication.

b. Create a one-way forest trust so that Cengage trusts Course Technology. Use forest-wide authentication.

c. Create a one-way forest trust so that Course Technology trusts Cengage. Use selective authentication.

d. Create a one-way forest trust so that Cengage trusts Course Technology. Use selective authentication.

20. Your company is implementing a consolidation of two forests into a single forest. Both forests are using the forest functional level of Windows Server 2008. You have downloaded and installed ADMT v3 on a domain controller in the target forest. However, ADMT is failing to migrate user accounts. What needs to be done?

    a. The forest functional level needs to be reduced to Windows Server 2003.

    b. The domain functional level needs to be raised to Windows Server 2008.

    c. SID filtering needs to be disabled.

    d. Use ADMT v3.1.

21. Your company is implementing a consolidation of two forests into a single forest. The forest functional level of both forests is Windows Server 2003. After migrating some test users from one forest to the target forest, you realize that the user accounts can't access resources from the original forest. What must be done to allow users to access those resources?

    a. Enable SID filtering.

    b. Migrate SID history.

    c. Raise the forest functional level of the target forest to Windows Server 2008.

    d. Raise the forest functional level of the source forest to Windows Server 2008.

22. Your company is implementing a consolidation of two forests into a single forest. The forest functional level of both forests is Windows Server 2003. After migrating some test users from one forest to the target forest, you realize that the user accounts can't access resources from the original forest. You have verified that SID history is included in the accounts in the target domain. What else should be done?

    a. Enable SID filtering.

    b. Disable SID filtering.

    c. Raise the forest functional level of the target forest to Windows Server 2008.

    d. Raise the forest functional level of the source forest to Windows Server 2008.

23. Your company has a forest named Cengage.com. You have acquired another company named CourseTech and you want to merge all of the resources into the Cengage forest. What should you do?

    a. Run ADUC from a DC in CourseTech.

    b. Run ADUC from a DC in Cengage.

    c. Run ADMT from a DC in CourseTech.

    d. Run ADMT from a DC in Cengage.

24. You are planning to migrate users from another domain to your domain after a company merger. Users in that domain commonly log on with their e-mail address. After the migration has been completed, you want to give users the ability to log on with the same user name in your domain that they used in their original domain. What should you create?

    a. Create an MX record in DNS.

    b. Create an alternative UPN suffix.

c. Migrate SID history.

d. Enable SID filtering.

25. Your organization is considering an upgrade of the existing Windows Server 2003 forest to a Windows Server 2008 forest. Which of the following factors will affect the upgrade? (Choose all that apply.)

a. Time

b. Resources and funding

c. Application compatibility

d. All of the above

Case Projects

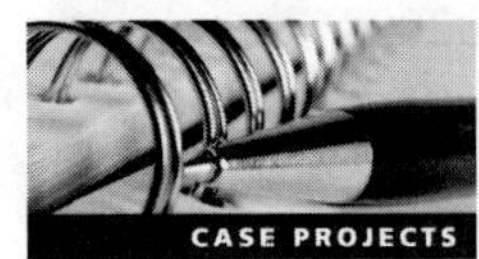

Case Project 1-1: Designing a Forest

You are redesigning a Windows Server 2003 forest that includes three domains. The different domains were created to support three different password policies. You want to consolidate the forest to the least number of domains. What's the minimum number of domains that can be used in the design? Explain your answer.

Case Project 1-2: Choosing Domain and Forest Functional Levels

You are planning the consolidation of a four-domain forest into a single-domain forest. The final solution must support multiple account lockout policies. The forest currently includes Windows Server 2003 domain controllers and Windows Server 2000 member servers. What must be done to support the plan? Explain your answer.

Case Project 1-3: Designing Forests for Autonomy

Cengage has acquired another company named Course Technology. Currently, Cengage is in one forest and Course Technology is configured as a separate forest. You are asked to design a solution that will provide data autonomy for each company. How would you design the enterprise? Explain your answer.

Case Project 1-4: Choosing a Trust

Your company recently created a partnership with another company to work on a joint project. Both companies are independent from each other, and both companies have multidomain forests configured with a forest functional level of Windows Server 2003. The companies will be sharing resources during this project. You need to design a plan in which a specific set of users in the other company can access specific servers in your enterprise. What should you do?

chapter 2

Designing Physical Topology

After reading this chapter and completing the exercises, you will be able to:

- Plan and implement sites and site links
- Design the plan to support a remote branch office
- Understand operations master roles
- Be able to transfer and seize operations master roles
- Plan and implement read-only domain controllers (RODCs)

The physical topology of Active Directory includes the sites, subnets, and wide area network (WAN) links. These elements exist outside of Active Directory, but you can (and should) teach Active Directory about them. The primary tool you use is Active Directory Sites and Services.

Once Active Directory has been configured with sites, subnets, and site link objects, different site-aware applications are optimized, which ensures that clients will access servers in their site when available, instead of accessing servers over slower WAN links.

The design of branch offices includes many considerations. Read-only domain controllers (RODCs) can be used in remote offices with limited physical security or when local administrators need to be given limited permissions. You can optimize the logon process for users by adding a global catalog server to the domain controller (DC) in the remote office or by enabling Universal Group Membership Caching on the site.

When deploying DCs, it's important to understand the different operations master roles hosted by some domain controllers. These roles can affect your planning of the global catalog and the use of RODCs. You should know how many roles exist in a forest and a domain, how to locate the role holders, and how to transfer and seize the roles.

Implementing Sites

A **site** is defined as a well-connected group of hosts or subnets. It's common for a small business to have all of its computers and servers in the same building and connected via a single local area network (LAN). This arrangement is considered a site; single-location businesses have only one site.

However, many businesses have more than one location. As an example, a business could have its primary office in Virginia Beach, but then create a satellite office in Norfolk. The connection between these two offices uses some type of wide area network (WAN) link.

Figure 2-1 shows this two-site configuration. The Virginia Beach office and the Norfolk satellite office could each be internally connected with a 1 Gbps LAN. But, between the sites, they are not well-connected. Instead, the WAN link is something less than 1 Gbps.

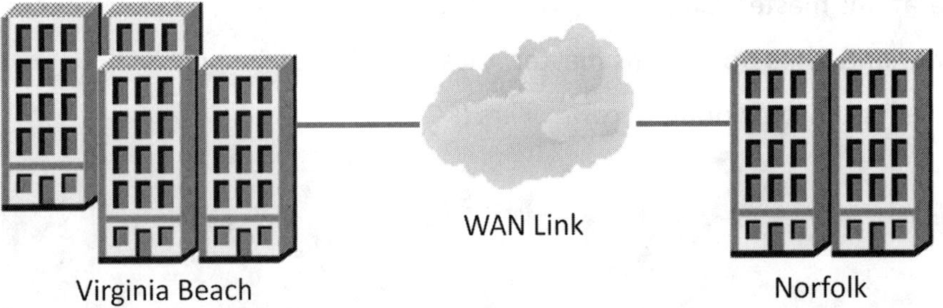

Figure 2-1 A two-site business configuration

Courtesy Course Technology/Cengage Learning

The WAN link speed could be a slow 56 Kbps, a quick T1 at 1.5 Mbps, or some other speed. However, the important point to recognize is that the typical WAN link speed is significantly less than the speeds within each site.

With this understood, we can expand the definition of sites. In addition to being a group of well-connected hosts or subnets, a site is connected to another group of well-connected hosts or subnets by a slower WAN link. The WAN link is represented by a site link object in Active Directory.

Site and Site Link Benefits

When sites, subnets, and site links are created, you gain several benefits. These include:

- Logon optimization
- Replication optimization
- Access to site data by site-aware applications

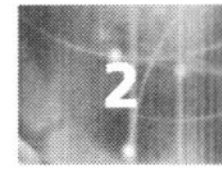

Logon Optimization

Clients use the Netlogon service to log on to a domain. Consider a user logging on to a computer in Norfolk, as shown in Figure 2-2. When the user logs on, which DC is preferable? DC1 or DC2?

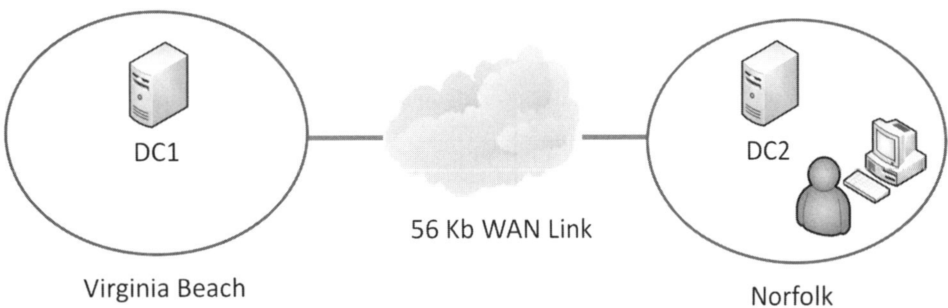

Figure 2-2 Netlogon process in two-site enterprise
Courtesy Course Technology/Cengage Learning

The obvious answer is DC2. If the Netlogon service contacts DC1 to log on, the traffic must traverse the much slower 56 Kbps WAN link. If Netlogon uses DC2, it's within a well-connected site and the process is much quicker. However, the answer isn't obvious to Active Directory—at least not by default.

You must complete several steps so that the Netlogon service knows which DC to contact. These steps assume that a physical location exists in the remote location, that it has one or more subnets, and that it contains one or more domain controllers. Take the following steps:

- Create a site object in Active Directory to correspond to each location
- Create subnet objects in Active Directory to represent the actual subnets that exist in the remote location
- Move the domain controller object to the newly created site in Active Directory

Remember that the site, subnet(s) and domain controller(s) already exist. You are using Active Directory to create objects that represent the actual location (site), and the subnet(s) and domain controller(s) in the location. This is similar to creating a user object that relates to a real person, or a computer object that relates to a physical computer. When you create a user object or site object, obviously you aren't creating a real person or physical location.

Replication Optimization

Another benefit of configuring sites, subnets, and site connectors is to optimize Active Directory **replication** between sites. Data replicated between domain controllers includes all the additions, changes, and modifications of objects, such as when a user is added or a password is changed. The amount of data replicated is variable and largely depends on the size of an organization.

As a reminder, replication between domain controllers within the same site occurs within 15 seconds for the original change. The change is then sent to other domain controllers within 3 seconds; within 30 seconds, all domain controllers have the change. This replication between domain controllers within a site is not compressed and uses a notification process.

However, replication between domain controllers in different sites offers several benefits:

- **Replication data is compressed.** It takes significantly less bandwidth to replicate compressed Active Directory data. If the replicated data is more than 32 Kb, it is compressed to about 40 percent of the original size, which can be significant in slow or heavily used WAN links.

- **Replication is scheduled.** You can restrict replication to occur only during specific times of the day or only on specific days of the week, and you can configure how often replication occurs. By default, replication between sites is scheduled to occur every 180 minutes, 7 days a week. However, you can change the default schedule, as shown in Figure 2-3. This example schedule has been changed to replicate every 180 minutes, but only between the hours of 6 p.m. and 6 a.m.

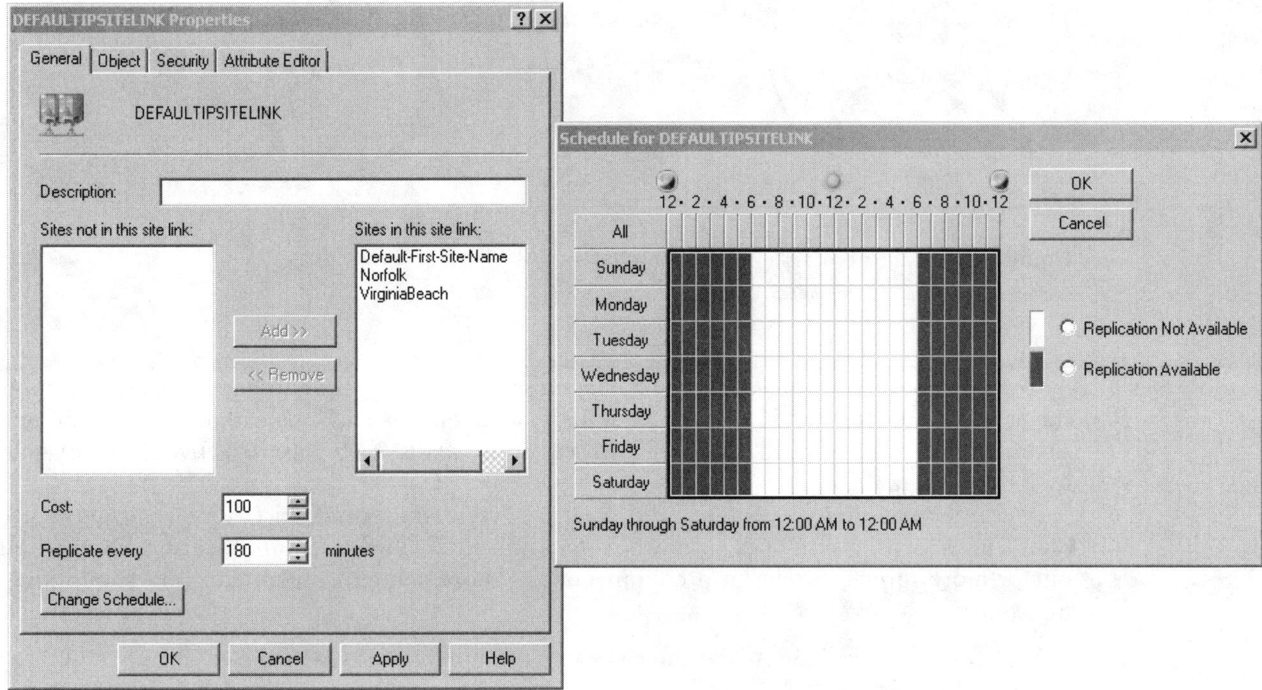

Figure 2-3 Scheduling site replication

Courtesy Course Technology/Cengage Learning

Replication between sites occurs without notification. Within a site, domain controllers notify replication partners that they have a change, and the receiving domain controller only requests the change if it doesn't already have the change. However, between sites the changes are replicated based on the schedule. The notification process isn't used; instead, changes are sent when the scheduled time arrives.

- **Replication can be directed.** Another significant benefit is the ability to control the path in which replication occurs. Figure 2-4 shows a three-site organization with three site links. You can see that the optimum path between Norfolk and Chesapeake is indirectly through Virginia Beach using the 512 Kbps links. However, Active Directory will use the direct path between Norfolk and Chesapeake with the much slower 56 Kbps link unless the site link properties are modified.

The compression occurs automatically. However, you need to configure the properties of the site link to control the replication schedule (as shown) and the path of replication. The replication path is manipulated by controlling the Cost value of the site link.

The Cost value is manipulated on the same page as the schedule. To access this page, right-click the site link and select Properties. Cost doesn't relate to a money value, but instead is used to identify the best path using a least-cost algorithm.

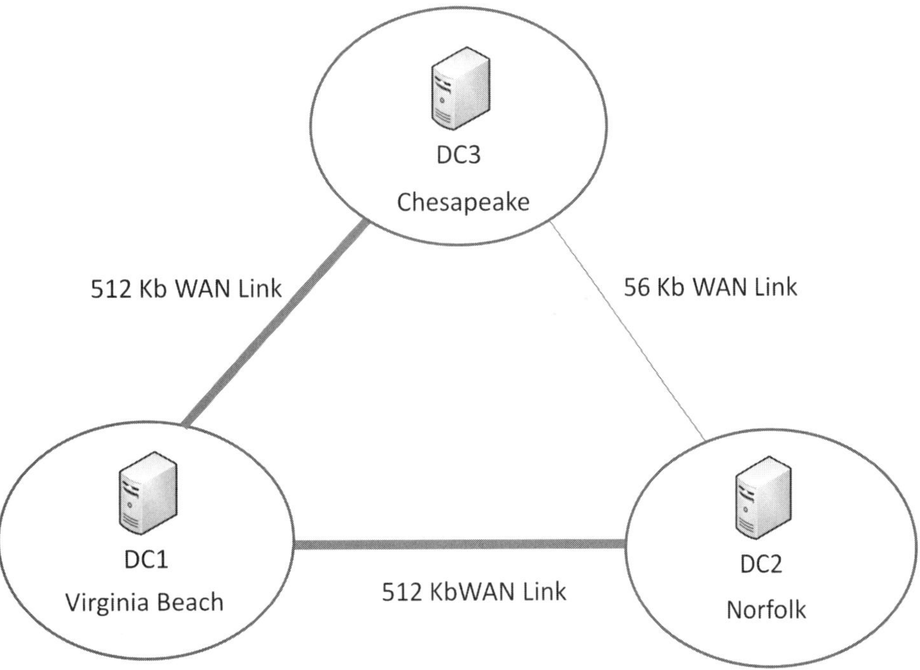

Figure 2-4 Controlling replication traffic in three-site enterprise
Courtesy Course Technology/Cengage Learning

By default, the cost of each site link is set to 100. Active Directory uses a least-cost algorithm to identify the path it uses. Using the default setting, the cost using the direct path between Chesapeake and Norfolk is 100, and the cost through Virginia Beach is 200 (a cost of 100 between Norfolk and Virginia Beach plus a cost of 100 between Virginia Beach and Chesapeake). When the default settings are used, Active Directory will attempt to replicate using the slower, 56 Kbps path because it has a lesser cost—100 instead of 200.

However, if the cost of the Chesapeake-to-Virginia Beach link is reduced to 25, and the cost of the Virginia Beach-to-Norfolk link is also reduced to 25, the combined path would have a cost of 50. Active Directory would use this path to replicate Active Directory data between Norfolk and Chesapeake. Figure 2-5 shows the paths with the new costs.

You can use any numbers between 1 and 99999 for the Cost value, but make sure that your choices adequately reflect the environment. If your fastest link is a T1, you can assign it as a 10 (the least cost). You then may assign a 512 Kbps partial T1 a cost of 100 and a 56 Kbps link a cost of 1000.

For any future site links you add, you'll need to follow the same strategy. Another T1 must have a cost of 10, and another 56 Kbps link must have a cost of 1000. Additionally, if you add a 256 Kbps link, it needs to have a cost between the 100 assigned to the 512 Kbps link and the 1000 assigned to the 56 Kbps link.

Using Sites for Site-aware Applications

Many applications and services are site-aware. A **site-aware application** can determine its own Active Directory site membership (and location) and connect to other servers in the same site.

The e-mail application Microsoft Exchange is one of many examples of a site-aware server application. Exchange frequently queries a global catalog server, and because Exchange is site-aware, it can locate a global catalog server in the same site.

Distributed File System (DFS) is also site-aware. You can use DFS to store copies of the same data in DFS folders in multiple sites. When users connect, they will automatically connect to the DFS folder in their own site instead of accessing the data over a slow WAN link.

DFS replication is an effective technology that can be used to replicate and synchronize data between multiple sites. Once DFS is configured, changes are detected and automatically replicated to all DFS servers.

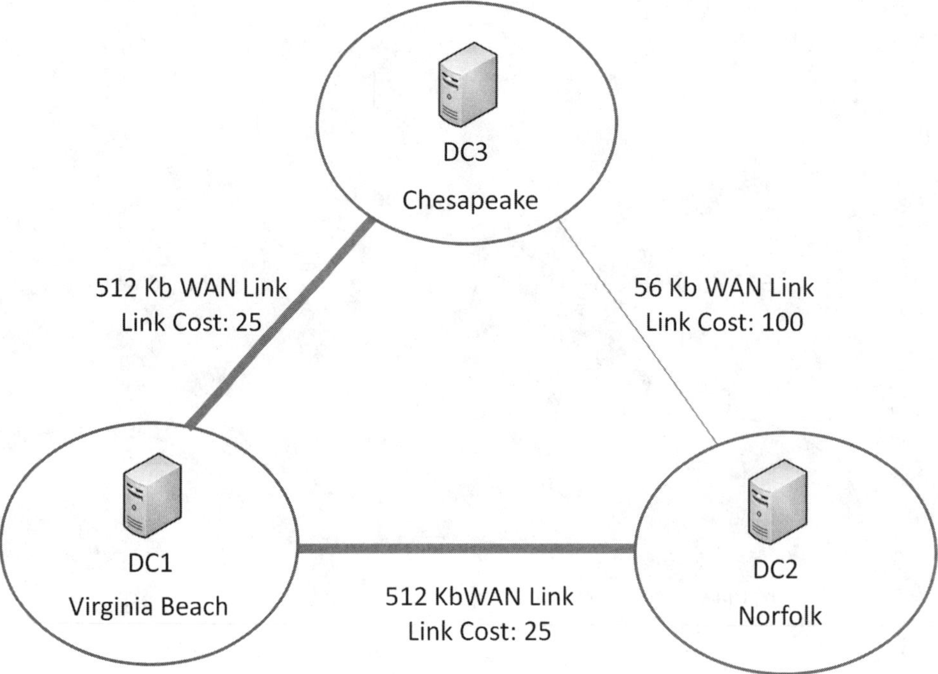

Figure 2-5 Controlling replication traffic by adjusting the cost of the link

Courtesy Course Technology/Cengage Learning

DFS includes two key topics worth mentioning here:

- **DFS namespace.** A DFS namespace is used to group shared folders from different servers into a logically structured namespace. This namespace appears to the user as a single shared folder with nested subfolders. The user can access the namespace and easily access all of the shared folders without knowing (or needing to know) that the folders are located on multiple servers.
- **DFS replication.** DFS replication allows DFS namespaces to be stored on multiple servers using a multiple-master replication scheme. The data within the DFS namespace can be stored on multiple servers (one in each site, for example) and each DFS server can accept changes to the data. DFS replication will keep the folders synchronized in all of the servers.

While not as common, you also can create a separate site to control queries by site-aware applications that query Active Directory. In other words, if you have an application server that frequently queries Active Directory, you can control which domain controller it queries by creating a site and placing the application server and domain controller in this site.

Active Directory applications use Lightweight Directory Access Protocol (LDAP) queries to query domain controllers, and these queries add to the load of a domain controller. You can separate these queries by "tricking" Active Directory into thinking that a separate site exists. Imagine that you have a single domain in a single well-connected site. Your business uses a site-aware application that frequently performs LDAP queries, and you want to ensure that this application only queries a specific domain controller. You could take the following steps to implement this strategy.

- Create a separate subnet on your network. Configure TCP/IP so that the domain controller and application server are located on this subnet.
- Open Active Directory Sites and Services and create a site (perhaps named AppSite) and a subnet that corresponds to the first subnet you created.
- Link the subnet to the site and move the domain controller to the site in Active Directory Sites and Services.

At this point, all LDAP queries by this application server would be directed at the domain controller in the site you created. No other site-aware applications or computers are on this subnet, so this domain controller would not be queried for anything else.

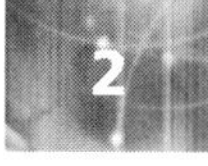

Creating Sites and Subnets

The physical locations of an enterprise include one or more subnets. However, Active Directory doesn't know about these locations by default. Instead, you must teach Active Directory what sites, subnets, and site links exist by creating site objects, **subnet objects**, and site link objects. The primary tool you use is Active Directory Sites and Services.

While separate physical locations have many different benefits, the focus with Active Directory sites is only on the communication with domain controllers from site-aware applications. If a domain controller is not placed in the remote location, you wouldn't need to create an Active Directory site to represent the remote location.

You can open Active Directory Sites and Services via the Administrative Tools menu. In Figure 2-6, Active Directory Sites and Services is shown with the default site and a single domain controller.

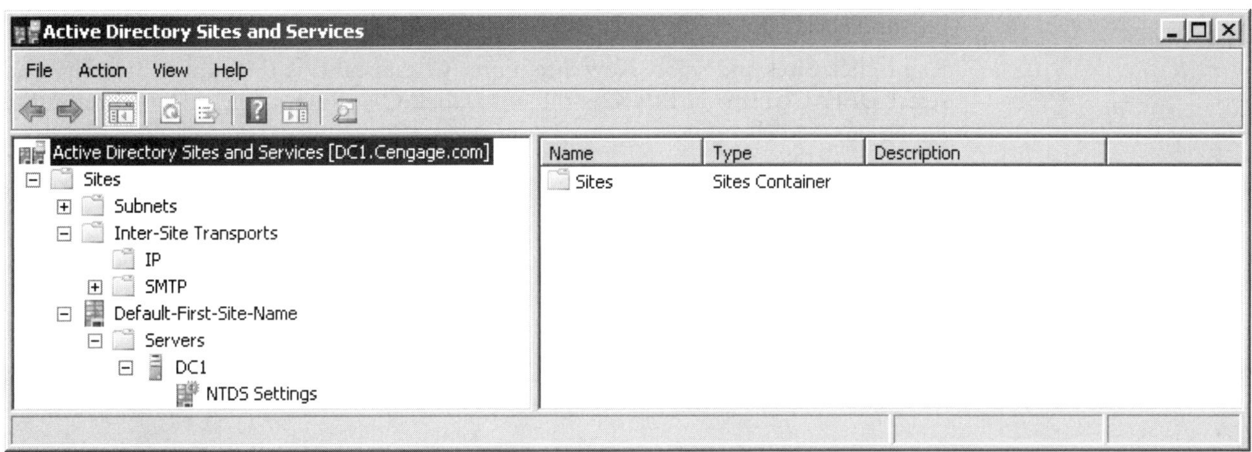

Figure 2-6 Active Directory Sites and Services

Courtesy Course Technology/Cengage Learning

Active Directory Sites and Services has little awareness of the actual environment by default when Active Directory is first installed. It doesn't have any subnets, has only one site link (named DEFAULTSITEIPLINK) in the Inter-Site Transports\IP node, and one site (named Default-Site-First-Name). When DCpromo is run on any server to promote it to a domain controller, the server will automatically be placed in this site.

If sites have been configured before DCpromo is run on a member server, DCpromo will automatically add the domain controller object to the site where it is located. It identifies the server's subnet based on the TCP/IP configuration data, and then queries Active Directory to determine the site where the subnet is located. If the sites and subnets have not been configured, the domain controller object must be manually moved to the site using Active Directory Sites and Services.

In conclusion, if your organization includes multiple locations, you can add the sites, subnets, and site links using Active Directory Sites and Services. Activity 2-1 shows you how to add sites and subnets.

Activity 2-1: Creating Sites and Subnets

Time Required: 20 minutes
Objective: Create sites and subnets to mimic an actual enterprise, and move a domain controller to a site.

Description: Your organization has a primary location in Virginia Beach, and recently added a location in Norfolk and another in Chesapeake. The Virginia Beach location has a single subnet of 192.168.1.0/24, the Norfolk location has a single subnet of 192.168.15.0/24, and the Chesapeake location has a single subnet of 192.168.22.0/24. You need to create sites and subnets in Active Directory to mimic the physical locations. This lab uses DC1, which is hosting the Cengage.com domain you created in Chapter 1.

1. Log on to **DC1** with the domain **Administrator** account and a password of **P@ssw0rd.**
2. Start **Active Directory Sites and Services** via the **Administrative Tools** menu.
3. Click the plus (+) icon to open the **Sites** node and select **Default-First-Site-Name.** Right-click **Default-First-Site-Name** and select **Rename.** Rename the site **VirginiaBeach.**
4. Right-click **Sites** and select **New Site.** Enter **Norfolk** as the name of the site and select **DEFAULTIPSITELINK** as the link. Click **OK.** Review the information in the dialog box and click **OK.**
5. Right-click **Sites** and select **New Site.** Enter **Chesapeake** as the name of the site and select **DEFAULTIPSITELINK** as the link. Click **OK.** Review the information in the dialog box and click **OK.**
6. Right-click **Subnets** and select **New Subnet.** Enter **192.168.1.0/24** and select the **VirginiaBeach** site, as shown in Figure 2-7. Click **OK.**

The /24 in the IP address is referred to as CIDR notation and indicates that the first 24 bits in the IPv4 address are 1s. It is equivalent to a subnet mask of 255.255.255.0. Each 255 in the subnet mask is represented with eight 1s in binary; because there are three 255s in the subnet mask, there are 24 binary 1s.

7. Right-click **Subnets** and select **New Subnet.** Enter **192.168.15.0/24** and select the **Norfolk** site. Click **OK.**
8. Right-click **Subnets** and select **New Subnet.** Enter **192.168.22.0/24** and select the **Chesapeake** site. Click **OK.**
9. Click the plus (+) icon to open the **Servers** node under the Virginia Beach site. Notice that DC1 is currently in this site because it was previously the Default-First-Site-Name.
10. Right-click **DC1** and select **Move.** Select the **Norfolk** site and click **OK.** Browse to the **Norfolk Servers** node and note that DC1 is now in this site. While these steps show you how to move the domain controller, the system won't work properly if left this way. DC1 has an IP address of 192.168.1.10/24, and that subnet is in Virginia Beach, not Norfolk. You need to move DC1 back to Virginia Beach.
11. Right-click **DC1** and select **Move.** Select the **VirginiaBeach** site and click **OK.** Browse to the **VirginiaBeach Servers** node and note that DC1 is back in this site.

Creating Site Links

A **site link object** is created in Active Directory Sites and Services to represent the actual WAN links used to connect different sites. So far, the organization described in this chapter has only one WAN link between Virginia Beach and Norfolk, and it has a default name of DEFAULTIPSITELINK. As locations and sites are added, you'll often add more site links.

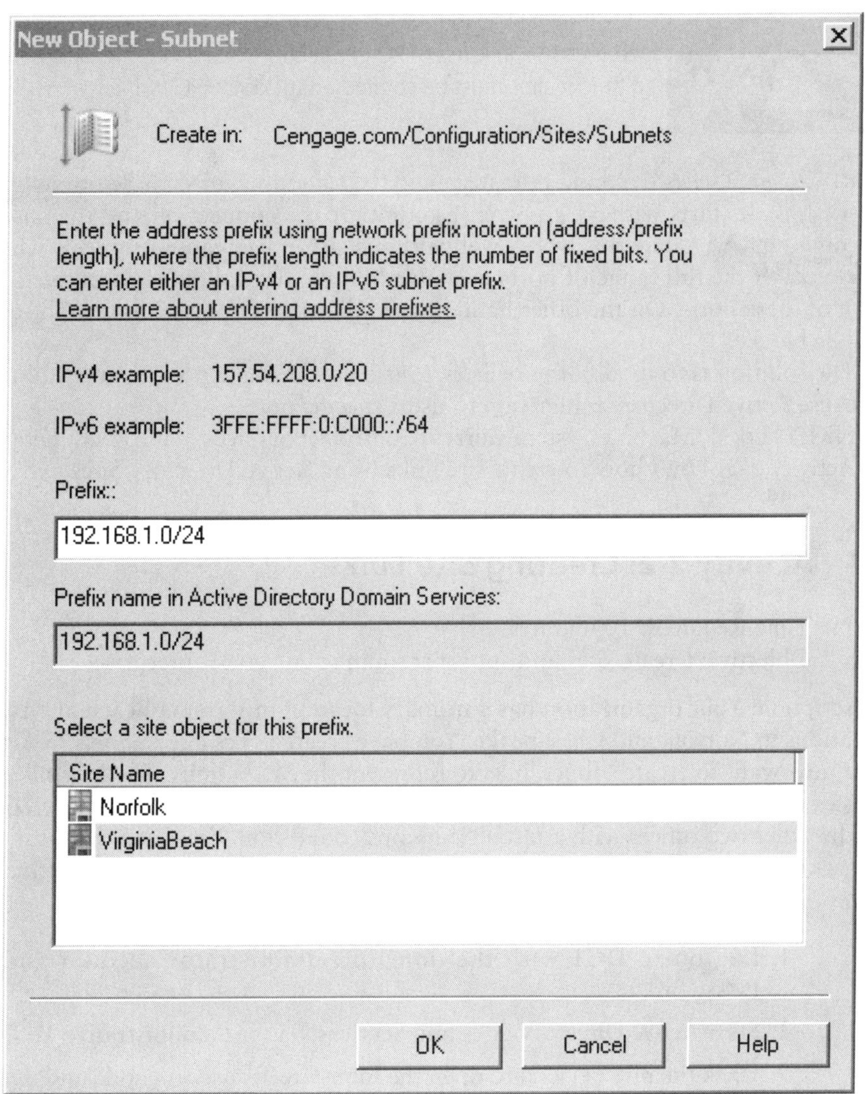

Figure 2-7 Adding a subnet and assigning it to a site

Courtesy Course Technology/Cengage Learning

If all of the WAN links are identical, you can use the DEFAULTIPSITELINK to represent each of the WAN links. For example, if you have one headquarters office, and two remote offices and all locations are connected via identical 256 Kbps links, you can use the same Active Directory site link for the WAN links. Usually, though, the WAN link connections are different and you'll create different site links to represent them.

Two types of site links exist:

- **IP.** The **IP site link** is commonly referred to as the **RPC over IP site link.** It uses a Remote Procedure Call (RPC) connection to establish a synchronous connection with a domain controller in the remote site. This is the most commonly used site link object.
- **SMTP.** A **SMTP site link object** is rarely used, but it can be if the WAN links aren't reliable and the targets are in different domains. Simple Mail Transport Protocol (SMTP) site links are only used to replicate differences in the configuration, schema, and application partitions of Active Directory, but never the domain partition. In other words, they cannot be used to replicate data within the same domain. SMTP uses asynchronous connections and is much more complex than RPC over IP site links. One of SMTP's significantly different requirements is the need to install and configure a certificate authority (CA).

The IP site link is sometimes called the RPC site link. It's important to realize that this link uses RPC connections, and that firewalls between the different sites must be configured to allow RPC traffic.

RPC over IP uses dynamic port mapping to communicate with domain controllers over the IP site link. It starts with TCP port 135 to initiate the connection and then uses different ports to communicate. While this works well within a site, it can cause problems when going through a firewall. If the full range of ports is enabled on the firewall, it exposes the firewall to risks on each of these ports. On the other hand, if the full range of ports is not enabled, communication will be blocked.

The solution is to modify the registry to use only a single port. Set the following registry key to cause Active Directory replication to use a specific port:

HKEY_Local_Machine\System\CurrentControlSet\Services\NTDS\Parameters\TCP/IP Port

Activity 2-2 shows how to create site links using Active Directory Sites and Services.

Activity 2-2: Creating Site Links

Time Required: 10 minutes
Objective: Create sites and subnets to mimic an actual enterprise.

Description: Your organization has a primary location in Virginia Beach and two remote locations in Norfolk and Chesapeake. You have created sites and subnets in Active Directory, and now want to create subnet links to represent the WAN links. The Norfolk and Chesapeake offices are connected with a slow 56 Kbps connection, but the Virginia Beach office is connected to the other two offices with a faster 512 Kbps connection. You need to adjust the cost to ensure that the connections are used properly. This activity assumes that Activity 2-1 was completed.

1. Log on to **DC1** with the domain **Administrator** account and a password of **P@ssw0rd.**
2. Start **Active Directory Sites and Services** via the **Administrative Tools** menu.
3. Click the plus (**+**) icon to open the **Inter-Site Transports** node and select **IP**. Right-click **IP** and select **New Site Link.** Name the site link **VB-Norfolk.** Select the **VirginiaBeach** and **Norfolk** sites and click **Add.** Your display will look similar to Figure 2-8. Click **OK.**
4. Right-click **IP** and select **New Site Link.** Name the Site Link **VB-Chesapeake.** Select the **VirginiaBeach** and **Chesapeake** sites and click **Add.** Click **OK.**
5. Right-click **IP** and select **New Site Link.** Name the Site Link **Norfolk-Chesapeake.** Select the **Norfolk** and **Chesapeake** sites and click **Add.** Click **OK.**
6. Right-click the **VB-Chesapeake** site link and select **Properties.** Change the **Cost** to **25,** as shown in Figure 2-9. Click OK.
7. Right-click the **VB-Norfolk** site link and select **Properties.** Change the **Cost** to **25** and click **OK.**

Understanding Bridgehead Servers

Each site has one domain controller designated as a **bridgehead server.** The bridgehead server is the only domain controller that accepts and transfers replicated data within the site. The bridgehead server then replicates the data to other domain controllers within the site (if any exist).

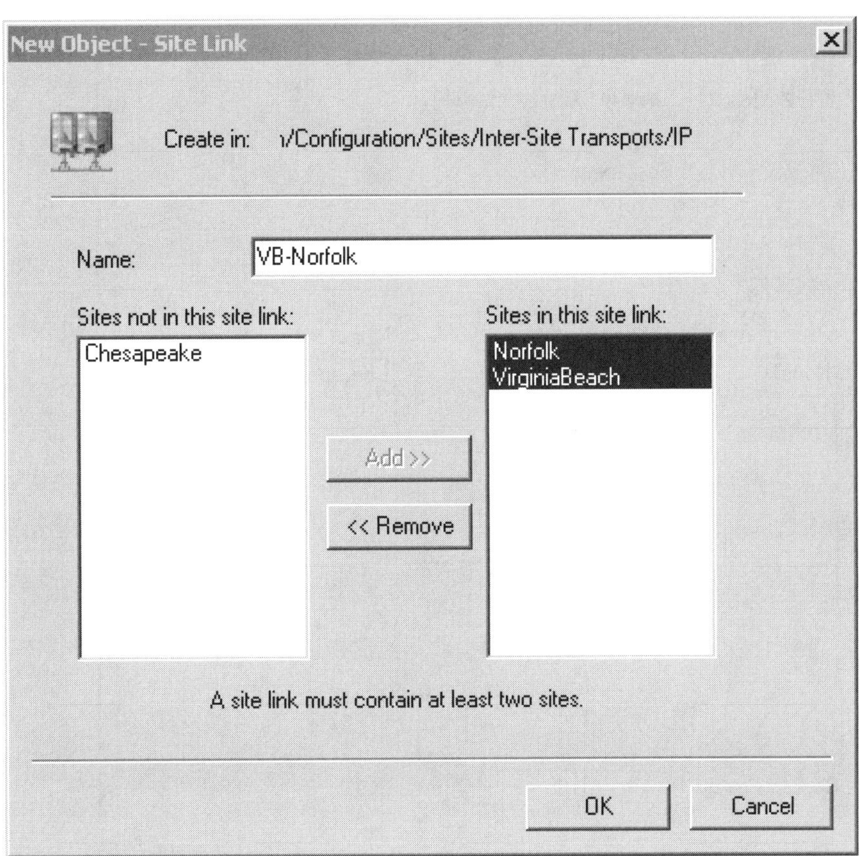

Figure 2-8 Creating a site link
Courtesy Course Technology/Cengage Learning

The **Inter-Site Topology Generator (ISTG)** is an Active Directory process that runs in the background on a domain controller in the site and automatically designates the bridgehead server within a site. If the designated bridgehead server fails, the ISTG automatically detects the failure and designates another domain controller to be the bridgehead server.

To determine which server has been designated as the bridgehead server, you can execute the following command from the command prompt on a domain controller in the site: **Repadmin /bridgeheads**.

By default, you don't have any control over which domain controller is designated as a bridgehead server. However, you can designate a **preferred bridgehead server.**

The logic of selecting preferred bridgehead servers can be confusing. You'd think that you would pick a domain controller to be a preferred bridgehead server because you specifically want that domain controller to assume the role, but that is not quite true. Instead, you pick domain controllers to be preferred bridgehead servers to specifically *exclude* another domain controller from ever assuming that role.

Imagine that a site has four domain controllers named DC1, DC2, DC3, and DC4. DC4 is an older server, and monitoring shows that during normal operation, it's close to the peak of resource usage. DC4 will run acceptably under normal conditions, but if the ISTG designates it as the bridgehead server for the site, DC4 can become overloaded when replicating with other sites.

You can't explicitly exclude this domain controller from being a bridgehead server, but you can select the other domain controllers as preferred bridgehead servers. Figure 2-10

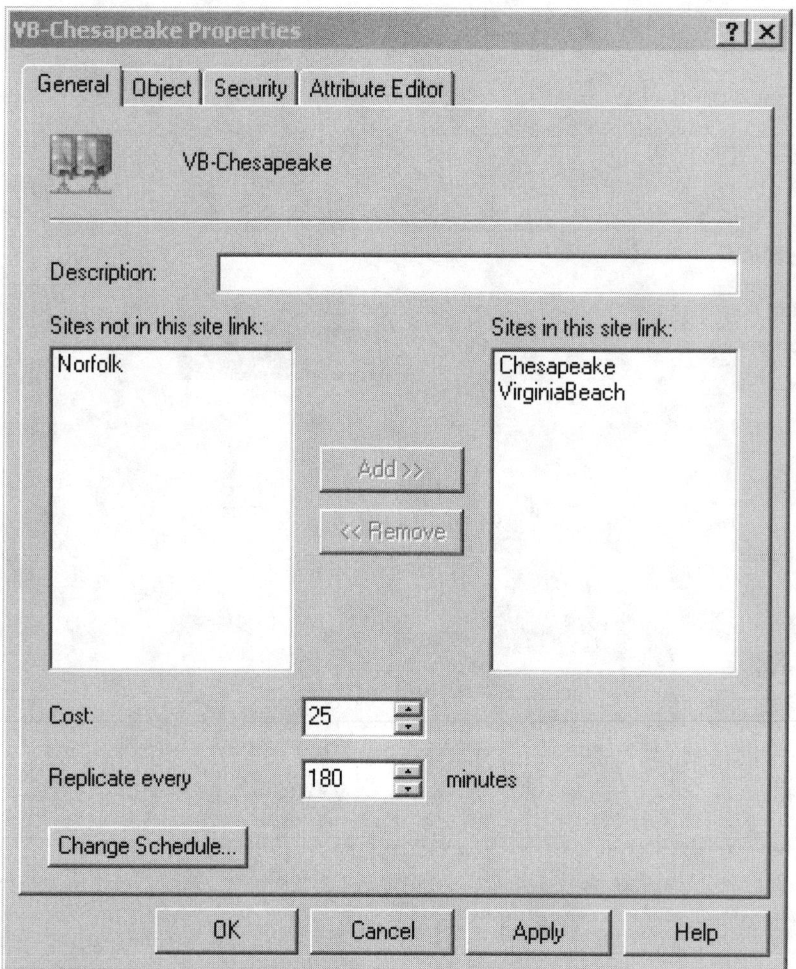

Figure 2-9 Changing the cost for a site link
Courtesy Course Technology/Cengage Learning

shows the property page for DC1 within Active Directory Sites and Services. IP is selected as the transport and then the Add button is clicked to designate DC1 as a preferred bridgehead server.

There's a drawback to this method, though. If the server you designate as a preferred bridgehead server goes down, the ISTG will not designate any other domain controllers as bridgehead servers unless they are also designated as preferred bridgehead servers. In other words, if DC1 is the only preferred bridgehead server in the site and it fails, the site will no longer receive and transmit inter-site replication traffic.

Therefore, when you designate one domain controller as a preferred bridgehead server, you should always designate at least one more to be a preferred bridgehead server. The ISTG will then designate one of the domain controllers to be a bridgehead server; if it fails, the ISTG will designate the other domain controller as the bridgehead server.

For the site with the four domain controllers (DC1, DC2, DC3, and the older DC4), you would designate DC1, DC2, and DC3 as preferred bridgehead servers. The ISTG will only designate DC1, DC2, or DC3 (but never DC4) as a bridgehead server.

Full Mesh Replication Topology

Most organizations will implement a **full mesh replication topology**. In this topology, each site can replicate with every other site. The full mesh replication topology is recommended for organizations that have 10 or fewer sites.

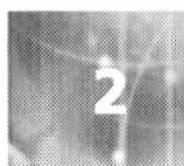

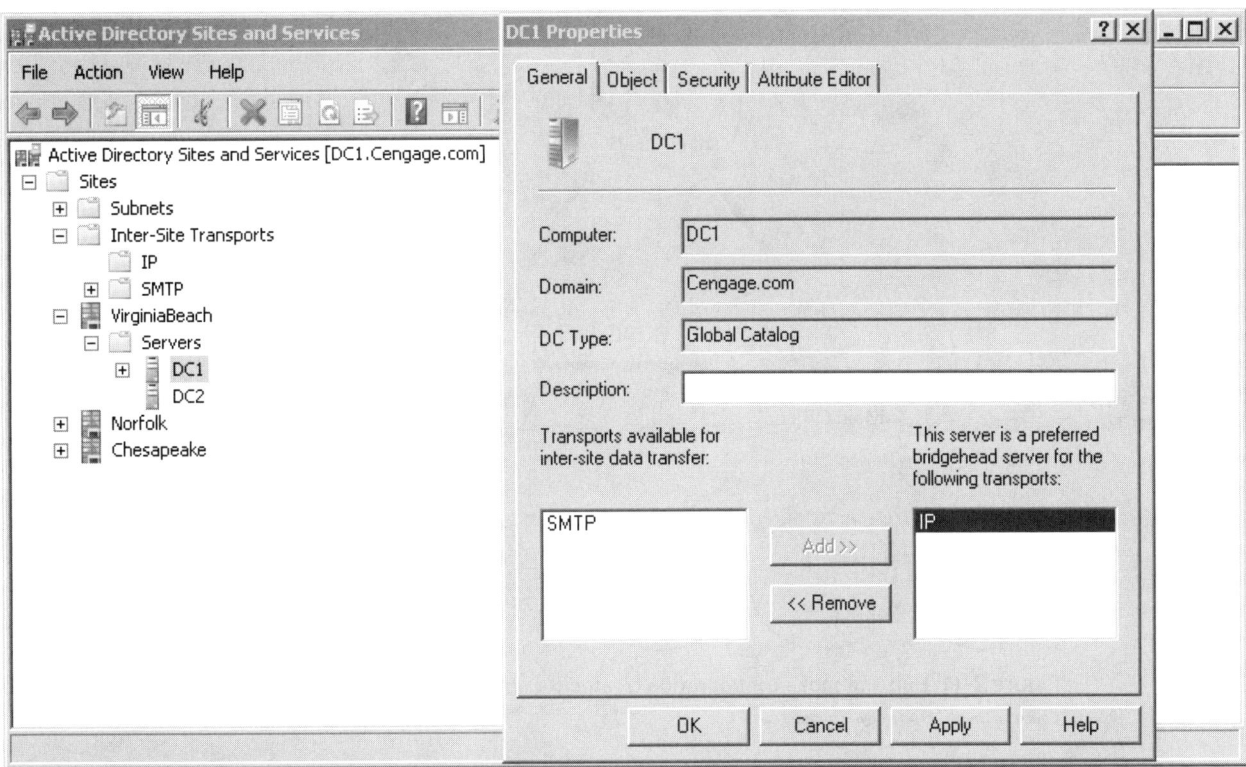

Figure 2-10 Designating a server as a preferred bridgehead server

Courtesy Course Technology/Cengage Learning

Site links are transitive by default. In other words, if Site A can replicate with Site B and Site B can replicate with Site C, Site A can also replicate with Site C through Site B. This normally works well for most organizations because site link bridging is enabled. However, you can remove the transitive nature of site links by disabling site link bridging, as shown in the next section.

Optimizing Replication with Hub and Spoke Sites

A **hub and spoke replication topology** is often used when you have relatively fast connections between regional sites, but slower connections to outlying sites. The outlying sites are often connected administratively to a regional headquarters, and the regional headquarters would typically have the faster connections.

Figure 2-11 shows a possible hub and spoke configuration that can be created for an organization with a main office, two regional headquarters, and multiple satellite offices. In the figure, the main office is configured as the hub for three satellite offices, and for each of the regional offices. Further, the regional office is configured as a hub for the two regional satellite offices.

As mentioned previously, site links are transitive by default. In other words, Regional HQ A has a direct link with the Main Office and Regional HQ B, and it also has indirect links with each of the satellite offices. Therefore, it's possible for regional satellite office 3 or 4 to replicate with Regional HQ A, which can result in duplicate replication.

You should consider disabling **site link bridging** when using a hub and spoke configuration for replication. When site link bridging is disabled, you must manually create any site link bridges that you want, but it gives you greater control over the site links used for replication.

Disabling site link bridging can prevent duplicate replication from occurring. Duplicate replication is not a problem with just three or four sites, but if many sites exist, a site can receive the same replicated data several times over a slow WAN link.

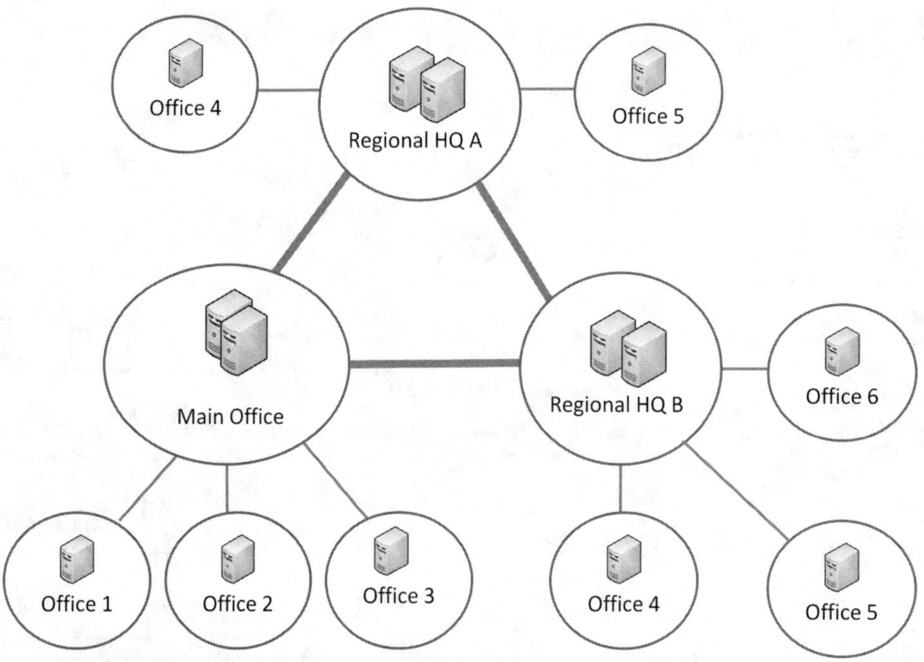

Figure 2-11 Hub and spoke configuration created for replication

Courtesy Course Technology/Cengage Learning

You can disable site link bridging by right-clicking IP in the Inter-Site Transports node of Active Directory Sites and Services. You would then deselect the Bridge all site links option shown in Figure 2-12.

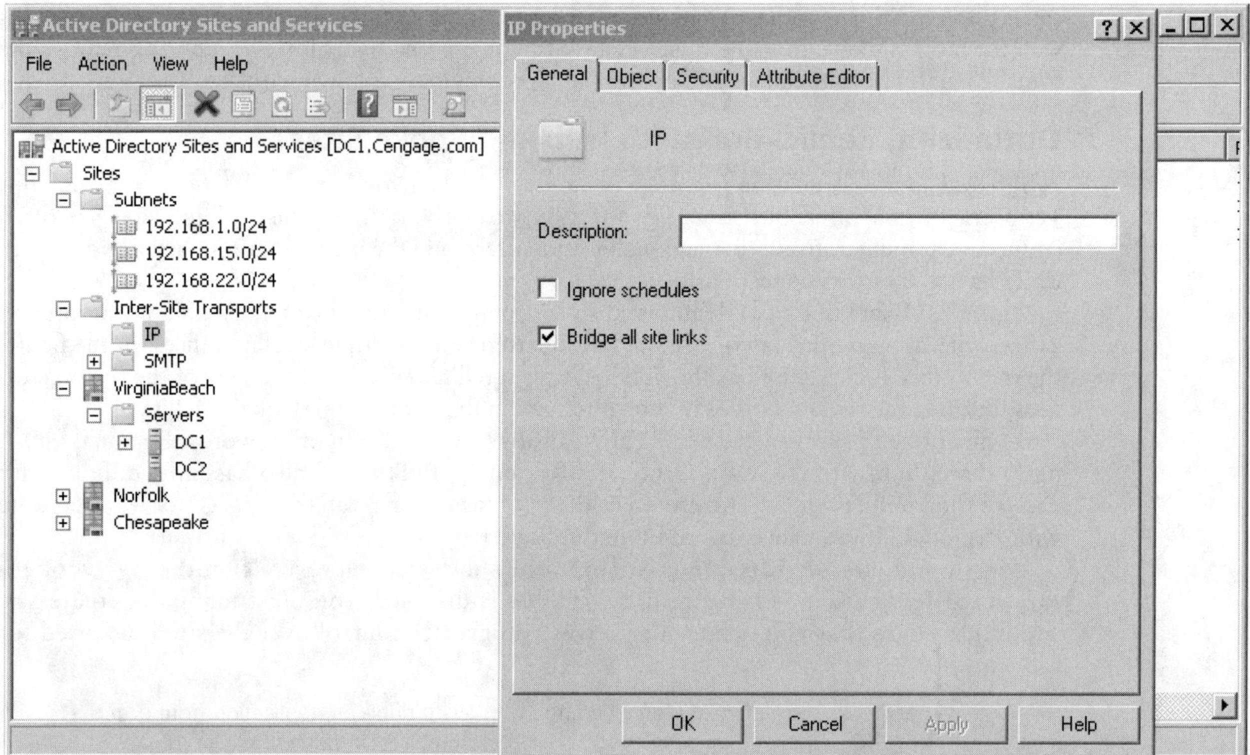

Figure 2-12 Disabling site link bridging

Courtesy Course Technology/Cengage Learning

If you do disable site link bridges, you'll need to manually create any site link bridges that you want to be transitive. For example, if you want Office 1 to replicate with Office 2 via the Main Office (from Figure 2-11), you'll need to create a manual site link bridge using Active Directory Sites and Services.

Designing the Branch Office

If your organization has multiple large physical locations, you create the subnet and **site objects**, place domain controllers (DCs) in the site, and configure the properties of the site link. This decreases the time needed for users to log on and ensures that users have access to local server resources even if the WAN link goes down.

However, what if the other locations aren't that large? In other words, what if you have a smaller branch office? The design of branch offices requires multiple questions to consider:

- Should a domain controller be placed in the site?
- Should the domain controller be a writable DC or a read-only DC (RODC)?
- Should the site include a DNS server?
- Should the DC be a global catalog server or should Universal Group Membership Caching be enabled?

All of these are important considerations. Before jumping into them one by one, it's useful to review the logon process. When a user (named Sally for this example) logs on, several steps occur behind the scenes. Look at Figure 2-13 when examining these steps.

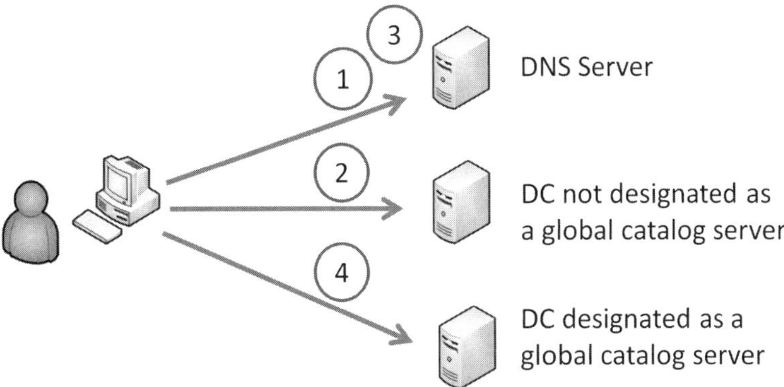

Figure 2-13 Reviewing the logon process
Courtesy Course Technology/Cengage Learning

1. After Sally enters her credentials (such as a user name and password), the Netlogon service will query DNS looking for a domain controller. It uses service location records in DNS (SRV records) to locate a DC in the same site.
2. The credentials are then passed to the DC and the process of building the token begins. Sally's token includes her SID and the SID of each group that includes her as a member. This DC will add the SIDs of global and domain local groups that include Sally as a member (but not universal groups because this DC is not a global catalog server).

Remember that universal group membership is only contained in the global catalog. Global and domain local group membership data is contained in every domain controller, but not universal group membership data. Additionally, not every DC is necessarily a global catalog server.

3. To complete the building of the token, the Netlogon service queries DNS to locate a global catalog server. It uses SRV records to identify a DC that is also a global catalog server. If one is located in the same site, it will be used. If a global catalog server is not located in the same site, another one will be located.
4. The global catalog server is contacted and the universal group membership information is identified. The SID for any universal groups that include Sally as a member is then added to the token, and the logon process finishes.

When Universal Group Membership Caching is enabled on a site, the Netlogon process recognizes that it can retrieve universal group membership information from the local domain controller instead of locating a global catalog server. Universal Group Membership Caching is covered in greater depth later in this chapter.

While these steps adequately explain the process, a couple of fine points are worth noting:

- **Logging with cached credentials.** If Sally has successfully logged on to the domain using her computer at least once before, her credentials are cached on the computer. If a DC is not available to authenticate her the next time she logs on, she can still log on using these cached credentials.
- **Cached credentials only provide local access.** When cached credentials are used, they only allow users to access resources on their local system. Sally will not be able to access any resources that require domain credentials.
  - If Sally was using a mobile computer, she could still log on to her computer while traveling and disconnected from the network. Or, if Sally was in a remote office with unreliable connectivity, she could still log on even if the WAN link was down.
  - This option also provides an added layer of security. Consider a user's account that has just been disabled because the user was fired. If he removed the NIC cable and logged on using cached credentials, the system wouldn't know his account was disabled, which creates a possible vulnerability. He could then reconnect the NIC cable and try to access resources on the network, such as company files located on a share. However, because cached credentials won't allow access to any domain resources until the account has been properly authenticated, this is not a risk.
- **Logon is prevented if a global catalog server can't be located.** Because the Netlogon process can't complete the creation of Sally's token if a global catalog server can't be located, her logon is prevented. This prevents another possible vulnerability. Imagine that Sally is a member of the U_Sales universal group, and the group has been explicitly denied permissions to a resource such as a share. If the universal group membership information wasn't available and the user was allowed to log on without it, she may be able to access the share even though access should be denied.

The following sections cover these points in more detail.

Deciding to Place a DC in a Remote Office

When you examine the logon process, focus on the important decision of whether to place a DC in a remote office or not. This decision isn't automatic, and it can affect capabilities and user experiences in the remote offices.

Placing a domain controller in a site provides two benefits:

- **Clients can log on to a DC in the site without using a WAN link.** This decreases the logon time required for users in the site.
- **Site-aware applications such as Distributed File System (DFS) will be optimized.** Users will access DFS data within their site (if it exists) without needing to cross the WAN link. Logon traffic remains within the site.

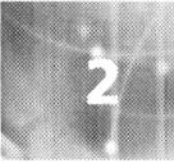

Consider the differences when a DC is placed in a site versus when it is not.

1. If a DC is not placed in the remote office, users must log on over the WAN link. If the WAN link is slow or not reliable, logon times may take a long time. If you have only five users in the site, this may be acceptable. As more users are added to a site, more traffic is generated and users might complain about the slow logon times, so the organization can choose to add a DC to the remote office.

2. If a DC is placed in the remote office, logon times will be quicker. Additionally, a server hosting DFS data could be replicated to the site.

If a DC is not placed in the remote office, you can still control which DCs a user will access when logging on. For example, you may want users in a remote office to log on using a DC in the main office. You can create a subnet object for the remote office and place it in the site object for the main office.

While the remote office subnet is not physically located at the main office, Active Directory doesn't know that. The Netlogon service will use the subnet of the client logging on to query DNS to locate a DC in the same site.

Deciding on a Writable DC or an RODC

Once you decide to place a DC in the site, you need to determine if it will be a normal **writable DC** or a **read-only domain controller (RODC)**. RODCs are a new feature in Windows Server 2008 and can be used in a branch office when a writable domain controller is not feasible.

Before Windows Server 2008, there were reasons you should *not* place a domain controller in a branch office: security and manpower.

- **Security**. If the branch office didn't have adequate physical security, placing a DC there presented a significant risk. If the DC was stolen, the attacker could gain access to administrator passwords. With unrestricted access to a DC, it's just a matter of time before the passwords would be cracked.
- **Manpower**. If the site didn't have IT personnel with adequate expertise to be placed in a domain administrators group, an organization wouldn't place a DC there.

RODCs overcome both of these issues. Unlike a writable DC, the RODC does not hold account passwords by default. Domain administrators can designate which passwords to hold on the DC, such as the users in the remote site. By default, user account passwords (most notably privileged users, such as those in the Domain Admins or Administrators groups) are not stored on the RODC.

RODCs also support a local Administrator role, providing Administrator role separation. Writable DCs do not have a local administrator. If a user needs to manage and administer the RODC, but should not have any permission in the domain, his user account can be added to the local Administrator role.

You can read more about RODCs later in this chapter.

Including DNS with the DC

Whenever possible, you should have the DC also host the role of Domain Name System (DNS) server. If you look back at Figure 2-13 and the explanation of the logon process, you can see that DNS is a central player. If a DNS server is not in the site, DNS queries will have to go over the WAN link.

When preparing for Microsoft exams, you should remember that Active Directory Integrated (ADI) DNS zones are often recommended. Microsoft has done a good job of making DNS easier to manage when it is ADI, and it works well; technically, it's a good choice. ADI DNS must be running on a domain controller, which must be running a Windows Server product. DNS could be hosted on a non-Microsoft system such as UNIX. However, it can't be ADI if hosted on a non-Microsoft system.

DNS zone transfers are included in Active Directory replication when the DNS server is configured with ADI zones. When the DNS server is hosted on a domain controller in another site, it enjoys the same benefits as other replication—the replicated data is compressed and can be scheduled.

Adding the Global Catalog or Enabling Universal Group Membership Caching

The last question you should answer is whether the DC should be a global catalog (GC) server or if **Universal Group Membership Caching** should be enabled. Remember the logon process described earlier. The Netlogon process requires access to universal group membership data. This data is hosted on a global catalog server, but you can also configure a site to cache universal group membership data.

When considering the global catalog server in a site, you actually have three choices:

- **Do not make the DC a global catalog server or enable Universal Group Membership Caching.** Users will have to access a global catalog server over the WAN link. This is the least desirable choice, but it is the default setting.
- **Make the DC a global catalog server.** If the organization has only one domain, the easiest solution is to make all DCs global catalog servers. It doesn't result in additional replicated data. However, if the organization has multiple domains, the global catalog will hold additional data, and replicated global catalog data can overload the WAN link. If the WAN link is reliable and has plenty of available bandwidth, this is the best choice. However, if the WAN link is unreliable or very little bandwidth is available, you should enable Universal Group Membership Caching.
- **Enable Universal Group Membership Caching on the site.** If you choose not to make the DC a global catalog server, you should enable this option. One significant benefit is that global catalog replication will be minimized in a multi-domain environment when Universal Group Membership Caching is enabled.

Although there are three choices, the first one simply indicates that the global catalog wasn't considered in the design. You should choose either to make the DC a global catalog server or enable Universal Group Membership Caching. This ensures that users can log on if the WAN link fails.

You can make any domain controller a global catalog server using Active Directory Sites and Services. Select the server in the Sites \ *SiteName* \ Servers \ *ServerName* node. Right-click NTDS Settings for the server and select Properties. Figure 2-14 shows the NTDS Settings Properties page for DC2. It is not currently a global catalog server, but it becomes one when you check the Global Catalog box and click OK.

Enabling the global catalog option on a server will result in replication of the global catalog data to the server. Depending on the size of the global catalog and available bandwidth, this could take a long time, and could affect the performance of the network.

When Universal Group Membership is cached on a site, a DC in the site caches this data once it is retrieved. For example, when Sally logs on the first time, her universal group membership information is retrieved from a global catalog server. The DC in the site caches the universal group membership information for Sally. The next time Sally logs on, the data is retrieved from cache instead of querying a global catalog server.

Remember the following points about Universal Group Membership Caching:

- **It is enabled on a per-site basis.** Enabling it on one site doesn't affect the functionality of other sites. It is enabled using Active Directory Sites and Services.

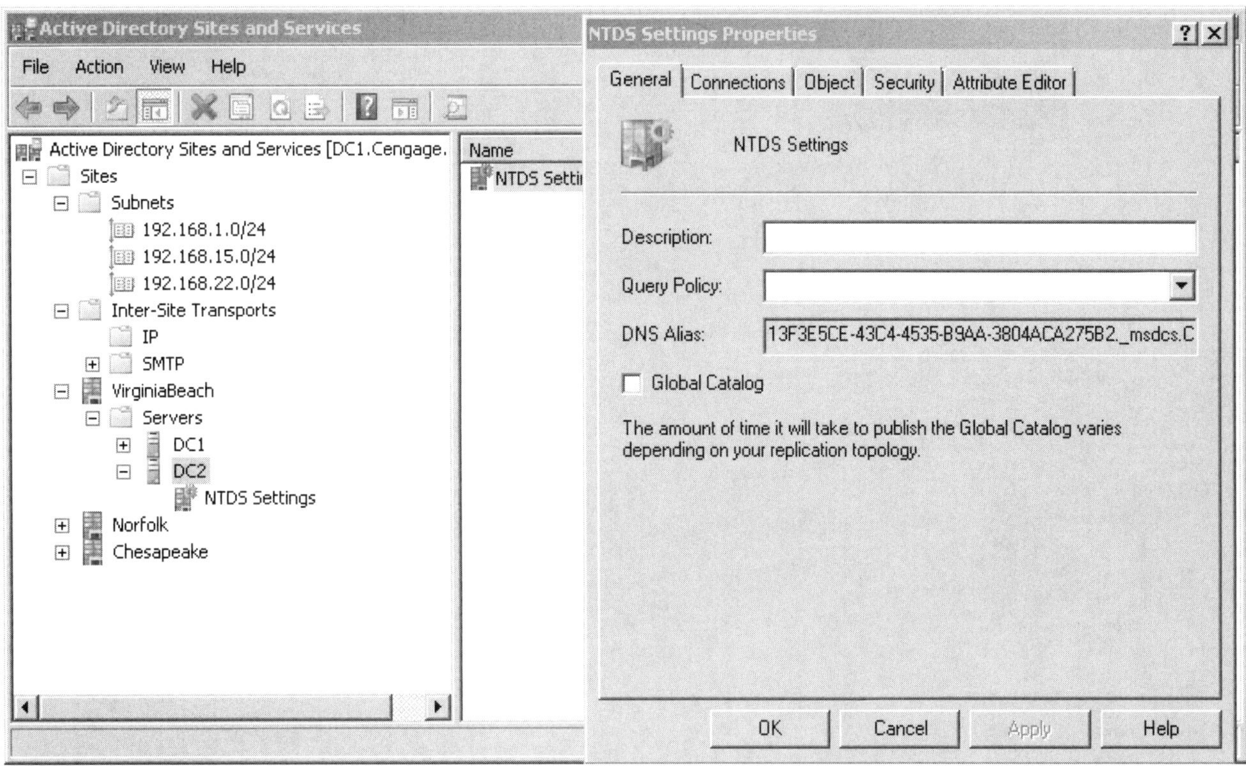

Figure 2-14 Designating a DC as a global catalog server

Courtesy Course Technology/Cengage Learning

- **The cached data is automatically renewed every 8 hours by default.** The DC in the site will query a global catalog server for changes in the cached universal group membership data and update the cache with current data. This 8-hour interval starts after the last refresh or after the last reboot.
- **Cached data will expire in 7 days.** If a DC can't reach a global catalog server to retrieve updates, the cached data will be considered stale. Users will no longer be able to log on with the cached data, but will instead need to contact a global catalog server.

Activity 2-3: Enabling Universal Group Membership Caching on a Site

Time Required: 10 minutes
Objective: Enable Universal Group Membership Caching on a site.

Description: You have recently reviewed design requirements for sites in your enterprise. You have decided to enable Universal Group Membership Caching for the Chesapeake site. This lab assumes that the Chesapeake site was created in Activity 2-1.

1. Start **DC1** and log on with the domain **Administrator** account and a password of **P@ssw0rd.**
2. Start the **Active Directory Sites and Services** console via the **Administrative Tools** menu.
3. Browse to the **Chesapeake** site in the **Sites** container.
4. Right-click **NTDS Site Settings** and select Properties.

The NTDS Site Settings provide access to different properties than the NTDS Settings for a server. For this step, ensure that you access the NTDS Site Settings for the site.

5. Select the check box next to **Enable Universal Group Membership Caching,** as shown in Figure 2-15. Click **OK.**
6. Close all open windows.

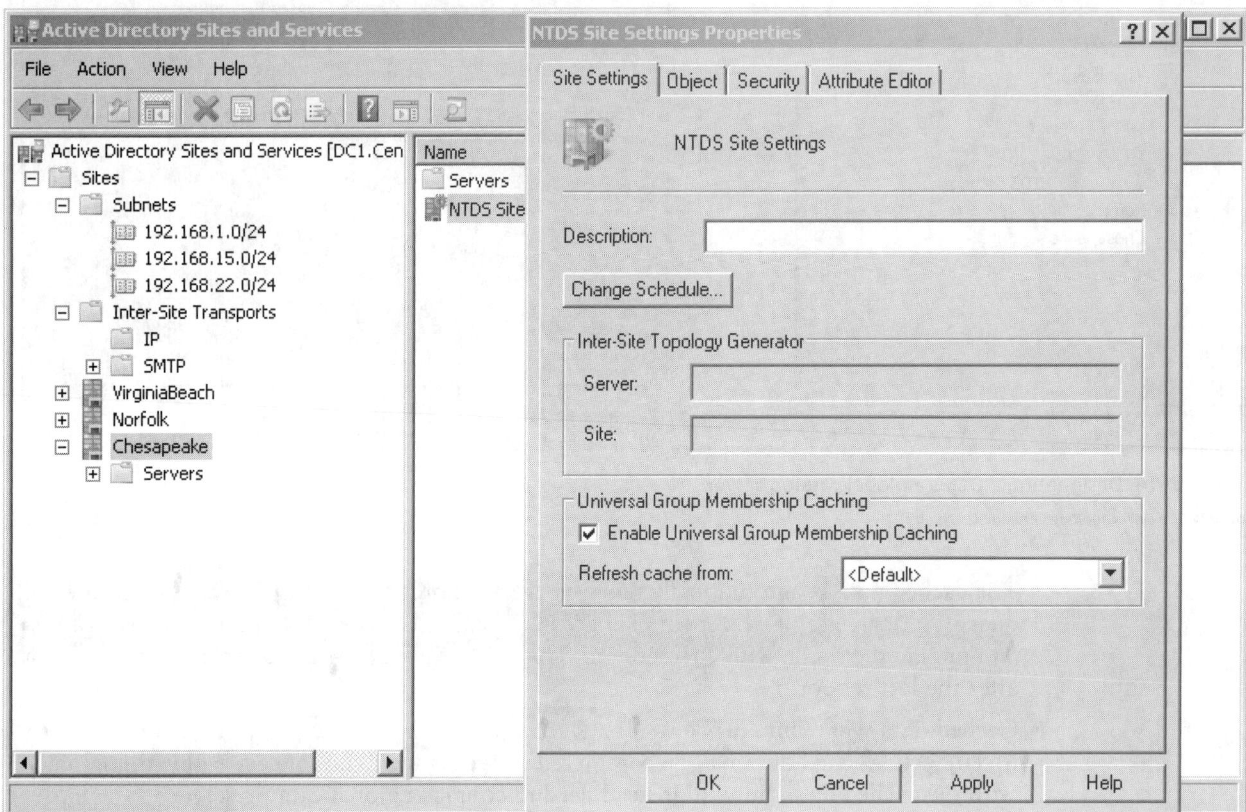

Figure 2-15 Enabling Universal Group Membership Caching

Courtesy Course Technology/Cengage Learning

Understanding Operations Master Roles

Domain controllers work as multi-masters with loose convergence. As multi-masters, they are all equal (for most functions) and each domain controller can accept changes and write those changes to the Active Directory Domain Services (AD DS) database. Loose convergence means that given enough time, all of the changes made to one domain controller (DC) will eventually make it to all other domain controllers.

However, as Napoleon said in Orwell's *Animal Farm*, "some are more equal than others." Similarly, some DCs perform additional roles or functions and are more equal than other DCs. Five **operations master roles** are held by different DCs in the enterprise.

These roles have been called Flexible Single Master Operations (FSMO, pronounced *fizz-mo*) masters, but Microsoft has replaced the term *FSMO* with *operations masters* in some documentation. Many tools, such as the NTDSUtil command-line utility, still refer to these as FSMO roles.

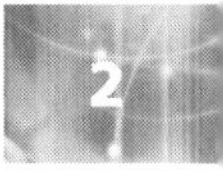

The five operations master roles are:

- **Schema master**. This is the only DC that has write permissions on the schema. When extending the schema, you must be able to reach the schema master and you'll often log on to the DC holding the schema master role. Only members of the Schema Admins group can modify the schema. Only one schema master exists in a forest.
- **Domain naming master**. The DC hosting the domain naming master role manages the addition and removal of domains, and the addition and removal of application directory partitions. If this DC is not available, you won't be able to create or remove domains using DCpromo, or create or remove application directory partitions. Only one domain naming master exists in a forest.
- **RID master**. This master manages the pool of available RIDs and issues banks of RIDs to other domain controllers. The RID master ensures that each relative identifier (RID) is unique. Domain controllers create security identifiers (SID) using these unique RIDs, which ensures that all the SIDs in a domain are unique. The RID master issues banks of about 500 new RIDs to DCs at a time. When the DC runs low, it requests more RIDs. Every domain in the forest holds one RID master.
- **PDC emulator**. The PDC emulator manages time synchronization and password changes in the domain. It's common to synchronize the DC holding the PDC emulator role with an external time source. All DCs in the domain synchronize their time with the PDC emulator, and all clients synchronize their time with the DC that authenticates them. Password changes are replicated to the PDC emulator using urgent replication. This ensures that if a user changes her password on one domain controller, she can log on to the domain even if she accesses a different domain controller that hasn't received the password change via replication yet. Every domain in the forest holds one PDC emulator.

The PDC emulator role must be hosted on a Windows Server 2008 domain controller to support read-only domain controllers (RODCs) in the domain. RODCs handle passwords differently than other domain controllers.

- **Infrastructure master**. This master updates cross-domain group-to-user references. It ensures that changes made to object names from objects in another domain are accurately reflected in the group membership information. For example, if a user's name is changed in domain A, the infrastructure master in domain B ensures that this name is accurately reflected in all of the domain B groups where the user is a member. The infrastructure master role is meaningless in a single-domain forest because there are no changes from another domain to update. Every domain in the forest holds one infrastructure master.

It's important to remember that the infrastructure master will not function properly if it is located on a DC that is also a global catalog server.

The easiest way to identify the role holders for all of the operations master roles in the forest and a domain is by executing the following command at the command-prompt:

`Netdom query fsmo`

The output will look something like this:

```
Schema Master            DC1.Cengage.com
Domain naming master     DC1.Cengage.com
PDC                      DC1.Cengage.com
RID pool manager         DC1.Cengage.com
Infrastructure master    DC1.Cengage.com
```

Figure 2-16 identifies the different operations master roles in a forest. Because this is a single forest, it includes one schema master and one domain naming master. Each domain also holds individual roles of RID master, PDC emulator, and infrastructure master. It's important to know how many of these roles exist in a domain and in a forest.

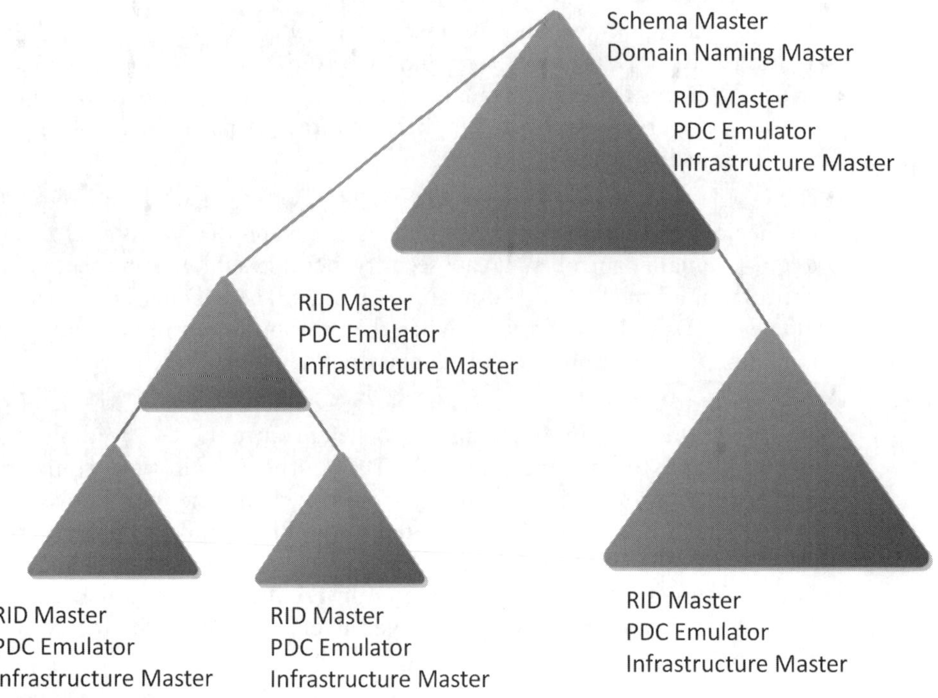

Figure 2-16 Identifying operations master roles in a forest

Courtesy Course Technology/Cengage Learning

The figure has one schema master and one domain naming master. This five-domain forest includes five RID masters, five PDC emulators, and five infrastructure masters.

The first domain controller in the forest will hold all five roles. The first domain controller in each domain will hold the three domain controller roles. However, you can transfer the roles to other domain controllers.

The Infrastructure Master and the Global Catalog

The infrastructure master will not work if it is on a DC designated as a global catalog server. It helps to understand how the global catalog works to understand this limitation. The global catalog includes a listing of all objects (and a subset of their attributes) in the entire forest. When an object name changes (Sally Smith changes to Sally Johnson, for example), the global catalog receives this name change and any DCs hosting the global catalog are also aware of the name change. Other DCs in the domain are unaware of the name change until the infrastructure master notifies them.

The infrastructure master will periodically query the global catalog to see if any names listed in the global catalog have changed. It only checks for object names from other domains that are members of groups in its domain. For example, if Sally Smith in domain A has been added to the G_Sales global group in domain B, the infrastructure master in domain B will periodically check whether the name of Sally Smith has changed. The infrastructure master in domain A would not perform this check because Sally Smith is in domain A.

However, if the infrastructure master is also the global catalog server, it will learn of the name change when the global catalog is replicated to it. The infrastructure master will never query the global catalog server and find differences, and other DCs in the domain will never be updated with the name changes.

A subtle point is worth mentioning here. While the infrastructure master will not work properly if it's on a global catalog server, you can get around this problem. If all domain controllers are also designated as global catalog servers, the infrastructure master isn't needed because every domain controller learns of the changes when it receives the global catalog. The challenge with this approach is that replicating the global catalog to all domain controllers can take excessive bandwidth.

Operations Masters and the ADPrep Tool

The Active Directory Preparation (ADPrep) tool was covered in Chapter 1. As a reminder, and to help you link these two topics, the ADPrep tool sometimes needs to be run on domain controllers holding specific operations master roles.

- **ADPrep /ForestPrep** should be run on the domain controller holding the schema master role for the forest.
- **ADPrep /DomainPrep** (and **ADPrep /DomainPrep /GPPrep**) should be run on the domain controller holding the infrastructure master role.
- **ADPrep /RODCPrep** can be run on any domain controller in the forest.

Transferring Operations Master Roles

Occasionally, you'll need to transfer roles from one domain controller to another. For example, you might need to implement the design of Active Directory or respond to maintenance needs.

As an example, you know that the infrastructure master won't work properly in a multi-domain environment if it's on a DC that is also a global catalog server. However, the first DC promoted in a domain will hold all three of the domain operations master roles, and will be a global catalog server. When you promote another server to a domain controller, you could transfer the infrastructure master role to the other server.

Most organizations design their DCs so that all operations master roles are hosted on a single DC. This isn't a requirement, but it makes the design simpler. If the domain has three DCs in the same site, one would typically hold all of the roles, and the other two would be configured as global catalog servers.

After your design is implemented, you might need to transfer the roles to perform maintenance. For example, if the domain controller designated as the RID master is being taken down to perform extensive maintenance, you could transfer the role to another DC. This would ensure that RIDs could still be issued while the original DC is down.

Active Directory Users and Computers is used to transfer the RID master, PDC emulator, and infrastructure master from one DC to another. When transferring roles, you would log on to the target DC—the DC that will hold the role after it has been transferred.

Figure 2-17 shows the Active Directory Users and Computers tool on DC2 being used to access the operations masters page. This page is accessed by right-clicking the domain name (Cengage.com in the figure) and selecting Operations Masters.

In the figure, the RID tab is selected, but you can just as easily select the PDC tab or the Infrastructure tab to transfer the roles. The figure shows that DC1 is currently holding the role. Because you're logged on to DC2, DC2 is selected in the lower text box. By clicking the Change button, the role will be transferred to DC2.

Active Directory Domains and Trusts is used to transfer the domain naming master role, and Active Directory Schema is used to transfer the schema naming master.

The Active Directory Schema tool is not available as an MMC snap-in by default. It must be registered before it appears. You can register the Active Directory Schema snap-in with the following command:

```
regsvr32 schmmgmt.dll
```

You can execute the command from the command prompt or from the Start Search text box. After it is executed, the Active Directory Schema snap-in can be added to an MMC.

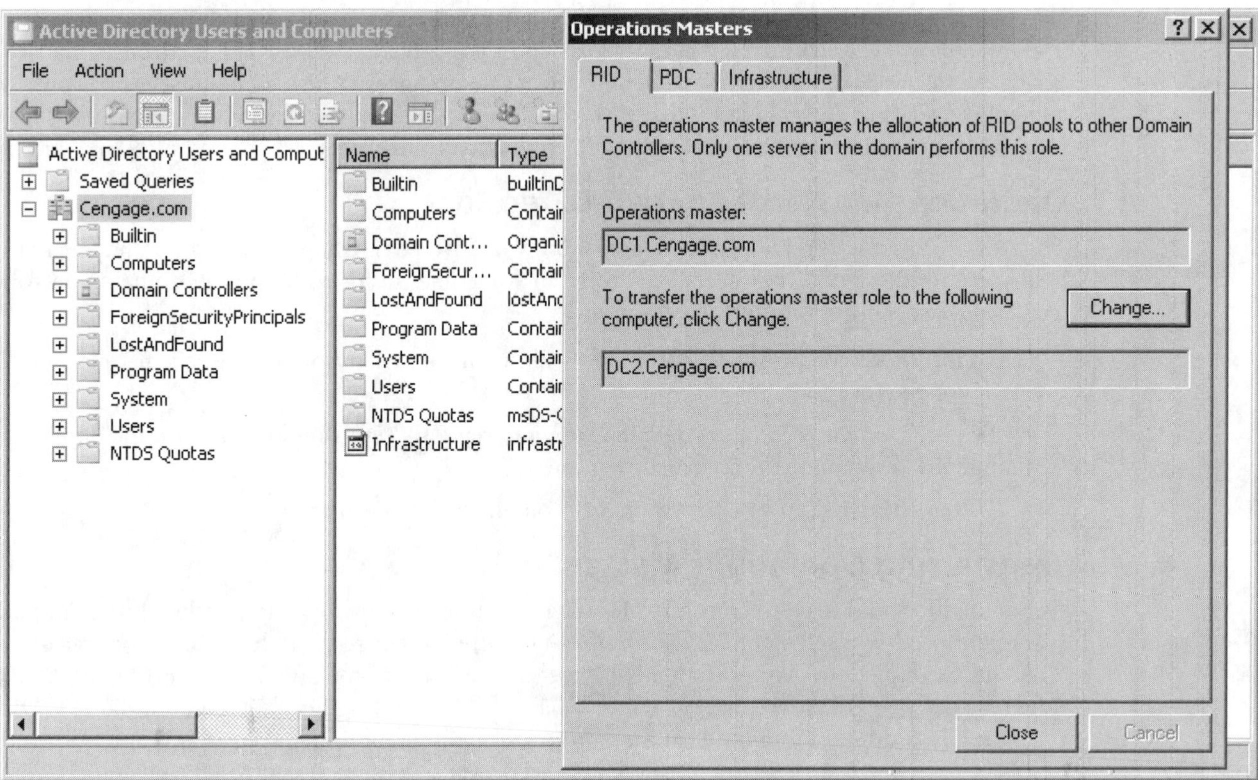

Figure 2-17 Identifying operations master roles in the domain

Courtesy Course Technology/Cengage Learning

In order to logically transfer the roles, both DCs must be up and operational. If they are not, the transfer will fail, but you can choose to seize the roles.

Seizing Operations Master Roles

If a DC fails while holding a role and you need to have another DC assume the role, you can seize the role. Seizing a role is a drastic action and should only be done as a last resort after verifying that you can't transfer the role.

Sometimes you can wait before seizing the role. For example, if an RID master fails but will be up after parts are received in a day or two, you may not need to seize the role. The RID master issues banks of about 500 RIDs to other DCs, so even if the RID master fails, other DCs will still be able to create additional objects using the available RIDs previously received from the RID master.

To view how many RIDs are available in the current RID pool for a DC, execute the following command from the command prompt on the DC:

```
dcdiag /test: ridmanager /v
```

The RidManager results include the range of the current pool issued to the DC (such as 2100 to 2599) and the value of the next RID to be used (such as 2101). These results can tell you how many objects you can create on the DC before new RIDS are needed.

You would use the **NTDSUtil** command-line tool to seize a role. This valuable shell utility has many layers, and as you access different layers of the shell, different capabilities are available.

When using NTDSUtil to seize a role, you log on to the target DC. The FSMO Maintenance subshell is used to connect to the target server, and then to seize the role. NTDSUtil will first try to transfer the role before seizing it, and will only seize it if the transfer fails.

Activities 2-4 and 2-5 lead you through the process of modifying your lab environment to a single-domain forest with two domain controllers. In Activity 2-6, you'll logically transfer a role and seize a role.

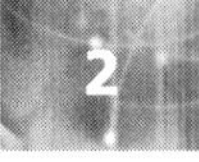

Activity 2-4: Removing Active Directory on DC2

Time Required: 15 minutes
Objective: Run DCpromo to remove Active Directory from a server.

Description: You previously hosted a forest named CT.com, but all the objects in this forest have been migrated into your primary forest. You now need to remove Active Directory from the last domain controller in the forest. This lab is designed to remove Active Directory from DC2, which was created in Chapter 1.

1. Start **DC1** and **DC2**. Log on to **DC2** with the domain **Administrator** account and a password of **P@ssw0rd**.
2. Click **Start**, type **DCpromo** in the **Start Search** text box, and press **Enter**.
3. Click **Next** on the **Welcome** page.
4. Review the information on the global catalog server, which is displayed in the popup dialog box. Click **OK**.

A global catalog server must exist in every domain within a forest. However, because this server is the last domain controller in the forest, a global catalog server is no longer needed in this domain (or this forest).

5. Select the check box to **Delete the domain because this server is the last domain controller in the domain**, as shown in Figure 2-18. Click **Next**.
6. Review the information on the **Application Data Partition** page. Click **Next**. Select the check box to **Delete All Application Directory Partitions on this Active Directory Domain Controller**. Click **Next**.
7. Enter **P@ssw0rd** in the **Password** and **Confirm Password** text boxes. This is the password for the **Administrator** account on the member server after Active Directory is removed. Click **Next**.
8. Review the information on the **Summary** page and click **Next**. Select the **Reboot on Completion** check box. When DCpromo finishes, the server will reboot.

If DC2 was created in the Chapter 1 activity, it was created using an IP address of 192.168.1.20/24 for itself, and a DNS address of 192.168.1.10, which is the DNS server. These settings will be maintained by this lab, but you may want to double-check the NIC settings (using **IPConfig /all**) to prevent problems later.

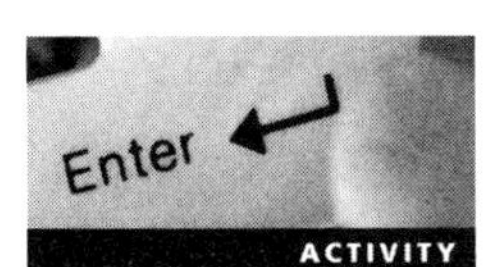

Activity 2-5: Creating a Replica Domain Controller

Time Required: 15 minutes
Objective: Run DCpromo on a second server in the domain to create a replica domain controller.

Description: You want to create a second domain controller and transfer FSMO roles to it. This lab assumes that you have a domain named cengage.com hosted by DC1, as created in Chapter 1, and that you have a second server named DC2 that does not have Active Directory installed.

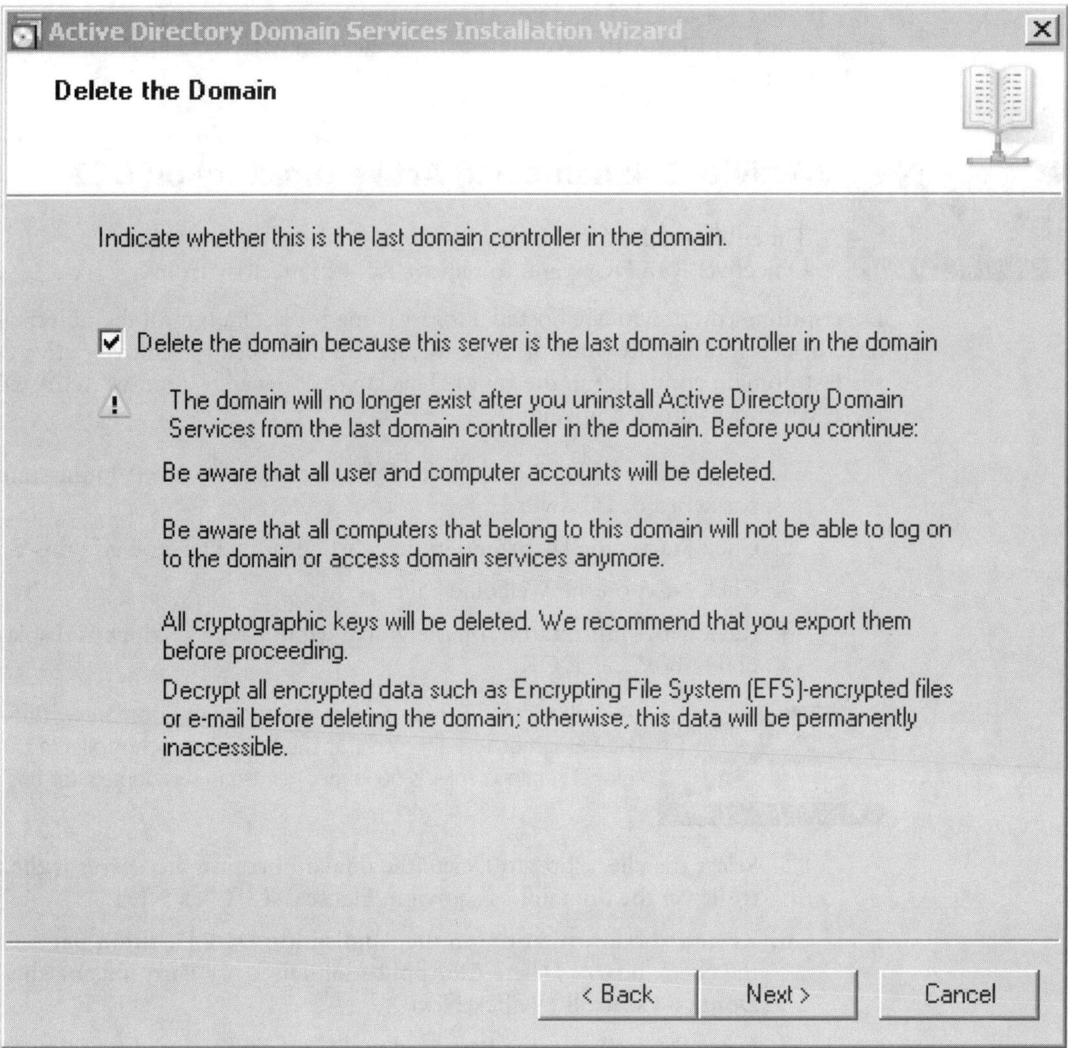

Figure 2-18 Deleting the last domain controller in the domain

Courtesy Course Technology/Cengage Learning

1. Ensure that both **DC1** and **DC2** are started. Log on to **DC2** with the local **Administrator** account and a password of **P@ssw0rd**.
2. Click **Start**, type **DCpromo** in the **Start Search** text box, and press **Enter**.
3. Click **Next** on the **Welcome** page. Click **Next** on the Operating System Compatibility page.
4. Select **Existing Forest**. Ensure that **Add a Domain Controller to an Existing Domain** is selected. Click **Next**.
5. Enter **cengage.com** as the name of the domain. Click **Set**. Type **Administrator** as the user name and enter a password of **P@ssw0rd**. Click **OK**. Click **Next**.
6. **Cengage.com** will be selected on the **Select a Domain** page. Click **Next**.
7. Select the **VirginiaBeach** site, which was created earlier in this chapter. Click **Next**.
8. On the **Additional Domain Controller Options** page, deselect **Global Catalog** and click **Next**. If you're using the same DC2 from Chapter 1, DNS will already be installed on this server.

9. A dialog box similar to that shown in Figure 2-19 will appear, indicating a conflict with the global catalog. Click **Do not transfer the infrastructure master role to this domain controller. I will correct the configuration later**. A later activity will explain how to transfer the infrastructure role.

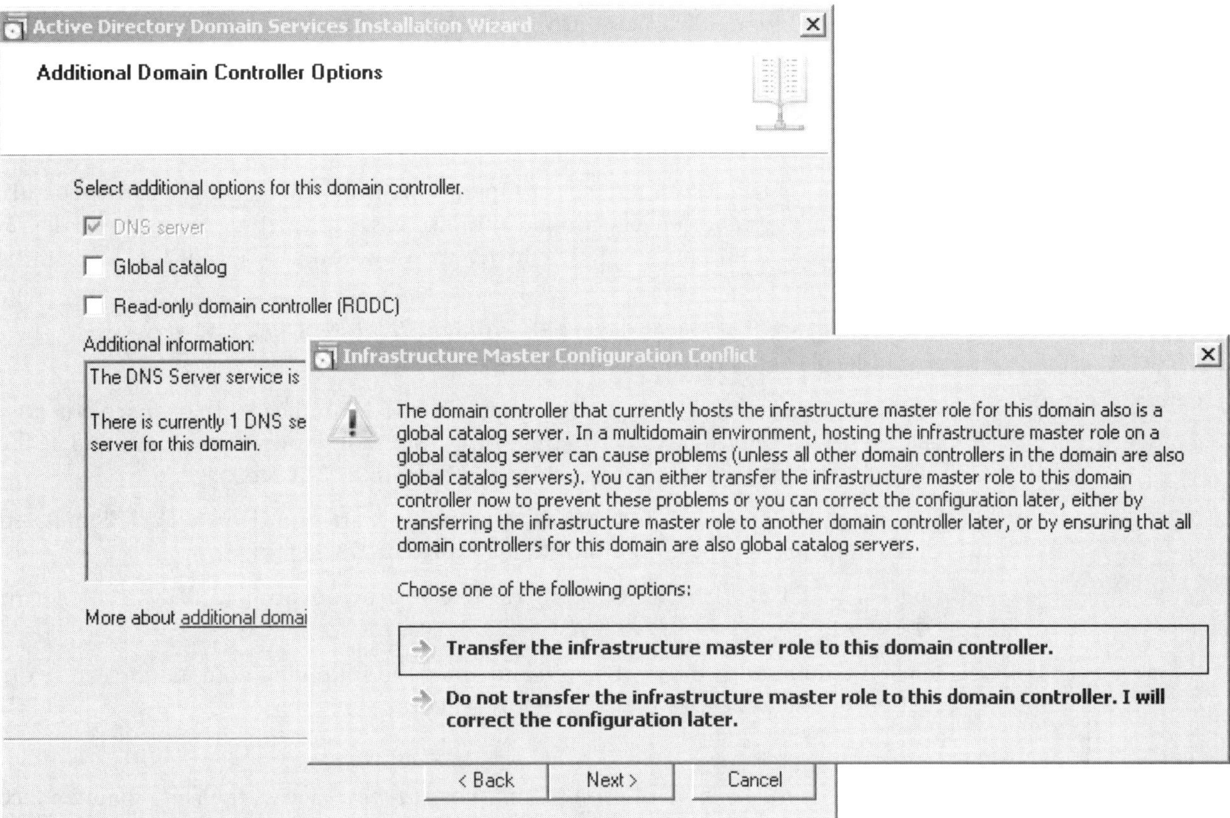

Figure 2-19 Infrastructure master conflict with global catalog warning

Courtesy Course Technology/Cengage Learning

10. Review the information on the **Delegation for the DNS Server** page, and click **Yes** to continue. This notification is normal.
11. Accept the default locations on the **Location for Database, Log Files, and SYSVOL** page and click **Next**.
12. Enter **P@ssw0rd** in the **Password** and **Confirm Password** text boxes. Click **Next**.
13. Review the information on the **Summary** page. Click **Next**. Select the check box to **Reboot On Completion**. When DCpromo finishes, the system will automatically reboot.

Activity 2-6: Transferring and Seizing the Infrastructure Master Role

Time Required: 20 minutes

Objective: Identify the operations master role holders, transfer a role, and seize a role.

Description: You need to document the role holders in your forest. After documenting the roles, you decide to transfer the infrastructure master role to DC2 in your domain. After you've verified that the transfer is successful, you decide to simulate a failure of DC2 and seize the role using DC1. This lab assumes that Activities 2-1 through 2-5 have been completed, and that the Cengage.com domain exists with two domain controllers (DC1 and DC2).

1. Ensure that both **DC1** and **DC2** are started. Log on to **DC2** with the domain **Administrator** account and a password of **P@ssw0rd.**
2. Click **Start**, type **cmd** in the **Start Search** box, and press **Enter** to open a command prompt.
3. Enter the following command at the command prompt to view all of the current operations masters in your forest:

   netdom query fsmo
4. Start **Active Directory Users and Computers** from the **Administrative Tools** menu.
5. Right-click **Cengage.com** and select **Operations Masters**. Select the **Infrastructure** tab. DC1.Cengage.com should be the current operations master and DC2. Cengage.com should appear in the lower window, indicating that the role can be transferred to DC2.
6. Click **Change.** Click **Yes** in the confirmation dialog box. Click **OK** in the dialog box that indicates the transfer was successful.

   At this point, **Active Directory Users and Computers** indicates that the role is now held by DC2. You can also verify this with the **netdom query fsmo** command at the command prompt. Click **Close** to close the **Operations Masters** page.
7. Shut down DC2 to simulate a failure by selecting **Start, Shut Down**. Enter **Simulated Crash** in the Comment box of the Shutdown Event Tracker window.
8. Log on to **DC1** with the domain **Administrator** account and a password of **P@ssw0rd.**
9. Open a command prompt on DC1 and enter the following command to start the NTDSUtil shell tool with the **NTDSUtil** prompt:

   ```
   NTDSUtil
   ```
10. Type **roles** at the **NTDSUtil** prompt and press **Enter** to access the **fsmo maintenance** prompt.
11. Type **connections** at the **NTDSUtil** prompt and press **Enter** to access the **server connections** prompt.
12. Enter the following command to connect to the target server (DC1).

   ```
   connect to server dc1.cengage.com
   ```

   This command binds a connection to DC1 using the same administrator credentials you used to log on to DC1.
13. Type **quit** and press **Enter**. This command doesn't actually quit the program, but instead exits the **server connections** prompt and brings you back to the **fsmo maintenance** prompt.
14. Enter the following command to seize the infrastructure master role:

   ```
   seize infrastructure master
   ```

   When prompted to confirm the request, click **Yes**. See Figure 2-20.

   NTDSUtil will first try to contact DC2 to logically transfer the role. Because DC2 is down, this attempt will fail. NTDSUtil will then initiate a seizure. The results will look similar to Figure 2-21.

   At first glance, you might think an error occurred because half of the output reports details on the error. However, these reports are expected because DC2 cannot be contacted.
15. Close the command prompt and any open windows.

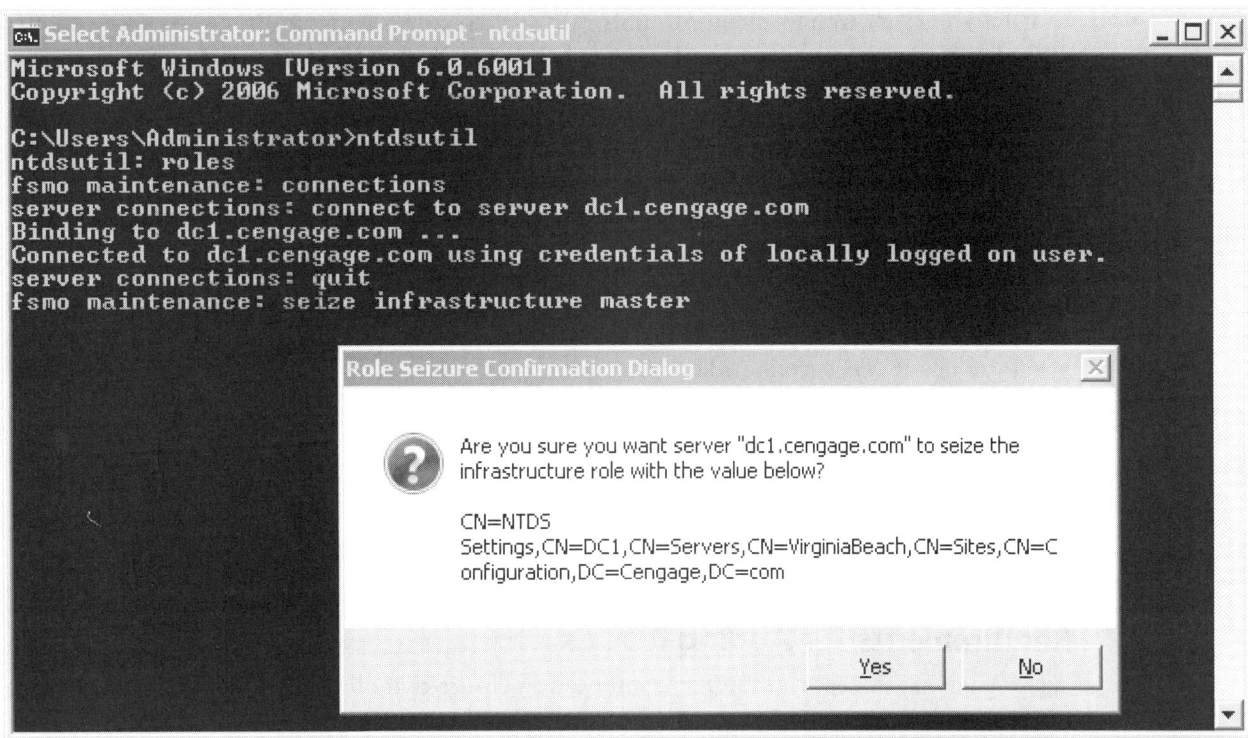

Figure 2-20 Verifying the role seizure action

Courtesy Course Technology/Cengage Learning

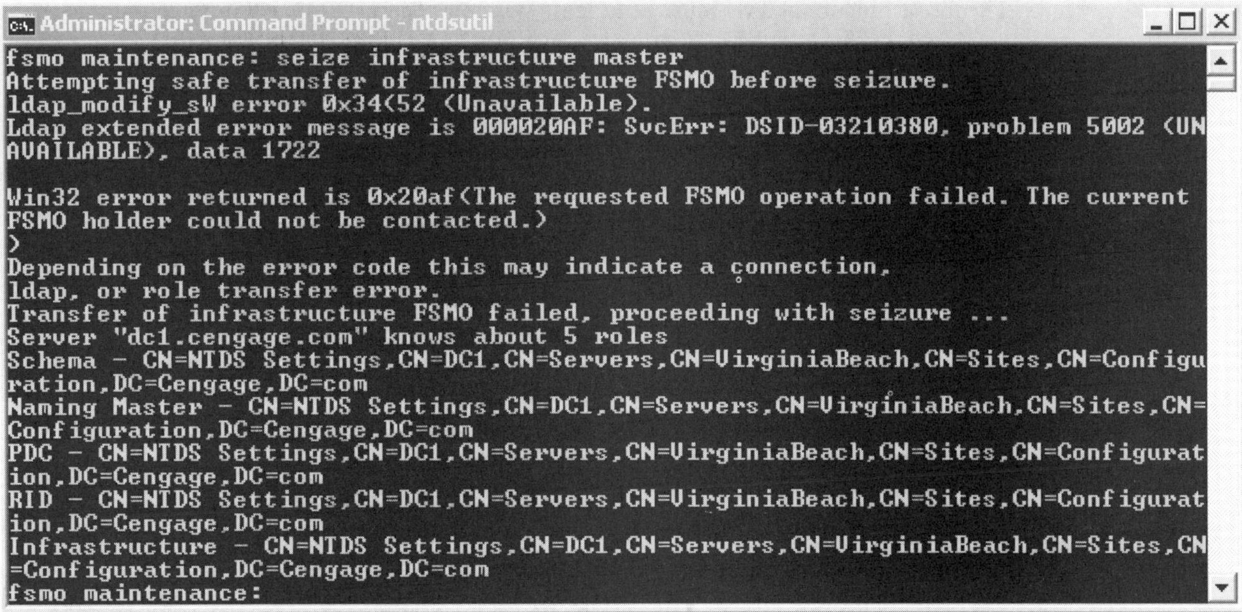

Figure 2-21 Successful seizure of the role using NTDSUtil

Courtesy Course Technology/Cengage Learning

Using RODCs

Read-only domain controllers (RODCs) are a new feature in Windows Server 2008. As mentioned earlier in the chapter, you can place a writable DC or an RODC in a remote office. The RODC provides increased security because the administrator passwords are not stored on an

RODC. You also can implement Administrator role separation on an RODC to allow administrators in the remote office to manage the RODC without granting them permissions in a domain account.

Most other functions of the RODC work just as they work on a regular DC. For example, Active Directory will still apply Group Policy objects (GPOs), just as Group Policy is applied anywhere else. Users in the remote office will be affected by the default domain policy. Additionally, a GPO could be applied to the site hosting the RODC, or to an OU that contains the users and computers in the site.

This section covers the following RODC topics:

- Requirements for adding RODCs
- Installing RODCs from media
- Server Core and RODCs
- Prestaging an RODC
- RODC passwords
- RODC filtered attribute set
- Local Administrators role on an RODC

Requirements for Adding RODCs

When planning to deploy an RODC, you need to ensure that all of the following requirements for RODCs have been met:

- **RODCs can only be installed on Windows Server 2008 or greater.** You cannot install Windows Server 2008 on a Windows Server 2003 system, but it is possible to install an RODC on Windows Server 2008 R2.
- **The forest functional level must be at least Windows Server 2003.** All domain controllers must be running on at least Windows Server 2003 and all domains in the forest must be raised to at least the domain functional level of Windows Server 2003.
- **ADPrep /RODCPrep must be run in the forest.** It only needs to be run once and can be run on any domain controller in the forest. This command was covered in more depth in Chapter 1.
- **At least one Windows Server 2008 writable domain controller must exist.** An RODC can only replicate data with a DC hosted on a Windows Server 2008 domain controller. This domain controller should be placed in an adjoining site to minimize replication across multiple site links. If site link bridging is not disabled, the RODC can still connect with the Windows Server 2008 DC if it's not in an adjoining site.
- **The DC holding the PDC emulator operations role must be running Windows Server 2008.** The PDC emulator handles password changes, and it must be hosted on a Windows Server 2008 domain controller so that it can properly handle password changes initiated by clients connected to an RODC.

Installing RODCs from Media

The **install from media (IFM)** option is available when you promote a server to a domain controller using the advanced options. The IFM option allows a server to get a copy of Active Directory from media (such as CD, DVD, or USB drive) instead of replicating the data over a WAN link.

Normally, when a member server is promoted to a DC, it replicates all of the Active Directory information from another DC in the domain. Within a well-connected site, this works well. However, when the new DC is in a remote site connected via a slow WAN link, this can be a problem. If the WAN link is slow, or highly utilized, the promotion could take an unacceptably long time and affect the performance of the link for other users. You have two options to avoid replicating data across the WAN link:

- **Promote the server in the same site as another DC and manually transport it to the remote site.** This might work well if the branch office is relatively close and the server hasn't been delivered to the branch office yet. However, if the server is in another city or another state, or has already been delivered to the branch office, the extra man-hours required for this option aren't justified.

- **Use the IFM option.** The IFM option allows you to transport only the media that holds the Active Directory data. You could deliver the media yourself if the office is relatively close, or mail it if necessary (though you should take extra security precautions if it's mailed).

IFM is created using the NTDSUtil command. Open a command prompt with administrative permissions on a writable DC and enter the following commands:

```
Ntdsutil
Activate instance ntds
Ifm
Create rodc c:\DCpromo
```

These commands create an ntds.dit file in the C:\DCPromo\Active Directory folder.

You can also create installation media for a full installation (not an RODC) for a server that will be deployed in a remote office. Instead of using **Create rodc c:\DCpromo** as the command, the command is **Create full c:\DCpromo**.

You can then select installation media when running DCpromo using the advanced installation options. You'd start by selecting the check box to Use advanced mode installation from the Welcome page, as shown in Figure 2-22.

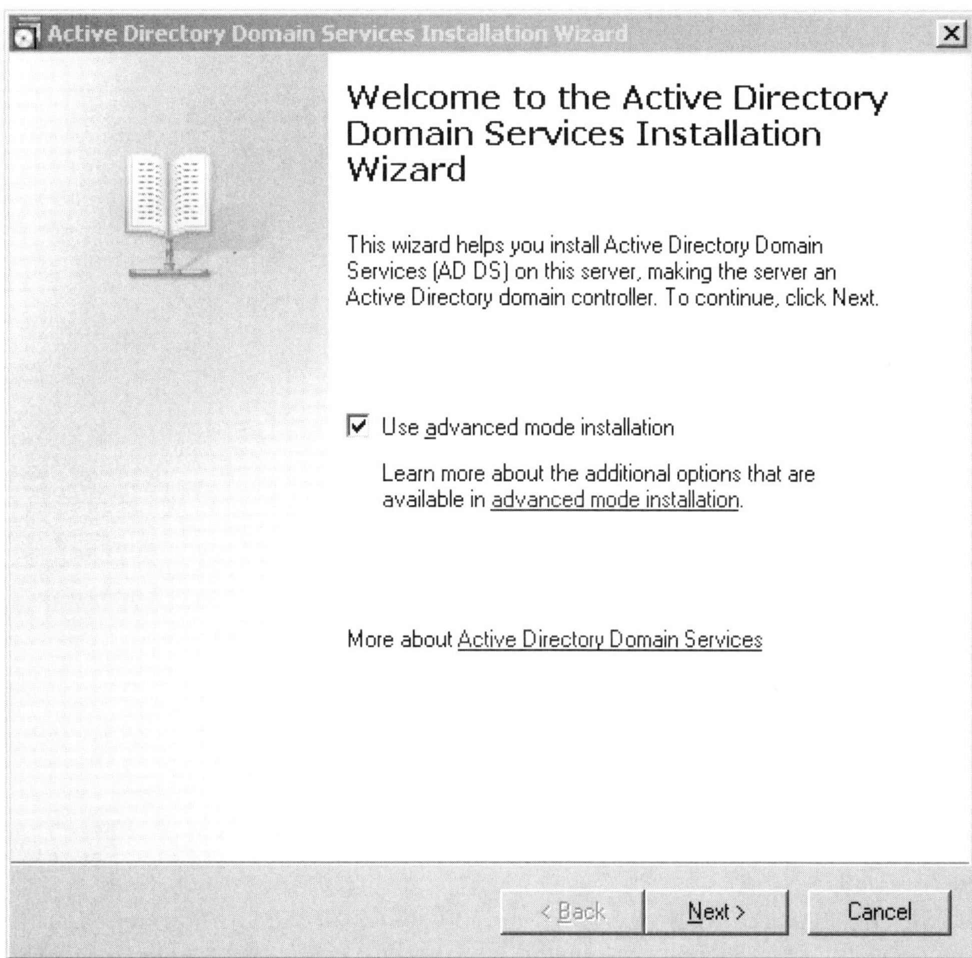

Figure 2-22 Selecting advanced options in DCpromo

Courtesy Course Technology/Cengage Learning

Later in the wizard, you'll see the Install from Media page, as shown in Figure 2-23. You can browse to the location of the folder that holds the ntds.dit file. In the figure, the C:\IFM folder is identified as the location because it holds the Active Directory folder created by NTDSUtil (containing the ntds.dit file). This location could just as easily be on a CD, DVD, or USB drive.

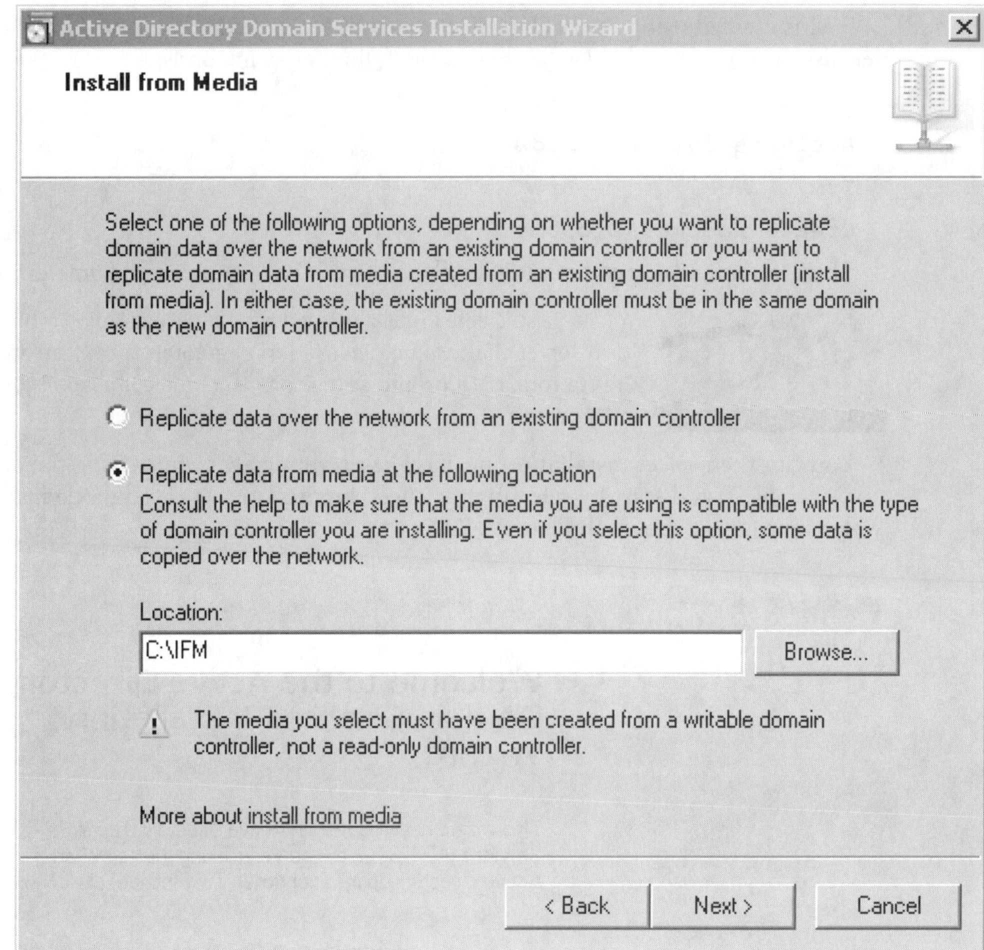

Figure 2-23 Specifying the location of the media

Courtesy Course Technology/Cengage Learning

Server Core and RODCs

If you're considering deploying an RODC into a branch office, you may also consider deploying it with Server Core. A **Server Core** installation of Windows Server 2008 is a limited installation that includes the command prompt but does not include the Windows graphical user interface (GUI). All administration is performed at the command prompt, or remotely once remote administration has been configured.

A basic tenet of hardening a server is to disable or remove all unneeded services and protocols. If the service or protocol is not running, it cannot be attacked. As an example, if a malware worm is wreaking havoc on all servers hosting the FTP service, a server that isn't hosting the FTP service isn't vulnerable. Microsoft introduced Server Core to drastically limit the services and protocols on a server, as one of many methods of hardening a server.

Server Core in Windows Server 2008 does not support PowerShell, which seems odd because Server Core is a command-line interface and PowerShell is an enhanced command-line tool. However, PowerShell requires the installation of .NET, and .NET is not included in a Server Core installation.

Windows Server 2008 R2 includes PowerShell in the Server Core installation, but Windows Server 2008 does not include it.

You can promote a server running Server Core to a domain controller and to an RODC. You'll have to create an answer file to do so, but it's relatively easy to create DCpromo answer files. Simply start DCpromo on another server and answer the questions from the wizard. When you reach the Summary page, instead of clicking Next, click the Export settings button to create an answer file. Figure 2-24 shows this button on the Summary page.

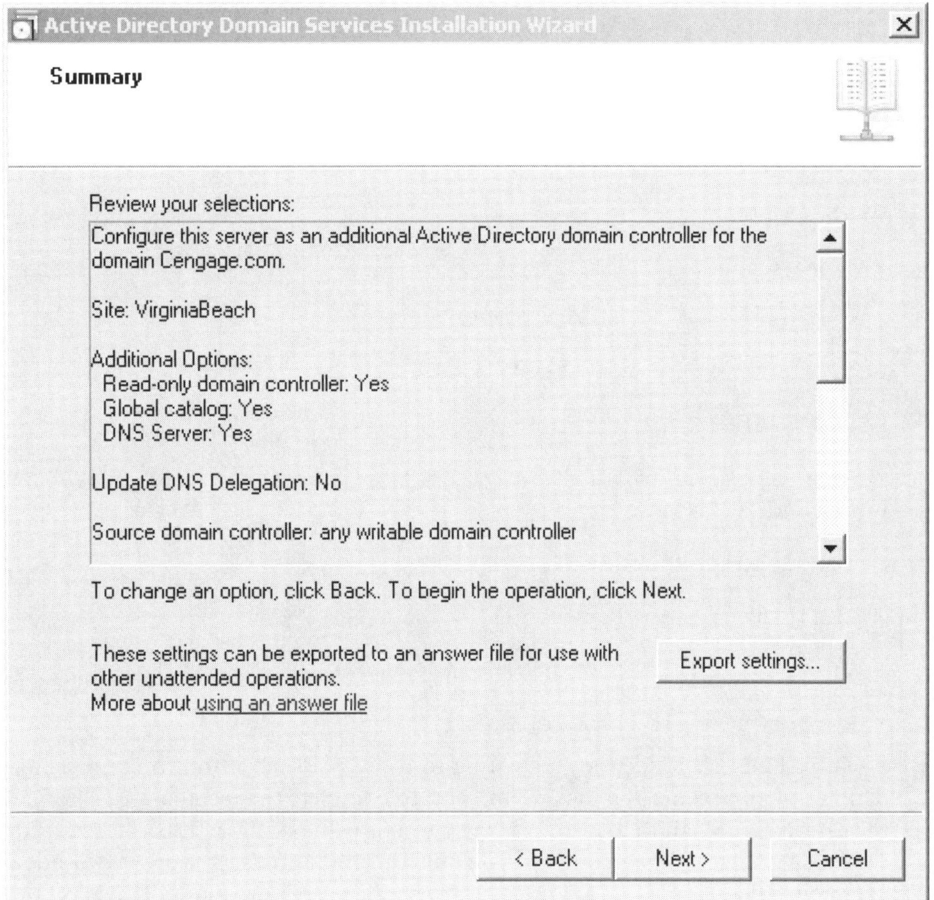

Figure 2-24 Exporting settings to an answer file from DCpromo

Courtesy Course Technology/Cengage Learning

The following listing shows a sample answer file created by this process.

```
; DCPROMO unattend file (automatically generated by DCpromo)

; Usage:

;   DCPromo.exe /unattend:C:\DCPromo\unattend.txt

;

; You may need to fill in password fields prior to using the unattend file.

; If you leave the values for "Password" and/or
"DNSDelegationPassword"

; as "*", then you will be asked for credentials at runtime.
```

```
;
[DCInstall]
; Read-Only Replica DC promotion
ReplicaOrNewDomain=ReadOnlyReplica
ReplicaDomainDNSName=Cengage.com
SiteName=Chesapeake
InstallDNS=Yes
ConfirmGc=Yes
CreateDNSDelegation=No
UserDomain=Cengage.com
UserName=*
Password=*
DatabasePath="C:\Windows\NTDS"
LogPath="C:\Windows\NTDS"
SYSVOLPath="C:\Windows\SYSVOL"
; Set SafeModeAdminPassword to the correct value prior to using the
unattend file
SafeModeAdminPassword=
; Run-time flags (optional)
; CriticalReplicationOnly=Yes
; RebootOnCompletion=Yes
```

Three lines are bolded in this listing to draw your attention to them. You can enter the credentials of an account that has permission to complete the installation. Alternatively, if you leave the **UserName=*** and **Password=*** lines with a value of an asterisk (*), the administrator using this answer file will be prompted to enter the credentials of a user with adequate permission. You must add a password for the directory services restore mode. This password is added in the **SafeModeAdminPassword=** line.

The following activity shows how to create an RODC. You can do this lab on any server that is not a domain controller. If DC2 is used, you can use Activity 2-4 to remove Active Directory from DC2 and then use the following activity to make DC2 an RODC. However, when using Activity 2-4, do not check the box in step 5 to delete the domain because the server is the last domain controller in the domain.

Activity 2-7: Creating an RODC

Time Required: 15 minutes
Objective: Run DCpromo to promote a server to a read-only domain controller (RODC).

Description: You want to deploy an RODC to a branch office in Chesapeake. The DC in the branch office will be hosted on a Server Core installation of Windows Server 2008, so you'll need to run DCpromo from the command line. You'll first create the unattend answer file for DCpromo and then test it by running it on a server. You'll later give the answer file to a technician in the branch office to run on that server.

1. Log on to a member server with the **Administrator** account and a password of **P@ssw0rd.** This could be a separate member server created specifically for this lab, or DC2 after Active Directory is removed using Activity 2-4. If using Activity 2-4, do not check the box in step 5 to **Delete the domain because this server is the last domain controller in the domain.**
2. Click **Start,** type **DCpromo** in the Start Search box, and press **Enter.**
3. Click **Next** on the **Welcome** page.
4. Review the information on the **Operating System Compatibility** page and click **Next.**
5. Select **Existing Forest** and ensure that **Add a Domain Controller to an Existing Domain** is selected. Click **Next.**
6. Enter **Cengage.com** as the name of your domain on the **Network Credentials** page. Select **Alternate Credentials** and then click **Set.** Enter the name and password of an account in the **Domain Admins** group. Click **OK.** Click **Next.**
7. Select **Cengage.com** on the **Select a Domain** page and click **Next.**
8. Deselect the check box to **Use The Site That Corresponds to the IP Address of This Computer** on the **Select a Site** page. Select the **Chesapeake** site. Click **Next.**
9. On the **Additional Domain Controller Options** page, select **Read-only domain controller** (RODC), as shown in Figure 2-25. Notice that this page is also selecting the

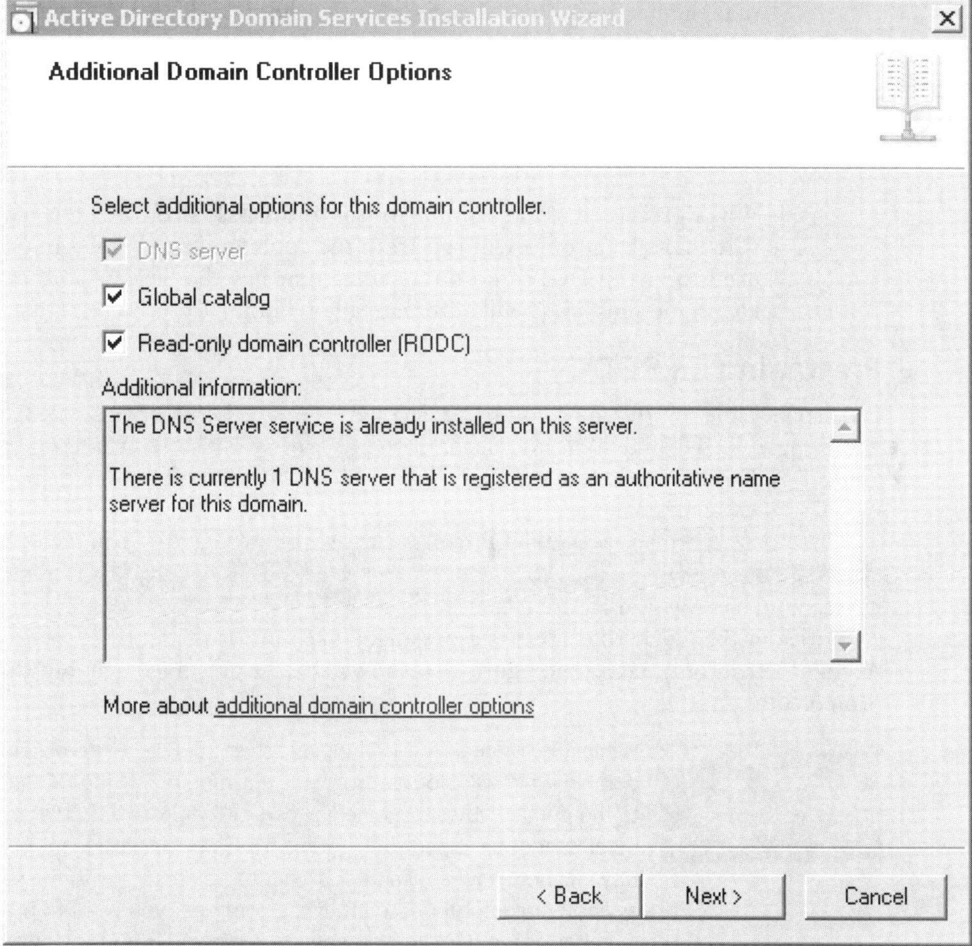

Figure 2-25 Selecting RODC as an additional domain controller option

Courtesy Course Technology/Cengage Learning

DC as a **Global catalog** server. If you choose not to make the server a global catalog server, you should enable Universal Group Membership Caching on the site where the RODC will be placed. Click **Next.**

10. Click **Next** on the **Delegation of RODC Installation and Administration** page. Because you are completing the installation of the RODC yourself, you will not need to designate a group or user.
11. Accept the default settings on the **Location for Database, Log Files and SYSVOL** page. Click **Next.**
12. Enter **P@ssw0rd** in the **Password** and **Confirm Password** text boxes. Click **Next.**
13. Review the information on the **Summary** page and click **Export Settings.**
14. Click **Browse Folders** and browse to the C: drive. Click **New Folder** and name the folder **DCpromo.** Select the **DCpromo** folder. Enter **Unattend.txt** as the filename and click **Save.** Click **OK** in the notification dialog box that indicates the file has been successfully exported.
15. Click **Cancel** on the **Summary** page. Click **Yes** to confirm that you want to cancel DCpromo.
16. Open a command prompt by clicking **Start** and selecting **Command Prompt.**
17. Enter the following command from the command prompt to open the unattend.txt file.

    ```
    notepad c:\DCPromo\unattend.txt
    ```

18. Move to the **SafeModeAdminPassword=** line and add the password of **P@ssw0rd** so that the line looks like this: **SafeModeAdminPassword=P@ssw0rd.** Close **Notepad.** When prompted, click **Save** to save your changes.
19. Enter the following command from the command prompt to run DCpromo using the unattend.txt file you've created.

    ```
    DCPromo.exe /unattend:C:\DCPromo\unattend.txt
    ```

20. When prompted, enter **Administrator** and **P@ssw0rd** for the **Network Credentials.** Click **OK.** DCpromo will run from the command line. This same procedure can be used to install DCPromo on a server that has the Server Core installation. When DCpromo finishes, it will automatically reboot.

Prestaging an RODC

It's also possible to prestage a computer account in Active Directory before the RODC is added. A **prestaged RODC** is a computer account that is created in Active Directory and designated as an RODC. This is done before the RODC computer is added to the domain and before DCpromo is run.

When the account is prestaged, it starts the DCpromo wizard. You can start the wizard by right-clicking the Domain Controllers OU and selecting Pre-create Read-only Domain Controller account, as shown in Figure 2-26.

Notice in the figure that DC3 is a prestaged account. It is identified as an Unoccupied DC Account (Read-only, GC). The figure also shows DC2, a prestaged account that has since been promoted to an RODC.

While it is common for a Windows Server 2008 server to be joined to the domain when DCpromo is run, it is not required. If the DC is not joined to the domain, it will be joined as part of the process. However, the computer cannot be joined to the domain before it is prestaged. Active Directory will not allow a computer account to be added with the same name as another computer account. If the computer you want to prestage is a member of the domain, you need to remove it from the domain by joining a workgroup before prestaging the computer.

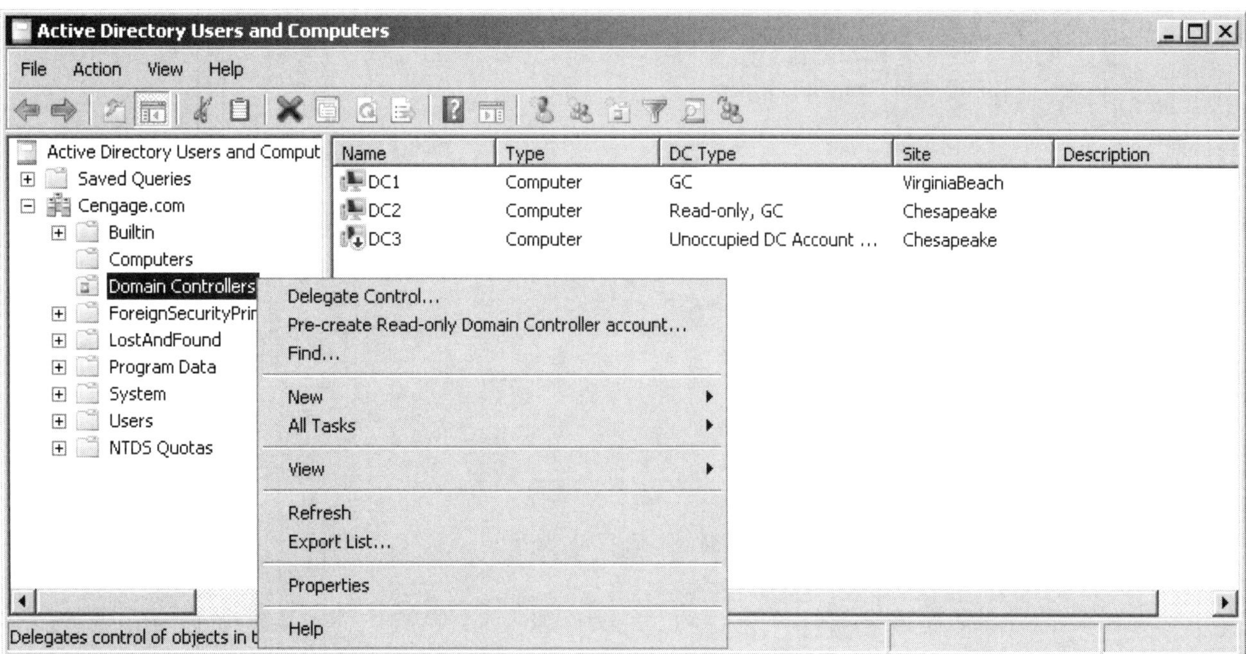

Figure 2-26 Beginning the prestaging of an RODC

Courtesy Course Technology/Cengage Learning

The DCpromo wizard has a lot of familiar pages and questions, but it will also require two additional details you don't normally use in DCpromo.

- **You will need to provide the name of the computer.** When DCpromo is run on the prospective RODC, it will query Active Directory to see if this name exists and if it's a prestaged RODC. If so, it will use the information from the prestaged account to include much of the information for DCpromo. Figure 2-27 shows the screen where you provide the computer name.
- **You will need to provide a user or group that can complete DCpromo.** This group will be delegated appropriate rights and permissions to complete the execution of DCpromo on the prospective RODC. Figure 2-28 shows the page where you identify the user or group that will finish DCpromo.

Once the wizard has been completed, anyone in the delegated group can run DCpromo on the prestaged computer to complete the installation. They don't need to be in the Domain Admins group, but only in the designated group when the wizard was run. Notice that this group will also have local administrator permissions on the RODC. You'll see later in this section how you can add any user to the **local Administrators role** after DCpromo has been run on the new RODC.

DCpromo will detect that the user is not a member of the Domain Admins group and indicate that DCpromo may fail. However, as long as the user is a member of the delegated group, DCpromo will succeed.

RODC Passwords

A primary benefit of an RODC is that passwords are not stored on the server, which is especially important for administrator accounts. If the RODC is compromised or stolen, an attacker cannot discover the passwords for these important accounts. Passwords are controlled via three methods:

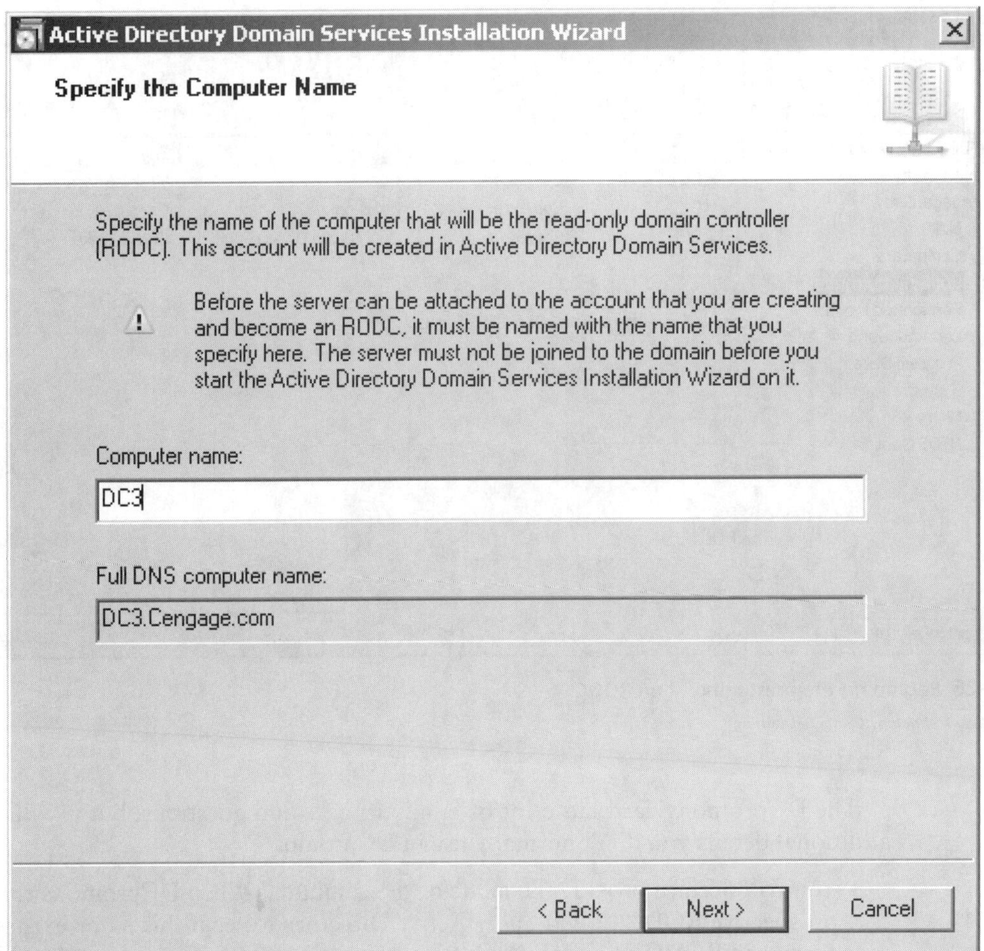

Figure 2-27 Specifying the computer name of the prestaged RODC

Courtesy Course Technology/Cengage Learning

- **Password Replication Policy.** This applies to a specific RODC. You can add specific users or groups here and specify Allow or Deny. The Allow setting means the password can be stored on the RODC, and Denied means the password will not be stored on the RODC.
- **Allowed RODC Password Replication Group.** This Active Directory group applies to all RODCs. Passwords for users in this group will be stored on the RODC.
- **Denied RODC Password Replication Group.** This Active Directory group applies to all RODCs. Users in this group are not prevented from logging on to an RODC, but their passwords will not be stored on the RODC.

The Deny setting takes precedence. You may have learned this from NTFS permissions, and it applies here. If a user is in a group that would allow his password to be stored on the RODC and in another group that would deny his password from being stored on the RODC, Deny "wins." The password will not be stored on the RODC.

Figure 2-29 shows the Active Directory properties for DC2, which is an RODC. You can access this page within Active Directory Users and Computers by expanding Domain Controllers, right-clicking the RODC, and selecting Properties. The Password Replication Policy tab is selected and the default selections are shown.

Notice that all of the key administrator groups have a policy setting of Deny. If any members of any of these groups logged on to this RODC, they would be authenticated by a writable DC but their passwords would not be cached or replicated to the RODC. By default, the only

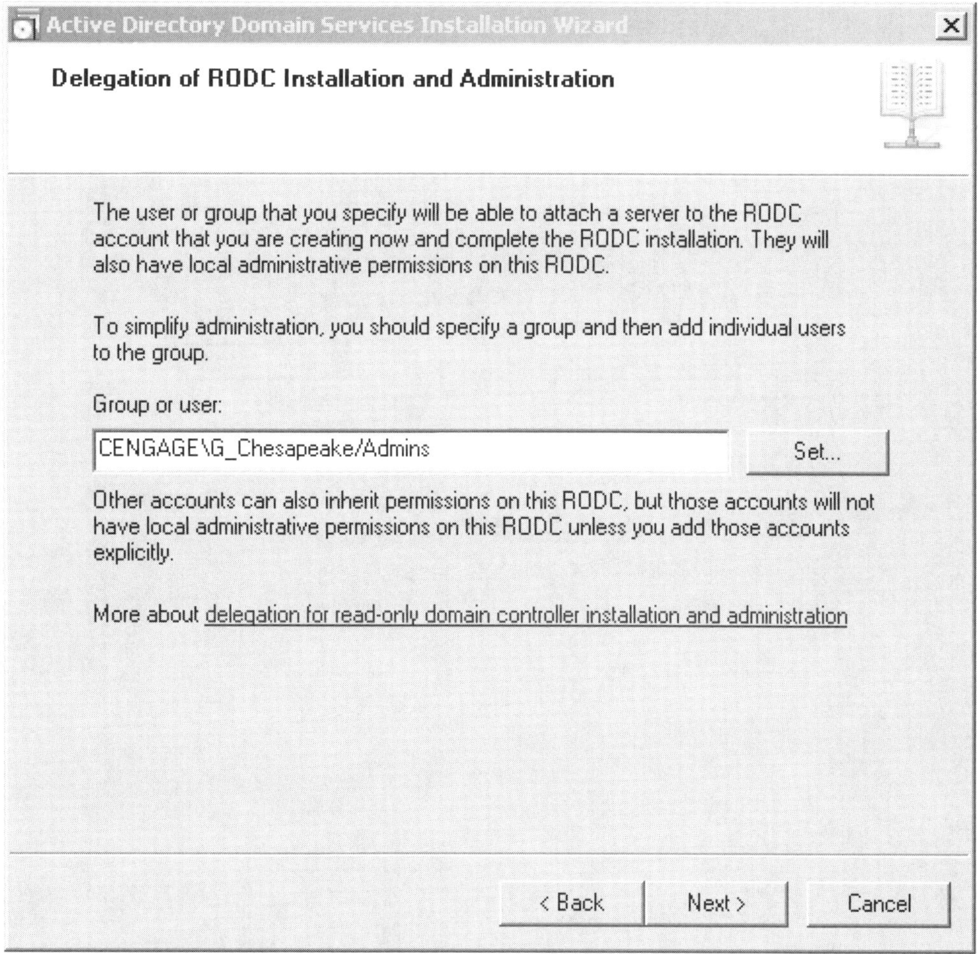

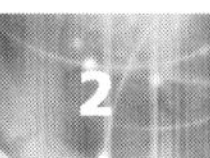

Figure 2-28 Identifying the user or group that will complete DCpromo

Courtesy Course Technology/Cengage Learning

passwords that can be replicated (or cached) to this server are those from users in the Allowed RODC Password Replication Group.

You can add more groups. As shown in the figure, the G_ChesapeakeBranchOfficeUsers group is added. This group includes the user accounts of all the users in the Chesapeake office.

Figure 2-30 shows the Allowed RODC Password Replication Group, which is located in the Users container in Active Directory Users and Computers. The G_RemoteOfficeUsers group has been added. Adding a group to the Allowed RODC Password Replication Group could be useful if the organization had users that traveled from one remote office to another.

When configured this way, the users in the G_RemoteOfficeUsers group will have their passwords replicated and cached on the RODC. If bandwidth is lost between the main office and the remote office, these users can still log on because their passwords are on the RODC. However, no other passwords will be stored on this server.

RODC Filtered Attribute Set

You can extend the schema to accommodate additional data storage within Active Directory. As an example, an application could store encryption keys or passwords as an attribute within a user account. While this works well in most instances, it presents a risk when RODCs are implemented, unless you add the items to the **RODC filtered attribute set** to identify attributes that should not be stored on the RODC.

Remember, a prime reason to use an RODC is that physical security isn't as strong in a remote office as it may be at the main headquarters of an organization. There's a risk that the RODC

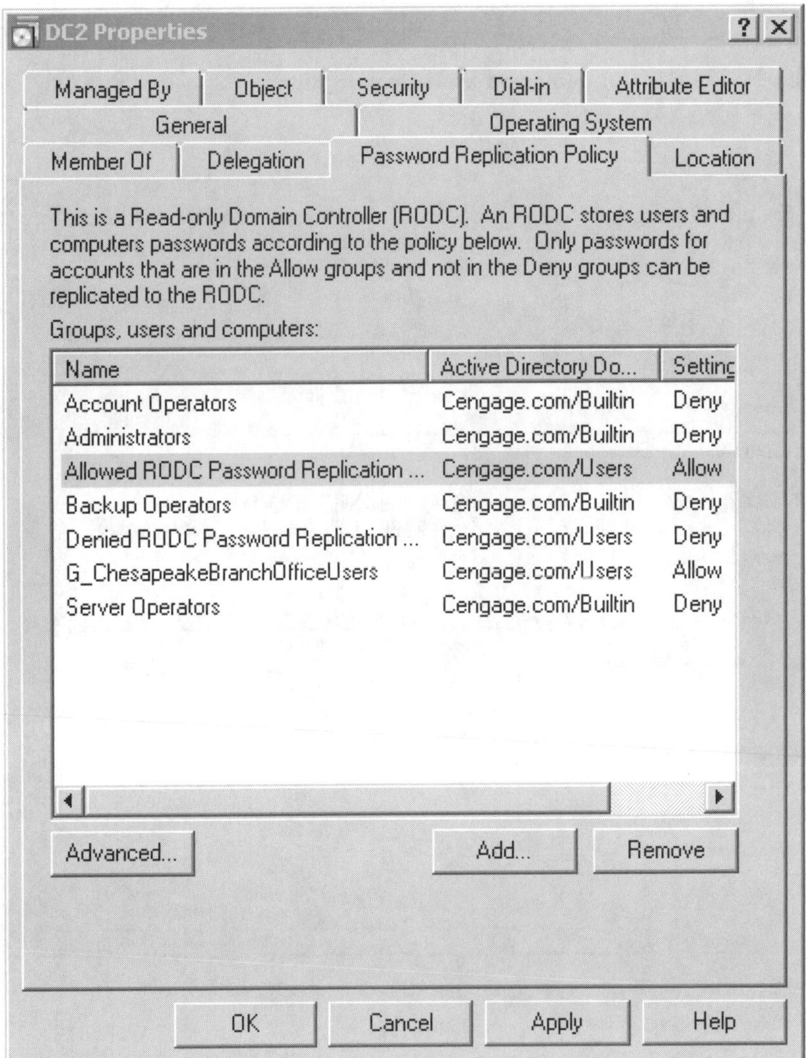

Figure 2-29 The Password Replication Policy for a specific RODC

Courtesy Course Technology/Cengage Learning

may be stolen or compromised. If it is, only minimal password data is available on the server, so the loss will have less of an impact on the organization.

If an application is storing sensitive data such as encryption keys or passwords in other attributes, the data will be stored on the RODC. Active Directory doesn't know this data is sensitive, so you must take steps to keep it from being stored on the RODC.

The RODC filtered attribute set is predefined. It includes several attributes that are marked as confidential. If your organization has added any Active Directory attributes that should not be replicated to RODCs, you should take the following two steps:

- **Add the attributes to the RODC filtered attribute set.** This prevents it from being replicated to any RODCs in the forest.
- **Mark the attribute as confidential.** This removes the ability for regular users to read the data.

These attributes can be modified by using the LDAP Data Interchange Format (LDIF) tool to modify the search flags of the attribute. When the 10th bit (0x200) is set to a 1, it adds the attribute to the RODC filtered attribute set. When the 7th bit (0x080) is set to a 1, it marks the attribute as confidential.

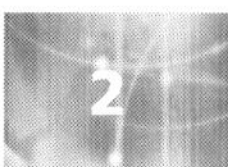

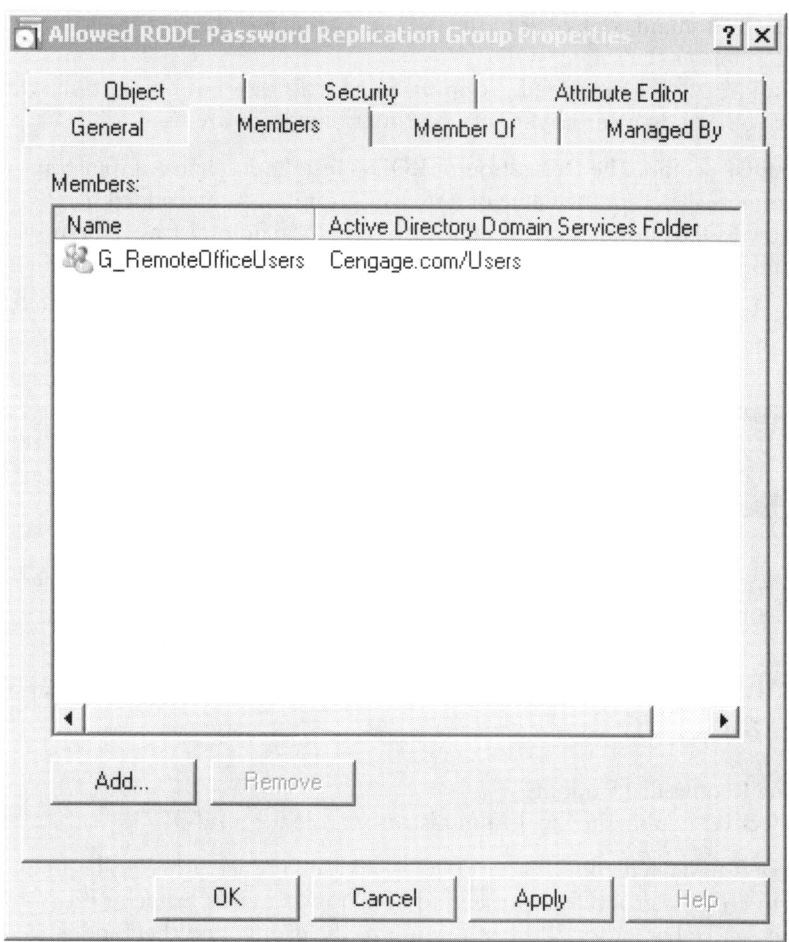

Figure 2-30 The Allowed RODC Password Replication group applies to all RODCs

Courtesy Course Technology/Cengage Learning

If you add 0x200 and 0x80, you get a hexadecimal value of 0x280 and a decimal value of 640. LDIF expects a decimal value, so you would add the decimal value of 640 to the existing search flag value.

Once the attribute has been added to the RODC filtered attribute set and marked as confidential, it will no longer be replicated to RODCs.

Local Administrators Role on an RODC

You can implement Administrator role separation on an RODC. In other words, you can enable the local Administrators role on an RODC by adding a user or group to that role. This user will then have the associated permission on the RODC to do regular maintenance, such as adding drivers or performing backups. However, the role membership will not grant the user any administrative rights or permissions in the domain.

When a server is promoted to a domain controller, the local database of users and groups is no longer available in Computer Management. This includes the local Administrators group. Instead, all accounts are managed through Active Directory Users and Computers, and permissions granted here apply to the entire domain. However, it is possible to enable the local Administrators role.

It's worth comparing the Server Operators group with the local Administrators role. You can add users or groups to the Active Directory Server Operators group, and they will have sufficient rights and permissions to administer *any* domain controllers without permissions to modify Active Directory. Notice the subtlety here: a member of the Server Operators group can administer *any* domain controller in the domain, while members of the local Administrators role can only administer the *single* RODC.

You can identify the delegated group or user for RODC administration when you create the RODC, or you can do so afterward. Two primary methods are used.

- **During DCpromo.** The Delegation of RODC Installation and Administration screen in DCpromo will accept the name of a user or group. Accounts added here will be able to complete the RODC installation and will also have local administrative permissions after the installation is complete. If using an answer file, the /DelegatedAdmin parameter is also used.
- **Using Active Directory Users and Computers.** View the properties of the RODC via the Domain Controllers OU. Select the Managed By tab and add a group account.

The Directory Services Utilities tool (**DSMgmt.exe**) is mentioned in some documentation as a method to enable Administrator role separation on the RODC. However, this tool is not recommended because it only stores the data locally on the RODC. Using Active Directory Users and Computers is the preferred method.

Activity 2-8 shows you how to add a user to the local Administrators role with Active Directory Users and Computers.

Activity 2-8: Configuring Administrator Role Separation for an RODC

Time Required: 15 minutes
Objective: Enable the local Administrators role for an RODC.

Description: You have deployed an RODC to a branch office. Alice will administer this RODC. You need to create a group to represent administrators in this branch office, create an account for Alice in Active Directory, add her account to the group, and then add a group to the local Administrator role on the RODC. She will then be able to perform maintenance on the RODC without having administrative permissions in the domain.

1. Ensure that both **DC1** and the RODC are started. Log on to **DC1** with the **Administrator** account and a password of **P@ssw0rd**. The Administrator account is a member of the Domain Admins group, which is required for this activity. Start **Active Directory Users and Computers** via the **Administrative Tools** menu.
2. Right-click the **Users** container and select **New User.** Enter **Alice** in the **First Name** and **User Logon Name** text boxes. Click **Next.**
3. Enter **P@ssw0rd** in the **Password** and **Confirm Password** text boxes. Click **Next.** Click **Finish.**
4. Right-click the **Users** container and select **New Group.** Enter **G_BrOfficeAdmins** as the name of the group. Ensure that both **Global** and **Security** are selected and click **OK.**
5. Double-click the **G_BrOfficeAdmins** group. Select the **Members** tab and click **Add.** Enter **Alice** as the object name and click **OK.** Click **OK** again.
6. Browse to the **Domain Controllers OU.** Double-click **DC2** to access the properties page. Select the **Managed By** tab.
7. Click **Change.** On the Select User or Group page, click **Object Types.** Select the check box next to **Groups** and click **OK.**
8. Enter **G_BrOfficeAdmins** as the Object Name and click **OK.** Your display will look similar to Figure 2-31. Click **OK.**
9. Close all open windows.

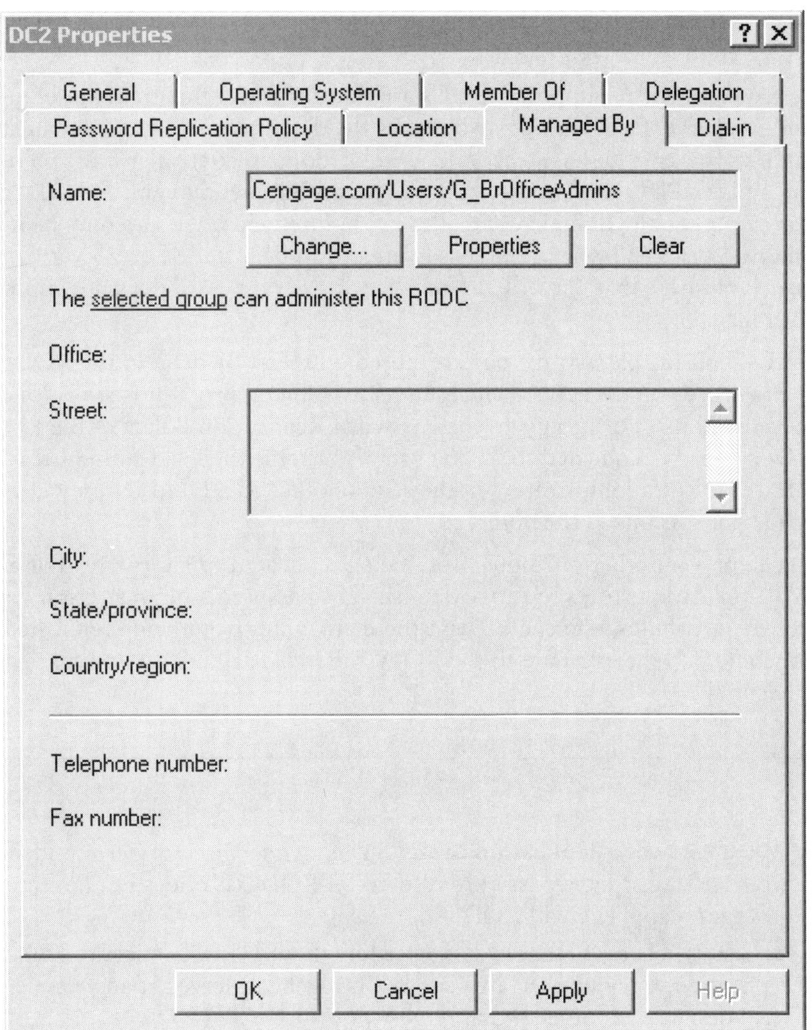

Figure 2-31 Adding a group to the local Administrators role on an RODC

Courtesy Course Technology/Cengage Learning

Chapter Summary

- A hub and spoke replication topology is often used when several key locations are connected with faster WAN connections. These key locations are connected to several smaller locations with slower WAN connections. When a hub and spoke replication topology is used, site link bridging should be disabled.
- Placing a DC in a remote office will improve logon times for users in that office and ensure that they can still log on if the WAN link fails. If a DC is placed in a remote office, it should also be a DNS server.
- When a DC is placed in a remote office, it should either be designated as a global catalog server or the site should have Universal Group Membership Caching enabled. If the DC is operating in a single-domain forest, the DC should be a global catalog server. If the DC is operating in a multi-domain forest and you want to minimize replication over the WAN link, enable Universal Group Membership Caching.
- Every forest has one schema master and one domain naming master. Every domain has one RID master, one PDC emulator, and one infrastructure master. In a multi-domain forest, the infrastructure master should not also be a global catalog server. If RODCs will

be deployed, the PDC emulator must be on a Windows Server 2008 server. Roles can be transferred to other DCs or seized.

- The requirements to support RODCs are that the forest functional level must be at least Windows Server 2003 (which also means the domain functional level must be at least Windows Server 2003). At least one writable domain controller must be running in the domain and the PDC emulator must be running Windows Server 2008. ADPrep/RODCPrep must be run on any domain controller in the forest. RODCs can only be installed on Windows Server 2008 (or greater) servers. It can be installed on Server Core for added security, but note that Server Core in Windows Server 2008 does not support Windows PowerShell.
- RODCs limit the passwords that are stored on them. By default, the RODC will not store any passwords on the server, which limits its vulnerability if it is stolen or compromised. You can add users or groups to the Password Replication Policy of the RODC to allow passwords to be replicated to it. You can also enable the local Administrators role on an RODC to allow administrators in the remote office to administer an RODC without being granted permissions in the domain.
- You can prevent other attributes from being replicated to an RODC. For example, if an LDAP application stores sensitive data such as passwords or encryption keys in Active Directory attributes, you can prevent these attributes from being replicated to the RODC. You would add the attribute to the RODC filtered attribute set and mark the attribute as confidential.

Key Terms

Allowed RODC Password Replication Group This Active Directory group identifies the only users or groups that can have passwords stored on RODCs. It does not have any members by default. This group applies to all RODCs.

Bridgehead server The DC that is designated by the ISTG to connect to DCs in other sites and perform replication. Only one DC in a site is a bridgehead server at any time. If this DC fails, the ISTG will designate another DC in the list.

Denied RODC Password Replication Group This Active Directory group identifies the users or groups that cannot have passwords stored on RODCs. Several groups (such as Administrators, Account Operators, and others) are members of this group by default. This group applies to all RODCs.

Distributed File System (DFS) A file services technology that is used to create DFS Namespaces and that uses DFS replication. A DFS namespace is used to group shared folders from different servers into a logically structured namespace. DFS replication allows DFS namespaces to be stored on multiple servers (such as one in each site), and it keeps all of the servers synchronized.

Domain naming master One of the forest operations master roles. The DC hosting this role manages the addition and removal of domains, and the addition and removal of application directory partitions. Only one domain naming master exists in a forest.

DSMgmt A command-line tool that can be used to manage and administer Active Directory Domain Services. It can be used to enable the local Administrators role on an RODC.exe

Full mesh replication topology Each site can replicate with every other site. It is generally recommended when an organization has 10 or fewer sites.

Hub and spoke replication topology A site design used when an organization has faster network connections between major hubs and slower network connections with outlying offices. When used, site link bridging is often disabled.

Infrastructure master One of the domain operations master roles. The infrastructure master updates cross-domain group-to-user references. It ensures that changes made to object names from objects in another domain are accurately reflected in the group membership information. The infrastructure master should not be the global catalog server in a multi-domain environment. Every domain in the forest holds one infrastructure master.

Install from media (IFM) An advanced option that can be used when promoting a server using DCpromo. It allows DCpromo to obtain the database information from a file instead of replicating it from another DC. It can be useful when promoting a server to a DC in a remote office without using a slow WAN link.

Inter-Site Topology Generator (ISTG) The ISTG is responsible for managing different processes related to replication of data between sites. The ISTG designates the bridgehead server within the site.

IP site link The IP site link represents a WAN link. It uses a Remote Procedure Call (RPC) connection to establish a synchronous connection with a domain controller in the remote site. It requires firewalls between the sites to allow RCP traffic. It is also referred to as RPC over IP.

Local Administrators role A role that can be enabled on an RODC in a remote site to grant local users rights and permissions to administer an RODC. It does not include any rights or permissions in the domain. It is enabled by adding a user account to the role. The DSMgmt tool can be used to add users to a role.

NTDSUtil A shell command-line tool used to manage and manipulate Active Directory Domain Services. It can be used to create the data used with the install from media (IFM) feature and seize operations master roles.

Operations master roles These five roles that can be held by DCs are also called flexible single master operations (FSMO) roles. The five roles are schema master, domain naming master, RID master, PDC emulator, and Infrastructure master.

Password Replication Policy Every RODC has this policy, which defines what users or groups can have their passwords stored on the RODC. It doesn't have any members by default, but it would typically be populated with the users or groups of users working in the remote office hosting the RODC.

PDC emulator One of the domain operations master roles. The PDC emulator manages time synchronization and password changes in the domain. If an RODC is needed in the domain, the PDC emulator must be running on Windows Server 2008. Every domain in the forest holds one PDC emulator.

Preferred bridgehead server A manually designated bridgehead server. The ISTG will normally designate any DC as a bridgehead server, but when a preferred bridgehead server has been designated, the ISTG will only pick preferred bridgehead servers. If you designate one DC as a preferred bridgehead server, you should always designate at least one more.

Prestaged RODC A computer account created in Active Directory Users and Computers with information used by DCpromo. It allows DCpromo to be started by an administrator with elevated permissions and finished by an administrator with lesser permissions. The computer account is designated as an unoccupied RODC account.

Read-only domain controller (RODC) A DC that limits the passwords replicated to it (or cached on it). You can specify what passwords are cached on the DC. You can also enable the local Administrators role to allow users in a remote office to administer the RODC without having any rights or permissions in the domain.

Replication The process of sending Active Directory additions, deletions, and modifications between DCs.

RID master One of the domain operations master roles. The RID master manages the pool of available RIDs and issues banks of RIDs to other domain controllers. RIDs are used to create SIDs, and the RID master ensures that all RIDs are unique within the domain, which ultimately ensures that all SIDs are unique in the domain. Every domain in the forest holds one RID master.

RODC filtered attribute set Any attributes added to this attribute set and marked as confidential will not be stored on the RODC.

RPC over IP site link Also known as an IP site link object. It's named IP in Active Directory Sites and Services, but is commonly referred to as RPC over IP in documentation.

Schema master One of the forest operations master roles. This is the only DC that has write permissions on the schema. When extending the schema, you must be able to reach the schema master. Only one schema master exists in a forest.

Server Core A Windows Server 2008 edition that only includes the command prompt instead of the full graphical user interface. It enhances security by reducing the attack surface; only the most necessary services and protocols are installed.

Site A group of well-connected hosts or subnets. Sites are typically connected to each other through slower wide area network (WAN) links.

Site-aware application An application or service that can determine what site it is in and optimize connections with other hosts in the same site.

Site link bridging A feature that allows site links to be transitive. In other words, if Site A can replicate with Site B and Site B can replicate with Site C, Site A can also replicate with Site C. Site link bridging is enabled by default, but is typically disabled in a hub and spoke topology to limit duplicated replication.

Site link object An Active Directory object that represents a wide area network (WAN) link used to connect two or more sites. Site link objects can be either IP (RPC over IP) or SMTP. Site link properties can be configured to control when replication occurs and to control the cost or priority of site links.

Site object An Active Directory object that represents a site. A site is a location that includes well-connected hosts or subnets. Site objects are commonly created in Active Directory to represent remote offices and branch offices.

SMTP site link object A site link object used to replicate configuration, schema, and application partitions using an asynchronous connection. It cannot be used to replicate data within the same domain.

Subnet object An Active Directory object that represents a subnet in a site. Subnet objects are associated with site objects to help site-aware applications identify locations.

Universal Group Membership Caching An option that can optimize logon times for users within a site. The option is chosen instead of making the DC a global catalog server in a multi-domain environment to limit replication of the global catalog.

Writable DC A normal DC. When discussing read-only DCs (RODCs) and normal DCs, normal DCs are referred to as writable DCs.

Review Questions

1. Your company includes one main office and three remote offices connected via slow WAN links. You're planning to deploy domain controllers to the remote offices to decrease the time needed for users to log in from these remote offices. What needs to be done to support this plan?
   a. Create at least one subnet object and at least one site object for each remote office. Link the subnet objects to their respective site objects. Move a domain controller to each site.
   b. Create at least one subnet object and at least one site object for each remote office. Link a GPO to each site object.
   c. Create at least one subnet object for each site and place the subnet objects in the Default-First-Site-Name site. Move a domain controller to each remote office.
   d. Add RODCs to each remote office.

2. Your company has a line-of-business (LOB) application hosted on a server named Srv1. Srv1 frequently performs LDAP queries. The business is hosted in a single domain in a single well-connected network. You want all of these queries to be executed only against a domain controller named DC5. What should you do?
   a. Designate DC5 as a global catalog server.
   b. Designate DC5 as a PDC Emulator.
   c. Designate DC5 as the bridgehead server.
   d. Create a site and place DC5 and Srv1 in this site.
3. You are asked to help an organization design its replication topology. The organization has three major regional offices with fast WAN connections between them. Each regional office has between 5 and 10 remote offices connected with slower links. Every office currently has at least one domain controller. Your design should not affect logon times for any users. What should you include in the design?
   a. Multiple sites with site link bridging enabled
   b. All domain controllers moved to only the regional offices
   c. Hub and spoke replication topology
   d. Universal Group Membership Caching enabled in the regional offices
4. Your organization has several sites scattered throughout the country. Several regional headquarters offices oversee regional satellite offices. Replication has been configured to occur using a hub and spoke configuration, with each of the regional headquarters offices configured as hubs. You want to prevent the satellite offices from replicating with any locations other than their hubs. What should you do?
   a. Enable site link bridging on each hub site. Disable site link bridges for satellite office links.
   b. Enable site link bridging for all sites. Create site link bridges for satellite office links.
   c. Disable site link bridging on each hub site. Disable site link bridges for satellite office links.
   d. Disable site link bridging for all sites. Create site link bridges for satellite office links.
5. Your company has recently added a site for a remote office and placed a domain controller in the site. You've added a subnet, site, and site link in Active Directory for this remote office, and moved the domain controller to the site. However, you've recently learned that replication traffic is not occurring. What is the likely problem?
   a. Universal Group Membership Caching is not enabled.
   b. The default cost is being used.
   c. The default schedule is being used.
   d. The firewall is not passing RPC traffic.
6. Your company has recently added a remote office. The domain is using Windows Server 2008 domain controllers. You've added a domain controller to the remote office to improve logon times for users in this office. What else needs to be done to ensure that users in the remote office use this domain controller to log on instead of logging on over the WAN link?
   a. Move the domain controller to the remote office's OU.
   b. Make the domain controller a global catalog server.
   c. Create a subnet object and a site object in Active Directory.
   d. Enable Universal Group Membership Caching.

7. Your organization includes two forests, as shown in Figure 2-32. How many operations master roles are in your organization?

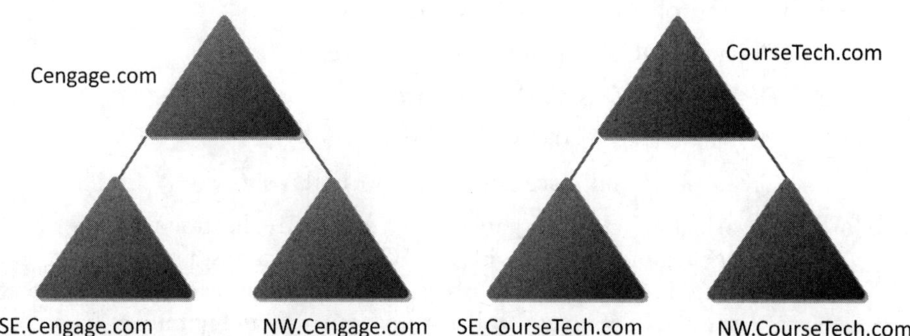

Figure 2-32 Organization with two forests

Courtesy Course Technology/Cengage Learning

   a. 1 schema master, 1 domain naming master, 6 RID masters, 6 PDC emulators, 6 infrastructure masters
   b. 2 schema masters, 2 domain naming masters, 6 RID masters, 6 PDC emulators, 6 infrastructure masters
   c. 6 schema masters, 6 domain naming masters, 6 RID masters, 6 PDC emulators, 6 infrastructure masters
   d. 2 schema masters, 2 domain naming masters, 4 RID masters, 4 PDC emulators, 4 infrastructure masters

8. You want to run the ADPrep /DomainPrep /GPPrep command to update the Resultant Set of Policy (RSOP) tool. Where should you run it?
   a. Any DC in the domain
   b. Any DC in the domain that is a global catalog server
   c. On the DC holding the role of schema master
   d. On the DC holding the role of infrastructure master

9. One of your domain controllers (DC1) recently suffered a catastrophic failure. DC1 was holding each of the operations roles for the domain. You are preparing to migrate over 500 user and computer objects from another domain. What should you do to ensure that you can create these objects?
   a. Seize the RID master role.
   b. Transfer the RID master role.
   c. Seize the infrastructure master role.
   d. Transfer the infrastructure master role.

10. Your organization has a remote office that was recently configured as a site. An Active Directory site was created, a subnet was created, and a domain controller was placed at the remote office using an IP address in the office's subnet. The domain controller is hosting an ADI DNS zone. Users complain that they sometimes are unable to log on. You determine that the problem occurs when the WAN link goes down, but the DC is still operational. What should be done?
    a. Enable the site as a global catalog server, or enable Universal Group Membership Caching on the DC.
    b. Enable the DC as a global catalog server, or enable Universal Group Membership Caching on the site.

c. Configure ADI reverse lookup zones for the DNS server.

d. Reconfigure the DC as an RODC.

11. Your multi-domain organization has a remote office and you are designing a plan to place a DC at the site to minimize logon times for the users. The remote office will support 20 users. You want to ensure that replication traffic is minimized. What should you include in the plan?

a. Enable Universal Group Membership Caching on the site.

b. Make the DC a global catalog server.

c. Configure the DC as an RODC.

d. Install the DC on a server core installation of Windows Server 2008.

12. You are an administrator in a single-domain forest that includes only Windows Server 2003 domain controllers. The forest functional level is currently Windows Server 2003. You are considering deploying an RODC on a Windows Server 2008 server to a branch office. Before you can deploy the RODC, what must be done? Select all that apply.

a. Raise the domain functional level to Windows Server 2008.

b. Raise the forest functional level to Windows Server 2008.

c. Run ADPrep /ForestPrep.

d. Run ADPrep /DomainPrep.

e. Run ADPrep /RODCPrep.

f. Add a writable DC running Windows Server 2008.

g. Transfer the PDC Emulator role to a DC running Windows Server 2008.

13. Your organization recently added two branch offices with about 20 users in each office. The offices are connected via slow WAN links and logon times are sometimes unacceptably long. You are planning to deploy a DC into each of the offices. You want to ensure that the DCs placed in these offices only hold passwords of users in the offices. What should you do?

a. Enable Universal Group Membership Caching for the sites hosting the offices.

b. Create the DCs with the IFM option.

c. Use a fine-grained password policy for the users in the remote offices.

d. Create RODCs for the remote offices.

14. Your organization recently added a branch office connected via a WAN link. You're planning to add a domain controller to the branch office to minimize the time it takes for users to log on over the WAN link. You also plan to add the Windows PowerShell feature. Your plan should provide the best possible security for this domain controller. What should you do?

a. Install the DC as an RODC on Windows Server 2008 Server Core.

b. Install the DC as an RODC on a full installation of Windows Server 2008.

c. Install the DC as a writable DC on Windows Server 2008 Server Core.

d. Install the DC as a writable DC on a full installation of Windows Server 2008.

15. Your organization uses a custom application that stores extra passwords for users in Active Directory in a user attribute. You are planning to deploy an RODC to a remote office and you want to ensure that these passwords are not stored on the RODCs. What, if anything, should you do?

a. Nothing. Passwords will not be stored on the RODC.

b. Add the attribute to the RODC's Password Replication Policy.

c. Add the attribute to the RODC's Denied RODC Password Replication Group.

d. Add the attribute to the RODC filtered attribute set and mark the attribute as confidential.

16. Your organization is currently running a single-domain forest in the forest functional level of Windows Server 2003. Some DCs are running Windows Server 2003 and some DCs are running Windows Server 2008. The organization includes a remote office currently hosting a domain controller on a Windows Server 2003 server. You want to convert the DC in the remote office from a writable DC to an RODC. What should you do?
    a. Upgrade the DC in the remote office to Windows Server 2008, run DCpromo to remove Active Directory, and then run DCpromo to promote it to an RODC.
    b. Upgrade the forest functional level to Windows Server 2008, run DCpromo on the DC in the remote office to remove Active Directory, and then run DCpromo to promote it to an RODC.
    c. Upgrade all domain controllers to Windows Server 2008 and upgrade the forest functional level to Windows Server 2008. Run DCpromo on the DC in the remote office to remove Active Directory and then run DCpromo to promote it to an RODC.
    d. Use NTDSUtil to change the DC in the remote office from a writable DC to an RODC.
17. Your organization recently added a branch office connected via a WAN link. You're planning to add a domain controller to the branch office to minimize the time it takes for users to log on over the WAN link. Your plan should provide the best possible security for this domain controller. What should you do?
    a. Install the DC as an RODC on Windows Server 2008 Server Core.
    b. Install the DC as an RODC on a full installation of Windows Server 2008.
    c. Install the DC as a writable DC on Windows Server 2008 Server Core.
    d. Install the DC as a writable DC on a full installation of Windows Server 2008.
18. You are planning to promote a member server to a domain controller in a remote office. The remote office is connected via a slow WAN link, so you want to minimize the traffic over the WAN link when the server is promoted. What should you do?
    a. Ensure the server is configured with Server Core.
    b. Promote it as an RODC.
    c. Ensure that ADI DNS is added when the DC is promoted.
    d. Use the IFM option.
19. Your organization recently added a branch office connected via a WAN link. Administrators at the office perform all the maintenance, including adding user and computer accounts to the domain. Occasionally the WAN link fails and no one can log on to the domain. You plan on creating an Active Directory site and placing a domain controller in the remote office so users can log on even if the WAN link fails. You want to make sure the administrators can still maintain the accounts if the WAN link fails. What should you do?
    a. Ensure that the DC is a writable DC.
    b. Ensure that the DC is an RODC.
    c. Ensure that the DC has Universal Group Membership Caching enabled.
    d. Ensure that the site is configured as a global catalog server.
20. Your organization is within a single-domain forest. It includes four branch offices connected to the headquarters office via WAN links. Each branch office has been configured as a site and hosts a domain controller. Several shares are hosted at headquarters and regularly accessed by users at headquarters and the branch offices. When the WAN link fails, users at the remote office are no longer able to access the shares. You need to implement

a solution that will allow users to access the data from these shares even if the WAN link fails. What should you do?

a. Implement WSUS.
b. Implement FRS.
c. Implement DFS.
d. Implement WDS.

Case Projects

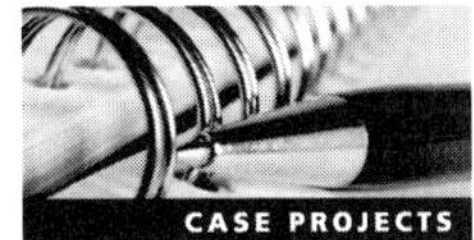

Case Project 2-1: Designing a WAN Replication Topology

You are hired as a consultant to design the replication topology for a major organization. The organization currently has four major regional offices throughout the country, and each regional office is connected to three remote offices. The design needs to ensure that users in all remote offices can easily log on. The major offices are connected with fast WAN connections, and the remote offices are connected with slower WAN connections. Remote offices should be allowed to replicate with each other through the regional office, but remote offices connected to one regional office should not be able to replicate with another regional office. Draw the replication design and describe how it would be configured.

Case Project 2-2: Determining a Logon Strategy for the Global Catalog

You are reviewing the design for the deployment of a site in your multiple-domain forest. A DC will be placed in the site, but you see no mention of the GC in the plan. You want to address this by ensuring that users can log on even if the WAN link is down, but you also want to minimize replication traffic. What should you include in the design and why?

Case Project 2-3: Adding a DC to a Remote Office

You are planning to add a DC to a remote office within a multi-domain forest. The remote office has limited physical security and your plan should consider this. The bandwidth to the site is very slow and close to capacity. You need to limit the use of bandwidth when you promote the server to a DC, and limit the use of bandwidth by the DC during normal operation. What should you include in the plan? Explain your answer.

Case Project 2-4: Planning Deployment of an RODC

You are planning to deploy an RODC to a remote office in your single-domain forest. The remote office has limited physical security and you don't want to grant users in the remote office any elevated permissions. You want a user in the remote office to be able to promote the server to an RODC, but you do not want to grant the user any domain permissions. What should you do and why?

chapter 3

Designing and Implementing DNS

After reading this chapter and completing the exercises, you will be able to:

- Understand Domain Name System (DNS) improvements in Windows 2008
- Understand the basics of DNS
- Plan and implement DNS Zones
- Create DNS records to support different clients
- Design replication scope using different Active Directory partitions

Windows Server 2008 includes several improvements to DNS that sometimes warrant upgrading DNS servers to Windows Server 2008, depending on DNS design requirements. Even with the improvements, though, much of DNS is the same as it was in earlier versions of Windows.

As mentioned in Chapter 2, DNS is tightly intertwined with Active Directory. You can't have an Active Directory domain without having DNS. The most important element of DNS, as it relates to Active Directory, is the service location (SRV) records. These records are created by default, but you can prevent generic (non-site-specific) records from being created to optimize organizations with multiple sites, such as an organization configured using a hub and spoke replication topology, as mentioned in Chapter 2.

DNS still supports multiple zone types, including primary zones, secondary zones, Active Directory-integrated (ADI) zones, stub zones, and the new GlobalNames zone (GNZ). Both forward and reverse lookup zone files are supported to provide name-to-IP address resolution and IP address-to-name resolution. Windows DNS servers commonly host A, AAAA, SRV, SOA, NS, MX, CNAME and PTR records. You'll need to know when to create different zones when designing DNS. Some zones are better suited for specific needs than others.

Also, if you're using ADI zones, you'll need to consider the replication scope. DNS zone data is replicated to DNS servers hosting ADI zones as an Active Directory partition. You can choose to replicate the zone data to all DNS servers in the domain using the ForestDNSZones application partition or using the DomainDNSZones application partition.

You'll learn about all of these concepts in this chapter.

Improvements in Windows Server 2008 DNS

Windows Server 2008 introduced several improvements with DNS. Some of them are obvious and will be covered in depth, but others are subtle and can provide significant improvements for specific designs.

The following improvements are available if DNS is hosted on Windows Server 2008:

- **GlobalNames zones.** DNS can be configured to resolve single-label names that have historically been resolved by Windows Internet Name Services (WINS) servers. WINS servers are used to resolve NetBIOS names, but if your organization is eliminating WINS, a **GlobalNames zone (GNZ)** can be implemented to resolve names for legacy clients or applications. This is especially important if an organization is migrating to an IPv6 network because IPv6 does not support WINS. GNZs are covered in more depth later in this chapter.
- **IPv6 support.** DNS now fully supports the 128 bit IPv6 addresses.
- **RODC support.** It's possible to host a read-only zone on a read-only domain controller. RODCs were covered in depth in Chapter 2.
- **Background zone loading.** Windows Server 2003 DNS servers could sometimes take up to an hour to reboot when it had to load a significant number of zones. Windows Server 2008 DNS servers load the zone data in the background, allowing the DNS servers to reboot quickly.

Upgrade your DNS servers to Windows Server 2008 to take advantage of these improvements. While most are obvious enhancements you'll see when configuring DNS, the background zone loading feature is a significant yet subtle improvement. If your DNS servers host 10 or more zones and they take a long time to reboot, consider upgrading them to Windows Server 2008 to improve the reboot times.

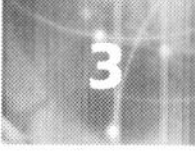

Name Resolution in a Domain

Name resolution plays an important part of the communications in any network. In short, name resolution is used to resolve names to IP addresses, but it does more. Name resolution in a domain is primarily provided by a Domain Name System (DNS) server. DNS is used to do the following:

- Resolve names to IP addresses using A or Host records (forward lookups)
- Resolve IP addresses to names using pointer (PTR) records (reverse lookups)
- Locate domain controllers using service location (SRV) records
- Locate mail servers using mail exchange (MX) records
- Resolve single-label names using GlobalNames zones

While DNS is of primary importance in a domain, it isn't the only type of name resolution in use. Before digging in too deep, it's worthwhile to review the basics of the different types of computer names and different types of name resolution.

Computer Names

Two types of computer names are used in networks: **NetBIOS names** and **host names.** NetBIOS names have been used longer in Microsoft networks.

- **NetBIOS names.** A NetBIOS name is 16 bytes long. The first 15 bytes are readable characters and the 16th is a hidden byte that identifies a service running on the system.
- **Host names.** A host name can be up to 255 characters, all of which are readable. When the host name is combined with the domain name, it becomes a fully qualified domain name (FQDN). As an example, a computer with a host name of DC1 in a domain named Cengage.com has an FQDN of dc1.cengage.com. Host names are used on any TCP/IP network, including the Internet.

Although a computer can be named with as many as 255 characters, the name is truncated to the first 15 characters to determine the host name. As long as networks are using NetBIOS names, you have a theoretical limit of 15 characters for host names within a network. This limit ensures that the truncated name isn't the same on any two computers.

As an example, consider two computers named CengageVirginiaBeachServer1 and CengageVirginiaBeachServer2. Both are legitimate host names. However, when the names are truncated to the first 15 characters, both computers will be named CengageVirginia, which isn't acceptable in a network. Because of this, you will see computers in networks named with only 15 characters or less, even though DNS may be the primary method of name resolution.

NetBIOS names were used primarily with Windows NT 3 and NT 4, but because Dynamic DNS was added in Windows 2000 Server, the use of NetBIOS continually decreases.

Name Resolution Methods

DNS isn't the only method of name resolution. Seven different types of name resolution can be used within a network. Table 3-1 shows the three name resolution methods that are primarily used with host names.

An application or service determines what type of name resolution is used. In other words, when an application needs to resolve a name, it assumes that the name is either a host name or a NetBIOS name. Increasingly, applications and services on Windows Server 2008 networks assume that the name is a host name and attempt the host name resolution methods first. Some legacy applications still assume that the name is a NetBIOS name and attempt the NetBIOS name resolution methods first.

Table 3-1 Name resolution methods used with host names

Method	Notable Features
DNS server	Clients receive the IP address of the DNS server from DHCP or their local TCP/IP configuration Clients automatically register their names and IP addresses using dynamic DNS Clients and applications can query DNS to resolve the names to IP addresses DNS can also resolve IP addresses to host names using reverse lookups SRV records are used in DNS to locate servers hosting specific services
Hosts file	This is a text file located in the *%systemroot%\System32\drivers\etc* folder A default IPv4 entry of 127.0.0.1 is resolved from localhost A default IPv6 entry of ::1 is resolved from localhost Other entries can be added Any entries in the hosts file are immediately placed in the host cache and used prior to querying DNS
Host cache	The host cache can be viewed with the command IPConfig /DisplayDNS Names resolved by DNS are temporarily stored in this cache DNS cached entries can be removed with the command IPConfig /FlushDNS

Table 3-2 shows the different name resolution methods primarily used with NetBIOS names. The server used to resolve NetBIOS names in a Microsoft environment is Windows Internet Name Service (WINS). Usage of NetBIOS names has been significantly reduced over the years, so the need for WINS servers is also decreasing. However, most current networks still include a WINS server, at least for the time being.

Table 3-2 Name resolution methods used with NetBIOS names

Method	Notable Features
WINS server	Clients receive the IP address of the WINS server from DHCP or their local TCP/IP configuration Clients automatically register their names and IP addresses with WINS Clients and applications can query WINS to resolve names to IP addresses WINS can also be queried to identify servers hosting specific services
LMHosts file	This is a text file located in the *%systemroot%\System32\drivers\etc* folder It does not have any default entries and is rarely used anymore
NetBIOS cache	The NetBIOS cache can be viewed with the command NBTStat /c

If you're counting, we've only covered six methods of name resolution: three for host names and three for NetBIOS names. The seventh method of name resolution is broadcast. As a last resort, a client often will just broadcast the name to the network, asking if any other client has the same name. If a client has the broadcasted name, it will respond with its IP address. Remember, though, broadcasts are not passed through routers, so a broadcast name resolution method will only work within a subnet.

DNS Zones, Zone Files, and Zone Resource Records

DNS includes zones, files, and resource records. It's important to understand the components of each when designing and implementing a DNS solution within an organization. A key point is that DNS is required for an Active Directory Domain Services (AD DS) environment. Without DNS, clients will not be able to log on, and applications using LDAP queries will fail because domain controllers cannot be located.

Figure 3-1 shows the DNS console for a DNS server hosting the Cengage.com zone. In the figure, the Cengage.com forward lookup zone is selected and the records in the zone are displayed. You can access the DNS console via the Administrative Tools menu.

The **DNS zone** defines a namespace. If a DNS server has a DNS zone, it can authoritatively answer queries for hosts in that zone or with that common namespace. In other words, the DNS server is the authority for the namespace; if there is a host with a given host name, the

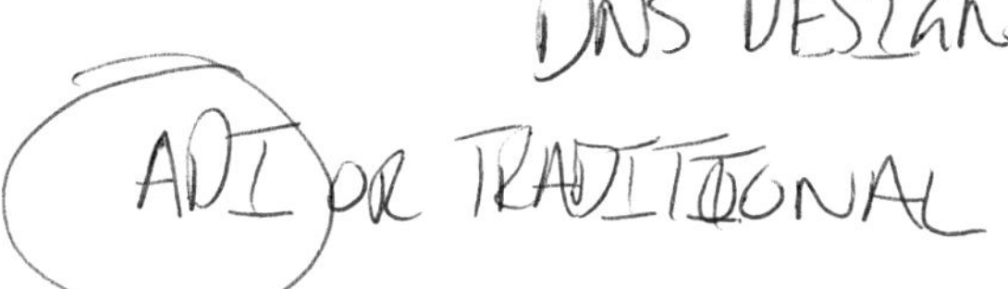

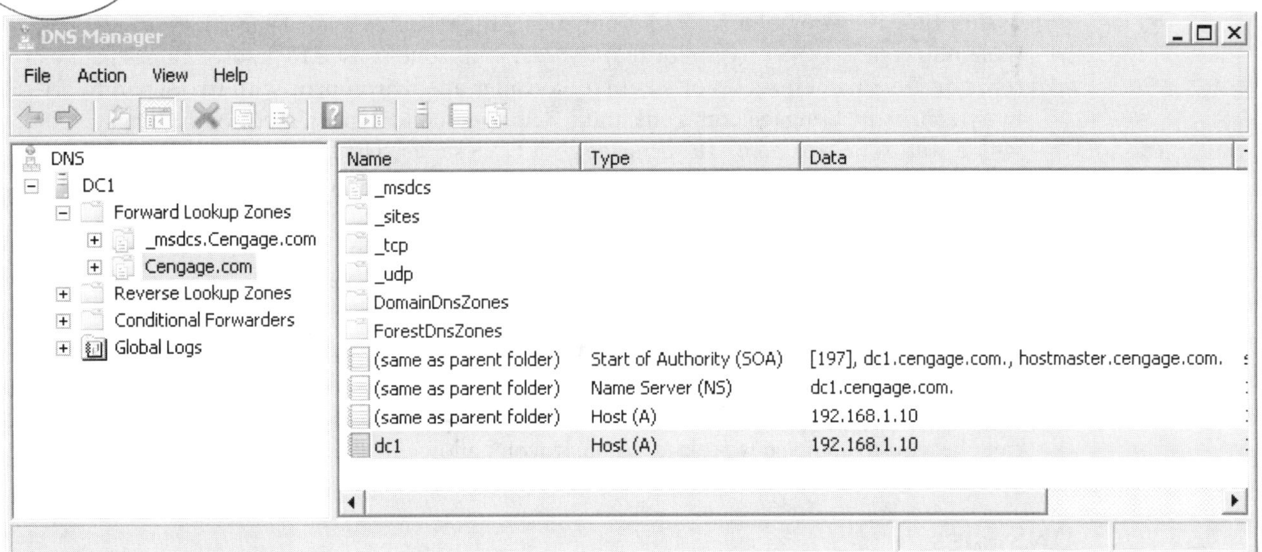

Figure 3-1 Viewing the DNS console

Courtesy Course Technology/Cengage Learning

authoritative DNS server knows it and can respond with an IP address. A DNS server will hold forward and/or reverse lookup zone files, and these files will contain individual records.

While DNS is heavily used on the Internet, this chapter focuses on how DNS is used within an Active Directory domain, because you'll be tested on this topic when taking the 70-647 exam. Remember that a DNS zone namespace directly correlates to the Windows domain. For example, DNS will have a Cengage.com namespace for the Cengage.com domain.

DNS Zones

A DNS zone is the namespace where a DNS server can resolve names. As an example, a DNS server could have a zone for Cengage.com. It can then resolve names in the Cengage.com namespace. Several types of DNS zones are available in Windows Server 2008:

- **A primary DNS zone** is a master copy of a zone. With traditional DNS servers, the master copy of the zone is the only writable copy of the zone; only one server can host a primary zone for any namespace. When ADI zones are used, multiple servers can host primary zones.
- A **secondary DNS zone** is a read-only copy of a zone used for fault tolerance and load balancing. A secondary zone can only be created if a primary zone exists. Changes are made to the primary zone (the master copy) and copied to the secondary zone using zone transfers. Secondary zones are only used with traditional DNS servers. If all DNS servers are using ADI zones, secondary zones are not used. However, if other DNS servers are hosting ADI zones, it's still possible to have a traditional secondary DNS zone.
- An **Active Directory-integrated (ADI) primary zone** is hosted on a domain controller, and zone transfers are integrated into Active Directory replication. Unlike traditional DNS, which allow only one primary (or only one master), ADI zones use multiple primary ADI zones with the same multi-master model used on domain controllers. Only primary zones can be ADI zones. In an Active Directory environment, it's common to host DNS on domain controllers and make all DNS servers ADI.

Microsoft highly recommends the use of ADI zones for DNS. ADI zones work well, reduce administrative workload, and provide extra security. For example, you can only use secure dynamic updates with ADI zones. An ADI zone can only be hosted on a domain controller.

- A **stub zone** is a copy of a zone that only hosts the resource records necessary to identify the authoritative DNS servers for that zone. A stub zone is used to resolve names between separate DNS namespaces. For example, consider an environment with two separate primary zones: the Cengage.com zone and a delegated child zone named south.Cengage.com with a stub zone created on the cengage.com DNS server. The stub zone in the Cengage.com domain will automatically be updated if changes are made in the child zone. This can improve name resolution because DNS servers in the Cengage.com zone automatically know what servers to query to resolve names in the south.Cengage.com zone. A stub zone can also be used when a corporate merger requires that DNS servers for different namespaces resolve names for clients in both namespaces.
- **GlobalNames zones** (GNZs) are new to Windows Server 2008 and allow DNS to resolve single-label names (such as NetBIOS names). A GNZ can be used to help an organization move to DNS as the primary name resolution method and remove WINS from the network. A GNZ can't be used to completely replace WINS. It won't allow the dynamic name registration of NetBIOS names as a WINS server does. Instead, all records in the GNC are created manually.

DNS Files

A DNS zone includes one or two files: forward lookup zone files for name-to-IP address resolution and reverse lookup zone files for IP address-to-name resolution. Just as you'd expect, a forward lookup zone holds a forward lookup file, and a reverse lookup zone holds a reverse lookup file. These files hold the actual records for the zone.

A caching-only DNS server can be created that does not hold any zone files or any zone data. Instead of holding copies of zone data, a caching-only DNS server is configured with forwarders and conditional forwarders to query other DNS servers. It then caches the results of these queries and provides the results to clients when queried again.

A forward lookup zone file is required for a zone and is defined when the zone is created. A reverse lookup zone is optional. If the zone is created without the reverse lookup zone file, it can't do reverse lookups, but it will still work for most uses.

- **Forward lookup zone file.** This file includes records to support name-to-IP address resolution. In other words, the name is provided and DNS responds with an IP address. The primary records used to provide forward lookup zones are A (or host) records for IPv4 addresses or AAAA records for IPv6 addresses. Most other records are also supported in, and located in, a forward lookup zone file. Besides A and AAAA records, you'll also see SRV, NS, MX, SOA, and CNAME records in a forward lookup zone file. All of these records are described in the next section.
- **Reverse lookup zone file.** This file is used to provide a name when an IP address is provided. This file is frequently used for security purposes to ensure that a host isn't impersonating another host. The IP address is included in the packet and used to query DNS to verify that the name provided is the same as the name registered with DNS. The primary records you'll see in reverse lookup zones are PTR records.

DNS Resource Records

Zone files hold zone resource records. Each of the record types has a specific purpose. Any single zone file will not hold all of these records, but you are likely to see the following record types in DNS server within an Active Directory domain:

- An **A record** (also called a host record) is used to resolve a name to an IPv4 address. A records can be manually created or created with the dynamic updates process.
- An **AAAA record** is used to resolve a name to an IPv6 address. AAAA records can be manually created or created with the dynamic updates process.

- A **service location (SRV) record** is used to locate a server running specific services. SRV records are extremely important in an Active Directory environment and are discussed in more depth later in this chapter. SRV records are created automatically by the Netlogon service on the domain controller hosting DNS.
- The **start of authority (SOA) record** is used by DNS and other services, such as DHCP and the dynamic updates process. It includes information that identifies the primary server for the zone, an e-mail address for someone who is responsible for the zone, and information used by secondary zone DNS servers on zone transfer times.
- **Name server (NS) records** identify DNS servers in the zone. An NS record can be created manually. The DCpromo service creates an NS record when DNS is included in the promotion of a server as a DNS server.
- A **mail exchange (MX) record** is used to find mail servers. These records are most commonly used to locate servers running Microsoft Exchange in a Microsoft domain environment. MX records must be created manually. If they aren't created, the Exchange server will not receive e-mails.
- An **alias record** is also known as a canonical name (or CNAME) record. They can be created to allow a single server to be resolved to the same IP address with multiple names. For example, if a Web server has a name of Server1 but you also want it to be known as Web1, you can create an alias record. Alias records must be created manually.
- **Pointer (PTR)** records are used for reverse lookups. In other words, a client can provide the IP address, and if the PTR record exists, DNS will respond with the name associated with the IP address. PTR records are only found in reverse lookup zones, and reverse lookup zones are optional. In other words, not all DNS servers have reverse lookup zones and PTR records, but the DNS servers will still operate without problems.

When preparing for the 70-647 exam, be aware of the different types of records, especially the ones that need to be created manually, such as MX, NS, and alias records.

Activity 3-1: Creating an A Record and an MX Record in DNS

Time Required: 15 minutes
Objective: Create an A record and an MX record in DNS.

Description: Your organization recently added a Microsoft Exchange server. You want to ensure that this server can be located, so you need to create an A record and an MX record for it. The mail server has been named Mail1 and has an IP address of 192.168.1.50/24. DNS is hosted on DC1, which is the domain controller for your Cengage.com domain.

1. Log on to DC1 with the domain **Administrator** account and a password of **P@ssw0rd.**
2. Start **DNS** via the **Administrative Tools** menu.
3. Expand **Forward Lookup Zones**, then right-click **Cengage.com** and select **New Host (A or AAAA)**.
4. Enter **Mail1** as the **Name**. Notice that the **Fully qualified domain name** (**FQDN**) is automatically filled in. Enter the IP address as **192.168.1.50**. Your display will look similar to Figure 3-2. Click **Add Host**.
5. A dialog box appears, indicating that the host record was successfully created. Click **OK**. Click **Done**.
6. Right-click **Cengage.com** and select **New Mail Exchanger** (**MX**). Enter **Mail1** in the **Host or Child Domain** text box. Notice that the FQDN is automatically filled in.

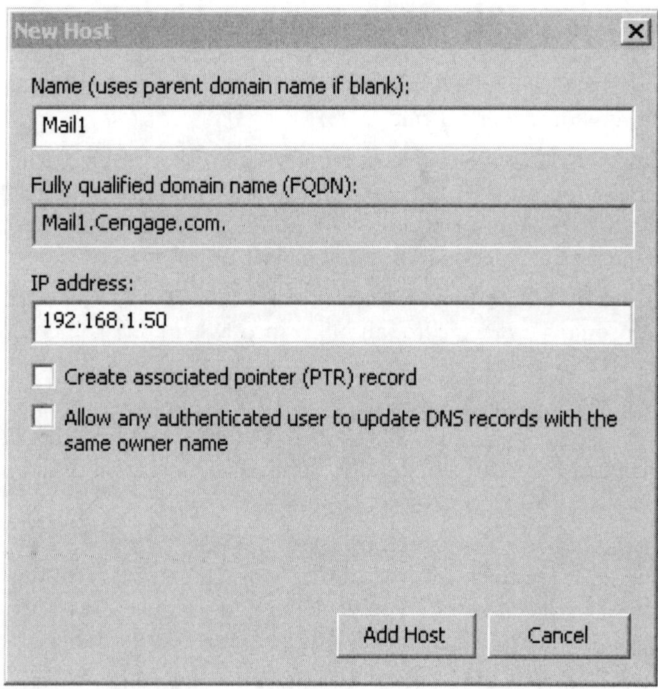

Figure 3-2 Creating an A record

Courtesy Course Technology/Cengage Learning

7. Click **Browse**. Double-click **DC1**. Double-click **Forward Lookup Zones**. Double-click **Cengage.com**. Select the **Mail1** Host (A) record, as shown in Figure 3-3.

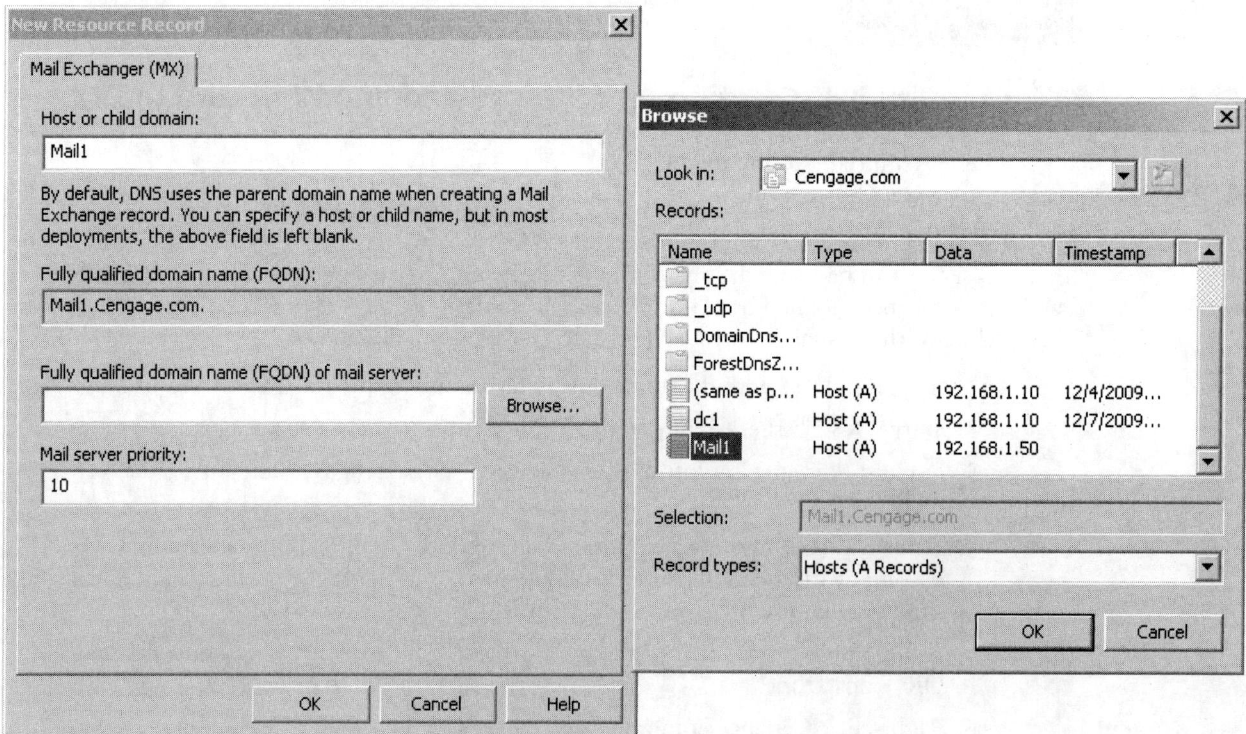

Figure 3-3 Creating an MX record

Courtesy Course Technology/Cengage Learning

8. When multiple mail servers are used, the **Mail Server Priority** can be manipulated, but you can accept the default priority of **10**. Click **OK**. At this point the display will look similar to Figure 3-4. Notice that **Mail1** has two records. The MX record doesn't have an IP address, but instead points to the A record. Both records are used in conjunction to locate the server.

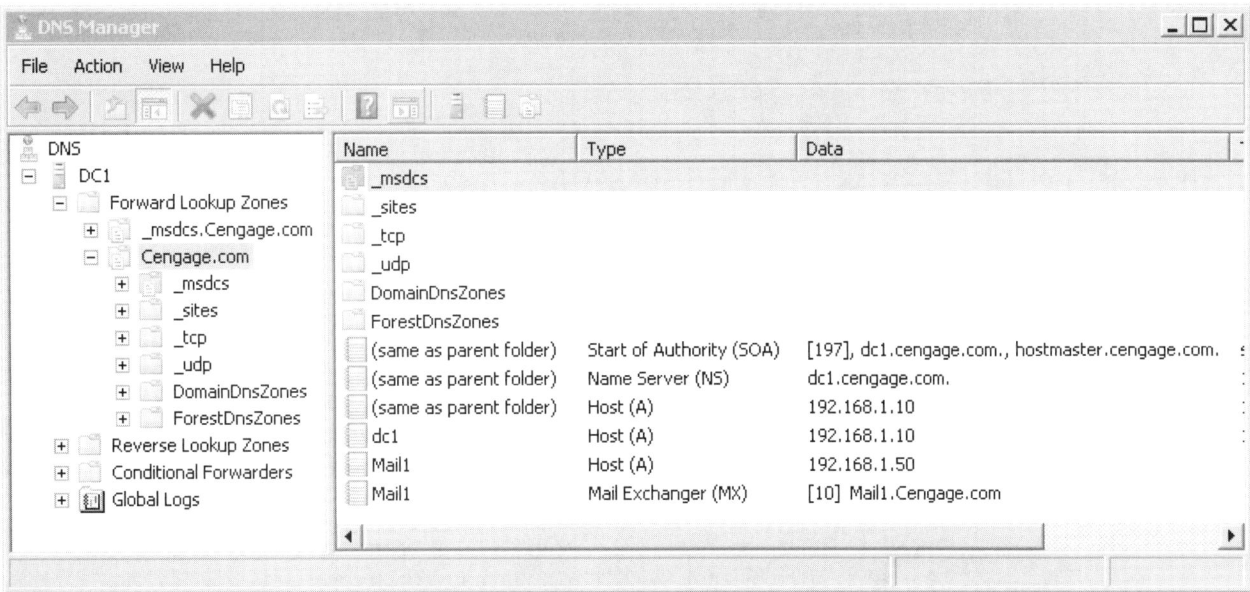

Figure 3-4 A and MX records created in DNS

Courtesy Course Technology/Cengage Learning

While this exercise shows how MX records are created within a network, these records also need to be created in other networks. For example, if you want your mail server to be located by other mail servers outside of your network, the DNS server used by these servers must be updated. This usually entails getting your Internet Service Provider (ISP) to create MX records to locate your mail server.

Understanding Dynamic Update and Secure Dynamic Update

Both A and PTR records are often updated automatically in DNS using a process known as **Dynamic Update**. For best security, secure dynamic updates should be enabled. **Secure dynamic updates** require that the DNS server is hosted on a domain controller and that a primary ADI zone is being used.

Several items need to exist or be configured to support dynamic updates:

- The client must be configured to use DHCP.
- DHCP options must include the address of the DNS server.
- The DNS server must be configured to allow dynamic updates (either Secure Only, or Nonsecure and Secure).

Figure 3-5 shows what happens with dynamic updates when all the pieces are configured. Dynamic updates work by default for any clients running Windows 2000 or later and start when the client turns on. The DHCP client and DHCP server exchange four packets with the client, and ultimately accept the TCP/IP configuration information offered by the DHCP server. The four packets are DHCP Discover, DHCP Offer, DHCP Request, and DHCP Acknowledge; they are frequently referred to as the DORA process, after the initial letters of the four DHCP packets.

The TCP/IP configuration information includes items such as the IP address, subnet mask, default gateway, and the address of a DNS server. The client then sends a request to the DNS server

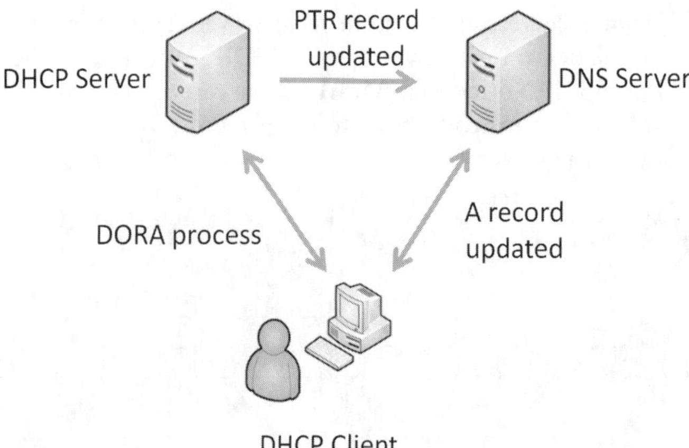

Figure 3-5 DNS dynamic updates

Courtesy Course Technology/Cengage Learning

to register its name and IP address by creating an A record, or an AAAA record if IPv6 is being used. A short time later, the DHCP server sends a request to update the PTR record for the server.

Dynamic Update allows A, AAAA, and PTR records to be updated automatically without any intervention. While dynamic updates are not unique to Microsoft DNS, secure dynamic updates are. They will only work on a Microsoft server hosting ADI DNS on a domain controller.

It's important to remember that secure dynamic updates can only be enabled on an Active Directory-integrated (ADI) zone, and a zone can only be ADI if DNS is hosted on a domain controller.

Secure dynamic updates will update the DNS records just as nonsecure dynamic updates will, but with two important benefits:

- **Only domain clients can update records.** When a client attempts to update DNS, the first attempt is refused. The client will then attempt a secure update, which will only succeed for clients with accounts in Active Directory.
- **You can set permissions on zones and records.** When Secure Dynamic Update is enabled, a security tab appears for zones and records. You can assign permissions to specific groups or users.

Activity 3-2: Configuring Secure Dynamic Updates on DNS

Time Required: 20 minutes

Objective: Configure and verify that secure updates are enabled on DNS.

Description: You are hosting DNS on a domain controller and want to verify that secure dynamic updates are enabled. DNS is hosted on DC1, which is the domain controller for your Cengage.com domain.

1. Log on to **DC1** with the domain **Administrator** account and a password of **P@ssw0rd.**
2. Start DNS via the Administrative Tools menu.
3. Right-click **Cengage.com** and select **Properties**. Your display should look similar to Figure 3-6.

   When you choose to add DNS with DCpromo, it configures the zone as Active Directory-integrated and sets Dynamic updates to Secure only, as shown in the figure. You can also see that a Security tab exists on this property page.
4. Click the **Change** button to the right of **Type: Active Directory-Integrated.** Deselect the check box next to **Store the Zone in Active Directory**. Click **OK**. When asked if

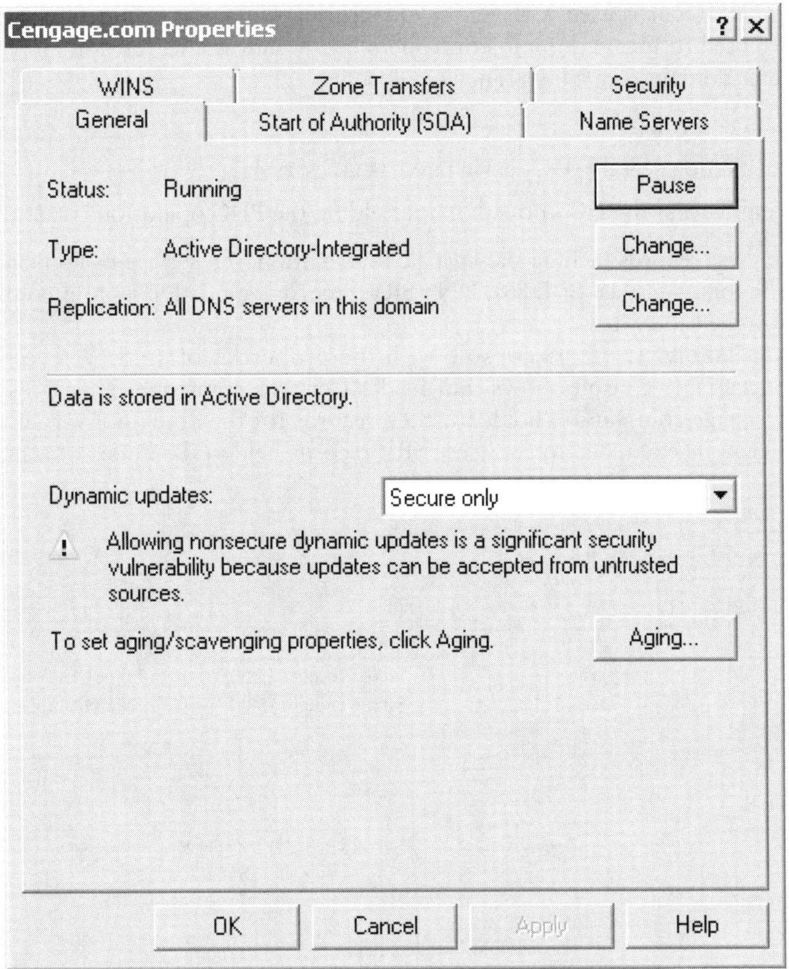

Figure 3-6 Verifying that secure updates are enabled on DNS

Courtesy Course Technology/Cengage Learning

you no longer want the zone to be Active Directory-integrated, click **Yes.** Click **OK** to dismiss the properties page.

5. Right-click **Cengage.com** and select **Properties**. Notice that when the **Type** is set to **Primary, Dynamic updates** is changed to **None** and the **Security** tab disappears.
6. Click the drop-down box next to **Dynamic updates**. Notice that you can't select **Secure only** when the zone isn't Active Directory-integrated.
7. Click the **Change** button to the right of **Type: Primary**. Select the check box next to **Store the Zone in Active Directory**. Click **OK.** When prompted if you want the zone to be Active Directory-integrated, click **Yes.**
8. Select **Secure only** from the drop-down box next to **Dynamic updates.** Click **OK** to dismiss the properties page.

DNS and Active Directory

Active Directory Domain Servers and DNS are so tightly intertwined that many people recommend checking DNS if you're having a problem with Active Directory. It's often said that 75 percent of Active Directory problems can be directly attributed to DNS. It's not that DNS is unreliable—far from it. However, the importance of DNS is sometimes overlooked.

The primary records used with Active Directory are the service location (SRV) records. SRV records are used to locate domain controllers in a Windows Server domain running Windows 2000 or later domain controllers. They can locate:

- Domain controllers
- Global catalog servers (DCs designated as GC servers)
- PDC emulators (the DC in the domain holding the PDC operations master role)

Further, these records include site-specific information. If a service or application is site-aware (such as the logon service or DFS), DNS SRV records help it locate and connect to a domain controller in the same site.

Figure 3-7 shows the DNS console with the properties of an SRV record displayed. The left side of the DNS console shows the _msdcs.Cengage.com zone. This is a subdomain of the domain (Cengage.com), and it holds the SRV records for the domain. Every node in the _msdcs subdomain can be expanded to show the SRV records held in the node.

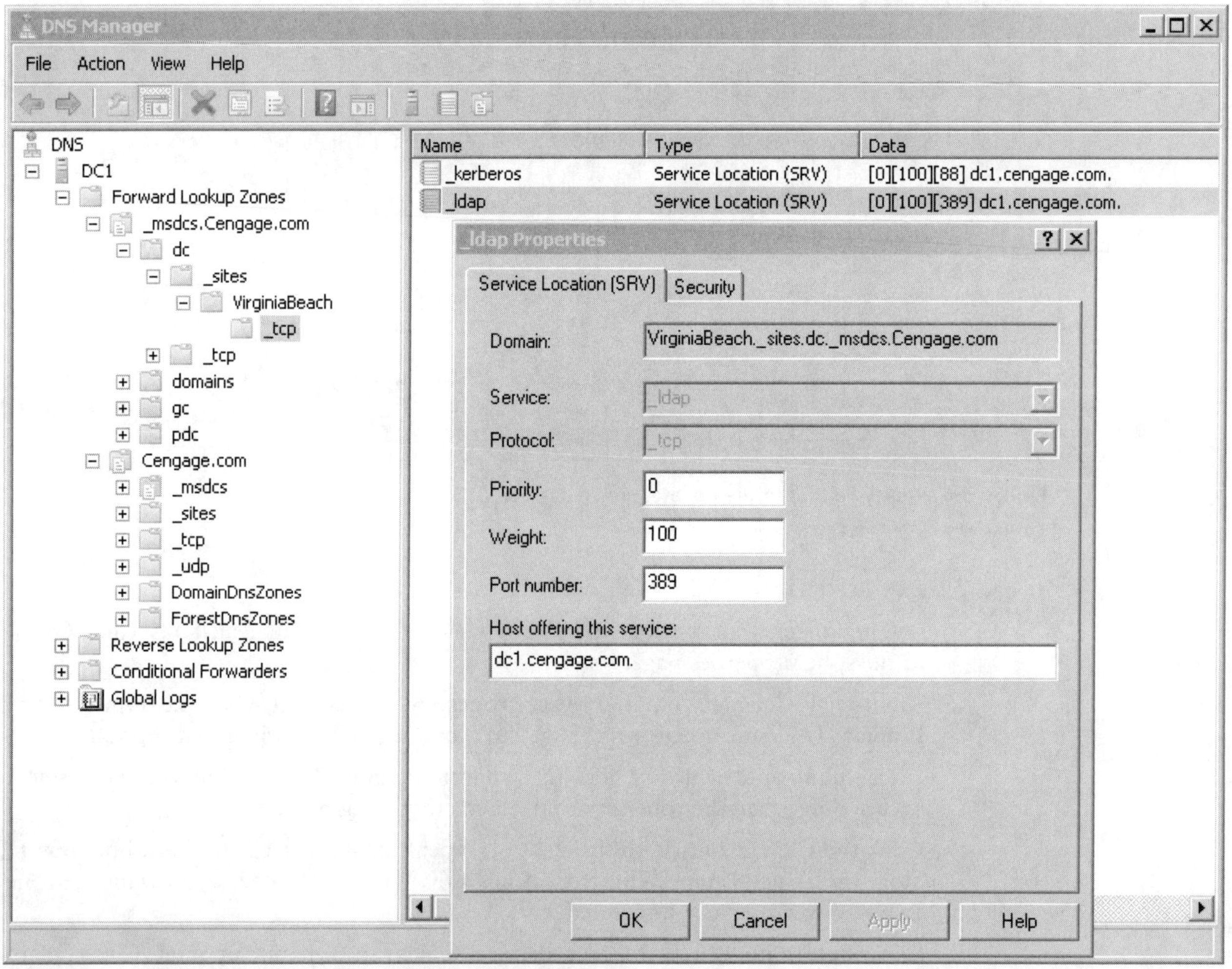

Figure 3-7 SRV records in the Windows Server 2008 DNS console

Courtesy Course Technology/Cengage Learning

Occasionally the SRV records don't appear in the DNS console. The service responsible for registering these SRV records is Netlogon. You can execute the following two commands from the command line to have the Netlogon service register the records: **Net Stop Netlogon** and **Net Start Netlogon**.

The properties of the _ldap record are shown in the figure. The Service property identifies the service running on the domain controller (DC). You'll see one of four services:

- **_ldap.** This identifies the server as a lightweight directory access protocol (LDAP) server, which will respond to LDAP queries. All Windows 2000 Server or later DCs will be identified by an _ldap record so that any DC can respond to any LDAP queries.
- **_kerberos.** This identifies the server that hosts the Key Distribution Center (KDC) used for the Kerberos protocol. Kerberos is the primary authentication protocol used on all Windows 2000 and later domains. All Windows 2000 Server or later DCs will be identified by a _kerberos record so that any DC can respond to any Kerberos queries.
- **_gc.** This identifies the server as a global catalog (GC) server. The GC server hosts a copy of the global catalog. Any Windows 2000 Server or later DCs can be designated as a GC server, and at least one DC in every domain must be a GC.
- **_kpasswd.** This identifies the server as a password change server. All Windows 2000 Server or later DCs will be identified by a _kpasswd record so that any DC can respond to password change requests.

These SRV records comply with RFC 2782, a standards document that can be implemented by any DNS server (not only Windows Server 2008 DNS servers). However, Microsoft adds the record to locate the DC hosting the PDC emulator role. The PDC emulator responds to LDAP queries and is registered with an LDAP record.

The following listing shows the SRV records created automatically for a single-domain forest with three sites (Virginia Beach, Chesapeake, and Norfolk). Notice that the first set of records are not site-specific, but many of the records are specific for a site in the organization. This is important for the next section.

```
_ldap._tcp.Cengage.com. 600 IN SRV 0 100 389 DC1.Cengage.com.

_ldap._tcp.pdc._msdcs.Cengage.com. 600 IN SRV 0 100 389
DC1.Cengage.com.

_ldap._tcp.gc._msdcs.Cengage.com. 600 IN SRV 0 100 3268
DC1.Cengage.com.

_ldap._tcp.a4e870c5-7ee6-4eab-8480-9ef5e2b8aa3a.domains._msdcs.
Cengage.com. 600 IN SRV 0 100 389 DC1.Cengage.com.

049204d1-8163-438f-b314-7f3e9da56f59._msdcs.Cengage.com. 600 IN CNAME
DC1.Cengage.com.

_kerberos._tcp.dc._msdcs.Cengage.com. 600 IN SRV 0 100 88
DC1.Cengage.com.

_ldap._tcp.dc._msdcs.Cengage.com. 600 IN SRV 0 100 389
DC1.Cengage.com.

_kerberos._tcp.Cengage.com. 600 IN SRV 0 100 88 DC1.Cengage.com.

_gc._tcp.Cengage.com. 600 IN SRV 0 100 3268 DC1.Cengage.com.

_kerberos._udp.Cengage.com. 600 IN SRV 0 100 88 DC1.Cengage.com.

_kpasswd._tcp.Cengage.com. 600 IN SRV 0 100 464 DC1.Cengage.com.

_kpasswd._udp.Cengage.com. 600 IN SRV 0 100 464 DC1.Cengage.com.

_ldap._tcp.DomainDnsZones.Cengage.com. 600 IN SRV 0 100 389
DC1.Cengage.com.
```

```
_ldap._tcp.ForestDnsZones.Cengage.com. 600 IN SRV 0 100 389
DC1.Cengage.com.

_ldap._tcp.VirginiaBeach._sites.Cengage.com. 600 IN SRV 0 100 389
DC1.Cengage.com.

_ldap._tcp.VirginiaBeach._sites.gc._msdcs.Cengage.com. 600 IN SRV 0
100 3268 DC1.Cengage.com.

_kerberos._tcp.VirginiaBeach._sites.dc._msdcs.Cengage.com. 600 IN SRV
0 100 88 DC1.Cengage.com.

_ldap._tcp.VirginiaBeach._sites.dc._msdcs.Cengage.com. 600 IN SRV 0
100 389 DC1.Cengage.com.

_kerberos._tcp.VirginiaBeach._sites.Cengage.com. 600 IN SRV 0 100 88
DC1.Cengage.com.

_gc._tcp.VirginiaBeach._sites.Cengage.com. 600 IN SRV 0 100 3268
DC1.Cengage.com.

_ldap._tcp.VirginiaBeach._sites.DomainDnsZones.Cengage.com. 600 IN
SRV 0 100 389 DC1.Cengage.com.

_ldap._tcp.VirginiaBeach._sites.ForestDnsZones.Cengage.com. 600 IN
SRV 0 100 389 DC1.Cengage.com.

_ldap._tcp.Norfolk._sites.DomainDnsZones.Cengage.com. 600 IN SRV 0
100 389 DC1.Cengage.com.

_ldap._tcp.Norfolk._sites.ForestDnsZones.Cengage.com. 600 IN SRV 0
100 389 DC1.Cengage.com.

_ldap._tcp.Chesapeake._sites.DomainDnsZones.Cengage.com. 600 IN SRV 0
100 389 DC1.Cengage.com.

_ldap._tcp.Chesapeake._sites.ForestDnsZones.Cengage.com. 600 IN SRV 0
100 389 DC1.Cengage.com.

Cengage.com. 600 IN A 192.168.1.10

gc._msdcs.Cengage.com. 600 IN A 192.168.1.10

DomainDnsZones.Cengage.com. 600 IN A 192.168.1.10

ForestDnsZones.Cengage.com. 600 IN A 192.168.1.10
```

You can view a listing of all SRV records that are automatically created on your DNS server. The records are located in the *%systemroot%\System32\config* folder in a file named netlogon.dns.

Using Non-Site-Specific SRV Records

While most organizations can use the SRV records created by default, larger organizations sometimes require you to manipulate the creation of some SRV records.

As an example, consider Figure 3-8. This organization is configured in a hub and spoke replication topology because the main office and the regional headquarters office are connected with a faster WAN connection (T1), but the other offices are connected with slower WAN connections (56 Kbps). The hub and spoke replication topology was covered in greater depth in Chapter 2.

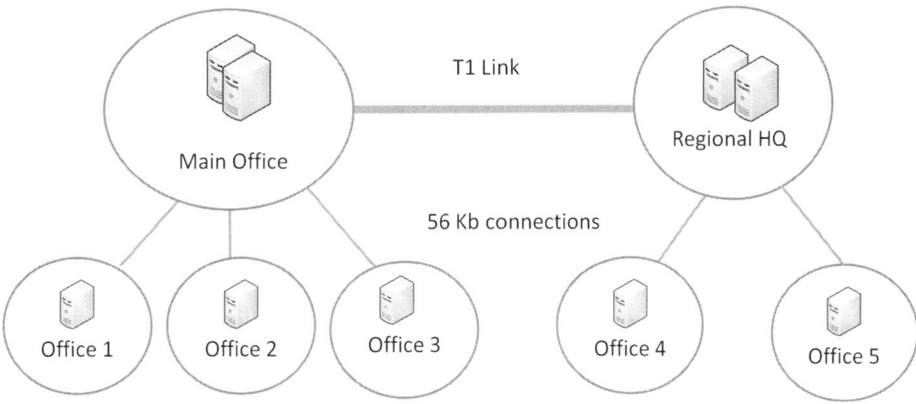

Figure 3-8 A multiple-site organization in a hub and spoke replication topology
Courtesy Course Technology/Cengage Learning

With the sites created and the default SRV records used, clients in Office 5 will log on using the DC in Office 5. However, what if the DC in Office 5 fails? To what DC *should* the clients connect for authentication? Looking at the diagram, you can see that only DCs in the main office or regional office should be used. If a DC from any other outlying office is used, authentication will have to traverse two slow 56 Kbps WAN links.

As a review, here's what happens by default when a user tries to log on in Office 5 and the DC in Office 5 is down:

- First, the Netlogon service queries DNS for a DC.
- A site-specific record is used to identify a DC in the Office 5 site.
- It's discovered that the DC in Office 5 is not reachable.
- A **generic (non-site-specific) DNS record** is used to identify any DC in the domain.

All DCs have both site-specific and non-site-specific records (generic records) created by default. The generic records don't have any prioritization related to them, so it's just as likely that the client will try to use a DC in Office 1 as a DC in the regional office. Clearly, this isn't desirable; the traffic has to go over two 56 Kbps links.

However, you can control the creation of these generic records to control which DCs are used when a DC in the site goes down. Specifically, you can prevent all of the DCs in the outlying offices from registering non-site-specific SRV records. If you prevent these generic SRV records from being created in each of the outlying offices, only DCs in the main office or the regional HQ office will be used if a DC in any site fails.

Configure DCs in outlying sites so that they do not create generic (non-site-specific) SRV records and to ensure these DCs are not used as a backup. Only DCs with the fastest WAN links should be allowed to create non-site-specific SRV records in organizations that use a hub and spoke replication topology.

The primary method used to prevent generic records from being created is Group Policy. The Group Policy node is: Computer Configuration, Policies, Administrative Templates, System, Net Logon, DC Locator DNS Records. The setting is: DC Locator DNS Records Not Registered by the DCs. The entry for Group Policy is shown in the following text. Even though the text spans two lines, it should be entered as a single line.

```
LdapIpAddress  Ldap  Gc  GcIPAddress  Kdc  Dc  DcByGuid  Rfc1510Kdc

Rfc1510Kpwd  Rfc1510UdpKdc  Rfc1510UdpKpwd  GenericGc
```

Each item in the entry is separated by a space, and is a mnemonic that refers to a specific record that is not to be created. Table 3-3 matches the mnemonic with the associated record that will not be created when properly configured.

Table 3-3 Mnemonics and records associated with generic (non-site-specific) records

Mnemonic	Record Type	Record
LdapIpAddress	A	<DnsDomainName>
Ldap	SRV	_ldap._tcp.<DnsDomainName>
Gc	SRV	_ldap._tcp.gc._msdcs.<DnsForestName>
GcIpAddress	A	_gc._msdcs.<DnsForestName>
Kdc	SRV	_kerberos._tcp.dc._msdcs.<DnsDomainName>
Dc	SRV	_ldap._tcp.dc._msdcs.<DnsDomainName>
DcByGuid	SRV	_ldap._tcp.<DomainGuid>.domains._msdcs.<DnsForestName>
Rfc1510Kdc	SRV	_kerberos._tcp.<DnsDomainName>
Rfc1510Kpwd	SRV	_kpasswd._tcp.<DnsDomainName>
Rfc1510UdpKdc	SRV	_kerberos._udp.<DnsDomainName>
Rfc1510UdpKpwd	SRV	_kpasswd._udp.<DnsDomainName>
GenericGc	SRV	_gc._tcp.<DnsForestName>

Table 3-4 shows the mnemonics of site-specific records that will be created even if you configure the DCs so that generic records are not created. Notice that most of these records include "AtSite," indicating clearly that they are site-specific records.

Table 3-4 Site-specific SRV mnemonics and SRV records

Mnemonic	Record Type	Record
DcAtSite	SRV	_ldap._tcp.<SiteName>._sites.dc._msdcs.<DnsDomainName>
Pdc	SRV	_ldap._tcp.pdc._msdcs.<DnsDomainName>
GcAtSite	SRV	_ldap._tcp.<SiteName>._sites.gc._msdcs.<DnsForestName>
GenericGcAtSite	SRV	_gc._tcp.<SiteName>._sites.<DnsForestName>
DsaCname	CNAME	<DsaGuid>._msdcs.<DnsForestName>
KdcAtSite	SRV	_kerberos._tcp.dc._msdcs.<SiteName>._sites.<DnsDomainName>
LdapAtSite	SRV	_ldap._tcp.<SiteName>._sites.<DnsDomainName>
Rfc1510KdcAtSite	SRV	_kerberos._tcp.<SiteName>._sites.<DnsDomainName>

Interestingly, Microsoft documentation indicates that you should modify the Default Domain Controllers Group Policy object (GPO) to ensure these records are not created on specific domain controllers. However, the Default Domain Controllers GPO applies to all GPOs in the domain. As an alternative, you can create a separate GPO and link it to the specific sites hosting the domain controllers where you don't want the generic records created.

Activity 3-3 shows you how to create a GPO, configure it to prevent generic (non-site-specific) records from being created, and link that GPO to a site.

Activity 3-3: Preventing Generic SRV Records from Being Registered

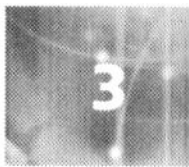

Time Required: 20 minutes
Objective: Prevent generic records from being created on DCs in a site.

Description: Your organization is preparing to create a hub and spoke replication topology. You are implementing the site named RemoteOffice. You want to ensure that if a DC in another site fails, clients will not be able to connect to DCs in the RemoteOffice site. This lab requires that DC1 is hosting the Cengage.com domain, which was created in Chapter 1.

1. Log on to **DC1** with the domain administrator account and a password of **P@ssw0rd.**
2. Start **Group Policy Management** via the **Administrative Tools** menu.
3. If necessary, expand Forest, Domains, and Cengage. Right-click **Group Policy Objects** and select **New.** Name the GPO **Prevent Generic Record Creation.** Click **OK.**
4. Right-click the **Prevent Generic Record Creation GPO** and **select Edit.**
5. Browse to the **Computer Configuration, Policies, Administrative Templates, System, Net Logon, DC Locator DNS Records** node.
6. Double-click the **DC Locator DNS Records Not Registered by the DCs** setting to access the **Properties** page.
7. Select **Enabled.** Enter the following text into the Mnemonics text box. Even though the text spans two lines, enter it in the text box as a single line.

```
LdapIpAddress Ldap Gc GcIPAddress Kdc Dc DcByGuid Rfc1510Kdc

Rfc1510Kpwd Rfc1510UdpKdc Rfc1510UdpKpwd GenericGc
```

These are the same mnemonics listed in Table 3-3. You can enter them using the table or the previous text, but be sure to enter a space after each mnemonic. You may want to enter the text in Notepad and then copy and paste it into the text box.

Your display should look similar to Figure 3-9. Click OK and close the Group Policy Management Editor.

8. Return to the **Group Policy Management** console. Right-click **Sites** and select **Active Directory Sites and Services** to start the Active Directory Sites and Services console.
9. Right-click **Sites** and select **New Site.** Name the site **RemoteOffice** and select the **DEFAULTIPSITELINK.** Click **OK.** Review the information in the dialog box and click **OK.** Close **Active Directory Sites and Services.**
10. Return to the **Group Policy Management** console. Right-click **Sites** and select **Show Sites.** Click the check box for the **RemoteOffice** site to select it. Click **OK.**
11. Click **Sites.** Right-click the **RemoteOffice** site and select **Link an Existing GPO.** Select the **Prevent Generic Record Creation** GPO you created earlier. Click **OK.**

No DCs exist in the RemoteOffice site yet, but when DCs are placed there, this GPO will prevent them from creating generic (non-site-specific) DNS records. This same GPO could be linked to all of the remote office sites, but should not be linked to the main office site or to any main hubs implemented in a hub and spoke replication topology.

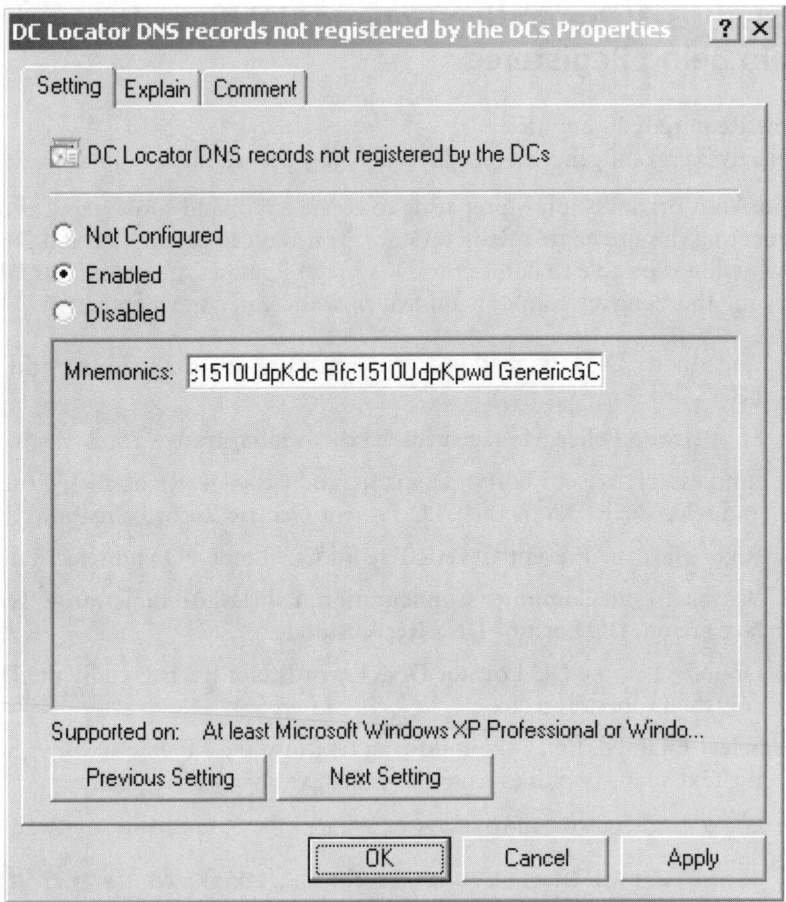

Figure 3-9 Configuring Group Policy to prevent the creation of non-site-specific records

Courtesy Course Technology/Cengage Learning

Designing DNS Zones

Earlier in this chapter you learned about the available DNS zones, but you should also know when these zones are used. Different DNS designs call for the use of different DNS zones. Admittedly, for most Active Directory designs, you'll want to configure all DNS servers as Active Directory-integrated primary zones, but sometimes you'll use other choices.

As a reminder, you can choose from the following available zones:

- ADI Primary Zones
- Primary Zones
- Secondary Zones
- Stub Zones
- GlobalNames Zones

Primary Zones

A primary zone is also referred to as a standard primary zone, and the server that hosts the primary zone is called the master server. It hosts the only writable copy of the DNS zone data. Standard primary zones are used with traditional DNS and will most often be seen when DNS is hosted on a non-Microsoft server such as a UNIX server. However, Microsoft servers can also host standard DNS zones.

The primary situation in which you would use a primary zone on a Microsoft server (over an Active Directory-integrated zone) is when the DNS server must be hosted on a member server—a server that is not a domain controller.

If a DNS server is configured with a primary zone and you need to create an additional DNS server, it must be configured as a secondary zone (or a standard secondary zone). Multiple DNS servers cannot host the same primary standard zone (unless the primary zones are configured as Active Directory-integrated).

The following activity shows how to create a primary zone.

Activity 3-4: Creating a Primary Zone

Time Required: 10 minutes
Objective: Create a primary zone on an existing DNS server.

Description: Your organization will be adding a new domain named CourseTech.com. To prepare for this domain, you musts add a primary zone named CourseTech.com to an existing DNS server. This lab requires that DC1 is hosting the Cengage.com domain.

1. Log on to **DC1** with the domain **Administrator** account and a password of **P@ssw0rd**.
2. Start **DNS** via the **Administrative Tools** menu.
3. Browse to the **Forward Lookup Zones** node. Right-click **Forward Lookup Zones** and select **New Zone**.
4. Review the information on the **Welcome** page and click **Next**.
5. On the **Zone Type** page, select **Primary zone**, as shown in Figure 3-10.

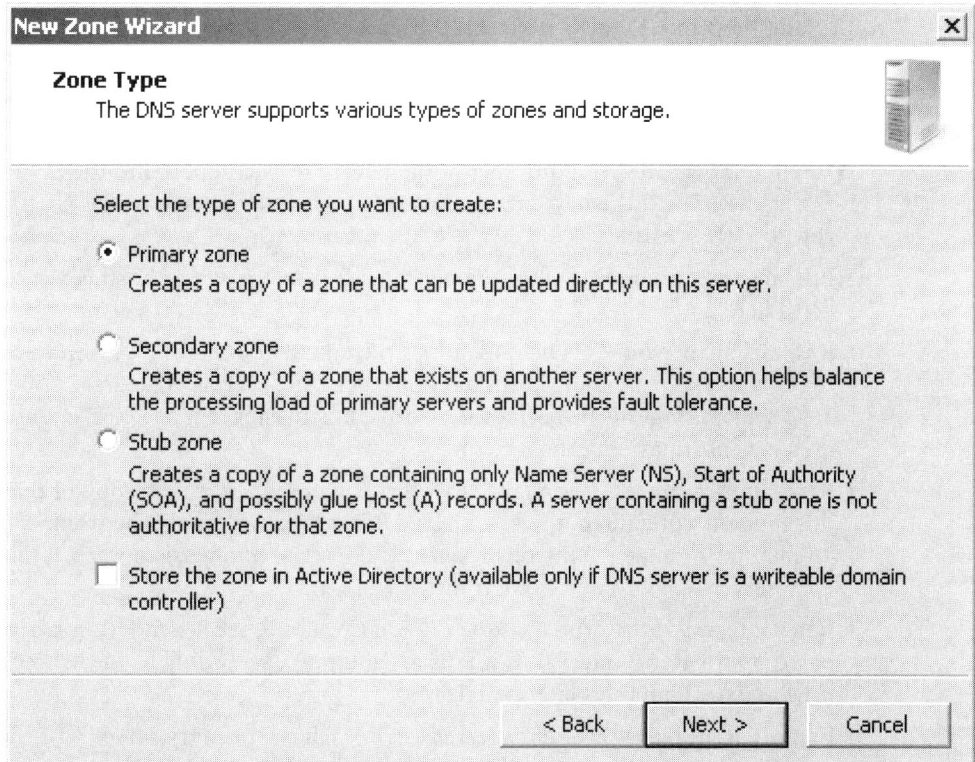

Figure 3-10 Creating a primary zone from the DNS console

Courtesy Course Technology/Cengage Learning

Ensure that **Store the zone in Active Directory** is not selected, which ensures that this zone is a standard primary DNS zone and not an ADI primary zone. Click **Next.**

6. Enter **CourseTech.com** on the **Zone Name** page. Click **Next.**
7. On the **Zone File** page, accept the default options and click **Next.** This selection creates a new file named CourseTech.com.dns to host the zone data.
8. Change the **Dynamic Update** page to select **Allow Both Nonsecure and Secure Dynamic Updates.** Click **Next.**

Because this zone is not an ADI zone, secure dynamic updates are not supported. However, a standard primary zone does support regular dynamic updates (which are referred to on this page as nonsecure dynamic updates).

9. Review the information on the completion page and click **Finish.**
10. Right-click the **CourseTech.com** zone and select **New Host (A or AAAA).** Enter **SRV1** as the name and **10.80.5.5** as the IP address. Click **Add Host.** Review the information in the dialog box that indicates the record was created and click **OK.** Click **Done.**

In the next activity, you will create a standard secondary DNS zone using this standard primary DNS zone as the master. Once successfully created, you'll be able to see this record transferred to the secondary DNS server.

Configuring Zone Transfers

Data within the DNS zone could be valuable if obtained by attackers outside the organization. Therefore, DNS data is protected from inadvertent disclosure by protecting zone transfers.

When using primary and secondary DNS servers, data is transferred between the servers using a process of zone transfers. Zone transfers are managed with the start of authority (SOA) record and the Zone Transfer settings. Both are accessible from the properties of the zone.

A server hosting a secondary zone will periodically request a new copy of the SOA record and use it in the zone transfer process. Figure 3-11 shows the Start of Authority (SOA) tab that includes the information from the SOA record. The tab has the following fields:

- **Serial number.** The serial number in the new SOA is compared to the SOA of the secondary DNS server. If the new serial number is higher, the secondary DNS server will initiate a zone transfer request.
- **Primary server.** The FQDN of the master server or the server hosting the primary zone is listed here.
- **Responsible person.** This field identifies the e-mail address of a person to contact in case of problems. It is used most often on Internet DNS servers. The first period is replaced by an @ when using this field. In other words, hostmaster.cengage.com is listed, but it is interpreted as hostmaster@cengage.com.
- **Refresh interval.** The secondary DNS server will request a new copy of the SOA based on this time. As configured, the secondary DNS server will query the primary server every 15 minutes for a new copy of the SOA. If the serial number is different, the secondary DNS server will initiate a zone transfer.
- **Retry interval.** If the primary server doesn't respond, the secondary server will keep trying based on the Retry Interval. If it fails at 1:00 p.m., according to the setting in Figure 3-11, it will retry 10 minutes later at 1:10 p.m.
- **Expires after.** If the secondary server can't reach the primary server past the expiration time, it will consider its records stale and will no longer respond to queries.
- **Minimum (default) TTL.** Manually created records will have a default time to live (TTL) specified by this setting.

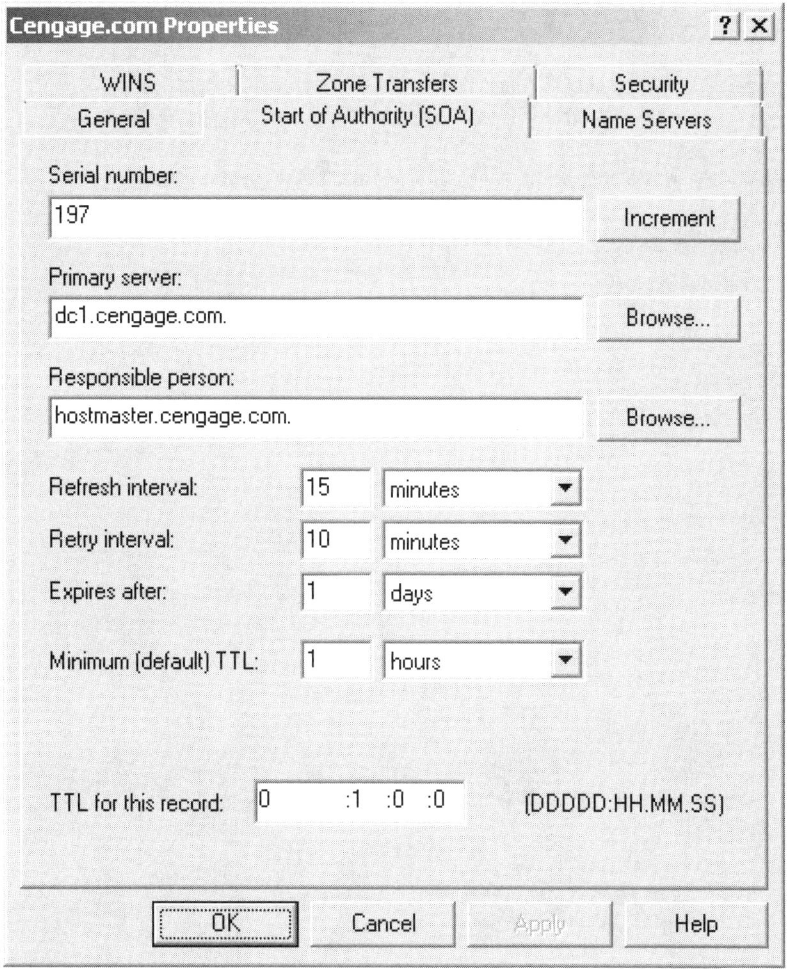

Figure 3-11 Viewing the SOA record

Courtesy Course Technology/Cengage Learning

- **TTL for this record.** The TTL for the SOA record is established with this setting. As shown, it has a TTL of one day.

The Zone Transfers tab is used to specify which DNS servers can participate in zone transfers. Figure 3-12 shows the settings for this tab. By default, Allow zone transfers is not selected; this is the most secure setting, but it is not very useful if you need to transfer zone data to a secondary DNS server.

When Allow zone transfers has been checked, you can select one of the following three choices.

- **To any server.** This is the least secure setting, and should not be used in a production environment.
- **Only to servers listed on the Name Servers tab.** NS records can be added by adding the server in the Name Servers tab. If the server is listed there, zone transfers are allowed. This is the most common selection when non-ADI zones are used.
- **Only to the following servers.** You can manually add the servers with this selection.

If zone transfers have not been configured, the secondary zone servers will fail when they try to initiate zone transfers or retrieve a copy of the SOA.

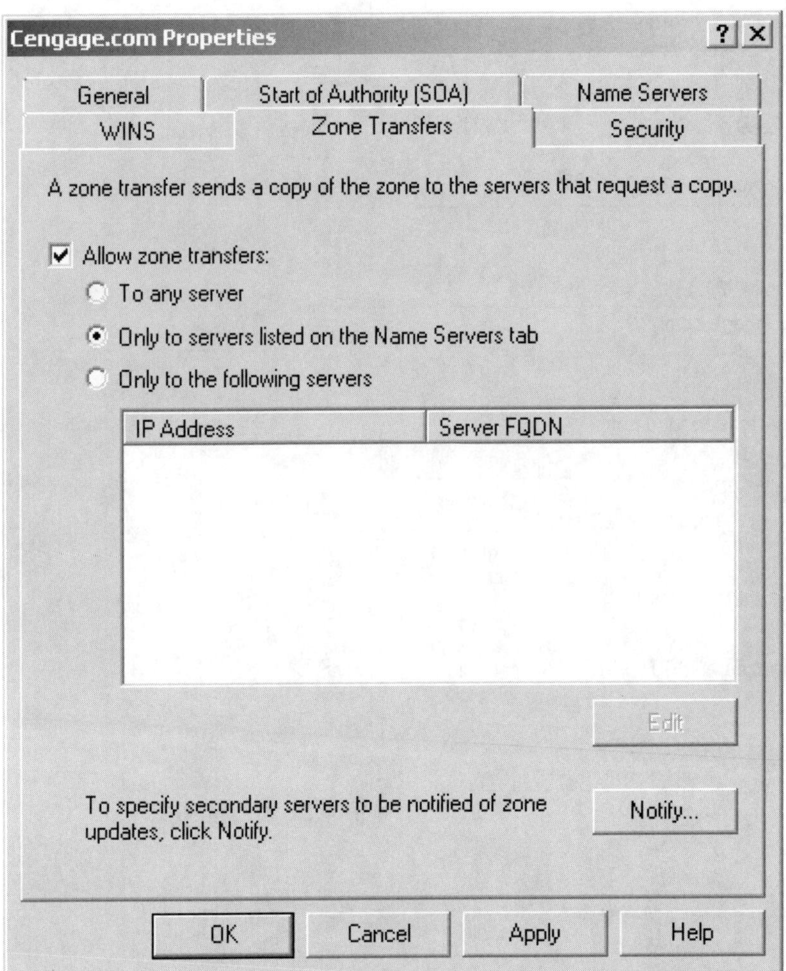

Figure 3-12 Configuring zone transfers

Courtesy Course Technology/Cengage Learning

One easy way to check whether zone transfers are allowed to a server is to use the NSLookup command. You need to be logged on to the secondary server and enter the following two lines from the command prompt.

```
NSLookup

ls cengage.com
```

Entering the first line (NSLookup) takes you to the NSLookup shell command with the NSLookup prompt of >. The second line (ls cengage.com) is used to list all of the records in the Cengage.com domain. The following listing shows the output:

```
C:\Users\Administrator>nslookup

Default Server: dc1.cengage.com

Address: 192.168.1.10

> ls cengage.com

[dc1.cengage.com]

 Cengage.com.           A       192.168.1.10

 Cengage.com.           NS      server = dc1.cengage.com

 _msdcs                 NS      server = dc1.cengage.com
```

```
Appl                A      192.168.1.150
Contracting         NS     server = dc3.contracting.cengage.com
DC3.Contracting     A      10.80.50.20
dc1                 A      192.168.1.10
DomainDnsZones      A      192.168.1.10
ForestDnsZones      A      192.168.1.10
Mail1               A      192.168.1.50
South               NS     server = dc2.south.cengage.com
DC2.South           A      192.168.1.20
>
```

If zone transfers are authorized to the server where you're logged on, it will list all of the records on the primary server. On the other hand, if zone transfers are not authorized, the response will be "Query Refused."

If the DNS server does not have a reverse lookup zone, NSLookup will time out after the initial NSLookup command. However, NSLookup will still work. It's unable to identify the name of the DNS server without a reverse lookup zone, but NSLookup will still list the records in the zone.

Secondary Zones

A secondary zone is also referred to as a standard secondary zone. If your organization has a DNS server hosting a standard primary server and you want to add more DNS servers in the zone, they must host standard secondary DNS zones.

A benefit of a secondary DNS server is the ability to provide fault tolerance and load balancing for clients in the network. As an example, your organization could have 1000 client computers with two DNS servers. DNS1 has an IP address of 192.168.1.10 and DNS2 has an IP address of 10.80.5.7. You could configure half of the clients to use DNS1 as their preferred DNS server and use DNS2 as the alternate DNS server, as shown in Figure 3-13.

The other half of the clients would be configured to use DNS2 as the preferred DNS server and DNS1 as the alternate DNS server. This solution provides both load balancing and fault tolerance.

- **Load balancing.** When both DNS servers are running normally, the load is balanced between both DNS servers, with half the clients using one DNS server and half using the other DNS server. As long as the preferred DNS server provides a response, the alternate DNS server is never queried.
- **Fault tolerance.** If either DNS server develops a fault, the network can tolerate it. If the failed DNS server for any client is configured as the preferred DNS server, the client will query the alternate DNS server when it fails to get a response from the preferred DNS server.

Multiple primary ADI DNS servers provide the same fault tolerance and load balancing capabilities as a primary DNS server and multiple secondary DNS servers. When more than one DNS server is added, the clients should be configured to spread the load between the different DNS servers, and should be configured with alternate DNS servers. This is easy to do in the DHCP scope options.

The following activity shows how to create a secondary zone.

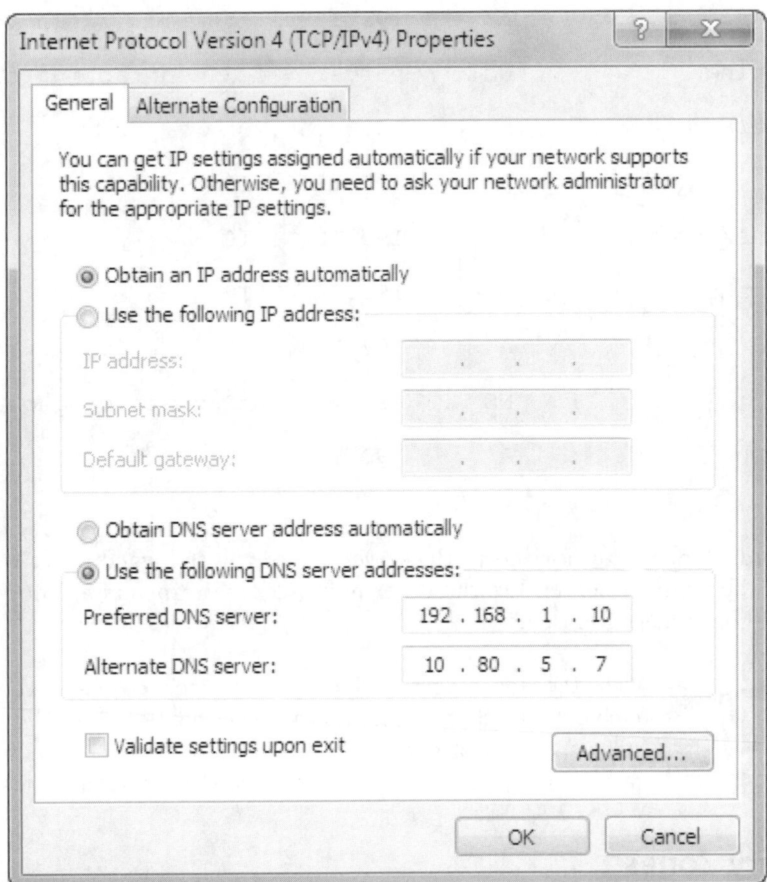

Figure 3-13 Local area connection configured with preferred and alternate DNS servers

Courtesy Course Technology/Cengage Learning

Activity 3-5: Creating a Secondary Zone

Time Required: 20 minutes

Objective: Create a secondary DNS zone.

Description: Your organization currently has a DNS server hosting the standard primary DNS zone of CourseTech.com. You need to add a standard secondary DNS zone to another member server. This lab requires DC1, which was used to create a standard primary DNS zone in the previous activity, and another server that is a member of the domain. The other server can be DC2, which was used in previous chapters.

1. Ensure that both **DC1** and **DC2** are started.

If you've done all the labs in the book to this point, DC2 is currently a read-only domain controller. The following step removes Active Directory from DC2.

2. Remove Active Directory from DC2 using the following steps.
   a. Log on to **DC2** with the domain **Administrator** account and a password of **P@ssw0rd**. Click **Start**, type **DCpromo** in the **Start Search** box, and press **Enter**.

b. Click **Next** on the **Welcome** screen. If prompted that the domain controller is a global catalog server, click **OK**.

c. Do not check the box on the **Delete the Domain** page to delete the domain. Click **Next**.

d. Type **P@ssw0rd** in the **Password** and **Confirm Password** boxes. Click **Next**.

e. Review the information on the **Summary** page and click **Next**.

f. Select the **Reboot on Completion** check box. Active Directory will be removed and the server will reboot.

3. After DC2 reboots, log on with a domain Administrator account. Verify that the NIC is configured to use DC1 for DNS by performing the following steps.

   a. Click **Start**, right-click **Network**, and select **Properties**.

   b. Click **Manage Network Connections**.

   c. Right-click **Local Area Connection** and select **Properties**.

   d. Select **Internet Protocol Version 4** (TCP/IPv4) and select **Properties**.

   e. Configure the Preferred DNS server as **192.168.1.10**.

   f. Click **OK** and close all open windows.

4. If the DNS role is not installed on DC2, use steps 5 through 7 to add it. If DNS is already available on the **Administrative Tools** menu, you can skip these steps and start on step 8.

5. Start **Server Manager** via the **Administrative Tools** menu.

6. Select **Roles** and click **Add Roles**. Click **Next** on the **Before You Begin** page.

7. Select **DNS Server** on the **Select Server Roles** page. Click **Next** on the **DNS Server** page. Click **Install** on the **Confirm Installation** page. When the installation is complete, click Close.

8. Start **DNS** via the **Administrative Tools** menu.

9. Expand DC2. Right-click **Forward Lookup Zones** and select **New Zone**. Click **Next** on the **Welcome** page.

10. Select **Secondary Zone** on the **Zone Type** page. Click **Next**.

11. On the **Zone Name** page, enter **CourseTech.com**. Click **Next**.

12. The **Master DNS Servers** page appears. Enter the **IP Address** of DC1 (**192.168.1.10**) and press the **Tab** key. Your display will look similar to Figure 3-14. Click **Next**.

    The IP address may not resolve to DC1 immediately, but it will resolve as long as both computers are in the same network and can ping each other.

13. Review the information on the **Completion** page and click **Finish**.

14. Select the **CourseTech.com** zone. The system will indicate an error. By default, the primary zone created on DC1 is not allowing zone transfer traffic.

15. Log on to **DC1** with the **Administrator** account and a password of **P@ssw0rd**. Start the **DNS** console via the **Administrative Tools** menu.

16. Locate the **CourseTech.com** zone created in the previous exercise and select **Properties**.

17. Select the **Name Servers** tab and click **Add**. Enter **DC2.Cengage.com** in the **Server Fully Qualified Domain Name** text box and click **Resolve**. Click **OK**. Your display should look like Figure 3-15. This step creates an NS record to identify DC2 as a DNS name server.

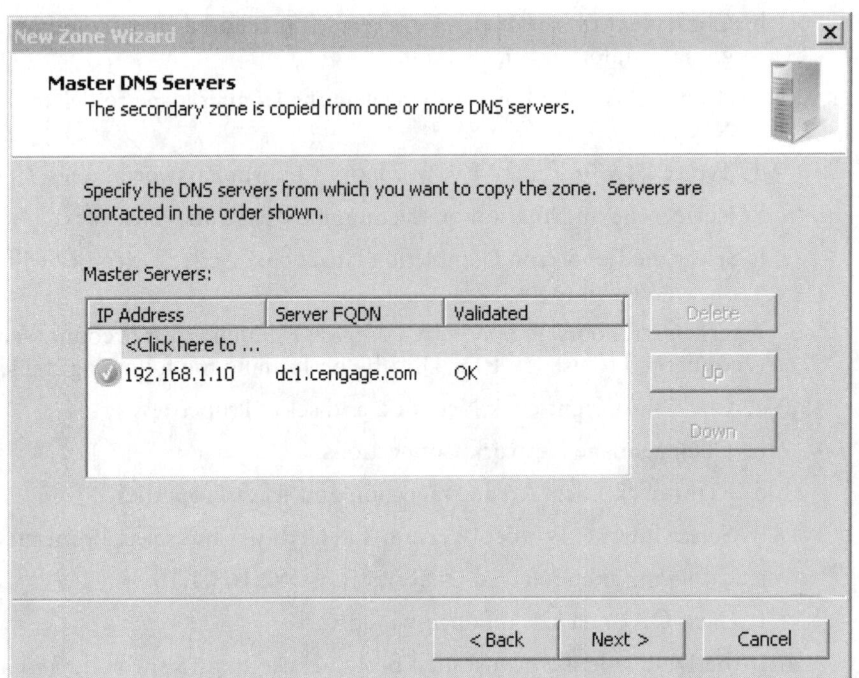

Figure 3-14 Configuring a secondary DNS zone with the IP address of the master server

Courtesy Course Technology/Cengage Learning

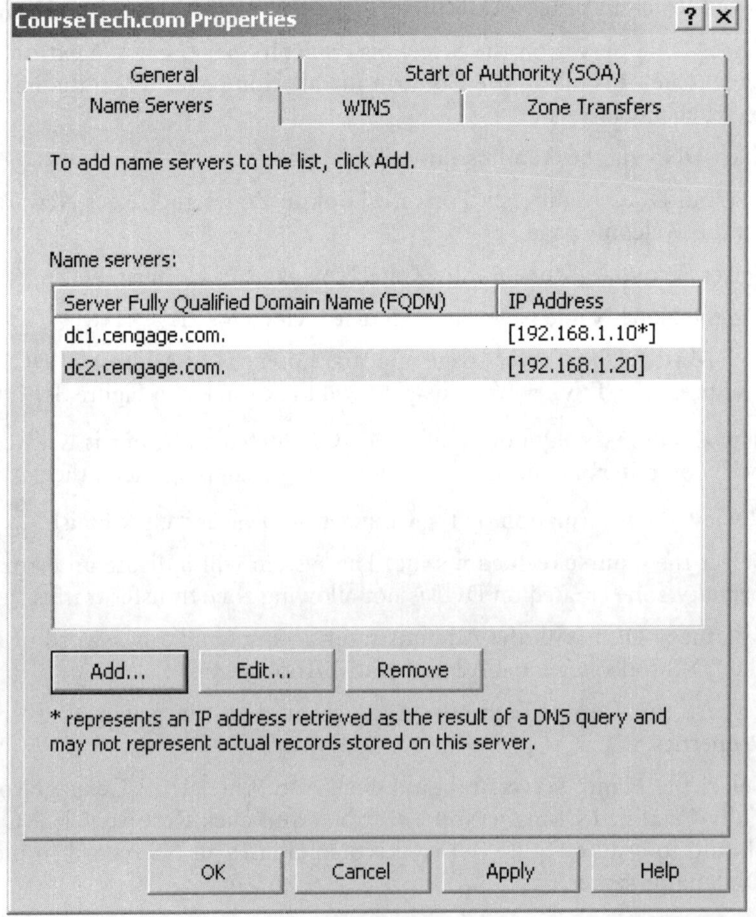

Figure 3-15 Adding an NS record to DNS

Courtesy Course Technology/Cengage Learning

18. Select the **Zone Transfers** tab. Verify that **Allow Zone Transfers** and **Only To Servers Listed on the Name Servers Tab** are both selected. Click **OK**.
19. Return to **DC2**. Right-click **CourseTech.com** and select **Transfer From Master**. Press the **F5** key to refresh the display. You should see that records replicated from DC1 appear on this server, including the SRV1 record created in the previous activity.

ADI Primary Zones

Active Directory-integrated (ADI) primary zones, sometimes just called ADI zones, can be used when DNS is hosted on a domain controller. Because ADI zones provide so many benefits, they should be used whenever possible. You cannot host an ADI zone if either of the following conditions exist.

- **When a standard primary zone is hosted on a member server**. ADI zones are only supported on DCs. If the DNS server is not hosted on a DC, it cannot support ADI zones. You can only add a secondary standard primary zone, not an ADI zone, to this DNS configuration.
- **When a standard primary zone is hosted on a domain controller**. If DNS is located on a DC, it can still host a standard primary zone (instead of an ADI primary zone). If this is the case, you can only add a secondary standard primary zone.

However, if you move DNS to a domain controller and create the zone as an ADI zone instead of a standard primary zone, you'll enjoy the following benefits:

- **Secure dynamic updates are supported.** This feature was discussed earlier in this chapter; it ensures that only clients with accounts in the domain can update DNS records.
- **Zone data is transferred to other ADI zones through Active Directory replication.** Zone transfers do not need to be configured or managed.
- **Replicated zone traffic is encrypted.** Active Directory replication traffic is encrypted by default. Because DNS ADI zone transfer traffic is replicated as part of the Active Directory replication process, it is automatically encrypted.
- **Multiple writable DNS servers can host the same primary zone if they are also ADI.** All ADI DNS servers can host primary zones if they are all ADI.
- **Individual security permissions can be applied to zones and records.** Granular control over zones and records is possible using traditional access control lists.

If a standard primary zone has been created on a domain controller, it's relatively easy to convert the zone to an ADI zone. The following activity shows you how.

Activity 3-6: Converting a Primary Zone to an ADI Zone

Time Required: 10 minutes
Objective: Convert a primary zone to an ADI zone.

Description: Your organization has recently reviewed internal security and has decided to convert all DNS zones hosted on domain controllers to ADI zones. DC1 currently hosts a standard primary zone named CourseTech.com. You need to convert this zone to an ADI zone. This activity assumes that a standard primary zone named CourseTech.com exists on DC1. This was created on Activity 3-4 earlier in this chapter.

1. Log on to **DC1** with the domain **Administrator** account and a password of **P@ssw0rd**.
2. Start **DNS** via the **Administrative Tools** menu.
3. Browse to the **Forward Lookup Zones** node and select **CourseTech.com**. Right-click **CourseTech.com** and select **Properties**.

4. Ensure that the **General** tab is selected. The **Type** should be set to **Primary**. Click **Change**.
5. On the **Change Zone Type** page, select the check box next to **Store the Zone in Active Directory**. Click **OK**. When asked if you want the zone to become Active Directory integrated, click **Yes**.

   Dynamic Updates aren't configured when changing from a standard primary zone to an ADI zone.
6. The **General** tab will show that the **Type** has changed to **Active Directory Integrated**. Change the **Dynamic Updates** setting to **Secure Only**. Click **OK**.

If desired, you can create another record in the DC1 DNS console and then verify that it is transferred to the secondary zone in DC2. The transfer will occur after 15 minutes by default, but you can force the transfer on DC2 by right-clicking the zone on DC2 and selecting Transfer From Master.

GlobalNames Zones

A GlobalNames zone (GNZ) is new in Windows Server 2008, and can be used to resolve single-label names. A single-label name mimics a NetBIOS name. The primary reason to include a GNZ in DNS is to support legacy applications using NetBIOS names after migrating to an IPv6 network in a multi-domain forest. IPv6 does not support NetBIOS names.

In older Windows operating systems before Windows 2000, the primary method of name resolution in a network was Windows Internet Naming Service (WINS), and NetBIOS was the primary type of name used. Since Windows 2000, DNS use for name resolution has steadily increased, and host names are used much more often than NetBIOS names.

WINS allows clients to dynamically register their names, similar to how dynamic update allows DHCP clients to dynamically update host names in DNS. Once NetBIOS names are registered in WINS, any client can query WINS to resolve the names of registered clients to IP addresses, just as any client can query DNS to resolve host names to IP addresses.

A significant difference between a GNZ and WINS is that a GNZ doesn't support automatic registration of clients. In other words, you must manually create all of the records in the GNZ. Because of this, a GNZ isn't intended to replace WINS, but instead is intended to aid in the retirement of WINS.

GNZ records are CNAME (or alias) records that point to an A (or AAAA) record contained in the primary zone. The CNAME record is created in the specialized GlobalNames zone.

A GNZ isn't really needed in a single-domain forest, due to how the DNS suffix search order is used. As an example, imagine that you have a single-domain forest named Cengage.com and a server named App1. App1 will have an FQDN of App1.Cengage.com within DNS. If a client in the Cengage.com domain tries to connect to App1 using a single-label name of App1, the suffix will be appended to create an FQDN of App1.Cengage.com.

You can achieve the same functionality in a multiple-domain environment by adding suffixes to the client's TCP/IP configuration. Figure 3-16 shows the IPv6 Local Area Connection properties for a Windows 7 client with multiple DNS suffixes added to the client.

When these additional suffixes are used, the clients will search each suffix in the order listed. Imagine that App1 is not in the root domain of Cengage.com, but instead is in training.south.Cengage.com. The client will first try to resolve App1.Cengage.com, then app1.north.Cengage.com, then app1.south.Cengage.com, and so on, until finally it comes to training.south.Cengage.com, which is not shown in the figure because it's 25th in the list.

While adding suffixes for one or two domains may be an acceptable solution, it's not a good solution for a forest with many domains. Adding all of these suffixes in a multiple-domain environment can affect the performance of the clients because each suffix must be searched. If a GNZ is used instead, the suffix search list doesn't need to be added to all clients.

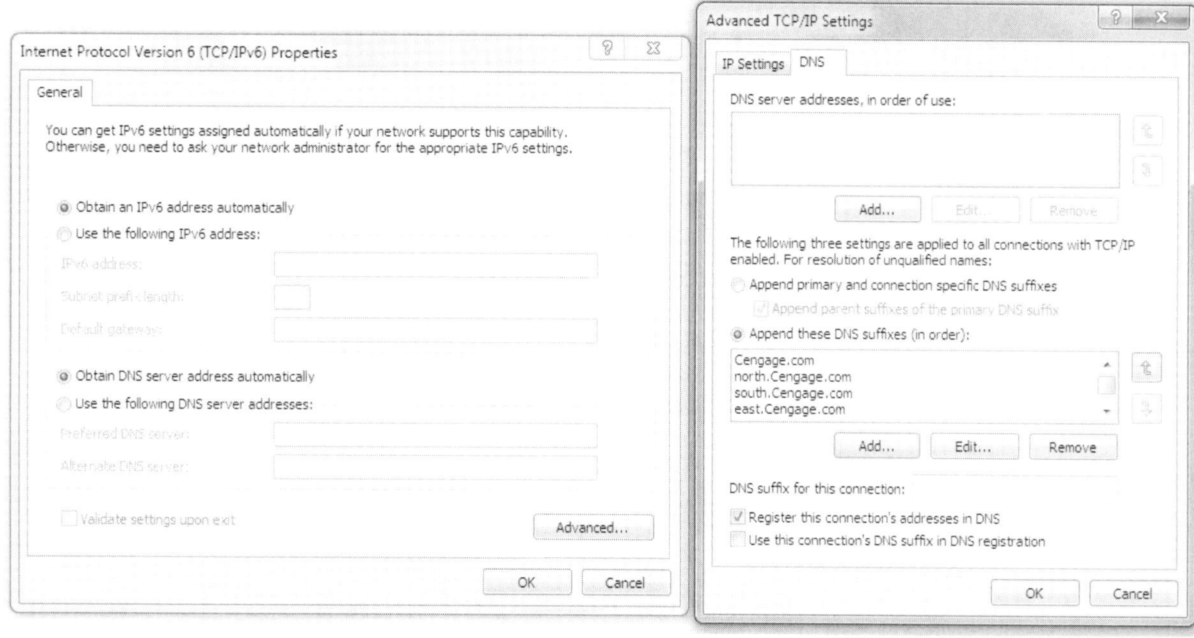

Figure 3-16 Additional DNS suffixes added to a client

Courtesy Course Technology/Cengage Learning

GlobalNames zone functionality is not enabled on a DNS server by default. Instead, you must first enable it using the command-line program DNSCmd. The full command is:

```
Dnscmd ServerName /config /Enableglobalnamessupport 1
```

If the server name is DC1, then the command is:

```
Dnscmd DC1 /config /Enableglobalnamessupport 1
```

After the command is entered, the screen will display the following text:

```
Registry property EnableGlobalNamesSupport successfully reset.

Command completed successfully.
```

Once the functionality is enabled on the server, you can create a primary zone called GlobalNames. Just as any zone hosted on a domain controller can be designated as an ADI zone, you can also designate a GlobalNames zone as ADI.

The following activity shows how to implement a GlobalNames zone on a DNS server.

Activity 3-7: Enabling and Creating a GlobalNames Zone

Time Required: 10 minutes
Objective: Enable GNZ functionality, create a GNZ, and add a GNZ record.

Description: Your organization is preparing to migrate to an IPv6 network. A legacy application accessed with a NetBIOS name is still used by clients. Clients need to be able to connect to the server using a single-label name of App1. You need to help prepare your network to support the migration by enabling GNZ functionality on the DNS server, creating the GNZ zone, and adding the record for App1. This activity can be completed on DC1, which hosts Cengage.com.

1. Log on to **DC1** with the domain **Administrator** account and a password of **P@ssw0rd.**
2. Open a command prompt and enter the following command.

   ```
   Dnscmd DC1 /config /Enableglobalnamessupport 1
   ```

Notice the two consecutive s's in /Enableglobalnamessupport. If spaces were added, it would read "Enable GlobalNames Support."

After you press Enter, the screen will display the following text to indicate success:

```
Registry property EnableGlobalNamesSupport successfully reset.
Command completed successfully.
```

3. Start **DNS** via the **Administrative Tools** menu.
4. Browse to the **Forward Lookup Zones** node. Right-click the **Cengage.com** domain and select **New Host (A or AAAA)**. Enter the Name **App1** on the **New Host** page and enter an IP address of **192.168.1.140**. Click **Add Host**. Click **OK** when notified that the record was created and click **Done**.

   This is the record of the server that is used by NetBIOS clients. You'll later create a CNAME record in the GlobalNames zone that will link with this record.
5. Right-click **Forward Lookup Zones** and select **New Zone**. Click **Next** on the **Welcome** page.
6. Ensure that **Primary Zone** and **Store the Zone In Active Directory** are both selected on the **Zone Type** page. Click **Next**.
7. Accept the default selection of **To All DNS Servers In This Domain**. Click **Next**.
8. Enter **GlobalNames** as the **Zone name**. Your display will look similar to Figure 3-17. Click **Next**.

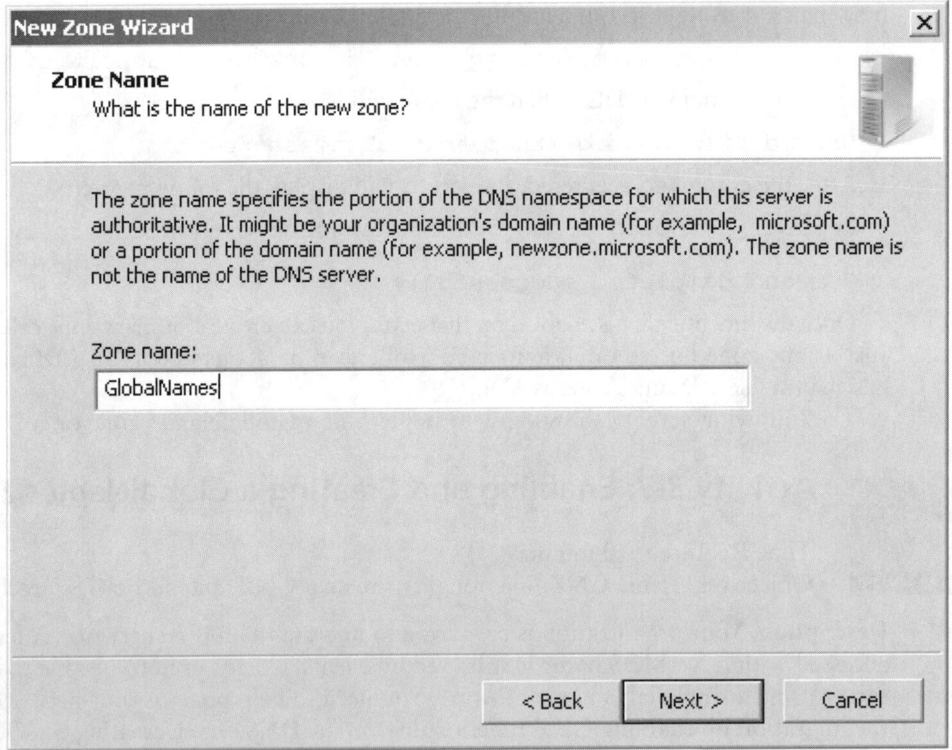

Figure 3-17 Adding a GlobalNames zone

Courtesy Course Technology/Cengage Learning

The primary zone name is not case sensitive. In other words, you can use the name "GlobalNames," "globalnames," or "GLOBALNAMES." However, spelling counts. Names such as "GlobalName" or "GlobaNames" will not work.

9. Accept the default **Dynamic Update** method of **Allow Only Secure Dynamic Updates** and click **Next**.
10. Review the information on the **Completion** page and click **Finish**.
11. Right-click the **GlobalNames** zone and select **New Alias (CNAME)**. Enter **App1** as the **Alias Name**.
12. Click **Browse**. Double-click **DC1**. Double-click **Forward Lookup Zones**. Double-click **Cengage.com**. Select the **App1** record and click **OK**. Click **OK** to create the record.

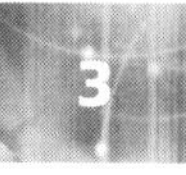

Stub Zones

Stub zones are used to store information about other zones hosted by other authoritative DNS servers. They are most commonly used to store information about a child zone associated with a child domain to reduce administrative effort. They can also be used to store information on DNS between two trusting domains that aren't in a parent/child relationship. When the stub zone is created, changes to DNS servers in the related zone are automatically transferred to the DNS server hosting the parent domain.

As a reminder, DNS zones are directly associated with Active Directory. Any DNS server can host multiple zones associated with multiple domains. As an alternative, delegated zones can be created and associated with child domains.

Consider Figure 3-18. DNS1 is configured to host the Cengage.com zone and DNS2 is configured to host the south.Cengage.com zone as a delegated subdomain. After the delegated subdomain is created, it's possible to create a stub zone. The stub zone is created on DNS1 and holds information on the delegated subdomain.

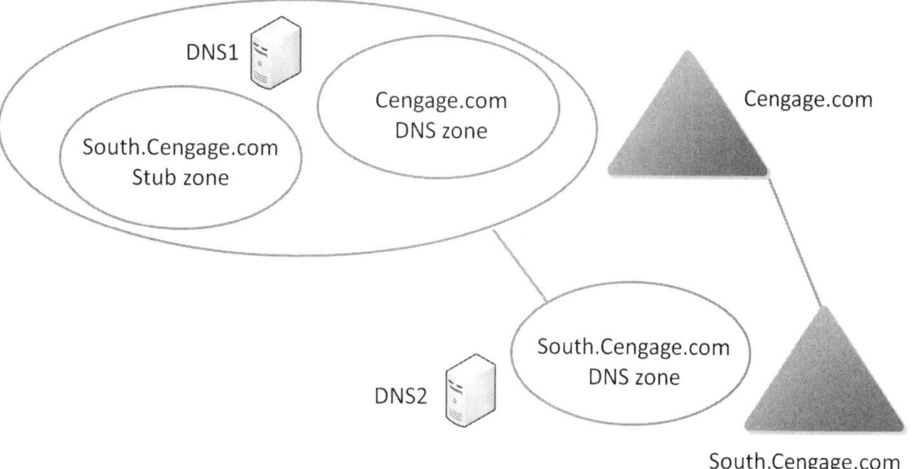

Figure 3-18 DNS zones in a multiple-domain environment
Courtesy Course Technology/Cengage Learning

When the stub zone is created, it will have three records:

- **Start of Authority (SOA) record.** This record provides key information on the zone.
- **Name Server (NS) record.** This record identifies the DNS server that is authoritative for the zone.
- **A (Host) record.** This record identifies the IP address of the DNS server.

If additional DNS servers are added to the delegated subdomain, the stub zone will hold two more records for each DNS server: the NS record and the A record. Stub zones provide several benefits:

- **Simplified DNS administration.** A stub zone will replicate a list of DNS servers that are authoritative for the child domain with little administrative effort.
- **Improved host name resolution.** DNS servers automatically use recursion to query DNS servers listed in the stub zone. In other words, when a DNS server receives a query for a

name in the child domain, it automatically knows the details on the authoritative DNS server for the child domain.

Add stub zones in the parent domain to simplify administration for delegated subdomains. When the stub zone is created, administrators don't have to create and manage conditional forwarders for delegated child domains.

Activity 3-8: Creating a Stub Zone for a Delegated Subdomain

Time Required: 45 minutes
Objective: Create a stub zone.

Description: Your organization wants to create a child domain named south.Cengage.com. After the domain is created, they want to ensure that administration of DNS records is minimized. You have been assigned to create a stub zone for this child domain. You will first promote a server in the child domain to automate the creation of the delegated subdomain. You will then create a stub zone in the DNS console for the root domain DNS server. This activity uses DC1 (which hosts Cengage.com) and DC2, which is a member server in Cengage.com.

1. Ensure that **DC1** and **DC2** are started.
2. After DC1 is fully booted, log on to **DC2** with the domain **Administrator** account and a password of **P@ssw0rd.**
3. Click **Start**, type **DCpromo**, and press **Enter**. Select **Next** on the **Welcome** page and select **Next** on the **Operating System Compatibility** page.
4. Select **Existing Forest** and **Create a New Domain in an Existing Forest**. Click **Next.**
5. Click **Next** on the **Network Credentials** page. If you aren't logged on to DC2 with the domain Administrator account, you'll need to change the credentials.
6. Enter **South** in the **Single-label DNS Name of the Child Domain** text box. The **FQDN** of the **Parent Domain** should already be configured as **Cengage.com**. Note that the FQDN of the child domain is created as south.Cengage.com. Click **Next**.
7. Click **Next** on the **Select a Site** page. If the Next button is dimmed, deselect the check box to **Use the Site That Corresponds to the IP Address of This Computer.** Ensure that **DNS** and **Global Catalog** are selected as **Additional Domain Controller Options.** Click **Next.**
8. Accept the default settings on the **Location for Database, Log Files, and SYSVOL** page. Click **Next.**
9. Enter **P@ssw0rd** in the **Password and Confirm Password** text boxes for the **Directory Services Restore Mode Administrator Password.** Click **Next.**
10. Review your selections on the **Summary** page and click **Next**. Select the check box to **Reboot on Completion.**
11. After **DC2** reboots, log on to **DC1** with the domain **Administrator** account and a password of **P@ssw0rd.**
12. Start **DNS** via the **Administrative Tools** menu. Browse to the **Forward Lookup Zones** node and click the plus (**+**) icon next to **Cengage.com** to open it. Your display will look similar to Figure 3-19. Notice that the folder icon for South within Cengage.com is dimmed. Additionally, the NS record within it identifies the DNS server as DC2.
13. With the delegated subdomain created, you can now create a stub zone to point to this domain. Right-click **Forward Lookup Zones** and select **New Zone.**
14. Select **Stub Zone** and click **Next.**

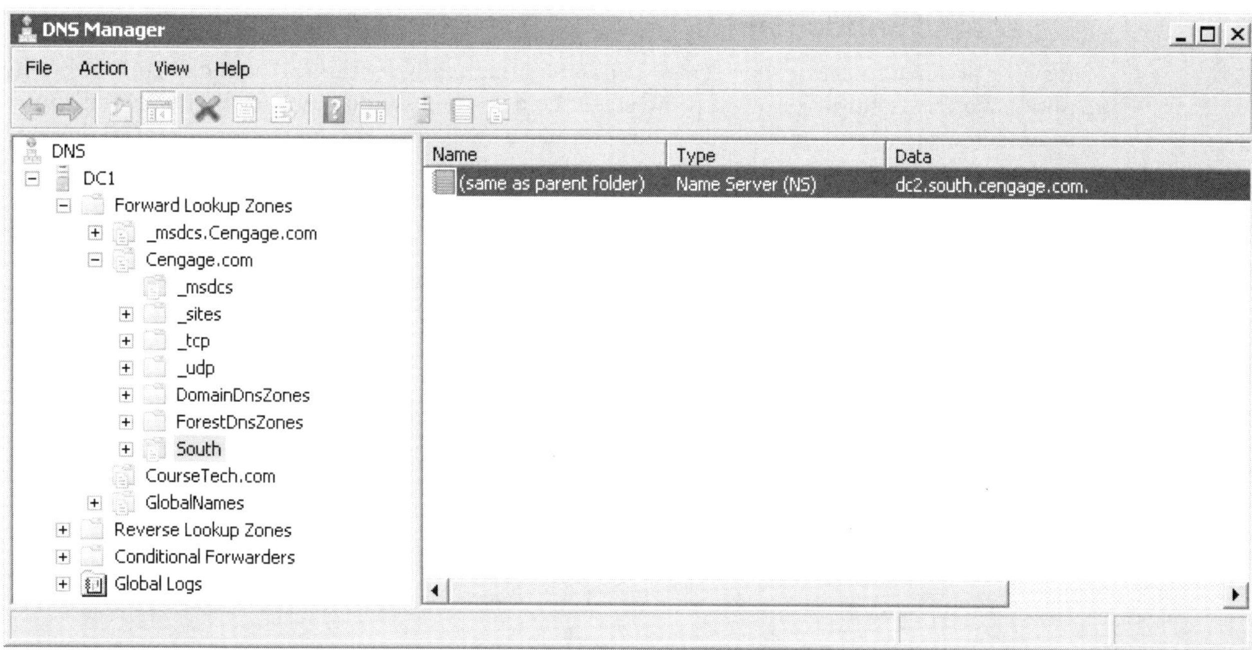

Figure 3-19 The South delegated subdomain is automatically created by DCpromo

Courtesy Course Technology/Cengage Learning

15. Click **Next** on the **Active Directory Zone Replication** page. Enter **south.Cengage.com** as the **Zone Name**. Notice that this is the same name as the FQDN of the child domain, and the FQDN of the delegated subdomain. Click **Next**.
16. On the **Master DNS Servers** page, enter the IP address of **DC2** as **192.168.1.20**. Click **Next**. Review the information on the **Completion** page and click **Finish**. You'll be returned to the DNS console. Figure 3-20 shows the DNS console with both the delegated subdomain zone (South within the Cengage.com zone) and the stub zone (south.cengage.com).

You can see the three records frequently called the glue record: the SOA, NS, and A records.

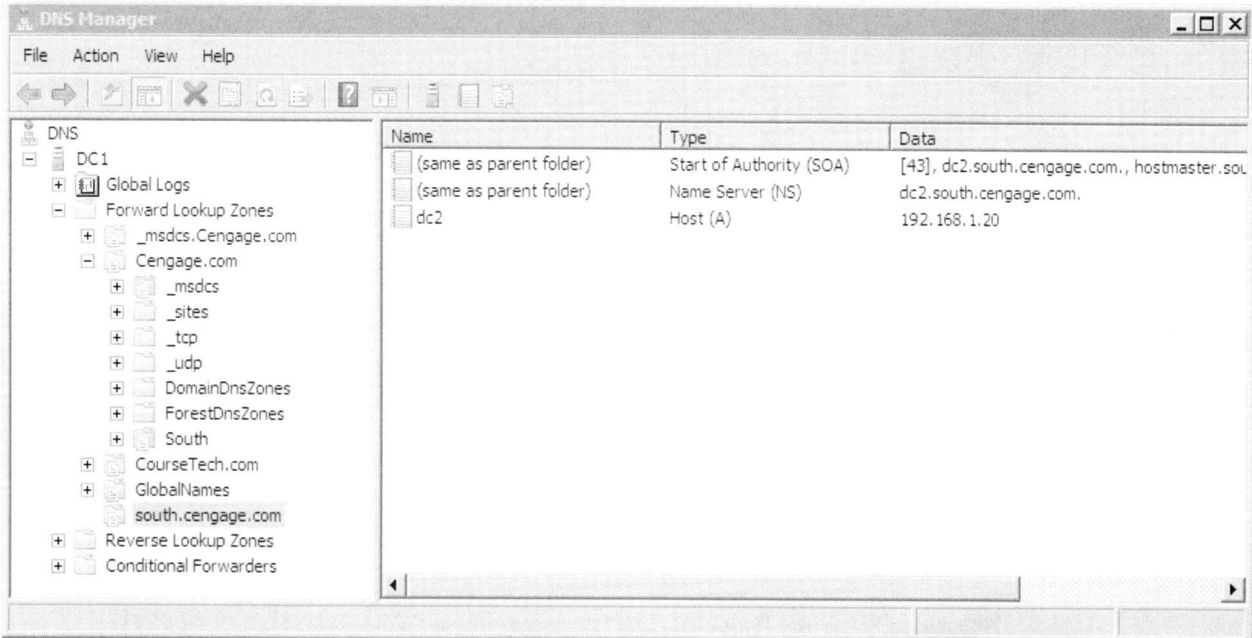

Figure 3-20 The south.cengage.com stub zone with the three records identifying the authoritative DNS server

Courtesy Course Technology/Cengage Learning

Delegated Subdomain

It's also possible to create a delegated subdomain manually (without running DCpromo). This option can be useful if you want to prestage the delegated subdomains, or if your organization is already created with multiple domains but has grown large enough that you want to delegate name resolution to some of the domains to different DNS servers.

The following activity shows how you can create a delegated subdomain manually.

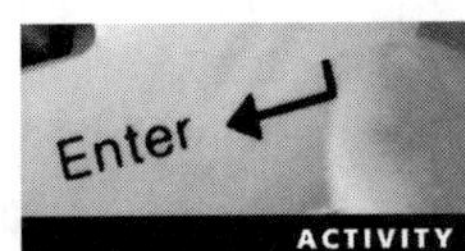

Activity 3-9: Manually Creating a Delegated Subdomain

Time Required: 10 minutes
Objective: Create a delegated subdomain manually within DNS.

Description: Your organization is planning to add an additional child domain to the Cengage.com domain. The child domain will be named Contracting and the DNS server will be hosted on DC3, which has not been created yet. You are assigned to create the delegated subdomain in DNS. You can use DC1 to accomplish this task.

1. Log on to **DC1** with the domain **Administrator** account and a password of **P@ssw0rd.**
2. Start **DNS** via the **Administrative Tools** menu.
3. Right-click **Cengage.com** and select **New Delegation.**
4. Click **Next** on the **Welcome** page.
5. Enter **Contracting** as the **Delegated domain** on the **Delegated Domain Name** page. Your display will look similar to Figure 3-21. Click **Next.**

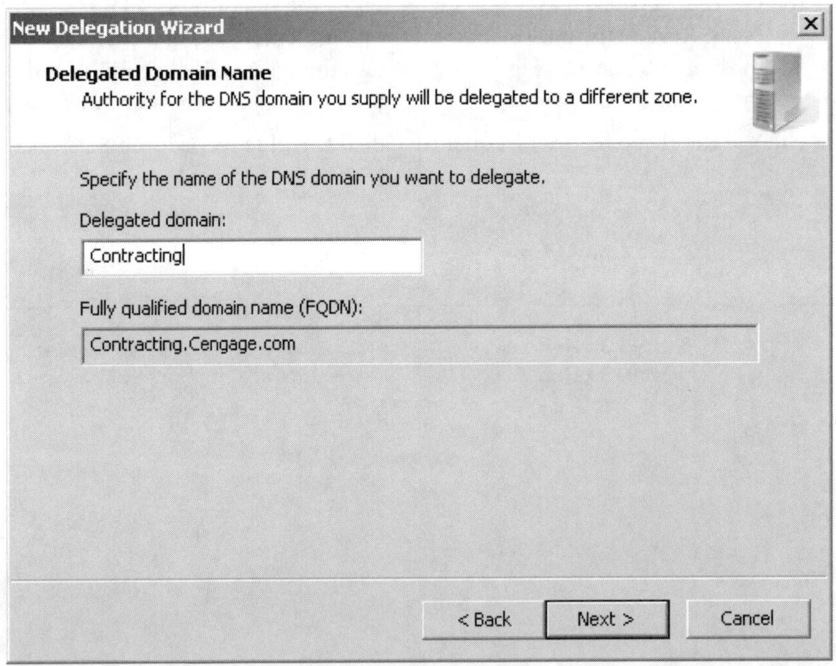

Figure 3-21 Naming the delegated domain
Courtesy Course Technology/Cengage Learning

Because a server named DC3 with an IP address of 10.80.5.20 doesn't exist at this point, the following step will indicate a timeout when DNS tries to validate the server. This is a normal response, so you can still complete the lab.

6. On the **Name Servers** page, click **Add**. Enter **DC3.Contracting.Cengage.Com** as the **Server Fully Qualified Domain Name**. Click in the IP address area and enter **10.80.5.20**. Press the **Tab** key. Click **OK**. Click **Next** on the **Name Servers** page. Click **Finish**.

At this point, the Contracting delegated subdomain will be created. You can tell it's a delegated subdomain because it is dimmed.

Designing Zone Replication Scope

When you use Active Directory-integrated (ADI) zones, you also can choose the replication scope. Remember, zone transfers for ADI zones are handled as part of Active Directory replication, so in this context, the replication scope only refers to DNS zone data.

Windows Server 2003 introduced Active Directory partitions. This allows any LDAP application to store data in a separate partition, which can then use the Active Directory infrastructure to replicate the partition to other domain controllers. That's exactly what ADI DNS zones do in Windows Server 2003 and later domain controllers. The DNS zone data is stored in a separate partition and replicated as part of Active Directory replication.

When designing a DNS solution, the important question is where you want the zone data to be replicated. You can choose to have it replicated to all DNS servers in the forest, to all DNS servers in the domain, or to all domain controllers in the domain.

The replication scope options are accessed on the properties page of the zone by clicking the Change button next to Replication, as shown in Figure 3-22.

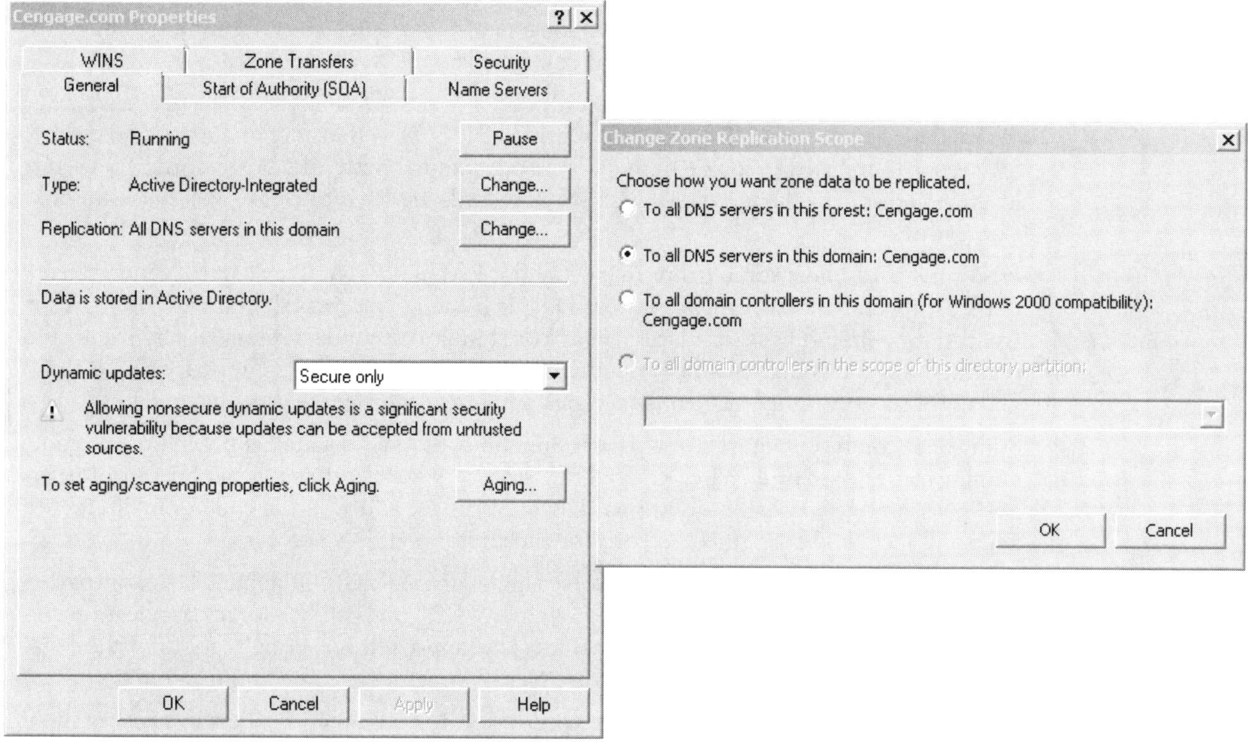

Figure 3-22 Configuring zone replication scope

Courtesy Course Technology/Cengage Learning

By default, you have three choices for the replication scope:

- **To all DNS servers in this forest.** This choice will replicate the zone data to all Windows Server 2003 and later DNS servers (running on domain controllers) in the forest. This is the best choice if you want to ensure that any ADI DNS server in the forest can resolve any names in any domain in the forest. This option uses the application partition named **ForestDNSZones** partition.

- **To all DNS servers in this domain.** This choice will replicate the zone data to all Windows Server 2003 and later DNS servers (running on domain controllers) in the domain. This is the best choice if you want to limit replication between domain controllers in different domains. This option uses the application partition named **DomainDNSZones** partition, and is the default choice.
- **To all domain controllers in this domain.** This option is used for backward compatibility to Windows 2000 Server domain controllers. Because Windows 2000 domain controllers don't support application partitions, you must use this option if any of your DNS servers are hosted on Windows 2000 Server domain controllers.

A fourth option is also available ("To all domain controllers in the scope of this directory partition"). However, as you can see in Figure 3-22, this option is dimmed. You must first create an application partition, and then DNS servers hosting the zone must be enlisted in the partition.

Chapter Summary

- Several improvements to DNS are introduced with Windows Server 2008. These improvements include background zone loading to improve boot times, GlobalNames zones to resolve single-label NetBIOS names in the absence of WINS, IPv6 support, and RODC support.
- The two types of computer names are NetBIOS names and host names. NetBIOS names are created by truncating the host name to the first 15 characters, and they are typically resolved by WINS. The usage of WINS is being reduced in most networks. Host names are resolved by DNS servers; they can be as long as 255 characters, but are usually limited to only 15 characters to remain backward compatible with NetBIOS names.
- Windows Server 2008 DNS servers host all of the typical DNS records. A (and AAAA) records provide name-to-IP address resolution. The SOA is the start of authority record. SRV records are used to locate domain controllers in the network. MX records are used to locate Microsoft Exchange servers. CNAME records are used to create aliases for hosts in the network.
- DNS servers can host standard primary, standard secondary, Active Directory-integrated (ADI), stub, and GlobalNames zones. If DNS is hosted on servers that are not domain controllers, they should host standard primary or standard secondary zones. If DNS is hosted on a domain controller, it can be ADI and take advantage of Active Directory replication and extra security. Only ADI zones can be configured with secure dynamic updates.
- Stub zones can be configured in a parent domain zone for delegated subdomains to reduce administrative overhead. When created, the stub zone will host as few as three records (the SOA, NS, and A records). If additional DNS servers are added in the child domain, the stub zone will include the NS and A record for each additional DNS server.
- GlobalNames zones can be used to resolve single-label (NetBIOS) names. This approach is useful if the organization is planning to remove WINS, but still has legacy applications or servers that need to resolve NetBIOS names. This approach is especially useful if the organization wants to migrate to IPv6 because NetBIOS names are not supported in IPv6.
- Generic or non-site-specific records are used to locate domain controllers in another site if the domain controller in the current site fails. While this provides fault tolerance with Active Directory, it can sometimes have unintended effects in a domain with multiple sites. You can use a GPO to prevent the creation of these generic records to ensure that domain controllers in specific sites are not used.
- You can control the zone replication scope by selecting either ForestDNSZones or DomainDNSZones application partitions. The ForestDNSZones application partition can be used to replicate DNS zone data to all ADI DNS servers in a multiple-domain forest, and to ensure that each DNS server can resolve names for any DNS server in any domain.

Key Terms

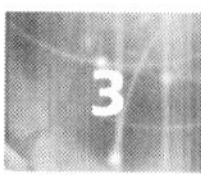

A and AAAA record An A record (also called a host record) is used to resolve a name to an IPv4 address. An AAAA record is used to resolve a name to an IPv6 address. A and AAAA records can be manually created or created with the dynamic updates process.

Active Directory-integrated (ADI) zone This zone is hosted on a domain controller, and zone transfers are integrated into Active Directory replication. Unlike traditional DNS, which allow only one primary (or only one master), ADI zones use multiple primary ADI zones with the same multi-master model used on domain controllers.

Alias (CNAME) record An alias record is also known as a canonical name (or CNAME) record, and is created on DNS so that a server can be resolved to an IP address with more than a single name.

DNS zone A namespace where a DNS server can resolve names. Zone data is stored either in forward lookup zone files or reverse lookup zone files.

DomainDNSZones An application partition used in ADI zones that causes zone data to be replicated to all DNS servers in the domain. This partition is useful if you want to limit the replication of zone data between DNS servers in different domains.

Dynamic Update The process of allowing clients to automatically create or update their A record on DNS.

ForestDNSZones An application partition used in ADI zones that causes zone data to be replicated to all DNS servers in the forest. This partition is useful if you want all DNS servers to be able to resolve host names for any domain in the forest.

Generic (non-site-specific) DNS records DNS records that can be used to locate domain controllers in any site. These records are created by default and are useful in a multi-site environment. If a DC fails in a site, generic (non-site-specific) records are used to allow clients to connect to any DC in the organization. In large organizations you can prevent these records from being created in specific sites using a GPO.

GlobalNames zone (GNZ) This option can be used to resolve NetBIOS or single-label names. It's useful if an organization wants to completely eliminate WINS, such as when the organization migrates to IPv6.

Host name A computer or server name that can be up to 255 characters. Host names are resolved to IP addresses using DNS.

MX records A mail exchanger record used to locate a mail server. In Microsoft networks, an MX record will point to a Microsoft Exchange server.

Name resolution The process of resolving a name to an IP address. DNS is used to resolve host names to IP addresses and WINS is used to resolve legacy NetBIOS names.

NetBIOS names A 16 byte name in which the first 15 characters are readable and the 16th is a hidden byte that identifies a service running on the system. NetBIOS names are traditionally resolved by WINS servers, but can be resolved by a GlobalNames zone. NetBIOS names are not supported in IPv6.

NS record A name server (NS) record identifies a DNS server in a DNS zone. NS records can be created manually or automatically when DCpromo is run.

Pointer (PTR) records These records are used for reverse lookups providing IP address-to-name resolution. PTR records are only found in reverse lookup zones, and reverse lookup zones are optional.

Primary DNS zone A master copy of a zone hosted on a traditional (non-ADI) DNS server. With traditional DNS servers, the master copy of the zone is the only writable copy of the zone; only one server can host a primary zone for any namespace.

Secondary DNS zone A read-only copy of a zone used for fault tolerance and load balancing. A secondary zone can only be created if a primary zone exists. Changes are made to the primary zone (the master copy) and copied to the secondary zone using zone transfers.

Secure Dynamic Update Dynamic update with security. Only authenticated clients in the domain can create or update DNS records. Secure dynamic updates are only supported in ADI zones.

Service location (SRV) records These DNS records are used to locate domain controllers in a domain. SRV records can be site specific (allowing site-aware applications to locate a DC in the site) and non-site-specific (allowing applications to locate any DC anywhere in the domain). SRV records are created automatically by the Netlogon service on the domain controller hosting DNS.

SOA record The start of authority record used by DNS and other services, such as DHCP and the dynamic update process. It includes information about the zone, such as the primary server for the zone and information used by secondary zone DNS servers on zone transfer times.

Stub zone A mini-zone that only hosts information about another zone hosted on another DNS server. In Windows Server environments, a stub zone is used to hold information on delegated subdomains.

Review Questions

1. Your enterprise has a single forest with 15 domains. All DNS servers are hosted on domain controllers running Windows Server 2003, and use ADI zones. When these DNS servers need to be rebooted to install an update or for other maintenance, they can take as long as an hour to start. You want to improve the performance of boot times of DNS servers. What should you do?
   a. Ensure that all DNS servers are using the ForestDNSZones partition.
   b. Change all the zones to GlobalNames zones.
   c. Add stub zones to each DNS server.
   d. Upgrade the DNS servers to Windows Server 2008.
2. Two new Windows Server 2008 servers were recently added to your organization. They have been named CengageServerRoom1SrvA and CengageServerRoom1SrvB. However, some users are unable to access these servers. What should be done to resolve this problem?
   a. Register the server names and IP addresses in WINS.
   b. Register the server names and IP addresses in DNS.
   c. Reduce the length of the names to 15 characters or less.
   d. Create host records in DNS for the servers.
3. You have recently installed a Microsoft Exchange mail server and configured your Windows Server 2008 network to use it. Testing shows that users are able to send e-mails back and forth between themselves. However, e-mails are not being received from the Internet. What is the likely problem?
   a. You need to add an MX record to your DNS server to identify the mail server.
   b. You need to get your ISP to add an MX record to their DNS server to locate your mail server.
   c. You need to add a CNAME record to your DNS server to identify the mail server.
   d. You need to add an SRV record to your DNS server to identify the mail server.
4. Your organization has recently begun implementing a new domain that is isolated from the Internet for security purposes. The primary domain includes WINS, DNS, DHCP, and domain controllers, but the isolated domain only hosts a single server, which hosts a DNS, DHCP, and domain controller on a separate subnet. Figure 3-23 shows a sample of how clients are configured for TCP/IP.

   Testing shows that these clients are not able to access the domain or resolve names in the isolated network. What is the likely problem?

a. WINS needs to be added to this isolated network.
b. The DNS address must be manually entered.
c. DHCP is not configured to provide DNS addresses.
d. You need to move all clients to the same subnet as the server.

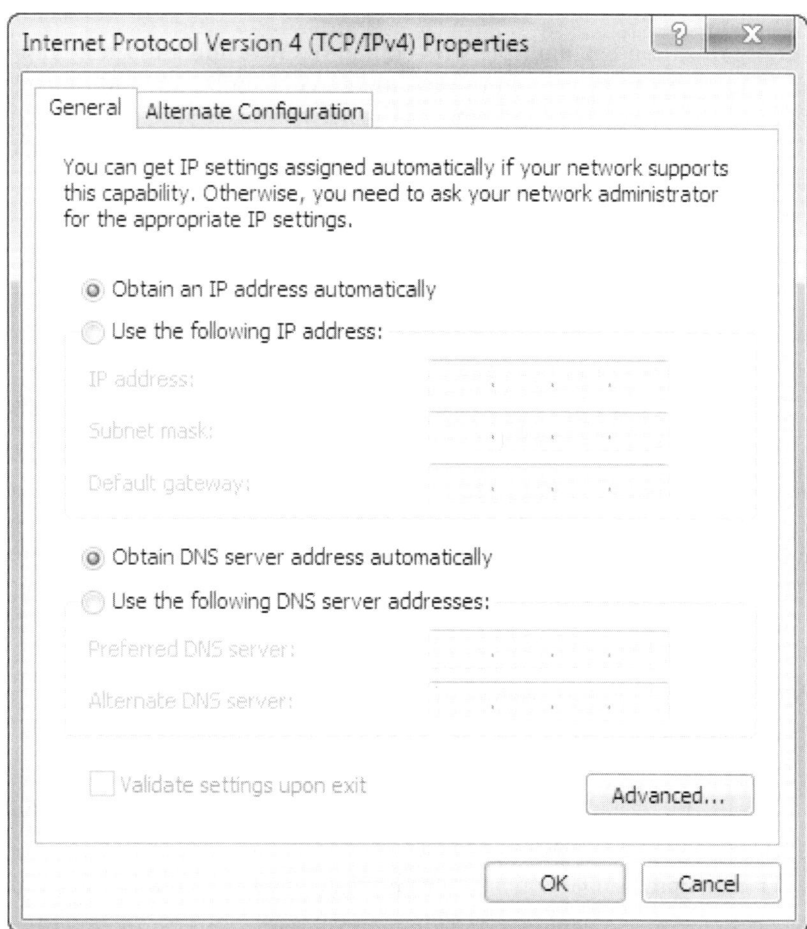

Figure 3-23 Local Area Connection properties

Courtesy Course Technology/Cengage Learning

5. Your enterprise is using a single-domain forest in the Windows Server 2003 forest functional level. The company is planning to add two remote offices, and you are considering a design plan to deploy domain controllers to these offices. You want to ensure that secure dynamic updates are supported in the remote offices. What should you include in the plan?
   a. Update the forest to the forest functional level of Windows Server 2008.
   b. Use stub zones for the remote offices.
   c. Ensure that the headquarters office uses primary zones and that the remote offices use secondary zones.
   d. Ensure that only ADI zones are used.
6. Your organization has multiple sites configured in a hub and spoke replication topology. You recently learned that after a DC failed in a remote office, clients connected to DCs in other remote offices. You want to ensure that clients only connect to DCs in the main hub sites if a DC fails in a remote office site. What should be done?
   a. Configure the network to create generic (non-site-specific) records for DCs in the main sites.

b. Configure the network not to create generic (non-site-specific) records for DCs in the main sites.

c. Configure the network to create generic (non-site-specific) records for DCs in the remote office sites.

d. Configure the network not to create generic (non-site-specific) records for DCs in the remote office sites.

7. Your organization has multiple sites configured in a hub and spoke replication topology. It includes two major regional offices configured as hubs, and multiple remote offices connected to each hub. You are designing the network to ensure that clients in remote offices will never be able to authenticate with DCs in other remote offices, and to ensure that clients in either of the two major offices will never be able to authenticate with DCs in any of the remote offices. What should you do?

   a. Create a GPO to prevent DCs in the remote offices from registering generic DNS records. Link the GPO to the remote office sites.

   b. Create a GPO to prevent DCs in the remote offices from registering generic DNS records. Link the GPO to the two regional office sites.

   c. Ensure that each DC in the remote office is also a global catalog server.

   d. Ensure that each DC in the remote office is not a global catalog server.

8. You are reviewing your organization's logical structure and DNS connectivity. The organization has three major offices and several smaller offices connected to each major office. Each office has at least one DC in it. Most of the offices are connected to each other with T1 lines, but one of the smaller offices is connected using a 56K connection. You want to ensure that the only clients who can connect to DCs in this office are the clients in the office. What should you do?

   a. Change the DC to an RODC.

   b. Change the registry on the DC to prevent the creation of non-site-specific DNS records for the DC.

   c. Modify the Default Domain Controllers GPO to prevent the creation of non-site-specific DNS records.

   d. Enable Universal Group Membership Caching for the site.

9. You are preparing to deploy a domain controller to a remote office. The DC will host DNS and DHCP. You want to ensure that only secure updates are allowed on the DNS server. What should you include in the plan?

   a. Ensure that DNS hosts a stub zone for the remote office.

   b. Ensure that DNS hosts an ADI zone.

   c. Create a GlobalNames zone for the remote office.

   d. Configure the DC as an RODC.

10. Your organization consists of a single-domain forest. The main office hosts two domain controllers on Windows Server 2008, and DNS is hosted on two member servers running Windows Server 2003. A remote office in your organization has recently grown large enough that the company has decided to add a domain controller to the office. You are reviewing the design plans and realize that a DNS server is not included. What should you ensure is added to the design plans?

    a. Ensure that the remote office DC is configured with an ADI zone.

    b. Ensure that the remote office DC is configured with a standard primary zone.

    c. Ensure that the remote office DC is configured with a standard secondary zone.

    d. Ensure that the remote office DC is configured with a GlobalNames zone.

11. Your company has a single domain of about 500 users. DNS is hosted on a member server. Recently the DNS server failed for a period of time, causing significant problems until it was restored. You need to implement a fault-tolerant solution for DNS. What should you do?
    a. Add the DNS role to another server and configure a standard secondary DNS zone.
    b. Add the DNS role to another server and configure a standard primary DNS zone.
    c. Add the DNS role to another server and configure a reverse lookup DNS zone.
    d. Add the DNS role to another server and configure an ADI DNS zone.
12. You are an administrator in a large enterprise hosted in a single forest with 20 child domains. DNS servers are running on Windows Server 2008 servers. The organization is using WINS running on Windows Server 2003 servers to connect to a few legacy servers using NetBIOS names. The organization is considering migrating to IPv6, but wants to ensure that access to these legacy servers is retained. What should be done to support the migration?
    a. Upgrade the WINS servers to Windows Server 2008.
    b. Convert the enterprise to a two-domain forest.
    c. Convert the zones to ADI.
    d. Configure a GNZ on DNS.
13. An administrator has created a GlobalNames zone on a DNS server named DNS1. He has named the zone GlobalNames and created it as a primary zone. However, testing indicates that the zone is not being used. What is the likely problem?
    a. The zone name needs to be GlobalName.
    b. The zone needs to be a standard secondary zone.
    c. The server needs to be configured with the following command:
       `dnscmd DNS1 /config /Enableglobalnamessupport 1.`
    d. The server needs to be configured with the following command:
       `NSLookup DNS1 /config /Enableglobalnamessupport 1.`
14. Cengage is a large organization configured in a single forest of 18 domains. Users connect to several internal Web servers using single-label names that are currently resolved by WINS. Cengage is planning to migrate to IPv6 in the near future. What should be done to support this plan?
    a. Remove the Web servers.
    b. Remove the WINS servers.
    c. Implement a GNZ.
    d. Implement a stub zone.
15. Your company is planning a reorganization that will separate several different business units. Each of the units has its own domain, configured as child domains within the same forest. Administrators in the child domains will have full administrative control; as the plan is phased in during the first year, several changes are expected to DNS servers for the child domains. You are asked to design a DNS solution that will minimize the effort required to maintain name resolution. What would you suggest?
    a. Configure stub zones in the root domain.
    b. Configure stub zones in the child domains.
    c. Configure each child domain with secondary zones.
    d. Configure each child domain with ADI DNS zones.
16. You have been asked to prepare DNS for the addition of a new domain. Your organization currently has a one-domain forest named Cengage.com. You are adding a new domain

named RnD.Cengage.com. Cengage.com has two ADI DNS servers and RnD will host DNS on a member server. What should be done to prepare DNS before adding the new domains?

a. Add a stub zone on the DNS server in the RnD domain.

b. Create a delegated subdomain on the RnD server. Add a standard primary zone to the DNS servers in the root domain.

c. Create a delegated subdomain on the ADI DNS servers in the root domain. Create a standard primary zone on the RnD DNS server.

d. Create a GNZ on the Cengage.com DNS servers and a GNZ on the RnD DNS servers.

17. You are troubleshooting DNS issues between a primary DNS server named DNS1 and a secondary DNS server named DNS2 in a domain named Cengage.com. You suspect that transfers are not occurring and you want to compare a list of records on the secondary servers with a list of records on the primary server. Using NSLookup, you enter **ls cengage.com** from the NSLookup prompt. The response is "Query Refused." What is the likely problem?

    a. Your account has not been granted security permissions on the primary zone hosted on DNS1.

    b. Network problems are preventing DNS2 from connecting to DNS1.

    c. DNS1 has not been configured for zone transfers.

    d. DNS2 has not been configured for zone transfers.

18. You are reviewing the DNS design for your organization. You have one forest with two domains and two sites with a domain functional level of Windows Server 2008. The root domain is hosted in the Virginia Beach site, and the child domain is hosted in the San Francisco site. DNS is hosted on domain controllers in each site, and the DNS zones are ADI. You want to ensure that DNS servers in each site can resolve names for both sites. What should you do?

    a. Configure the zones using the ForestDNSZones partition.

    b. Configure the zones using the DomainDNSZones partition.

    c. Configure the network to create generic (non-site-specific) records for DCs.

    d. Configure the network not to create generic (non-site-specific) records for DCs.

19. Your organization hosts a two-domain forest and includes two sites, with each site hosting its own domain. Each site includes two domain controllers and each of the DCs hosts ADI DNS. You want to ensure that the DNS servers in each site can resolve names without querying the DNS servers in the other site. What should you do?

    a. Enable a GNZ in each site.

    b. Create stub zones in each site.

    c. Configure the zones using the To All DNS Servers in the Domain replication scope option.

    d. Configure the zones using the To All DNS Servers in the Forest replication scope option.

20. Your organization has one forest with two domains and two sites. Each site has its own domain controllers hosting ADI DNS on Windows Server 2003 servers. The two sites are connected with a slow link. You want to limit the replication of DNS zone data between the sites without affecting the performance of DNS. What should you do?

    a. Configure the zones using the DomainDNSZones partition.

    b. Configure the zones using the ForestDNSZones partition.

    c. Upgrade the servers to Windows Server 2008.

    d. Convert the zones to standard primary zones.

Case Projects

Case Project 3-1: Adding Microsoft Exchange to an Organization

You are planning to add a Microsoft Exchange server in your organization, and are designing the implementation plan. You know that you'll need to run a program that modifies the schema of the forest before the first Microsoft Exchange server is added. What, if anything, should be done to DNS to support the Exchange server?

Case Project 3-2: Preparing for Secure Dynamic Update

Security has become increasingly important within your organization. You are assigned to ensure that the DNS servers operate in the most secure manner. The DNS servers are currently hosted on Windows Server 2003 servers, and they are also running DHCP. You need to ensure that all zone data replicated between DNS servers is encrypted, and that only secure dynamic updates are allowed. What should you do? Explain your answer.

Case Project 3-3: Deploying DCs to Remote Sites

Your organization is preparing to deploy a domain controller in each of two remote sites. These domain controllers will be used by site-aware applications and services in the sites. You want to ensure that these domain controllers are not used by any clients outside of the site. What should you do and how can you do it?

Case Project 3-4: Designing the Replication Scope

Your organization has five different sites connected via WAN links that have a lot of available bandwidth. The root domain is hosted at the main office, and each outlying office has its own domain hosted in its own site. Every location has one DNS server and one domain controller. Some of the servers are Windows 2000 Server, some are Windows Server 2003, and some are Windows Server 2008. You want to ensure that each site's DNS server can resolve the name of any host in the forest without querying other DNS servers. What should you do?

chapter 4

Designing and Implementing Group Policy

After reading this chapter and completing the exercises, you will be able to:

- Design Organizational Units to support an administrative model
- Understand Group Policy basics
- Design a Group Policy strategy
- Configure different Group Policy settings
- Configure advanced GPO settings
- Implement fine-grained policies using a password settings object

Group Policy is a powerful tool used to manage users and computers within a domain. With a little bit of planning, you can design a Group Policy strategy that can deploy applications, lock down computers, and reduce the total cost of ownership for computers in your organization.

You can apply Group Policy objects (GPOs) to sites, domains, and Organizational Units (OUs). The area where a GPO is applied is called the scope of the GPO. It's important to understand the basics of both OUs and GPOs when designing a GPO strategy. Any GPO design will be created to manage and control clients by applying settings. While a few settings are covered in this chapter, it's more important to understand the strategy of how the settings are applied.

Advanced GPO strategies include the use of Block Inheritance, Enforced, and loopback processing settings. Block Inheritance can be applied to an OU, Enforced can be applied to a GPO, and loopback processing can make a computer's settings take precedence over the logged-on user's settings. GPOs can also be filtered by modifying the GPO's permissions so they apply to different groups.

Fine-grained policies allow you to create separate password policies or account lockout policies to apply to different groups in the organization. These policies are applied by creating password settings objects (PSOs) and linking the PSO groups.

All of these concepts are covered in this chapter.

Designing Organizational Units

Chapter 1 covered the design of the forest and domains to achieve different goals. Within a domain, you can create Organizational Units (OUs) to support data autonomy. There are two important reasons to use OUs:

- **Managing with Group Policy**. Group Policy objects hold **Group Policy** settings. GPOs can be created and linked to sites, domains, and OUs within a domain. By creating separate OUs and placing user and computer objects in the OUs, you can use GPOs to provide administrative control over the objects.
- **Delegation of control**. You can delegate full control or individual permissions for any OU to any individual user or group. You can then grant data autonomy to a group of users, allowing them to control the data (the objects) in their OU.

Recall from Chapter 1 that the structure of Active Directory Domain Services (AD DS) is designed to support autonomy and isolation goals. Isolation of AD DS can only be achieved by creating a completely separate forest. Service autonomy of AD DS can only be achieved by creating separate domains. Data autonomy can be achieved by creating separate domains (which also provides service autonomy), or by creating separate OUs.

Using OUs for Group Policy

Group Policy Objects (GPOs) can be linked to sites, domains, and OUs. GPOs are covered in much more depth later in this chapter, but at this point you probably already know that Group Policy can be used to manage users and computers. You can set different security policies, configure standards, restrict usage, deploy applications, and much more. By organizing users and computers in OUs, you can manage all of them with a single OU.

Sites were covered in Chapter 2, but as a reminder, sites are well-connected groups of hosts or subnets that often represent branch offices or remote offices. Chapter 3 included an activity that created a GPO for a site used to restrict the creation of generic (non-site-specific) DNS records.

Figure 4-1 shows an example of how OUs could be created in a domain. In the figure, OUs have been created for several departments; child OUs are shown within the Sales OU.

You can create a GPO and then link it according to where you want it applied. If you want the GPO applied to users and computers in a site, you can link the GPO to the site. If you want it applied

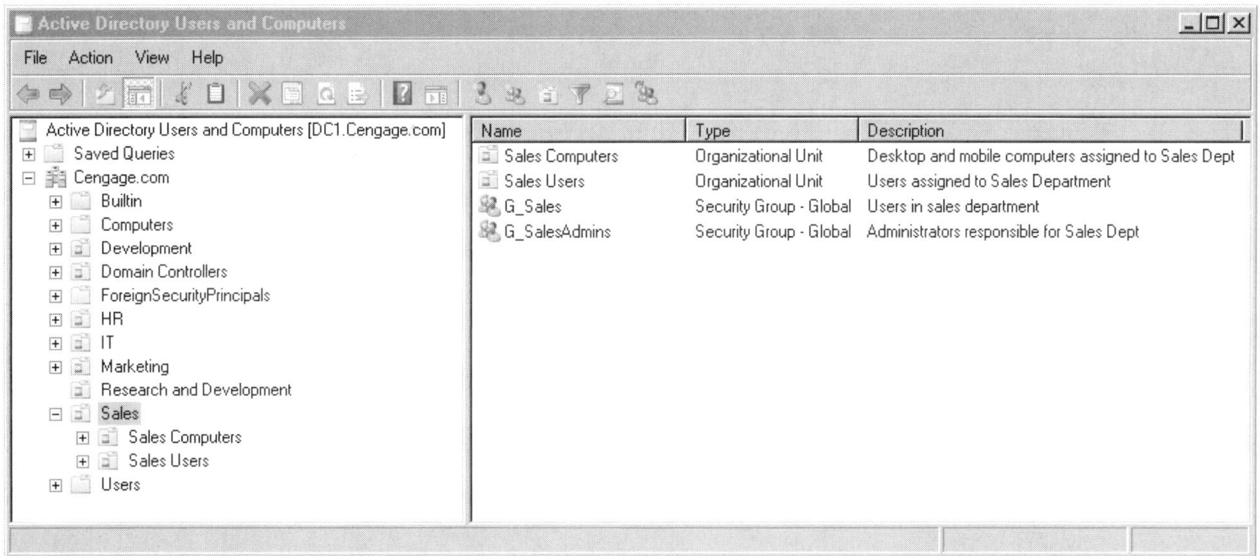

Figure 4-1 An example of how OUs can be created within a domain

Courtesy Course Technology/Cengage Learning

to users and computers in a domain, link it to the domain. If you want it applied to a group of users and computers in an OU, you link the GPO to the OU.

GPOs cannot be linked to either the Users container or the Computers container. A GPO can only be linked to a site, a domain, or an OU. Even though you can't link a GPO directly to the Users or Computers containers, a GPO applied to the domain will still apply to all users and computers in the domain, including users and computers in the Users and Computers containers. You just can't link a GPO directly to the Users or Computers containers so that it applies only user objects in these containers.

Using OUs to Delegate Control

Often, administrative tasks will be delegated to administrators to perform tasks specific to their area of responsibility. For example, administrators could be assigned to support users in the Sales department. When a new person is hired, these administrators may be asked to create the user and computer accounts. When users forget their passwords or lock themselves out of their account, these administrators should be able to help.

Of course, these administrators need appropriate permissions and privileges to help the users in the Sales department, but not to manipulate accounts for users in other departments or elsewhere in the domain. If your only consideration was to give the administrators permissions, you could add their accounts to the Domain Admins group and they'd be able to do anything in the domain. However, this ignores the basic security principle of least privilege by granting the administrators much more rights and privileges than is necessary.

Instead, you'd create an OU for users in the Sales department and use the **Delegation of Control Wizard** to delegate appropriate permissions. This wizard is available within Active Directory Users and Computers. Figure 4-2 shows how to start this wizard by right-clicking the OU.

Imagine you have created a global group named G_SalesAdmins and placed the Sales administrator's accounts into this group. You can then use the Delegation of Control Wizard to grant this group appropriate permission on the Sales OU. Of course, the Sales OU would need to hold all of the users, computers, and other objects for the Sales department to make this strategy work.

Additionally, you could create other groups and other OUs for other departments. A G_MarketingAdmins global group could be created and delegated permission to manage the Marketing OU, the G_HRAdmins global group could be created and delegated permission to manage the HR OU, and so on.

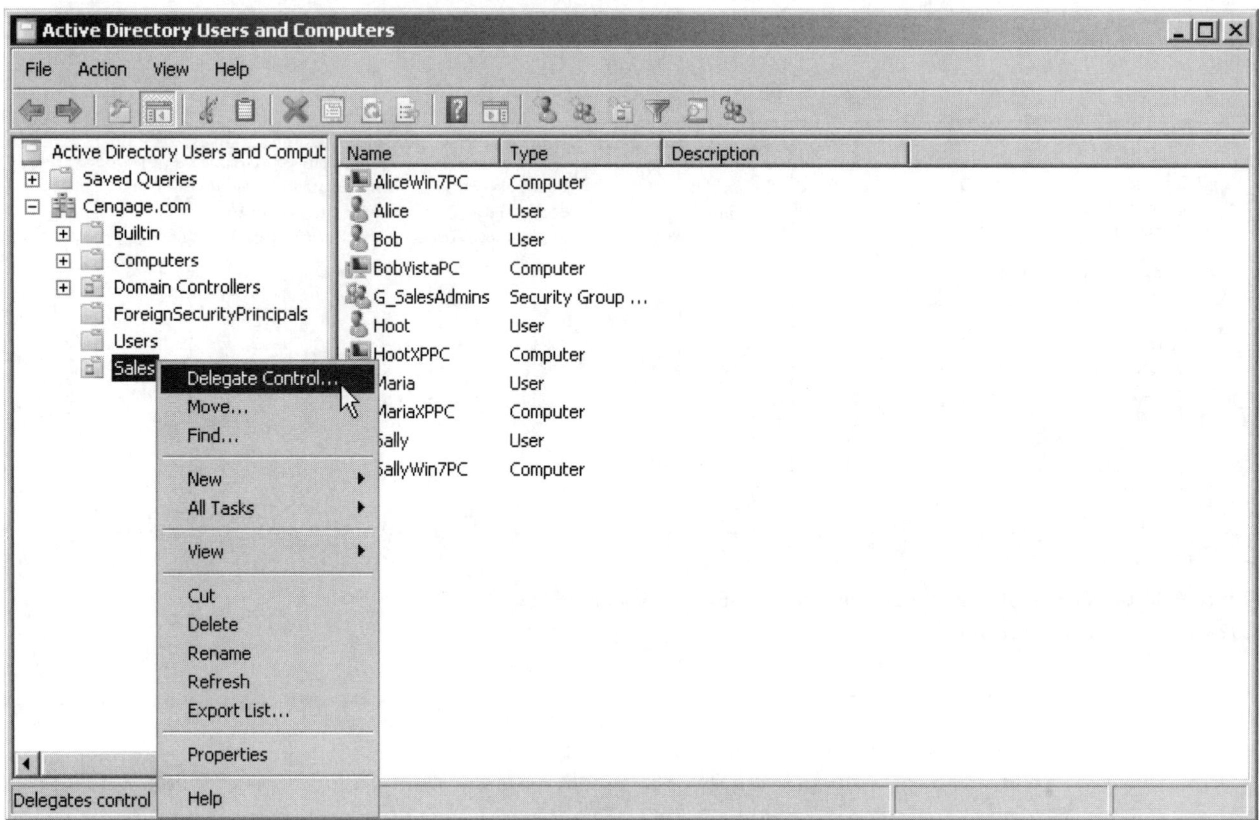

Figure 4-2 Starting the Delegation of Control Wizard

Courtesy Course Technology/Cengage Learning

With this in mind, if you have specific users or groups to whom you want to delegate administrative control, you need to create OUs. The users, computers, groups, and other Active Directory objects can be moved to the OU, and then you can easily delegate control. It's also possible to delegate control at the domain level. However, when you do so, you'll grant permissions throughout the entire domain.

The following activity shows how to use the Delegation of Control Wizard.

Activity 4-1: Delegating Control with the Delegation of Control Wizard

Time Required: 15 minutes

Objective: Use the Delegation of Control Wizard to delegate permissions to reset user passwords.

Description: You want to grant a user named Betty permissions to administer all of the users in the Sales department. Other users may also need these permissions, so you plan to grant the permission to a global group named G_SalesAdmins and place Betty's account into the global group. You need to create an OU named Sales, a user account for Betty, and the G_SalesAdmins global group. After placing the user in the group, you will delegate control to this group. This activity should be performed on DC1, which was created and used in earlier chapters.

1. Start **DC1** and log on with the domain **Administrator** account.
2. Open the **Active Directory Users and Computers** console via the **Administrative Tools** menu.

3. Right-click the domain and select **New, Organizational Unit.** Name the OU **Sales** and click **OK.**
4. Create a user account by right-clicking the **Sales** OU and selecting **New, User.** Enter **Betty** in the **First Name** and **User Logon Name** text boxes. Click **Next.** Enter **P@ssw0rd** in the **Password** and **Confirm Password** text boxes. Click **Next.** Click **Finish.**
5. Create a global group by right-clicking the **Sales** OU and selecting **New, Group.** Name the group **G_SalesAdmins.** Ensure that the **Group Scope** is set to **Global** and that the **Group Type** is set to **Security.** Click **OK.**

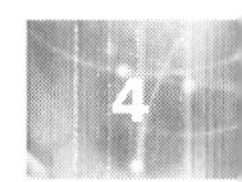

6. Add the Betty user account to the G_SalesAdmins group. Double-click the **G_SalesAdmins** group to access the properties page and select the **Members** tab. Click **Add.** Enter **Betty** and click **OK.**
7. Right-click the **Sales** OU and select **Delegate Control.** Click **Next** on the **Welcome** page.
8. Click **Add** on the **Users or Groups** page. Enter **G_SalesAdmins** to add this group and click **OK.** Click **Next.**
9. Select the check box next to **Reset user passwords and force password change at next logon,** as shown in Figure 4-3. Click **Next.** Click **Finish.**

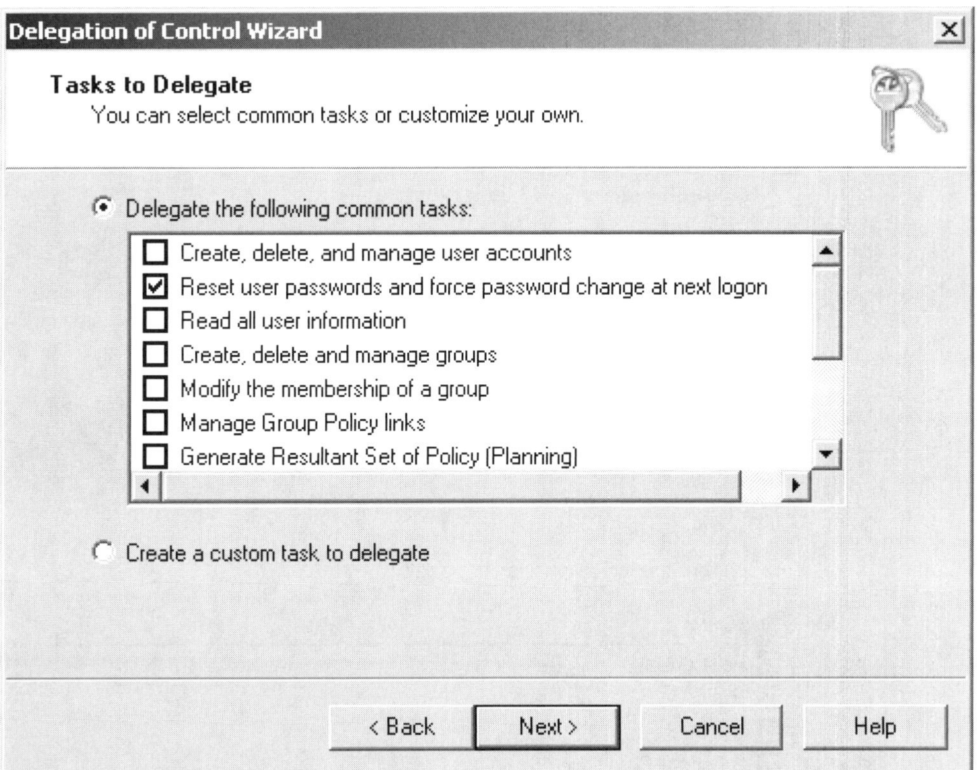

Figure 4-3 Delegating permissions to change passwords

Courtesy Course Technology/Cengage Learning

10. Close all open windows.

At this point, users in the G_SalesAdmins group can reset passwords for any users in the Sales OU. Users in this group do not have permissions anywhere else in the domain. The following activity can be used to expand this group's control over the OU by granting Full Control permissions.

Activity 4-2: Delegating Full Control with the Delegation of Control Wizard

Time Required: 10 minutes
Objective: Use the Delegation of Control Wizard to delegate full control over an OU.

Description: The G_SalesAdmins group has permissions to change passwords, but the company has determined that the group needs full control permissions in the OU. You need to use the Delegation of Control Wizard to grant the group full control over the Sales OU. This activity assumes that the previous activity was completed; you used it to create the Sales OU and the G_SalesAdmins group on a domain controller in the domain. This activity should be performed on DC1.

1. Start **DC1** and log on with a domain **Administrator** account.
2. Open the **Active Directory Users and Computers** console via the **Administrative Tools** menu.
3. Right-click the **Sales** OU and select **Delegate Control.** Click **Next** on the **Welcome** page.
4. Click **Add** on the **Users or Groups** page. Enter **G_SalesAdmins** to add this group and click **OK.** Click **Next.**
5. Select **Create a Custom Task to Delegate** and click **Next.**
6. On the **Active Directory Object Type** page, accept the default selection of **This Folder, Existing Objects in This Folder and Creation of New Objects in This Folder.** Click **Next.** This ensures that permissions are inherited in any OUs that may be created within the Sales OU.
7. Click the **Full Control** check box. Notice that all the check boxes are selected, as shown in Figure 4-4. Click **Next.**

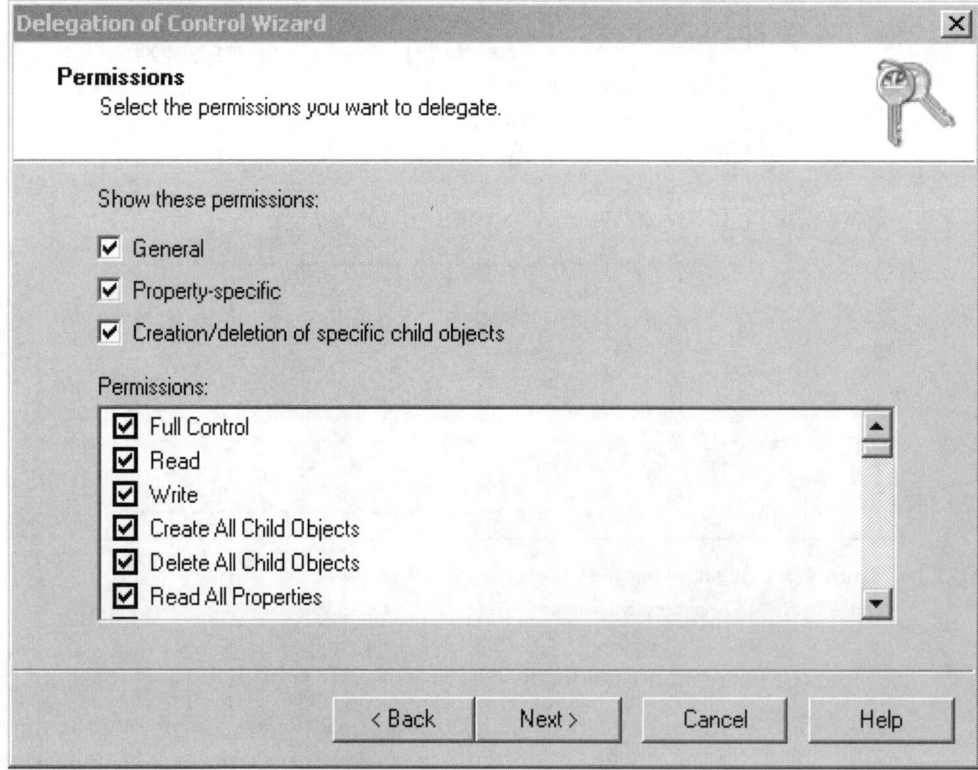

Figure 4-4 Delegating Full Control permissions to a group
Courtesy Course Technology/Cengage Learning

8. Click **Finish.** Close all open windows.

At this point, any users who are currently in the G_SalesAdmins global group (or any users added later to it) will be granted full control in the OU. They will be able to add objects to the OU, modify them, and delete them. If any child OUs are added to the Sales OU, the permissions will be inherited by the child OUs. However, the G_SalesAdmins group does not have any permissions for any other OUs in the organization or for any objects at the domain level.

Designing Organizational Units

Once you understand the two benefits and purposes of OUs, it becomes much easier to design the OUs for your organization. As a reminder, the only technical reasons to design OUs are to delegate control or manage objects using Group Policy.

It's not uncommon for administrators to create OUs to logically organize users and computers. For example, OUs may be created for each department or division in an organization even if separate GPOs aren't used, and even if separate groups are not being delegated permissions to the OUs. This decision is a matter of preference; it isn't based on technical reasons and isn't required. You could just as easily leave all the users in the Users container and leave all the computers in the Computers container, and they would work well.

However, if you want to delegate control for a specific set of users or computers, or deploy Group Policy to a specific set of users or computers, you'll need to design and create OUs. When considering the design of OUs, consider the following characteristics:

- **OUs are created for administrators' use.** Users will never see OUs so they don't have to follow a structure understood by the users.
- **OUs are completely separate from DNS.** The domain has a DNS namespace with specific rules and guidelines, but OUs do not interact with DNS at all. DNS does not need to be considered when designing OUs.
- **OUs are easy to modify.** It is difficult to change a domain or forest structure after implementation. However, OUs can be easily modified after deployment of AD DS. Objects within Active Directory can easily be moved by dragging and dropping them.

OUs should be named according to what they will contain, which enables administrators to easily understand the purpose of the OUs. Names such as OU1 for the Sales department and OU2 for the HR department will lead to confusion later.

OUs are often designed based on the organization's structure, the geographical layout of the organization, or a combination of the two. The choice of these three designs is based on the use of GPOs to manage the OUs, delegating control to OUs, and administrator preference.

- **Organizational Structure.** A simple OU design is based on the structure of the organization. In other words, there's an OU for every department such as Sales, Marketing, Human Resources, IT, and so on. If a department has multiple divisions, it's also possible to create child OUs within the departmental OUs to represent the divisions.
- **Geography.** Organizations with multiple sites often use OUs based on their locations. For example, an organization with sites in three cities could create three OUs with one for each city. Administrators in the OUs can then be delegated control to manage their OUs and create any child objects (including children OUs).
- **Hybrid.** A combination of both geography and organizational structure is used. Figure 4-5 shows an example of a hybrid design for an organization with three locations (Virginia Beach, Norfolk, and Chesapeake). While the figure shows child OUs for only the Norfolk location, each OU could have child OUs.

It's also possible to further refine the OU structure so that objects are separated in different OUs. In other words, each department OU could have an OU to store computers and another OU to store users.

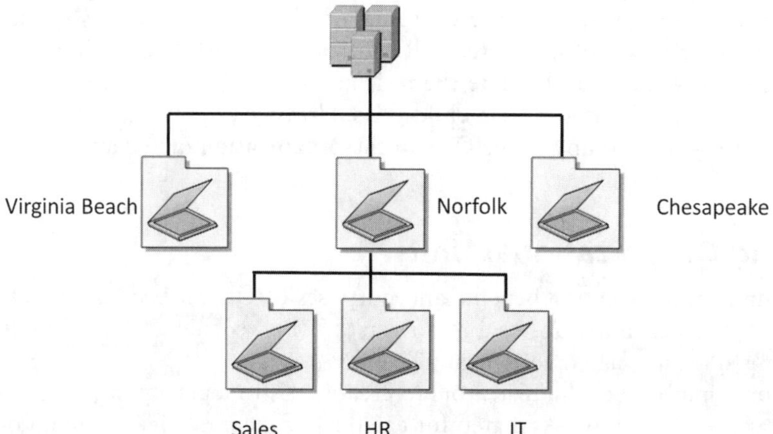

Figure 4-5 A hybrid OU design based on geography and the organizational hierarchy
Courtesy Course Technology/Cengage Learning

Designing Group Strategies

It's also important to understand and consider the design of group strategies. Whenever possible, permissions should be assigned to groups instead of users; while it takes a little longer to design and implement the groups, it significantly reduces administration in the long term.

As an example, the two earlier activities in this chapter granted Betty permissions to manage the Sales OU. However, instead of delegating control to Betty, a group was created, Betty's account was added to the group, and permissions were assigned to the group.

Imagine what would happen if Betty's account (instead of a group) was assigned permissions to manage the OU directly. Later, Betty's account (instead of a group) could also be assigned permissions on some NTFS folders and shares managed by the Sales department. Later still, Betty could be promoted and Joe might need to take over her job. You would now need to remember every location in which Betty was assigned permissions directly and modify each of these permissions to add Joe's account.

On the other hand, if Betty's account was added to the G_SalesAdmins group and the permissions were assigned to this group, Joe's account could be added to the group and he would have all the required permissions. After Joe was trained, Betty's account could be removed from the group and all of her access to data as a member of the G_SalesAdmins group could be removed.

Groups are identified by their group scope, and the following group scopes are supported in Windows Server 2008:

- **Universal.** Universal groups are used in a multiple-domain environment. They can include accounts or groups from any domain in the forest and they can be assigned permissions to any resource in any domain in the forest. Global groups can be added as members to universal groups. Universal groups can be added to domain local groups.
- **Global.** Global groups are used to organize users (or other global groups) in the same domain. You can only add members from the same domain, not other domains, but global groups can be assigned permissions to resources in any domain in the forest. Global groups can be added to both universal groups and domain local groups.
- **Domain local.** Domain local groups can be used to assign permissions to resources within the domain. They can include accounts or groups from any domain in the forest, but can only be assigned permissions for resources within the domain. Domain local groups can have global groups and universal groups as members.

As a reminder, universal group membership information is only contained in the global catalog. Modifying the universal group membership often can affect replication across slow WAN links.

To better imagine how groups can be added together, see Figure 4-6, which shows the different groups with arrows to illustrate what groups can (and can't) be added to each other. User accounts can be added to any of the group types, but the most common scenario is to add users to global groups to organize the users. It's also possible to assign permissions directly to users, though this strategy is not recommended.

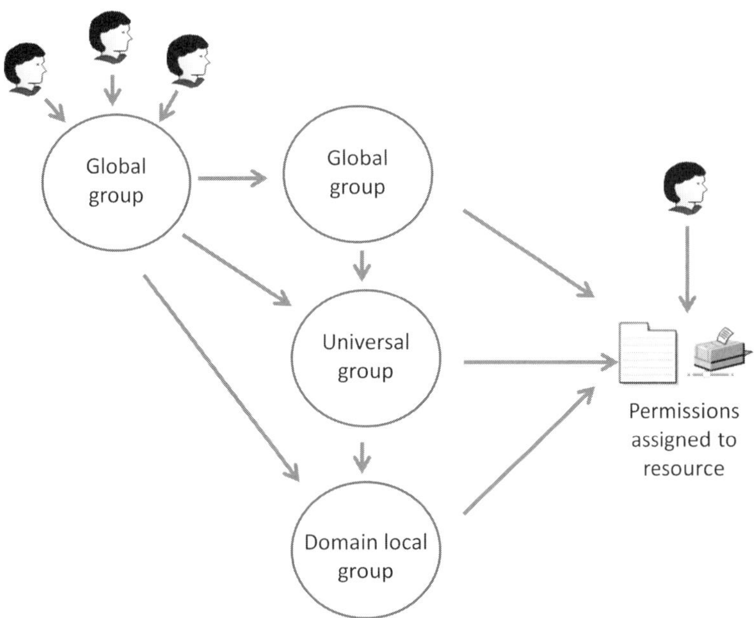

Figure 4-6 Understanding groups

Courtesy Course Technology/Cengage Learning

Global groups can be added to other global groups (commonly called nesting), added to universal groups, or added to domain local groups. It's possible to assign permissions to the global group directly, and this is often done in small organizations. Notice how the arrows point. You cannot go against the arrow to add a global group to a user, which admittedly seems silly. Likewise, you cannot go against the arrow to add universal groups or domain local groups to global groups.

Figure 4-7 shows a typical strategy using universal groups. Imagine two domains in a forest that have the same OU structure. Administrators in two separate domains need permissions

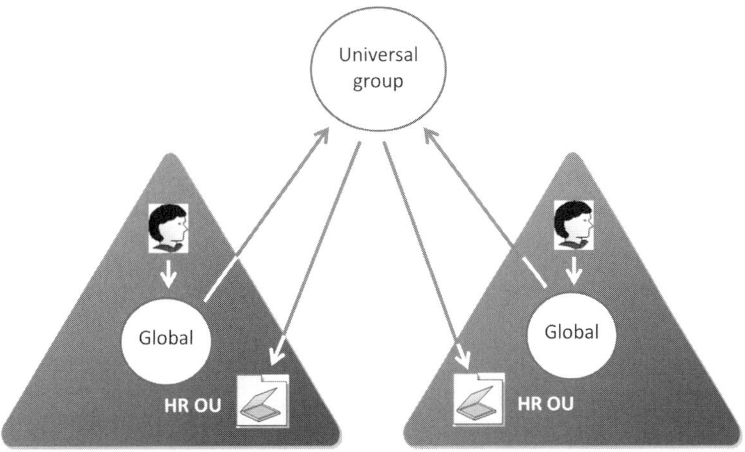

Figure 4-7 Group policy strategy using universal groups

Courtesy Course Technology/Cengage Learning

assigned to the HR OU in each of the domains. The way to assign these permissions is to add the global group that holds the administrator accounts in each domain to a universal group. You can then delegate control of each of the OUs (one in each domain) to the universal group.

While this figure shows only two domains to illustrate the point, the real strength of universal groups is realized with multiple domains. With only two domains, you could bypass the use of universal groups and instead delegate control to individual OUs in each domain. However, if your organization includes 5 or 10 domains, adding all of the global groups from all of the other domains becomes much more difficult to manage. The universal group will simplify this process with more domains.

Redirecting Placement of New Accounts

By default, all new computers that are joined to the domain are automatically added to the Computers container. Additionally, when user accounts are created without specifying the OU, they are placed in the Users container. However, it is possible to redirect the placement of new accounts. The two commands that you can use to redirect computer accounts and user accounts are **redircmp** and **redirusr**, respectively.

When a user account is created, the target OU is usually specified. However, some legacy methods of creating user accounts (such as the Net User command) can be used without specifying the target OU for the user account. The redirusr command only comes into play when the OU is not specified and a new default location is desired. It does not modify the target location of new user accounts when the target location is specified.

Both commands must be executed from a command prompt with administrative permissions, and both commands accept a **distinguished name (DN)** as a parameter.

Distinguished names are used to uniquely identify objects in any Lightweight Directory Access Protocol (LDAP)-based directory, such as Active Directory Domain Services (AD DS). DNs have formal structures; the three most common elements in a DN are CN, OU, and DC.

- **CN** (Common name). The common name can be used to identify individual users, or non-OU containers such as the Users or Computers container. A user named Sally would be identified with CN=Sally and the Users container would be identified with CN=Users.
- **OU** (Organizational Unit). The OU identifies the OU and can include nested OUs. OUs are listed with children OUs first and parents last. As an example, the Accounting OU could have two child OUs of AR and AP. The AR OU would be identified as OU=AR, OU=Accounting.
- **DC** (Domain Component). Each element of the domain name must be separated. For example, Cengage.com must be identified as DC=cengage, DC=com, not DC=cengage.com.

When put together, the full DN of the AR OU (a child of the Accounting OU) within the Cengage.com domain is: OU=AR, OU=Accounting, DC=Cengage, DC=com.

A common mistake when creating DNs is to list the OUs in the wrong order. Children OUs must be listed as the first OU in the DN, and parent OUs must be listed next. In the previous example, using a DN of OU=Accounting, OU=AR, DC=Cengage, DC=com would be incorrect because the AR OU is a child of Accounting and should be listed first.

If you want to ensure that all new computers joined to the Cengage.com domain are added to the NewComputers OU, you could use the following command:

```
redircmp OU=NewComputers, DC=Cengage, DC=com
```

Similarly, if you want to ensure that all users created without specifying a target OU are created in the New Users OU, you could use the following command:

```
redirusr OU=NewUsers, DC=Cengage, DC=com
```

Reviewing Group Policy Basics

Group Policy is a powerful tool that allows you to automate the management of users and computers in an organization. You can configure a setting once with a Group Policy object, link the GPO to a site, domain, or OU, and have it apply to all of the objects in the GPO's scope. Regardless of whether you have five users, 500, 5,000, or more, Group Policy will apply the setting to each object in its scope.

Even if you've learned about Group Policy before, it's worth reviewing some of the basics to ensure you get the most out of this chapter. In this section, you'll review:

- Group Policy scope
- Group Policy inheritance and order of precedence
- Group Policy setting categories
- Default Group policies
- Group Policy Management console
- Starter GPOs

Group Policy Scope

When a GPO is applied to a site, a domain, or an OU, it applies to all of the user and computer objects at that level. While this is simple on the surface, you should understand the subtleties.

When a GPO is applied to a site, it can affect one or more domains, only part of a domain, or an entire domain. As an example, consider Figure 4-8. The single domain on the left has four offices and four sites. GPO1 is being used to assign an Accounting application, and GPO1 is linked to Site 1 only. The Accounting application will only be deployed from this GPO to Site 1. GPO1 won't be applied to any user or computers anywhere else in the domain. It's common to use GPOs linked to sites to deploy applications. The application source files can be stored on a server in the same site, ensuring that the application is not deployed over a WAN link. It's also common to use site-linked GPOs to control the creation of non-specific DNS records, as you learned in Chapter 3.

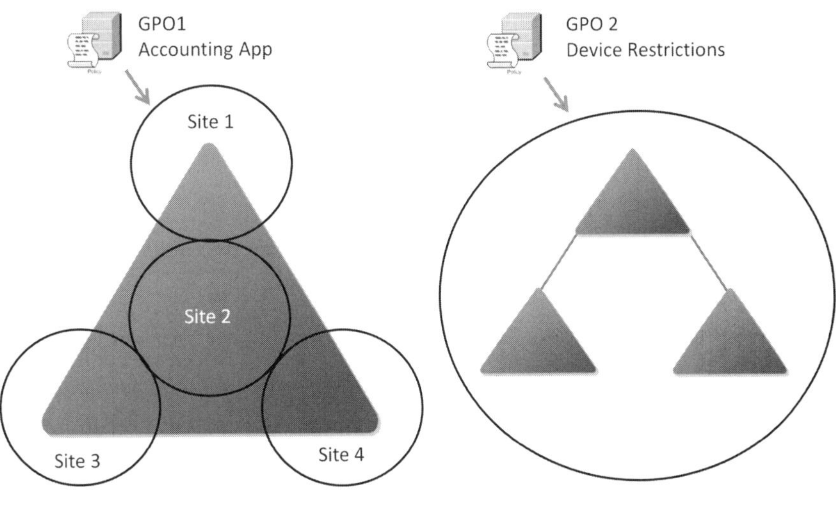

Figure 4-8 Comparing sites and groups with Group Policy

Courtesy Course Technology/Cengage Learning

The configuration on the right shows a multiple-domain forest contained within a single site. When a GPO is linked to this site, it will affect objects in all three domains. In the figure, GPO2 is used to implement device installation restrictions, and will affect all three domains because they are in the same site. This is the only way that a single GPO can affect multiple domains; GPOs applied to a parent domain are not inherited by child domains.

It's also possible to have a single domain in a single site. When configured this way, there is no difference between linking a GPO to the site or linking the GPO to the domain, though it's much more common to link the GPOs to the domain.

GPOs linked to the domain will apply to all objects in the domain, including objects in the Users and Computers container. As a matter of fact, the only way to apply Group Policy to users in the Users container or to computers in the Computers container is by linking a GPO to the domain.

As discussed earlier, it's also common to link GPOs to OUs. When a GPO is linked to an OU, it applies to all the objects in that OU, and by default, to all of the objects in children OUs. In other words, the scope of the GPO will be to that OU.

Consider Figure 4-9, which shows three GPOs. GPO1 is applied to the domain, and so it affects all users and computers in the domain (including users and computers in the Users and Computers containers).

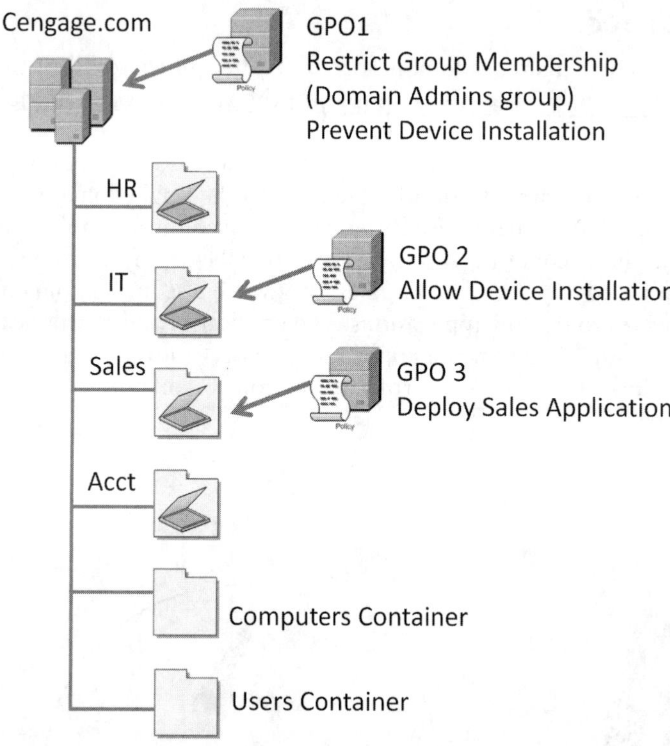

Figure 4-9 Identifying the scope of GPOs assigned to OUs
Courtesy Course Technology/Cengage Learning

GPO2 is being used to override the device installation policy for all users in the IT OU so that any users in this OU can install devices. GPO3 is being used to deploy a software application to users in the Sales OU, and only affects users in that OU.

While naming a GPO as GPO1 or GPO2 works well for explanatory purposes, actual GPOs are commonly named based on their purpose. For example, if a GPO is used to configure security settings, it could be called Generic Security Settings, while a GPO designed to ensure that clients use IPSec could be called IPSec. Such names make it easier to remember the purpose of the GPO.

But what happens if a user is promoted or transferred and their account is moved from the IT OU to another OU, such as the HR OU? At that point, GPO2 would "fall out of scope" for the user and GPO2 would no longer apply to the moved user account. Once Group Policy is refreshed for the user, only GPO1 is applied, and the policy to allow device installation is no longer applied.

Similarly, if a user is moved out of the Sales OU, the GPO for the software application falls out of scope. However, software can be handled differently. When software is deployed via a GPO, you have the option to "Uninstall this application when it falls out of the scope of management." If this option is selected, the software will be uninstalled. If the option is not selected, it will remain installed.

Uninstalling an application if it falls out of scope is one way to help manage software licenses. The application can be deployed to an OU, and when a user account is moved out of the OU, the application will automatically be uninstalled.

You'll see how to deploy an application in an activity later in this chapter. The activity also shows how to configure the option to uninstall the application if it falls out of scope.

GPO Inheritance and Order of Precedence

GPOs applied at the domain level will be inherited by all OUs in the domain and applied to the Users and Computers containers in the domain. GPOs applied to a parent OU will apply to all child OUs. All of this occurs because of GPO inheritance unless the **Block Inheritance** option is used. Block Inheritance is discussed in more depth later in the chapter.

GPO inheritance means that GPO settings applied at higher levels will be inherited and applied at lower levels. For example, imagine a parent OU named Sales and a child OU named Users. If a GPO is applied at the parent OU that sets Internet Explorer proxy settings, you don't need to create another GPO for the child OU. The settings are inherited.

The **GPO order of precedence** refers to how Group Policy is applied and what settings take precedence if there are problems with two conflicting settings. For example, one GPO may prevent device installations while another GPO allows device installations. The order of precedence is:

- Site
- Domain
- Parent OUs
- Children OUs

In other words, assuming GPOs exist at each of the levels, the site GPO will be applied first. Next, the domain GPO is applied. If there isn't a conflict with the settings, all of the settings from both the site GPO and the domain GPO are applied. If there is a conflict, the domain GPO setting will take precedence because it is applied last. Other settings from the site GPO that don't conflict with the domain GPO will still be inherited.

Next, GPOs will be applied to parent OUs; if there are any conflicts with the domain or site GPO settings, the parent OU GPO setting will take precedence. Last, GPOs for children OUs will be applied; the children GPO settings will take precedence if there are any conflicts with settings from previously applied GPOs.

When applying GPOs, remember that the last GPO applied wins. The exception is if the Enforced option is used. The Enforced option is discussed later in the chapter.

Consider Figure 4-10. Each GPO has only one setting—to disable the Telnet service or enable it. Can you determine the state of the Telnet service in the IT OU, the Computers container, the Sales OU, and the Direct OU (direct sales), which is a child of the Sales OU?

GPO1 applies to the domain, so all OUs and containers will have this GPO applied to them first. The IT and HR OUs and the Computers and Users containers don't have any other GPOs applied, so GPO1 takes precedence.

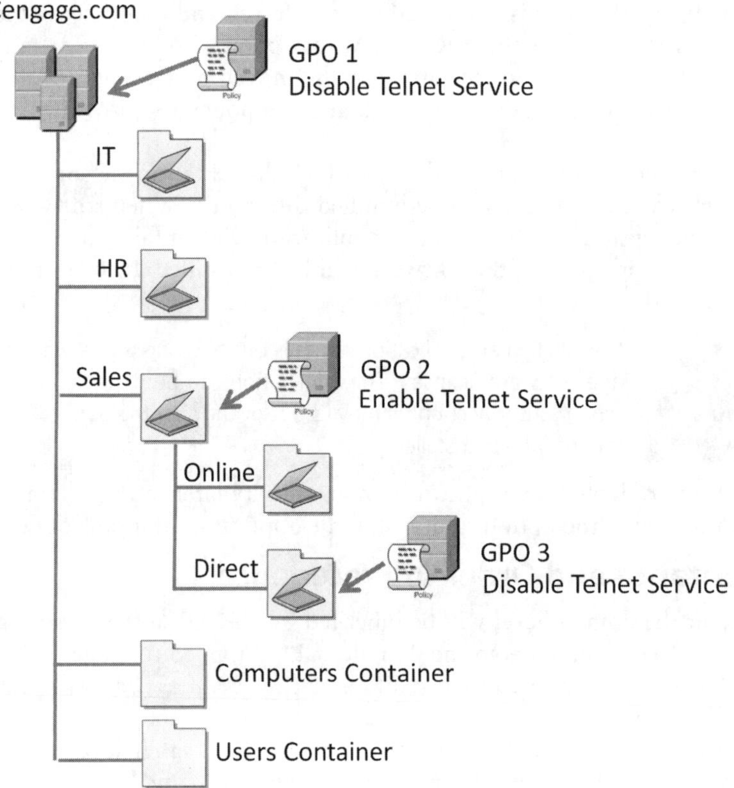

Figure 4-10 Group Policy and order of precedence

Courtesy Course Technology/Cengage Learning

The Sales OU has GPO2 applied, which is inherited by the Online sales and Direct sales OUs. Because there is a conflict between GPO2 and GPO1, in which GPO1 disables the Telnet service but GPO2 enables it, the last one applied (GPO2) wins for the Sales OU and the Online OU. The Direct sales OU has GPO3 applied, which disables the Telnet service. For objects in this OU, GPO3 will take precedence and the Telnet service will be disabled. In summary:

- IT OU: Telnet service disabled (GPO1 wins)
- Computers container: Telnet service disabled (GPO1 wins)
- Sales OU: Telnet service enabled (GPO2 wins)
- Direct OU: Telnet service disabled (GPO3 wins)

Group Policy Setting Categories

There are hundreds of GPO settings, and you'll never learn them all unless that's all you do. Most administrators instead learn how GPOs work and then start building on their knowledge of GPOs as they gain experience. Instead of trying to learn all GPO settings, a better goal is to understand how they work and then study the details of a few as they appear. Some of the commonly used categories of GPO settings are:

- **Software settings.** You can use these settings to automate the deployment of applications within the network. Applications can be assigned to users or computers or published to users. Deploying applications with GPOs will be covered in greater depth later in this chapter.
- **Windows settings.** Windows settings include the ability to have scripts run at certain times, configure a wide variety of security settings, and implement a TCP/IP-based Quality of Service policy to throttle outbound traffic.

- **Security settings.** Security settings are a part of the Windows settings, but are important enough to mention separately. You can configure account policies (such as password and account lockout policies), local policies, restricted group policies, system services policies, Windows firewall policies, and much more.
- **Administrative templates.** Administrative templates are used to manage many of the interfaces, such as Control Panel, Network, Printers, System, and other Windows components. Settings in this category are frequently included when Group Policy is used. As a simple example, you can block a user's ability to install devices using settings in the Administrative Templates category. Settings in this category usually modify the registry. Administrative templates are released by Microsoft in the Administrator Template file format (ADMX), which improved multi-language support for Administrative Templates.
- **Preferences.** Preferences allow you to set and configure different settings on users' computers. However, unlike other GPO settings, users can override the preferences and configure the settings to meet their own needs. Examples of some preference extensions include folder options, mapped drives, printers, scheduled tasks, services, and Start menu settings.

Default Group Policies

When you promote your first server in the domain to a domain controller, two default Group Policy objects are created: the **Default Domain policy** and the **Default Domain Controllers policy.** They have several different settings, mostly related to security, that provide a starting point. Each of these policies can be modified, and additional group policies can be added, but it's important to be aware of these two.

Figure 4-11 shows the **Group Policy Management console** (GPMC) opened to the Default Domain policy. The Settings tab is selected so you can view the settings of the Default Domain

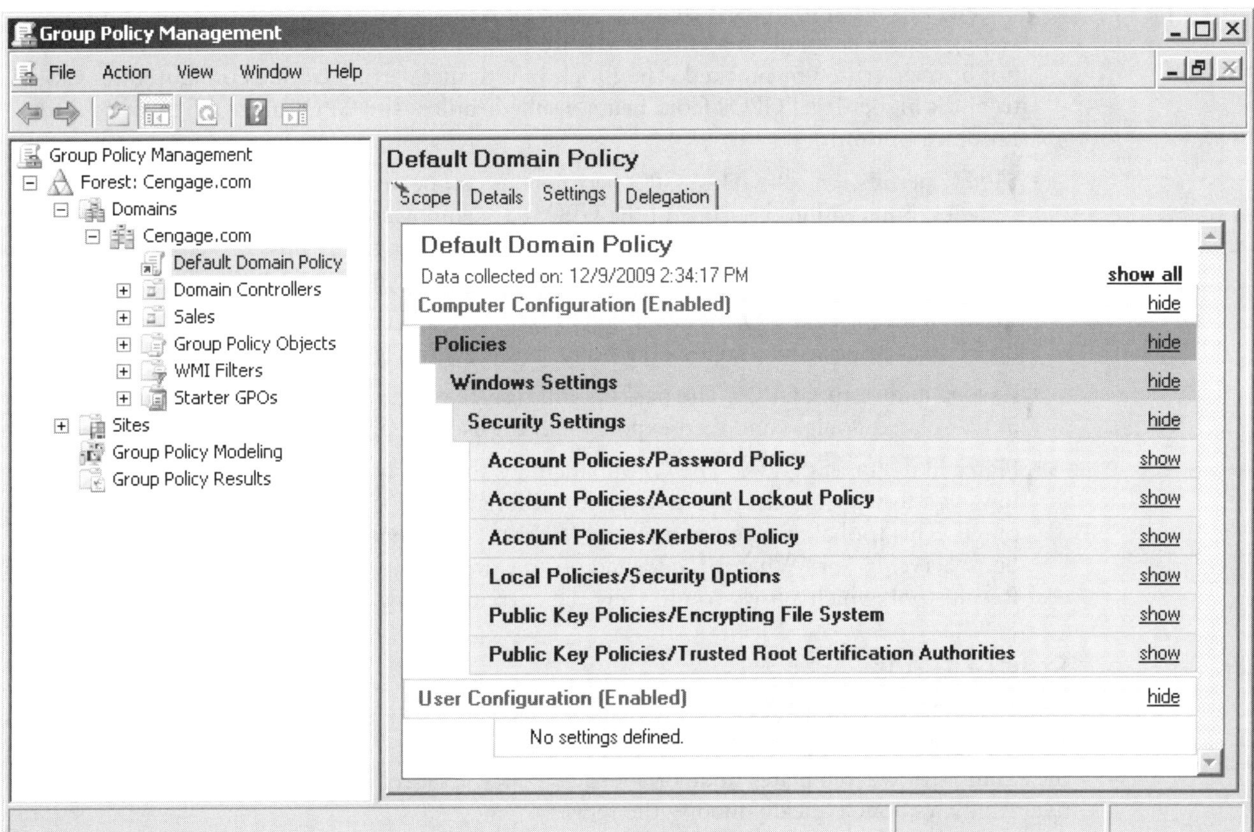

Figure 4-11 Group Policy Management console showing Default Domain policy

Courtesy Course Technology/Cengage Learning

policy. Notice that this policy only has settings in the Computer Configuration node, and more specifically, only in the Windows Settings, Security Settings node. The other default policy is the Default Domain Controllers policy, shown linked to the Domain Controllers OU.

- The Default Domain policy is linked at the domain level and applies to all users and computers in the domain. Settings in this policy will apply to users in the Users container and to computers in the Computers container, and to all users and computers in any OU.
- The Default Domain Controllers policy is linked to the Domain Controllers OU. This policy has more stringent security applied to add a stronger layer of security for domain controllers. When DCpromo is run, it will move the promoted server into this OU. Domain controllers should not be removed from this OU; if they are, this policy will no longer apply to them.

Group Policy Management Console

The primary tool used to create and manipulate Group Policy is the GPMC. This tool is available via the Administrative Tools menu on domain controllers. The GPMC can be used to do the following:

- **Create and modify GPOs.** The GPMC is the primary tool used to create GPOs. Any GPO can be modified by right-clicking the GPO and selecting Edit to start the Group Policy Management Editor.
- **Link and unlink GPOs.** GPOs can be linked or unlinked to sites, domains, and OUs using the GPMC.
- **Enable and disable GPOs.** GPOs can be enabled and disabled. A disabled GPO can still be linked, but the settings will not be applied.
- **Modify advanced options such as Enforced and Block Inheritance.** The GPO **Enforced** setting can be enabled on a GPO to ensure that the GPO settings are enforced and cannot be overwritten or blocked. The Block Inheritance setting can be configured on OUs to block higher-level GPOs from being applied (unless the GPOs are configured with the Enforced option).
- **Modify permissions on GPOs.** GPO permissions can be modified so that they only apply to certain groups within the scope of the GPO. For example, a GPO linked to an OU would normally apply to all users and computers in the OU, but the permissions could be modified to apply the GPO only to a specific global group. This is commonly called filtering the GPO.
- **View the settings of GPOs.** When a GPO is selected, a Settings tab can be selected to view the actual settings configured by the GPO, as shown in Figure 4-11.
- **Backup and restore GPOs.** The backup and restore tools allow you to create and test GPOs in an isolated domain and then export them for use in a production domain.
- **Plan and document GPOs.** The GPMC includes the Group Policy Modeling tool, which allows you to view the effective settings for different users if they log on from different computers. This tool allows you to answer "What if" questions, such as "What if Sally logged on to Server1?" or "What if Joe logged on to Client5"? It also includes the Group Policy Results tool, which allows you to view the current settings applied to users and computers.

Starter GPOs

Starter GPOs are templates of GPOs that can accelerate the use of GPOs in an organization. They are collections of preconfigured Administrative templates, and only include settings within the Administrative Templates node of a Group Policy. As a reminder, settings in the Administrative Templates node typically modify the registry.

You can create your own Starter GPOs, or download preconfigured Starter GPOs and add them to the GPMC. Once added, you can use these Starter GPOs to create new GPOs with these preconfigured settings.

It's important to realize that Starter GPOs are not actual GPOs that can be linked anywhere. Instead, they are only templates that can be used to create new GPOs. Additionally, it's not possible to import a Starter GPO into an existing GPO.

The following activity can be used to add Starter GPOs to your GPMC console. This activity uses the VistaStarterGPOs.msi, which is available from the Microsoft download site (*www.microsoft.com/downloads*). This file includes four Starter GPOs:

- **Windows Vista EC Computer.** This GPO includes Administrative Template settings recommended to apply to the Computer node for Enterprise Clients.
- **Windows Vista EC User.** This GPO includes Administrative Template settings recommended to apply to the User node for Enterprise Clients.
- **Windows Vista SSLF Computer.** This GPO includes Administrative Template settings recommended to apply to the Computer node for Specialized Security Limited Functionality.
- **Windows Vista SSLF User.** This GPO includes Administrative Template settings recommended to apply to the User node for Specialized Security Limited Functionality.

Activity 4-3: Applying a Starter GPO

Time Required: 15 minutes
Objective: Install and implement Starter GPOs.

Description: You want to create a GPO template that can be used to create other GPOs. You plan to use Microsoft-provided Starter GPOs and create GPOs from them. This activity should be run on DC1, which is used throughout the book. This activity assumes that you have already downloaded the VistaStarterGPOs.msi file. You can get this file by going to Microsoft's download site (*www.microsoft.com/downloads*) and searching on "Starter GPOs."

When using virtual machines, such as with Microsoft Virtual PC, you should download files using the host system and then copy the files to the virtual machine instead of trying to reconfigure the virtual PC for Internet access. If you reconfigure the virtual environment for Internet access, it will affect the activities.

1. Start **DC1** and log on with the domain **Administrator** account.
2. Start **Windows Explorer** and browse to the location of the **VistaStarterGPOs.msi** file. Double-click the file to start it. Click **Next** on the **Welcome** page.
3. Review the information in the **License Agreement** and select **I Agree**. Click **Next**.
4. On the **Select Installation Folder** page, accept the default location of *C:\Program Files\Microsoft Group Policy\StarterGPOs*. Select **Everyone** and click **Next**. Click **Next** on the **Confirm Installation** page. After the installation is complete, click **Close**.
5. Open the **Group Policy Management console** via the **Administrative Tools** menu. Expand **Forest, Domains, Cengage.com.** Select the **Starter GPOs** node. If this is the first time you've selected this node, you'll need to click the **Create Starter GPOs Folder** button.
6. Click the **Load Cabinet** button. Click **Browse for CAB** and browse to the *C:\Program Files\Microsoft Group Policy\StarterGPOs* folder. Select the **Windows Vista EC User** cabinet file and click **Open**. Your display will look similar to Figure 4-12. Click **OK**.
7. Click the **Load Cabinet** button again. Select the **Windows Vista EC Computer** cabinet file and click **Open**. Click **OK**.
8. Right-click the **Windows Vista EC User** Starter GPO and select **New GPO from Starter GPO**. Name the GPO **Default Vista User**. Click **OK**. At this point, you have

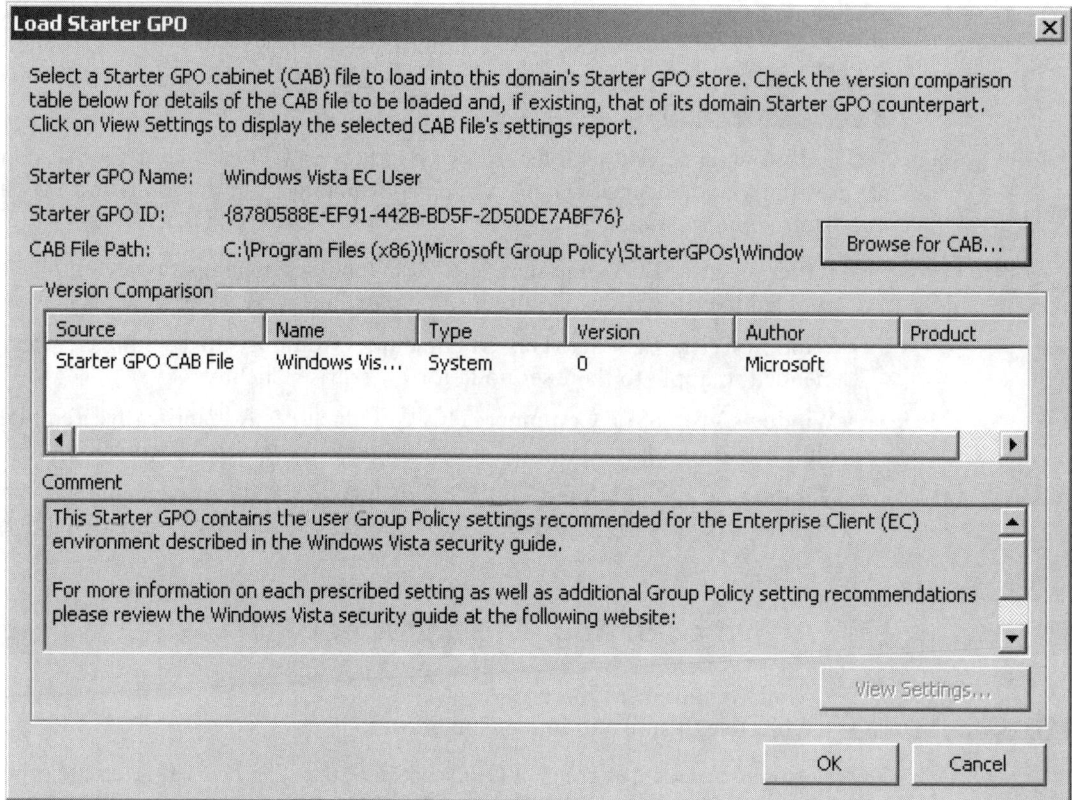

Figure 4-12 Adding a Starter GPO cabinet file to the GPMC

Courtesy Course Technology/Cengage Learning

created a new GPO, but it is not linked to anything so it will not be applied. However, you can still view the settings of the GPO.

9. Expand the **Group Policy Objects** node and select the **Default Vista User** GPO. Select the **Settings** tab. If you receive a message that content is being blocked by Internet Explorer Enhanced Security Configuration, click Close. At this point, you can browse through the settings imported from the Starter GPO. Your display will look similar to Figure 4-13.

   While the GPO currently only includes the settings from the Starter GPO, you can add more settings to this GPO to meet your needs.

10. You can also create a new GPO using a Starter GPO as a template. Right-click **Group Policy Objects** and select **New**. Name the GPO **Default Vista Computer** and select the **Windows Vista EC Computer** Starter GPO from the **Source Starter GPO** drop-down box. Click **OK**.
11. Select the **Default Vista Computer** GPO and select the **Settings** tab. Notice that the only settings from this GPO are in the Computer Configuration node of the GPO.
12. Close all open windows.

Group Policy Settings

As mentioned previously, there are hundreds of Group Policy settings. You can't learn them all at once and this section certainly won't address them all. However, several specific Group Policy settings are mentioned and alluded to in the 70-647 exam objectives. Knowing these settings will build on your knowledge of other GPO settings you probably learned while studying for earlier Microsoft MCITP exams.

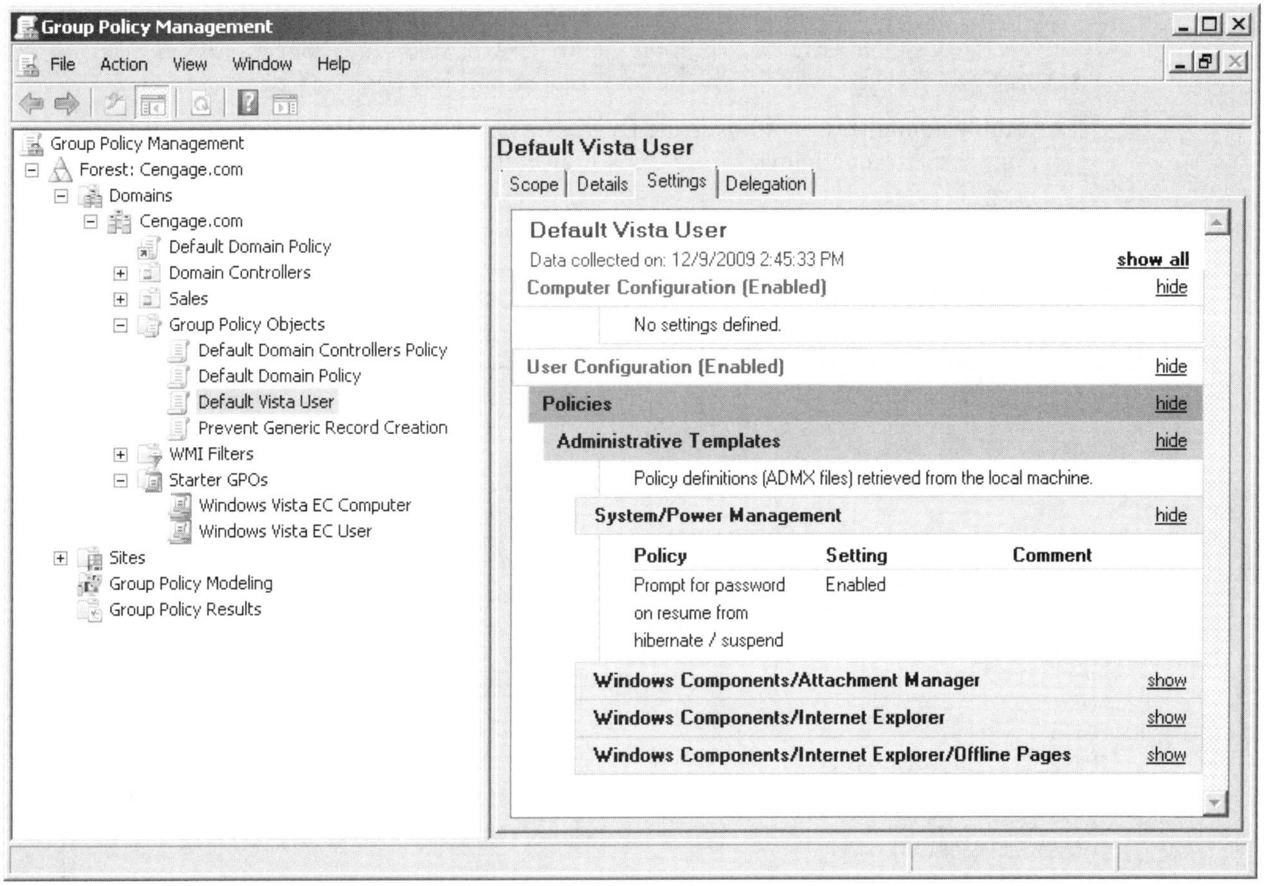

Figure 4-13 Viewing the Starter GPO settings

Courtesy Course Technology/Cengage Learning

Some Group Policy settings are covered in other chapters. For example, when covering DNS in Chapter 3, it was appropriate to show how a GPO can be used to prevent non-site-specific SRV records from being created for a specific site. In Chapter 7, you'll see how to use a GPO to enhance an auditing policy.

Some of the specific Group Policy settings covered in this section are:

- Device installation restrictions
- Restricting group membership
- Deploying applications
- Internet Explorer proxy settings
- Implementing printer location policies
- Configuring IPSec settings

Device Installation Restrictions

One of the most risky devices in an organization is USB flash drives. They can easily be infected with malware, which can easily be transported between unprotected computers (such as a user's home computer) and protected computers within the network. Additionally, portable USB disks can be plugged into systems and quickly copy gigabytes of sensitive information. A disgruntled employee could easily copy this data and store the removable drive in his pocket. Understanding these risks, many organizations seek ways to control device installation.

Group Policy provides several settings that can restrict the installation of devices and/or device drivers. These settings are located in the Computer Configuration, Policies, Administrative Templates, System, Device Installation, Device Installation Restrictions node:

- **Allow administrators to override Device Installation Restriction policies.** When this setting is enabled, administrators can still install devices even if other policy settings prevent it.
- **Allow installation of devices using drivers that match these device setup classes.** Setup classes have predefined globally unique identifiers (GUIDs). For example, the GUID of a USB flash drive is {4d36e967-e325-11ce-bfc1-08002be10318}, which can be specified to allow the installation of new device drivers for this class. The Setup Class of devices can be viewed using Device Manager. Figure 4-14 shows a USB device that was selected via Device Manager on a Windows 7 system. The drop-down box has many properties you can select, but the Device Class GUID is shown.

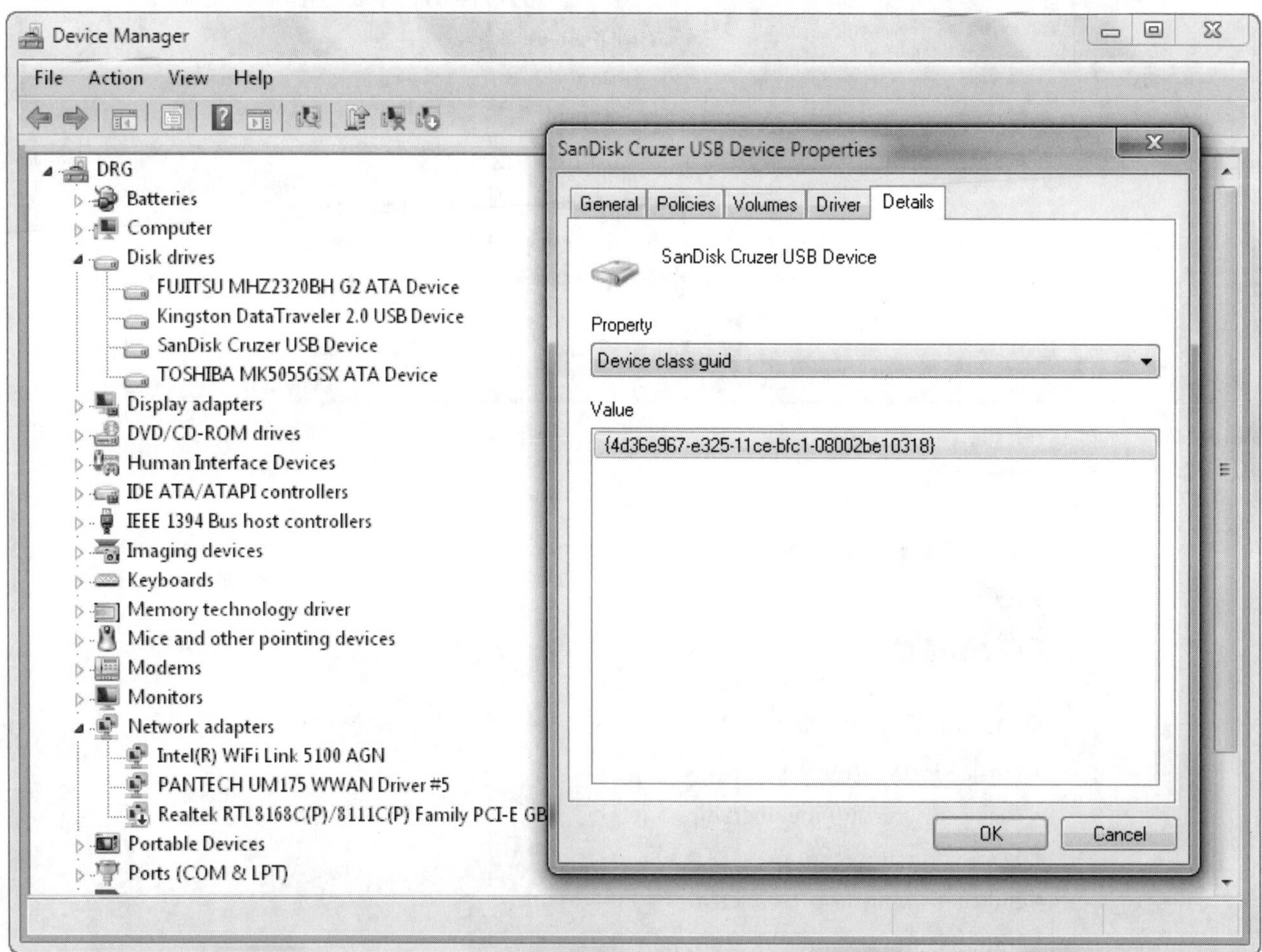

Figure 4-14 Identifying a Device Class GUID using Device Manager

Courtesy Course Technology/Cengage Learning

- **Prevent installation of devices using drivers that match these device setup classes.** The same setup classes that can be allowed can also be prevented.
- **Display a custom message when installation is prevented by policy (balloon text).** A display message such as "Installation of this device is not authorized" can be configured to appear if a user tries to use a restricted device.

- **Display a custom message when installation is prevented by policy (balloon title).** You can specify the title of the balloon notification.
- **Allow installation of devices that match any of these device IDs.** You can specifically allow certain devices using their device IDs. This is similar to how you can use the setup classes, but the device IDs are more specific. The device IDs can be located in the detailed properties of the device by selecting the Hardware IDs property.
- **Prevent installation of devices that match any of these device IDs.** You can specifically prevent the installation of devices that match certain device IDs.
- **Prevent installation of removable devices.** This setting will apply to all removable devices equally.
- **Prevent installation of devices not described by other policy settings.** This setting will prevent the installation of any devices that aren't specifically allowed by the following Group Policy settings: "Allow installation of devices using drivers that match these device setup classes," or "Allow installation of devices that match any of these device IDs."

Device IDs can be used to identify and approve hardware purchased by the company. For example, the company could purchase USB flash drives that are encrypted and locked with biometrics so that only users with registered fingerprints can use them. Another example might be company-issued, USB-based PDA or smart phone docking stations. However, the use of all other USB drives could be prevented.

Note that settings in this policy can prevent the installation of new devices, but these settings won't stop the use of devices that have already been installed. Another group of settings can be used in both the Computer Configuration and User Configuration nodes to restrict usage of removable storage devices. Figure 4-15 shows these settings.

You can access these settings in the Policies, Administrative Templates, System, Removable Storage Access node. As a simple example, you can enable the Removable Disks, Deny Write Access setting to prevent users from writing to removable storage devices.

Restrict Group Membership

The Restrict Group Membership setting is useful to control the membership of any group in Active Directory. Once configured, Group Policy will check the membership of the group. If an extra member has been added, Group Policy will remove the member. If a member that should be in the group has been removed, Group Policy will add the member.

Consider the Domain Admins group, which is often a highly protected group. It's not uncommon for a company security policy to state that only specific employees or specific accounts can be a member of this group. You can simply add the Domain Admins group as a restricted group in a GPO, and then add the authorized users. Each time the GPO is applied, the membership of the GPO will be checked and adjusted if necessary.

As a reminder, Group Policy is normally applied every 90 to 120 minutes (90 minutes with a random offset of 30 minutes). For domain controllers, Group Policy is normally applied every 5 minutes. However, you can always cause Group Policy to be immediately refreshed using the following command from the command prompt:

```
GPUpdate /force
```

Any groups can be managed using Restrict Group Membership, including built-in groups such as the Domain Admins or Enterprise Admins groups, and groups created by administrators in the domain.

The following activity shows how to create a GPO to implement Restricted Groups.

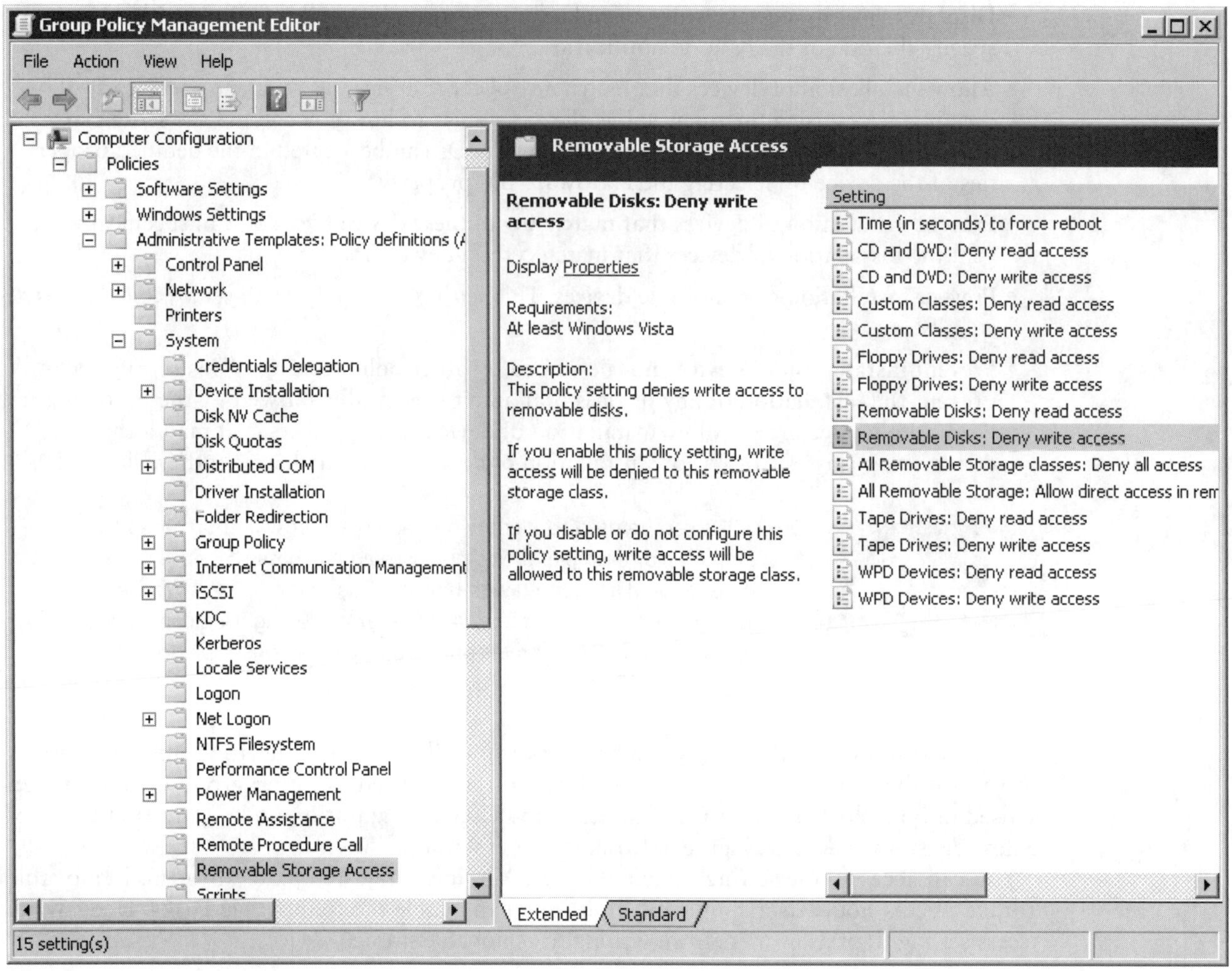

Figure 4-15 Controlling the use of removable storage devices
Courtesy Course Technology/Cengage Learning

Activity 4-4: Implementing Restricted Groups

Time Required: 15 minutes
Objective: Create a GPO to restrict group membership.

Description: Company policy states that only the domain Administrator account should be in the Domain Admins group. You are assigned to create a GPO to enforce this policy. This activity should be run on DC1, which is used throughout the book.

1. Start **DC1** and log on with a domain **Administrator** account.
2. Open the **Group Policy Management console** via the **Administrative Tools** menu.
3. Right-click the domain and select **Create a GPO in this Domain, and Link it Here.** Name the new GPO **Restricted Groups**. Click **OK**.
4. Right-click the new **Restricted Groups** policy and select **Edit**. Browse to the Computer Configuration, Policies, Windows Settings, Security Settings, Restricted Groups setting. Right-click **Restricted Groups** and select **Add Group.**
5. Enter **Domain Admins** as the group name. Note that you can also browse and search for the group. Click **OK**.

6. Click the **Add** button next to **Members of this group**. Click **Browse**. Type **Administrator** and click **Check Names**. Click **OK** after the name has been verified. Click **OK** to add the Administrator as the member of the group. Your display will look similar to Figure 4-16. Click **OK** to apply the setting.

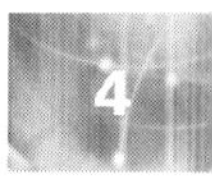

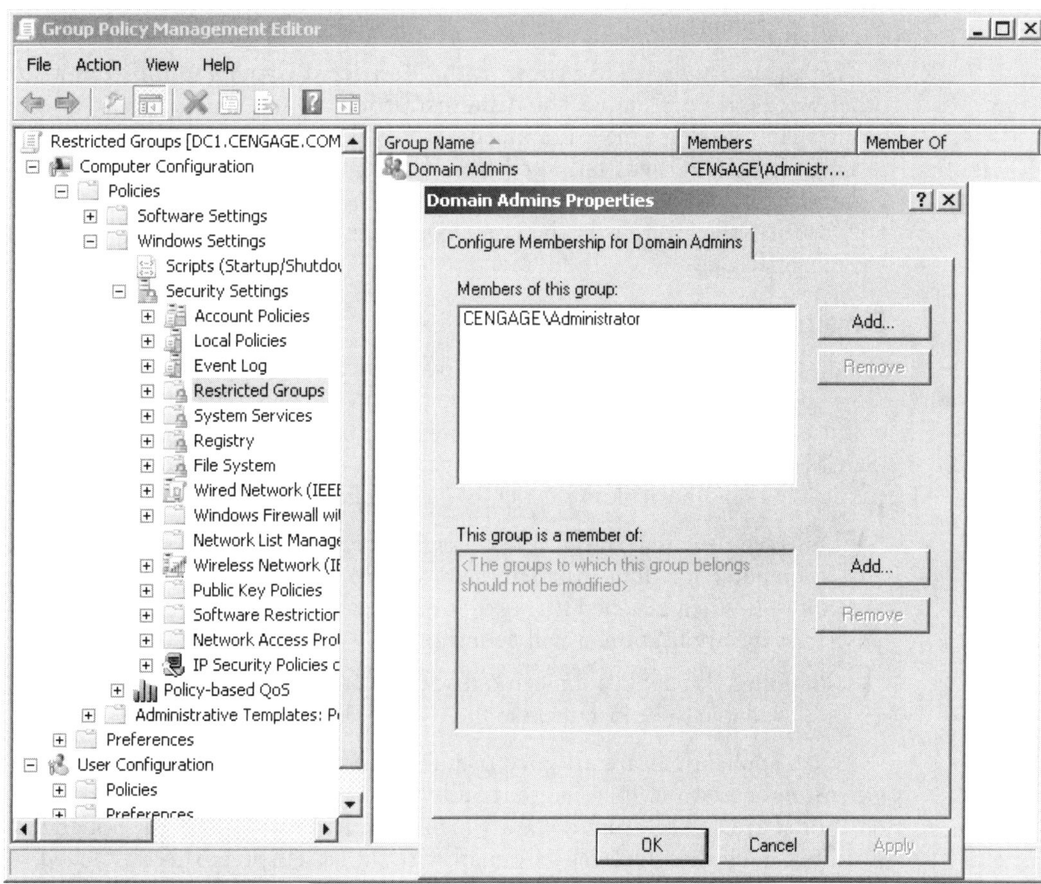

Figure 4-16 Restricting the membership of the Domain Admins group

Courtesy Course Technology/Cengage Learning

By default, only the Administrator account is a member of the Domain Admins group, so this GPO will not change the settings from the default. However, if you've added other user accounts to the Domain Admins group, this setting will remove them. If you want other accounts to be members, you can add them here.

7. Open **Active Directory Users and Computers** via the **Administrative Tools** menu. Browse to the **Users** container. Right-click the **Domain Admins** group and select **Properties**.
8. Select the **Members** tab. Only the **Administrator** account is a member.
9. Click **Add**. Enter **Guest** and click **Check Names**. Click **OK** after the name has been verified. Click **Apply**. Notice that you're allowed to add another account even though a Group Policy has been configured to restrict the group membership. Click **OK** to close this page.

   You can immediately reopen the page to confirm that the Guest account is still there. However, when the GPO is reapplied (every 90 to 120 minutes by default), the Restricted Groups setting will remove the Guest user.

10. Open a command prompt and execute the **GPUpdate /force** command, which forces the GPOs on this system to be reapplied.
11. Return to **Active Directory Users and Computers**. Right-click the **Domain Admins** group and select **Properties**. Select the **Members** tab. You'll see that the **Guest** account has been removed after the Group Policy was refreshed with the GPUpdate /force command.

While this activity didn't show it, the Restricted Groups setting will also add accounts. In other words, if you remove the Administrator account, the GPO will automatically add this group again the next time it is applied.

Last, if the GPO was unlinked from the domain and applied to another OU (such as the Domain Controllers OU), it would not have any effect. The group must be in the scope of the OU. Because the group is in the Users container, the GPO needs to be linked to the domain to have an effect.

Deploying Applications

Group Policy can also be used to deploy applications as long as they are packaged as a Windows Installer file (.msi), a transform file (.mst), or a patch file (.msp). While large organizations will use more sophisticated enterprise applications like System Center Configuration Manager (SCCM) to deploy applications, any organization can use Group Policy to deploy applications. Applications can be deployed using two methods:

- **Assigned.** An application can be assigned to either users or computers. When assigned to a computer, it will be installed the next time the system is booted after the GPO has been applied. When assigned to a user, it will be advertised on the Start menu. When the user starts the application, it will be installed.
- **Published.** An application can only be published to a user, not a computer. When published, it's available to be installed via the Control Panel.

When applications are assigned or published to users, they can also be installed through file extension activation. Imagine that Sally is assigned the Microsoft Excel application, but she has not started Excel from the Start menu yet. At this point, even though it's assigned, it's not installed. Sally then receives an e-mail with an Excel spreadsheet attached. When she double-clicks the attachment, the system recognizes it as an Excel spreadsheet, and recognizes that Excel has been assigned but hasn't been installed yet. Excel will then be installed.

In a multiple-site environment, it's common to deploy applications by linking GPOs to sites. Consider Figure 4-17. In the figure, the same accounting application is being deployed, but with two GPOs. This prevents users in Site 1 from downloading the application from Site 2.

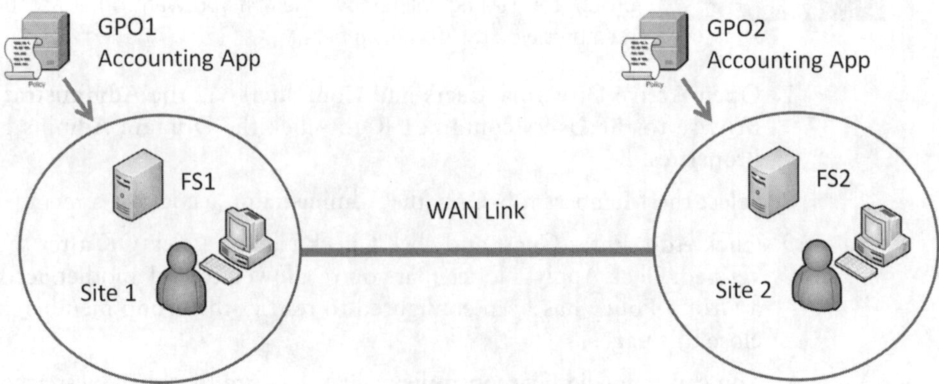

Figure 4-17 Deploying the same application to different sites

Courtesy Course Technology/Cengage Learning

GPO1 is linked to Site 1, so it applies to all users and computers in Site 1 only. GPO1 identifies the server named FS1 as the source of the application, so when the application is installed for clients in Site 1, it's retrieved from a server in their site. Similarly, GPO2 is linked to Site 2 and identifies FS2 as the source of the application files.

The following activity shows how an application can be deployed to users in an OU and how you can ensure that the application is uninstalled if the user is moved out of the scope of the GPO.

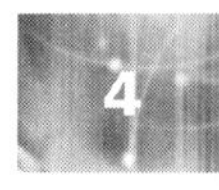

Activity 4-5: Deploying an Application

Time Required: 15 minutes
Objective: Create a GPO to deploy an application.

Description: Starter GPOs need to be available on all domain controllers in the domain. This will ensure that administrators who create GPOs can use available starter GPOs. You have downloaded the VistaStarterGPOs.msi file, and need to create a GPO linked to the Domain Controllers OU to assign this installer file to all domain controllers. You also want to ensure that if a domain controller is demoted, it will no longer have the Vista Starter GPOs installed. This activity should be run on DC1, which is used throughout the book.

When using virtual machines, such as with Microsoft Virtual PC, you should download files using the host system and then copy the files to the virtual machine.

1. Start **DC1** and log on with a domain **Administrator** account.
2. Open **Windows Explorer** and create a folder named **Apps** at the root of the C: drive. Copy the VistaStarterGPOs.msi installation file to this folder.
3. Right-click the **Apps** folder and select **Share**. Select **Everyone** from the drop-down box and click **Add** to add the **Everyone** group with the **Reader Permissions** level. Click **Share**.
4. Review the information on the **File Sharing** page. Notice that the Universal Naming Convention (UNC) path to the share is in the format of \\servername\sharename. If you're using DC1 as the server, the share will be \\DC1\Apps. Click **Done**.
5. Open the **Group Policy Management console** via the **Administrative Tools** menu.
6. Right-click the **Domain Controllers OU** and select **Create a GPO in this Domain, and Link it Here**. Name the new GPO **Starter GPOs for Windows Vista**. Click **OK**.

   Because this GPO is linked to the Domain Controllers OU, it will only assign the application to domain controllers in this OU. Other servers in the organization will not receive the application.
7. Right-click the **Starter GPOs for Windows Vista** GPO and select **Edit**.
8. Browse to the **Computer Configuration, Policies, Software Settings, Software** installation node. Right-click **Software Installation** and select **New, Package**.
9. Enter the UNC path of the share you created in the **File Name** box. If you're using DC1, this will be **\\DC1\Apps**. Click **Open**. Select the **VistaStarterGPOs.msi** file. Click **Open**. Notice that Published is dimmed. Applications can only be assigned to computers.
10. Select **Advanced** and click **OK**.
11. The properties page of the GPO appears. Select the **Deployment** tab and select the check box to **Uninstall this application when it falls out of the scope of management**. Your display will look similar to Figure 4-18.

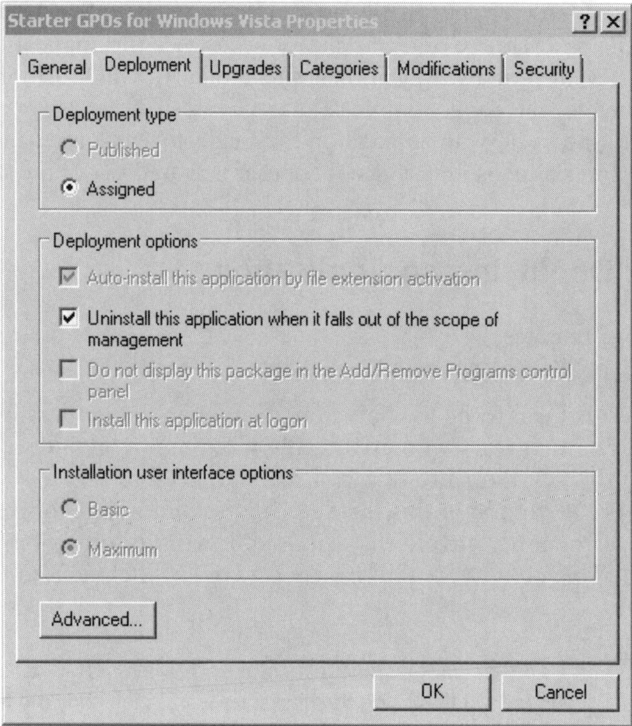

Figure 4-18 Deploying the same application to different sites

Courtesy Course Technology/Cengage Learning

This setting ensures that if the domain controller is demoted, this starter GPO will be removed. Click **OK**.

12. Close all open windows.

Internet Explorer Proxy Settings

It's common for many organizations to use a proxy server for Internet access. Clients within the network send their requests for Internet access to the proxy server, and the proxy server acts as the middleman to retrieve the data from the Internet. When the data is returned to the proxy server, it sends the data to the client. Proxy servers provide several benefits for an organization:

- **Network Address Translation (NAT).** The proxy server will have one or more public addresses connected to the Internet and accept connections from internal computers with private addresses. The NAT protocol on the proxy server translates private addresses to public addresses and public addresses back to private.
- **Caching is used to conserve bandwidth usage.** Retrieved data is cached on the proxy server; when another request for the same data is received, it is presented from the cache, instead of being retrieved again. For example, if Sally performs some research on the Internet and pulls up a page on Cengage.com, the page will be cached on the proxy server. If Joe later pulls up the same page, the proxy server presents the cached data instead of retrieving the same page from the Internet again.
- **Site access restrictions.** A proxy server can be configured so that users are prevented from going to specific Web sites. For example, if company policy states that users should not use gambling sites, the proxy server can prevent access to gambling sites.

Because proxy servers offer so many benefits, they are often used in corporate networks. However, clients need to be configured to use them. As an example, Figure 4-19 shows the proxy server

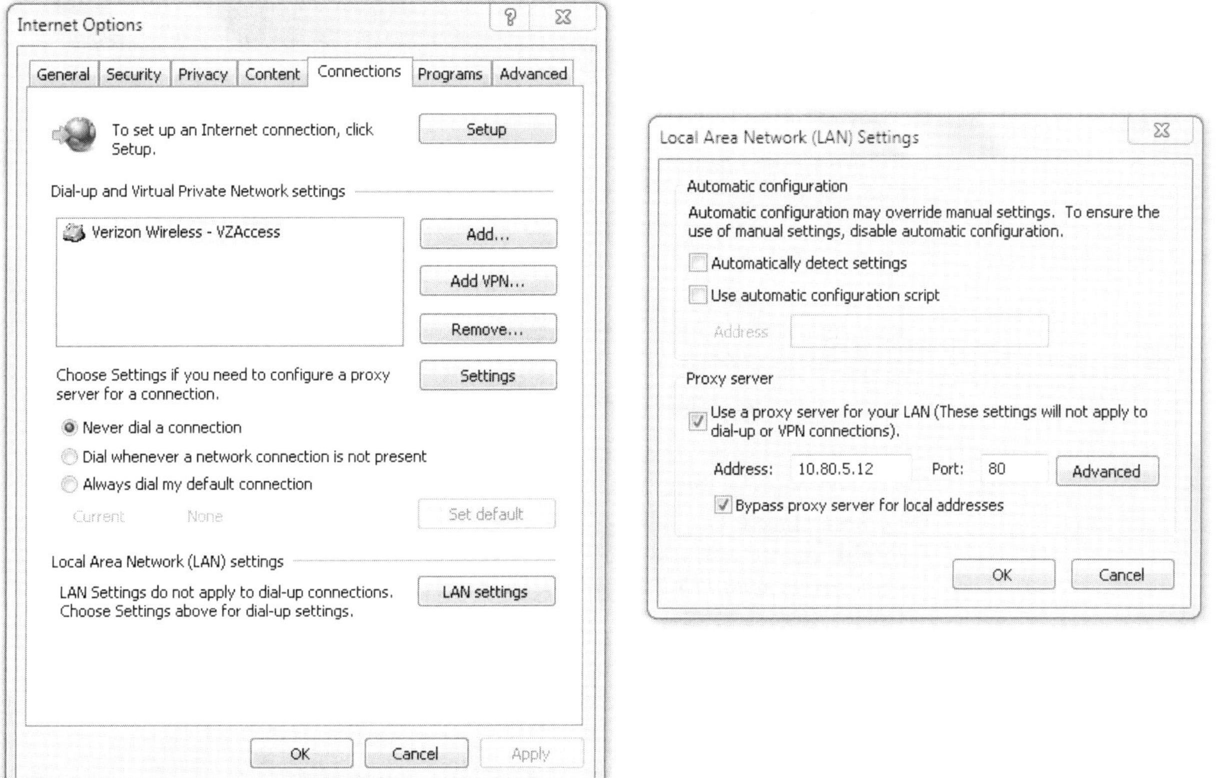

Figure 4-19 Configuring a proxy server on IE

Courtesy Course Technology/Cengage Learning

settings for Internet Explorer. The Internet Options page can be accessed by selecting Tools and then Internet Options in Internet Explorer, selecting the Connections tab, and clicking the LAN Settings button. You can then enter the proxy server data on the Local Area Network (LAN) Settings page. That's a lot of steps on just a single computer. Imagine if you had to do the same for 500 computers in your network. Without Group Policy, this would not be an easy task.

Fortunately, Group Policy settings allow you to easily configure the proxy settings for multiple clients. The following activity shows you how to configure these settings.

Activity 4-6: Implementing Internet Explorer Proxy Server Settings

Time Required: 15 minutes

Objective: Create a GPO to implement Internet Explorer (IE) proxy server settings.

Description: Users in the Atlanta site should be using a server named PS1 as their proxy server. This server has an internal private IP address of 10.80.5.12. You are asked to create a GPO and link it to the Atlanta site to automate the setting of the IE proxy server settings. This activity should be run on DC1, which is used throughout the book.

1. Start **DC1** and log on with a domain **Administrator** account.
2. Open the **Group Policy Management console** via the **Administrative Tools** menu.
3. Right-click **Sites** and select **Active Directory Sites and Services** to start the tool.
4. Within **Active Directory Sites and Services**, right-click **Sites** and select **New Site.** Name the site **Atlanta** and select **DEFAULTIPSITELINK** as the link. Click **OK.** Review the information in the dialog box and click **OK.** Close **Active Directory Sites and Services.**

This activity does not completely configure the site, but creates it just to show how to link a GPO to a site. Chapter 2 covered the complete configuration of a site.

5. Return to the **Group Policy Management console.** Right-click **Sites** and select **Show Sites.** Select the check box next to the **Atlanta** site and click **OK.** Right-click the **Atlanta** site. Notice that you can't create and link a GPO here, but must instead create the GPO separately and then link it.
6. Expand the nodes in the GPMC to access the **Group Policy Objects** container. Right-click **Group Policy Objects** and select **New.** Enter **IE Proxy** as the name and click **OK.**
7. Right-click the **IE Proxy** GPO and select **Edit.**
8. Browse to the **User Configuration, Policies, Windows Settings, Internet Explorer Maintenance, Connection** node of the Group Policy.
9. Double-click **Proxy Settings** to access the **Properties** page. Select the check box to **Enable proxy settings** and enter an IP address of **10.80.5.12.** Ensure that **Use the same proxy server for all addresses** is checked. Your display will look like Figure 4-20. Click **OK.**

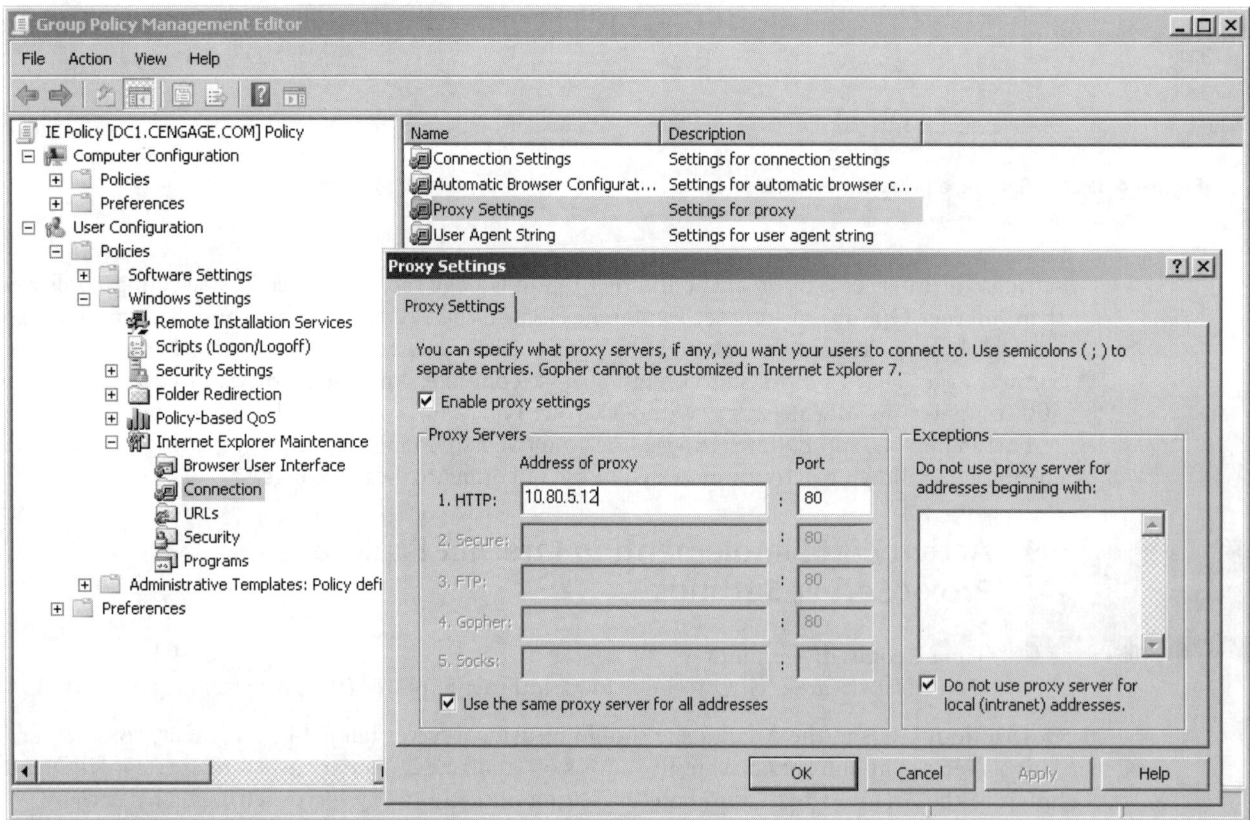

Figure 4-20 Configuring proxy server settings via a GPO

Courtesy Course Technology/Cengage Learning

10. Close the **Group Policy Management Editor** window. The GPO has been created and configured, but it's not linked to anything yet.
11. Return to the **Group Policy Management console.** Under Sites, right-click the **Atlanta** site and select **Link an Existing GPO.** Select the **IE Proxy** GPO you just created and click **OK.**

The IE Proxy GPO will now apply to all users in the Atlanta site, but only to users in the Atlanta site. Because you haven't configured the Atlanta site, it won't have any effect on your domain. In a production environment, you would link the GPO to an active site that has been fully configured.

Printer Location Policies

Printer location policies can be implemented to provide users with a list of printers that are close to them in an office. It's possible to search for printers that have different capabilities, such as color printing or double-sided printing. However, it's not useful for someone in San Francisco to get a listing of printers in Chicago.

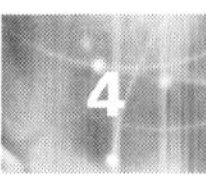

When Printer Locations are implemented via Group Policy, searches will only return a list of printers close to the user (as long as site and subnet objects have been configured correctly). Additionally, users will be able to see the location of the printer in the search results.

The primary Group Policy setting to enable printer locations is called "Pre-populate printer search location text." It is located in the Computer Configuration, Policies, Administrative Templates, Printers node, as shown in Figure 4-21.

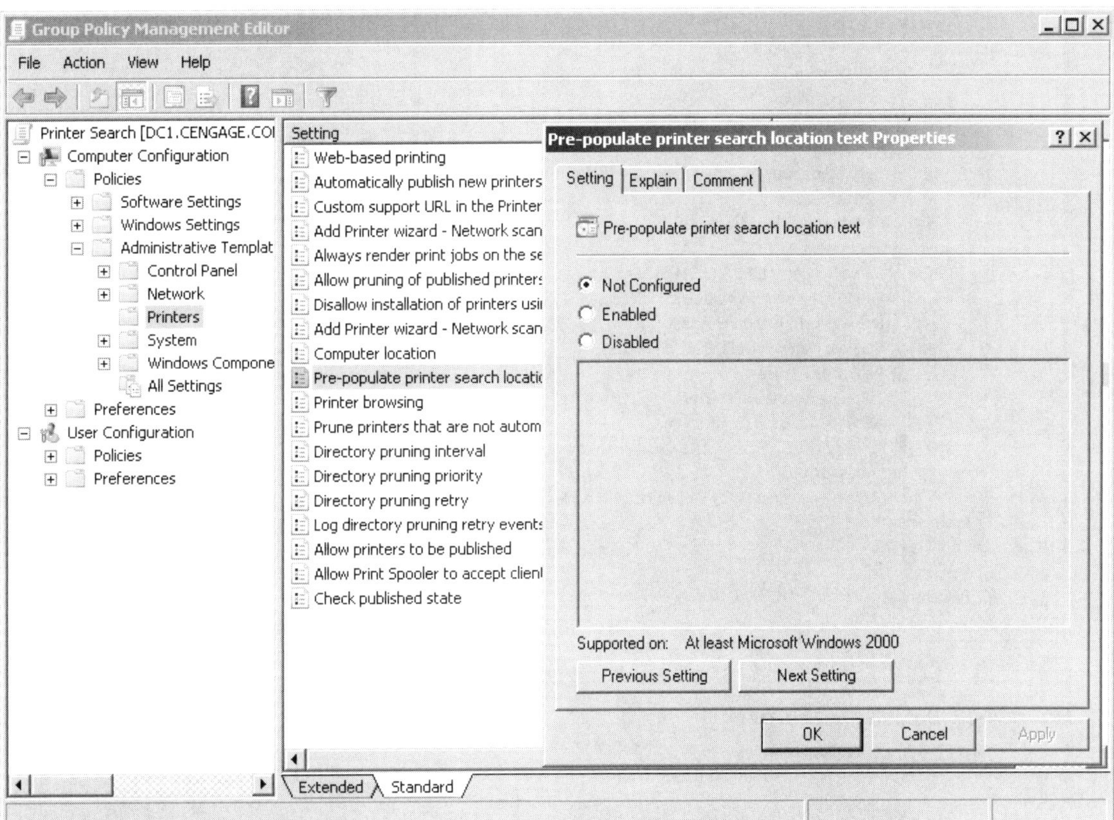

Figure 4-21 Configuring printer location settings

Courtesy Course Technology/Cengage Learning

Configuring this setting to Enabled enables the Location Tracking feature. This Group Policy setting must be enabled. Several other steps are required:

- Ensuring that the network IP Addressing corresponds to the physical layout
- Site and subnet objects created in Active Directory Sites and Services must match the actual sites in the organization
- A naming convention following a format of location\location (such as city\building or building\floor) that is entered in the sites, subnets, and printer properties.

IPSec

Internet Protocol Security (IPSec) is a protocol that can be used to provide both confidentiality and authentication when data is transmitted on a network. It provides confidentiality by encrypting the data using Encapsulated Security Payload (ESP) and provides authentication with an Authentication Header (AH). IPSec can be used with Network Access Protection (NAP), and will be mentioned in Chapter 5.

Figure 4-22 shows the three IPSec policies that are available by default in a domain. Any of these policies can be assigned by right-clicking it and selecting Assign. Only one policy can be assigned at a time.

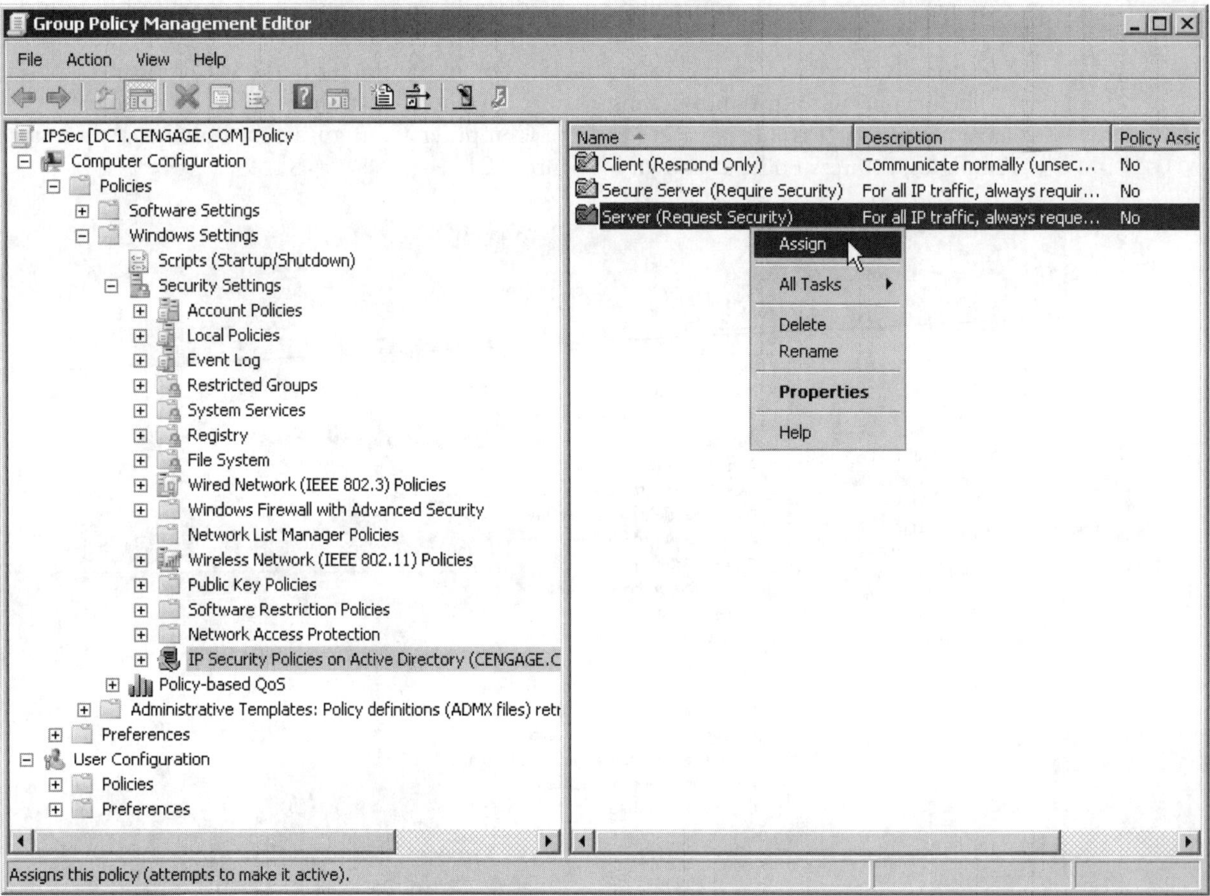

Figure 4-22 Default IPSec policies

Courtesy Course Technology/Cengage Learning

The three default policies are:

- **Client (Respond Only)**. Clients configured with this policy will be able to communicate with other hosts on the network with IPSec, but they will never initiate an IPSec session.
- **Server (Request Security)**. Clients configured with this policy will always try to initiate an IPSec session. However, they will be able to communicate even if the other host can't negotiate an IPSec session.
- **Secure Server (Require Security)**. Clients configured with this policy will always try to initiate an IPSec session. If the other host cannot negotiate an IPSec session, clients with this policy will refuse the connections.

When IPSec is needed, it's not uncommon to configure a GPO at the domain level with the Client (Respond Only) GPO so that all clients can communicate using IPSec. Then, any specific systems (such as servers hosting proprietary data) will have a GPO applied with the Server (Require Security) IPSec policy. The two combined policies ensure that the secure servers will always use IPSec, and that any clients within the domain can negotiate IPSec.

Manipulating GPO Deployments with Advanced Options

While most GPO designs can use the standard methods, occasionally the default settings won't work. In these situations, you can use some of the advanced options, but only as a last resort. If you start using these advanced options for all of your deployments, your Group Policy design will quickly become complex and hard to manage.

You can use the following advanced options:

- Enforcing GPOs
- Blocking Inheritance
- Filtering GPOs
- Loopback processing

Blocking Inheritance

Sometimes, you might not want inherited Group Policies to apply to an OU. For example, an OU may have a special purpose, and you want to prevent GPOs from applying to users or computers in this OU. This can be achieved by setting the Block Inheritance.

Figure 4-23 shows how you can configure the Block Inheritance setting. You can tell that the setting has been enabled because the Research and Development OU has an icon of a blue circle with a white exclamation mark. You can also see the check mark next to Block Inheritance when you right-click the OU; this is not checked by default.

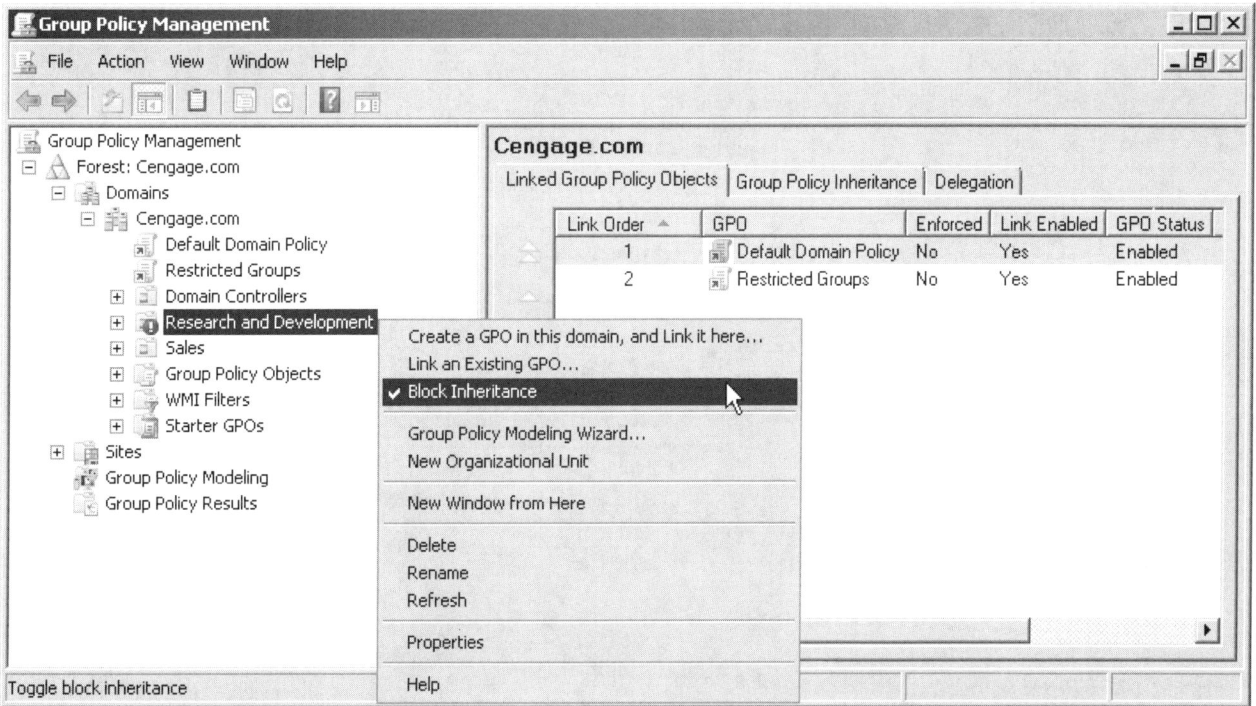

Figure 4-23 Configuring Block Inheritance

Courtesy Course Technology/Cengage Learning

The two policies configured at the domain level in the figure (the Default Domain policy and the Restricted Groups policy) will not apply to this OU. When considering a Group Policy design using Block Inheritance, you should remember several points:

- **You can only block inheritance at the OU level.** This option is not available on GPOs.
- **All inherited GPOs are blocked.** You can't pick and choose which GPOs are blocked. When Block Inheritance is selected, it will block all GPOs (except GPOs that are configured with the Enforced option).
- **GPOs applied directly to the OU will still apply.** Block Inheritance only affects the GPOs that are normally inherited. It's still possible to link GPOs directly to the OU.

While you'll rarely use this option, you should be aware that it is available for some special circumstances.

Enforcing GPOs

You often configure policies in your environment that you do not want to be overwritten due to conflicts or be blocked by the Block Inheritance setting. Remember, if there are any conflicts with GPOs, the last GPO applied wins. In other words, a GPO set at the domain level can be overwritten by a GPO at the OU level.

As an example, you may want to restrict the use of USB devices for all users in the domain, so you create a GPO to do this. However, if you've also delegated full control for administrators for an OU, they can create their own GPOs to allow the use of the devices, or even to block inheritance of all GPOs. Because a GPO applied to an OU is applied after the GPO applied to the domain, the OU GPO settings will win, allowing users in the OU to use USB devices—unless you use the Enforced option.

Figure 4-24 shows how you can configure the Enforced option. You can see that the Default Domain policy is enforced by the small lock icon on the policy and by the check mark next to Enforced.

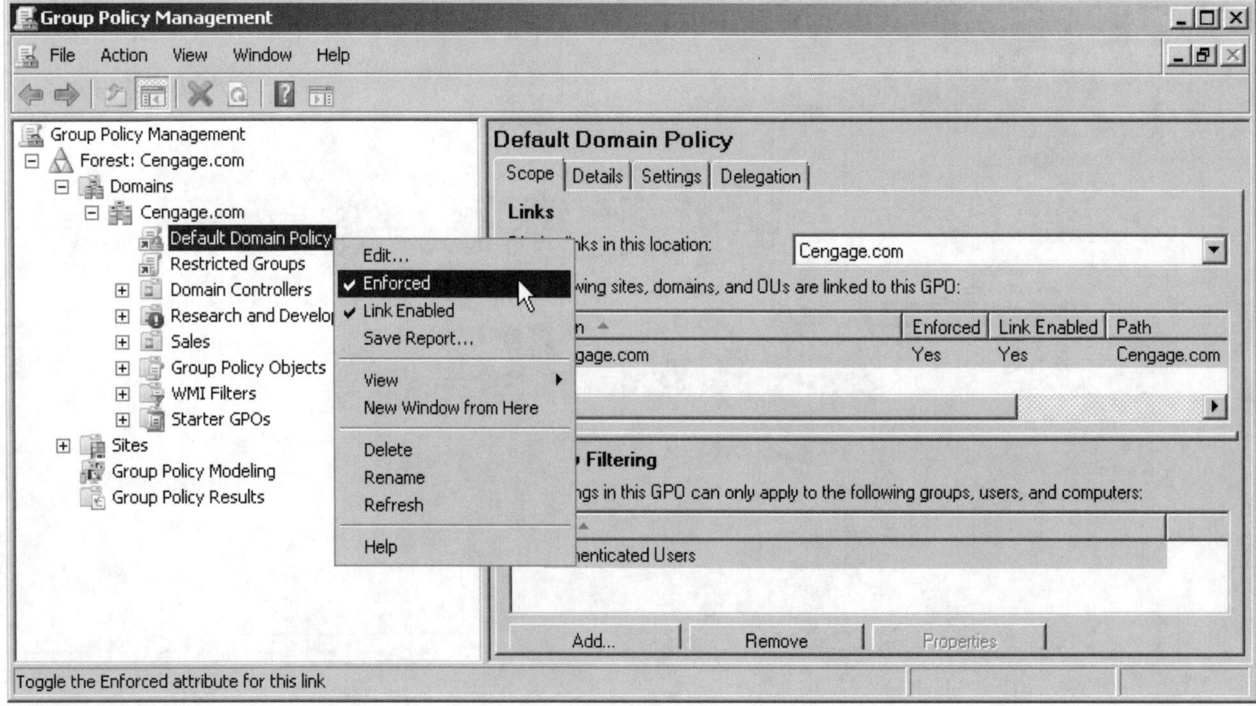

Figure 4-24 Configuring the Enforced option

Courtesy Course Technology/Cengage Learning

You should remember two points about the Enforced option.

- **Enforced can only be set on a per-GPO basis.** It can't be set on an OU or at the domain level.
- **The settings in the enforced GPO cannot be overwritten or blocked.** Conflicting settings in lower-level GPOs will not be used (though non-conflicting settings in these lower-level GPOs will still be used). The Block Inheritance setting on an OU will not block a GPO with the Enforced setting enabled.

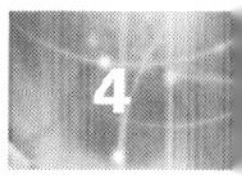

Filtering GPOs

When a GPO is created, it is configured to apply to the Authenticated Users group by default. Every user who can successfully log on to the domain is added to this group when they log on, so the GPO will apply to all users who are in the scope of the GPO. However, you can filter which groups have permissions for a GPO.

You filter a GPO when you want to apply a GPO to a select group of users based on group membership. For example, if you only want to apply the GPO to a specific group of users in an OU, you would link the GPO to the OU, but filter it based on a select group of users. These users must be in a global group.

When filtering GPOs, the two most important permissions to understand are:

- **Read.** Users who have this permission can read the policy. This allows the Group Policy settings to be accessed so that it can be processed by their systems.
- **Apply Group Policy.** When users have the Apply Group Policy and Read Policy permissions applied, the policy will apply to them.

Figure 4-25 shows the underlying permissions for a GPO. This page can be accessed by clicking the Advanced button of the Delegation tab. The figure shows the default permissions (Allow Read and Allow Apply Group Policy) applied to the Authenticated Users group.

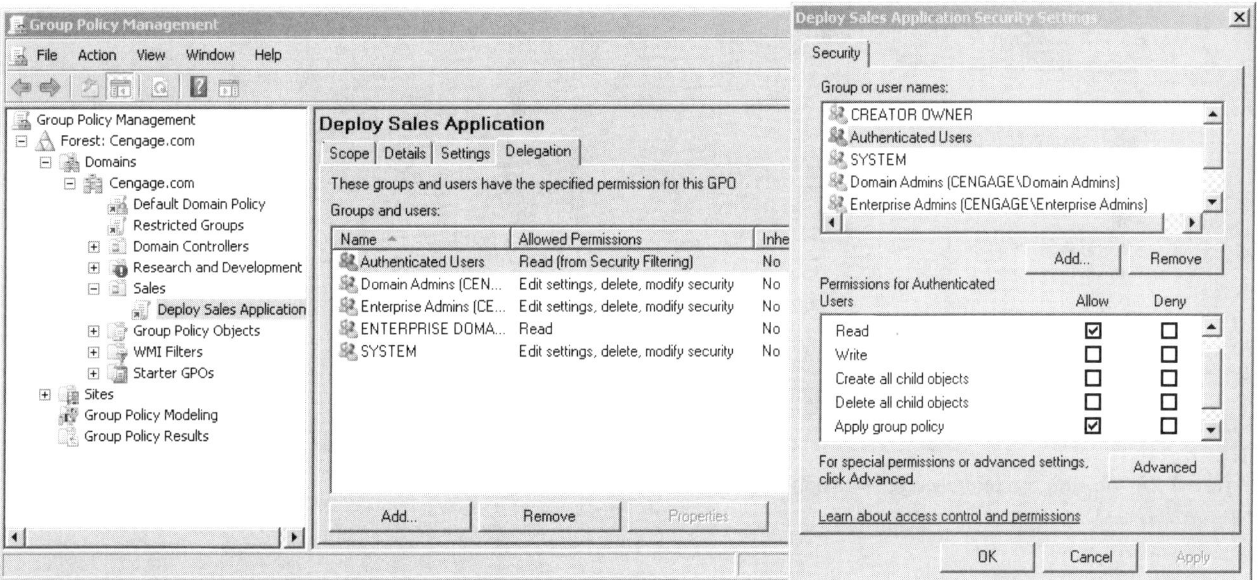

Figure 4-25 Viewing the underlying permissions for a Group Policy

Courtesy Course Technology/Cengage Learning

Administrators (such as members of the Domain Admins or Enterprise Admins groups) have other permissions on the GPO, but because any user who can log on is automatically a member of the Authenticated Users group, this GPO will apply to any user (including users in the Domain Admins and Enterprise Admins groups) in the scope of the GPO. If the GPO is linked to the domain, it applies to all the users in the domain.

The GPO can be filtered in two ways:

- **Select Deny for Apply Group Policy.** For example, if you don't want this policy to apply to users in the Domain Admins group, select Deny for Apply Group Policy. Just as Deny takes precedence with NTFS and other permissions, Deny takes precedence with the Apply Group Policy permission. This must be done from Advanced permissions, as shown in Figure 4-25.
- **Remove the Authenticated Users group and add another group.** If you don't want the GPO to apply to all users, remove the Authenticated Users group and add another group. For example, if you want to deploy an application to a select group of users in a global group, you can remove the Authenticated Users group and add this target group. You would then ensure that the Read and Apply Group Policy permissions are set to Allow for this target group.

While you can use the Advanced permissions page to manually assign permissions (see Figure 4-25), you don't need this page to remove the Authenticated Users group and add another group.

Figure 4-26 shows how the Scope tab of the GPO can be used for this purpose. In the figure, the Deploy Sales Application GPO is selected. The goal is to have this application deployed to members of the G_SalesMgrs group. This group is in the Sales OU, but many other users are in the Sales OU, and they should not receive the application.

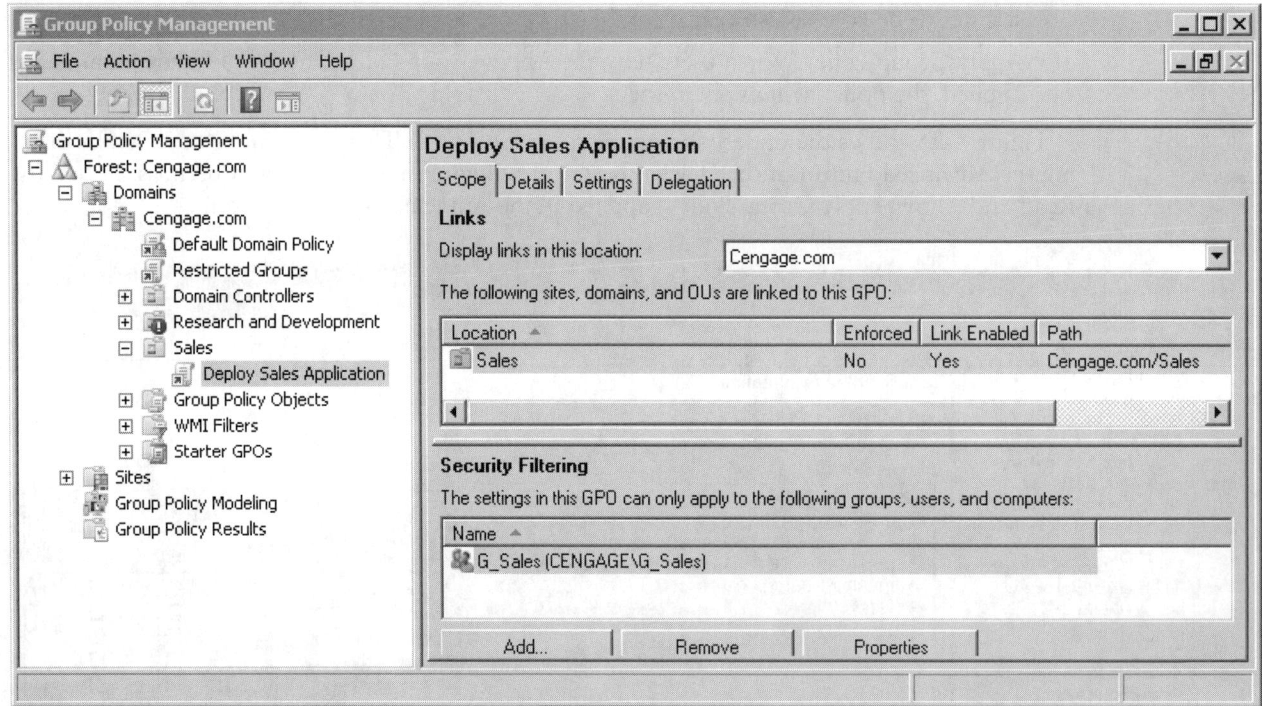

Figure 4-26 Viewing the underlying permissions for a Group Policy

Courtesy Course Technology/Cengage Learning

Normally, only the Authenticated Users group is in the Security Filtering area. However, you can remove the Authenticated users group by selecting it and clicking Remove. You can then add another group by clicking Add. In the figure, the G_SalesMgrs group has been added and the Authenticated Users group has been removed. At this point, the G_SalesMgrs group would have the Read and Apply Group Policy permissions assigned, but not the Authenticated Users group. The GPO is filtered for all users except those in the G_SalesMgrs group.

The following activity shows how you can filter a GPO.

Activity 4-7: Filtering a GPO

Time Required: 20 minutes
Objective: Configure a GPO to apply only to a specific group.

Description: You need to ensure that access to the Control Panel is hidden for all users in the domain except for users in the Domain Admins group. You will deploy a GPO at the domain level to achieve this, and then filter it using the Domain Admins group. This activity should be run on DC1, which is used throughout the book.

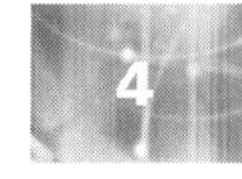

1. Start **DC1** and log on with a domain **Administrator** account.
2. Start the **Group Policy Management console** via the **Administrative Tools** menu.
3. Right-click the domain and select **Create a GPO in this Domain, and Link it Here.** Name the GPO **Disable Control Panel** and click **OK.**
4. Right-click the **Disable Control Panel** GPO and select **Edit.** Browse to the **User Configuration, Policies, Administrative Templates, Control Panel** node. Locate the **Prohibit Access to the Control Panel** setting and double-click it. Select **Enabled** and click **OK.**
5. Close the **Group Policy Management Editor.**
6. Open a command prompt and enter the following command to force the GPO to be applied:

   ```
   GPUpdate /force
   ```

   If a message appears, indicating that the computer needs to be restarted, click **N** to continue.
7. Enter the following command to verify that the GPO is applied:

   ```
   GPResult /r /scope User
   ```

   This command will display the resultant set of policy (RSOP) summary data for the computer configuration. The Applied Group Policy Objects listing will look like this:

   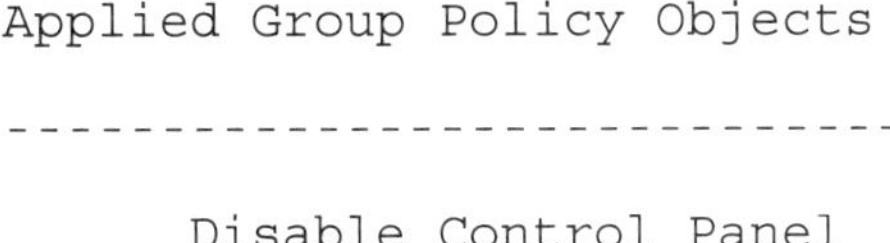

   ```
   Applied Group Policy Objects
   -----------------------------
          Disable Control Panel
   ```

   This listing verifies that the policy is being applied. You could also try to access the Control Panel, but it's not available.
8. Return to the **Group Policy Management console.** Select the **Disable Control Panel** GPO and select the **Delegation** tab. Click the **Advanced** button (in the lower-right portion of the screen).
9. On the **Disable Control Panel Security Settings** page, select the **Domain Admins** group and select the check box for **Deny** next to **Apply group policy**, as shown in Figure 4-27. Notice that the Domain Admins group has other permissions set to Allow, which allows any member of this group to manage the GPO. However, with Deny Apply Group Policy selected, the GPO will not apply to members of the Domain Admins group.
10. Click **OK** to apply the **Deny Apply Group Policy** setting. Review the information in the **Windows Security** dialog box and click **Yes.**

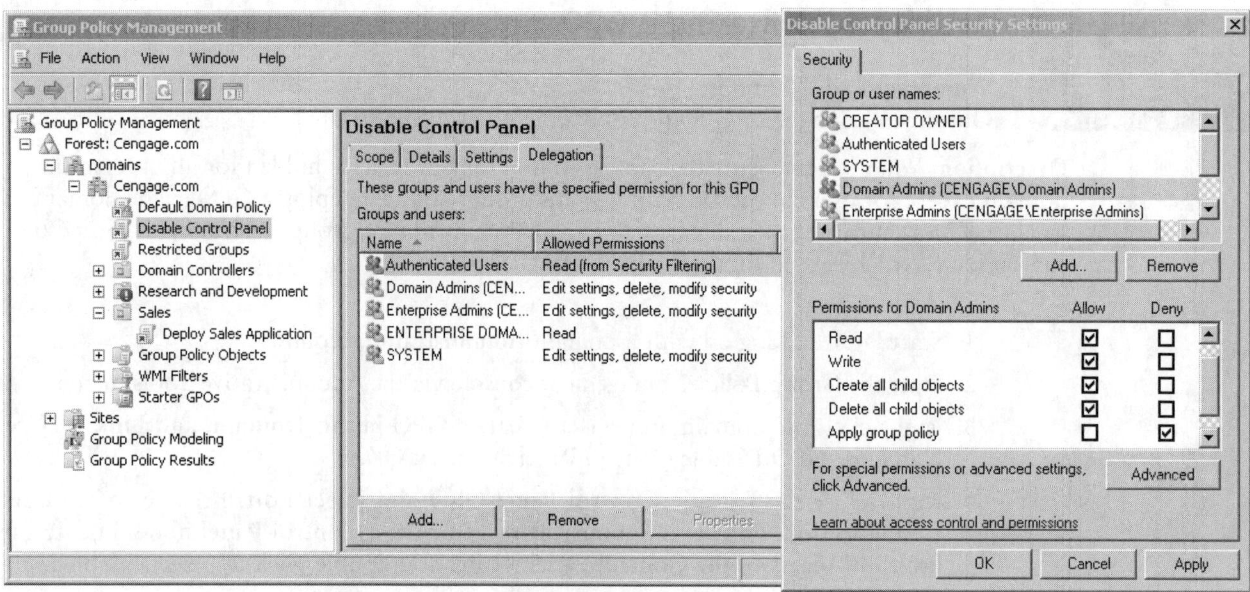

Figure 4-27 Filtering the Domain Admins group for a GPO

Courtesy Course Technology/Cengage Learning

11. Return to the command prompt and enter the following command to force the GPO to be applied:

    `GPUpdate /force`

    If a message appears, indicating that the computer needs to be restarted, click **N** to continue.

12. Enter the following command to verify that the GPO is no longer applied:

    `GPResult /r /scope User`

    You'll see that the group policy is no longer in the Applied Group Policy Objects listing. Instead, it will be in the filtered listing and look something like this:

```
The following GPOs were not applied because they were
filtered out

----------------------------------------------------------

Disable Control Panel

Filtering:  Denied (Security)
```

    If you click Start, you'll also see that the Control Panel has been returned to the Start menu.

13. Return to the **Group Policy Management** console. Right-click the **Disable Control Panel** GPO and select **Link Enabled** to disable it.

14. Close all open windows.

WMI Filtering

Windows Management Instrumentation (WMI) filtering can also be used to control how GPOs are applied. WMI allows the inspection of systems to look for specific conditions on a computer, and is widely used with scripting. When a WMI filter is used with a GPO, the GPO is only applied if the WMI filter condition is met. As an example, if an application needs 400 MB of free disk space, the WMI filter can check for this requirement before applying the GPO and installing the application.

WMI filters work on any computers running Windows XP or later (but not Windows 2000). As long as the computers are Windows XP or later, you can even create a WMI filter to identify the operating system. They are created by first building a WMI query using the WMI Query Language (WQL). WQL is very similar to SQL queries, but has its own set of objects that can be queried. Once a WMI filter is created, it can be applied to a GPO, but you can only apply one WMI filter to any GPO.

The most common use of WMI filters is for exception management. In other words, if you want the GPO to apply to all the computers in its scope *except* specific ones, you could create a WMI filter to meet the condition of the exceptions. For example, if your environment includes Windows XP, Windows Vista, and Windows 7 computers, you could create a WMI filter to identify Windows XP computers. This WMI filter could be linked to a GPO so that the GPO applies to all computers except Windows XP computers.

Loopback Processing

The last advanced GPO option covered in this section is **loopback processing**. This setting allows the GPO settings for a computer to override the settings applied to a user.

Any computer can have multiple GPOs applied, based on the site, domain, or OU of a computer object. If there are any conflicts, the last GPO applied wins (assuming there aren't any other advanced GPO options being applied).

Similarly, a user can also have multiple GPOs applied. Depending on where the user object is located, it can also have multiple GPOs applied. If there are conflicts, the last GPO applied wins.

Think about this for a moment. What happens last: the computer booting or the user logging on? Obviously, a user can't log on unless the computer boots, so the user logs on last. If there are any conflicts between the GPOs applying to the computer and the GPOs applying to the user, the user settings take precedence because the GPOs applying to the user are applied last.

However, in some situations this isn't desirable. For example, consider a computer placed in a public place for company employees. It could be in a break room that employees use for personal reasons, such as checking Web-based e-mail or surfing the Web during lunch. The following GPOs could be applied for a public computer and a user in the IT Admins group.

- **Public Computer**. GPO1 is applied to ensure tight security for this computer.
- **Sally, in the IT Admins group**. GPO2 is applied to unlock most of the settings locked down on the public computer.

If you want the public computer to stay locked down no matter who accesses it, you can use loopback processing. Figure 4-28 shows the Group Policy Loopback Processing Mode setting. It's located in the Computer Configuration, Policies, Administrative Templates, System, Group Policy node.

Note that the Loopback Process mode has two possible settings when enabled.

- **Replace**. When Replace is selected, all of the user's settings will be completely replaced.
- **Merge**. When Merge is selected, any of the user's computer settings that do not conflict with GPO settings will still apply. Any GPO settings that conflict with the computer GPO settings will be overwritten.

Fine-Grained Account Policies

A significant addition to Windows Server 2008 is the ability to use fine-grained account policies, which allow an organization to have more than one account policy within a single domain. This might not seem like a big deal, but it is for administrators coming from Windows Server 2003 domains. Before Windows Server 2008, if you needed a group of users to have a more stringent account policy, you had to create a separate domain.

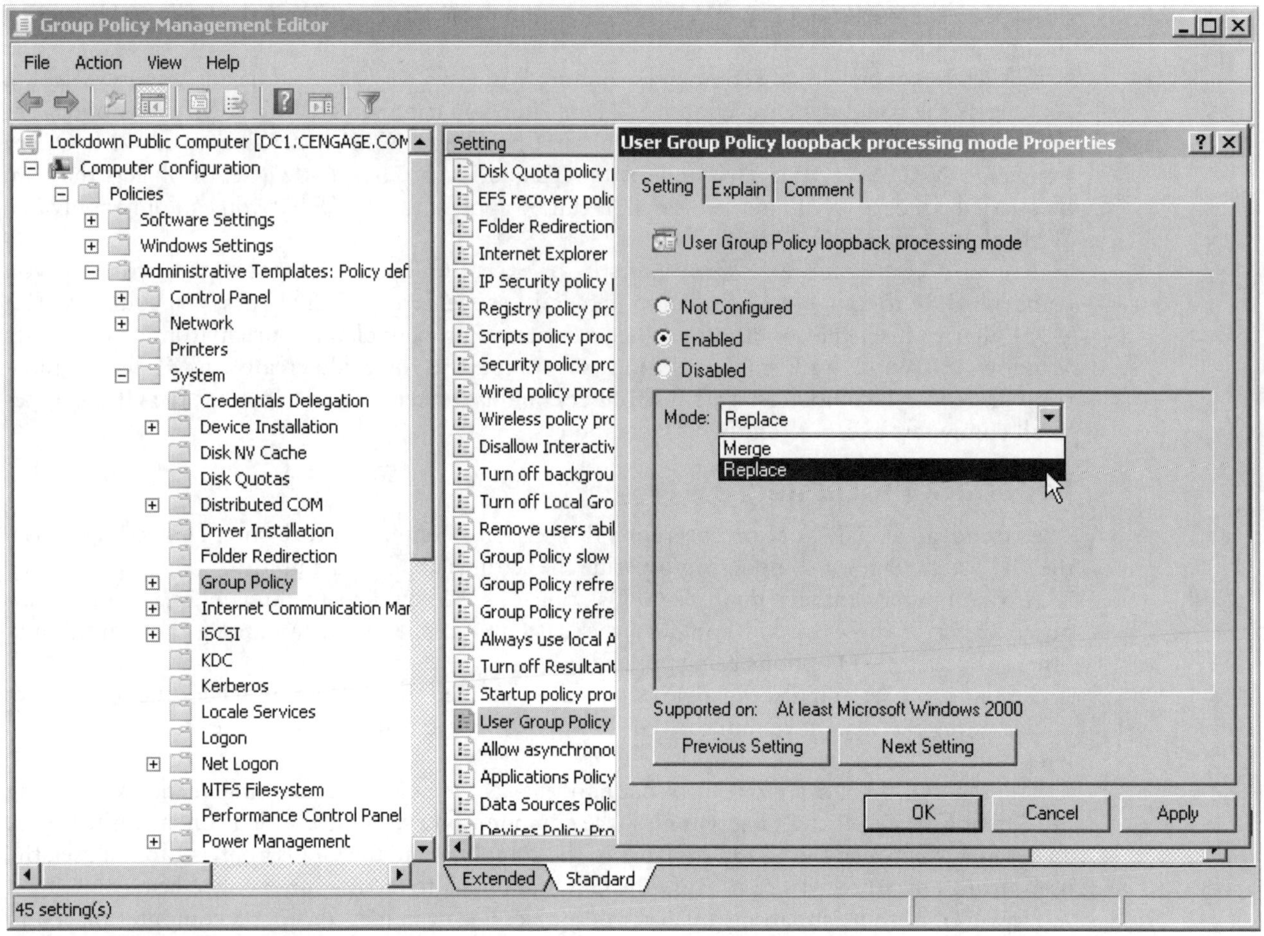

Figure 4-28 Using loopback processing

Courtesy Course Technology/Cengage Learning

Imagine that your organization had 10 researchers working on highly valuable data, and the company dictated that these users needed passwords of at least 15 characters. Either you had to create a policy to ensure that *all* users in the organization used passwords of at least 15 characters (not a popular option for regular users), or you created a separate domain for these 10 researchers.

Figure 4-29 shows the account policies within the Default Domain policy for a domain. Account Policies settings are traditionally only configured in the Default Domain policy, but they could be configured in another policy applied to the domain.

Account policies are only applied to domain accounts when the GPO is applied at the domain level. Nothing stops you from configuring Account Policies settings in a GPO applied to an OU, but these settings will not affect domain accounts.

Account policies are specific settings within Group Policy. They include three groups of settings:

- **Password Policy.** The Password Policy includes items such as minimum age and minimum password length. For regular users, a password length of 8 characters is often considered adequate. For accounts with greater access or with access to highly valuable data, a password length of 15 characters is often recommended.
- **Account Lockout Policy.** The Account Lockout Policy includes the account lockout duration, threshold, and the time to reset the account lockout counter.

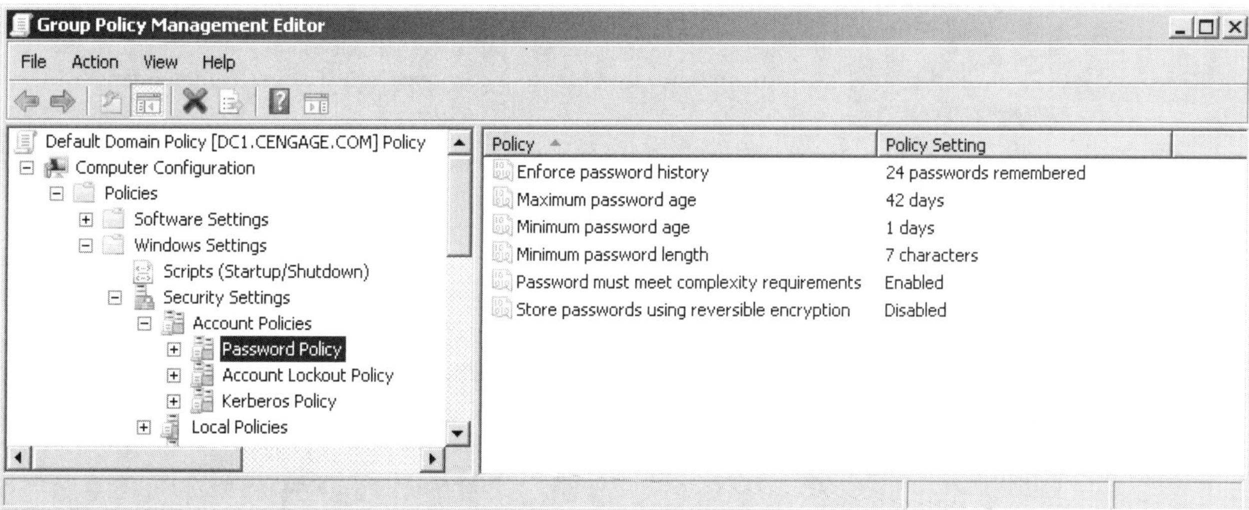

Figure 4-29 Account policies configured in the Default Domain policy

Courtesy Course Technology/Cengage Learning

- **Kerberos Policy.** The Kerberos Policy is used to modify settings for Kerberos, which is the authentication protocol used by Active Directory. It's not common for these settings to be manipulated, and organizations very rarely require two separate Kerberos policies.

Requirements for Fine-Grained Policies

Recall from Chapter 1 that when you raise the domain functional level to Windows Server 2008, you can support fine-grained policies. This can allow some organizations to consolidate multiple-domain forests to single-domain forests. Of course, this also requires that all domain controllers in the domain must be running at least Windows Server 2008.

If you can consolidate a multiple-domain forest to a single domain, you will ease the administrative workload.

If you currently have extra domains that were specifically designed to support extra account policies, you can take the following steps:

- Upgrade all DCs in the target domain to Windows Server 2008.
- Raise the domain functional level to Windows Server 2008.
- Create a fine-grained policy.
- Migrate the accounts to the target domain.
- Delete the older domain.

A password settings object (PSO) is created to implement a fine-grained policy. You must be a member of the Domain Admins group to create a PSO.

Creating Fine-Grained Policies

Fine-grained policies are created in a two-step process. First, you create a PSO and then you link the PSO to a group. While it's possible to link the PSO to individual users, it is not recommended, just as assigning permissions to individual users is not recommended. Whenever possible, use groups instead of users to ease the long-term administrative workload.

PSOs can be created using the Active Directory Service Interfaces Editor (ADSI Edit) tool. ADSI Edit can be used to query, view, and edit any objects and attributes in Active Directory Domain Services.

It's also possible to script the creation of PSOs with the LDIFDE tool (Lightweight Directory Access Protocol Data Interchange Format Directory Exchange). However, because the creation of PSOs is often a one-time occurrence, it's easier to use ADSI Edit.

When creating a PSO, several attributes must be entered. These are marked as "mustHave" attributes, so you won't be able to continue until you enter some value. Table 4-1 lists these attributes and some acceptable values. Note that time values are entered in a d:hh:mm:ss format, as in days, hours, minutes, seconds.

Table 4-1 PSO "mustHave" attributes

Attribute	Acceptable Values
msDS-PasswordSettingsPrecedence	Anything greater than 0 (only used if more than one PSO applies)
msDS-PasswordReversibleEncryptionEnabled	True or False (False recommended)
msDS-PasswordHistoryLength	0 through 1024 (24 commonly used)
msDS-PasswordComplexityEnabled	True or False (True recommended)
msDS-MinimumPasswordLength	0 through 255 values of 8 to 15 often used
msDS-MinimumPasswordAge	Time value in d:hh:mm:ss format. 1 day is 1:00:00:00
msDS-MaximumPasswordAge	Time value in d:hh:mm:ss format. 30 days is 30:00:00:00
msDS-msDS-LockoutThreshold	0 through 65,535 (values of 3 and 5 commonly used)
msDS-LockoutObservationWindow	Time value in d:hh:mm:ss format. 30 minutes is 0:00:30:00
msDS-LockoutDuration	Time value in d:hh:mm:ss format. 30 minutes is 0:00:30:00

The following activity shows how a PSO can be created and applied to a group.

Activity 4-8: Creating and Applying a PSO

Time Required: 45 minutes

Objective: Create and apply a password settings object (PSO).

Description: Researchers in your two-domain forest are required to have more stringent password policies. A separate domain was previously created to support enforcing this requirement with Group Policy, but you want to migrate these users back to the original domain and remove the second domain. You recently upgraded the domain functional level to Windows Server 2008. You need to create a group for these users, create a PSO with the more stringent policy, and link the PSO to the group. This activity should be run on DC1, which is used throughout the book.

1. Start **DC1** and log on with a domain **Administrator** account.
2. Start **Active Directory Users and Computers** via the **Administrative Tools** menu. Right-click the **Users** container and select **New, Group.** Name the group **G_Researchers.** Ensure that **Global** and **Security** are selected and click **OK.**
3. Click **Start,** type **ADSI** in the **Start Search** text box, and press **Enter** to start the **ADSI Edit** tool.
4. Right-click **ADSI Edit** and click **Connect To.** Enter the name of the domain (**Cengage .com** if using the labs in this book) in the **Name** box. Click **OK.**
5. Double-click **Cengage.com** to expand it. Double-click **DC=Cengage, DC=com.** Double-click **CN=System.** Select the **CN=Password Settings Container**, as shown in Figure 4-30.

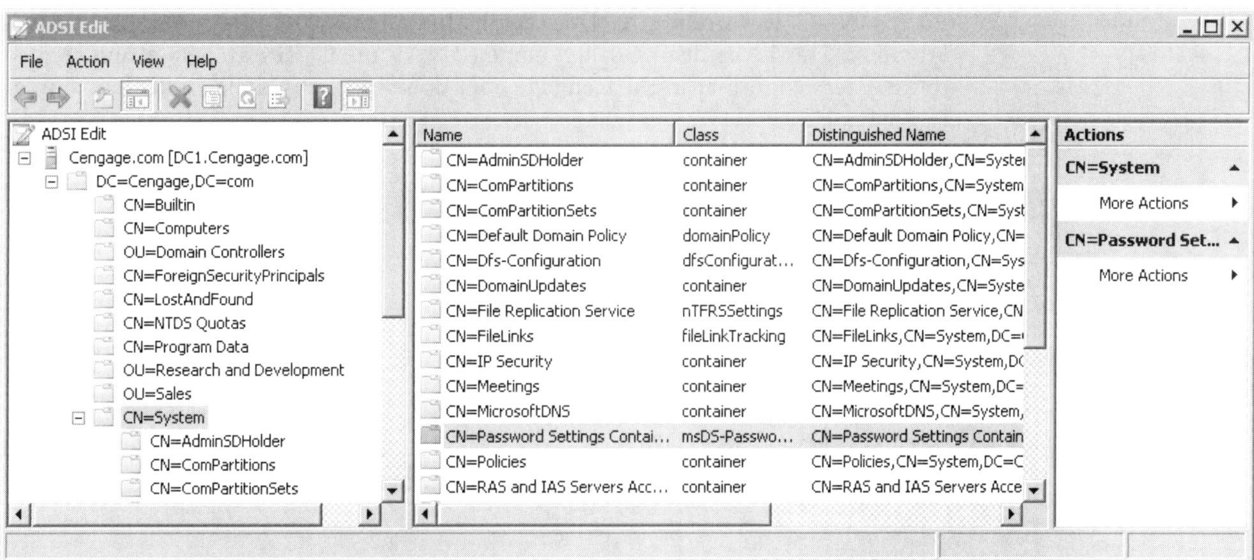

Figure 4-30 Accessing the Password Settings Container in ADSI Edit

Courtesy Course Technology/Cengage Learning

6. Right-click the **CN=Password Settings Container** and select **New, Object**. The **msDS-PasswordSettings** object will be the only available class. Click **Next**.
7. Enter **psoResearchers** for the cn (common name) attribute. Click **Next**.
8. Enter a value of **10** for the **msDS-PasswordSettingsPrecedence** attribute. This setting can be used to set a priority if multiple PSOs apply. Click **Next**.
9. Enter **False** for the **msDS-PasswordReversibleEncryptionEnabled** attribute. This setting prevents passwords from being stored using reversible encryption. Click **Next**.
10. Enter a value of **24** for the **msDS-PasswordHistoryLength** attribute. This setting prevents users from reusing any of the past 24 passwords. Click **Next**.
11. Enter **True** for the **msDS-PasswordComplexityEnabled** attribute. This setting ensures that passwords meet the complexity requirements. Click **Next**.
12. Enter **15** for the **msDS-MinimumPasswordLength** attribute. This setting ensures that passwords will be at least 15 characters. Click **Next**.
13. Enter **1:00:00:00** for the **msDS-MinimumPasswordAge** attribute. This setting ensures that passwords can't be changed before a day has passed. Click **Next**.
14. Enter **30:00:00:00** for the **msDS-MaximumPasswordAge** attribute. This setting ensures that passwords must be changed at least every 30 days. Click **Next**.
15. Enter **5** for the **msDS-msDS-LockoutThreshold** attribute. Accounts will be locked out if the wrong password is entered 5 times in a row. Click **Next**.
16. Enter **0:00:30:00** for the **msDS-LockoutObservationWindow** attribute. This attribute identifies when the lockout threshold counter will be reset. If a user enters a wrong password, the count is 1, but the count will be reset to 0 after 30 minutes. Click **Next**.
17. Enter **0:00:30:00** for the **msDS-LockoutDuration** attribute. Accounts will be locked out for 30 minutes if the lockout threshold is exceeded. Click **Next**.

    The PSO is created. However, the PSO must be linked to a user or group before it is applied.
18. Click **More Attributes**.
19. Select **Both** from the **Select which properties to view** drop-down box.
20. Select **msDS-PSOAppliesTo** from the **Select a property to view** drop-down box.

21. Enter **CN=G_Researchers, CN=Users, DC=Cengage, DC=com** in the **Edit Attribute** box. This is the distinguished name (DN) of the G_Researchers group created in the Users container in the Cengage.com domain. Your display will look similar to Figure 4-31.

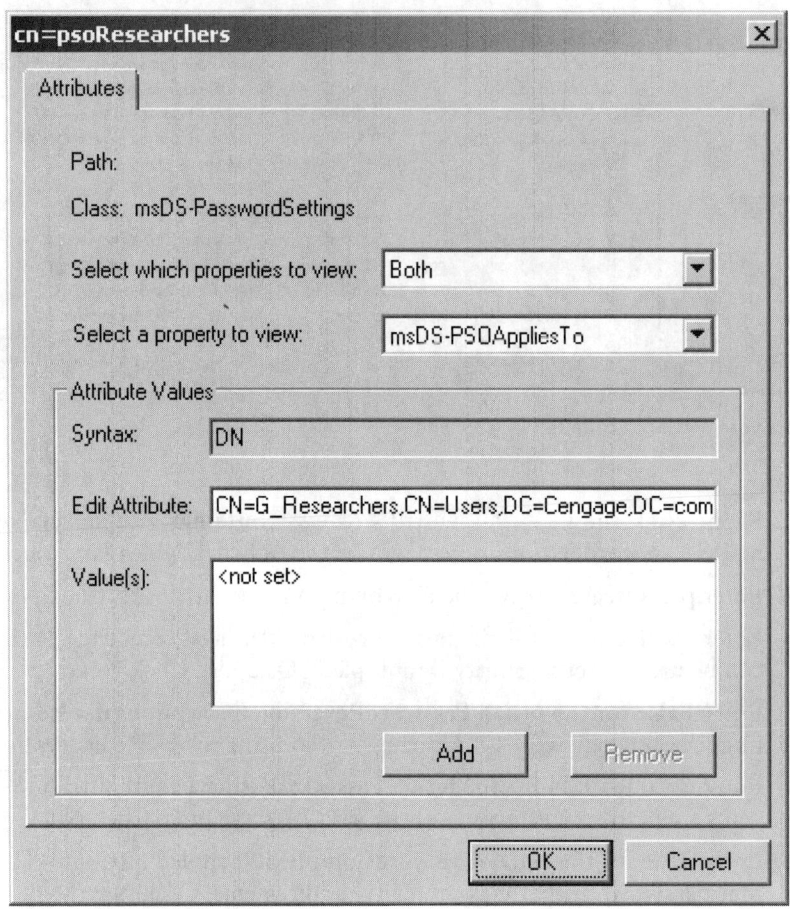

Figure 4-31 Linking the PSO to the G_Researchers group
Courtesy Course Technology/Cengage Learning

22. Click **Add** to add the DN as an attribute and link the group to the PSO. Click **OK**.
23. Click **Finish** in the **Create Object** dialog box.

At this point, the PSO is created, and the G_Researchers group is linked to it. All users added to the G_Researchers group will be affected by this PSO.

If you want to add more groups later, or modify the DN of the group you added, you can use ADSI Edit to browse to the same CN=Password Settings Container node. Right-click the PSO you created and select Properties. You can then modify the msDS-PSOAppliesTo property or any of the other properties that have been configured in the PSO.

Chapter Summary

- The two technical reasons to create an OU are to delegate control to a group of users and to apply GPOs. The Delegation of Control Wizard is used to delegate control of OUs to groups. The Group Policy Management console is used to manage GPOs.

- GPOs cannot be linked to the Users and Computers containers in Active Directory. These are not OUs; they are just containers.
- The redircmp and redirusr command-line commands can be used to redirect the default location of accounts. Computer accounts are normally created in the Computers container when a computer joins the domain, but the redircmp command can redirect new computer accounts to an OU that can be directly managed by a GPO.
- Group Policy objects (GPOs) can be linked to sites, domains, and OUs. When multiple GPOs are assigned and any of the settings have conflicts, the last setting applied wins. In other words, the settings of OUs take precedence over the settings in the site GPOs or domain GPOs.

- Two GPOs are created by default in a domain. The Default Domain policy applies to all objects in the domain. The Default Domain Controllers policy applies to the Domain Controllers OU, which holds all domain controllers by default. Both default policies can be modified.
- The Block Inheritance setting can be established on an OU to block all inherited OUs (except those configured with the Enforced option).
- The Enforced setting can be configured on a GPO to ensure that its settings are applied within the scope of the GPO. GPOs configured with Enforced cannot be overwritten by conflicting policies and cannot be blocked by the Block Inheritance setting.
- You filter GPOs by modifying the permissions. A GPO normally applies to the Authenticated Users group within the scope of the GPO, but the permissions can be changed so that the GPO is applied differently. The Deny Apply Group Policy permission can be configured so the policy does not apply to a group. Additionally, the Authenticated Users group can be removed and another group can be added to the GPO.
- Fine-grained policies can be implemented when the domain is in the domain functional level of Windows Server 2008. A password settings object (PSO) is created with ADSI Edit and applied to groups.

Key Terms

Block Inheritance A Group Policy option that can be applied to an OU. When enabled, GPO settings will not be inherited by any GPOs at higher levels unless a GPO has the Enforced GPO option enabled.

Default Domain Controllers policy A default Group Policy created when the domain is created. It applies to all objects in the domain controllers OU (which should be all the domain controllers in the domain as long as the domain controllers weren't moved).

Default Domain policy A default Group Policy created when the domain is created. It applies to all objects in the domain.

Delegation of Control Wizard A wizard used to delegate control and permissions in Active Directory Users and Computers. Permissions can be granted to groups at the domain and OU levels.

Distinguished name (DN) An LDAP name that uniquely identifies objects in Active Directory Domain Services (AD DS). DNs in AD DS typically have a domain component (DC), an OU component (OU), and a common name component (CN).

Enforced A Group Policy option that can be applied to a GPO. It will ensure that the GPO will be the winning GPO if any lower-level GPOs have conflicts. Additionally, it ensures that if an OU has the Block Inheritance policy set, the Enforced GPO will not be blocked.

GPO order of precedence The hierarchy of GPOs. GPOs are applied in the following order: site, domain, and OU. If there is a conflict, the settings that are applied last take precedence (unless the order is modified with the Enforced option or loopback processing).

Group Policy An administrative management tool that allows administrators to set a policy once in a Group Policy object (GPO) and apply the policy to all users in a domain, in an Organizational Unit (OU), or in a site. The GPO is linked to the site, domain, or OU using the Group Policy Management console (GPMC).

Group Policy Management console (GPMC) A management console used to manage Group Policy. You can create and link GPOs through the GPMC and manipulate different Group Policy settings.

Group Policy objects (GPOs) GPOs contain Group Policy settings and can be linked to sites, domains, and OUs.

loopback processing An advanced Group Policy setting. It makes Group Policy settings that apply to the computer take precedence over Group Policy settings that apply to the logged-on user.

redircmp A command-line tool that can be used to change the default location of newly created computers from the Computers container to a specified OU. This tool works when a computer account is created after the computer joins a domain.

redirusr A command-line tool that can be used to change the default location of newly created users from the Users container to a specified OU. This only works if the OU isn't specified when the account is created.

Windows Management Instrumentation (WMI) filtering A filtering tool that can be applied to GPOs. The tool makes the GPO apply only to computers that meet specific conditions. WMI filters use the WMI query language (WQL); only one WMI filter can be applied to a GPO.

Review Questions

1. You are creating the design of OUs for your company. The company has three departments: Sales, HR, and IT. Each department has one or more IT technicians assigned to manage all of the resources in the department. A global group has been created for each department as G_SalesAdmins, G_HRAdmins, and G_ITAdmins with the administrators in their respective groups. Each of these groups is a member of the Domain Admins group. You want to ensure that IT administrators can manage all of the resources in their department, but in no other departments. What should you do? (Choose two.)
    a. Create OUs for the three departments and delegate control of each group to their department OU only.
    b. Create OUs for the three departments and assign GPOs to each of the departments.
    c. Add each of the groups to the OU Admins group.
    d. Remove the department admin groups from the Domain Admins group.
2. You are designing an administrative solution for a three-domain forest. Each domain has a Sales OU and a group called G_SalesAdmins, which includes user accounts of administrators responsible for the sales department. You want to ensure that members of the G_SalesAdmins group in any domain can administer the Sales OU for each of the domains without compromising security. What should you do?
    a. Add the G_SalesAdmins group to the Domain Admins group in each domain.
    b. Add the G_SalesAdmins group from one domain to the G_SalesAdmins group in the other domain.
    c. Create a domain local group in one of the domains. Add each of the G_SalesAdmins groups to the domain local group. Delegate control of the domain local group to each of the OUs.
    d. Create a universal group. Add each of the G_SalesAdmins groups to the universal group. Delegate control of the universal group to each of the OUs.

3. You manage a one-domain forest. You want to ensure that any new computers in the domain automatically have GPO4 assigned to them, which ensures that the computer has extra security until its updates have been verified. GPO4 is linked to an OU named NewComputers. What should you do to ensure that GPO4 is applied to all new computers joined to the domain without affecting other computers?
   a. Direct personnel to add their computers to the NewComputers OU when they join the domain.
   b. Run the redirusr command.
   c. Run the redircmp command.
   d. Link GPO4 to the domain.
4. You are designing a plan that will use Group Policy in your domain. Several administrators will create GPOs that they'll link to OUs they manage. You want to ensure that each of these GPOs includes several basic settings. What should you use?
   a. Create a Starter GPO and import it into all of the other GPOs.
   b. Create a Starter GPO and use it as a template to create other GPOs.
   c. Create a GPO with the settings. Export a copy of this GPO and direct other administrators to import it into their GPOs.
   d. Modify the Default Domain policy GPO to include these settings.
5. You are an administrator for the Cengage.com domain, which includes a global group named G_DeptMgrs. Members of this group are managers of the different company departments, and this group has access to company documents that should not be shared with others. You are asked to create a solution to ensure that only department managers are members of this group. If anyone else is accidentally added, the person should automatically be removed. Your solution should require the least administrative effort. What would you do?
   a. Create a GPO to restrict group membership and link it to each of the department OUs.
   b. Create a GPO to restrict group membership and link it to the domain.
   c. Create a GPO to restrict group membership and apply a filter so that it only applies to members of the G_DeptMgrs group.
   d. Write a script to check the membership of the group and reconfigure it if it has been modified. Schedule the script to run on an hourly basis.
6. You are designing a Group Policy to deploy a desktop publishing application to users in the Publishing department within your company. All of these users are in a child OU named DTPub. Only 10 users should receive the application, and you want to ensure that the application is removed from their systems if they move out of the department. What should you do?
   a. Configure the GPO with filtering.
   b. Enable Block Inheritance on the DTPub OU.
   c. Configure the GPO to uninstall the application if it falls out of scope.
   d. Enable the Enforced option on the GPO.
7. You are designing GPOs for your domain and have created the following GPOs:
   - GPO1: Denies read and write access to USB flash drives
   - GPO2: Allows read and write access to USB flash drives

   Your domain includes several OUs, including the IT OU, the Sales OU, and the HR OU.

   You want to ensure that all users except those in the IT OU are prevented from using USB flash drives. What should you do?
   a. Link GPO1 to the domain and GPO2 to the IT OU.
   b. Link GPO2 to the domain and GPO1 to the IT OU.

   c. Link GPO1 to the domain and to the Users and Computers containers. Link GPO2 to the IT OU.
   d. Link GPO2 to the domain and use filtering so that it only applies to users in the IT OU.
8. Your single-domain forest includes three sites. Each site has access to the Internet through separate proxy servers. You need to design a GPO strategy that will configure the proxy server settings for all users in the domain. What should you do?
   a. Create a single GPO and link it to the domain.
   b. Create a single GPO and link it to each of the sites.
   c. Create three GPOs and link one to each site.
   d. Create four GPOs with one for each site and one for the domain.
9. You are designing GPOs for your domain and have created a GPO that will deny read and write access to USB flash drives. You want to ensure that this policy does not apply to users in the IT Admins group. About half of the users in the IT Admins group are in the IT OU. What should you do?
   a. Set Block Inheritance on the IT Admins group.
   b. Use Block Inheritance at the IT OU.
   c. Set Enforced at the IT OU.
   d. Filter the GPO.
10. Your administrative model includes several administrative groups. However, you need to ensure that only three specific users are members of the Domain Admins group. Members of the Domain Admins group are also members of the IT Admins group. If any more than the three users are mistakenly added to the Domain Admins group, you want to ensure that they are automatically removed. What should you do?
    a. Use GPO filtering on the Domain Admins group.
    b. Use GPO filtering on the IT Admins group.
    c. Use a GPO to restrict group membership of the Domain Admins group.
    d. Use a GPO to restrict group membership of the IT Admins group.
11. Your single-domain forest has an OU named Servers, which in turn has an OU named Financial Servers. Servers in the Financial Servers OU hold sensitive data. You're asked to create and apply a group policy to ensure that all data transferred with these servers is encrypted. What should you do?
    a. Create a GPO using the Server IPSec Policy. Apply this policy to the Servers OU.
    b. Create a GPO using the Server IPSec Policy. Apply this policy to the Financial Servers OU.
    c. Create a GPO using the Secure Server IPSec Policy. Apply this policy to the Servers OU.
    d. Create a GPO using the Secure Server IPSec Policy. Apply this policy to the Financial Servers OU.
12. Your domain includes users in the Consulting department who regularly travel, and users in the Sales and Training departments. OUs named Consulting, Sales, and Training have been created for each department, respectively. You need to design a GPO strategy that will prevent all users from using USB flash drives on computers, with the following exceptions:
    - Users in the Consulting department can use any USB flash drives.
    - Users in the Training department can use USB flash drives purchased by the company.

    What should you do?
    a. Create three GPOs. Link one to the domain to prevent use of the devices. Link a GPO to the Consulting OU to allow the use of devices, and link a GPO to the Training OU to allow the use of only specific devices.

b. Create three GPOs. Link one to the domain to prevent use of the devices. Link a GPO to the Training OU to allow the use of devices, and link a GPO to the Consulting OU to allow the use of only specific devices.

c. Create two GPOs. Link a GPO to the Consulting OU to allow the use of devices, and link a GPO to the Training OU to allow the use of only specific devices.

d. Create one GPO. Link it to the domain to prevent use of the devices. Use filtering to prevent the policy from applying to the Consulting OU or the Training OU.

13. Your company has a single domain with several offices configured as sites. The Miami location is one of the sites. You want to deploy an application to some of the users in the Miami location. These users are in a group named G_Mgrs. Other sites also have users in the G_Mgrs group. What should you do?

    a. Create a GPO and link it to the domain. Filter the GPO on the G_Mgrs group.

    b. Create a GPO and link it to the Miami site. Filter the GPO on the G_Mgrs group.

    c. Create a GPO and link it to the domain. Configure Block Inheritance for the G_Mgrs group.

    d. Create a GPO and link it to the Miami site. Configure Enforced for the G_Mgrs group.

14. Your organization is in a single-domain forest with multiple OUs that have been created for departments. Department personnel manage their own objects in their OUs. You want to install an application on all company computers using Group Policy. The application has one version for Windows XP and another version for Windows Vista and Windows 7. How should you design the GPOs to ensure that the correct application version is installed on the computers without affecting the current administrative model?

    a. Move all of the Windows XP computers to one OU and all of the Windows Vista and Windows 7 computers to another OU. Create two GPOs. Link the GPO with the Windows XP application version to one OU, and link the GPO with the other application version to the other OU.

    b. Create two GPOs. Associate two WMI filters to each GPO.

    c. Create one GPO with both versions of the application. Associate two WMI filters to the GPO.

    d. Create two GPOs with one for each version of the application. Associate a WMI filter with each GPO and link each GPO to the domain.

15. You are planning the GPO strategy for a group of computers that will be placed in the library. The computers will be secured with a GPO. You want to ensure that the GPO applied to the library computers takes precedence over any GPO applied to a user who logs on to a library computer. What should you do?

    a. Enable loopback processing.

    b. Enable Enforced on the OU where the GPO is applied.

    c. Disable Block Inheritance on the GPO.

    d. Configure the refresh time of the GPO to occur more frequently.

16. You are an administrator for a single-domain forest. The company has three locations configured as sites in Atlanta, Chicago, and New York. Each location has a separate OU named Atlanta, Chicago, and New York, respectively, but these OUs include clients hosted at the main location in Atlanta. You need to deploy an application to all users in the company, but want to reduce the amount of bandwidth used over WAN links. What should you do?

    a. Create a GPO to deploy the application and link it to the domain.

    b. Create three GPOs to deploy the application, with each GPO using a local server to host the application. Link a GPO to each OU.

   c. Create three GPOs to deploy the application, with each GPO using a local server to host the application. Link a GPO to each site.
   d. Create a single GPO to deploy the application. Link the GPO to each site.

17. Your enterprise includes two domains in the same forest: Cengage.com and Training.Cengage.com. The entire forest is located in a single location in Albany, New York. You need to deploy an application to all the client computers in the forest. What should you do?
   a. Create a GPO to deploy the application and link it to the forest.
   b. Create a GPO to deploy the application, link it to the parent domain Cengage.com, and enable inheritance to the child domain.
   c. Create a GPO to deploy the application and link it to the DefaultSiteName site.
   d. Create a GPO to deploy the application. Create a new OU in each domain. Link the GPO to the new OU.

18. You manage a small domain of about 100 users. All users and groups are in the Users container. You need to apply a GPO to users in the G_Marketing group. How should you proceed?
   a. Create a GPO and link it to the domain. Filter the GPO on the G_Marketing group.
   b. Create a GPO, link it to the Users container, and filter it based on the G_Marketing group.
   c. Create a GPO and link it to the G_Marketing group.
   d. Add an OU named Marketing. Create a GPO and link it to the Marketing OU.

19. You manage a single-domain forest in the forest functional level of Windows Server 2008. You want one group of administrators to manage all the users and computers in the Research and Development (R&D) department, and another group of administrators to manage all the users and computers in the rest of the company. Users in the R&D department should have more stringent password policies than other users. How can you achieve these goals with the least administrative effort?
   a. Create two domains. Place all the R&D objects in one domain and grant administrators rights in that domain. Leave the rest of the objects in the first domain and grant administrators rights in that domain. Create password policies in each domain.
   b. Create two OUs: R&D and Company. Delegate control of each OU to the appropriate groups. Set a domain policy for passwords. Create a PSO for the R&D department and link the PSO to a group that holds all of the users in the R&D department.
   c. Create two OUs: R&D and Company. Delegate control of each OU to the appropriate groups. Set a domain policy for passwords. Create a PSO for the R&D department and link the PSO to the R&D OU.
   d. Create two OUs: R&D and Company. Delegate control at the domain level for each of the groups. Set a domain policy for passwords. Create a PSO for the R&D department and link the PSO to a group that holds all of the users in the R&D department.

20. You are assisting a company in designing a plan to consolidate a two-domain forest into a one-domain forest. The second domain was originally created to support separate password policies. What should you ensure is included in the plant to support PSOs?
   a. The DC holding the PDC emulator must be running Windows Server 2008.
   b. All servers must be running Windows Server 2008.
   c. All DCs must be running Windows Server 2008.
   d. The forest functional level must be configured to Windows Server 2008.

21. You are designing a Group Policy strategy for your domain. GPO1 must be applied to all of the users in the domain except users in the Sales OU. GPO2 must only apply to users

in the Sales OU, and GPO3 must apply to all users in the domain. How should you apply these GPOs?

a. Link GPO1 and GPO3 to the domain. Link GPO2 to the Sales OU. Enable Block Inheritance on the Sales OU. Set Enforced on GPO3.

b. Link GPO1 and GPO3 to the domain. Link GPO2 to the Sales OU. Enable Block Inheritance on GPO2. Set Enforced at the domain.

c. Link GPO3 to the domain and GPO2 to the Sales OU. Link GPO1 to all OUs except the Sales OU.

d. Link GPO1 and GPO2 to all OUs. Link GPO2 to the Sales OU.

22. You want to deploy an application using a GPO. However, you only want the GPO to apply to users in the Sales department. Users in the Sales department are also in the Sales OU. What's the easiest way to deploy the application?

    a. Link the GPO to the Sales group.

    b. Link the GPO to the Sales OU.

    c. Link the GPO to the domain and filter the GPO based on the Sales group.

    d. Link the GPO to the domain and apply a PSO.

23. Your domain currently has a single-account lockout policy that locks out an account after five bad password attempts. The account will be locked out for 30 minutes. Users in the IT Admins OU are in a global group named G_IT Admins. You want to assign these users an account lockout policy that locks their account after three bad password attempts, and you want these accounts to remain locked until an administrator unlocks the account. You don't want to affect other users. What should you do?

    a. Modify the Default Domain policy.

    b. Create a GPO and assign it to the IT Admins OU.

    c. Create a PSO and link it to the G_IT Admins group.

    d. Create a PSO and link it to the IT Admins OU.

24. Your single-domain forest has two domain controllers running Windows Server 2003. The domain currently has a password policy applied to all users, requiring them to use passwords of at least 8 characters and to change their password every 60 days. You need to require any users in the Domain Admins or Enterprise Admins groups to have passwords of at least 15 characters and to change their password every 30 days. How can this be accomplished?

    a. Upgrade the DCs to Windows Server 2008. Update the domain functional level to Windows Server 2008. Update the forest functional level to Windows Server 2008. Create a PSO-enabled GPO and link it to the domain.

    b. Upgrade the DCs to Windows Server 2008. Update the domain functional level to Windows Server 2008. Create a PSO and link it to the domain.

    c. Upgrade the DCs to Windows Server 2008. Update the domain functional level to Windows Server 2008. Create a PSO and link it to the Domain Admins and Enterprise Admins groups.

    d. Upgrade the DCs to Windows Server 2008. Update the domain functional level to Windows Server 2008. Create a PSO-enabled GPO and link it to the Domain Admins and Enterprise Admins groups.

25. You manage a single-domain forest using Windows Server 2003 member servers and Windows Server 2008 domain controllers. The current domain functional level is Windows Server 2008. A password of a researcher in your organization was recently cracked and the account was accessed. You need to design a plan that will allow members of the Researchers

OU to have a separate password policy. You cannot change the operating system on any servers. What should be done?

a. Create a separate domain. Create a GPO with a more stringent password policy. Move researchers into this domain.

b. Create a GPO with a more stringent password policy and link it to the Researchers OU.

c. Create a PSO and link it to the Researchers OU.

d. Create a PSO and link it to a group that holds the researcher accounts.

Case Projects

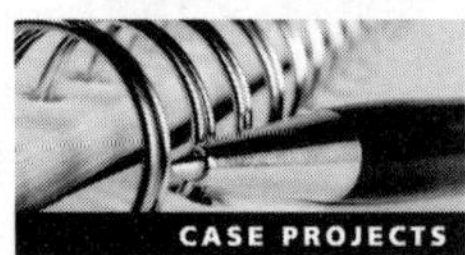

Case Project 4-1: Designing OUs

You are reviewing a design plan for an organization that will move to Windows Server 2008. They plan to create a one-domain forest. The organization has five departments named Sales, Marketing, Human Resources, Accounting, and Information Technology. Each department except Human Resources will have an administrator responsible for creating and managing all of the accounts in the department. Personnel in the IT department will manage the HR department resources. An accounting application will be deployed via Group Policy to about half the users in the Accounting department.

Create a design for the OUs used in this organization. Explain your answers.

Case Project 4-2: Designing GPOs

You are designing a Group Policy plan for your organization. The OU structure of the domain is shown in Figure 4-32. All groups for each department are held in the primary OU. In other words, all of the groups for the IT department (including the Tier 1 and Tier 2 divisions) are in the IT OU. All groups in the Accounting department are in the Acct OU. You need to use the existing OU structure and you can create as many GPOs as necessary. Your GPOs need to achieve the following goals:

- All users should be prevented from installing new devices on their system.
- All users in the Accounting department need to have an accounting application installed on their computers.
- Half of the users in the Accounts Receivable (AR) division are in a global group named G_Auditors and need to have a specialized line-of-business (LOB) application installed on their systems.
- Membership in the G_Auditors group should be controlled through Group Policy.

Identify the GPOs you'll create and where they will be linked. Generically identify what the GPO will do, such as install an application. It's not necessary to provide the details of the actual settings.

Case Project 4-3: Server Postinstallation Tasks

You need to design a Group Policy strategy that will allow you to have GPO1 apply to all the users and computers in the domain, except for the objects in the Sales OU. GPO2 needs to be applied to all objects in the domain without exceptions. GPO3 needs to be applied to all the objects in the Public OU, and the settings for the computers in the OU should take precedence over settings for individual users. What would you implement?

Case Project 4-4: Designing Multiple Password Policies

Your organization is in a single-domain forest that runs in the Windows Server 2003 domain functional level and Windows Server 2003 forest functional level. Servers and domain controllers are running both Windows Server 2003 and Windows Server 2008 operating

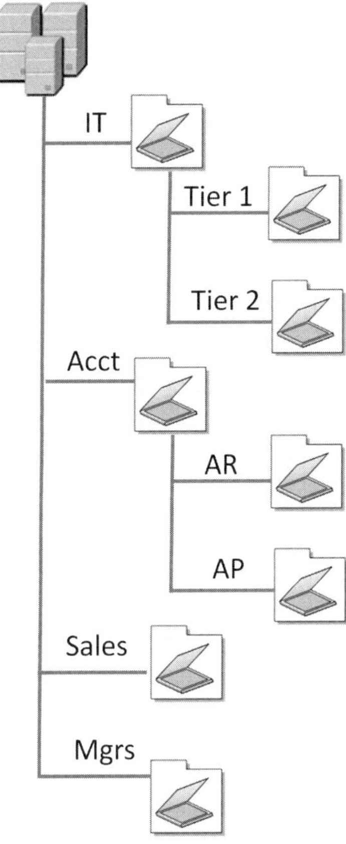

Figure 4-32 Case project OU structure
Courtesy Course Technology/Cengage Learning

systems. The current password policy requires users to have 8-character passwords and to change their passwords every 60 days. Management would like to impose a policy that requires administrators in the Domain Admins, Enterprise Admins, or IT Admins groups to have a password of 15 characters and to change it every 30 days. What needs to be done to support this plan?

chapter 5

Designing Remote Access and Terminal Services Strategies

After reading this chapter and completing the exercises, you will be able to:

- Design a network access solution
- Identify the best tunneling protocol to use with a VPN
- Identify the components of Network Access Protection
- Design a NAP solution to meet specific goals
- Choose the appropriate NAP enforcement method
- Plan for the deployment of Terminal Services
- Identify the purpose and use of different Terminal Services components
- Plan for Terminal Services licensing

Workers are often mobile and need access to internal networks from external or remote locations. This is achieved by designing a remote access solution for dial-up or VPN access. The Network Policy and Access Services server role provides all the tools needed to plan and implement a remote access solution.

Network Policy and Access Services also includes tools for ensuring that clients meet specific health requirements. These tools, known as Network Access Protection, include several components for verifying that clients have a firewall enabled, that antivirus and antispyware software are installed and up to date, and that the clients are current with Microsoft updates. Noncompliant or unhealthy computers can be restricted to certain portions of the network to get updates or applications needed to become healthy. Healthy clients can be granted unrestricted access.

Terminal Services includes technologies that allow users to run applications or full-blown desktops on terminal servers. This can be useful to support thin clients and to allow applications to run on a wide variety of clients. Terminal Services requires client access licenses for each client connection, and any Terminal Services design must include details on Terminal Services licensing.

Readers should have been exposed to in-depth details for the topics in this chapter while preparing for the 70-643 exam. 70-643 is focused on configuring and the 70-647 exam is focused on designing and planning. The goal of this chapter isn't to dwell on configuration, but instead to provide the relevant information needed to create a successful design incorporating the configuration tools.

Designing Remote Access

Remote access technologies allow users to access a network from a remote location. As an example, users may regularly travel and require access to servers or other resources in the internal network while on the road. A **remote access server** can be used to provide this access.

Access to remote networks is provided through either a dial-up connection or a **virtual private network** (VPN) connection.

- **Dial-up**. The remote access client has a modem and access to a phone line, and the remote access server has at least one modem and is connected to a phone line. The client can dial in to the remote access server, which provides access to resources in the internal network.
- **VPN**. A VPN is used to provide access to a private network over a public network. The public network is most often the Internet, but it can also be semi-private leased lines. Tunneling protocols are used to tunnel through the public network to provide security.

Figure 5-1 shows how remote access could be implemented for both dial-up and VPN connections. In the figure, the remote access server is configured as both a VPN server and a dial-up server.

A remote access server has many names. When configured with both dial-up and VPN connections, it can be called a network access server. If it's configured with VPN connections only, it is commonly called a VPN server. A VPN server is just a more specific term for a remote access server, similar to how an SUV is a more specific term for an automobile. A remote access server configured with dial-up access only would not be considered a VPN server.

Notice that the remote access server is placed in the perimeter network between two firewalls, which is commonly called a demilitarized zone (DMZ). The VPN server needs two network interface cards (NICs); clients connect to one NIC with a public IP address, and the second NIC connects to the internal network. Going through the firewall is often a challenge in larger enterprises because specific ports must be opened to allow the traffic. It's not very difficult to open the ports, but security administrators that manage the firewall view every open port as an additional risk.

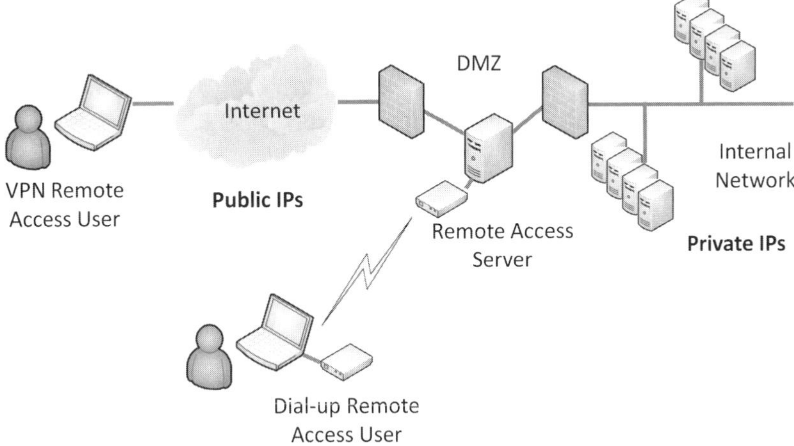

Figure 5-1 A remote access server configured for dial-up and VPN access

Courtesy Course Technology/Cengage Learning

Requests to modify existing security policies and open additional ports require a significant amount of justification. As an overall security practice, open ports are kept to a minimum.

It's also possible to have just a single firewall, with the remote access server either hosted on the Internet or on the internal network. Hosting the server on the Internet adds a lot of risk. If the remote access server is hosted on the internal network with just a single firewall, the firewall often uses network address translation (NAT) to translate the public IP addresses from the Internet to private IP addresses on the internal network.

Tunneling Protocols

When VPN connections are used, the traffic must pass through public networks, making them susceptible to eavesdropping or sniffing attacks unless the traffic is protected. A VPN connection uses a tunneling protocol to protect against attacks and provide the virtual private connection. A tunneling protocol encapsulates and encrypts the traffic between the client and the back-end network so that the traffic isn't readable on the public network.

Windows Server 2008 provides three choices for tunneling protocols:

- **Point-to-Point Tunneling Protocol (PPTP)** is the oldest of the three VPN tunneling protocols. It uses Microsoft Point-to-Point Encryption (MPPE) to encrypt the data.
- **Layer 2 Tunneling Protocol (L2TP)** uses IPSec to secure the connection. IPSec provides significantly better security than MPPE used with PPTP. However, NAT will corrupt IP packets protected with IPSec, so if the VPN connection must pass through a connection using NAT, L2TP/IPSec cannot be used.
- **Secure Socket Tunneling Protocol (SSTP)** uses Hypertext Transfer Protocol (HTTP) over a Secure Sockets Layer (SSL) connection to secure the connection. SSTP is the newest of the three tunneling protocols. HTTP over SSL is commonly referred to as HTTPS and uses port 443 by default. This option is much more secure than PPTP and more flexible than L2TP/IPSec.

Choosing a Tunneling Protocol

When designing a VPN solution, you'll need to identify the tunneling protocol(s) that you'll use. The three tunneling protocols have different strengths and weaknesses that will affect your choice. Design considerations for all three protocols are shown in Table 5-1.

Before Windows Server 2008, L2TP/IPSec was recommended as the first solution unless you needed to go through NAT. If NAT was used, you could weaken security and use PPTP, but it was recognized as a less than ideal solution. SSTP provides a more secure and flexible alternative than PPTP.

Table 5-1 Choosing a tunneling protocol

	Client support	Public key infrastructure (PKI)	Security provided	Firewall access
PPTP	All currently supported Windows clients (Windows 2000 and newer) support PPTP.	PPTP doesn't require the use of certificates, so a PKI is not needed.	Data confidentiality by encryption. PPTP does not include data integrity, data authentication, or machine authentication.	PPTP uses TCP port 1723. It is not affected by NAT.
L2TP/ IPSec	All currently supported Windows clients (Windows 2000 and newer) support L2TP/IPSec.	L2TP uses IPSec for security. Certificates are recommended for IPSec authentication and a PKI is required to issue the certificates. While it's possible to use a shared key (shared secret or shared password) with IPSec, it isn't as secure and isn't recommended for a production server.	Data confidentiality, data integrity, data authentication, and machine authentication. Confidentiality is provided by encrypting the data. Data integrity and data authentication provide assurances that the data has not been modified in transit. Machine authentication provides assurances that the data is being received from a specific system. Of the three choices, L2TP/IPSec is the most secure.	Because IPSec is corrupted by NAT, the VPN traffic must be configured so it is not going through a network device with NAT installed. This is easily achievable when the remote access server is placed in a DMZ.
SSTP	Only Windows Vista SP1 or newer clients are supported. Windows XP clients cannot use SSTP.	SSTP uses SSL to secure the connection, and SSL requires a certificate from a PKI.	Data confidentiality, data integrity, and data authentication. This provides more security than PPTP, but it does not include the machine authentication provided by L2TP/IPSec.	SSTP uses HTTPS, which uses port 443 by default, so port 443 needs to be open on the firewall to support SSTP. If a Web server is already being hosted by the company, this port is probably already open, making SSTP easier to implement.

Adding the Remote Access Service on Windows Server 2008

You can create a network access solution using the **Network Policy and Access Services** role on Windows Server 2008. This role includes multiple services used for remote access, routing, RADIUS, and Network Access Protection.

Figure 5-2 shows the available services for Network Policy and Access Services. The Remote Access Service is the primary service used to allow remote users to connect to a private network using either dial-up or VPN connections. You can see that the role has several other available services.

Other available services in the Network Policy and Access Services role are:

- **Network Policy Server (NPS)**. The NPS service can be added to allow the server to act as a Remote Authentication Dial-in User Service (RADIUS) or to enforce **Network Access Protection (NAP)**. Both RADIUS and NAP will be explored in more depth later in this chapter.
- **Routing**. The Routing service allows the server to act as a router. While it is possible to use this service to configure a Windows Server 2008 server as a router, it's rare to do so exclusively. A dedicated hardware router is much more efficient and affordable than a full-blown server configured as a router.
- **Health Registration Authority (HRA)**. The HRA is used in conjunction with a NAP solution. It can be used to issue health certificates for clients if a client meets certain conditions predetermined by the administrator. The HRA gets certificates from a certification authority (CA).
- **Host Credential Authorization Protocol (HCAP)**. The HCAP can be used to integrate Cisco's Network Access Control Server with Microsoft's NAP solution.

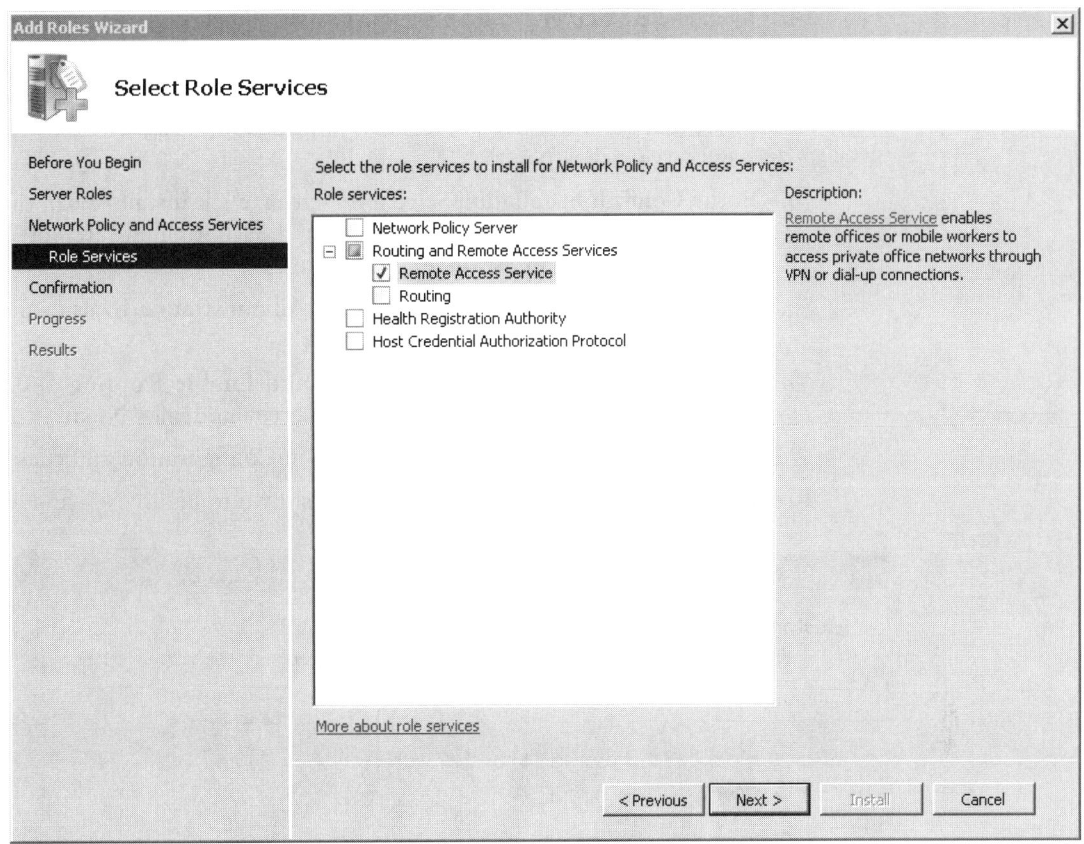

Figure 5-2 Adding the Remote Access Service
Courtesy Course Technology/Cengage Learning

You can use Activity 5-1 to add the Network Policy and Access Services role with only the Remote Access Service. Once this service is added, you'll be able to view, add, and configure network access policies.

Activity 5-1: Installing the Remote Access Service

Time Required: 20 minutes
Objective: Install the Remote Access Service in preparation for creating a remote access solution.

Description: You are planning to add a VPN server to your network and need to add the Network Policy and Access Services role with the Remote Access Service. This activity can be performed on DC1, which was created and used in earlier chapters.

While it's OK to install the Remote Access Service on a domain controller in a test environment, you would not do so in a production environment. A remote access server would be accessible from the Internet, but making the domain controller accessible from the Internet makes it unnecessarily susceptible to attacks. If an attacker can gain access to the domain controller and crack administrative accounts, he can compromise the entire domain.

1. Start **DC1** and log on with the **Administrator** account.
2. Start **Server Manager** via the **Administrative Tools** menu.
3. Select **Roles** and click **Add Roles**. Review the information on the **Before You Begin** screen and click **Next**.

4. On the **Select Server Roles** screen, select the check box next to **Network Policy and Access Services.** Click **Next** twice.
5. Select the check box next to **Remote Access Service** on the **Select Role Services** screen. Notice that several other services can be added, but they are not needed for a remote access server. Click **Next.**
6. On the **Confirm Installation Selections** screen, click **Install.** When the installation has been completed, click **Close.** At this point, the **Routing and Remote Access** console is available on the **Administrative Tools** menu.
7. Start **Routing and Remote Access** via the **Administrative Tools** menu. Notice that the service is installed, but not yet configured.
8. Right-click **DC1** and select **Configure and Enable Routing and Remote Access.** Review the information on the **Welcome** screen and click **Next.**
9. On the **Configuration** screen, select **Custom Configuration** and click **Next.**
10. Select **VPN access** and **Dial-up access,** as shown in Figure 5-3, and click **Next.**

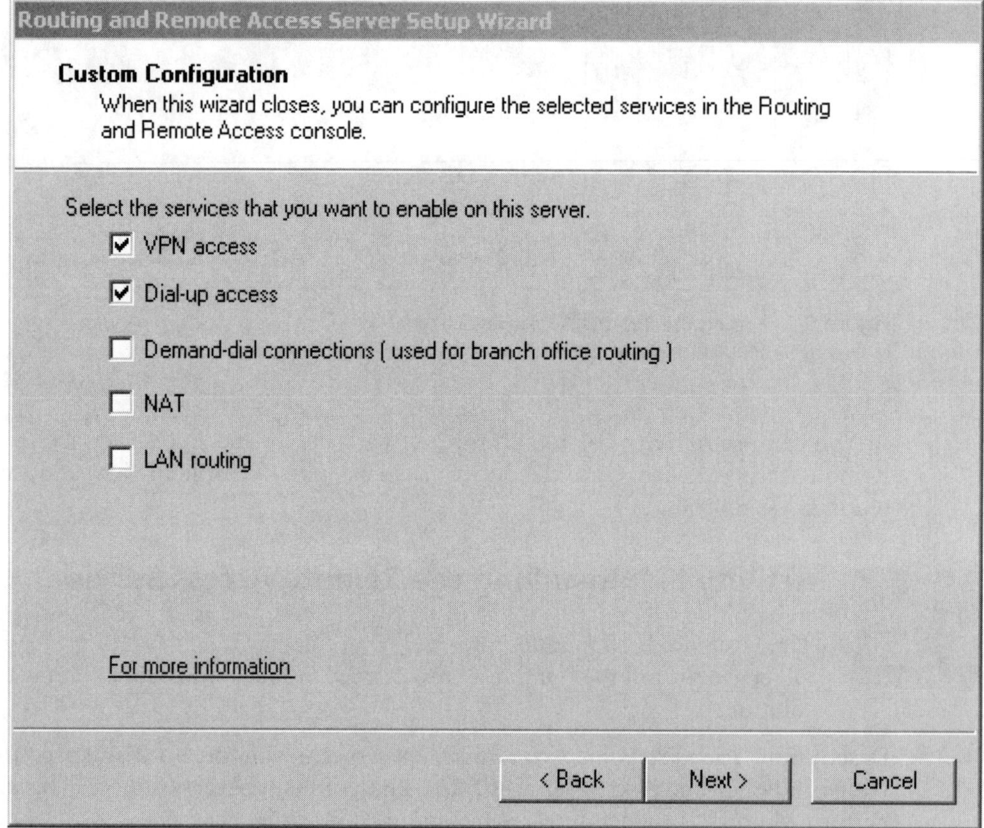

Figure 5-3 Configuring the remote access server for both VPN access and dial-up access
Courtesy Course Technology/Cengage Learning

11. Review the information on the **Completion** screen and click **Finish.** When prompted to start the Routing and Remote Access service, click the **Start Service** button.

Network Access Policies

A **network access policy** is used to determine which users are granted access to a remote access server. In previous versions of Windows Server, the policies were configurable from the Routing and Remote Access console. In Windows Server 2008, the policies are accessible using the Network Policy Server console.

Policies have four primary components:

- **Conditions.** One or more conditions can be configured for any policy, and the condition(s) determine if the policy is used. Conditions can include membership in a group, day and time of a connection, IP addresses used, and more. If the condition is met, the policy is used and no other policies are checked. If the conditions of a policy are not met, the next policy is checked. If conditions are not met for any policy, access is not granted.

The order of the policies is important to consider when designing remote access. Only one policy will be used for any connection, and the policy used is determined by the first policy that meets the conditions. For example, if the first policy has a single condition of any time of any day in the week, and the policy denies access, access will be denied for all connections and no other policies will be checked. Similarly, if no policies exist, the conditions of a policy cannot be met and access will be denied.

- **Permissions.** Permissions can be set to Allow or Deny within the policy to control access to the remote access server. Figure 5-4 shows how the policy permissions can be overridden by checking Access is determined by User Dial-in properties. This setting causes the permissions set in the Active Directory user account (on the dial-in tab of the user's properties) to be used instead. By default, this check box is unchecked, causing the user account dial-in properties to be ignored.

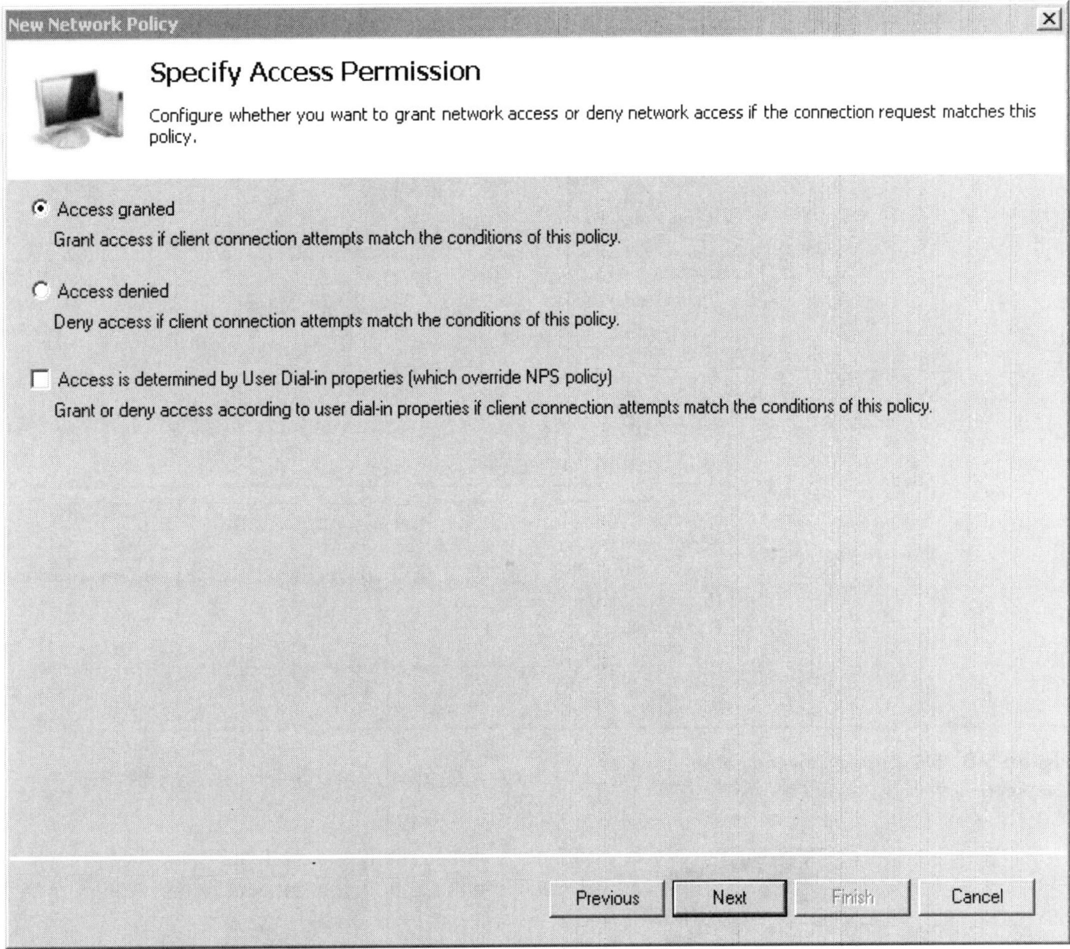

Figure 5-4 Network access policy permissions

Courtesy Course Technology/Cengage Learning

- **Constraints.** Constraints specify other settings that must be met for the connection, including the authentication method used, idle timeout settings, session timeout settings, and more. All the constraints must be met for the connection. If a constraint is not met, the connection is stopped. For example, if the client was not able to use the authentication method required by the server, the connection would be refused. Or, if the client exceeded the idle timeout period, the connection would be disconnected.
- **Settings.** Additional settings are applied to the connection once the conditions and constraints are met.

When the Remote Access Service is added, two default policies are added. Figure 5-5 shows the two default policies that are available in the Network Policy Server (NPS) console. The icon of the white X in the red circle indicates that each policy is configured to deny access. In other words, access to the server will not be granted by either default policy unless it is modified. Notice also that the processing order is set to 999998 and 999999. If any policies are added, they will have a processing order with a lower number, and will be used before the default policies unless the order is modified.

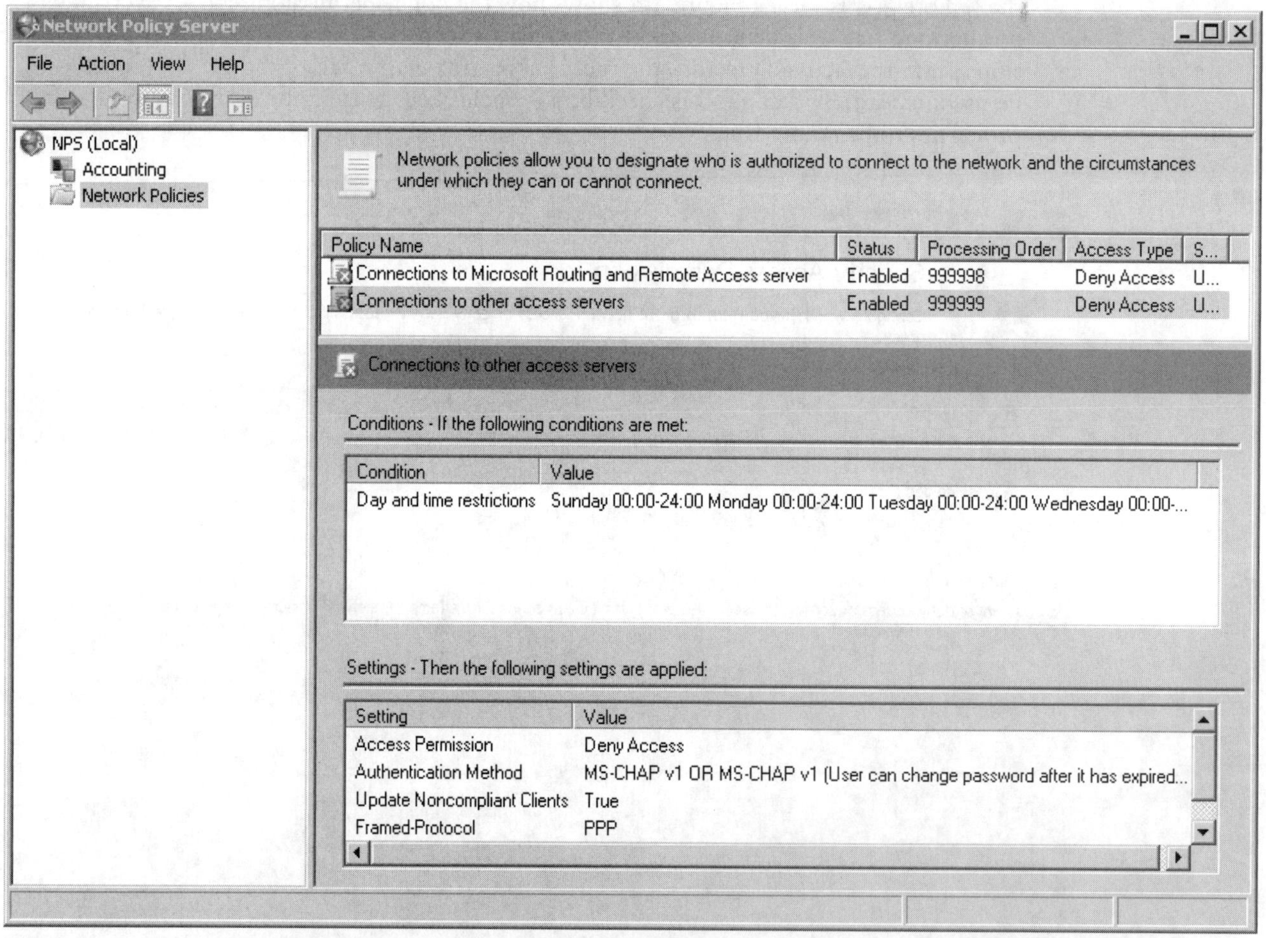

Figure 5-5 NPS console showing default policies

Courtesy Course Technology/Cengage Learning

The NPS console has many more capabilities when the NPS service is added. You'll see this later in the Network Access Protection section.

The following activity shows how to add a basic policy to provide access for a remote access server.

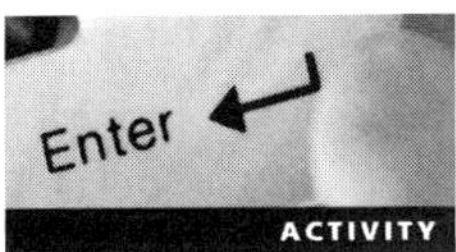

Activity 5-2: Adding a Network Access Policy

Time Required: 15 minutes
Objective: Add a network access policy to support VPN users.

Description: You have added a VPN server and you want to allow domain users to connect Monday through Friday between 7 a.m. and 7 p.m. You need to add a policy to support this plan. This activity should be performed on DC1, which was used in the previous activity.

1. Start **DC1** and log on with the **Administrator** account.
2. Start **Routing and Remote Access** via the **Administrative Tools** menu.
3. Expand the server and select **Remote Access Logging and Policies.** Right-click **Remote Access Logging and Policies** and select **Launch NPS** to start the NPS console.
4. Right-click **Network Policies** and select **New.**
5. Type **Domain Users** as the **Policy Name.** Select **Remote Access Server (VPN-Dial up)** as the **Type of Network Access Server** and click **Next.**
6. On the **Specify Conditions** screen, click **Add.** Select **User Groups** and click **Add.** Click **Add Groups.** Type **Domain Users** and click **OK** twice.
7. On the Specify Conditions screen, click **Add** again. Scroll down and select the **Day and Time Restrictions.** Click **Add.** Select the timeframe between 7 a.m. and 7 p.m. Monday through Friday, as shown in Figure 5-6, and then click **Permitted.** Click **OK.** On the Specify Conditions screen, click **Next.**

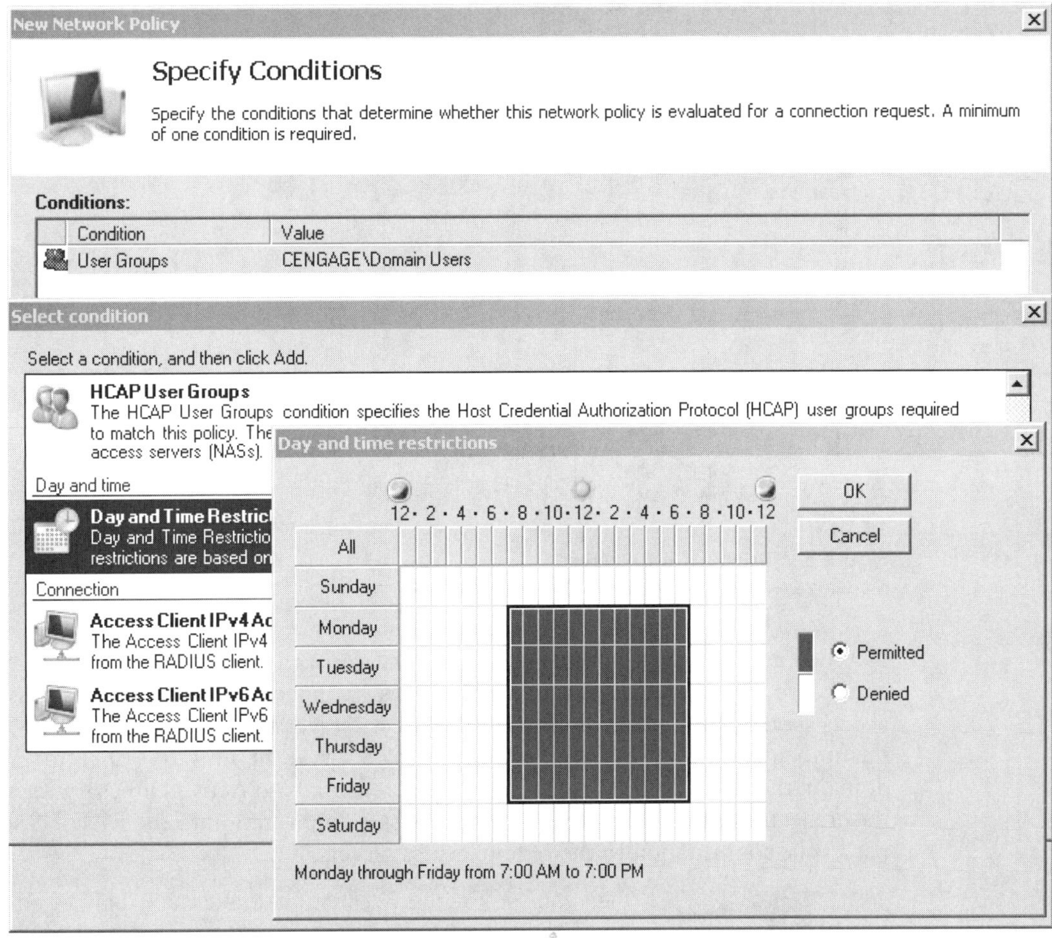

Figure 5-6 Configuring a day and time restriction for a network policy
Courtesy Course Technology/Cengage Learning

8. On the **Specify Access Permissions** screen, accept the default setting of **Access Granted.** Click **Next.**
9. Review the information on the **Configure Authentication** screen. Accept the default authentication methods and click **Next.**
10. Review the information on the **Configure Constraints** screen. Accept the default settings and click **Next.**
11. Review the information on the **Configure Settings** screen. Accept the default settings and click **Next.**
12. Review the information on the **Completing New Network Policy** screen and click **Finish.**

Using a RADIUS Server

A **Remote Authentication Dial-in User Service (RADIUS)** server can be used for central authentication and logging. A Windows Server 2008 server can be used as a RADIUS server by adding the NPS service, which is part of the Network Policy and Access Services. You don't need a RADIUS server if you have only one remote access server. However, if you have multiple remote access servers, it can be valuable. Consider Figure 5-7, which shows four remote access servers.

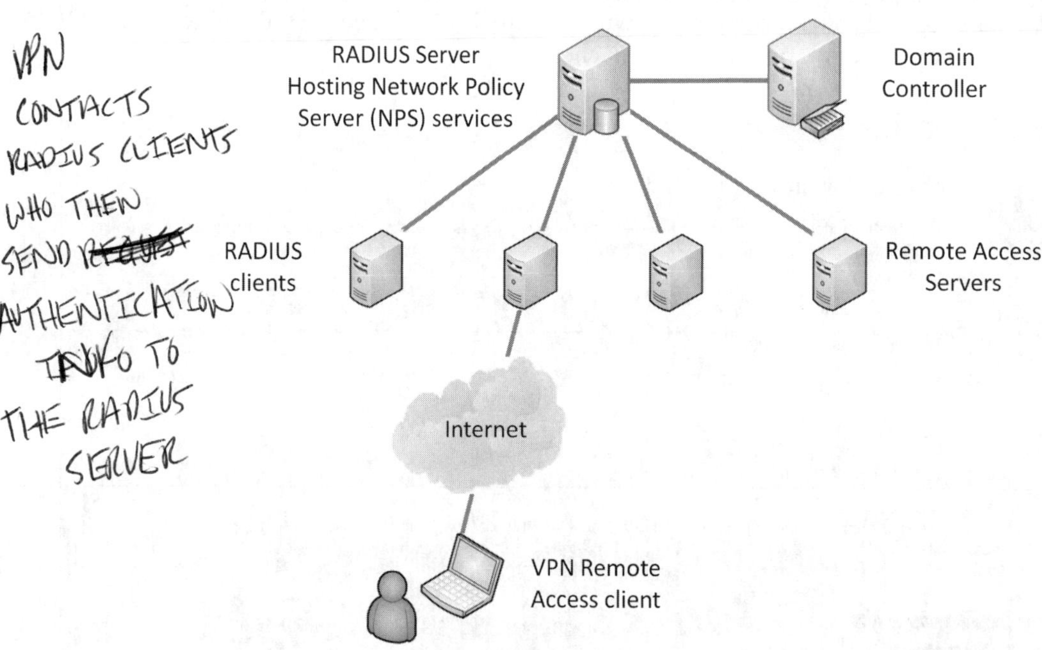

Figure 5-7 Using a RADIUS server
Courtesy Course Technology/Cengage Learning

When using multiple remote access servers, you can use a single RADIUS server. Clients can connect to any remote access server. When they connect, authentication is passed to the remote access server from the client. The remote access server then acts as a RADIUS client and passes the authentication information to the RADIUS server. In an Active Directory Domain Services domain, the RADIUS server will pass these credentials to Active Directory for authentication. If the credentials are valid, Active Directory passes confirmation to the RADIUS server, which then passes the confirmation to the remote access server.

When you see the term "client," you normally think of an end-user system. However, the remote access servers are clients of the RADIUS servers, so they are also known as RADIUS clients.

Users can access any remote access server and experience the same level of service. In addition to providing centralized authentication, the RADIUS server can provide the following:

- **Centralized logging.** Instead of each remote access server maintaining separate logs for remote access clients, all logs can be maintained on the RADIUS server.
- **Centralized policies.** When a RADIUS server is configured to be used for authentication, only the policies on the RADIUS server are used. If a change is required in any network access policy, you can modify the policy on the RADIUS server; you don't need to modify it on each remote access server.

You can add the Network Policy and Access Services role with the NPS service to a Windows Server 2008 server. The NPS service can be used to allow the server to act as a RADIUS server. Each remote access server would then be configured to use the RADIUS server.

Figure 5-8 shows the Routing and Remote Access console with the properties of a remote access server. The Security tab is selected.

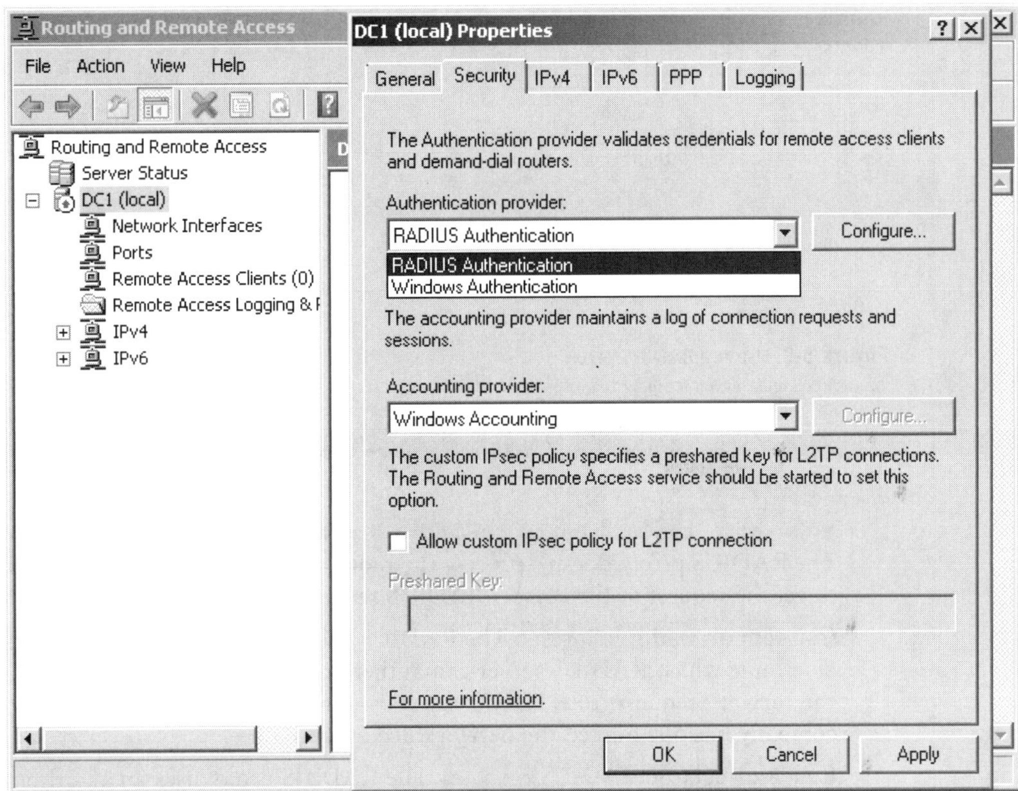

Figure 5-8 Configuring a remote access server for RADIUS authentication

Courtesy Course Technology/Cengage Learning

Windows Authentication and Windows Accounting are selected by default. If a RADIUS server is used, RADIUS Authentication and RADIUS Accounting are selected. You then add information about the RADIUS server so the remote access server can connect to it.

Using a RADIUS Proxy

In organizations that use several RADIUS servers, a **RADIUS proxy** server can be implemented as a central switching or routing point. All RADIUS client requests will go through the RADIUS proxy, which determines which RADIUS server should handle the request.

Remember that a single remote access server can serve multiple end-user clients and a single RADIUS server can support multiple remote access servers (configured as RADIUS clients). If the organization needs more than one RADIUS server, it is supporting a significant number of end users.

Figure 5-9 shows how a RADIUS proxy would be configured within a network. Clients will still connect with a remote access server normally. However, the remote access server forwards authentication requests to a RADIUS proxy instead of directly to the RADIUS server. The RADIUS proxy then sends the authentication request to the appropriate RADIUS server.

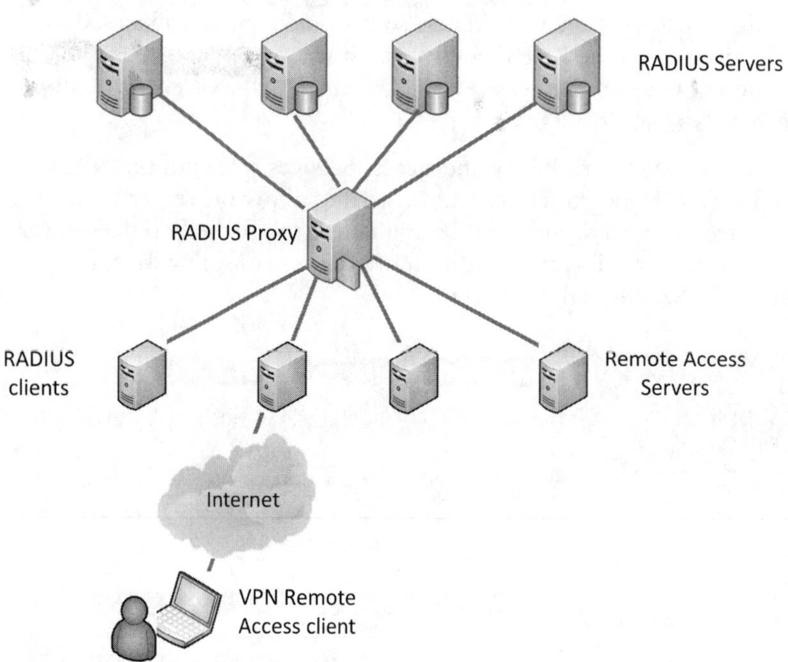

Figure 5-9 Using a RADIUS proxy
Courtesy Course Technology/Cengage Learning

When considering the use of a RADIUS proxy, you should keep the following points in mind. The RADIUS proxy:

- **Will receive requests from remote access servers and forward them to a RADIUS server.** The RADIUS proxy doesn't process the requests itself, but instead just acts as the gateway to get the request to the correct RADIUS server.
- **Can support multiple forests.** The RADIUS proxy can analyze the connection request and determine which RADIUS server can authenticate the requests. The RADIUS proxy server can forward requests to RADIUS servers in different forests. This ability is valuable when a company has outsourced the network access solution.
- **Can load-balance RADIUS requests.** The RADIUS proxy uses an algorithm to dynamically balance the load between multiple RADIUS servers.
- **Can interact with non-Microsoft environments.** The RADIUS proxy can forward requests to RADIUS servers that use something other than Microsoft Active Directory for authentication.

Network Access Protection

Network Access Protection (NAP) is new in Windows Server 2008, and can be used to provide added layers of protection for a network. In short, NAP ensures that any supported client that connects to a network is healthy. It can be used in conjunction with a remote access solution, or by itself within a network.

From a security perspective, remote access clients are the hardest to secure. Within a network, administrators can secure the computers with Group Policy; ensure that they regularly receive updates, have anti-malware software installed, and have virus signatures updated regularly; and perform a myriad of other checks and controls.

However, clients that connect via remote access are not necessarily controlled by the administrators. There's no guarantee that the clients have the firewall enabled, that current updates are installed, that up-to-date anti-malware is installed, or that clients are otherwise secured—unless you use NAP. With NAP, you can design a policy that specifies the requirements for a healthy client. When the supported client connects, it can be inspected to see if it meets the requirements; if it does, the client will be issued a health certificate.

Additionally, NAP can help you protect more than just remote access clients. It can extend this protection to clients connecting internally, depending on the components used. Overall, NAP has the following goals:

- **Health state validation.** NAP can identify what is considered healthy for a client and validate a client that has met the health requirements.
- **Network access limitation.** If a client does not meet health requirements, access to the network can be completely restricted or limited to an isolated portion of the network. This isolated portion is used to house remediation servers.
- **Automatic remediation.** Clients that are not compliant with the policy can become compliant without user intervention.
- **Ongoing compliance.** Clients are periodically checked to ensure that they continue to meet the health state. If a computer becomes noncompliant, the health state can be lost and network access can be limited.

Components of NAP

The architecture of a NAP solution has many different components. Refer to Figure 5-10 as you read about these components. This discussion focuses on using NAP for a VPN connection, but later in the chapter, you'll see how NAP can be used to enforce other connections.

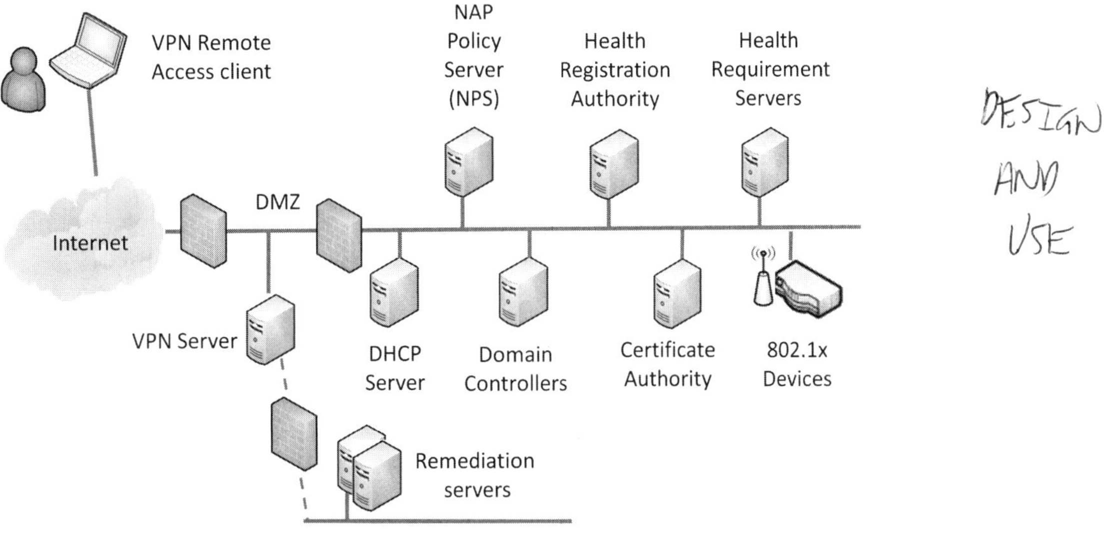

Figure 5-10 Components of a NAP solution
Courtesy Course Technology/Cengage Learning

- **NAP clients.** Clients need to be running Windows XP SP3, Windows Vista SP1, or Windows 7 to support the health validation process. Compatible clients have **System Health Agents (SHAs)** that regularly inspect the system and **System Health Validators (SHVs)** that can provide a **System Statement of Health (SSoH)**. The SSoH includes information such as how Microsoft updates are performed, the state of the firewall, and the state of anti-malware software. In the figure, the remote access client is the NAP client.

The client SHV monitors the settings in the Windows Security Center for Windows XP SP3 and Windows Vista. In Windows 7, the Action Center is monitored.

- **VPN server.** This is a Windows Server 2008 server with the Routing and Remote Access service installed and configured as a VPN server.
- **NAP servers.** Two servers are involved in the enforcement of a NAP policy: the NPS and a Health Registration Authority (HRA). These servers need to be running at least Windows Server 2008. It is possible to have a single server host both services.
- **NPS.** A Windows Server 2008 server with the NPS service added as part of the Network Policy and Access Services role. Policies are defined on this server for NAP clients and server-based SHVs can be configured on the NPS. The NPS server is also called the NAP health server in some documentation. NPS is not necessarily a separate server, but instead a server that holds the policies used to define health.
- **HRA.** A Windows Server 2008 server with the HRA service added as part of the Network Policy and Access Services role, and the Internet Information Services (IIS) role. Clients send their SSoH to the HRA server. If the client's SSoH indicates that the client is in compliance with the policy, the HRA obtains a health certificate from a certification authority (CA) and sends it to the client. The NAP server and CA must be installed on the network for the HRA to operate.

Chapter 6 covers the components of a public key infrastructure (PKI), including certificate services and CAs.

- **Health Requirement Servers.** These servers are used by clients to remain healthy. For example, a Windows Server Update Services (WSUS) server can be used to download updates, or a file server may host antivirus or antispyware application software that can be downloaded and installed. These servers are also referred to as remediation servers.
- **DHCP.** Dynamic Host Configuration Protocol (DHCP) servers are used to dynamically provide TCP/IP configuration information such as IP addresses, subnet masks, default gateways, the address of DNS, and more. NAP can be used with DHCP enforcement to ensure that only compliant computers receive TCP/IP configuration information.
- **802.1x.** 802.1x devices such as wireless access points or Ethernet switches can be controlled using 802.1x enforcement. If a client is not considered healthy, access through the devices can be controlled.
- **Domain controllers.** An NPS architecture can work with or without Active Directory Domain Services. However, if clients will be granted access to resources in a restricted network, it's very likely that the resources will be protected using Active Directory accounts.
- **Restricted network and remediation servers.** If a client is not determined to be healthy, access to the internal network is restricted. Instead, clients will only have access to a restricted network that includes remediation servers, which have the resources necessary to make the client healthy. For example, a remediation server may include antivirus software with up-to-date definitions.

Figure 5-10 shows separate servers used for the different services, but remember that it's possible to have multiple services hosted on a single server. As an example, a single server could host the NAP Policy Server, the HRA, and the CA. In the activities that follow in this chapter, the NPS services are added to the same server that hosts Remote Access Services.

Adding the NPS Service

The NPS service is separate from the remote access service, though both are part of the same Network Policy and Access Services role. An earlier activity led you through the process of installing and configuring the Remote Access Services service. You also created a policy using a scaled-down version of the NPS console.

After you add the NPS service, the NPS console expands to include additional capabilities, including the ability to configure the server System Health Validators, configure the Remediation Server Groups, and create Health Policies. The following activity shows how to add the NPS service.

Activity 5-3: Adding the Network Policy Server Service

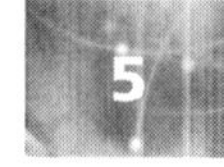

Time Required: 10 minutes

Objective: Add the NPS service to a server hosting the Network Policy and Access Services role.

Description: You are planning to design a NAP solution for your network and need to add the NPS service to a VPN server. This activity should be performed on DC1, which was used in the previous activity.

1. Start **DC1** and log on with the **Administrator** account.
2. Start **Server Manager** via the **Administrative Tools** menu.
3. Select **Roles** and scroll down to the **Network Policy and Access Services** role. Click **Add Role Services.**
4. On the **Select Server Role Services** screen, select the check box next to **Network Policy Server**. Click **Next.**
5. Click **Install** on the **Confirm Installation Selections** screen. Click **Close** when the installation is complete.
6. Start **Network Policy Server** via the **Administrative Tools** menu. If you expand the nodes, your display will look similar to Figure 5-11.

   This is the same NPS console that you accessed in an earlier lab from the Routing and Remote Access console, but you may notice more capabilities when the NPS service is added.
7. Expand the **Policies** node and select **Network Policies.** This node holds the policies from the remote access server. You'll see the two default policies and the Domain Users policy you created in an earlier activity.
8. Close all open windows.

System Health Agents, Validators, and NAP Agents

The System Health Agents (SHAs), System Health Validators (SHVs), and NAP agents are important elements of the health policy. They work together to provide a statement of health for the client.

SHAs regularly perform system health updates on the client based on checks identified in SHVs. These updates are published in the form of a Statement of Health (SoH) to the NAP agent. The NAP agent collects an SoH from different SHAs and creates a System Statement of Health (SSoH), which is passed to the NAP enforcement client when requested.

The NAP agent service is periodically run to gather information and build the SSoH. The service is set to Manual by default. If it is disabled, the system will no longer be able to gather information from the SHAs and will not be able to create the SSoH.

The majority of this process is automated on the client. However, the server also includes at least one SHV that can be configured and manipulated. You can configure the NPS to enforce or not enforce individual settings for any SHV.

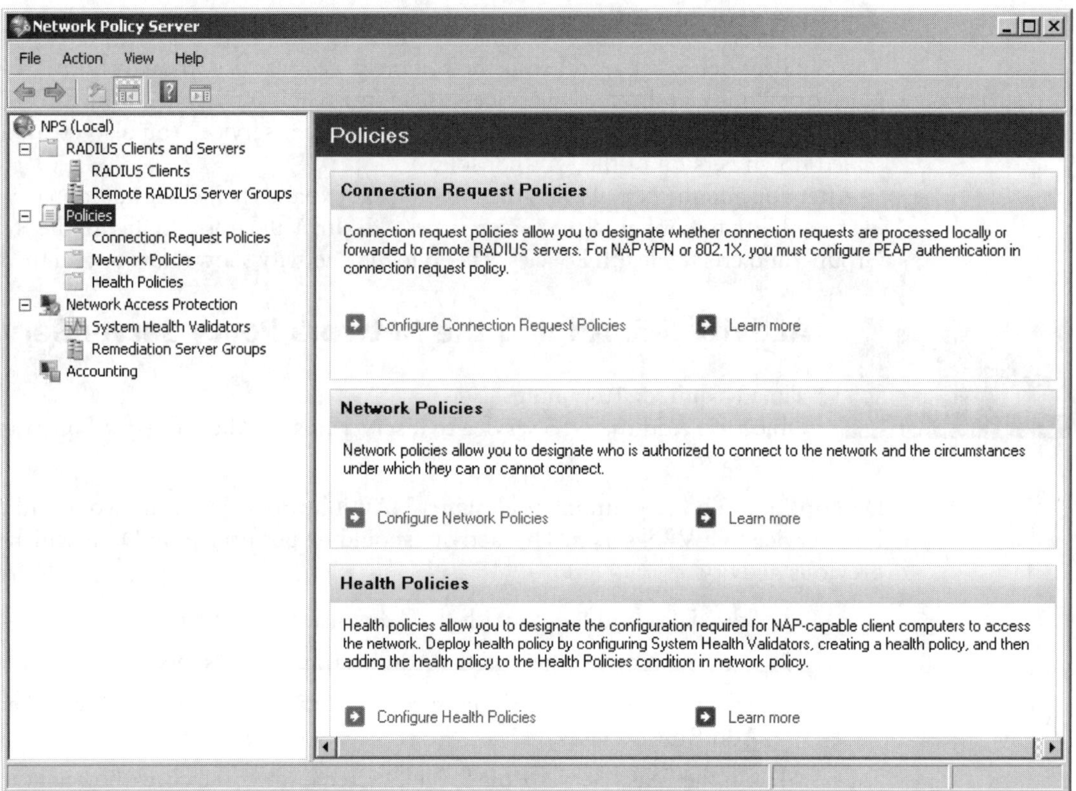

Figure 5-11 Accessing the NPS console
Courtesy Course Technology/Cengage Learning

NPS includes the built-in Windows SHV, but it is possible to add more SHVs. Microsoft has made Application Programming Interfaces (APIs) available for third-party developers to create additional SHVs, but they do not appear in the NPS console by default.

Figure 5-12 shows the Windows Security Health Validator properties with the Windows Vista tab displayed. It can be configured to check for all of the individual settings, or the administrator can check any combination.

- **Firewall.** When checked, a firewall must be enabled for all network interface cards. The firewall can be the Windows Firewall or another third-party firewall recognized by the Windows Security Center. If the third-party firewall isn't recognized by the Windows Security Center, this check will fail.
- **Virus Protection.** Antivirus software recognized by the Windows Security Center needs to be installed and enabled. If this option is selected, you should also select Antivirus is up to date to ensure that antivirus signature definitions are current.
- **Spyware Protection.** Anti-spyware software recognized by the Windows Security Center needs to be installed and enabled. If this option is selected, you should also select Antispyware is up to date to ensure that signature definitions are current.
- **Automatic Updating.** This option ensures that the client is configured to automatically download and install automatic updates from Microsoft's update site.
- **Security Update Protection.** This setting is only used for clients configured to receive their updates from a Windows Server Update Services (WSUS) server. When a WSUS server is being used, you can configure which updates are required (such as critical updates, important updates, and so on).

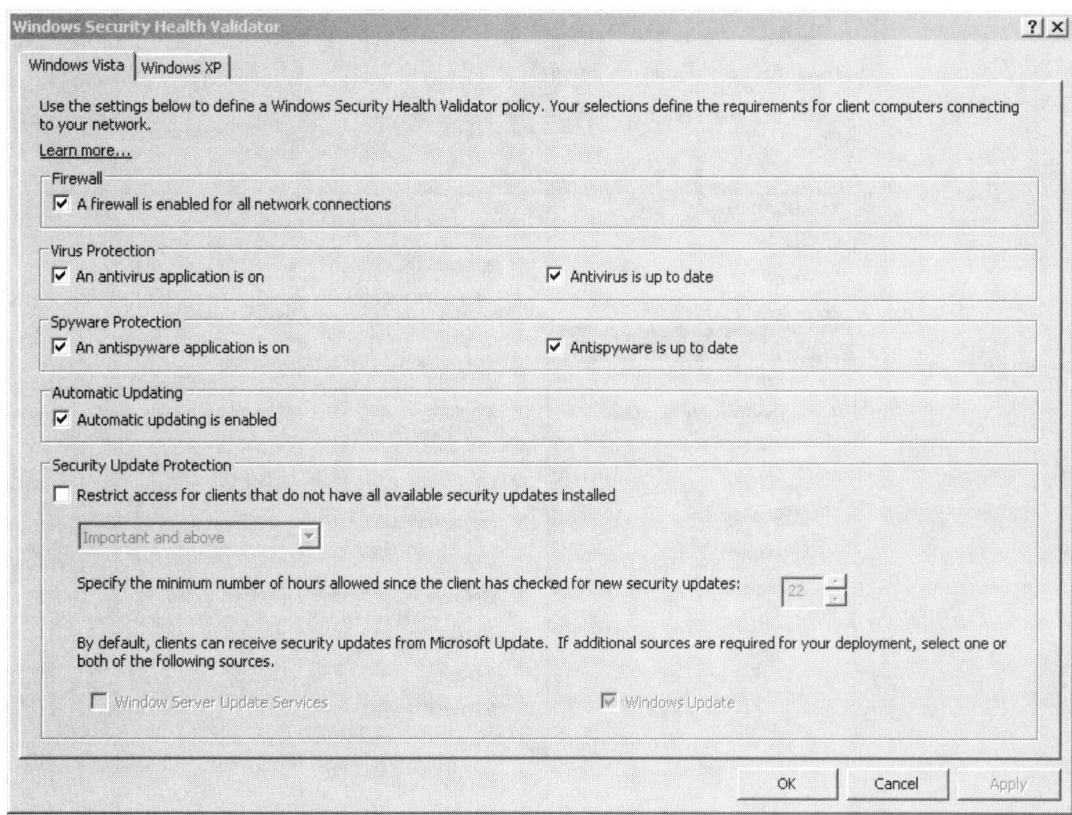

Figure 5-12 Configuring an SHV policy
Courtesy Course Technology/Cengage Learning

If NAP autoremediation is enabled, the SHV can direct the noncompliant client to enable a specific security solution to ensure that the client becomes compliant. For example, if the client is found to be noncompliant because the firewall is not enabled, the SHV can direct the client to enable the Windows firewall. This occurs without any user action.

Autoremediation also applies to:

- **Spyware protection.** Windows Defender will be enabled.
- **Automatic Updating.** Microsoft Update is enabled and configured for automatic downloading and installation of updates.
- **Security update protection.** Updates are downloaded from the configured WSUS server and installed.

Autoremediation is enabled by default when a network policy is created. Figure 5-13 shows the Domain Users network access policy created earlier in this chapter, with the Settings tab selected. The Autoremediation settings are at the bottom of the screen.

Activity 5-4: Configuring the Windows Security Health Validator

Time Required: 10 minutes
Objective: Use the NPS console to configure the Windows Security Health Validator.

Description: Your network includes Windows XP SP3 and Windows Vista SP1 clients. You want to ensure that the clients pass all checks for the Windows Security Health Validator. This activity should be performed on DC1, which was used in the previous activity.

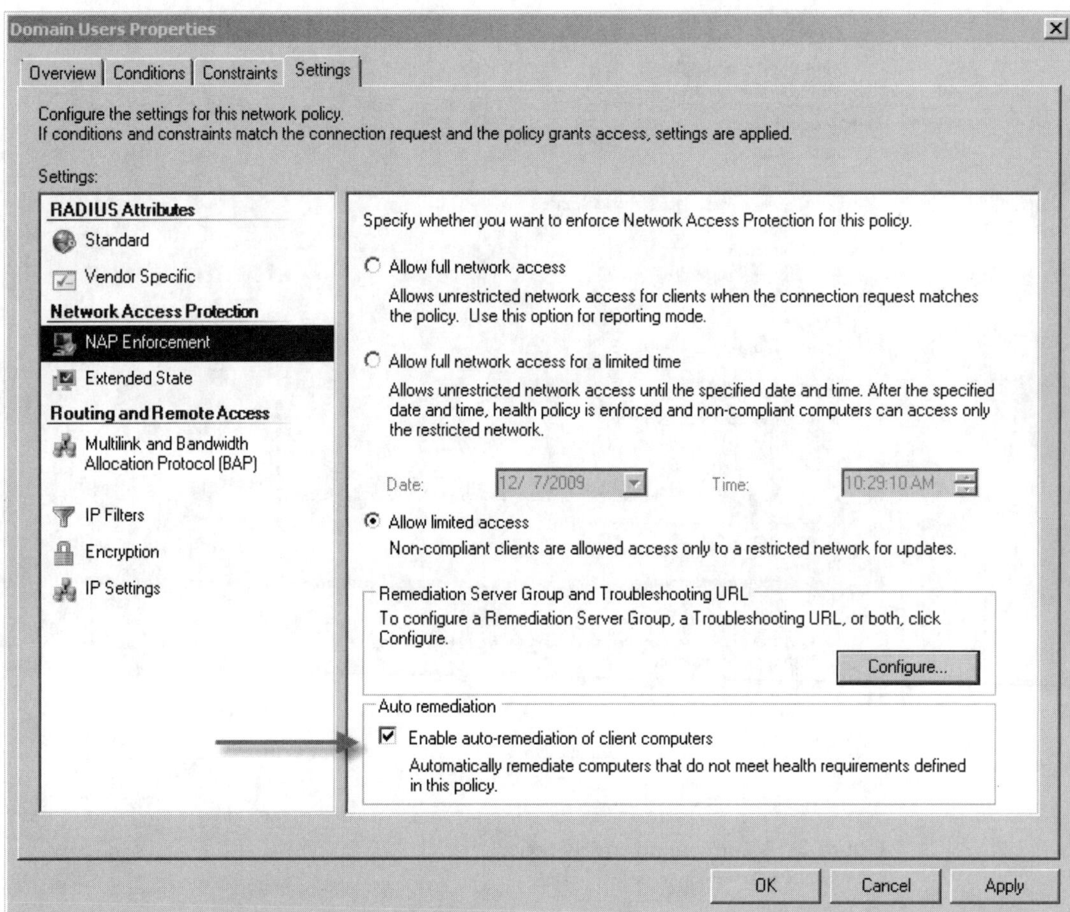

Figure 5-13 Autoremediation enabled for a network access policy

Courtesy Course Technology/Cengage Learning

1. Start **DC1** and log on with the **Administrator** account.
2. Start **Network Policy Server** via the **Administrative Tools** menu.
3. Expand the **Network Access Protection** node. Notice that there is only one SHV (the Windows Security Health Validator). Right-click the **Windows Security Health Validator** on the right and select **Properties**. Your display will look similar to Figure 5-14.

   Notice that you can configure any of these error code resolution selections to Compliant or Noncompliant. For example, if either the System Health Agent or the System Health Validator cannot contact a required service (such as the Windows Firewall service), the client will be found noncompliant by default.
4. Click the **Configure** button. The **Windows Security Health Validator** screen opens, as shown previously in Figure 5-12. Ensure that the following settings are enabled:

   Firewall—A Firewall is enabled for all network connections

   Virus Protection—An antivirus application is on. Antivirus is up to date

   Spyware Protection—An antispyware application is on. Antispyware is up to date

   Automatic Updating—Automatic updating is enabled
5. Click **OK** to accept the configuration. Click **OK** again on the Settings screen.

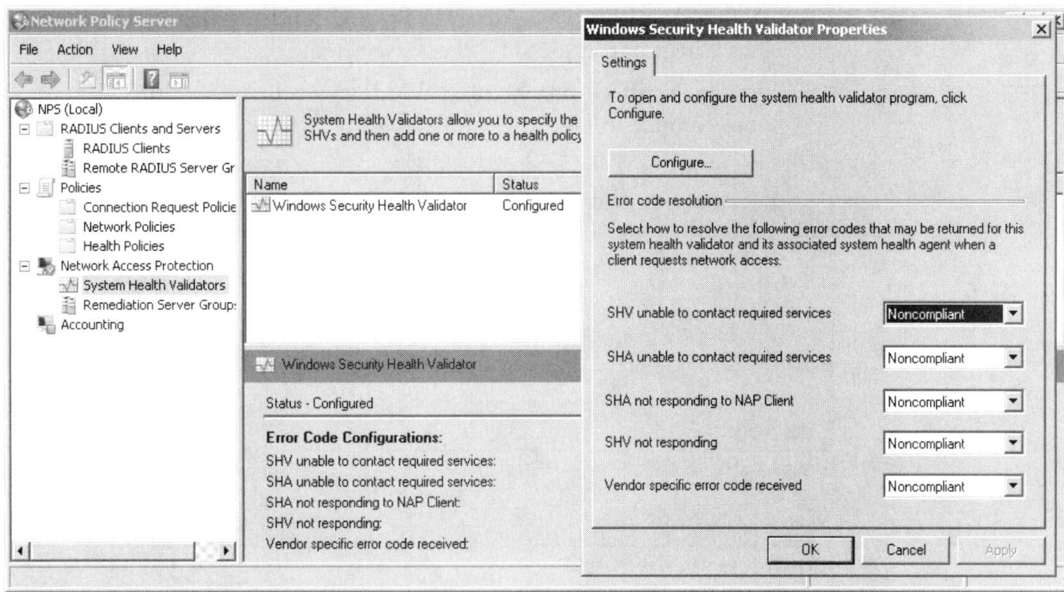

Figure 5-14 Windows Security Health Validator error code resolution
Courtesy Course Technology/Cengage Learning

Creating a Health Policy

After the SHV is configured, you can create a health policy. The health policy will use one of the SHV policies, but only one SHV policy (the Windows Security Health Validator) is included by default.

You can also choose how the SHV checks are interpreted. Most of the time, you will configure the health policy to ensure that the client passes all SHV checks. However, you have a lot of flexibility in how the SHV checks are interpreted. You can choose any of the following:

- Client passes all SHV checks
- Client fails all SHV checks
- Client passes one or more SHV checks
- Client fails one or more SHV checks
- Client reported as transitioned by one or more SHV checks
- Client reported as infected by one or more SHV checks
- Client reported as unknown by one or more SHVs

The following activity shows how to create a health policy with the NPS console.

Activity 5-5: Creating a Health Policy

Time Required: 10 minutes
Objective: Use the NPS console to create a health policy.

Description: You are designing a NAP solution and want to ensure that only clients that pass all SHV checks are allowed access. You need to create the health policy for the SHV checks. This activity should be performed on DC1, which was used in the previous activity.

1. Start **DC1** and log on with the **Administrator** account.
2. Start **Network Policy Server** via the **Administrative Tools** menu.
3. Expand the **Policies** node. Right-click **Health Policies** and select **New**.

4. Name the policy **Pass All SHV**. Ensure that the **Client SHV Checks** drop-down menu has **Client passes all SHV checks** selected.
5. Select the check box next to **Windows Security Health Validator**. Your display will look similar to Figure 5-15. Click **OK**.

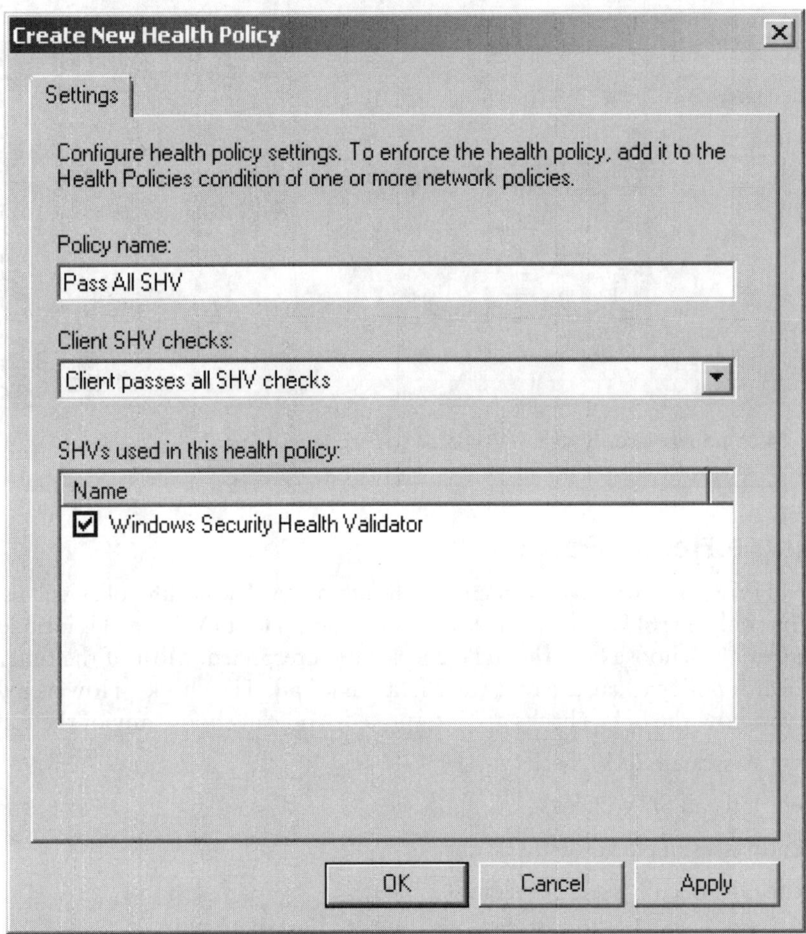

Figure 5-15 Creating a new health policy named Pass All SHV
Courtesy Course Technology/Cengage Learning

6. Close all open windows.

Creating a Remediation Server Group

If the client is not compliant, it's common to restrict its access to only specific servers. This is done by creating a Remediation Server Group. The group includes the names and IP addresses of the servers that hold the applications and/or updates that can be used to bring the client into compliance. This group can include any number of servers.

Conceptually, the servers in the Remediation Server Group are often represented as being physically isolated from the rest of the network. However, because the policy will restrict the client's access to only the listed servers, these servers may be on the intranet and regularly accessed by internal clients. For example, if a WSUS server is used internally, it's not necessary to create another WSUS server for the VPN clients.

The following are examples of servers that may be included in the Remediation Server Group list:

- **Antivirus servers.** Some corporate editions of antivirus software can be used to deploy antivirus software and updates to client computers.
- **WSUS servers.** WSUS servers can be used to deploy updates to clients instead of using Microsoft Updates.
- **Network Infrastructure servers.** DNS servers and domain controllers may be needed for clients to authenticate with remediation servers to access the resources.

Activity 5-6: Creating a Remediation Server Group

Time Required: 10 minutes
Objective: Use the NPS console to create a Remediation Server Group.

Description: You are designing a NAP solution and want to ensure that clients that don't meet the health policy can only access the domain controller named DC1 (which is running DNS), a WSUS server named WSUS1, and a file server named Apps1 that hosts applications you can download. This activity should be performed on DC1, which was used in the previous activity.

1. Start **DC1** and log on with the **Administrator** account.
2. Start **Network Policy Server** via the **Administrative Tools** menu.
3. Expand the **Network Access Protection** node. Right-click **Remediation Server Group** and select **New**.
4. Enter **Remediate** as the **Group** name.
5. Add **DC1**. Click **Add**. Enter **DC1** as the **Friendly Name**. Enter **192.168.1.10** as the **IP Address** and click **OK**.

The following steps add nonexistent servers to the Remediation Server Group. If you enter the name WSUS1 in the IP Address or DNS Name text box and click the Resolve button, it will return an error because the record doesn't exist in DNS. In a production environment, you would add the details for servers that actually exist; if the server has a record in DNS, the Resolve button would work.

6. Add **WSUS1**. Click **Add**. Enter **WSUS1** as the **Friendly Name**. Enter **192.168.1.15** as the **IP Address** and click **OK**.
7. Add **Apps1**. Click **Add**. Enter **Apps1** as the **Friendly Name**. Enter **192.168.1.16** as the **IP Address** and click **OK**. Your display will look similar to Figure 5-16. Click **OK**.
8. Close all open windows.

Configuring Network Policy Settings

After the Network Policy Server and health policies are configured, you can configure network access policies. Health and NAP policy settings can be configured on the conditions of a policy and on the settings of a policy.

As a reminder, the conditions of a policy determine if the policy will be used. If you specify a health policy for a client as a condition and the client is not compliant with the health policy, the computer will not use the policy. If you are using only a single network access policy, this is a good way to ensure that only compliant computers will connect. However, because the connection is refused, clients will not be able to access remediation servers.

Several policy conditions are relevant to Network Access Protection. Figure 5-17 shows the Conditions tab of the Domain Users policy created earlier in this chapter. The Add button was clicked and the display was scrolled down to the Network Access conditions shown in the figure.

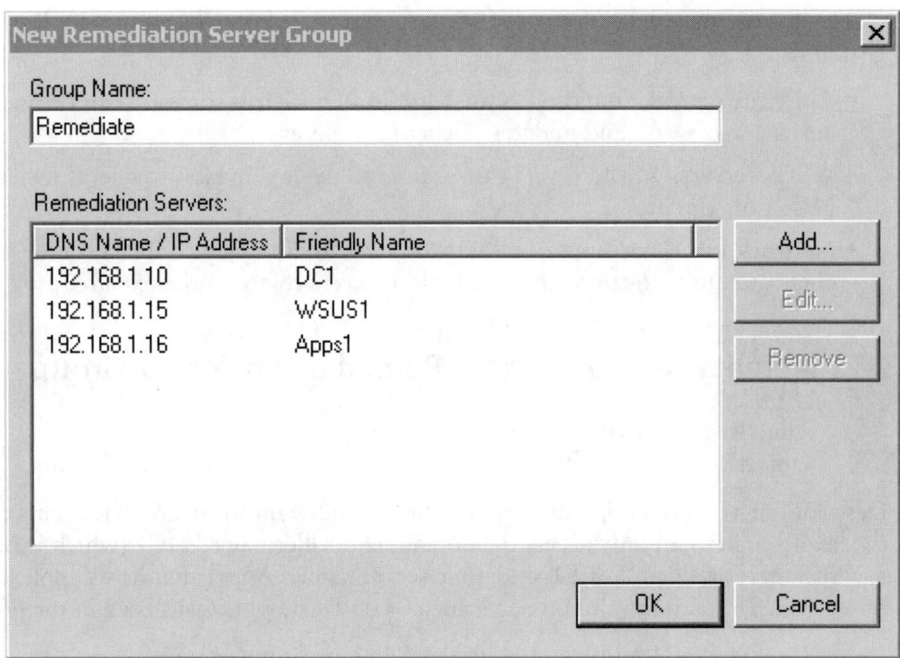

Figure 5-16 Creating a new Remediation Server Group
Courtesy Course Technology/Cengage Learning

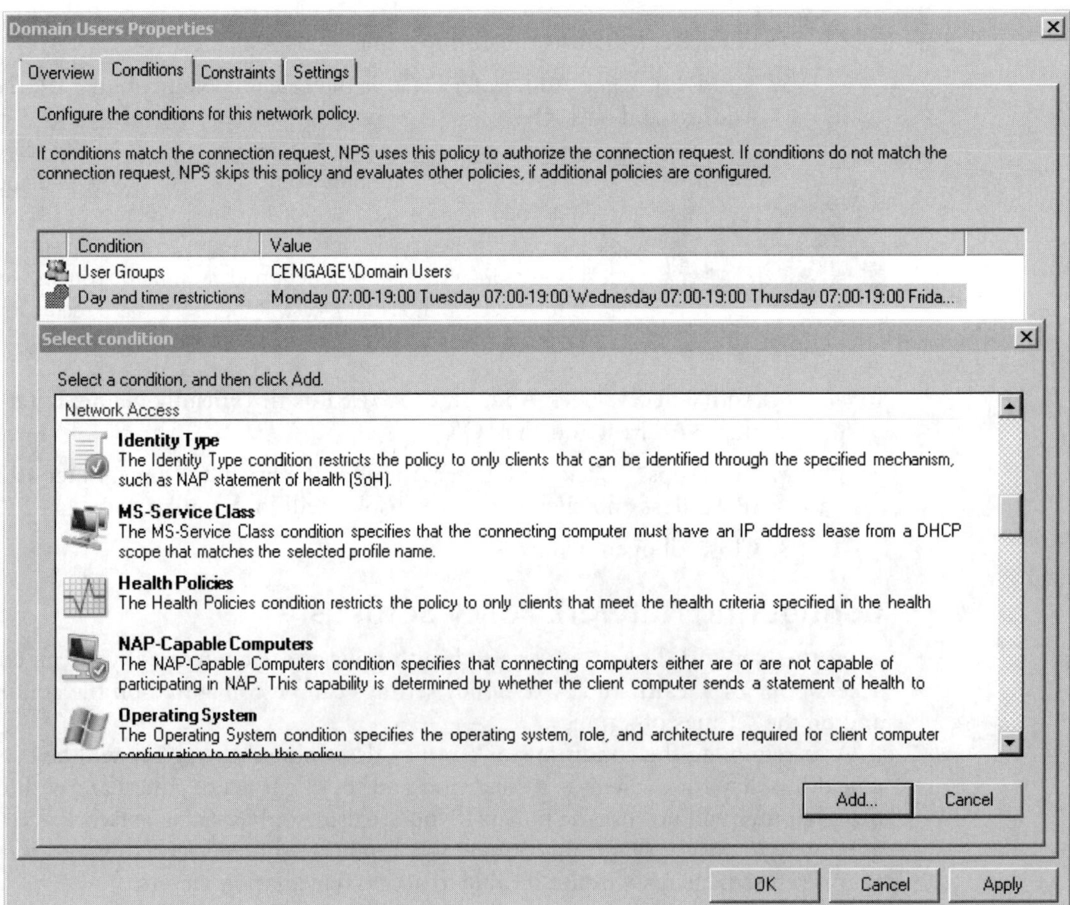

Figure 5-17 Identifying network policy conditions
Courtesy Course Technology/Cengage Learning

The following conditions are relevant to network access:

- **Identity Type.** This condition can be used to specify that the policy will only apply to clients that can be identified through a specific mechanism. NAP will use a machine health check.
- **MS-Service Class.** You can specify that only clients that have received a specific DHCP lease will meet the condition. The DHCP lease is identified by the profile name specified in the DHCP scope. Figure 5-18 shows a DHCP scope configured with a Profile Name of MobileUsers. You would specify MobileUsers as the Profile Name in this condition.

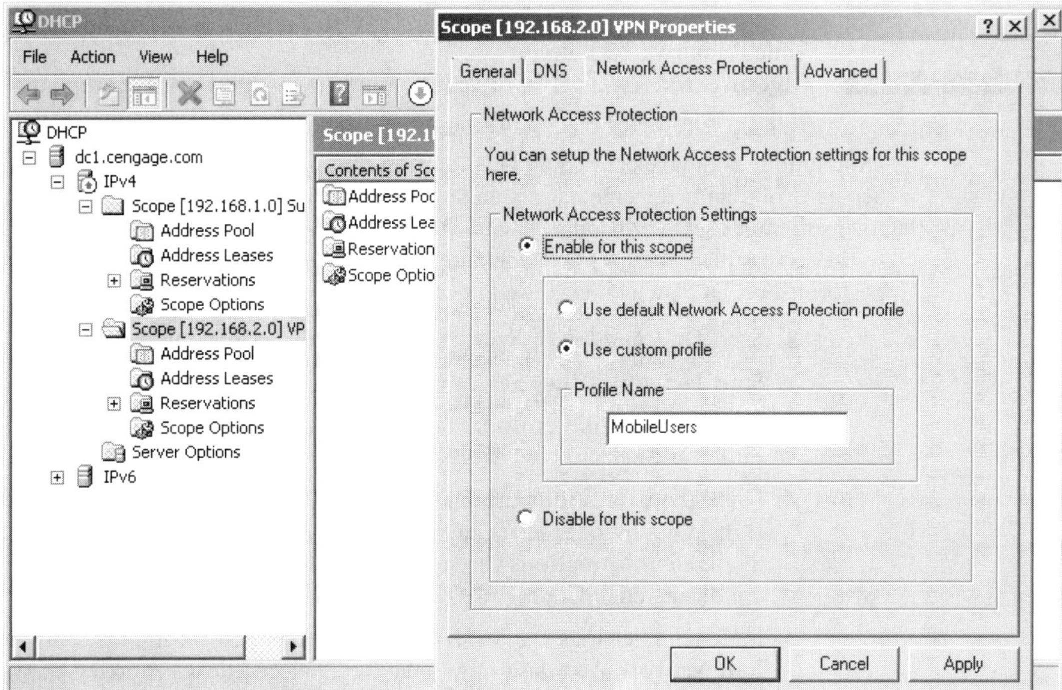

Figure 5-18 DHCP scope configuration
Courtesy Course Technology/Cengage Learning

- **Health Policies.** You can select a health policy that has been created. For example, earlier activities included the Pass All SHV health policy. If you selected this condition, you could select the Pass All SHV policy from the drop-down menu.
- **NAP-Capable Computers.** This condition can be used to specify whether the policy applies only to computers that are NAP-capable or not NAP-capable. Remember, Microsoft client computers that are NAP-capable are running Windows XP SP3, Windows Vista SP1, and Windows 7.
- **Operating System.** This condition allows you to specify the operating system version, the newest installed service pack, the operating system role (client or server), the architecture (x86, x64, or ia64), and/or the operating system build.
- **Policy Expiration.** You can use this condition to specify a date and time when the policy has expired and is no longer evaluated.

It's also possible to use NAP without specifying NAP as a condition in a network access policy. If you want the noncompliant clients to be able to access remediation servers after connecting, you can configure the settings of the network access policy. The settings apply only when the conditions of the policy are met. Two settings are related to NAP on the settings of a policy:

- **NAP Enforcement.** You can specify whether noncompliant computers are allowed full network access, full network access for a limited amount of time, or limited access specified by a Remediation Server group.

Network policy settings enable full network access by default. If you want to restrict access for noncompliant computers, you need to configure the NAP Enforcement setting.

- **Extended State.** These settings only need to be configured if you're using NAP with Cisco Network Admission Control. Otherwise, it can be left with the default setting of <Blank>.

The following activity leads you through the steps needed to configure a policy to use NAP.

Activity 5-7: Configuring a Network Access Policy with NAP

Time Required: 15 minutes

Objective: Modify a network access policy to ensure that noncompliant computers have only restricted access.

Description: You have created a NAP solution that includes a restricted network. A Remediation Server Group named Remediate includes specific servers used for health remediation. You want to ensure that users who connect with the Domain Users network access policy can only connect to the servers identified in the Remediate group if they are noncompliant. This activity should be performed on DC1, which was used in the previous activity.

1. Start **DC1** and log on with the **Administrator** account.
2. Start **Network Policy Server** via the **Administrative Tools** menu.
3. Expand the **Policies** node. Select **Network Policies**. Right-click the **Domain Users** policy and select **Properties.**
4. Click the **Conditions** tab and click **Add.** Scroll down to the **Network Access** conditions. One by one, select each Network Access condition and click **Add.** Review the available information. Click **Cancel** on each condition. After you have viewed each condition, click **Cancel.**
5. Select the **Settings** tab. Select **NAP Enforcement.** Notice that by default, the **Allow Full Network Access** setting is selected. Select **Allow Limited Access.**
6. Click **Configure.** Select the **Remediate** Remediation Server Group from the drop-down menu, as shown in Figure 5-19.

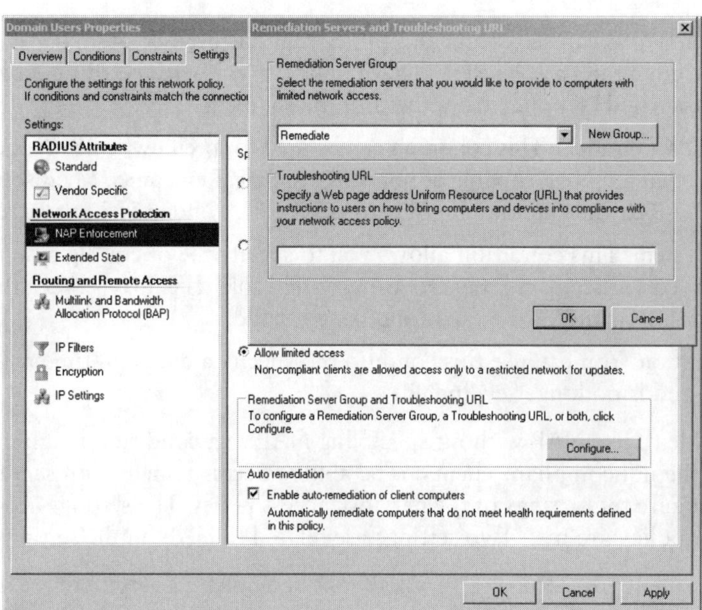

Figure 5-19 Selecting the Remediation Server Group for limited network access

Courtesy Course Technology/Cengage Learning

Notice that it's also possible to add a URL for a Web site. This Web site could be created to instruct users on how to bring their clients into compliance with the policy. Click **OK**.

7. Click **OK** to close the **Domain Users** properties screen.
8. Close all open windows.

Other NAP Enforcement Methods

The majority of this section has focused on using **VPN enforcement**—in other words, ensuring that VPN clients meet specific health requirements prior to allowing access to a network. However, Network Access Protection includes support for three other methods of enforcement. Each method can be used individually, or they can be used together to form a comprehensive solution.

The three other methods of NAP enforcement are:

- DHCP enforcement
- 802.1x enforcement
- IPSec enforcement

DHCP Enforcement

DHCP enforcement is used to ensure that a client is compliant prior to issuing TCP/IP configuration information. Noncompliant computers could be issued a DHCP lease that gives them access to a restricted network.

A Dynamic Host Configuration Protocol (DHCP) server issues leases to DHCP clients; these leases may include an IP address, subnet mask, default gateway, and addresses of DNS and WINS servers. Normally, a DHCP client only has to turn on and broadcast a DHCP Discover message to receive the lease. With DHCP enforcement, additional checks are performed prior to issuing the lease.

Health policy requirements are enforced when a client requests a DHCP lease, renews a lease, and periodically while it has a lease. Users can manually assign the TCP/IP configuration and bypass DHCP, so DHCP enforcement is considered a weak method of NAP enforcement.

802.1x Enforcement

802.1x enforcement is used with managed switches and wireless access points to control access and ensure that traffic stays within a limited network. For example, a large LAN could include several subnets; some of these subnets could include clients and servers that have more sensitive data. The subnets with sensitive data could be identified with an 802.1x policy as a restricted network.

802.1x (not 802.1x enforcement) is an authentication protocol used for port-based access for network devices. It's designed to provide extra protection for protected or limited-access networks. In essence, it ensures that the clients are authenticated prior to granting access to the network.

When 802.1x enforcement is used, it ensures that clients are compliant with the policy prior to providing access to the restricted network. A fully compliant computer could be granted unlimited access, while noncompliant computers could be denied access to the restricted network or limited access on the LAN. Restricted networks can be identified by:

- **A limited access profile using access control lists (ACLs).** These ACLs include IP packet filters on the network device to grant or deny access, and can be used to grant access only to specific subnets and even to specific IP addresses.
- **Virtual LAN identifiers (VLAN IDs).** These ensure that traffic with the VLAN ID is restricted to the VLAN. Traffic isn't allowed out of the VLAN, and unwanted traffic isn't allowed in.

802.1x cannot be used on unmanaged network devices. Unmanaged devices don't have any configuration or options. For example, an unmanaged switch will work as a switch; if you plug it in, it will learn the physical addresses of clients connected to specific ports and make internal connections. However, an unmanaged switch does not have any advanced capabilities. A managed switch (or other managed network device) has software that can be manipulated and is generally understood to be more intelligent.

IPSec Enforcement

IPSec enforcement is used to ensure that communications with computers are protected with IPSec. IPSec was mentioned in Chapter 4; you learned how to configure a Group Policy object to force clients to use IPSec. As a reminder, IPSec is used to encrypt data (using the Encapsulating Security Payload) and to digitally sign data using an Authentication Header.

While it's easier to configure IPSec for a large number of clients with a GPO, you can also configure clients individually without a GPO. Additionally, clients aren't required to be in a domain to use IPSec; clients can use it within a workgroup.

Some of the benefits of IPSec protected data transfers are:

- **Confidentiality**. When IPSec encrypted data is intercepted, the attacker is unable to read it. This ensures data confidentiality and provides secure end-to-end communication.
- **Integrity**. The Authentication Header provides integrity. If any of the data is modified, the receiving end will know. This prevents an attacker from intercepting data, modifying it, and replaying it.
- **Authentication**. The Authentication Header provides assurances that the data was sent by a specific system with the use of a digital signature.

Another benefit of IPSec is that it can be used instead of 802.1x in a network that has unmanaged network devices. IPSec is the most secure form of NAP enforcement.

Planning for Terminal Services

Terminal Services (TS) is used to provide end users with access to individual applications or full desktop operating systems from almost any mobile device. The user connects to the terminal server and can run applications and use resources on it.

Microsoft changed the name of Terminal Services to Remote Desktop Services in Windows Server 2008 R2. It remains Terminal Services in Windows Server 2008.

A significant addition to Terminal Services in Windows Server 2008 is the use of **TS RemoteApp** programs. Once a TS RemoteApp program is configured on a TS server, users can run the application remotely instead of starting a complete desktop session. When a user executes a TS application, the application runs on the TS server. Keyboard, mouse, and display data is transferred back and forth between the user and the TS server.

It's still possible to support full desktop sessions on a TS server for older computers or thin clients. A thin client has minimal hardware resources, but has enough resources to connect to a TS server. The client can connect to the TS server and run a full Windows Vista desktop. Even though the session is running on the TS server, the user will see the Windows Vista desktop and can then run Windows Vista applications within this remote desktop.

A TS server can support multiple clients, and each client will have access to their session only. The server will need to have enough hardware resources (memory, processing power, disk capability, and network bandwidth) to support these clients.

Users connect to a terminal server using Remote Desktop Connection (RDC). RDC version 6.0 or newer is required to connect to a Windows Server 2008 terminal server, to take advantage of increased security with Terminal Services. Windows Vista comes with RDC 6.0, and Windows XP SP3 can use RDC 6.1.

RDC 6.0 or newer is needed to support Network Level Authentication (NLA). NLA plugs a security hole by ensuring that access to the terminal server is not granted until the client has been authenticated. If older clients are used, you must weaken security on the terminal server to support them.

Adding the Terminal Services Role

A limited version of Terminal Services is installed by default on Windows Server 2008 servers. The Terminal Services menu is available via the Administrative Tools menu. However, this menu is for administrative purposes, not for end users. If you want to implement Terminal Services for end users, you must add the Terminal Services role.

It's common for administrators to use the built-in Terminal Services feature to remotely administer servers. This feature is sometimes called Remote Desktop for Administration. Administrators can connect to the server and gain full access to the server's desktop. When using Terminal Services for administrative purposes only, you do not need a licensing server.

When adding the Terminal Services role, you'll have the choice of adding multiple supporting services, as shown in Figure 5-20. Some of these services require additional supporting services.

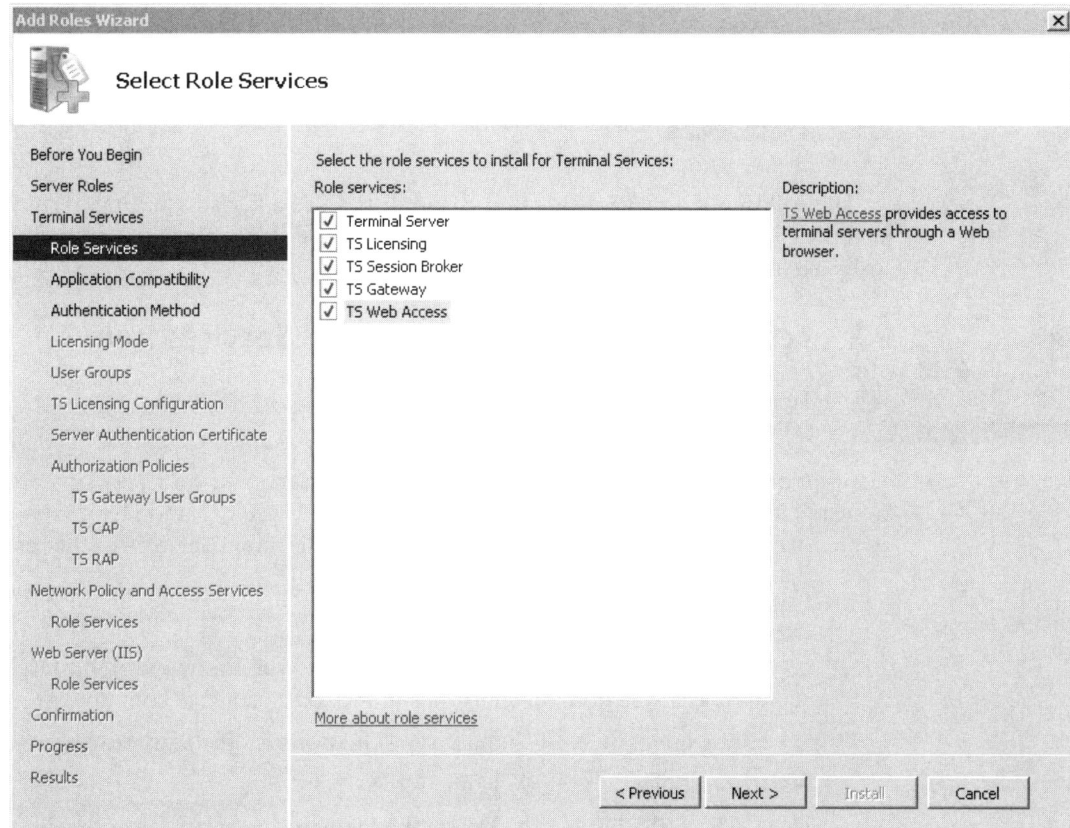

Figure 5-20 Adding Terminal Services role services

Courtesy Course Technology/Cengage Learning

The Terminal Services role services are:

- **Terminal Server service.** This is the primary service used to support Terminal Services. It allows the server to host Windows-based programs and full Windows desktops.
- **TS Licensing service.** This service manages TS client access licenses (TS CALs), which are required for all connections. A single TS licensing server can be used to support multiple TS servers, but the licensing server must be running on Windows Server 2008 to support Windows Server 2008 TS servers.
- **TS Session Broker service.** This service can be used to balance the load when multiple TS servers are used. Servers are configured in a **Terminal Services farm** and the Session Broker service will direct client connections based on their load. Additionally, if a client becomes disconnected from an active session and then tries to reconnect, the Session Broker service will ensure that the client reconnects to the server hosting the disconnected session.
- **TS Gateway service.** This service can be used in conjunction with a remote access solution to allow clients to connect to terminal servers over the Internet. This service requires several additional services and features to be installed. When using the Server Manager to add the service, you are automatically prompted to add the required services and features.
- **TS Web Access service.** This service allows clients to connect to terminal servers through a Web browser. The service is used with RemoteApp programs, and can be used either on the Internet or an internal intranet. Once configured, users can start the RemoteApp program by clicking a link in the Web browser; the application runs within the browser. This service also requires additional services and features to be installed; the Server Manager wizard automatically prompts you to add them.

It's not recommended to install Terminal Services on a domain controller (DC) because it exposes the DC to extra risks and may affect performance. The Remote Desktop Users group must be granted the Allow Log On Through Terminal Services right on a DC, but this step is not needed on member servers.

The following activity leads you through the process of installing Terminal Services on a server. It includes all of the services, except for the Licensing Server service, which will be installed later.

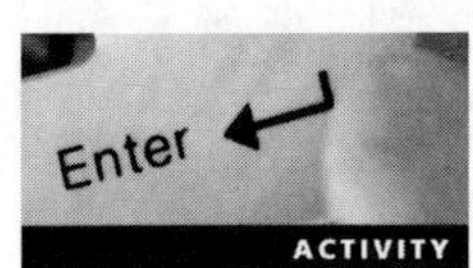

Activity 5-8: Adding the Terminal Services Role

Time Required: 60 minutes

Objective: Add Terminal Services to a server.

Description: You need to add Terminal Services to a server in your network, and have decided to install it on DC2. DC2 currently is hosting Active Directory and DNS, so you first need to remove Active Directory and DNS. You'll then add Terminal Services to the server.

1. Start **DC1** and **DC2**. After both servers have started, log on to **DC2** with an **Administrator** account.
2. Remove Active Directory from **DC2** using the following steps. DC2 was last configured as a sole domain controller in the south.cengage.com domain.

   a. Log on to **DC2**. Click **Start**, type **DCpromo** in the **Start Search** box, and press **Enter**.

   b. Click **Next** on the **Welcome** screen.

   c. Check the box on the **Delete the Domain** screen to delete the domain. Click **Next**.

   d. On the **Application Directory Partitions** screen, click **Next**.

   e. On the **Confirm Deletion** screen, click **Next**.

f. On the **Network Credentials** screen, click **Next**, and then click **Next** again to **Remove DNS Delegation.**

g. Type **P@ssw0rd** in the **Password** and **Confirm Password** boxes. Click **Next.**

h. Review the information on the **Summary** screen and click **Next.**

i. Select the **Reboot on Completion** check box. Active Directory will be removed and the server will reboot.

3. Remove DNS from **DC2** with the following steps.

a. Log on to **DC2**. If **Server Manager** doesn't start, open it via the **Administrative Tools** menu.

b. Select **Roles,** and click the **Remove Roles** link. Click **Next** on the **Before You Begin** screen.

c. Uncheck the boxes for **Active Directory Domain Services** and **DNS Server.** At this point, no boxes should be checked on this screen. Click **Next.**

d. Review the information on the **Confirm Remove Selections** screen and click **Remove.**

e. When the removal process is complete, click **Close.** When prompted to restart the server, click **Yes.**

f. After the server reboots, log on using the **Administrator** account. **Server Manager** will start and the removal process will be completed. When it finishes, click **Close.**

4. Ensure that DC2's network interface card is configured to use DC1 for DNS by taking the following steps.

a. Click **Start,** right-click **Network,** and select **Properties.**

b. Select **Manage Network Connections.**

c. Right-click **Local Area Connection** and **select Properties.**

d. Select Internet **Protocol Version 4** (**TCP/IP v4**) and select **Properties.**

e. Ensure that the **Preferred DNS Server** is set to an IP address of **192.168.1.10.**

f. Click **OK** and close all open windows.

5. Add **DC2** to the **Cengage.com** domain by taking the following steps.

a. Click **Start,** right-click **Computer,** and select **Properties.**

b. Click **Advanced System Settings.** Select the **Computer Name** tab. Click **Change.**

c. Select **Domain** in the **Member Of** section. Type **Cengage.com** and click **OK.**

d. Type **Administrator** and **P@ssw0rd** in the **Username** and **Password** text boxes, respectively. Click **OK.**

e. Click **OK** when the **Welcome** screen appears. Click **OK** to dismiss the dialog box that prompts you to restart the computer. Click **Close** and then click **Restart Now.**

f. After **DC2** reboots, log on with the domain **Administrator** account and a password of **P@ssw0rd.**

6. Start **Server Manager** via the **Administrative Tools** menu.

7. Select **Roles** and click **Add Roles.** Review the information on the **Before You Begin** screen and click **Next.**

8. Select the check box for **Terminal Services** and click **Next.** Review the information on the **Terminal Services** screen and click **Next.**

9. Select the check boxes for the **Terminal Server** and **TS Session Broker** services. Select the check box for the **TS Gateway** service. When you click this box, a dialog box will appear and your screen will look similar to Figure 5-21. Click **Add Required Role Services.**

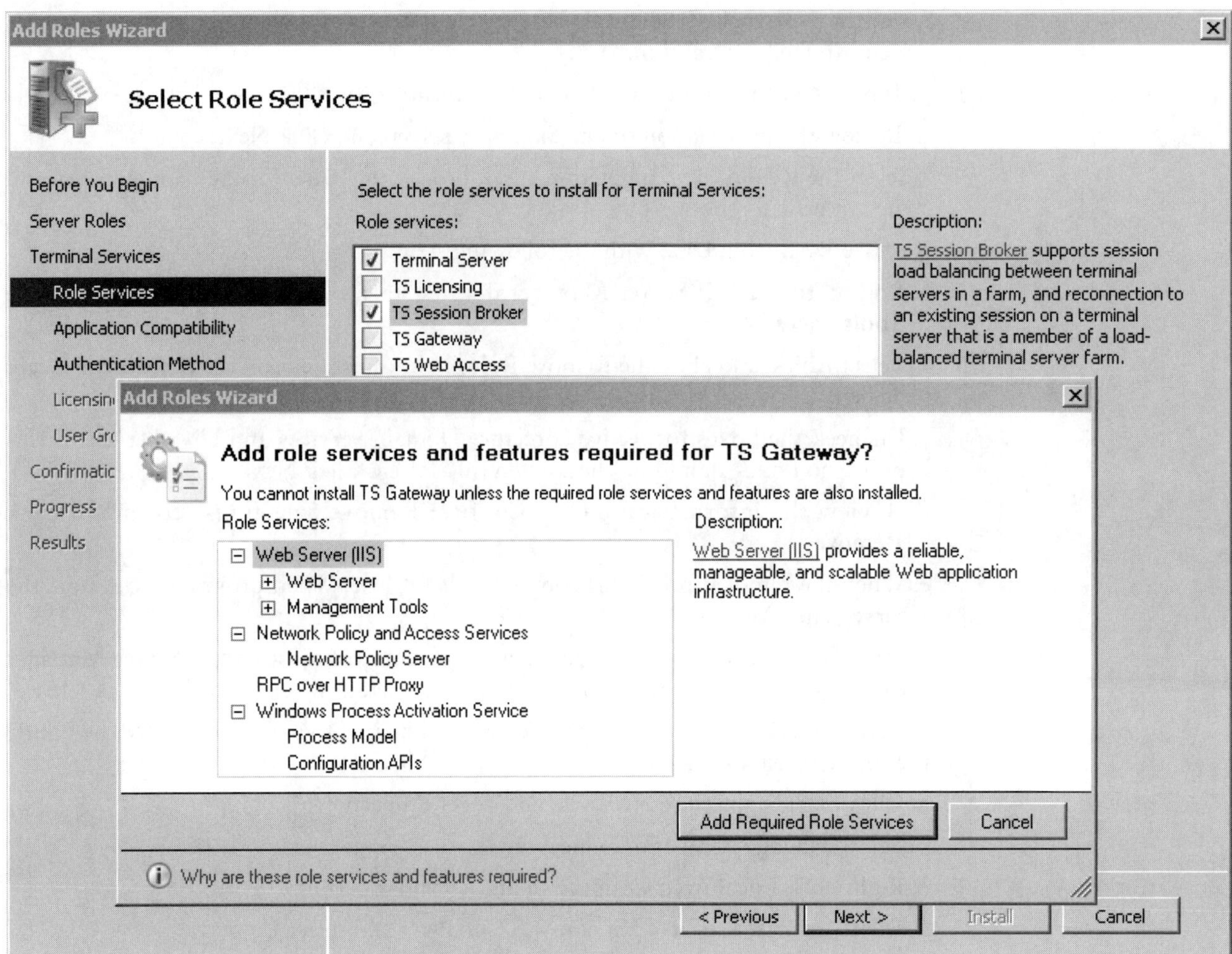

Figure 5-21 Adding supporting roles and features for TS Gateway

Courtesy Course Technology/Cengage Learning

10. Select the check box for the **TS Web Access** service. When you click this box, a dialog box will prompt you to add required services and features. Click **Add Required Role Services.** Click **Next.**
11. Review the information on the **Application Compatibility** screen and click **Next.**
12. Review the information on the **Network Level Authentication** screen. If any of your clients cannot run RDC 6.0 or greater, you will have to weaken security and select Do Not Require Network Level Authentication. Select **Require Network Level Authentication** and click **Next.**
13. Review the information on the **Specify Licensing Mode** screen. Licensing will be configured later in this chapter, so accept the default setting of **Configure Later** and click **Next.**
14. Users or groups need to be added to the local Remote Desktop Users group, but the Administrators group is already added. On a production server, you may add more user groups when adding the role or do it later. On the **Select User Groups Allowed Access To This Terminal Server** screen, click **Next.**
15. TS Gateway requires a certificate to be used for SSL encryption. In a production environment, you would obtain a certificate from a certification authority, but for a lab environment, you can use a self-signed certificate. Select **Create a Self-signed Certificate for SSL Encryption** and click **Next.**

16. Authorization policies are needed for TS Gateway; they will be explained later in this chapter. Select **Later** and click **Next.**
17. Review the information on the **Network Policy and Access Services** screen and click **Next.**
18. The **Network Policy Server** role service is selected by default. Accept this default selection and click **Next.**
19. Review the information on the **Web Server (IIS)** screen and click **Next.**
20. Several Web server services and features are selected by default. Accept these default selections and click **Next.**
21. Review your selections on the **Confirm Installation Selections** screen and click **Install.**

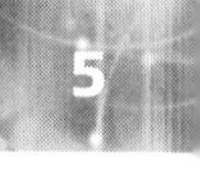

22. When the installation is complete, click **Close.** When prompted to restart the server, click **Yes.**
23. After the server reboots, log on with the domain Administrator account. Enter Cengage\Administrator to ensure that the domain Administrator account is used. **Server Manager** will start and the installation of **Terminal Services** will be completed. Click **Close.**
24. A special case exists in which Terminal Services sometimes finishes with the following error: "Attempt to configure terminal server failed with error code 0x80004005. Error HResult E_Fail has been returned from a call to a COM component." If this error occurs, use the following steps to overcome it.
    a. Start a **Microsoft Management Console** by clicking **Start,** typing **MMC** in the **Start Search** box, and pressing **Enter.**
    b. Select **File, Add/Remove Snap-in.**
    c. Select **Group Policy Object Editor** and click **Add.** Click **Finish.** Click **OK.**
    d. Expand the Group Policy nodes to access the **Computer Configuration, Administrative Templates, Windows Components, Terminal Services, Terminal Server, Connections** node.
    e. Double-click **Allow Users to Connect Remotely Using Terminal Services.** Change the setting to **Not Configured.** Click **OK.**
    f. Start the command prompt by clicking **Start, Command Prompt.**
    g. Type the following command and press **Enter.**

    ```
    gpupdate /force
    ```

    h. Remove the **Terminal Services** role using **Server Manager.**
    i. Redo Steps 5 through 22.
25. Close all open windows.

Configuring the Terminal Services Server

After you've added the Terminal Services role and the supporting services, you'll need to configure the server to accept connections by performing the following steps:

- **Configure the Remote Desktop connections to allow connections.** This option is accessible from the Remote tab of the System Properties page. If all of the clients are running RDC 6.0 or newer (Windows XP SP3, Windows Vista SP1, or newer), you can select the more secure setting to use Network Level Authentication.
- **Add users or groups to the local Remote Desktop Users group.** Users added to this group are granted the right to log on to the TS server.

The local Remote Desktop Users group is different from the domain Remote Desktop Users group. If you add users to the domain Remote Desktop Users group, they will not be able to connect to sessions on the terminal server.

Use the following activity to configure the TS server and test the connection.

Activity 5-9: Configuring the Terminal Services Server

Time Required: 15 minutes

Objective: Configure Terminal Services to accept remote connections and test the connection.

Description: After installing the Terminal Services role on DC2, you need to configure it to allow clients to connect. You need to create a user account named Dawn and configure the TS server to allow this user to connect to remote sessions. This activity will use both DC1 (the domain controller) and DC2 (the TS server).

1. Start **DC1** and **DC2**.
2. Log on to **DC1** with a domain **Administrator** account. Start **Active Directory Users and Computers.** Right-click the **Users** container and select **New, User.** Enter **Dawn** in the **First Name** and **User Logon Name** text boxes. Click **Next.**
3. Enter **P@ssw0rd** in the **Password** and **Confirm Password** text boxes. Deselect the check box for **User Must Change Password at Next Logon.** Click **Next.** Click **Finish.** Leave **DC1** as it is; you will return to it later in this activity.
4. Log on to **DC2** with an administrator account. Click **Start**, right-click **Computer**, and select **Properties.** Select **Remote Settings.** If the selections are not dimmed, go to step 5. If the selections are dimmed on the Remote Settings screen, close the screen by clicking Cancel and use the following steps to modify the Local Security Policy.

   a. Start a **Microsoft Management Console** by clicking **Start**, typing **MMC** in the **Start Search** box, and pressing **Enter.**

   b. Select **File, Add/Remove Snap-in.**

   c. Select **Group Policy Object Editor** and click **Add.** Click **Finish.** Click **OK.**

   d. Expand the Group Policy nodes to access the **Computer Configuration, Administrative Templates, Windows Components, Terminal Services, Terminal Server, Security** node.

   e. Double-click **Require User Authentication for Remote Connections.** Change the setting to **Not Configured.** Click **OK.**

   f. Start the command prompt by clicking **Start, Command Prompt.**

   g. Type the following command and press **Enter.**

   ```
   gpupdate /force
   ```

   h. Click **Start**, right-click **Computer**, and select **Properties.** Select **Remote Settings.**
5. On the **System Properties** screen, select **Allow connections only from computers running remote desktop with network level authentication** (more secure). If a dialog box appears, indicating that the **Remote Desktop Firewall Exception Will Be Enabled,** click **OK.** If the dialog box does not appear, use the following steps to verify the firewall exception is enabled.

   a. Click the link labeled **You Must Enable The Windows Firewall Exception for Remote Desktop.**

b. Review the information on the help screen and click the link labeled **Click to Open Windows Firewall.**

c. On the **Windows Firewall** screen, click **Change Settings.** Select the **Exceptions** tab.

d. Ensure that **Remote Desktop** and **Remote Administration** are both checked.

e. Click **OK** and close the **Windows Firewall** and **Help** screens.

6. Click **Select Users.** Click **Add.** Enter **Dawn** and click **Check Names.**

If you're logged on with the local administrator account, you'll be prompted to provide credentials in the domain. Enter Administrator and P@ssw0rd to give the credentials for the domain administrator account.

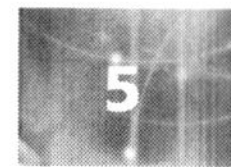

7. Click **OK.** At this point, your display will look similar to Figure 5-22. Click **OK** on the **Remote Desktop Users** screen. Click **OK** on the **System Properties** screen. Close the **System** screen.

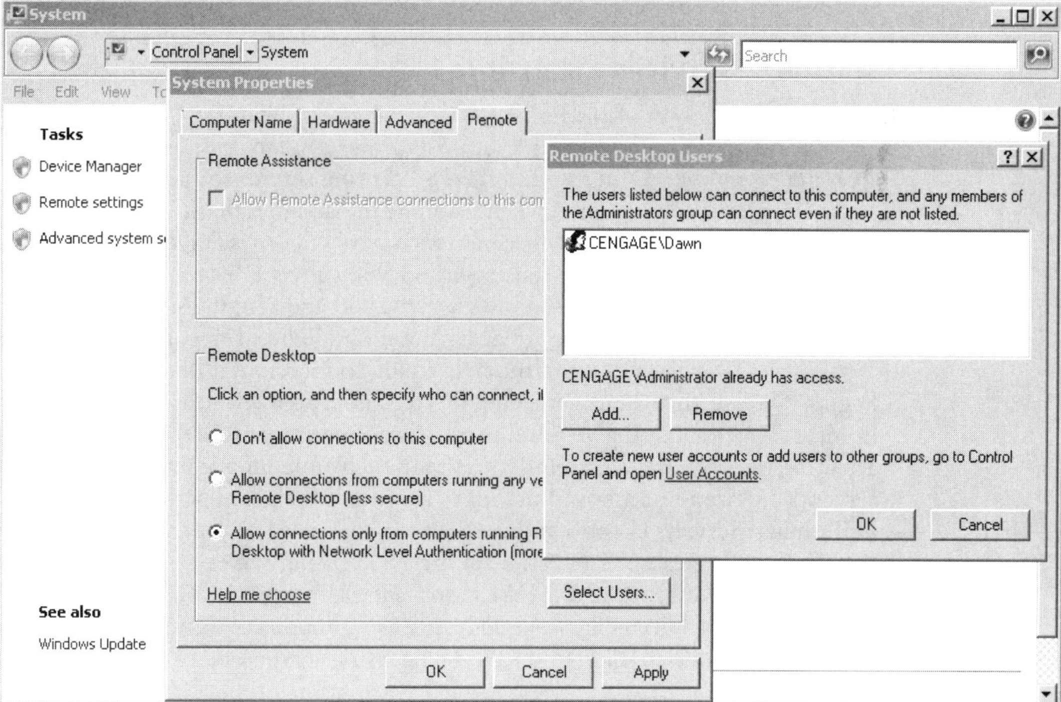

Figure 5-22 Configuring the TS server to accept connections
Courtesy Course Technology/Cengage Learning

8. Return to **DC1**. Click **Start, All Programs, Accessories, Remote Desktop Connection.**

9. Enter **DC2** as the **Computer Name** and click **Connect.** When prompted to enter your credentials, enter **Cengage\Dawn** as the **User Name** and P@ssw0rd as the **Password.** Click **OK.**

   After a moment, you will be logged on to a remote session on DC2.

10. Return to **DC1**. Click **Start, Administrative Tools, Terminal Services, Terminal Services Manager.** Select **DC2.** Your display will look similar to Figure 5-23.

    Notice that two sessions are displayed: the remote session from the user Dawn, and the console session with you logged on as an administrator.

11. Return to **DC2** and log off. Close all open windows in both **DC1** and **DC2.**

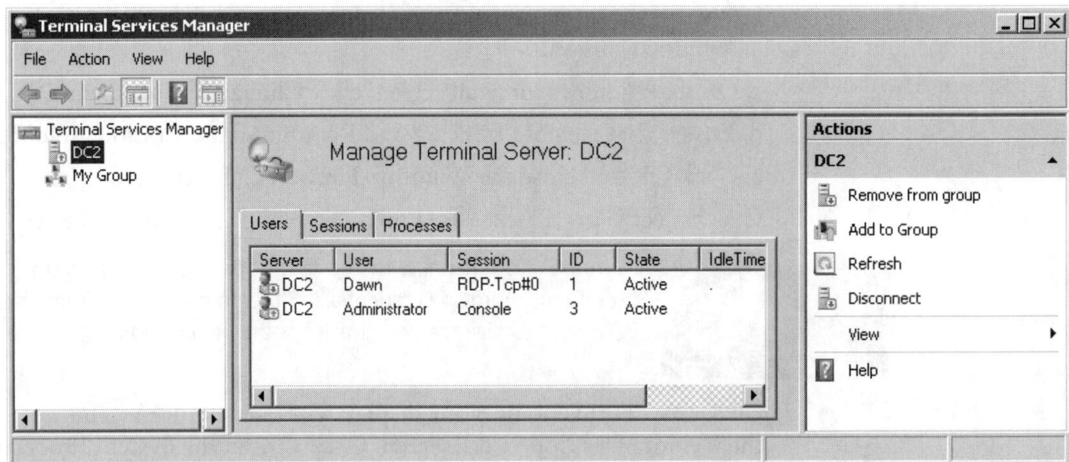

Figure 5-23 Viewing active connections on the terminal server

Courtesy Course Technology/Cengage Learning

Terminal Services Licensing

Every user or computing device that connects to a terminal server needs to have a Terminal Services client access license (TS CAL). TS CALs are managed and maintained on a Terminal Services licensing server. You can add the TS licensing service to the TS server or to another server.

An important consideration when planning the design is that the TS licensing server must be running on a Windows Server 2008 server to support Windows Server 2008 Terminal Services servers. A Windows Server 2008 TS licensing server will support Terminal Services servers running older operating systems, including Windows Server 2000 and Windows Server 2003, but Windows Server 2008 servers running Terminal Services cannot obtain licenses from an older TS licensing server.

When a TS server accepts the first client connection, a licensing grace period of 120 days begins. During this time, Terminal Services operates without a licensing server and without licenses. The goal is to give administrators enough time to deploy the licensing server without affecting the end users. Reminders appear each time an administrator logs on to the terminal server, with a report on how many days remain in the grace period.

Terminal Services clients can be either users or devices. When a client connects to a TS server, the TS server requests a TS CAL from the TS licensing server.

There are two types of TS CALs, and each is mapped to a licensing mode used on the TS server and the TS licensing server. The licensing mode configured on the TS server must match the licensing mode configured on the TS licensing server. The two types of CALs are:

- **TS per-device CALs.** Licenses are issued to devices and any number of users can use the device. When a device connects the first time, the TS license server issues a temporary license. When the device connects the second time, a permanent TS CAL is issued to the device (assuming a TS CAL is available).
- **TS per-user CALs.** Licenses are issued to users and users can access the TS server using any number of devices. Unlike per-device CALs, per-user CALs are not permanently issued to clients and are not tracked by the licensing server. The administrator is responsible for ensuring that enough licenses have been purchased.

The choice between per-device and per-user CALs depends on how your organization uses the computers, but in general, you have more flexibility when per-user is selected, especially if the users are mobile. With per-user CALs, users can connect using different devices, including mobile laptops. A single user could use a desktop PC at work and a mobile computer from home or on the road with a single per-user CAL.

Windows Server 2008 Terminal Services use a discovery process to locate TS licensing servers. If the TS licensing server is on the same server as the TS server, the TS server will automatically be able to discover the licensing server. However, if the licensing server is on a different server from the TS server, the discovery scope needs to be properly configured.

Figure 5-24 shows the selection screen to choose the discovery scope when you are adding the licensing server. In the figure, the Workgroup selection is dimmed because the server is joined to a domain.

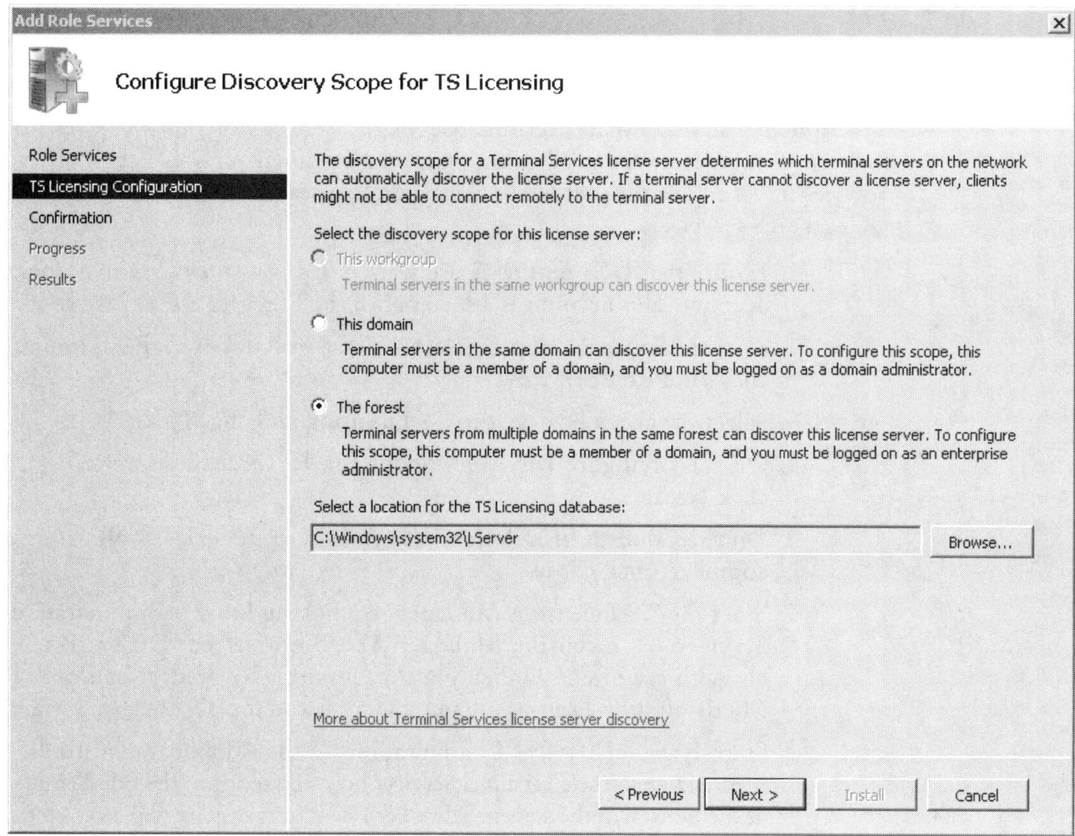

Figure 5-24 Choosing the discovery scope for TS licensing
Courtesy Course Technology/Cengage Learning

Three discovery scopes are available. For the easiest administration, you should use the forest discovery scope:

- **Workgroup discovery scope.** This scope is used when the TS servers are not in a domain, but in a workgroup. Other TS servers in the same workgroup can automatically discover the TS license server.
- **Domain discovery scope.** When this scope is selected, other TS servers in the domain can locate the TS licensing server as long as the server is in the same domain *and* the licensing server is on a domain controller. The domain discovery scope method is most valuable if you want to control which servers are used. You can use this method if you want to control which TS licensing server a TS server will use. For example, if your organization spans multiple sites across slower WAN links with TS servers in different sites, you can configure TS servers to use TS licensing servers in the same site.
- **Forest discovery scope.** When this scope is selected, TS licensing data is published to Active Directory Domain Services (AD DS). TS servers in the forest can then locate a TS licensing server anywhere in the forest, and do not need to be individually configured.

You must be logged on as a member of the Enterprise Admins group to configure forest discovery scope.

You can use the following activity to add and configure Terminal Services Licensing. This activity adds the server, but you won't be able to activate it until you actually purchase licenses.

Activity 5-10: Adding Terminal Services Licensing

Time Required: 20 minutes
Objective: Add Terminal Services Licensing to a TS server.

Description: You need to add Terminal Services Licensing to your TS server. You have decided to use per-user CALs; you need to configure the Terminal Services licensing server and Terminal Services server to use per-user CALs. This activity uses both DC1 (the domain controller) and DC2 (the TS server).

1. Ensure that **DC1** and **DC2** are started. Log on to **DC2** with a domain **Administrator** account. This account is a member of the Enterprise Admins group.
2. Start the **Server Manager**. Select **Roles**. Scroll down to the **Terminal Services** role and click **Add Role Services**.
3. Select the check box next to **TS Licensing** and click **Next**.
4. On the **Configure Discovery Scope for TS Licensing** screen, select **The Forest** and click **Next**.
5. On the **Confirm Installation Selections** screen, click **Install**. After the installation is complete, click **Close**.
6. Start the **TS Licensing Manager** by clicking **Start**, **Administrative Tools**, **Terminal Services**, **TS Licensing Manager**. You'll notice that DC2 is listed; it has a red circle with a white X, indicating that it isn't activated. It can only be activated with Microsoft after licenses are purchased. Close the **TS Licensing Manager**.
7. Start **Terminal Services Configuration** via the **Administrative Tools**, **Terminal Services** menu. Double-click **Terminal Services licensing mode** in the **Edit Settings**, **Licensing** section at the bottom of the screen. Select **Per User**. Your display will look similar to Figure 5-25.

   Notice that you can also specify which license server the terminal server will use by clicking **Use the specified license servers**. This option would be used when the discovery scope is set to **Domain** and TS licensing servers are not located on domain controllers.
8. Click **OK** to set the Licensing mode. If any sessions are active, a notification will appear, indicating that the change will not apply to the active user session. Click **OK**.
9. Close all open windows.

TS RemoteApp

TS RemoteApp programs can be configured on a TS server so that clients can run only the application on the server, instead of a full desktop session. When the application starts, it looks and feels to the user as if it's just another application running on the user's computer, instead of running in a remote session on a server. Because the applications are actually running on the server, they are easier to maintain.

Some of the benefits of using TS RemoteApp applications are:

- **For incompatible applications.** One of the biggest benefits of using TS RemoteApp is that it can allow users to run incompatible programs from a single computer. As an example, Microsoft Outlook 2003 and Microsoft Outlook 2007 couldn't run on the same system. However, a client could be running Microsoft Outlook 2003 on the local system, and then run Microsoft Outlook 2007 via TS RemoteApp.
- **To support remote users.** TS RemoteApp programs can be configured to support remote users either through a VPN or together with TS Gateway. The remote users may be working from home, traveling, or in remote offices. The application only needs to be maintained on the TS server.

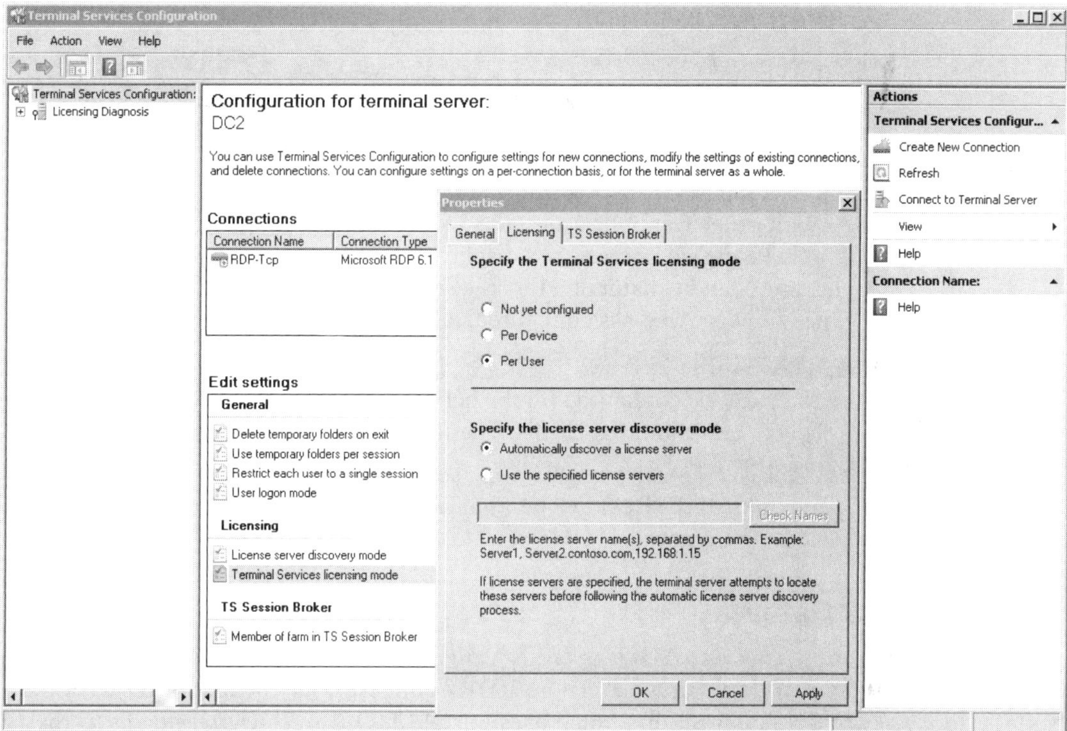

Figure 5-25 Choosing the Licensing mode
Courtesy Course Technology/Cengage Learning

- **For line-of-business (LOB) applications.** An LOB application is developed specifically for the company and is sometimes designed for a specific operating system. Instead of rewriting the application when a new operating system is deployed, the LOB application can be deployed as TS RemoteApp.
- **To support roaming users.** If users don't have dedicated computers but instead roam from one computer to another, the TS RemoteApp program can be made available to the user from any system without requiring the application to be installed on all systems.

Users can start TS RemoteApp applications using multiple methods:

- **Using a Remote Desktop Protocol (.rdp) file.** An administrator can create the .rdp file and distribute it manually or through Group Policy. Users then double-click the .rdp file to start the application.
- **Using .msi files.** Microsoft Windows installer (.msi) files can be created and distributed to clients manually or through Group Policy. When users double-click the shortcut to the .msi file (from their desktop or Start menu), the application is remotely started.
- **Through document activation.** Files are named with extensions that associate them with specific applications. For example, .xls and .xlsx are extensions for Microsoft Excel; .doc and .docx are extensions for Microsoft Word. Extensions of TS RemoteApp programs can be registered with Active Directory, and if a user double-clicks a file with the matching extension, the application will run.
- **From a Web browser.** When TS Web access is configured with Terminal Services, users can simply click a link in Internet Explorer to start the application.

If you'd like to see TS RemoteApp applications in use, consult Microsoft's step-by-step guide at *http://technet.microsoft.com/library/cc730673.aspx*. You can use this guide to add to the capabilities currently configured on the TS server.

TS Web Access

Terminal Services Web Access allows users to access TS RemoteApp programs via a Web browser or access complete desktops using Remote Desktop Web Connection. TS Web Access uses Microsoft's Internet Information Services (IIS) 7.0 as the Web browser. You can configure the TS server hosting the RemoteApp applications to host TS Web Access as well, or you can configure a separate server to run TS Web Access and IIS.

As with other TS applications, the TS RemoteApp program runs as a session on the TS server, with only keyboard, mouse, and display data being transferred back and forth to the client. The applications can be maintained on the server.

Once TS Web Access is configured, it provides several benefits, including:

- **Accessible via Internet or intranet.** Depending on your company's needs, the TS Web Access server can be configured on the perimeter network to serve Internet clients or placed internally to serve internal clients. The functionality is the same.
- **Requires minimal configuration.** TS Web Access can be configured with a simple Web page and links to the RemoteApp applications, or incorporated into a Windows SharePoint Services (WSS) portal.

TS Gateway

Terminal Services Gateway allows clients to remotely connect to TS servers using the Remote Desktop Protocol (RDP). The RDP connection is encapsulated within an HTTPS (HTTP over SSL) connection, which uses port 443. Once the user connects to the TS Gateway server via this secure connection, the TS Gateway server forwards the connection to a Terminal Services server.

Earlier in this chapter, you learned that the SSTP protocol is often used for VPNs because it allows clients to access a VPN server through port 443. HTTPS traffic is often allowed in networks, and firewalls often have port 443 open. Using port 443 might seem like a minor point, but in a production environment it's significant. The boundary protection administrators in charge of managing a firewall do not want to open new ports and add new vulnerabilities. Even when there's a valid reason to open a new port, it usually requires significant paperwork and justification, and approval is rarely automatic.

As an example, port 3389 is the standard port used for Terminal Services. If an administrator wanted to remotely administer a server using Terminal Services (without TS Gateway), port 3389 would need to be opened. Many organizations would simply decide that the risk was too great and keep the port closed. This took away the convenience of remote administration, but tighter security often results in less convenience.

However, with TS Gateway using port 443, additional open ports aren't needed (assuming port 443 is already open). Consider Figure 5-26. A user can use the Remote Desktop Connection client to connect to the TS Gateway server in the perimeter network. Once the user connects to the TS Gateway, the client's requests can be forwarded to the Terminal Services server.

TS Gateway can be integrated with Network Access Protection (NAP) to further enhance security in a network. As discussed earlier in this chapter, NAP can be used to ensure that clients meet specific health policies before being granted access to the network.

Terminal Services Authorization Policies for TS Gateway

TS Gateway requires two authorization policies when it's implemented. You're given an opportunity to add these policies when you add the TS Gateway role service, but you can also add them later:

- **Terminal Services connection authorization policy** (TS CAP). The **TS CAP** policy is used to specify the users or groups that are authorized to connect via TS Gateway.
- **Terminal Services resource authorization policy** (TS RAP). The **TS RAP** is used to specify the computers (based on computer groups) to which users can connect via TS Gateway.

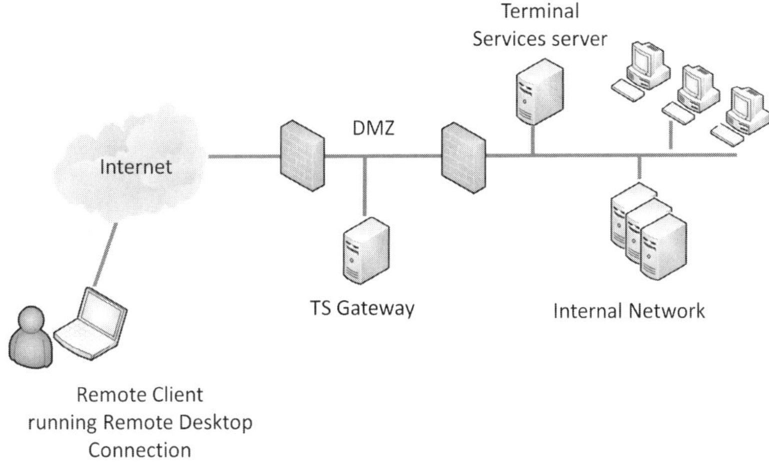

Figure 5-26 Designing Terminal Services with TS Gateway
Courtesy Course Technology/Cengage Learning

These policies work with an implicit deny principle. In other words, connections must be explicitly allowed. If your TS CAP and TS RAP do not specify that certain users can connect to certain computers, connections will not be allowed.

The following activity shows how to add a TS CAP and a TS RAP.

Activity 5-11: Configuring Connection Authorization Policies

Time Required: 30 minutes
Objective: Add a TS CAP and a TS RAP.

Description: Before TS Gateway will work, a TS CAP and a TS RAP must be configured. You need to configure a TS CAP to specify that only members of the Domain Admins group can connect, and configure a TS RAP to specify that members can only connect to DC1 or DC2. This activity uses both DC1 (the domain controller) and DC2 (the TS server).

1. Ensure that **DC1** and **DC2** are started. Log on to **DC2** with a domain **Administrator** account.
2. Start the **TS Gateway Manager** via the **Administrative Tools, Terminal Services** menu.
3. Expand the **Policies** node under the **DC2** server. Right-click **Connection Authorization Policies** and select **Create New Policy, Wizard.**
4. Select **Create a TS CAP and a TS RAP (recommended).** Click **Next.**
5. Type **Domain Admins** as the name for the **TS CAP.** Click **Next.**
6. On the **Requirements** screen, click **Add Group.** Type **Domain Admins** and click **OK.** If you're logged on with the local Administrator account instead of the domain Administrator account, you'll be prompted to provide credentials in the domain. Your display will look similar to Figure 5-27.

   Notice that you can also add computer groups here if you need to restrict access based on the computer and the user accounts. Click **Next.**
7. Review the information on the **Device Redirection** screen. You can modify whether users will be able to use local disk drives, printers, ports, and more. Because the TS server is configured for Network Level Authentication, you can accept the default setting of **Enable Device Redirection for All Client Devices.** Click **Next.**
8. Review the information on the **Summary of TS CAP Settings** screen and click **Next.**

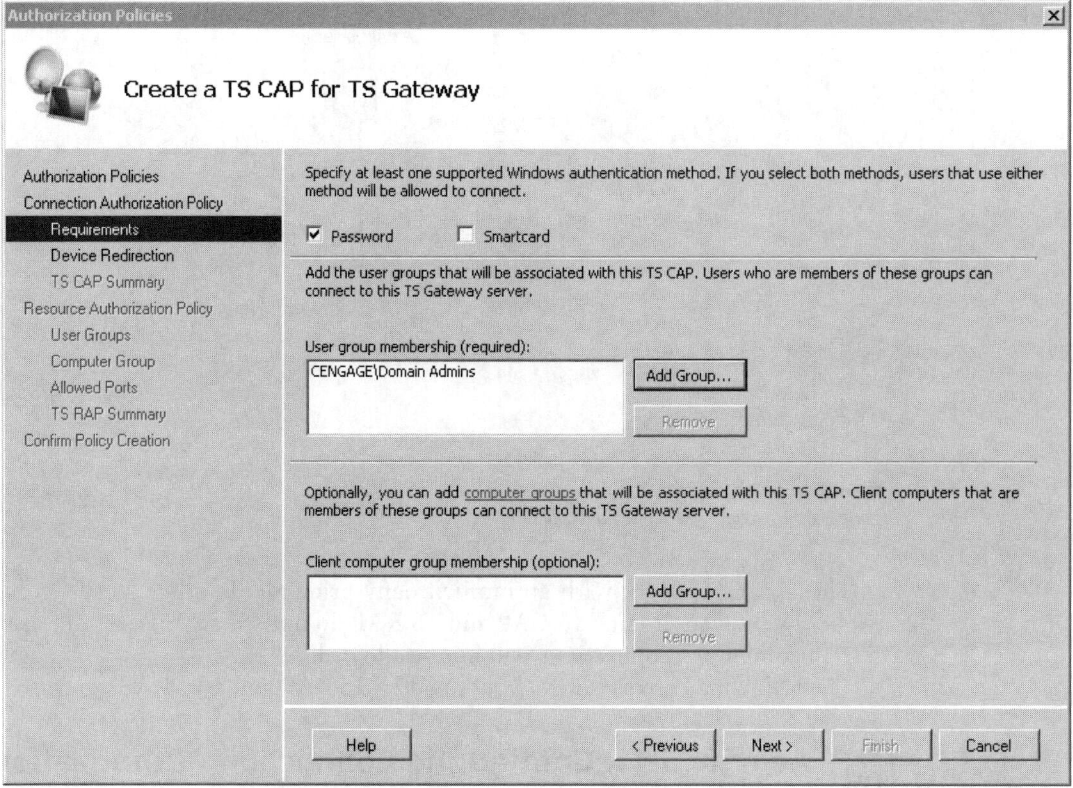

Figure 5-27 Creating a TS CAP for TS Gateway
Courtesy Course Technology/Cengage Learning

9. Type **DCs** as the name for the **TS RAP.** Click **Next.**
10. On the **User Groups** screen, accept the default setting of the **Domain Admins** group and click **Next.**
11. On the **Computer Group** screen, click **Select an existing TS Gateway-managed computer group, or create a new one.** Click **Next.**
12. Type **Domain Controllers** as the name of the group. Type **DC1** as the name of the server and click **Add.** Type **DC2** as the name of the server and click **Add.** Your display will look similar to Figure 5-28. Click **Next.**
13. Review the information on the **Allowed Ports** screen. This screen refers to the ports used to connect to the internal servers from the TS Gateway server (not the port used by external clients to access the TS Gateway server). Accept the default setting of **Allow Connections Only Through TCP Port 3389.** Click **Next.**
14. Review the information on the **Summary of TS RAP Settings** screen and click **Finish.**

TS Session Broker

In organizations with a large number of TS servers, it can be difficult to ensure that any single server doesn't become overloaded with requests while another server remains idle. Several methods are possible for balancing the load among multiple TS servers, but the most efficient method is with TS Session Broker.

It's common to use a basic method of load balancing, such as DNS round robin, with TS Session Broker. With DNS round robin, the DNS server is configured to resolve the name of the

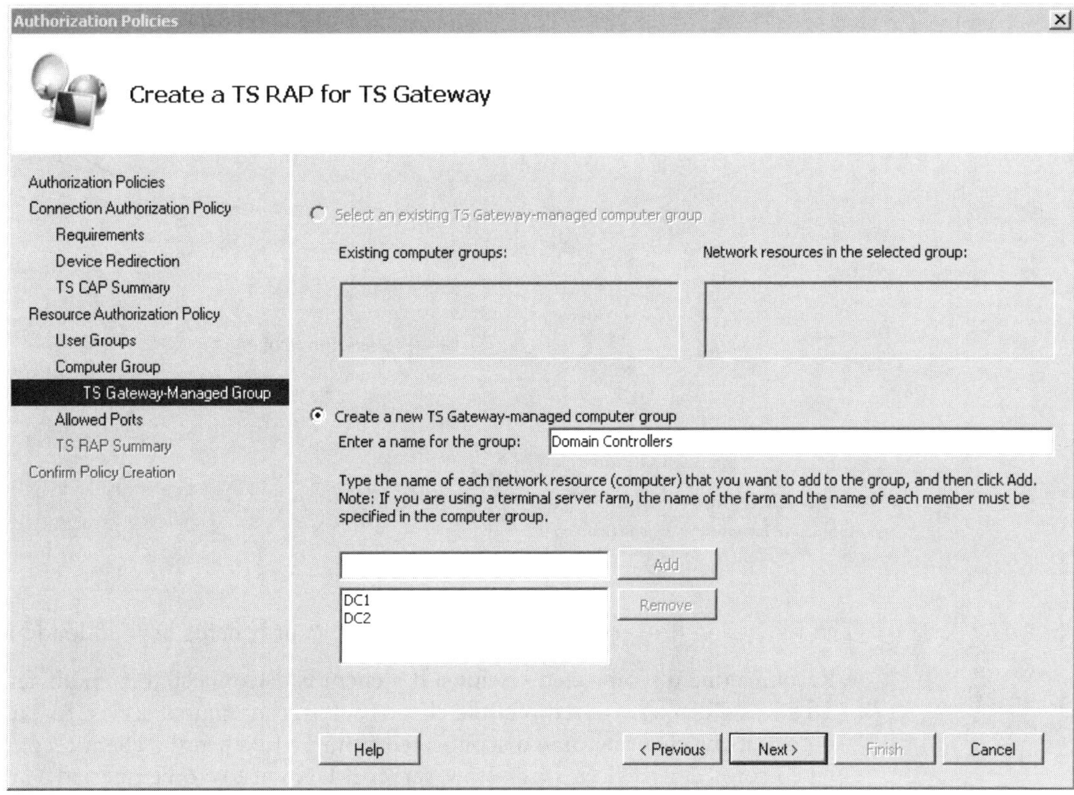

Figure 5-28 Creating a TS RAP for TS Gateway

Courtesy Course Technology/Cengage Learning

TS server farm to a different IP each time it is queried. The first query will return the IP address of the first server, the next query returns the IP address of the next server, and so on. After the IP address of the last server is returned to the client, DNS starts over. If the TS server farm has four TS servers, DNS will answer the first four queries with different IP addresses to send clients to different TS servers.

When multiple terminal servers are configured together to provide services, they are frequently referred to as a farm. This terminology is common for most vendors that have terminal server products, not just Microsoft.

After the basic load-balancing mechanism is used, TS Session Broker can be implemented to provide more advanced load balancing. Figure 5-29 shows how TS Session Broker can be used for load balancing in a Terminal Services farm.

1. The client will first query DNS for the IP address of a TS server in the TS server farm.
2. When a client first connects, it communicates with the TS server based on the IP address it received from DNS. For the figure, imagine that DNS gave the IP address for TS2.
3. This TS server (TS2) then communicates with the TS Session Broker, which is constantly monitoring the TS servers in the TS farm. The TS Session Broker identifies the TS server that has the fewest connections. For the figure, imagine that TS1 has the fewest connections at this time. The TS Session Broker passes this information back to TS2.
4. TS2 informs the client to connect to TS1 and the client then connects.

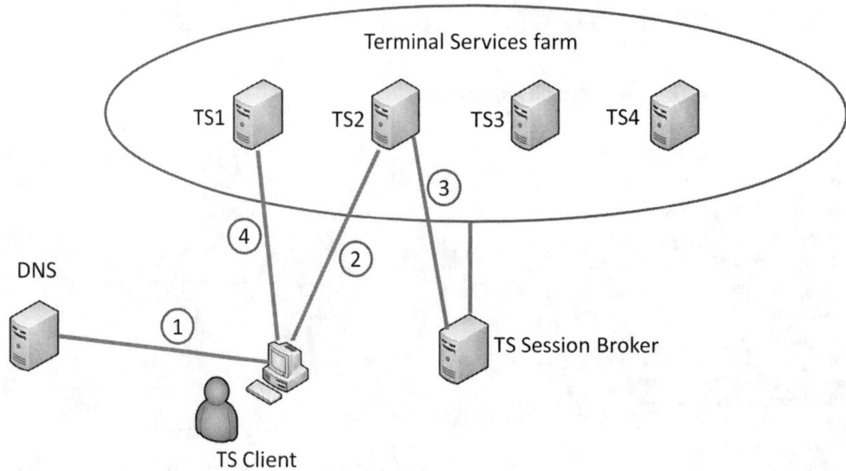

Figure 5-29 Using TS Session Broker for a TS farm
Courtesy Course Technology/Cengage Learning

The TS Session Broker includes two other significant benefits beyond load balancing:

- **Reconnecting disconnected sessions.** If a client is disconnected from an active session, the TS Session Broker will redirect the client back to the original server. As an example, suppose that the client became disconnected from TS1. When the client reconnects, it will first try to connect with TS2 (or another server if DNS needs to be queried again), and then TS2 will forward the request to the TS Session Broker. The TS Session Broker recognizes that the session is active on TS1 and sends this information back to TS2, which sends it to the client.
- **Servers can be weighted.** Weights can be assigned to TS servers to cause them to be assigned more often or less often. For example, if TS1 has twice as much resource power (CPU and RAM) as TS2, you could assign TS1 a weight of 200 and TS2 a weight of 100. TS1 will then be assigned twice as often as TS2.

Chapter Summary

- The Network Policy and Access Services role includes the Remote Access Service, which can be used to host a dial-up and VPN remote access server. VPN servers support PPTP, L2TP/IPSec, and SSTP tunneling protocols. PPTP is the oldest. L2TP/IPSec is more secure than PPTP, but cannot be used if the VPN connection must go through a NAT server. SSTP is the newest and most versatile tunneling protocol; SSTP uses SSL and connects through port 443.
- Network access policies are configured to grant access on remote access servers. Network access policies are a part of the Network Policy Server service. They include conditions, permissions, constraints, and settings. The first policy that meets all the conditions will be used; no other policies are used. If the remote access client cannot meet the conditions of any policy, access is denied.
- Remote Authentication Dial-in User Service (RADIUS) is used to provide centralized authentication for multiple remote access servers. Microsoft's Network Policy Server can be configured as a RADIUS server. When multiple RADIUS servers are used, a RADIUS proxy can be implemented to accept connections from remote access servers and forward them to the appropriate RADIUS server, even if the RADIUS servers are in different forests.

- Network Access Protection (NAP) is used to provide an added layer of protection. It can ensure that clients meet certain health requirements, such as having a firewall enabled, having antivirus and antispyware software installed and up to date, and having current Microsoft updates. NAP can be used with VPN clients (with VPN enforcement) and with DHCP enforcement, IPSec enforcement, and 802.1x enforcement.
- Clients must be running Windows XP SP3, Windows Vista SP1, or newer to support NAP. These clients have System Health Agents that run as part of the Network Access Protection Agent service. These agents determine the health of the system (such as whether the firewall is enabled) and report the status to a System Health Validator (SHV). The SHV creates a Statement of Health, and multiple Statement of Health reports are combined to create a System Statement of Health (SSoH). This SSoH is reported to a Health Registration Authority (HRA). If the SSoH meets the health requirements, the HRA requests a certificate from a certification authority and provides it to the client.

- DHCP enforcement is used to ensure that clients meet specific requirements prior to being granted a lease. 802.1x enforcement is used to restrict unhealthy clients to specific subnets or even specific servers using managed switches and/or wireless access points. IPSec enforcement is used to ensure that clients are using IPSec. IPSec provides secure end-to-end connections with encryption and digital signatures.
- Terminal Services (TS) is a group of technologies that allow clients to run applications and/or full operating system desktops on a remote server. The sessions are hosted on the server, and only the keyboard, mouse, and display data is transferred back and forth between the user and the TS server.
- TS licensing must be configured for TS servers. TS client access licenses (TS CALs) can be purchased on a per-user or per-device basis. When using per-user TS CALs, users can access the TS servers from multiple devices.
- TS licensing is configured with a discovery scope. The Workgroup discovery scope is used when the TS servers are not in a domain. The Domain discovery scope is used when TS servers are located in different sites and you want to specify which TS licensing server a TS server should use. The Forest discovery scope is used when you want TS servers to automatically locate the TS servers without any user interaction.
- TS Gateway allows clients to access internal TS servers from the Internet. The TS Gateway server is placed in the perimeter network and is accessible to clients using SSL over port 443. The TS servers are on the intranet.
- TS RemoteApp applications can be configured on the TS server. TS RemoteApp applications run within a session on the server, but appear to be running as a separate application on the user's desktop. TS Web Access can be used to allow clients to access TS RemoteApp applications via a Web browser.

Key Terms

802.1x enforcement Using Network Access Protection (NAP) to control access to subnets or individual systems based on specific health requirements. It is commonly used with managed switches and wireless access points.

DHCP enforcement Using NAP to ensure that DHCP clients meet specific health requirements prior to being issued a DHCP lease. DHCP enforcement is considered the least secure method of NAP enforcement because it can be overridden by the client by manually assigning an IP address.

Health Registration Authority (HRA) A service used in conjunction with a NAP solution to issue health certificates for clients. The HRA receives certificates from a certification authority (CA).

Host Credential Authorization Protocal (HCAP) A protocol that can be used to integrate Cisco's Network Access Control Server with Microsoft's NAP solution.

IPSec enforcement Using NAP to ensure that clients are using IPSec. IPSec can provide secure end-to-end communication and prevent replay of data between clients.

Layer 2 Tunneling Protocol (L2TP) A tunneling protocol used with VPN connections. L2TP uses IPSec to secure the connection. IPSec cannot pass through a connection using the network address translation (NAT) protocol.

Network access policy A policy used on a remote access server to determine which users are granted access. Policies include conditions, permissions, constraints, and settings. A policy is used when the conditions are met. If conditions are not met for any policy, access is not granted.

Network Access Protection (NAP) A group of technologies used to ensure that clients are healthy before being granted full network access. Health is determined by a health policy that can be configured by the administrator.

Network Policy and Access Services A Windows Server 2008 role that includes the following services: Network Policy Server, Remote Access Service, Routing, Health Registration Authority, and Host Credential Authorization Protocol.

Network Policy Server (NPS) A server hosting the NPS service used to enforce policies for both remote access and Network Access Protection.

Point-to-Point Tunneling Protocol (PPTP) A tunneling protocol used with VPN connections. PPTP uses Microsoft Point-to-Point Encryption (MPPE). It doesn't require a certification authority.

RADIUS proxy A server acting as a centralized routing point for multiple RADIUS servers. RADIUS clients contact the RADIUS proxy, which forwards the request to the appropriate RADIUS server.

Remote access server A server used to provide access to the internal network from a remote location. A remote access server can support dial-up connections, VPN connections, or both.

Remote Authentication Dial-in User Service (RADIUS) A server used for centralized authentication and logging for multiple remote access servers. A Network Policy Server can be configured as a RADIUS server.

Secure Socket Tunneling Protocol (SSTP) A tunneling protocol used with VPN connections. It uses HTTP over SSL (HTTPS) connections on port 443. It provides a higher level of security than PPTP and is more flexible than L2TP/IPSec.

System Health Agent (SHA) An agent that runs on clients as part of the Network Access Protection Agent service. The SHA regularly validates the health of a client and reports this to the System Health Validator.

System Health Validator (SHV) SHVs receive reports of health from System Health Agents and create a Statement of Health (SoH). SoHs are combined to create a System Statement of Health (SSoH). NAP servers can read the SSoH and choose to restrict or grant access based on the client's health.

System Statement of Health (SSoH) A compilation of individual Statement of Health reports created by System Health Agents and System Health Validators. SSOHs are passed to NAP servers when they exist in a network.

Terminal Services (TS) A group of technologies that allow clients to connect to a terminal server and run applications and/or full operating system desktops on the terminal server from the client computer.

Terminal Services connection authorization policy (TS CAP) A policy used with TS Gateway to specify which users or groups are authorized to connect.

Terminal Services farm A group of Terminal Services servers working together. The TS farm can be created to provide load balancing, fault tolerance, or both.

Terminal Services Gateway A TS service that can provide access to internal TS servers from the Internet. Clients connect to the TS Gateway server using HTTPS (on port 443), and the TS Gateway computer acts as a gateway to the internal TS server.

Terminal Services Licensing A TS service that runs on a server to manage TS client access licenses (TS CALs). TS CALs are purchased separately on a per-user or per-device basis.

Terminal Services RemoteApp An application that can be hosted on a TS server. When clients run the application, it appears to run on their system, but it is actually running in a session on the TS server.

Terminal Services resource authorization policy (TS RAP) A policy used with TS Gateway to specify which servers a client can connect with after being authorized by a TS CAP.

Terminal Services Session Broker A TS service that can provide load balancing support for multiple TS servers in a TS farm. TS Session Broker can also ensure that disconnected sessions are reconnected to the same server, and provide weighting to ensure that more powerful servers are used more often than less powerful servers.

Terminal Services Web Access A TS service that can allow clients to run TS RemoteApp programs from a Web browser. TS Web Access uses Internet Information Services (IIS).

Virtual private network (VPN) A private connection created over a public network such as the Internet. VPNs are commonly used to allow clients to access a work network from a remote location.

VPN enforcement Using NAP to ensure that VPN clients meet specific health requirements prior to being granted full access to a network. This method of NAP enforcement is used with remote access solutions.

Review Questions

1. You are planning to create a VPN server to provide network access for users at a subsidiary company. Users can access the Internet from the other company using HTTP and HTTPS; otherwise, connections through the firewall are restricted and you can't modify their firewall. What tunneling protocol should you use to allow these users to access the VPN server?
   a. PPTP
   b. HTTP
   c. L2TP/IPSec
   d. SSTP
2. You are configuring a remote access solution that includes five servers within an Active Directory domain. Four Windows Server 2008 servers are running Routing and Remote Access services to provide remote access. One Windows Server 2008 server is configured as a RADIUS server. You want to ensure that only users in the G_VPN global group are allowed to connect. What should you create?
   a. A network access policy on each of the five Windows Server 2008 servers.
   b. A network access policy on the four Windows Server 2008 servers configured as remote access servers.
   c. A network access policy on the Windows Server 2008 server configured as a RADIUS server.
   d. A network access policy configured as part of the default domain policy.
3. Your organization provides a remote access solution for multiple large companies that have outsourced remote access. You are considering adding a RADIUS proxy server to the design. What will a RADIUS proxy server do?
   a. Process connection requests directly from end users.
   b. Process connection requests directly from remote access servers.
   c. Process connection requests directly from RADIUS servers.
   d. Hold network access policies.

4. Your organization has created a VPN server and placed it in the perimeter network. It has been used successfully, but recently some computers have connected without having up-to-date antivirus definitions or recent Microsoft updates installed. You want to ensure that these computers cannot connect unless the issues are resolved. What should you do?
   a. Implement NAP.
   b. Configure the clients to use WSUS.
   c. Create a GPO and link it to the perimeter network.
   d. Add a RADIUS server.
5. You are designing a remote access solution with Network Access Protection (NAP). You want to include a NAP Health Registration Authority (HRA). What server is required on the network to support the HRA?
   a. RADIUS
   b. RADIUS proxy
   c. certification authority
   d. WSUS
6. A user running Windows Vista SP1 complains that he cannot connect to the network remotely. You verify that other clients can connect. After remoting into the client's system, you determine that the NAP Agent service is disabled. Is this a possible problem, and if so, why? (Choose all that apply.)
   a. No, this would not stop a client from connecting.
   b. Yes. The client will not be able to create an SHV.
   c. Yes. The client will not be able to create an SoH.
   d. Yes. The client will not be able to create an SSoH.
7. Why would you choose IPSec as a NAP enforcement method? (Choose all that apply.)
   a. IPSec provides secure end-to-end communication.
   b. IPSec can be used on unmanaged network devices.
   c. IPSec prevents the replay of data between clients.
   d. IPSec can be used to restrict data transfers based on VLAN IDs.
8. You are designing a NAP solution to ensure that clients can only connect to all resources on the network if they meet the following conditions:
   - They have antivirus software installed and it is up to date.
   - They have antispyware software installed and it is up to date.
   - They have current updates from Microsoft Update.
   - You need to ensure that managed switches on the network only allow clients to access a single server named NAP1 when they first connect. What NAP enforcement method should you use?

   a. DHCP
   b. 802.1x
   c. IPSec
   d. VPN
9. You are designing a NAP enforcement solution for clients in your network. All clients are running Windows SP1 or greater. Network switches used by the clients on the LAN are unmanaged. Users can postpone Windows Updates, and some clients postpone these updates

for weeks without installing them. You want to ensure that only computers with current updates can connect to the network. What NAP enforcement method should you use?

a. DHCP
b. 802.1x
c. IPSec
d. VPN

10. Your network is configured as a single-domain forest. You need to design a plan that prevents computers from having access to network resources if the Windows Firewall is not enabled on the computer, or if they are not running Windows XP SP3 or greater. What should you use?

a. Network Access Protection
b. The Default Domain Controllers GPO
c. The Default Domain GPO
d. RADIUS

11. You are considering a proposal to implement NAP. What is a valid reason to use NAP on a network? (Choose all that apply.)

a. Health state validation
b. Limiting network access
c. Automatically remediating clients
d. Ongoing compliance checks

12. Your organization has one Windows Server 2003 Terminal Services server running in a single-domain forest. This server has been running for over a year. The domain functional level is Windows Server 2003. You are planning to add another Terminal Services server running on Windows Server 2008. What else should be done to support this plan?

a. Raise the domain functional level to Windows Server 2008.
b. Raise the forest functional level to Windows Server 2008.
c. Install Terminal Services licensing on a Windows Server 2008 server.
d. Remove Terminal Services from the Windows Server 2003 server first.

13. You are designing Terminal Services for a single-domain forest. You plan to deploy multiple TS servers at the company's headquarters and a major regional office. Instead of using one TS licensing server for both locations, you plan to use two licensing servers installed on member servers. How should you configure the licensing servers?

a. Use Workgroup discovery scope.
b. Use Domain discovery scope.
c. Use Forest discovery scope.
d. Use Enterprise discovery scope.

14. You are considering a plan to deploy a single Terminal Services server in your single-domain forest. Users will use laptops while on the road and desktop computers while in the office. What licensing mode should you select?

a. Per user
b. Per device
c. Domain discovery
d. Forest discovery

15. Your organization installed two Terminal Services servers that have been running for several months. They are hosting TS RemoteApp applications that users run from their desktops. Suddenly, both servers stop accepting connections from clients. You are able to remote into the servers using an administrator account. What is the likely problem?
    a. Terminal Services Web Access has expired.
    b. Terminal Services Licensing hasn't been configured.
    c. Terminal Services Session Broker needs to be restarted.
    d. Terminal Services Gateway needs to be restarted.
16. You are designing a plan to support the creation of a new remote office for your company. The company has several legacy computers running Windows 2000 that can be used in this office, but the users need to run Windows Vista applications. You have a powerful server you can use, but there isn't money in the budget to purchase new computers right away. What can be done to support these users?
    a. Configure the server with the Terminal Services role.
    b. Configure the server with Remote Desktop for Administration.
    c. Deploy the applications using Group Policy.
    d. Deploy a domain controller with DNS to the site.
17. You are designing a Terminal Services solution that will allow users to access internal Terminal Services servers via the Internet using a TS Gateway server. You want to ensure that only users in the G_TSRemote group can connect via TS Gateway, and that they can only connect to specific servers. What should be created?
    a. A TS RAP for the servers only.
    b. A TS CAP for the users only.
    c. A TS CAP to specify the servers and a TS RAP to specify the users.
    d. A TS CAP to specify the users and a TS RAP to specify the servers.
18. Your organization includes users who frequently travel. These workers need access to an application that is hosted on a Terminal Services server on the internal network. You're asked to design a solution that will allow clients to run this application using an SSL connection. What would you recommend?
    a. Configure a TS Gateway.
    b. Configure TS Session Broker.
    c. Configure WSRM.
    d. Use a VPN with L2TP/IPSec.
19. Your company has a line-of-business application that is currently deployed to a client's computers. The company is planning to upgrade the computers from Windows XP to Windows 7, but testing indicates that the application will not run on Windows 7. What could be done to minimize the cost of running this application?
    a. Deploy the application using TS Gateway.
    b. Deploy the application as a TS RemoteApp.
    c. Deploy the application using TS Session Broker.
    d. Deploy the application with a TS CAP and a TS RAP.
20. Your network includes several Terminal Services servers. One of the servers is older, and has a slower processor and less memory, yet you've noticed that it sometimes has more active sessions than the other servers. Users have complained about the performance. You

want to implement a solution to ensure that sessions are distributed equally to the other TS servers and that the older TS server receives even fewer sessions. What should you do?

a. Implement TS Gateway. Assign a lower weight value to the older TS server.
b. Implement TS Gateway. Assign a higher weight value to the older TS server.
c. Implement TS Session Broker. Assign a lower weight value to the older TS server.
d. Implement TS Session Broker. Assign a higher weight value to the older TS server.

Case Projects

Case Project 5-1: Creating a Remote Access Solution

You need to design a solution that allows external clients with Internet access to access your internal network. The clients will use their computers in public places and when connected to other companies' networks. You've verified that the clients can make connections using HTTPS from the other company networks. What should you create and what protocols should you implement? Explain your answer.

Case Project 5-2: Network Access Policies

You are planning the design of remote access for a network. The clients that connect must be current with Microsoft updates and have a firewall enabled before being granted access to the network. What should be implemented, and what are the different client and server requirements to support the design? Explain your answer.

Case Project 5-3: Designing TS Licensing

Your organization has two primary locations in different cities. The locations are configured as separate sites within a single-domain forest. You are planning to deploy multiple Terminal Services servers to both sites. Most of the clients will be mobile users, and may access the TS servers remotely or from the internal network at either site. You want to minimize TS traffic across the WAN link. What type of TS CALs should you use and what discovery scope should be configured? Explain your answer.

Case Project 5-4: Balancing the Load

Your organization has several Terminal Services servers that are configured in a Terminal Services farm. Two of the servers are older and have less memory than the others. Currently, no method is used to load-balance the servers. You need to design a plan to provide load balancing and ensure that the older servers are used less than the newer ones. What should you do? Explain your answer.

chapter 6

Designing and Implementing a PKI

After reading this chapter and completing the exercises, you will be able to:

- Describe the different uses of a certificate
- Understand the major events in the life cycle of a certificate
- Differentiate between the types of certification authorities
- Install Active Directory Certificate Services
- Identify the uses of certificate templates
- Issue and revoke certificates
- Configure autoenrollment of certificates

A public key infrastructure (PKI) is used to issue and manage certificates. On the surface, a PKI is rather simple, but when you start digging, you'll see that a PKI is more complex. Certificates have a wide range of uses, such as identification, authentication, and encryption. Certificates are issued by different types of certification authorities, such as public and private, root and subordinate, enterprise and stand-alone.

You can implement a PKI in a Microsoft environment by adding the Active Directory Certificate Services (AD CS) server role. When AD CS is added to a domain as an enterprise certification authority, you have additional capabilities that can better control how certificates are issued to clients in your domain.

Some of the significant additions to Windows Server 2008 AD CS include the use of version 3 (V3) certificate templates for newer clients, autoenrollment of certificates, network device enrollment, and restricted enrollment agents. These capabilities are sure to be on the 70-647 exam. You'll learn about all of these new features and more in this chapter.

An Overview of PKI and Certificates

A **public key infrastructure** (**PKI**) includes all of the technologies needed to create, issue, manage, store, and revoke **certificates.** A PKI includes a **certification authority** (**CA**), which is the entity that issues the certificates. A CA can be a company such as VeriSign that issues certificates for use on the Internet, or it can be a software component, such as Microsoft's Certification Authority, that issues certificates. Notice that the primary purpose of a PKI focuses on certificates.

A CA is sometimes referred to as a certificate authority in some documentation. Public CAs such as VeriSign refer to themselves as a certification authority.

Before delving into the details of a PKI, it is worthwhile identifying what a certificate is and how it is used. Certificates are used for a wide variety of purposes, including:

- Creating secure sessions (such as with SSL)
- Digital signatures
- Authentication (clients and servers)
- Code Signing

Figure 6-1 shows the details of a Microsoft certificate that was retrieved from the **Trusted Root Certification Authorities store** of Internet Explorer.

You can view certificates in the Trusted Root Certification Authority through Internet Explorer. Start Internet Explorer, select the Tools menu, and click Internet Options. Select the Content tab and click the Certificates button. Select the Trusted Root Certification Authority tab to view all the certificates in this store. You can then select any of the certificates and click View to view the details.

The General tab includes information on the intended uses for the certificate, who it was issued to, and who issued it. Notice in Figure 6-1 that the certificate was issued to and by the same entity—Microsoft Root Authority. This is a self-signed certificate, and is identified as a root CA. Root CAs are covered in more depth later in the chapter.

The Details tab includes information such as the certificate version (V3), its serial number (a unique number used to identify the certificate), validity dates (1/10/1997 through 12/31/2020), and the public key. The public key is selected, and all 2048 bits are displayed in the bottom pane in hexadecimal.

The Certification Path tab identifies who issued the certificate (Microsoft Root Authority in Figure 6-1).

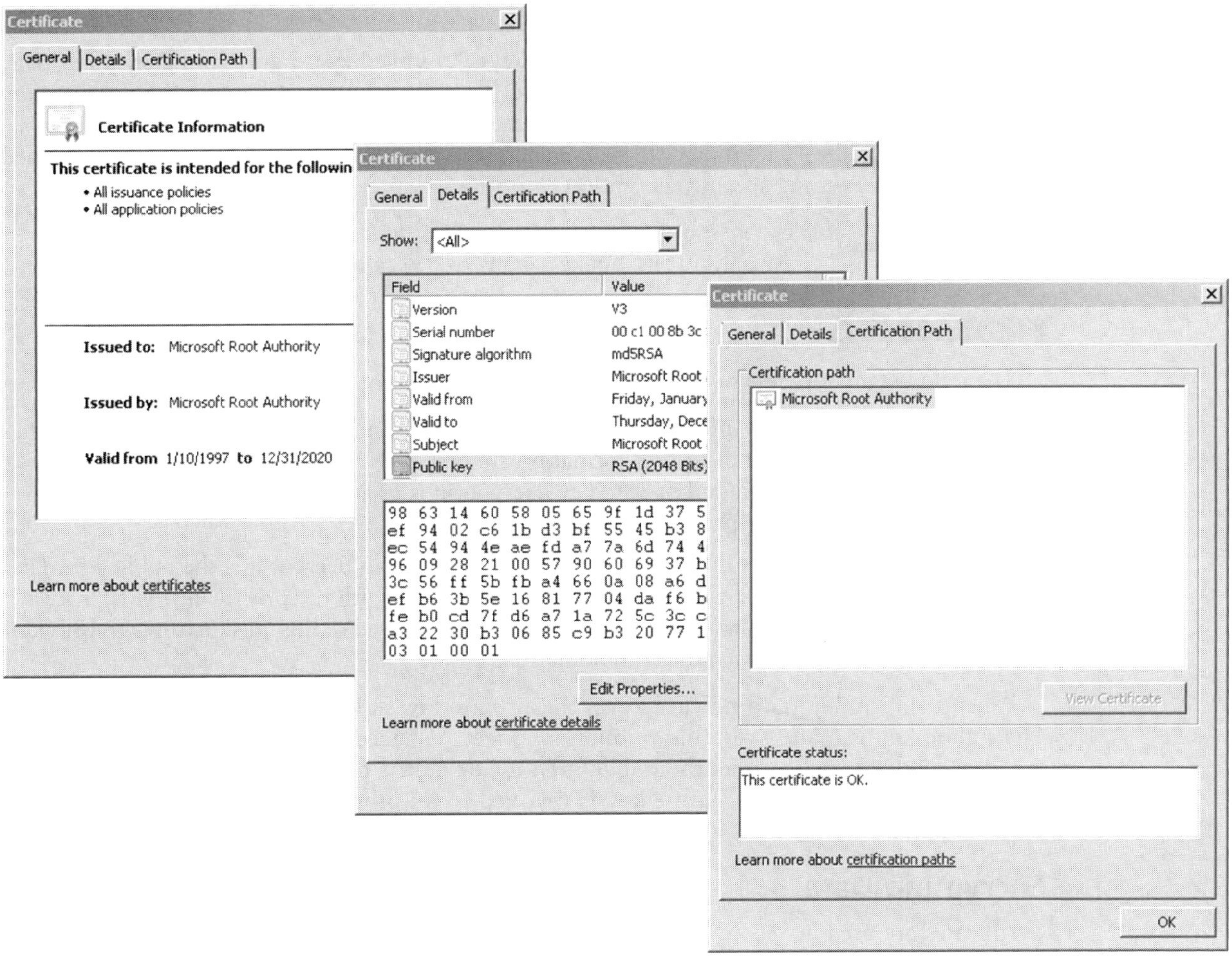

Figure 6-1 Viewing the details of a certificate

Courtesy Course Technology/Cengage Learning

Trusted Certification Authorities

Certificates are issued by a CA; some CAs are trusted and some are not. This is an important concept, because if the CA is trusted, then any certificates issued by the CA are also trusted. Similarly, if the CA is not trusted, the certificate is not trusted.

As an example, consider what happens when you try to pay for a store item by writing a check. You'll be asked to show some type of identification; for example, a driver's license is commonly used. Storekeepers will accept your license because they trust that the department of motor vehicles (DMV) has verified who you are before issuing the license.

On the other hand, if you purchased a cheap ID card from a questionable source and tried to use the ID to cash a check, the storekeeper would probably not accept it. Even if the source was a valid business, it wouldn't have the same level of built-in trust as a state DMV.

Many trustworthy public CAs exist, including VeriSign and Thawte. These companies sell certificates that are commonly used on the Internet. They provide Microsoft with their root certificate, and Microsoft places it into the Trusted Root Certification Authorities store. If the root certificate for a company is in this store, it is considered trusted (just as the DMV is trusted), and any certificates issued by this company are also considered trusted (like a DMV-issued driver's license).

Additionally, it's possible for a company to have an internal CA and deploy the root certificate to all the clients in the company. Clients will then trust all the certificates issued by the internal CA.

Public Key and Private Key

Certificates are used to embed and share **public keys.** A public key is part of a matched key pair; one key is called the public key and one key is called a **private key.** When a public/private key pair is used, one key encrypts the data and the other key decrypts the data. As a simple example, a public key could be 1234 and could be matched to a private key of 4321. These two matched keys work together using specific encryption algorithms.

Keys are much more complex than just four numbers. A small key may have only 40 bits, but keys embedded in certificates are often 2048 bits long.

The following two points highlight basic but important principles of a public/private key pair:

- **If a public key encrypts information, the only key that can decrypt it is the private key.** The same public key *cannot* decrypt information encrypted with the public key. This process of public key encryption and private key decryption is used in SSL sessions to start the encryption of data, which provides confidentiality.
- **If a private key encrypts information, the only key that can decrypt it is the public key.** The same private key *cannot* decrypt information encrypted with the private key. This process of private key encryption and public key decryption is used in digital signatures to provide authentication, integrity, and non-repudiation.

When using public and private keys, the private key is kept private and never shared. The public key is made available publicly and freely shared. If the private key is compromised or inadvertently shared, the public/private key pair is no longer considered secure. The certificate used to share the public key is revoked to let others know the key pair has been compromised.

Encrypting Data

Certificates are used in Secure Socket Layer (SSL) and Transport Layer Security (TLS) sessions to ensure that data can be encrypted and transmitted securely. Chapter 5 discussed the Secure Socket Tunneling Protocol (SSTP) and TS Gateway service. Each requires a certificate to support SSL. SSTP uses SSL to secure VPN sessions and TS Gateway uses SSL to secure Terminal Services sessions.

When a public and private key are used for encryption, the process is called asymmetric encryption. Asymmetric encryption is very secure, but is also resource intensive, requiring a lot of processing power.

On the other hand, symmetric encryption uses a single key (often referred to as a session key) to encrypt and decrypt the data. For example, a key of 1234 could be used to encrypt data. When the data needs to be decrypted, the same key of 1234 would be used. Symmetric encryption is much more efficient than asymmetric encryption, but the challenge is ensuring that both parties in the secure session know the single session key without allowing anyone else to discover it.

In short, that's the purpose of asymmetric encryption in SSL sessions: to privately share the single symmetric session key without allowing anyone else to discover it. Once the symmetric key is known by both parties in a connected session, symmetric encryption is used to encrypt and decrypt the entire session.

As an example, imagine that a user wants to buy something from Amazon using Internet Explorer as the Web browser. Figure 6-2 shows this process.

1. The user clicks the link to Check Out and an HTTPS session is requested.
2. The Amazon Web server sends back a certificate that holds the user's public key. Remember that this key is matched to a single private key that is always kept private on the Amazon server.

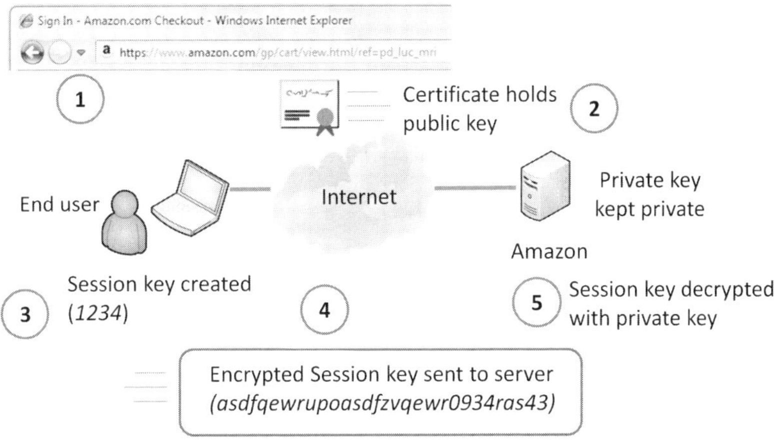

Figure 6-2 Starting an SSL session
Courtesy Course Technology/Cengage Learning

3. Internet Explorer on the client will then create a session key to be used to encrypt and decrypt the data for the symmetric portion of the session. Imagine that the session key is 1234 (though it will actually be much more complex). If this session key is sent across the Internet in clear text, it could be intercepted by an attacker, who could then use the key to decrypt the session.
4. Instead of sending the session key in clear text, Internet Explorer encrypts this key using the public key provided by the Amazon Web server. The encrypted session key could be *asdfqewrupoasdfzvqewr0934ras43*. If an attacker intercepts this encrypted session key, he will not be able to decrypt it, because he does not have Amazon's matching private key. The attacker will not be able to determine the actual session key.
5. Because the session key was encrypted with Amazon's public key, it can only be decrypted with the matching private key on the Amazon Web server. Once the Web server decrypts the encrypted session key, only the client and the server know the session key. The remainder of the session is encrypted and decrypted with this session key.

Some Internet Explorer users might wonder how this process can be secure if others have the same public key. The answer lies in one of the basic principles of asymmetric cryptography: If a public key encrypts information, the only key that can decrypt it is the private key, and no one else has access to the private key.

The session key is used for the entire session. Once the session is ended, either by closing the Web browser or inactivity on the page after a specified period of time, the session key is discarded. Because session keys are randomly created for each session, it is highly improbable that the same computer will use the same session key twice.

Digital Signatures

Another way to use a public/private key pair is with a **digital signature**. A digital signature provides authentication, integrity, and non-repudiation. Authentication provides assurances that the sender is who he appears to be, integrity provides assurances that the data has not been modified, and non-repudiation prevents the sender from later denying he took a specific action.

The perspective of the public and private keys is different when used for digital signatures. Instead of using the public key to encrypt and the private key to decrypt, the process works in reverse. The private key encrypts and the public key decrypts.

Consider Figure 6-3 when following the steps to create a digital signature. Imagine that Sally wants to send a message to Bob; she wants Bob to be assured that she sent the message and that

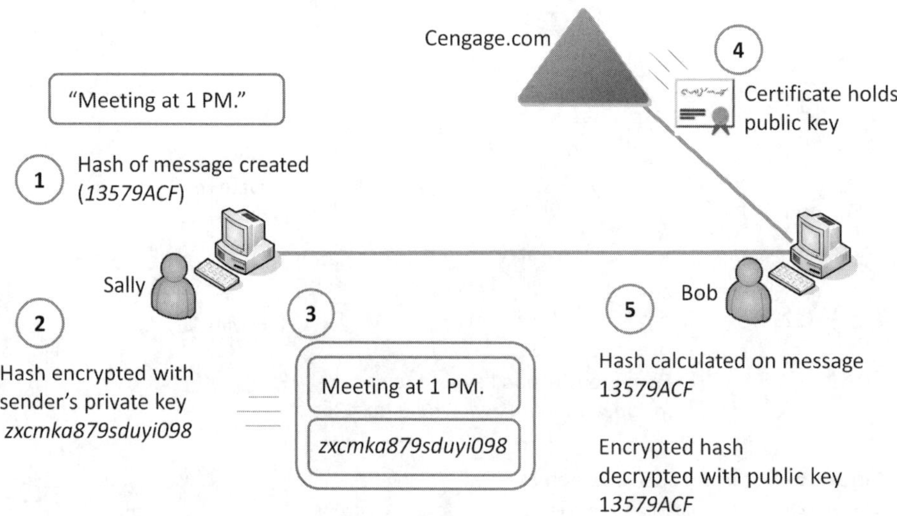

Figure 6-3 Using a digital signature
Courtesy Course Technology/Cengage Learning

it has not been modified. The message is simply "Meeting at 1 PM," but Sally wants to digitally sign it. She could use Microsoft Outlook within an Active Directory domain and simply click a button to create and attach the digital signature for her message.

1. First, the message is hashed. A **hash** is a number created by performing a hashing algorithm on data. As long as the data remains the same, the hashing algorithm will always produce the same hash as a result. Imagine that the hash is 13579ACF (though it would actually be more complex).
2. Next, the hash is encrypted with the sender's private key. The encrypted hash could be *zxcmka879sduyi098*.
3. The message and the encrypted hash of the message are sent to Bob.
4. Bob's client application (such as Microsoft Outlook) would receive the signed message and realize that the sender's public key is needed. It would query Active Directory to retrieve the sender's digital signature certificate, which includes the sender's public key.
5. The encrypted hash is decrypted with the sender's public key, giving the result of 13579ACF. The hash is then calculated on the original message ("Meeting at 1PM"), giving the result of 13579ACF. Both hashes should be the same.

This process provides several layers of security:

- **Authentication.** If the encrypted hash can be decrypted with the sender's public key, it must have been encrypted with the sender's private key. Because only the sender has access to the private key, you know definitively that it was sent by the sender. If the hash is encrypted using a different key (by someone trying to impersonate the sender), the decryption of the hash will fail and the receiver will get an error.
- **Integrity.** If the decrypted hash is the same as the hash that is recalculated on the message, the message has not been modified and has retained data integrity. If the two hashes are different, the message has lost data integrity. You won't know if data integrity was lost due to a network problem or a malicious attack that modified the message, but you do know that the message should not be trusted.
- **Non-repudiation.** Sally cannot believably claim that she did not send the message. Because the hash was decrypted with Sally's public key, it must have been signed by Sally's private key. Additionally, because only Sally would have access to her private key, no one else could have used it.

It's common to wonder how a message is kept secret using digital signatures. The answer is that the message is not really kept secret. The primary purpose of the digital signature is authentication. If the message needs to be kept confidential, it can be encrypted using the receiver's public key as a separate process. Any e-mail can be encrypted only, digitally signed only, or both encrypted and digitally signed.

Certificates and EFS

Microsoft's New Technology File System (NTFS) includes the Encrypting File System (EFS), which can be used by individual users to encrypt their data. EFS uses both asymmetric encryption (with a public and private key) and symmetric encryption (with a single session key). However, the asymmetric portion doesn't require a certification authority. Instead, the public and private keys are generated by the operating system.

The first time a user encrypts data using EFS, a public/private key pair is generated. These keys are stored on the user's local system within the user's profile and protected with the user's master key, which is only accessible when a user successfully logs on. When a user encrypts a file with EFS, the following steps are taken:

- The EFS service creates a symmetric encryption key known as a File Encryption Key (FEK). Symmetric encryption is used to encrypt the data because it is faster and more efficient than asymmetric encryption. This FEK is used to encrypt (and decrypt) the file.
- The FEK is encrypted with the user's public key and stored with the file.
- When a Data Recovery Agent (DRA) is designated (normally the domain administrator account), the FEK is also encrypted with the DRA public key and stored with the file.
- When a user needs to access the file, the user's private key is retrieved and used to decrypt the FEK. The decrypted FEK is then used to decrypt the file.
- If necessary, the DRA can recover the file. The DRA's private key is retrieved and used to decrypt the FEK, and the decrypted FEK is then used to decrypt the file.

A challenge with this configuration is that the user's public and private keys are stored in the user's profile. The public key and public key certificate are stored in the ...\SystemCertificates\My\Certificates folder of the user profile, and the private key is stored in the ....\Crypto\RSA folder. These keys are sufficiently protected with the user's master key. However, if the profile is deleted or corrupted, or the user just uses a different computer, the private key is no longer accessible and the data can no longer be decrypted.

Different operating systems store the profile in different paths, so the beginning path for profiles could be different. For example, Windows XP stores user profiles in the Documents and Settings folder, while Windows 7 stores the profiles in the Users folder.

Companies take one of two steps to prevent the loss of data due to encryption:

- **EFS is disabled via Group Policy.** This prevents curious users from encrypting their data just for the fun of it.
- **DRAs are enabled.** A DRA (often the administrator) is designated. The DRA can then recover data if the user's profile is lost.

Certificates and Smart Cards

A smart card is used for authentication. It is approximately the size of a credit card, and includes a microprocessor and a user certificate. A smart card combines two factors of authentication: something you have (the smart card) and something you know (like a PIN or user name and password). Smart cards are much more secure than a simple user name and password.

A CA can issue the certificates used for smart cards, but many other elements must exist within an organization before it can use smart cards. Hardware is needed to embed the certificate into the smart card when it is issued to clients. Additionally, workstations need the ability to read the smart card when a user logs on. All of these elements add cost for an organization.

Despite the trade-off with cost, smart cards are becoming much more common in the workplace, due to the added authentication security they provide. Even if a user loses the card, the finder cannot use it to log on (unless the user wrote his PIN on the card, which is not recommended).

Certificates and WinRM

Windows Remote Management (WinRM) is a standard used to remotely manage Windows servers. Using WinRM, you can execute command-line commands from one server against a remote server. The remote server needs to be configured to accept and respond to these commands using Windows Remote Shell (WinRS).

When the two clients are in the same forest, WinRM and WinRS traffic use HTTP over port 80 for communication. Encryption and authentication methods built into Active Directory, such as Kerberos Security Support Provider (SSP), are used to secure the connection. However, if the two clients are not in the same forest, WinRM will not function unless the traffic is secured using another method.

It's possible to secure WinRM/WinRS traffic using HTTPS. When this is done, a certificate needs to be issued to the server running WinRM. This certificate can be used for server authentication and to start an SSL session with HTTPS to secure the session.

Certificate Life Cycle Management

Certificate life cycle management involves the creation, issuing, managing, and revoking of certificates. Any CA (including Microsoft's Active Directory Certificate Services) needs to be able to support certificates for the entire life cycle.

Certificates are requested from the CA; these certificate requests need to be approved. Approval can be automatic using **autoenrollment**, or it might be manual—a CA manager might review the certificate request and approve or deny it. Once the request is approved, the certificate is enrolled; an enrolled certificate is managed by the CA for the entire life cycle.

The following sections cover these certificate life cycle events:

- Certificate enrollment
- Certificate revocation
- Certificate validation

Certificate Enrollment

Certificates can be requested in several ways, depending largely on the type of CA. For a public or stand-alone CA, the methods used to request the certificate involve direct user interaction. If the CA is an enterprise CA, the process can be automated. Certificates can be requested in the following ways:

- **Manually by copying files.** When using public CAs, the certificate request can be put into a specific format and saved as a certificate request file. This file can be forwarded to the CA for approval.
- **Using the Certificates snap-in.** The Certificates snap-in can be added to a Microsoft Management Console (MMC) and used to request certificates from an enterprise CA. You'll learn more about the Certificates snap-in later in this chapter.

- **Manually via Web enrollment.** Public CAs often have Web pages that clients can use to submit data for a certificate request. This option can also be set up within an enterprise CA to accept certificate requests for clients that do not have domain accounts.
- **Automatically using autoenrollment.** Certificate templates can be created, permissions assigned, and Group Policy configured to allow certificates to be automatically enrolled for users. Very little user interaction is required.

Certificate Revocation Lists

Certificates have validity dates that allow them to expire naturally. However, a certificate can be revoked prior to the expiration date. Revoked certificates are published by the CA via a **certificate revocation list (CRL)** using an X.509 version 2 certificate.

CRL is commonly pronounced as "crill."

Figure 6-4 shows a copy of the CRL published as a V2 certificate. It has only a single revoked certificate. Notice that the certificate is identified by the serial number; when the certificate is selected, details on the revocation are included.

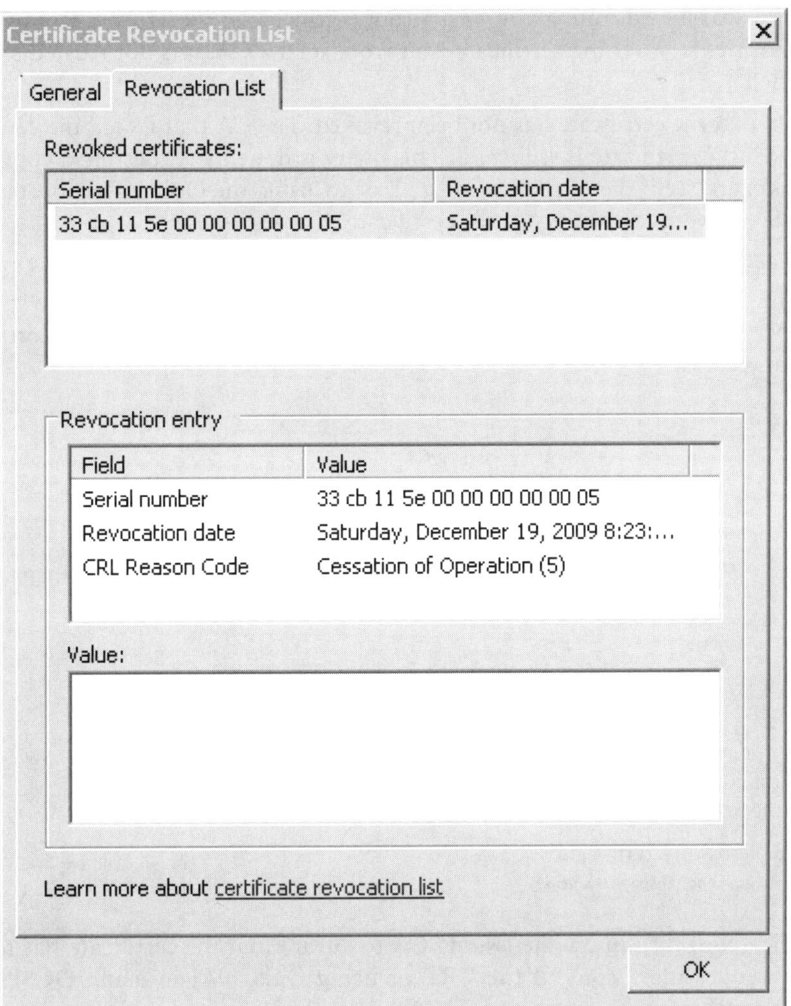

Figure 6-4 Certificate revocation list
Courtesy Course Technology/Cengage Learning

There are multiple reasons to revoke a certificate, but the primary reason would be if the certificate's private key became compromised. The private key should always remain private, but if someone other than the intended subject has access to the private key, it no longer provides the same protection. A certificate might also be revoked because a business affiliation has changed or privileges have been withdrawn.

The term "subject" in this context refers to a user, a smart card, a desktop or server computer, or other type of computing device.

The CRL can be published as a new CRL or a delta CRL. A new CRL is a complete listing of all certificates revoked by the CA. A delta CRL only includes the updates since the last time the CRL was published. Delta is a Greek letter used to indicate a change.

Validating the Certificate

If you recall the SSL session created with Amazon, as shown in Figure 6-2, something else was occurring. The client that initiated the secure session needed to be assured that the certificate it received from the server was trustworthy, and hadn't been compromised. To provide this security, two additional steps occur when the SSL session is started:

- **Verify that the certificate is issued from a trusted authority**. The certificate is checked to see if it was issued from a CA with a root certificate in the Trusted Root Certification Authorities store. If the certificate isn't from such a CA, it is not trusted and the user is notified.
- **Verify that the certificate has not been revoked.** The CA that issued the certificate is queried to see if the certificate is still valid. This query is done by requesting a copy of the CRL and checking to see if the certificate is listed, or by using the Online Certificate Status Protocol (OCSP) to verify the status of the certificate.

As an example, consider Figure 6-5. After the client requests an HTTPS session, the server returns the certificate with the embedded public key. The client receives the certificate and then checks the Trusted Root Certification Authorities store to verify that the certificate was issued from a trusted CA.

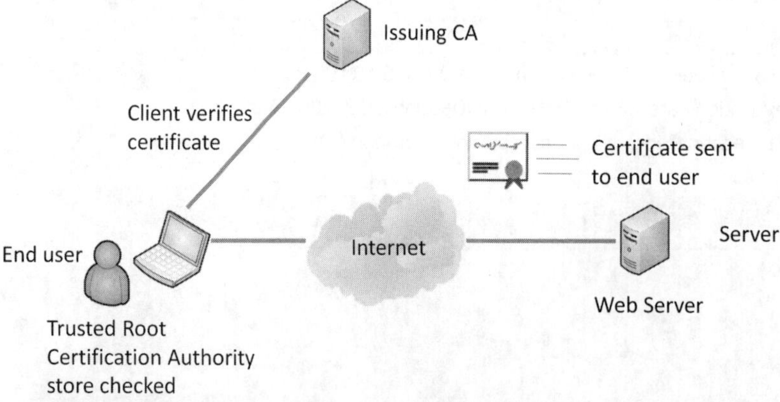

Figure 6-5 Verifying a certificate
Courtesy Course Technology/Cengage Learning

The client will then query the issuing CA to ensure that the certificate has not been revoked, either by requesting a copy of the CRL or using OCSP. When using OCSP, the client sends the serial number of the certificate. The CA will then respond with the status. As long as the certificate is valid and hasn't been revoked, the online responder will respond with a status of Healthy.

Types of Certification Authorities

When considering the design of a public key infrastructure, it's important to understand the different types of CAs:

- **Root CA vs. Subordinate CA.** The **root CA** is the first CA in the hierarchy. If additional CAs are added in the same trust path, they are referred to as **subordinate CAs.** If multiple levels are used in the hierarchy, the lowest-level CAs are commonly called issuing CAs.
- **Public CA vs. Private CA.** A **public CA** is trusted by Internet users, while a **private CA** is only trusted by users within a company. A public CA's root certificate is published to the Trusted Root Certification Authorities store for Internet users; certificates issued from a public CA are automatically trusted. Private CAs are internal to an organization and don't have their root certificates published to users outside the organization. If the certificate issued from the CA is not in the Trusted Root Certification Authorities store, then certificates issued by the CA are not trusted, resulting in an error. If external users need to use the certificates without errors, a certificate from a public CA is required.
- **Enterprise CA vs. Stand-alone CA.** An **enterprise CA** is heavily integrated with Active Directory and automates many of the tasks to clients in Active Directory. A **stand-alone CA** can be a member of Active Directory and can have some information published through Active Directory, but it can also be completely separate from a domain and kept as an offline CA.

When preparing for the 70-647 exam, ensure that you understand the purposes of the CA types and the differences between them.

All of these choices are explained in greater depth in the following sections.

Root vs. Subordinate CA (CA Hierarchy)

The first CA installed in a PKI is referred to as the root CA. The root CA uses a self-signed certificate for identity purposes. When a public company creates a root CA for the purposes of selling certificates, it must take additional steps following established business standards so that other companies trust them. However, within a domain, an enterprise administrator can create the root CA and choose to have clients throughout the enterprise automatically trust it.

A company can use just a single root CA and issue certificates to clients from this CA. However, if the organization is large, a CA hierarchy can be created, similar to the one shown in Figure 6-6. The root CA issues certificates to subordinate CAs, which can then issue certificates to the issuing CAs. The issuing CAs actually issue certificates to users and computers.

When a CA hierarchy is used, a trust path is created. If a client has a certificate from the root CA in the Trusted Root Certification Authorities store, it will trust certificates issued from any servers in the hierarchy. This makes the root CA quite valuable. If the root CA becomes compromised, all certificates issued by any CAs in the hierarchy are also considered compromised. All certificates would need to be revoked.

Public CA vs. Private CA

When your organization needs to use certificates, one decision you'll need to consider is whether to use a public CA or a private CA. A public CA is established publicly from a company such as VeriSign or Thawte, while a private CA is created internally. Certificates must be purchased from a public CA, but a company can create its own certificates if it manages a private CA.

Consider the following two scenarios as examples.

Imagine that Bob is using an e-commerce Web site that chose to cut costs and did not purchase a certificate, but instead created its own private CA. Bob decides to make a purchase, pulls out his credit card, and clicks Check Out to start an HTTPS session.

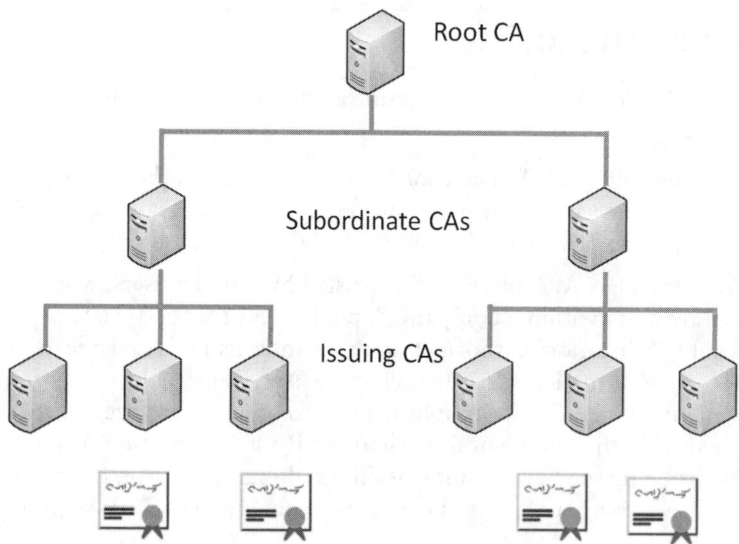

Figure 6-6 Using a CA hierarchy
Courtesy Course Technology/Cengage Learning

The Web site sends the certificate with its public key to start a secure SSL session. Internet Explorer (IE) checks the Trusted Root Certification Authorities store but doesn't find a certificate in the trust path, so it reports an error similar to the one shown in Figure 6-7. Bob sees all of these errors, so it's unlikely that he will continue with the purchase.

If a company is involved in e-commerce on the Internet, a certificate that is in the Trusted Root Certification Authorities store needs to be purchased from a public CA. If a certificate is purchased from a public CA in the trusted path, the user won't receive an error like the one in Figure 6-7.

On the other hand, imagine that a company wants to create a TS Gateway server so that employees can access TS RemoteApp applications on internal Terminal Services servers from external locations. TS Gateway would be needed; it requires a certificate so that an SSL session can be established. However, instead of purchasing a certificate from a public CA, the company can create an internal private CA using AD CS. This internal CA can be used to issue a certificate for TS Gateway. By default, the private CA does not have a certificate in the Trusted Root Certification Authorities store, so an error will occur.

However, employees can be provided directions on how to establish sessions through TS Gateway; one of the steps can display the error and explain what to do when the error appears. Because the employer is providing the access and the directions explain the error, including how to deal with it, users will continue.

If you control the end users' computers, you can use several methods to add the root CA's certificate to the Trusted Root Certification Authorities store with Group Policy. Users can also be given directions for how to add this certificate if their computers are not controlled with Group Policy.

When deciding between a public and private CA, consider the following points.

- **Trusted certificates.** An established public CA will have a root certificate in the Trusted Root Certification Authorities store. Certificates purchased from an established public CA are automatically trusted.
- **Certificate errors.** If you want to avoid errors, use certificates purchased from a public CA with a root certificate in the Trusted Root Certification Authorities store.
- **Cost vs. Convenience.** Certificates must be purchased from a public CA, but they are easy to implement. Certificates from a private CA have no direct charges, but the CA must be internally configured and implemented. If one certificate is needed, it's best to purchase it. If 100 certificates are needed internally, it's cheaper in the long run to create a CA.

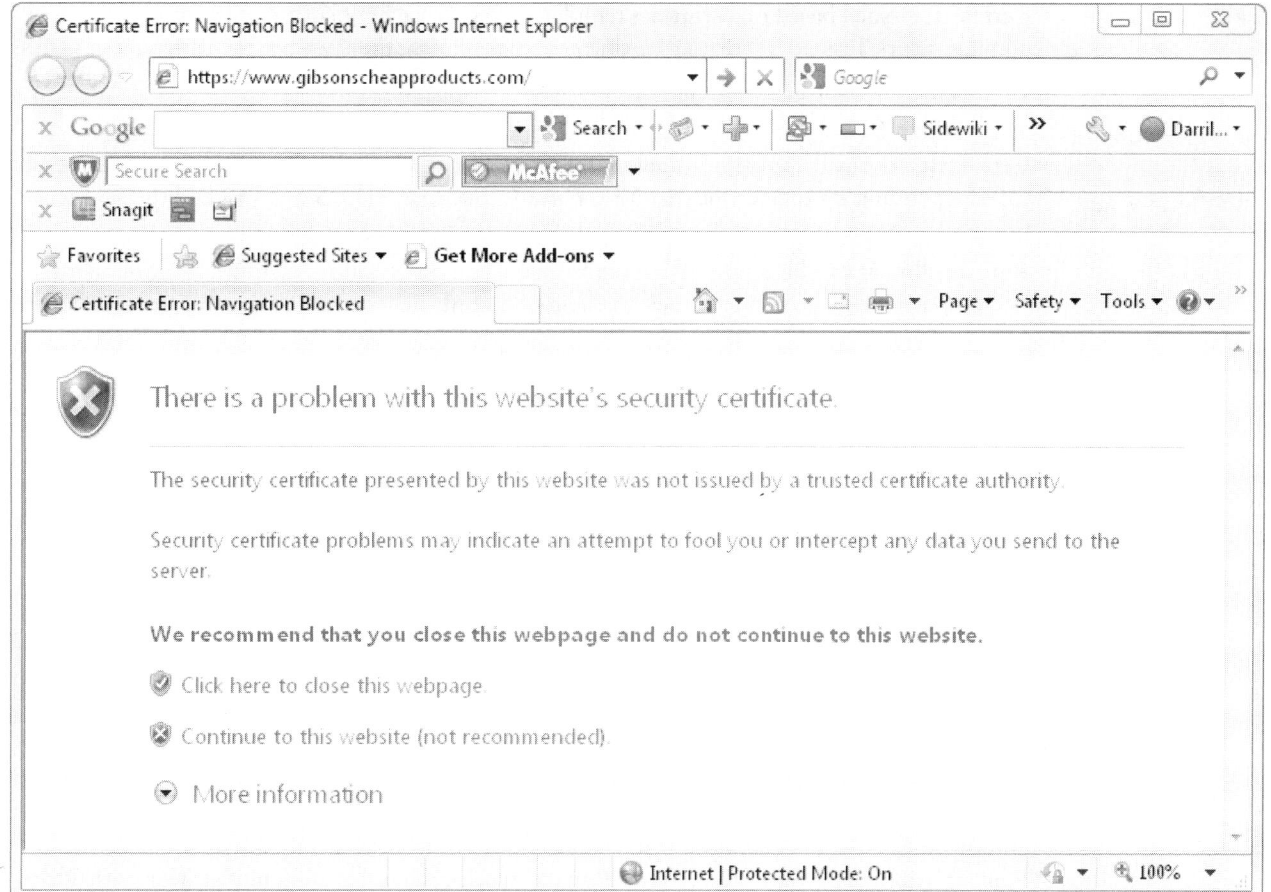

Figure 6-7 Error from an untrusted certificate
Courtesy Course Technology/Cengage Learning

Enterprise CA vs. Stand-Alone CA

The choice between an enterprise CA and a stand-alone CA largely depends on how much interaction your CA should have with Active Directory Domain Services (AD DS). An enterprise CA is heavily integrated with Active Directory, and can be used to automate many of the processes associated with deploying certificates to Active Directory clients. A stand-alone CA can be configured within a domain (or in a workgroup), and can be configured to automate some of the deployment of certificates. However, a stand-alone CA's integration with Active Directory is limited.

An enterprise CA would be used as a private CA, while a stand-alone CA could be used either as a public or private CA.

The following points describe an enterprise CA.

- **Must be in a domain.** Requires access to AD DS. Configuration data is stored in Active Directory.
- **Root certificate publication automatic.** Group Policy is automatically configured to distribute the trusted root certificate to clients. The root certificate is deployed to the end user's Trusted Root Certification Authorities store. Certificates issued by the enterprise root CA or any subordinate CAs will automatically be trusted by users and computers in the domain.
- **Certificate publication automatic.** Certificates and certificate revocation lists (CRLs) issued by the CA are automatically published to AD DS. The CA's root certificate and CRL are published in Active Directory.

- **Certificates issued based on certificate templates.** Certificate templates ease the workload of administrators. Instead of creating certificates from scratch, they can be created from templates.
- **Certificate data can be generated automatically.** Information needed for the certificate can be obtained from AD DS instead of being manually entered by the requestor.
- **Certificate approval can be automated.** Certificates can be approved manually or automatically, depending on the certificate and the needs. Because AD DS can validate the information on the requestor, the CA administrator doesn't need to verify the information.
- **Autoenrollment can be used with an enterprise CA.** Autoenrollment allows an administrator to configure certificates to be issued to clients without them having to request the certificates.

The following points describe a stand-alone CA. It differs from an enterprise CA in three major ways: interaction with AD DS is limited, certificate templates cannot be used, and autoenrollment is not possible.

- **AD DS not needed.** A stand-alone CA can be in a domain but it doesn't require AD DS.
- **Can be taken off-line.** A stand-alone CA can be removed from the network and placed in a more secure area.
- **Root certificate publication.** Group Policy can be configured to distribute the root certificate to users in the domain, but this does not normally occur automatically, as it does with an enterprise CA. As an exception, if the stand-alone root CA is installed by a member of the Domain Admins group or an administrator with Write access to a domain controller, the root certificate is automatically added to the Trusted Root Certification Authorities store for all users and computers in the domain.
- **Certificate publication.** Certificates and CRLs issued by the CA can be published to AD DS if it is connected to a domain, but this does not occur automatically, as it does with an enterprise CA. As an exception, if the stand-alone root CA is installed by a member of the Domain Admins group of the parent domain in a forest, or by an administrator with Write access to AD CS, then the stand-alone CA will publish the CRL to AD DS.
- **Certificate templates.** Stand-alone CAs do not use certificate templates.
- **Only manual certificate requests are allowed.** Information needed for the certificate must be manually entered by the requestor; the requestor must specify the type of certificate needed.
- **Certificates are manually approved.** Certificate requests are set to pending until an administrator verifies the information and approves the request.
- **Autoenrollment is not possible with a stand-alone CA.** Autoenrollment is only possible with certificate templates, which are not supported by stand-alone CAs.

Active Directory Certificate Services (AD CS)

Microsoft's **Active Directory Certificate Services** (**AD CS**) can be used to implement a PKI, including a fully functioning certification authority. When designing a plan to use AD CS, you should be aware of its capabilities and limitations with different versions of Windows Server 2008. You can't install AD CS on all versions, and the versions that do support AD CS don't always support all of its capabilities.

As a reminder, the editions of Windows Server 2008 are Web Edition, Standard Edition, Enterprise Edition, and Datacenter Edition. Web Edition is designed to be used as a Web server; it does not support Active Directory, including AD CS. The Standard Edition provides limited support for AD CS; both Enterprise and Datacenter provide full support. AD CS is not supported on Server Core editions of Windows Server 2008 (though AD CS is supported on Server Core editions of Windows Server 2008 R2).

Table 6-1 shows which components are supported by the various editions of Windows Server 2008.

Table 6-1 Supported AD CS components

Component	Standard Edition	Enterprise Edition	Datacenter Edition
Certificate Authority (CA)	Yes	Yes	Yes
Network Device Enrollment service	No	Yes	Yes
Online Responder service	No	Yes	Yes
CA Web enrollment support	Yes	Yes	Yes

Once the CA has been added to the Windows Server 2008 server, different features will be available, depending on the operating system edition. Table 6-2 shows the features supported on different editions.

Table 6-2 Supported AD CS features

Feature	Standard Edition	Enterprise Edition	Datacenter Edition
Customizable V2 and V3 templates	No	Yes	Yes
Key archival	No	Yes	Yes
Role separation	No	Yes	Yes
Delegated enrollment agent restrictions	No	Yes	Yes

When using Windows Server 2008 to host AD CS, you need to consider the capabilities of the operating system. For example, if you want to ensure that the server hosting AD CS remains highly available, you can configure a failover clustering solution. In short, a failover cluster consists of two or more servers that act as nodes. If one node fails, the other node can take over. Even if a single server suffers a catastrophic failure, the cluster ensures that another server in the cluster continues to provide the services. Failover clustering is discussed in more depth in Chapter 8.

Windows Server 2008 Enterprise and Datacenter editions both support failover clustering, but Windows Server 2008 Standard Edition does not.

Implementing AD CS

Certificates can be issued by AD CS and used for many different scenarios, including virtual private networks (VPNs), IPSec, Network Access Protection (NAP), wireless networks, EFS, smart cards, and more. A significant feature of AD CS is the ability to use certificate templates within an enterprise CA.

This section describes many of the implementation details of AD CS:

- Certificate templates
- Installing AD CS
- Certificate services administrative separation
- Online Responder service
- Issuing and revoking certificates
- Deploying trusted root certificates via Group Policy
- Automatic certificate enrollment
- Network Device Enrollment service
- Restricted enrollment agents

Certificate Templates

Certificate templates are used within an enterprise CA to create certificates based on preconfigured templates. Instead of creating a certificate from scratch, you can make a copy of the template. Additionally, existing templates can be modified to create new templates. The template includes the rules, settings, and formats used for certificates, including enrollment, use, renewal, and management. You cannot use certificate templates with a stand-alone CA.

Some commonly used certificate templates are:

- **User.** Used for e-mail, EFS, and client authentication. It provides both a signature and encryption.
- **Web server.** Proves the identity of a Web server and provides both a signature and encryption.
- **Root certification authority.** Proves the identity of a root CA and provides a signature.
- **OCSP response signing.** Used by the online responder to sign responses to certificate status requests.
- **IPSec.** Used by the IPSec protocol to sign, encrypt, and decrypt network communication.
- **Enrollment agent.** Used to request certificates on behalf of a user and provides a signature.
- **Enrollment agent (computer).** Used to request certificates on behalf of a computer and provides a signature.

The templates are stored in Active Directory Domain Services; when a certificate is requested, it is issued from the template.

Certificate template versions are different from certificate versions. Most certificates today are X.509 V3 certificates, except for certificate revocation list (CRL) certificates, which are X.509 V2 certificates. The versions of AD CS certificate templates have no direct relationship with the version of X.509 certificates.

The different versions of templates are:

- **V1 certificate templates.** V1 templates were introduced with Windows 2000 Server and are included for backward compatibility. When new templates are created from a V1 template, they are created as V2 or V3 templates.
- **V2 certificate templates.** Windows Server 2008 includes many default V2 templates that can be customized. Windows XP and newer clients support V2 certificates for autoenrollment. When templates are duplicated, Windows 2003 Server, Enterprise Edition is used to create a V2 template.
- **V3 certificate templates.** V3 templates add advanced cryptographic settings to the certificate, and can be used with Windows Vista and later clients. You cannot use V3 templates with Windows XP clients. When templates are duplicated, Windows Server 2008, Enterprise Edition is used to create a V3 template. You'll see this when you create a V3 template in Activity 6-2.

There is a subtle yet critical difference between V2 and V3 templates in AD CS. V3 templates use new cryptographic interfaces called Crypto Next Generation (CNG), which are different from the CryptoAPI interfaces used in V1 and V2 templates. The cryptographic interfaces make V3 certificate templates incompatible with Windows XP.

Figure 6-8 shows a copy of a new user template created as a V2 template, and Figure 6-9 shows a copy of a new user template created as a V3 template. Each template includes preconfigured properties. Notice that the V3 template has the extra Cryptography tab. This tab includes properties for the newer cryptography standards, known as Suite B cryptography.

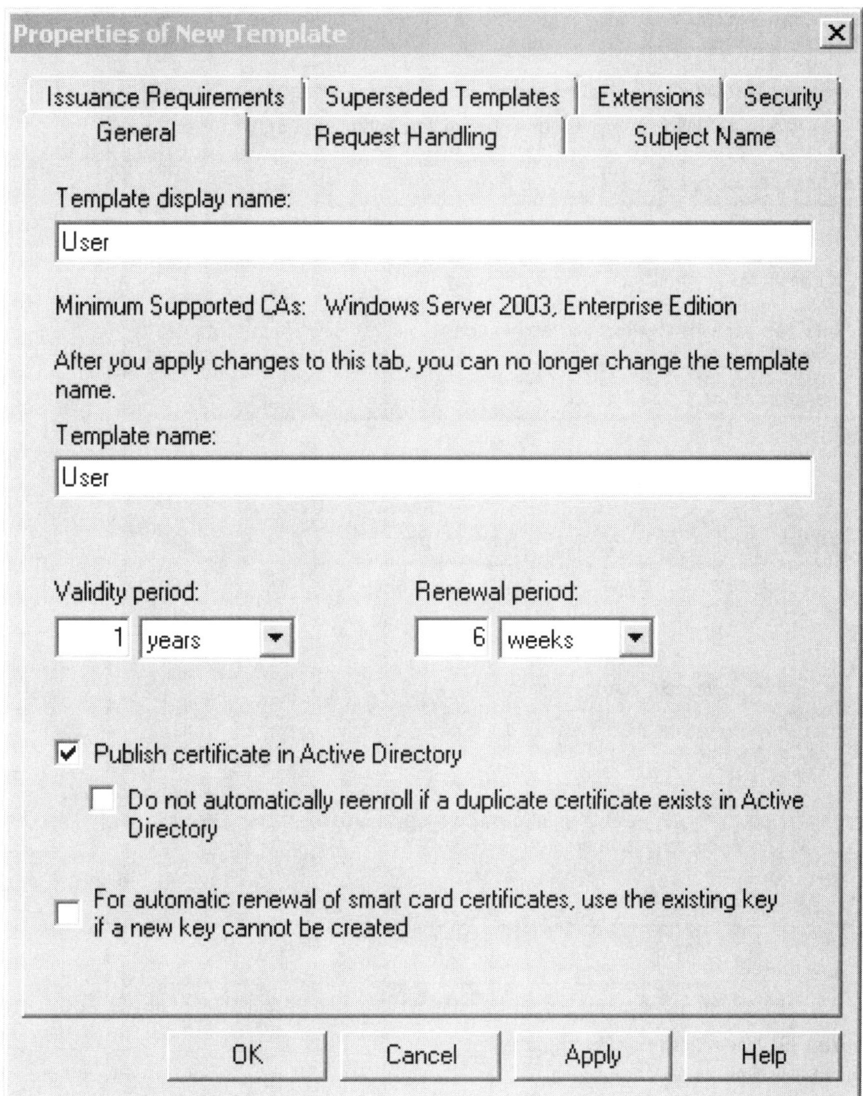

Figure 6-8 Properties of a V2 template
Courtesy Course Technology/Cengage Learning

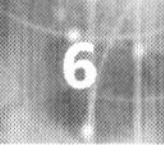

Installing Certificate Services

AD CS can be added as a role on a Windows Server 2008 server. As with other roles, you add the role using Server Manager.

An important consideration is that the name of the computer and the domain settings cannot be changed after adding AD CS. You can't add it or remove it from a domain, promote it to or demote it from a domain controller, or change the computer name. If you take any of these actions, AD CS will no longer function correctly. The only workaround is to uninstall AD CS, change the name or settings, and then reinstall it.

The CA name can have up to 64 characters. The name is typically a single-label name instead of a fully qualified domain name. For example, if you install the CA on DC1 in a domain named Cengage.com, you may name it Cengage-DC1-CA.

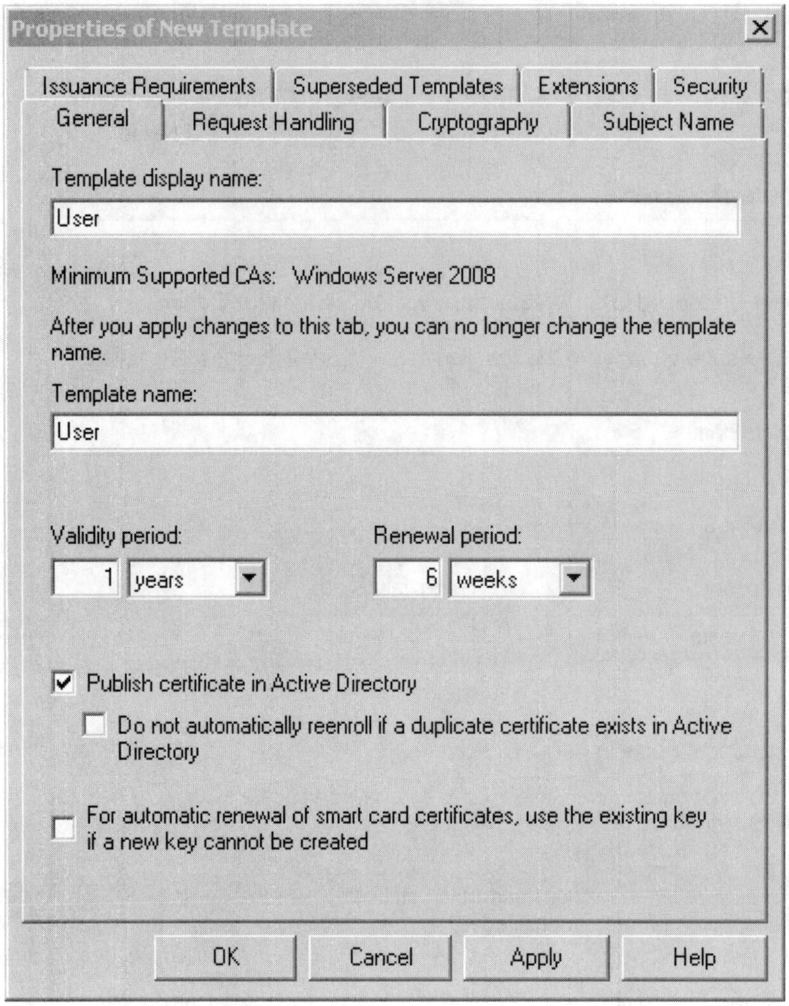

Figure 6-9 Properties of a V3 template
Courtesy Course Technology/Cengage Learning

AD CS has four role services:

- **Certification Authority.** The CA is used to issue and manage certificates.
- **Certification Authority Web Enrollment.** The **CA Web Enrollment** service uses Internet Information Services (IIS) to provide a Web interface that can be used to request and renew certificates, retrieve CRLs, and enroll smart card certificates.
- **Online Responder.** The **Online Responder** service is used to respond to certificate validation requests. It can provide copies of the CRL or respond to Online Certificate Status Protocol (OCSP) queries.
- **Network Device Enrollment Service.** This service is used to issue and manage certificates for network devices (such as routers) that don't have network accounts. This service cannot be installed at the same time as the CA. You can install the CA and add this service later.

Once you've installed AD CS, several Microsoft Management Consoles (MMCs) are available to manage AD CS:

- **Certification authority (CA).** This is the primary tool used to manage certificates, certificate enrollment, and certificate revocation.
- **Certificate templates.** This MMC can be used to duplicate and configure certificate templates. Issued certificates are commonly created from templates.

- **Online responder.** This MMC is used to manage the online responders that provide the CRL to requestors to validate certificates.
- **Enterprise PKI.** If an enterprise has more than one CA, this MMC can be used to manage all of them.
- **Certificates.** You can use the Certificates MMC to view and manage all of the certificate stores used by the computer, users, or services on a computer. This MMC is available before installing AD CS.

Activity 6-1: Installing Certificate Services

Time Required: 20 minutes
Objective: Add the Certificate Services role.

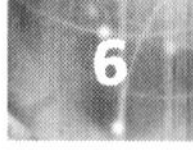

Description: You want to issue certificates to users and computers in your domain. You have decided to create an enterprise CA and need to install a root CA. The CA needs to be able to access Web enrollments and respond to OCSP requests, so you'll also add the Certification Authority Web Enrollment and Online Responder services. This activity should be run on DC1, which is used throughout the book.

1. Start **DC1** and log on with the domain **Administrator** account.
2. Open the **Server Manager** via the **Administrative Tools** menu.
3. Select **Roles**, and click **Add Roles**. Review the information on the **Before You Begin** screen and click **Next**.
4. Select **Active Directory Certificate Services**. Click **Next**.
5. Review the information on the **Introduction to Active Directory Certificate Services** screen and click **Next**.
6. Select the check box for **Certification Authority Web Enrollment**. A dialog box like the one shown in Figure 6-10 will prompt you to install the additional role servers needed to support the Certification Authority Web Enrollment service. Click **Add Required Role Services**.
7. Select the check box for **Online Responder**. Select the check box for **Network Device Enrollment Service** and read the error message that appears. You can't add this service at the same time that you add the Certification Authority service. Click **OK**. At this point, the **Certification Authority, Certification Authority Web Enrollment,** and **Online Responder** role services are checked. Click **Next**.
8. Select **Enterprise** as the type of CA. Click **Next**.
9. This is the first CA, so select **Root CA** and click **Next**.
10. On the **Set Up Private Key** screen, ensure that **Create a new private key** is selected. Click **Next**.
11. Accept the default settings on the **Configure Cryptography for CA** screen. The **Cryptographic Service Provider (CSP)** is **RSA#MicrosoftSoftware Key Storage Provider**, the **Key Character Length** is **2048** bits, and the **Hash Algorithm** is **SHA1**. Click **Next**.
12. On the **Configure CA Name** screen, accept the default name of **Cengage-DC1-CA** and the default **Distinguished Name Suffix** of **DC=Cengage, DC=com**. Click **Next**.
13. On the **Set Validity Period** screen, accept the default validity period of **5 Years**. Click **Next**.
14. Accept the default location of **C:\Windows\System32\CertLog** for the **Certificate Database** and **Certificate Log**. Click **Next**.
15. Review the information on the **Introduction to Web Server (IIS)** screen and click **Next**.

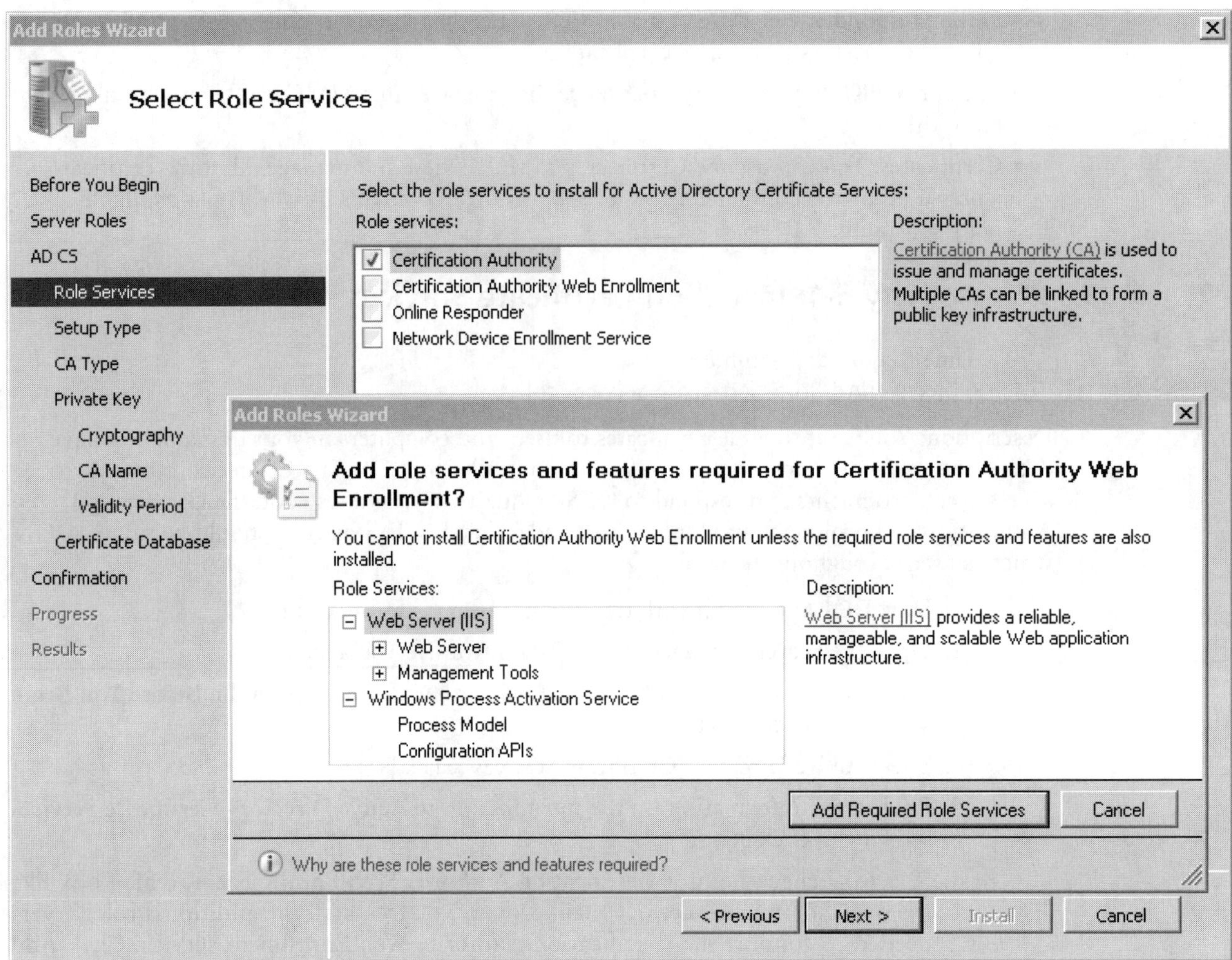

Figure 6-10 Adding the AD CS role services

Courtesy Course Technology/Cengage Learning

16. Accept the default role services selected on the **Select Role Services** screen and click **Next.**
17. Review the information on the **Confirm Installation Selections** screen and click **Install.**
18. When the installation is complete, click **Close.**
19. Open the **Certification Authority** from the **Administrative Tools** menu. Expand **Cengage-DC1-CA** and select **Issued Certificates.** You'll see one self-signed certificate.
20. Double-click the certificate and select the **Certification Path** tab. Your display will look similar to Figure 6-11.

    Notice that the certificate is issued to **DC1.Cengage.com** (the server) from the **Cengage-DC1-CA** (which is also on the server). This is a self-signed certificate.
21. Close all open windows.

Certificate Services Administrative Separation

AD CS includes several predefined roles that can be used for administrative separation. These roles are used within an organization to separate the permissions assigned to different CA administrators, based on the roles they perform within the CA.

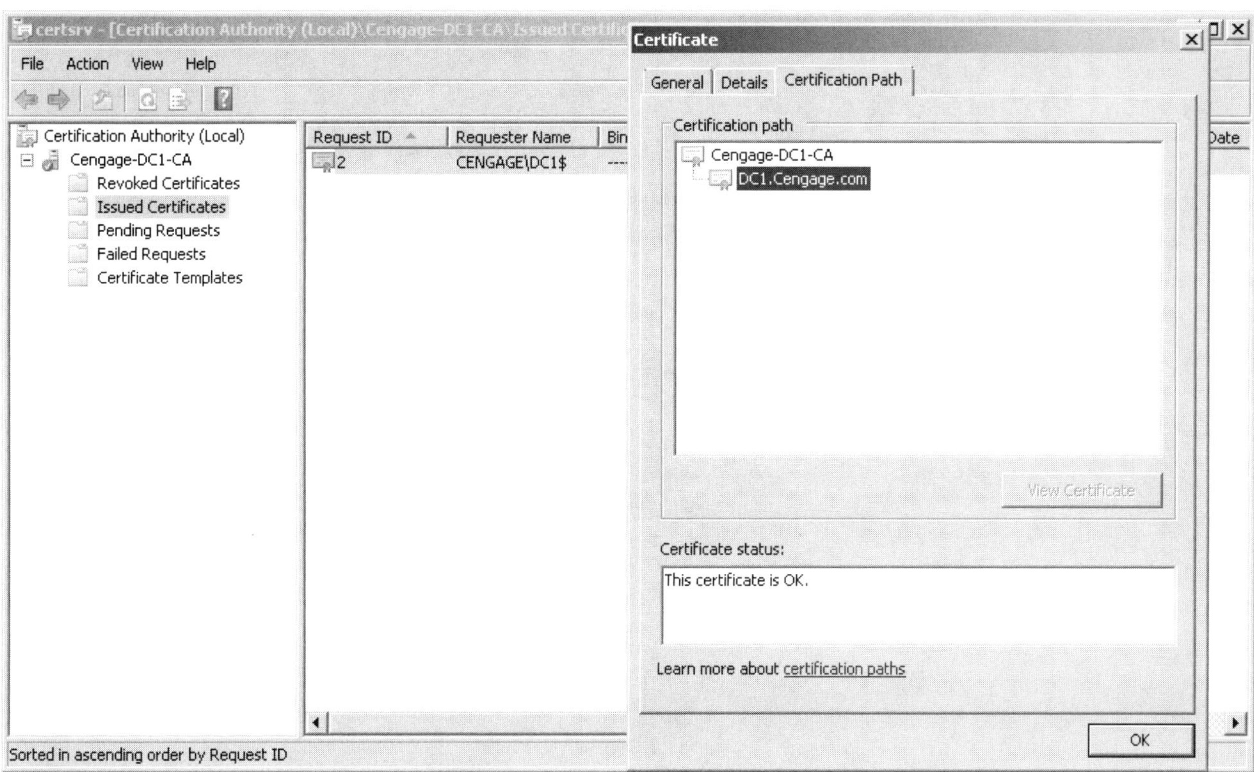

Figure 6-11 Viewing the self-signed certificate

Courtesy Course Technology/Cengage Learning

In a domain, you can add a user account to the Account Operators group or the Domain Admins group to grant specific rights and permissions. The user then has all of the permissions of the group. Similarly, you can assign a user to a role in AD CS to grant the user the rights and permissions of the role.

The permissions that can be assigned directly from the Certification Authority console are shown in Figure 6-12. The Enterprise Admins group is selected, and it has both Issue and Manage Certificates and Manage CA permissions.

- **Manage CA**. Permissions to configure and maintain the settings of the CA are granted. This does not include permissions to enroll and revoke certificates.
- **Issue and Manage Certificates**. Certificates can be enrolled and revoked. This does not include permissions to configure and maintain the CA.
- **Read**. Certificates can be viewed.
- **Request Certificates**. Certificates can be requested.

You can use role-based administration on both enterprise and stand-alone CAs. The predefined roles are granted one or more of the following permissions at the operating system level for the management of AD CS:

- **CA administrator**. Users in this role are granted the Manage CA permission and can configure and maintain settings on the CA. This includes the ability to assign any roles and renew the CA certificate.
- **Certificate manager**. Users in this role are granted the Issue and Manage Certificates permission and can approve certificate enrollment and revocation requests. This role is also called a CA officer.

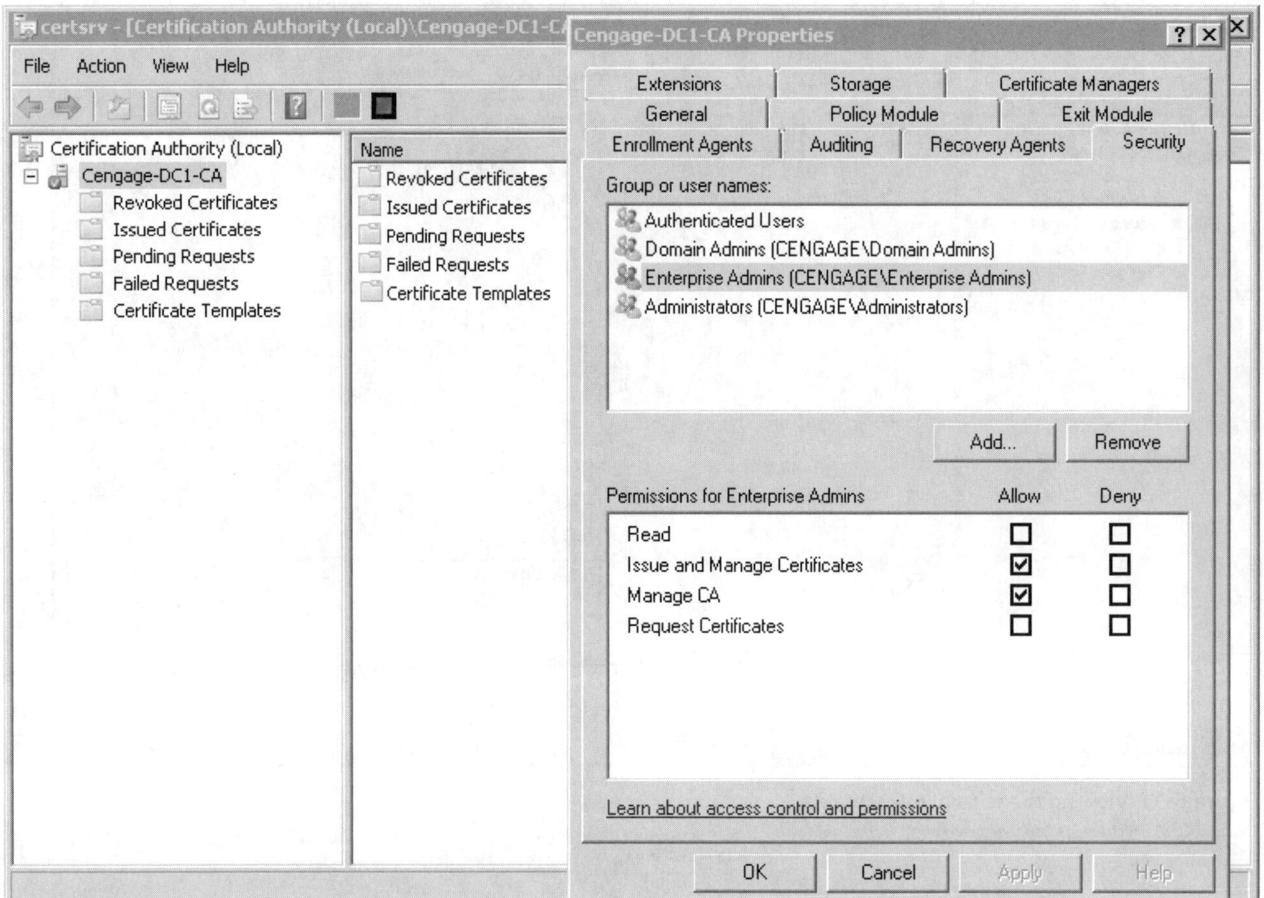

Figure 6-12 Security permissions for an enterprise CA
Courtesy Course Technology/Cengage Learning

- **Backup operator.** Users in this role are granted Backup File and Directories and Restore File and Directories permissions. The permissions are assigned at the operating system level.
- **Auditor.** Users in this role are granted the Manage Auditing and Security Log permissions. They can configure, view, and maintain audit logs. The permissions are assigned at the operating system level.

Enrollees is a Windows-based group, not an AD CS role, but you may see it in documentation. Users in the Enrollees group are granted Read and Enroll permission and are authorized to request certificates from a CA.

Online Responder Service

The Online Responder service provides certification revocation data to clients. The Online Responder console is added automatically when the Online Responder role service is added as part of the AD CS role. However, two additional steps need to be taken to configure the Online Responder service:

- **Add a certificate for the online responder.** This is created from the OCSP response signing template.
- **Configure the online responder to respond to requests.** The OSCP response signing certificate is associated with the online responder, which is configured to respond to revocation status requests. These steps can be completed using a wizard in the Online Responder console.

The following two activities show how to complete these two steps to configure the online responder.

Activity 6-2: Adding a Certificate for an Online Responder

Time Required: 45 minutes
Objective: Add a certificate for the Online Responder service.

Description: You have added an enterprise CA, and you want it to issue responses to requests for the certificate revocation list. Before the CA can be configured, you need to create an OCSP response signing certificate. This activity should be run on DC1, which is used throughout the book.

1. Start **DC1** and log on with the domain **Administrator** account.
2. Click **Start**, type **MMC** in the **Start Search** box, and press **Enter**.
3. Select **File, Add/Remove Snap-in.** Select the **Certificate Templates** and click **Add.** Select **Certificates** and click **Add.** Select **Computer Account** and click **Next.** Ensure that **Local Computer** is selected and click **Finish.** Click **OK.**

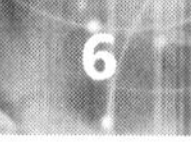

You can also access the Certificate Templates console from the Certification Authority console by right-clicking Certificate Templates and selecting Manage.

4. Select **Certificate Templates** and scroll down to the **OCSP Response Signing** certificate.
5. Right-click **OCSP Response Signing** and select **Duplicate Template.** Ensure that **Windows Server 2008, Enterprise Edition** is selected. Your display will look similar to Figure 6-13. Click **OK.**

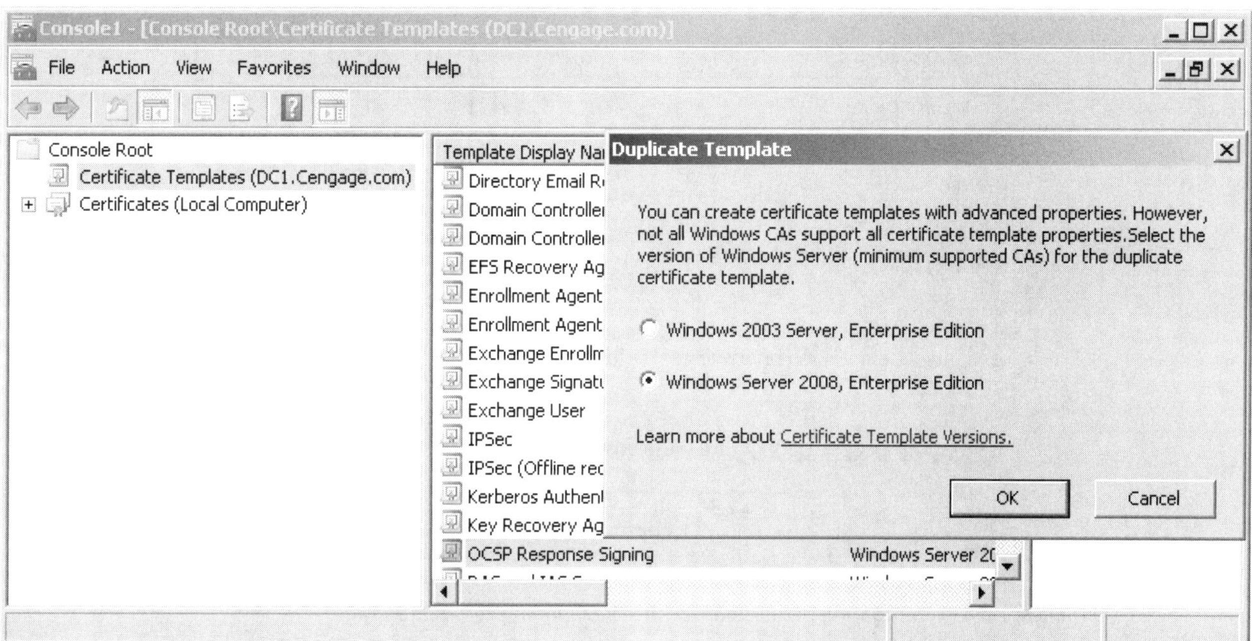

Figure 6-13 Creating a copy of a certificate template
Courtesy Course Technology/Cengage Learning

When Windows 2003 Server, Enterprise Edition is selected, a V2 template will be created. When Windows Server 2008, Enterprise Edition is selected, a V3 template will be created.

6. Type **DC1 OCSP Response Signing** as the **Template Display Name.** Click **OK.**

7. Right-click the **DC1 OCSP Response Signing** template and select **Properties**. Select the **Security** tab.
8. Click **Add**. In the **Select Users, Computers, or Groups** box, click the **Object Types** button. Select **Computers** and click **OK**. Type **DC1** and click **OK**.
9. Select the **Read, Enroll,** and **Autoenroll** check boxes. Your display will look similar to Figure 6-14. Click **OK**. Leave the **MMC** open. You will return to it later in this activity.

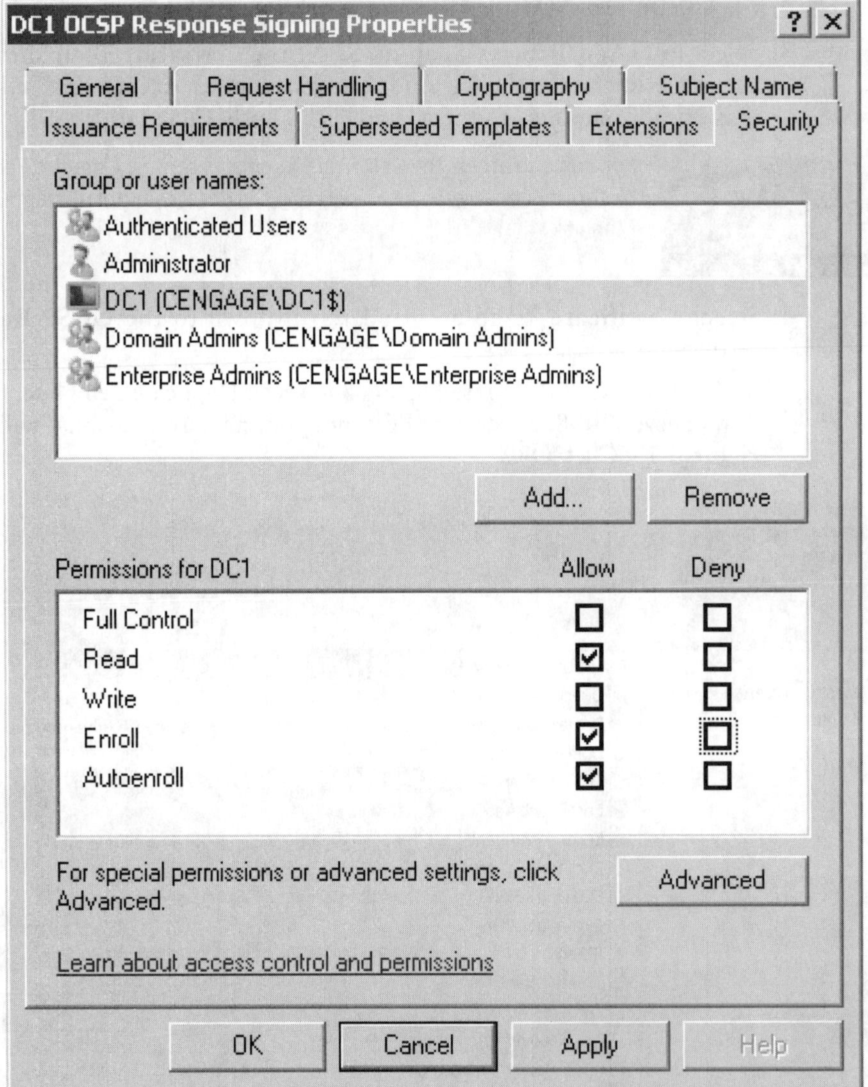

Figure 6-14 Configuring permissions for the OCSP signing certificate
Courtesy Course Technology/Cengage Learning

10. Start **Certification Authority** via the **Administrative Tools** menu. Select **Cengage-DC1-CA.** Right-click **Cengage-DC1-CA** and select **Properties**.
11. Select the **Extensions** tab. In the **Select Extension** drop-down list, click **Authority Information Access (AIA)**.
12. Click **Add**. Enter **http://dc1/ocsp** as the **Location**. Click **OK**.

13. Select the two check boxes to **Include in the AIA extension of issued certificates** and **Include in the online certificate status protocol** (**OCSP**) **extension.** Click **OK.** Your display will look similar to Figure 6-15. Click **OK.**

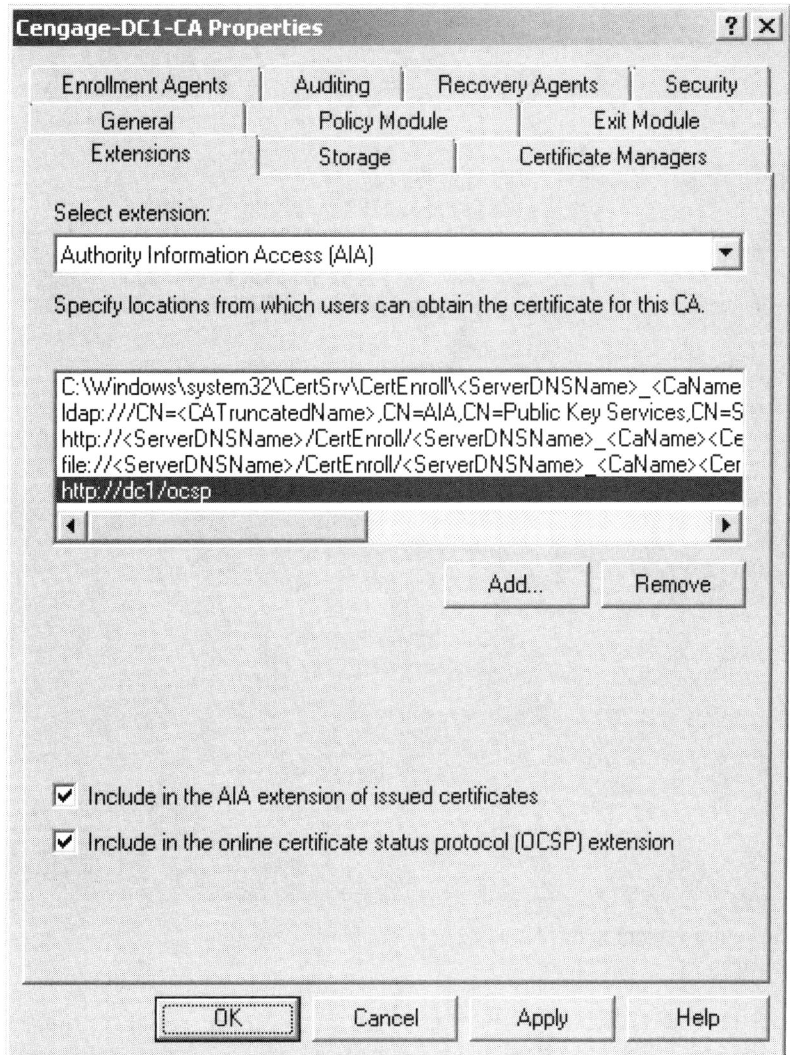

Figure 6-15 Configuring OCSP extensions
Courtesy Course Technology/Cengage Learning

14. You'll be prompted to restart **Active Directory Certificate Services.** Click **Yes.**
15. Expand **Cengage-DC1-CA.** Right-click **Certificate Templates** and select **New, Certificate Template to Issue.**
16. Select the **DC1 OCSP Response Signing** certificate from the **Enable Certificate Templates** screen. Click **OK.**
17. Select **Certificate Templates.** You'll see the **DC1 OCSP Response Signing** certificate that you just configured.
18. Return to the **MMC** you created earlier with the **Certificate Templates** and **Certificates** snap-ins. Expand **Certificates** in the **MMC.** Double-click **Personal** and double-click **Certificates.** In the Actions pane, click **More Actions.** Select **All Tasks** and **Request New Certificate.**

19. Review the information on the **Before You Begin** screen and click **Next.**
20. Select the **DC1 OCSP Response Signing** certificate, as shown in Figure 6-16. Click **Enroll.**

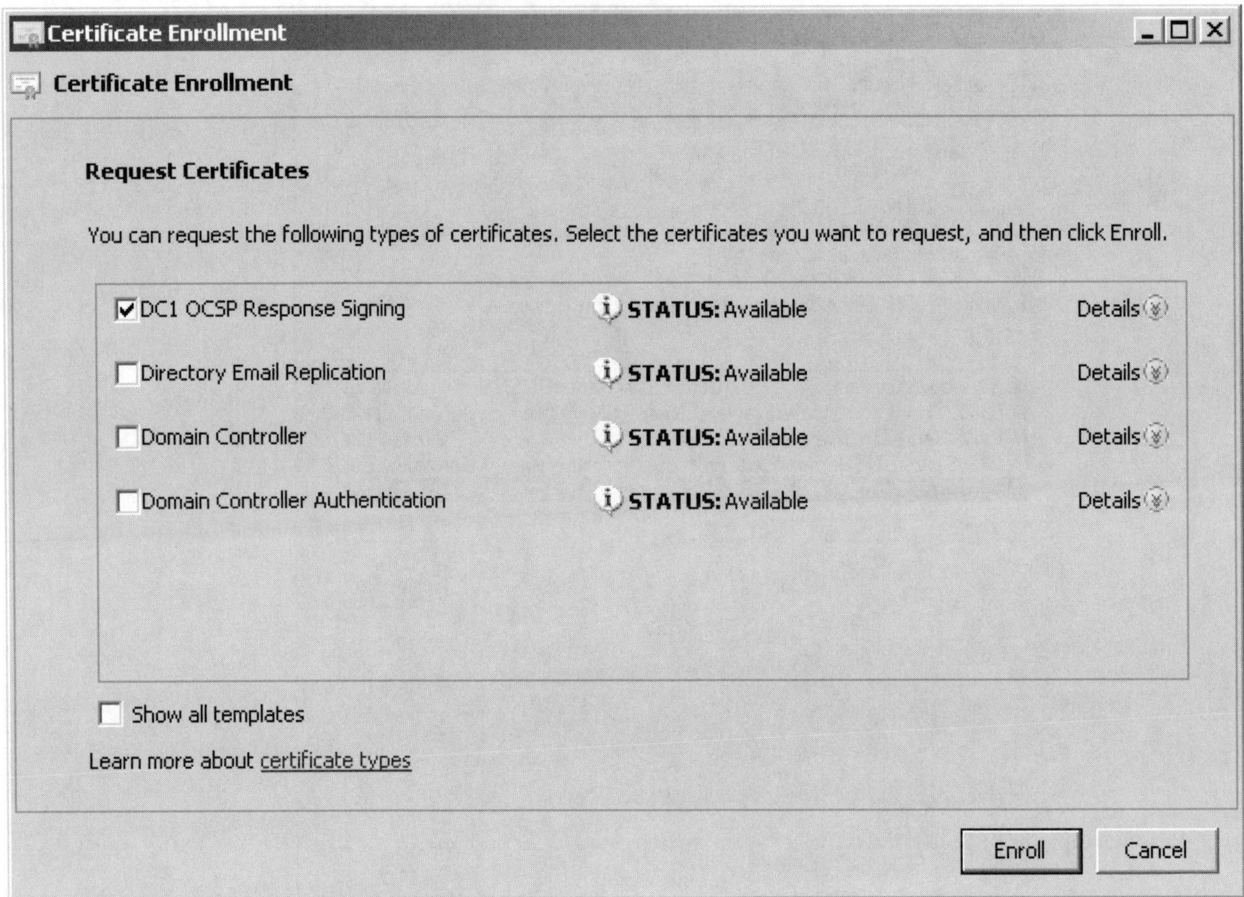

Figure 6-16 Enrolling the OCSP Response Signing certificate
Courtesy Course Technology/Cengage Learning

21. After the certificate has been enrolled, click **Finish**. You'll see the certificate as one of three certificates in the **Personal Certificates** store.
22. Scroll to the right in the main window that shows the certificates and locate the **Intended Purpose** column. Select the certificate that has an **Intended Purpose** of **OCSP Signing.** Right-click the **OCSP Signing Certificate** and select **All Tasks, Manage Private Keys.** Click **Add.**
23. Type **Network Service** and click **OK.** The **Network Service** account will be granted **Allow Full Control** permission. Click **OK.**
24. Close all open windows.

Once the certificate for the online responder has been added, you can configure the online responder. As a reminder, this role service was added when the AD CS role was added to DC1. Four steps are required to complete the configuration of the online responder:

- Specify a name for the new revocation configuration.
- Select a CA certificate to associate with the revocation configuration.
- Select a signing certificate to sign online responder responses.
- Configure the revocation provider that will process revocation status requests.

The following activity leads you through these steps.

Activity 6-3: Configuring the Online Responder

Time Required: 20 minutes
Objective: Configure the Online Responder service.

Description: You have added an enterprise CA, and you want it to issue responses to requests for the certificate revocation list. To prepare for this, you have created an OCSP response signing certificate. You now need to configure the CA to use this certificate and to respond to requests for the CRL. Afterward, you will test the CA's ability to issue a CRL. This activity should be run on DC1, which is used throughout the book.

1. Start **DC1** and log on with the domain **Administrator** account.
2. Open **Online Responder Management** via the **Administrative Tools** menu.
3. Select **Revocation Configuration.** Right-click **Revocation Configuration** and select **Add Revocation Configuration.**
4. Review the information on the **Getting Started** screen and click **Next.**
5. On the **Name the Revocation Configuration** screen, enter **DC1.Cengage.com.** Click **Next.**
6. On the **Select CA Certificate Location** screen, accept the default setting of **Select a Certificate for an Existing Enterprise CA.** Click **Next.**
7. Ensure that **Browse CA Certificates Published in Active Directory** is selected. Click **Browse.** Select the **Cengage-DC1-CA** certificate. Click **OK.** Click **Next.**
8. Check the **Select Signing Certificate** screen to ensure that it looks like Figure 6-17. If the previous activity was completed, this screen will be configured by default.

   Notice that the selected **Certificate Template** is **DC1OCSPResponseSigning,** which was created in the previous activity. Click **Next.**
9. On the **Revocation Provider** screen, click **Provider.**
10. In the **Base CRLs** box, select **http://dc1.cengage.com/CertEnroll/Cengage-DC1-CA.crl** and click **Edit.** Select the URL in the text box and press **CTRL+C** to copy it. You will paste this URL into Internet Explorer later to verify that the CRL can be accessed. Click **Cancel.**
11. Click **Cancel** again on the **Revocation Provider Properties** screen. Click **Finish.** The **Online Responder Configuration** screen will look similar to Figure 6-18, indicating that DC1.Cengage.com is working correctly.
12. Select **Internet Explorer** (**IE**) from the **Start** menu.
13. Paste or type the following URL into the address text box in IE: **http://dc1.cengage.com/CertEnroll/Cengage-DC1-CA.crl.** Press **Enter.**
14. Click **Add** in the **Internet Explorer** security dialog box. Click **Add** again and click **Close.** Paste or type the URL (**http://dc1.cengage.com/CertEnroll/Cengage-DC1-CA.crl**) into the address text box again and press **Enter.** Click **Open.** The **Certificate Revocation List** certificate will open; it should look similar to Figure 6-19.

    Notice that the CRL is a version 2 certificate, which refers to the X.509 version types. Most X.509 certificates are version 3 certificates, with the exception of the CRL.
15. Select the **Revocation List** tab, which shows all the revoked certificates for this CA. At this point, however, there are no revoked certificates. Click **OK.**
16. Close all open windows.

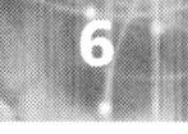

Issuing and Revoking Certificates

Once the CA is created, it can be used to issue certificates. Any certificates issued by the CA can be revoked. Once certificates are revoked, they can be published in the CRL as a version 2 certificate. Clients can then request a copy of the CRL to determine if a certificate is invalid. If a

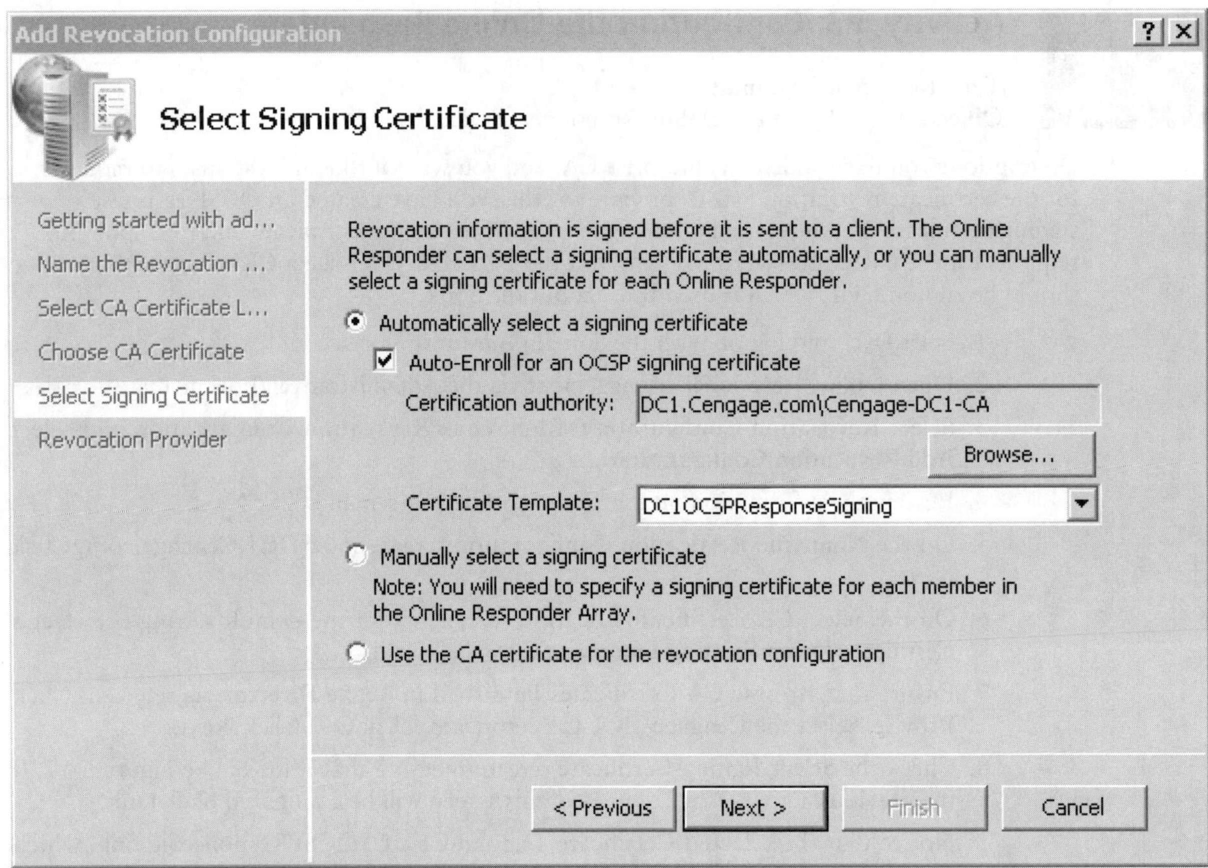

Figure 6-17 Select Signing Certificate screen
Courtesy Course Technology/Cengage Learning

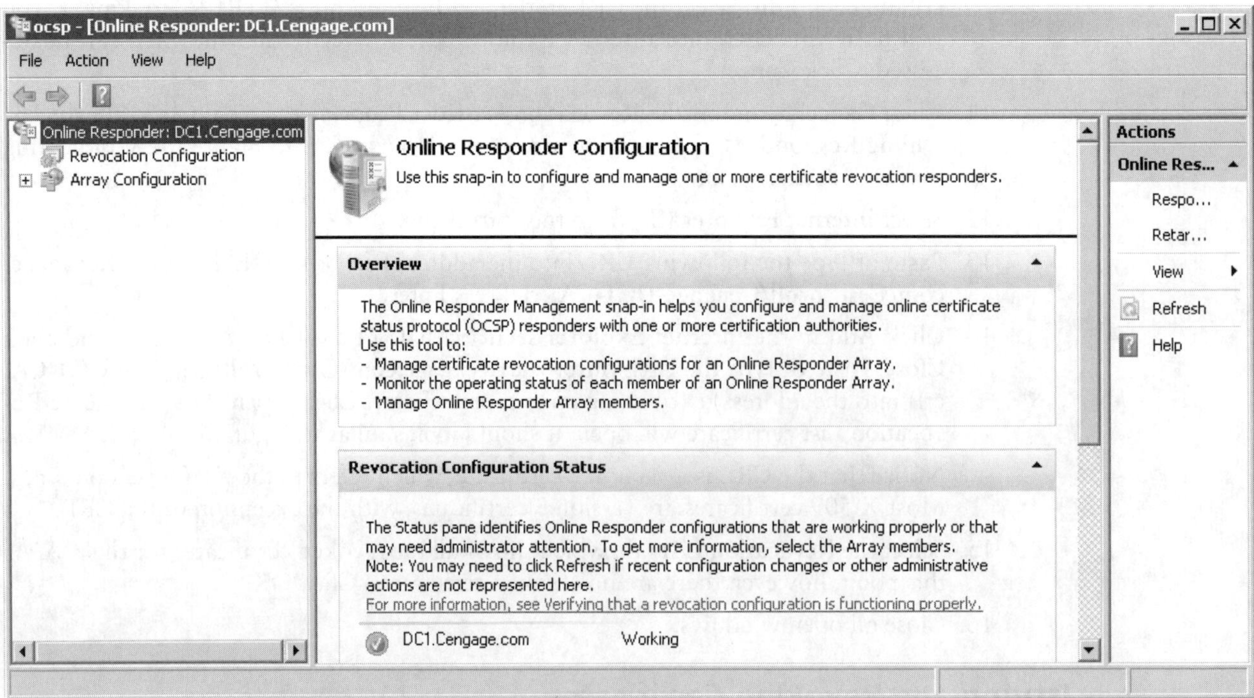

Figure 6-18 Online responder working correctly
Courtesy Course Technology/Cengage Learning

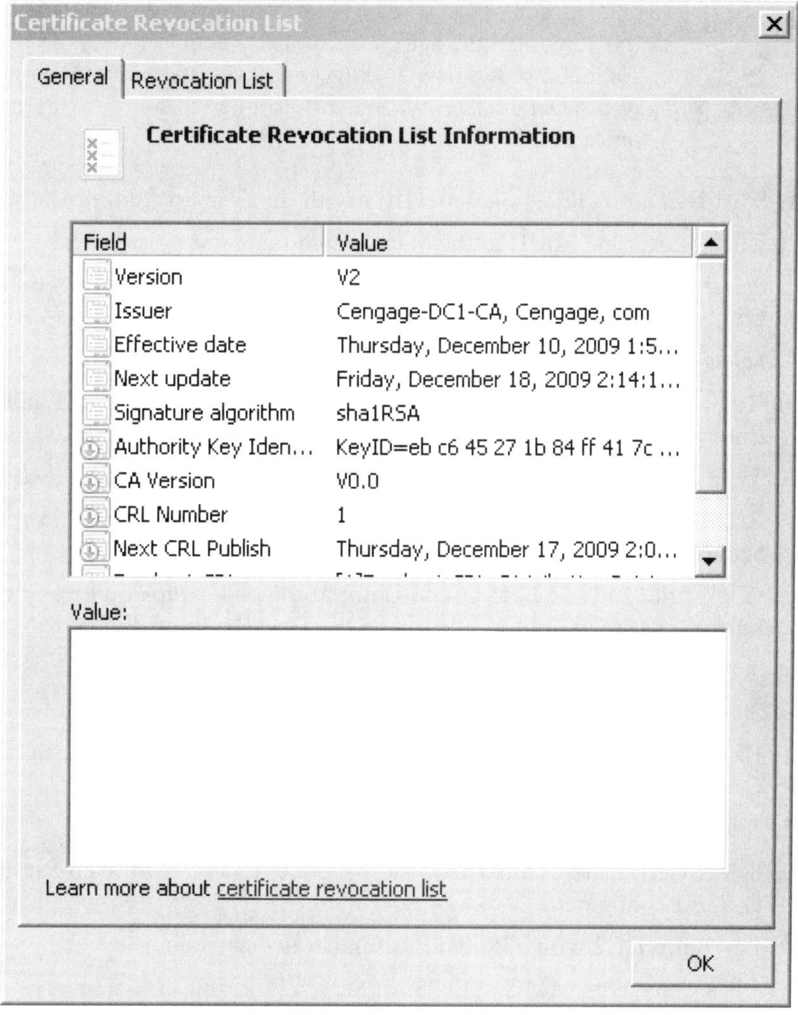

Figure 6-19 Viewing the CRL from the online responder
Courtesy Course Technology/Cengage Learning

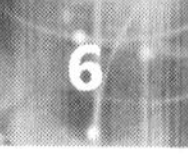

certificate's serial number appears on the CRL, the certificate is considered invalid and the user will see an error.

As mentioned previously, the CRL can be published as a new CRL, which is a complete listing of all certificates revoked by the CA, or it can be published as a Delta CRL, which lists only the changes since the last CRL publication. The publication timeframes for CRLs in AD CS are:

- **Full CRL.** AD CS publishes the full CRL once a week by default.
- **Delta CRL.** AD CS publishes a delta CRL once a day by default.

The following two activities show how to issue a certificate for a Web server and then revoke the certificate.

Activity 6-4: Issuing a Certificate for a Web Server

Time Required: 20 minutes
Objective: Issue a certificate.

Description: You have added an enterprise CA and you want to configure a certificate template to issue a certificate. This certificate is for a Web server that will be used as a TS Gateway server. This activity should be run on DC1 and DC2, which are used throughout the book.

DC2 doesn't actually need to be configured as a TS Gateway server. The purpose of this activity is to create a certificate that can be revoked, but it also shows how a certificate can be issued for a Web server. The Web server would need additional configuration to use the Web server certificate.

1. Start **DC1** and **DC2**. Log on to **DC1** with the domain **Administrator** account.
2. Click **Start**, type **MMC** in the **Start Search** box, and press **Enter**.
3. Select **File**, **Add/Remove Snap-in**. Select the **Certificate Templates** and click **Add**. Click **OK**.
4. Select **Certificate Templates** and scroll down to the **Web Server** certificate.
5. Right-click **Web Server** and select **Duplicate Template**. Select **Windows Server 2008, Enterprise Edition** to create a V3 certificate template. Click **OK**.
6. Type **TS Gateway Web Server** as the **Template Display Name**. Click **OK**.
7. Right-click the **TS Gateway Web Server** template and select **Properties**. Select the **Security** tab.
8. Click **Add**. In the **Select Users, Computers, or Groups** box, click the **Object Types** button. Select **Computers** and click **OK**. Type **DC2** and click **OK**.
9. Select the **Read**, **Enroll**, and **Autoenroll** check boxes. Click **OK**.
10. Start **Certification Authority** via the **Administrative Tools** menu.
11. Expand **Cengage-DC1-CA**. Right-click **Certificate Templates** and select **New**, **Certificate Template to Issue**.
12. Select the **TS Gateway Web Server** certificate. Click **OK**.
13. Select **Certificate Templates**. You'll see the **TS Gateway Web Server** certificate that you just configured.
14. Log on to **DC2** with a domain **Administrator** account.
15. Click **Start**, type **MMC** in the **Start Search** box, and press **Enter**.
16. Select **File**, **Add/Remove Snap-in**. Select **Certificates** and click **Add**. Select **Computer Account** and click **Next**. Ensure that **Local Computer** is selected and click **Finish**. Click **OK**.
17. Expand **Certificates** and select **Trusted Root Certification Authorities, Certificates**. Notice that the **Cengage-DC1-CA** root certificate has been published from Active Directory, so it is already in this store.
18. Select **Personal, Certificates**. Right-click **All Tasks, Request New Certificate**.
19. Review the information on the **Before You Begin** screen and click **Next**.
20. Select the check box for **TS Gateway Web Server**. Click the link for **More information is required to enroll for this certificate. Click here to configure settings.**
21. Ensure that **Full DN** is selected as the **Type** in the **Subject name** area. Enter **CN=DC2,DC=Cengage,DC=com** as the **Value** and click **Add**. Your display will look similar to Figure 6-20. Click **OK**. Click **Enroll**. After the certificate has been enrolled, click **Finish**.
22. Return to **DC1**. Start **Certification Authority** via the **Administrative Tools** menu.
23. Expand **Cengage-DC1-CA** and select **Issued Certificates**. Notice that the last certificate has a **Requestor Name** of **CENGAGE\DC2$**. You can double-click this certificate to view the details.
24. Close all open windows.

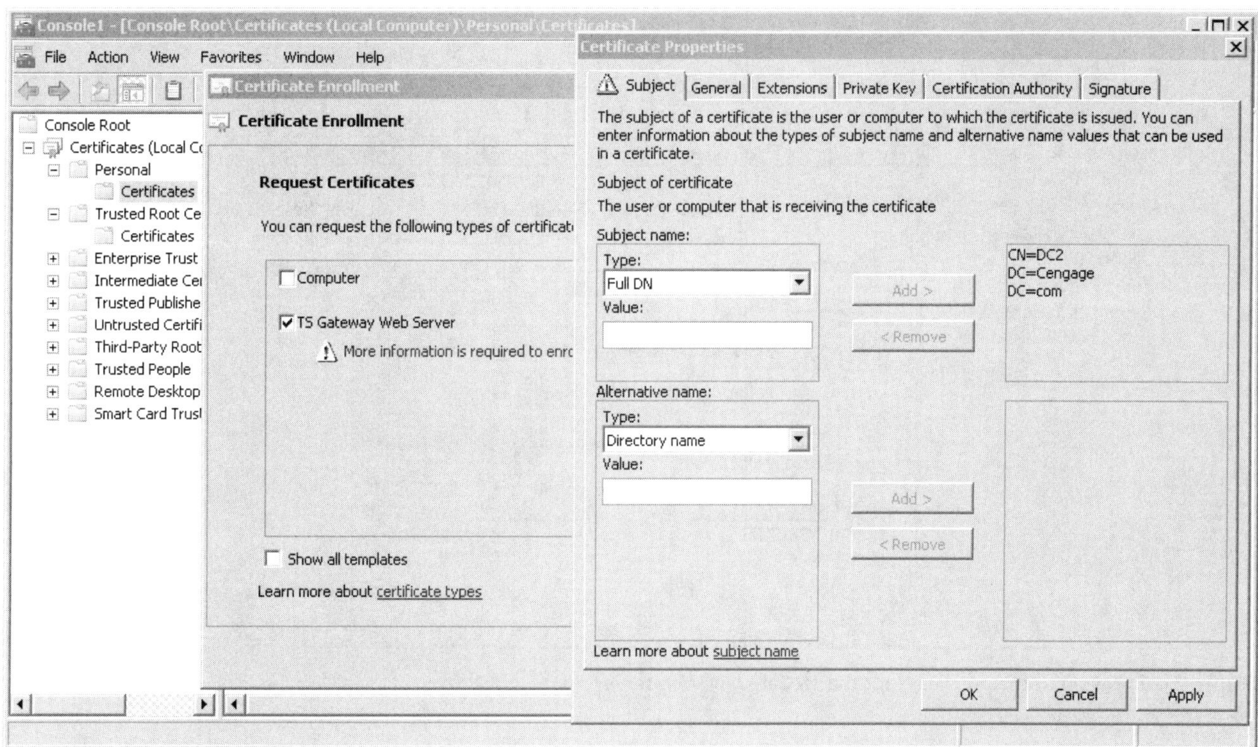

Figure 6-20 Adding the certificate for the TS Gateway Web server
Courtesy Course Technology/Cengage Learning

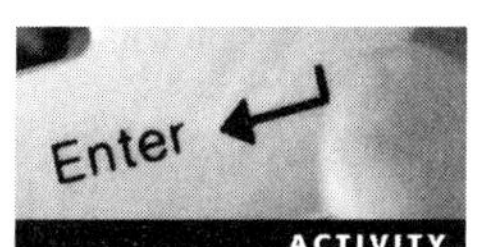

Activity 6-5: Revoking a Certificate

Time Required: 15 minutes
Objective: Revoke a certificate.

Description: The certificate that was previously issued to DC2 for TS Gateway is no longer needed. TS Gateway has been removed from DC2, and you have been asked to revoke the certificate. This activity should be run on DC1.

1. Start **DC1** and log on with the domain **Administrator** account.
2. Start **Certification Authority** via the **Administrative Tools** menu.
3. Expand **Cengage-DC1-CA** and select **Issued Certificates.**
4. Right-click the **TS Gateway Web Access** certificate (the last certificate that was issued) and select **All Tasks, Revoke Certificate.** Select **Cease of Operation** as the **Reason code.** Your display will look similar to Figure 6-21. Click **Yes.**

   You'll see that the certificate is no longer in the issued **Certificates** node.
5. Select **Revoked Certificates.** You'll see that the certificate you just revoked is listed.
6. Right-click **Revoked Certificates** and select **Properties.** Your display will look similar to Figure 6-22.

   Notice that the default **CRL publication interval** is set to 1 week. If you look at the CRL now, the revoked certificate will not be included. Click **OK.**
7. Right-click **Revoked Certificates** and select **All Tasks, Publish.** Ensure that **New CRL** is selected and click **OK.**
8. Right-click **Revoked Certificates** and select **Properties.** Select the **View CRLs** tab.

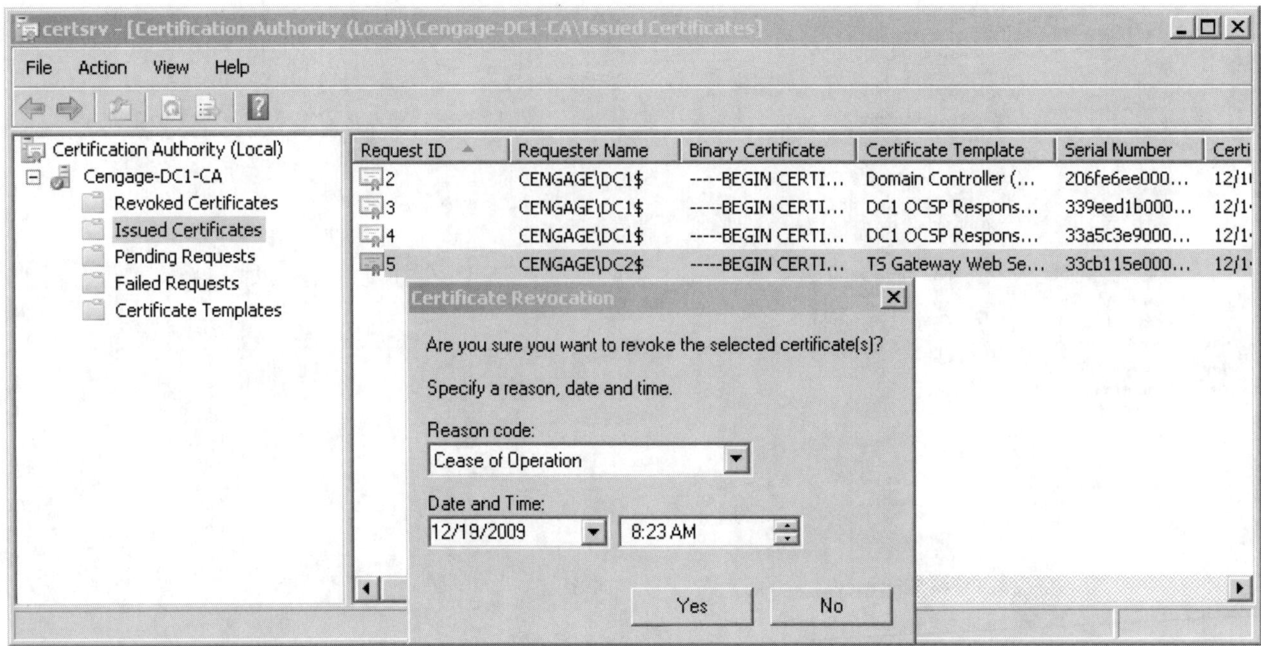

Figure 6-21 Revoking the certificate for the TS Gateway Web server

Courtesy Course Technology/Cengage Learning

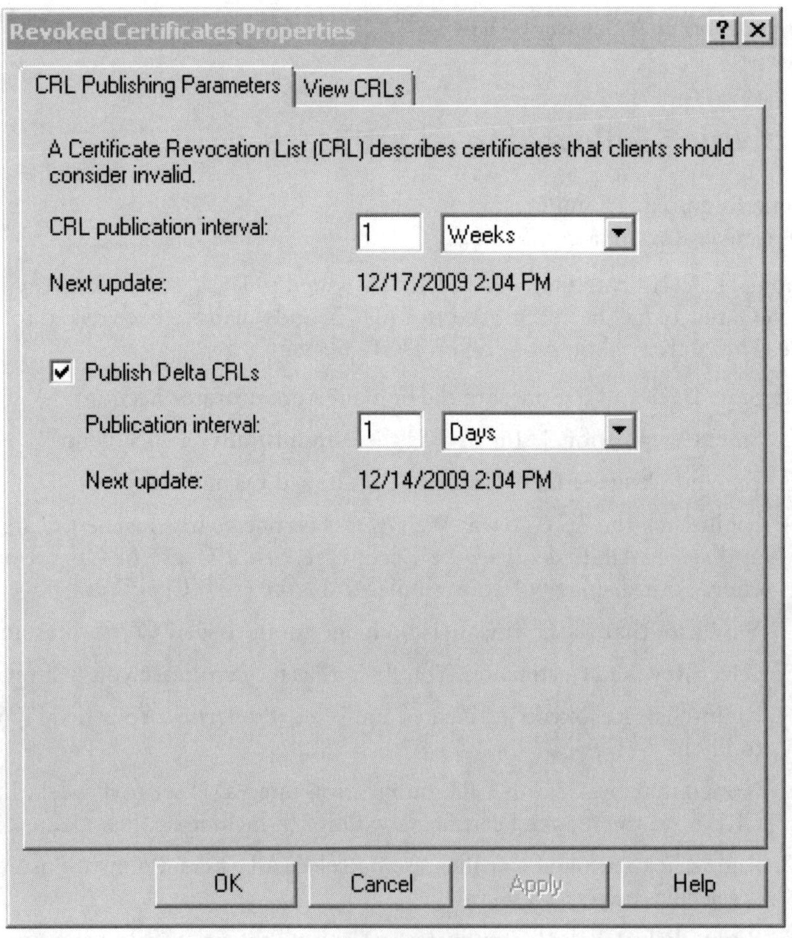

Figure 6-22 Viewing the CRL publishing parameters

Courtesy Course Technology/Cengage Learning

9. Select the **CRL** and click **View CRL**. Select the **Revocation List** tab. You'll see the certificate you just revoked listed by its **Serial Number**. Select the revoked certificate. You'll see that the **CRL Reason Code** is listed as **Cessation of Operation** (5). Your display will look similar to Figure 6-4 near the beginning of this chapter. Click **OK** twice.
10. Close all open windows.

Deploying Trusted Root Certificates via Group Policy

When using a stand-alone CA, you may want users in the organization to automatically trust certificates issued by the CA. If so, you can install a copy of the stand-alone root CA's certificate in the Trusted Root Certification Authorities store for the clients. If you only need to install a copy for one or two users, you can do it manually, but if you have several users, you can do it much more efficiently with Group Policy.

Group Policy was covered in much greater depth in Chapter 4. Recall that you can configure a single setting once with a Group Policy object (GPO) and have the setting apply to all the users and computers in the scope of the GPO. If you want it to apply to all users in the domain, the GPO can be linked at the domain level. If you want it to apply to all users in an OU, you can link it at the OU level.

The Group Policy setting is Trusted Root Certification Authority, and it's located in the Computer Configuration, Policies, Windows Settings, Security Settings, Public Key Policies, Trusted Root Certification Authorities node. Certificates imported to this Group Policy setting will be automatically deployed to the Trusted Root Certification Authorities store for clients in the scope of the GPO.

The following activity shows how to export a root CA certificate and then use GPO to deploy it.

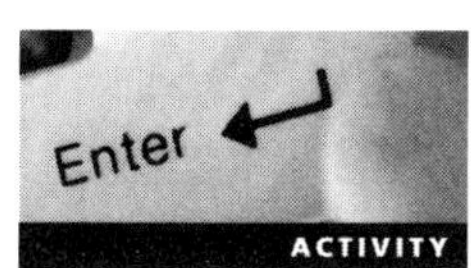

Activity 6-6: Deploying a Trusted Certificate with Group Policy

Time Required: 20 minutes
Objective: Deploy a trusted root certificate using Group Policy.

Description: Your organization has created a stand-alone CA. You want this certificate to be deployed to the Trusted Root Certification Authorities store for all users in the Development department. Users in the Development department will be placed in an OU named Development. You need to export the root CA certificate, create the Development OU, create a GPO to issue this certificate to the Trusted Root Certification Authorities store, and link it to the Development OU. This activity should be run on DC1.

These steps aren't needed for an enterprise CA because the root certificate for an enterprise CA is published automatically to the Trusted Root Certification Authorities store for all clients in the domain. However, these steps show how a certificate could be published if the CA was a stand-alone CA instead of an enterprise CA.

1. Start **DC1** and log on with the domain **Administrator** account.
2. Start **Certification Authority** via the **Administrative Tools** menu.
3. Right-click **Cengage-DC1-CA** and select **Properties**. Ensure that the **General** tab is selected and click **View Certificate**.
4. Select the **Details** tab. Your display will look similar to Figure 6-23.
5. Click **Copy to File**. Review the information on the **Welcome to the Certificate Export Wizard** screen and click **Next**. Accept the default setting of **DER Encoded Binary X.509 (.CER)** and click **Next**.
6. On the **File to Export** screen, click **Browse**. Create a folder named **Certificates** at the root of C: and select the folder. Enter **CengageRoot** as the **File Name** and click **Save**. Click **Next**.

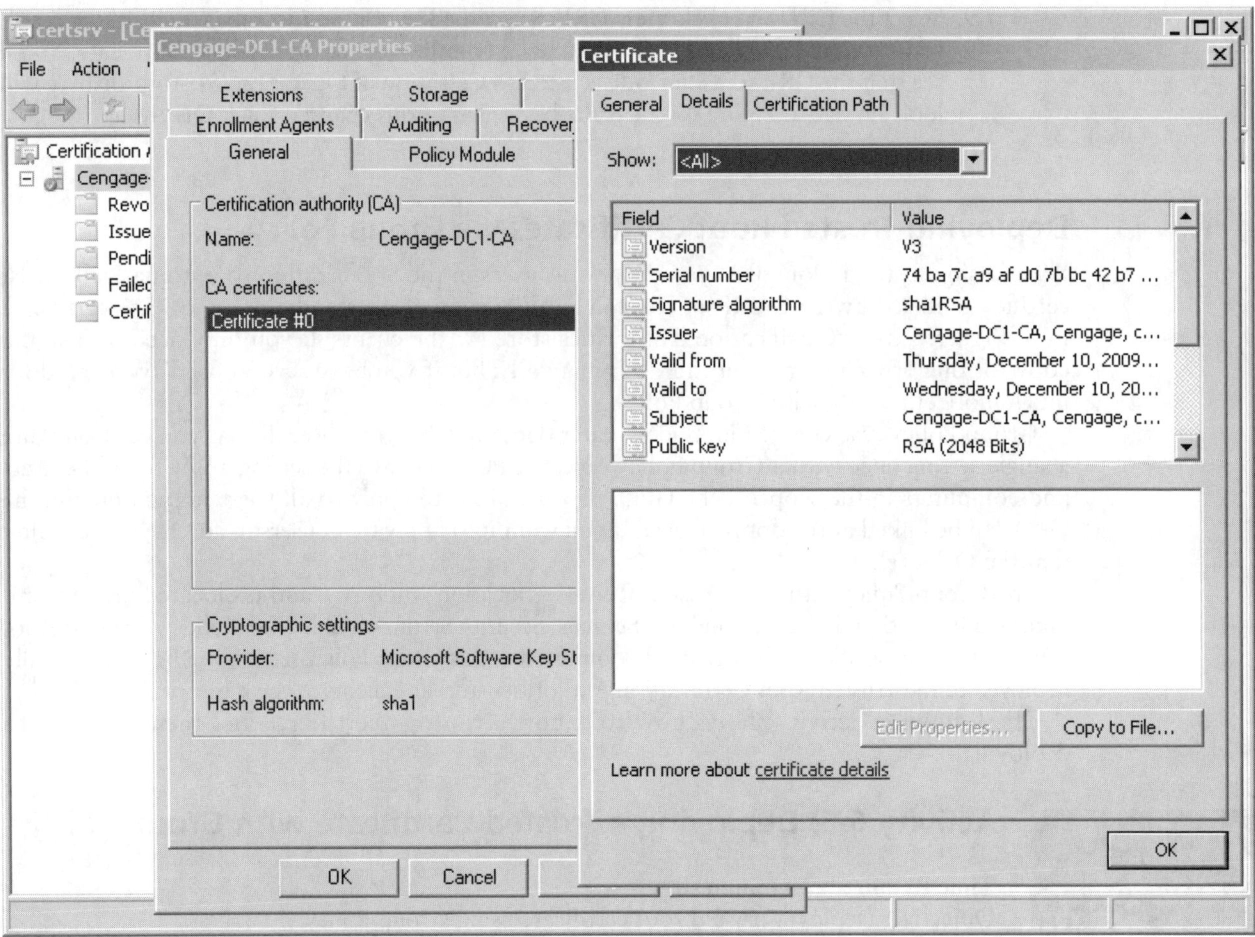

Figure 6-23 Exporting the root CA certificate
Courtesy Course Technology/Cengage Learning

7. Click **Finish** on the completion screen. Click **OK** in the dialog box that indicates the export was successful.
8. Close the **Properties** pages in **Certification Authority** by clicking **OK** twice.
9. Open **Group Policy Management** via the **Administrative Tools** menu.
10. Expand **Forest: Cengage.com, Domains,** and **Cengage.com.** Right-click **Cengage.com** and select **New Organizational Unit.** Name the OU **Development** and click **OK.**
11. Right-click **Development** and select **Create a GPO in This Domain, and Link It Here.** Name the GPO **Deploy Trusted Root Certificate.** Click **OK.**
12. Right-click the **Deploy Trusted Root Certificate** GPO and select **Edit.**
13. Open the **Computer Configuration, Policies, Windows Settings, Security Settings, Public Key Policies, Trusted Root Certification Authorities** node.
14. Right-click **Trusted Root Certification Authority** and select **Import.**
15. Review the information on the **Certificate Import Wizard Welcome** screen and click **Next.**
16. Click **Browse.** Browse to the **C:\Certificates** folder and select the **CengageRoot** certificate file created earlier. Click **Open.** Click **Next.**
17. Accept the default setting to **Place All Certificates in the Following Store (Trusted Root Certification Authorities)** and click **Next.** Click **Finish.** Click **OK.** Your display will look similar to Figure 6-24.
18. Close all open windows.

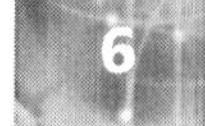

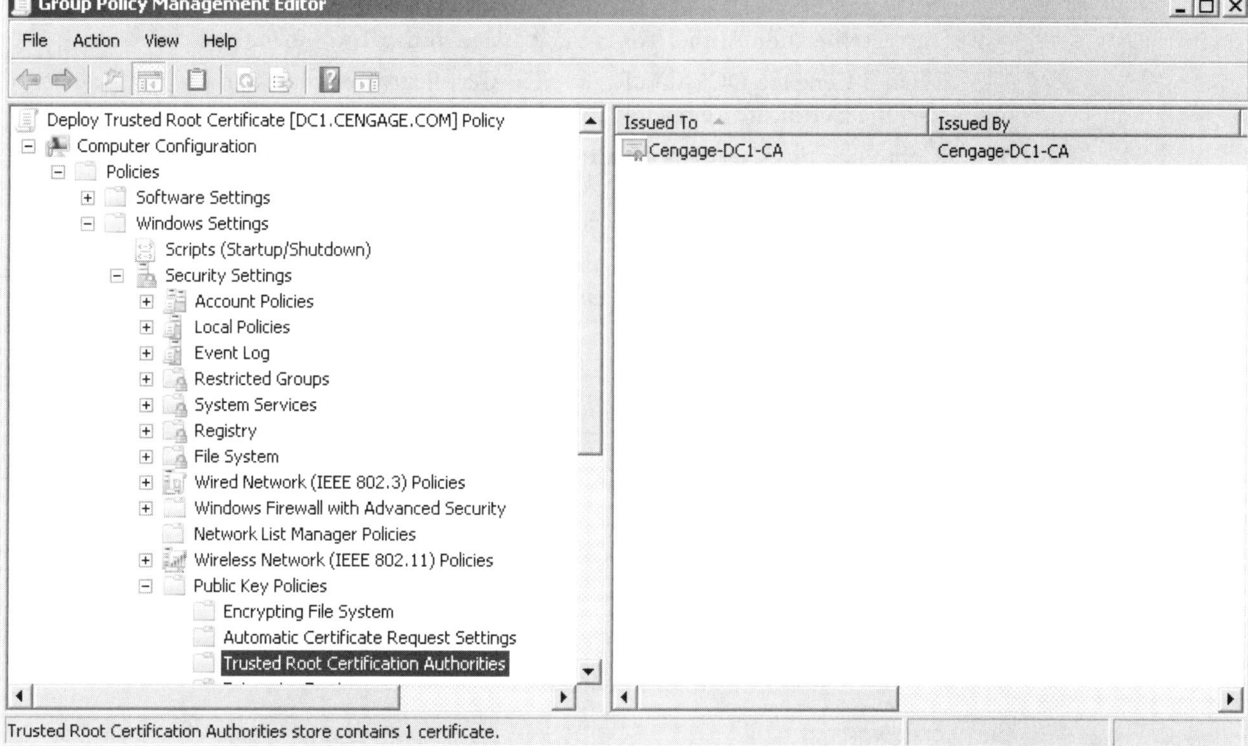

Figure 6-24 Root CA certificate added to GPO policy
Courtesy Course Technology/Cengage Learning

Automatic Certificate Enrollment

AD CS can be configured to automatically enroll, issue, and renew certificates without user action. This autoenrollment can be useful when a large number of certificates need to be issued to clients. Instead of an administrator taking action for each certificate, autoenrollment can be configured through the permissions of the certificate and enabled with Group Policy.

Autoenrollment is only available with an enterprise CA and can only be used with version 2 and version 3 certificate templates.

The permissions that must be assigned to the template are Read, Enroll, and Autoenroll. These permissions are assigned to the certificate template in the Certificate Templates console. The Group Policy setting is Certificate Services Client – Auto-Enrollment, and it is available in both the computer configuration and user configuration of Group Policy. You can find this setting in Policies, Windows Settings, Public Key Policies.

The following activity shows how to configure certificate autoenrollment.

Activity 6-7: Configuring Certificate Autoenrollment

Time Required: 15 minutes

Objective: Configure certificate template permissions and Group Policy to support autoenrollment.

Description: You need to issue user certificates to users in the Development OU. Instead of doing this manually, you want to use autoenrollment. You need to create a certificate template, configure the permissions for autoenrollment, and then configure a GPO for autoenrollment. This activity should be run on DC1.

1. Start **DC1** and log on with the domain **Administrator** account.
2. Start **Certification Authority** via the **Administrative Tools** menu.
3. Expand **Cengage-DC1-CA.** Right-click **Certificate Templates** and select **Manage** to start the **Certificate Templates** console.
4. Right-click the **User** template and select **Properties.** Select the **Security** tab. Notice that you can't assign the Autoenroll permission to this template because it is a V1 certificate template. Click **Cancel.**
5. Right-click the **User** template and select **Duplicate Template.** Ensure that **Windows 2003 Server, Enterprise Edition** is selected so that a V2 certificate template is created. Click **OK.**
6. Change the name of the template to **V2 User (includes XP)** and click **OK.**
7. Double-click the **V2 User (includes XP)** certificate template and select the **Security** tab. Select **Allow** for the **Read, Enroll,** and **Autoenroll** permissions. Your display will look similar to Figure 6-25. Click **OK.**

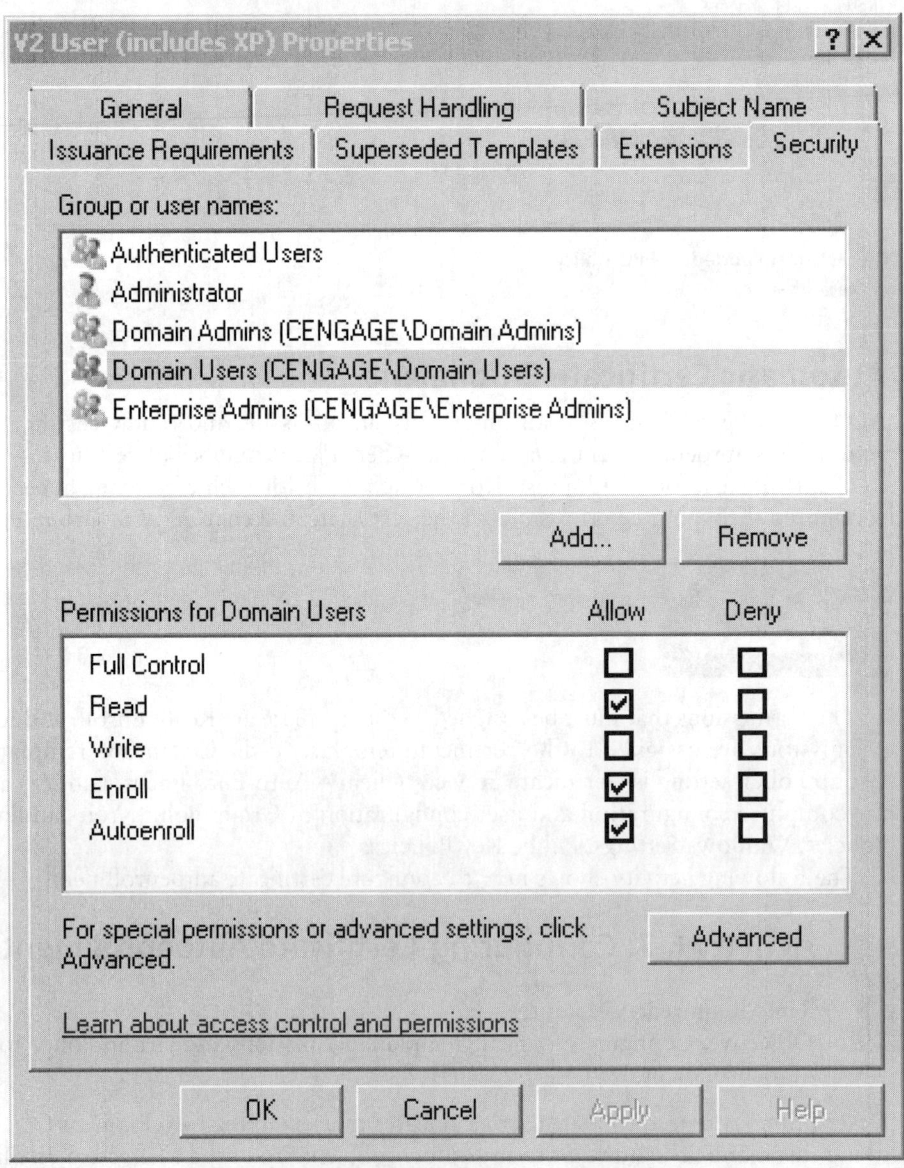

Figure 6-25 Configuring permissions for a certificate template

Courtesy Course Technology/Cengage Learning

8. Return to the **Certification Authority** console. Right-click **Certificate Templates** and select **New, Certificate Template to Issue**. Select the **V2 User** (**includes XP**) certificate and click **OK**.
9. Start **Group Policy Management** via the **Administrative Tools** menu.
10. Right-click **Development** and select **Create a GPO in This Domain, and Link It Here**. Name the GPO **Enable Certificate Autoenrollment**. Click **OK**.

While this lab will only enable autoenrollment for the users and computers in the Development OU, you could also enable it for all users in the domain by creating a new GPO and linking it to the domain, or by modifying the default domain policy.

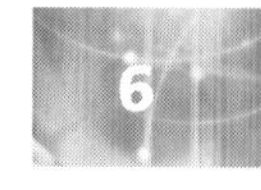

11. Right-click the **Enable Certificate Autoenrollment** GPO and select **Edit**. Browse to the **Computer Configuration, Policies, Windows Settings, Security Settings, Public Key Policies** node.
12. Right-click the **Certificate Services Client – Auto-Enrollment** GPO setting and select **Properties**. Change the **Configuration Model** to **Enabled**. Select the check boxes to **Renew expired certificates, update pending certificates, and remove revoked certificates**, and **Update certificates that use certificate templates**. Your display will look similar to Figure 6-26. Click **OK**.

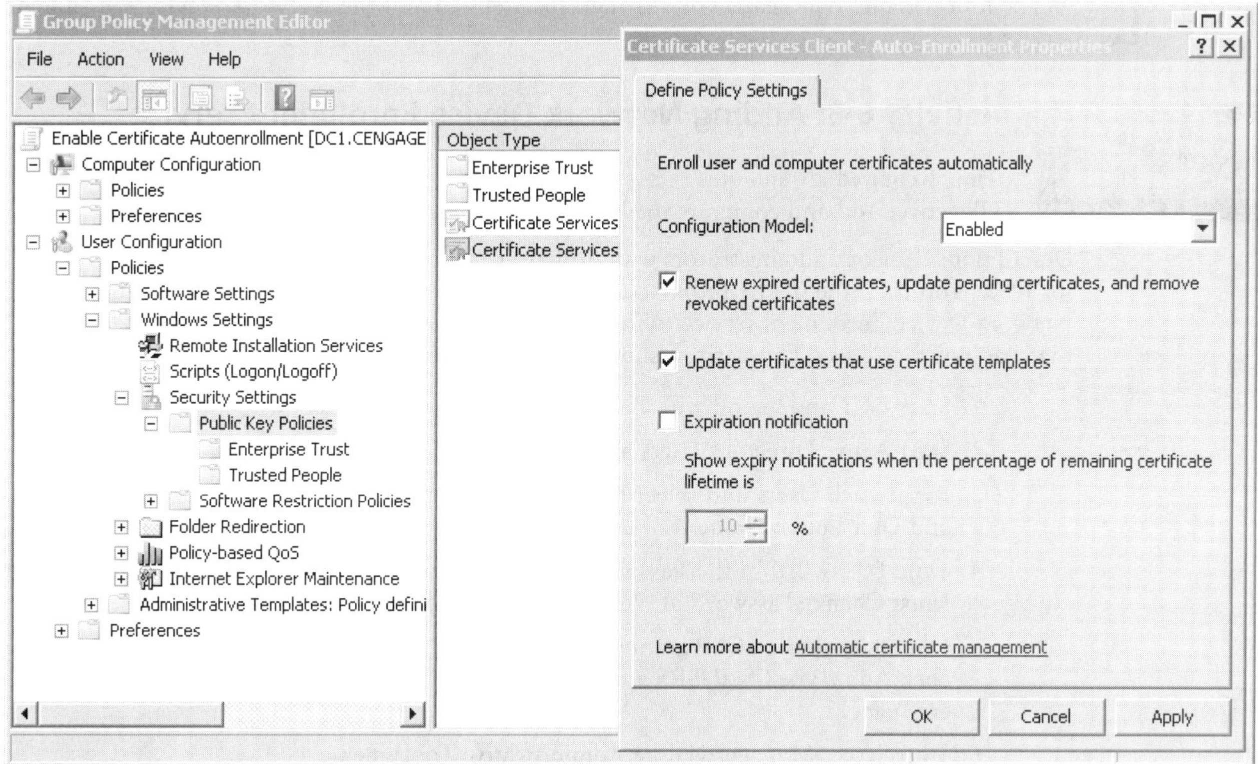

Figure 6-26 Configuring Group Policy for autoenrollment
Courtesy Course Technology/Cengage Learning

13. Close all open windows.

Network Device Enrollment Service

The **Network Device Enrollment** service is used to issue certificates to network devices such as routers that do not have accounts in Active Directory. It uses the **Simple Certificate Enrollment Protocol** (**SCEP**), which was specifically designed to support automatic request and retrieval of certificates for network devices. The network device must also support SCEP.

You can add the Network Device Enrollment service as an additional role service after the AD CS role has been added to a server. After it is installed, the service will provide the following benefits:

- Generates one-time enrollment passwords that can be used by administrators to enroll devices.
- Can submit SCEP certificate enrollment requests to a CA.
- Can retrieve enrolled certificates and forward them to the network device.

The Network Device Enrollment service uses a registration authority (RA) to accept the registration requests. The RA will use a default name of ServerName-MSCEP-RA. For example, if the service is added to DC1, the RA name will be DC1-MSCEP-RA.

Certificates issued to network devices can be used for identification or encryption. As an example, IPSec can be used to encrypt and digitally sign data that is processed by routers. IPSec requires certificates, and the Network Device Enrollment service can be used to issue the certificates to these devices for IPSec. As with most AD CS features, the Network Device Enrollment service is only available on AD CS when it's installed on the Windows Server 2008 Enterprise or Datacenter edition.

When adding the Network Device Enrollment service, you need to create a user account for the service. This account needs permissions in Internet Information Services (IIS), which are granted by placing the account in the IIS_IUSRS group.

The following activity leads you through the steps to add the Network Device Enrollment service.

Activity 6-8: Adding Network Device Enrollment service

Time Required: 20 minutes
Objective: Add and configure the Network Device Enrollment service.

Description: Network administrators want to have certificates issued to routers on the network for IPSec. You want the CA to automatically accept these requests, so you need to add the Network Device Enrollment service to the CA. You also need to add an account (named SCEP) that the service will use. This activity should be run on DC1.

1. Start **DC1** and log on with the domain **Administrator** account.
2. Start **Active Directory Users and Computers** via the **Administrative Tools** menu.
3. Right-click **Users** and select **New, User**. Enter **SCEP** as the **First Name, Full Name,** and **User Logon Name.** Click **Next.**
4. Type **P@ssw0rd** in the **Password** and **Confirm Password** text boxes. Deselect **User Must Change Password at Next Logon.** Click **Next.** Click **Finish.**
5. Double-click the **SCEP** account to access the **Properties** page. Select **Member Of** and click **Add.** Type **IIS_IUSRS** and click **OK.** Click **OK** to dismiss the user account property page.
6. Start **Server Manager** via the **Administrative Tools** menu.
7. Select **Roles.** Scroll down to the **Active Directory Certificate Services** role and click **Add Role Services.**
8. Select the **Network Device Enrollment Service** and click **Next.**
9. On the **Specify User Account** screen, click **Select User.** Type **SCEP** as the user name and **P@ssw0rd** as the password. Your display will look similar to Figure 6-27. Click **OK.** Click **Next.**
10. Accept the default name for the RA and click **Next.**
11. Accept the default cryptography information and click **Next.**

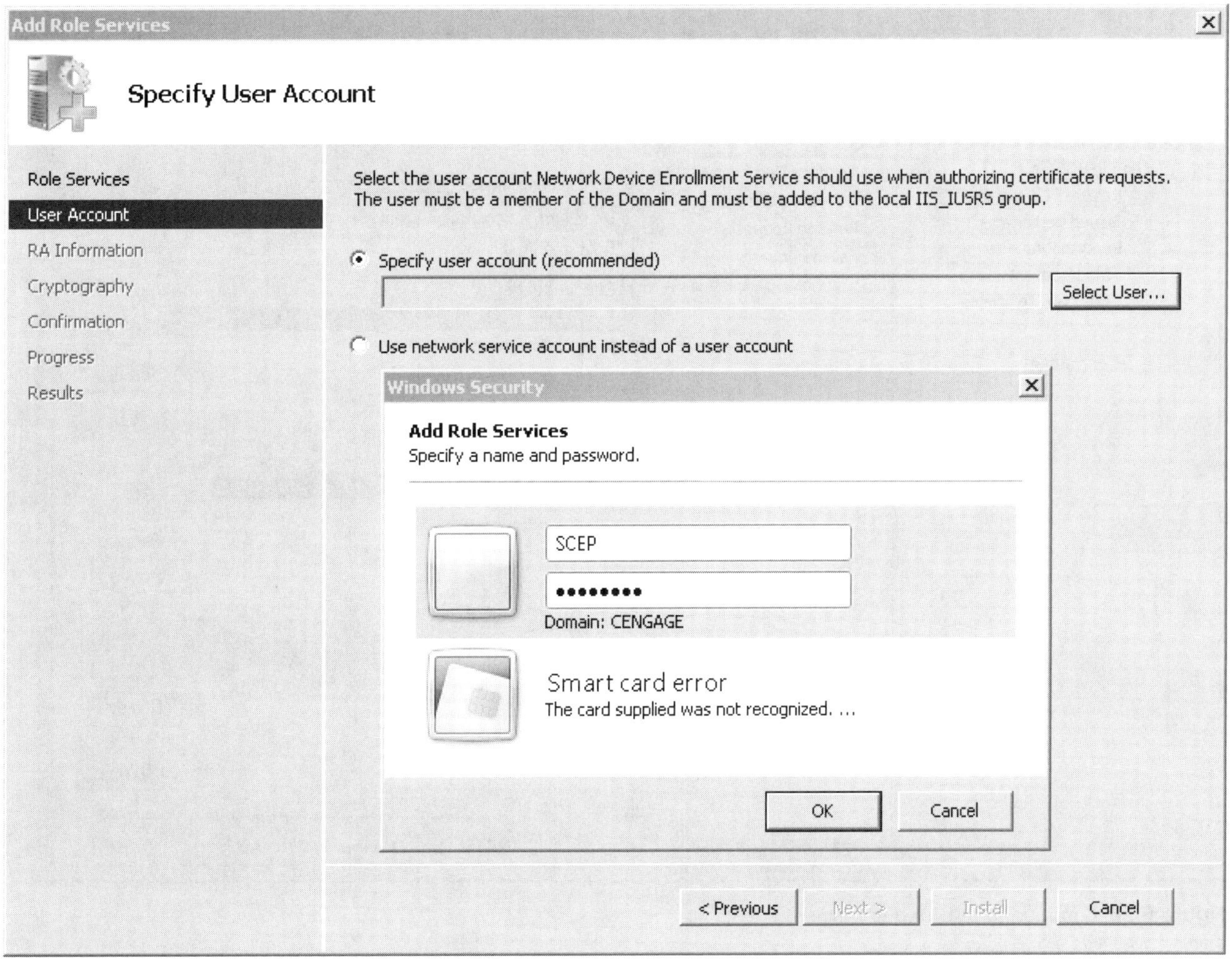

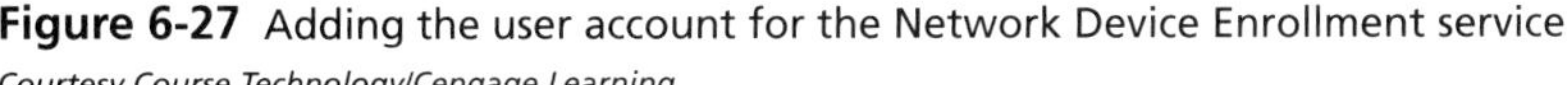

Figure 6-27 Adding the user account for the Network Device Enrollment service
Courtesy Course Technology/Cengage Learning

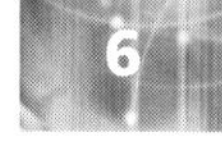

12. Review the information on the **Confirmation** screen and click **Install**. Once the installation is complete, click **Close**. As a reminder, configuration on the network devices using SCEP is also required.
13. Close all open windows.

Restricted Enrollment Agents

A significant addition to AD CS with Windows Server 2008 is the use of **restricted enrollment agents**. One or more people in an organization can be designated as restricted enrollment agents, and can then request certificates on behalf of users. The agent is called *restricted* because you can designate people as enrollment agents for specific templates.

Restrictions on enrollment agents can only be enforced on Windows Server 2008 or later CAs. They aren't supported on Windows Server 2003 CAs.

Figure 6-28 shows how restricted enrollment agents can be configured in Certification Authority for an enterprise CA. Users in the G_SmartCardRA group can request the Cengage Smartcard Logon certificate for any users in the Domain Users group.

In addition to modifying the properties of the CA to support enrollment agents, users in the delegated group also need to have valid enrollment certificates enrolled for their accounts.

The following activity shows how you can configure restricted enrollment agents for a specific certificate template.

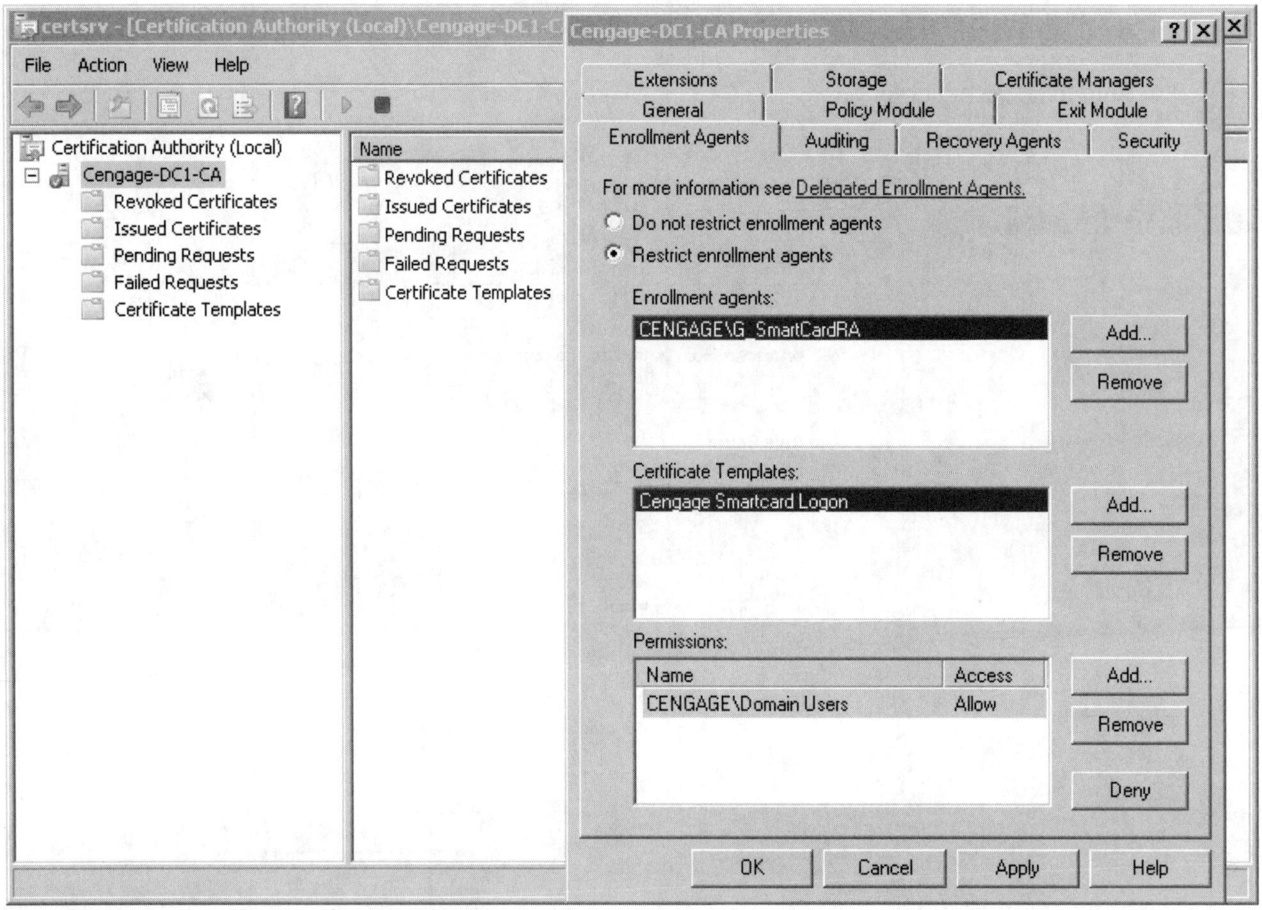

Figure 6-28 Configuring restricted enrollment agents

Courtesy Course Technology/Cengage Learning

Activity 6-9: Configuring Restricted Enrollment Agents

Time Required: 15 minutes

Objective: Configure restricted enrollment agents.

Description: Users in the G_SmartCardRA group need to be able to request and enroll smart card logon certificates for users in the domain. You need to create the global security groups (G_SalesITAdmins and G_Sales), create the Smartcard logon certificate template, and configure restricted enrollment agents. This activity should be run on DC1.

1. Start **DC1** and log on with the domain **Administrator** account.
2. Start **Active Directory Users and Computers** via the **Administrative Tools** menu.
3. Right-click **Users** and select **New, Group.** Enter **G_SmartCardRA** as the **Group Name.** Ensure that the **Group Scope** is set to **Global** and the **Group Type** is set to **Security.** Click **OK.**
4. Start **Certification Authority** via the **Administrative Tools** menu.
5. Expand **Cengage-DC1-CA.** Right-click **Certificate Templates** and select **Manage.**
6. In the **Certificate Templates** console, scroll down to the **Smartcard Logon** certificate template. Right-click the template and select **Duplicate Template.**
7. Select **Windows Server 2008, Enterprise Edition** and click **OK** to create a new V3 certificate template.
8. Name the new template **Cengage Smartcard Logon** and click **OK.**

9. Return to the **Certification Authority** console. Right-click **Certificate Templates** and select **New, Certificate Template to Issue**. Select the **Cengage Smartcard Logon** certificate and click **OK**.
10. Right-click **Cengage-DC1-CA** and select **Properties**. Select the **Enrollment Agents** tab.
11. Click **Restrict enrollment agents**. Review the information in the dialog box and click **OK**. Your display will look similar to Figure 6-29.

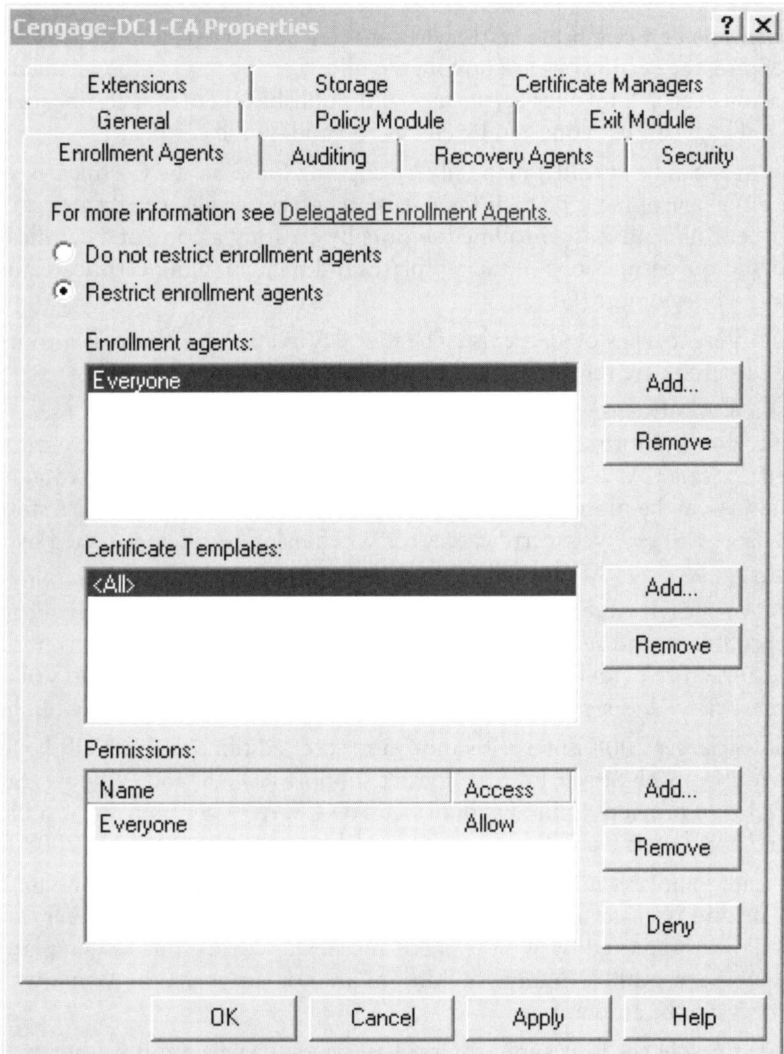

Figure 6-29 Default enrollment agents and templates
Courtesy Course Technology/Cengage Learning

12. Click **Add** next to **Enrollment Agents**. Type **G_SmartCardRA** and click **OK**. Select **Everyone** and click **Remove**.
13. Click **Add** next to **Certificate Templates**. Select the **Cengage Smartcard Logon** certificate template and click **OK**. Select **All** and click **Remove**.
14. Click **Add** next to **Permissions**. Type **Domain Users** and click **OK**. Select **Everyone** and click **Remove**.
15. Click **OK** to apply the changes.
16. Close all open windows.

Chapter Summary

- A public key infrastructure (PKI) is a group of technologies used to create, issue, manage, store, and revoke certificates. It includes a certification authority (CA), which actually issues the certificates. Certificates are used for authentication, encryption, identification, EFS, smart cards, and much more.
- Public key encryption uses a public/private key pair. Anything encrypted by one key in the pair can be decrypted by the other key in the pair. The public key is embedded in a certificate and the private key is kept private.
- The life cycle of a certificate starts when it is enrolled. Certificates have validity dates; when they expire, the certificates are no longer valid. Certificates can be revoked prior to the expiration. The CA revokes certificates and publishes them in a certificate revocation list (CRL), which can be requested by clients to validate the certificate.
- Certificates can be enrolled manually by copying files, via the Certificates snap-in, or by using a Web enrollment page. If the CA is an enterprise CA, certificates can be configured for autoenrollment. Autoenrollment works by creating a copy of a certificate template, modifying the permissions of the template, and then enabling certificate autoenrollment via a Group Policy object (GPO).
- Many different types of CAs exist. The first CA in a CA hierarchy is a root CA. Other CAs in the hierarchy are referred to as subordinate CAs.
- A public CA is trusted and would have its root CA certificate in end users' Trusted Root Certification Authorities store. Any certificates issued by a trusted CA are automatically trusted. Private CAs are used internally within an organization. The root certificate of a private CA can be placed in the Trusted Root Certification Authorities store. If this is not done, users will receive a certificate error when using certificates issued by the private CA.
- Microsoft's AD CS can be configured as an enterprise CA or a stand-alone CA. An enterprise CA is heavily integrated with Active Directory, and supports certificate templates, autoenrollment, and restricted enrollment agents. A stand-alone CA is not integrated with Active Directory by default, and doesn't support the advanced features of an enterprise CA. An enterprise CA is a private CA; a stand-alone CA could be either a public or private CA.
- Windows Server 2008 Enterprise and Datacenter editions support all the features of AD CS. Windows Web Server Edition doesn't support AD CS, and Windows Server 2008 Standard Edition provides limited support for AD CS. AD CS cannot be installed on Windows Server 2008 Server Core, but it can be installed on Windows Server 2008 R2 Server Core.
- Certificate templates are used in an enterprise CA, and reduce the amount of time necessary to create and issue certificates. V2 templates (identified as Windows Server 2003, Enterprise Edition) are supported by Windows XP and newer clients, but V3 templates (identified as Windows Server 2008, Enterprise Edition) are not supported by Windows XP. V2 and V3 templates can be autoenrolled.
- The AD CS role has four supporting role services. Certification Authority is the primary role service. Certification Authority Web Enrollment can be used to allow clients to enroll certificates via a Web interface. The Online Responder service is used to validate certificates when requested (such as by issuing a copy of the CRL). The Network Device Enrollment service is used to issue certificates to network devices using the Simple Certificate Enrollment Protocol (SCEP).
- AD CS provides role-based administration with four roles. The CA administrator is granted permission to manage the CA. The certificate manager can issue and manage certificates. The backup operator can back up and restore the CA. The auditor is granted Manage Auditing permission to view, configure, and maintain auditing logs.
- Restricted enrollment agents can allow a selected group of users permission to enroll specific certificate templates for specific users. Restricted enrollment agents are enabled and configured in AD CS.

Key Terms

Active Directory Certificate Services (AD CS) Microsoft's implementation of a certification authority. AD CS can be used as an enterprise CA or a stand-alone CA. When used as an enterprise CA, it supports certificate templates, autoenrollment, and restricted enrollment agents.

Authentication A process used to prove that entities and senders are who they claim to be. For example, users can provide a user name and password as authentication. Similarly, a digital signature is used to provide authentication and provide assurances that a user sent a message.

Autoenrollment A process used on an enterprise CA that allows certificates to be enrolled automatically without user intervention. Only V2 and V3 certificate templates can be autoenrolled. A copy of a template is created, permissions (Read, Enroll, and Autoenroll) are assigned to the template, and a GPO is used to enable autoenrollment.

CA Web Enrollment A service added to AD CS that allows clients to use a Web interface to request and renew certificates, retrieve certificate revocation lists (CRLs), and enroll smart card certificates.

Certificate A digital file issued by a CA that holds identifying characteristics for a subject. Certificates include a public key, and can be used for identification, encryption, authentication, smart cards, and much more.

Certificate revocation list (CRL) A list of certificates that have been revoked by a CA prior to the expiration of the certificate. A certificate is revoked when the primary key is compromised. A certificate can also be revoked for other reasons—for example, if it is no longer needed.

Certificate templates Templates are only available in an enterprise CA, and are used to create certificates instead of creating them from scratch. V2 templates and V3 templates can be autoenrolled. Windows XP cannot use V3 templates.

Certification authority (CA) An entity that issues certificates. A CA can be a company such as VeriSign or a software component such as Microsoft's Certification Authority.

Digital signature A cryptographic component that provides authentication, integrity, and non-repudiation. When an e-mail is digitally signed, it is hashed, and the hash is encrypted with the sender's private key. The receiver decrypts the encrypted hash with the sender's public key.

Enterprise CA An enterprise CA is heavily integrated with Active Directory, and automates many of the tasks for managing certificates in Active Directory. An enterprise CA would also be considered a private CA.

Hash A number created by performing a hashing algorithm against a file or message. Hashes are used to provide integrity. No matter how many times the hash is calculated, it will result in the same number, unless the file or message has been changed. If the recalculated hash is different, the file or message is no longer the same—it has lost integrity.

Network Device Enrollment A service available on AD CS that allows certificates to be automatically enrolled for network devices such as routers.

Non-repudiation A process that prevents a user from denying an action. Digital signatures provide assurances that a user sent a message, so that the user cannot believably deny sending the digitally signed message. Similarly, if a user is authenticated on a network and actions are logged by his user account, the user cannot believably deny that he performed the logged action.

Online Responder A service added to AD CS to respond to Online Certificate Status Protocol (OCSP) queries, which can be used to determine the status of a certificate.

Private CA A private CA is internal to an organization. The root certificate is not published to users outside the organization.

Private key One of two keys in a matched public/private key pair used with asymmetric encryption. When this key pair is used, one key encrypts the data and the other key decrypts the data. If a private key is compromised, the certificate that holds the matching public key is revoked and published in a CRL.

Public CA A public CA is used on the Internet. The public CA's root certificate is published to the Trusted Root Certification Authorities store for Internet users; certificates issued from a public CA are automatically trusted.

Public key One of two keys in a matched public/private key pair used with asymmetric encryption. When this key pair is used, one key encrypts the data and the other key decrypts the data. Public keys are embedded in a certificate and issued by a CA.

Public key infrastructure (PKI) A group of technologies used to create, issue, manage, store, and revoke certificates.

Restricted enrollment agents An available feature when AD CS is used as an enterprise CA. Restricted enrollment agents can allow a selected group of users permission to enroll specific certificate templates for specific users.

Root CA The first CA in a CA hierarchy. The root CA issues certificates to subordinate CAs, which issue certificates to end users, or a root CA is used without subordinate CAs and thus issues certificates for end users. Every CA hierarchy must have a root CA.

Simple Certificate Enrollment Protocol (SCEP) A protocol used with the Network Device Enrollment service to automatically issue certificates to network devices such as routers.

Stand-alone CA A stand-alone CA can be a member of Active Directory and can have some information published through Active Directory, but it can also be completely separate from a domain and kept as an offline CA. A stand-alone CA could be a public CA or a private CA.

Subordinate CA A child CA in a CA hierarchy. A subordinate CA is issued a certificate from a root CA (or a higher-level subordinate CA). Subordinate CAs are used in larger organizations but are not required.

Trusted Root Certification Authorities store The location on a computer where certificates for root CAs are stored. If a certificate for a root CA is stored here, all certificates issued by the root CA are trusted.

Review Questions

1. Your company has a single-domain forest running Windows Server 2008 servers. One of these servers is running AD CS. The company recently added a Web server to the perimeter network for external clients. Web developers want to allow users to establish a secure Web session without receiving any errors. What should be done?
   a. Issue a certificate from the AD CS server to the Web server.
   b. Create an enterprise root CA and issue a certificate from this CA to the Web server.
   c. Install a certificate from a public CA on the Web server.
   d. Purchase a trusted root certification authority and install a certificate from this CA on the Web server.
2. What is embedded in a smart card that provides authentication? (Choose two.)
   a. OCSP certificate
   b. User certificate
   c. Microprocessor
   d. NIC
3. You have been using Windows Remote Management (WinRM) and Windows Remote Shell (WinRS) to remotely manage a Windows Server 2008 Server Core server in your single-domain forest. You have recently installed Windows Server 2008 Server Core on a non-domain server, but you aren't able to remotely manage it with WinRM and WinRS. What needs to be done?
   a. The server must be added to the domain.
   b. AD CS must be added to the new Server Core server.
   c. Disable the firewall.
   d. Issue a certificate to the server and configure WinRM to use HTTPS.

4. You are designing the deployment of AD CS in your single-domain forest. Client computers in the domain include Windows XP, Windows Vista, and Windows 7. You want to support autoenrollment of certificates for all computers in the network. What should you include in the plan?
   a. Use V2 certificates.
   b. Use V3 certificates.
   c. Use V2 templates.
   d. Use V3 templates.
5. You are planning the design of AD CS in your single-domain forest. AD CS will be installed on a Windows Server 2008 server. Clients include Windows XP, Windows Vista, and Windows 7. Your plan should include automatic certificate enrollment for all clients. What elements should you include? (Choose two.)
   a. Create an enterprise CA as a root CA.
   b. Create a stand-alone CA as a root CA.
   c. Create an enterprise CA as a subordinate CA.
   d. Create a stand-alone CA as a subordinate CA.
   e. Use V2 templates.
   f. Use V3 templates.
6. Your single-domain forest has two servers. DC1 is a domain controller hosting AD DS. Cert1 is hosting AD CS. You are considering a plan to deploy computer certificates without any user intervention. What should be configured? (Choose two.)
   a. Configure the default domain policy on DC1.
   b. Configure the default domain policy on DC2.
   c. Configure the permissions on the V1 template on DC1.
   d. Configure the permissions on the V1 template on DC2.
   e. Create a copy of the V1 template on DC1. Configure the permissions on the template copy.
   f. Create a copy of the V1 template on DC2. Configure the permissions on the template copy.
7. Your organization is configured as a single-domain forest in the domain functional level of Windows Server 2008. Company policy states that user accounts and user profiles are to be deleted within 30 days of an employee leaving the company. An employee is trying to retrieve data that was encrypted with EFS by a previous employee who was terminated more than 30 days ago. What is needed to retrieve this data?
   a. The current employee's public key, which is stored in the employee's profile.
   b. The current employee's private key, which is stored in the employee's profile.
   c. The ex-employee's public key, which was stored in the employee's profile.
   d. The ex-employee's private key, which was stored in the employee's profile.
8. You are considering adding AD CS in your single-domain forest. The forest is currently operating at the forest functional level of Windows Server 2008. You want to ensure that AD CS remains highly available. What should you do?
   a. Install AD CS on a Windows Server 2008 Standard Edition server.
   b. Install AD CS on a Windows Server 2008 Enterprise Edition server.
   c. Install AD CS on two Windows Server 2008 Standard Edition servers.
   d. Install AD CS on two Windows Server 2008 Enterprise Edition servers.

9. Your organization is considering the deployment of certificates to internal clients. You are asked to identify the benefits of using an enterprise CA over a stand-alone CA. What are some valid points you could add? (Choose all that apply.)
    a. An enterprise CA will automatically publish the root certificate to clients via Group Policy. A stand-alone CA requires extra steps to publish the root certificate to clients.
    b. An enterprise CA can use V2 and V3 certificates, but a stand-alone CA cannot.
    c. An enterprise CA can use V2 and V3 certificate templates, but a stand-alone CA cannot use certificate templates.
    d. An enterprise CA is heavily integrated in Active Directory; a stand-alone CA is not.
    e. An enterprise CA can support all clients from Windows XP through Windows 7, but a stand-alone CA cannot support all clients.
    f. An enterprise CA supports autoenrollment; a stand-alone CA does not.
10. You have created an enterprise root CA on a Windows Server 2008 server and have decided to use rolc-based administration. Sally needs to be able to issue and manage certificates in the CA, including the ability to approve certificate enrollment and revocation requests. What role should be used to grant Sally all of the appropriate permissions?
    a. CA administrator
    b. Certificate manager
    c. Certificate administrator
    d. Auditor
11. You suspect that a certificate issued by a CA you manage has been compromised. What should be done?
    a. The certificate should be renewed.
    b. The certificate should be deleted.
    c. The certificate should be revoked.
    d. The certificate should be depreciated.
12. What does a CA use to inform clients of revoked certificates?
    a. Autoenrollment
    b. Restricted enrollment agents
    c. Network Device Enrollment service
    d. CRL
13. You are considering adding a stand-alone CA and making it a member server in your single-domain forest. Certificates issued by the CA will be used by internal and external clients. You want to ensure that certificates issued by this CA are automatically trusted by internal clients. What should you do?
    a. This is not possible.
    b. Use Group Policy to publish the root certificate to clients' Trusted Root Certification Authority.
    c. Use autoenrollment to publish the root certificate to clients' Trusted Root Certification Authority.
    d. Configure the stand-alone CA as a restricted enrollment agent.
14. You have configured a CA that has issued certificates to clients on the internal network and the Internet. Clients regularly use these certificates to digitally sign and encrypt e-mail. You want to ensure that any client that receives a certificate issued by this CA can validate the certificate. What should be configured to fully support this need?
    a. A CRL
    b. An online responder

c. A V2 certificate
d. A V2 certificate template

15. You manage an enterprise CA and want to configure autoenrollment of certificates from a certificate template. Certificates will be issued to all clients in the domain, which includes Windows XP, Windows Vista, and Windows 7 clients. What should be done to support this plan? (Choose two.)
    a. Create V2 duplicates of the desired certificate and assign Autoenroll permission.
    b. Create V3 duplicates of the desired certificate and assign Autoenroll permission.
    c. Create V2 duplicates of the desired certificate and assign Read, Enroll, and Autoenroll permissions.
    d. Create V3 duplicates of the desired certificate and assign Read, Enroll, and Autoenroll permissions.
    e. Create a GPO with the Certificate Services Client – Auto-Enrollment setting and link it to the Domain Controllers OU.
    f. Create a GPO with the Certificate Services Client – Auto-Enrollment setting and link it to the domain.

16. You manage an enterprise CA that is used to issue certificates to users and computers with a single-domain forest. Some certificates need to be created and issued to clients that do not have accounts in Active Directory. Your solution should use the least administrative effort. What should you use?
    a. Create a stand-alone CA to issue certificates.
    b. Create a public CA to issue certificates.
    c. Use Web page enrollment with the existing CA.
    d. Use Web page enrollment using a subordinate CA.
17. You manage AD CS running on Windows Server 2008 Enterprise Edition as an enterprise CA. Network administrators want to ensure that all routers on the network use IPSec, and you're asked to provide a solution that allows the routers to automatically request certificates. What would you suggest?
    a. Add the Network Device Enrollment service with SCEP support to the CA.
    b. Add the Network Device Enrollment service with SCEP to the routers.
    c. Add the SCEP service to the CA.
    d. Remove the Certification Authority service from the CA and add the Network Device Enrollment service.
18. You manage AD CS running on Windows Server 2008 Enterprise Edition as an enterprise CA. Network administrators want to enable device authentication for routers used on the network, and ask you for a solution to issue certificates to the routers. The routers support SCEP. What would you suggest?
    a. Change the CA to a stand-alone CA and add the Network Device Enrollment service.
    b. Create a subordinate CA and add the Network Device Enrollment service.
    c. Upgrade the server to Windows Server 2008 Datacenter Edition and add the Network Device Enrollment service.
    d. Add the Network Device Enrollment service to the existing CA.
19. You are an administrator for a single-domain forest with AD CS configured as an enterprise CA. End users use smart cards to log on. You want specific users in the HR department to be able to request and enroll the certificates for smart cards. What should you use?
    a. V2 certificate templates
    b. V3 certificate templates

c. Restricted enrollment agents
d. Role-based administration

20. Your organization is considering the use of smart cards for log-on purposes. Each user will be issued a smart card with an embedded certificate and use it to log on to computers in the domain. Currently, the plan is to implement AD CS in the domain and have users in the Certificate Managers role issue the certificates. However, the administrator in this role says this task should be delegated to other security professionals. How can this be done?
    a. Implement role-based administration.
    b. Add the other administrators to the certificate managers role.
    c. Add the other administrators to the certificate administrator role.
    d. Use restricted enrollment agents.

Case Projects

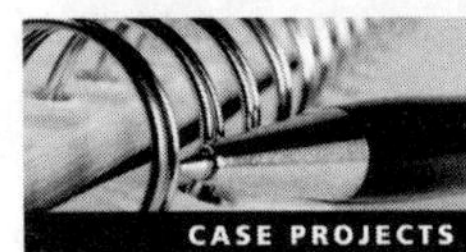

Case Project 6-1: Designing a Certificate Services Solution

Your organization is configured as a single-domain forest, and it wants to implement certificates to internal users and computers. After the CA is configured, autoenrollment will deploy the certificates to subjects without user interaction. Clients are running Windows XP, Windows Vista, and Windows 7. What type of CA should you deploy, and what should be used to deploy the certificates? CA types include root, subordinate, private, public, enterprise, and stand-alone. Explain your answer.

Case Project 6-2: Evaluating a Plan to Create a Stand-alone Root CA

Your organization is planning to deploy a Web server that will allow customers to purchase products. Customers should not see any certificate errors during this process. Management has asked you to evaluate the plan to support this server. The plan will create a stand-alone root CA and use this CA to issue a certificate for the Web server. How would you respond to management?

Case Project 6-3: Configuring Autoenrollment

Your organization is a single-domain forest with more than 5000 users. It includes a Windows Server 2008 Standard Edition server running AD CS that was originally created to issue certificates used by Web browsers. You want to enable autoenrollment of certificates to Windows XP, Windows Vista, and Windows 7 clients in the network. What needs to be done to support this plan? Your plan should address all of the issues necessary to enable autoenrollment.

Case Project 6-4: Issuing Certificates to Routers

AD CS is installed and operational on a Windows Server 2008 Standard Edition server. Network administrators want to have certificates issued to routers in the network. What needs to be done on the AD CS server and the routers to support this plan?

chapter 7

Securing Windows Server 2008 Servers

After reading this chapter and completing the exercises, you will be able to:

- Understand the basics of hardening a server
- Use the Security Configuration Wizard (SCW) to create a security policy
- Use Microsoft Baseline Security Analyzer (MBSA) for compliance auditing
- Design Windows Server Update Services (WSUS) for different scenarios
- Understand firewall usage in a perimeter network

When designing system security, you need to start by hardening the systems. A hardened system starts with a reduced attack surface; it is regularly audited to ensure that it remains secure and is kept up to date. You have several tools available to harden systems, including the Security Configuration Wizard and Microsoft Baseline Security Analyzer.

Within a network, systems are often kept up to date using Windows Server Update Services (WSUS). WSUS is used to download updates and deploy them to hosts within the network. WSUS is a free product that can be used in small networks within a single site, and in complex networks with multiple sites.

Networks that have Internet access must be protected with at least a single firewall. A perimeter network is provided by using two firewalls; this arrangement is often referred to as a demilitarized zone (DMZ). Microsoft's Internet Security Accelerator and Forefront Threat Management Gateway are both dedicated firewall applications that can be installed on a server.

All of these concepts are covered in this chapter.

Hardening a System

Hardening a system is the process of making it more secure from the default configuration; it is a very important consideration for server deployment. Years ago, security wasn't a primary concern, but with all the malware and persistent attacks on systems today, administrators need to consider security throughout the lifetime of a system.

System security should be considered in several distinct areas:

- **Reduce the attack surface.** A system should be deployed only with the required services and protocols. Unneeded services and protocols should be removed or disabled. The **Security Configuration Wizard (SCW)** and Group Policy can be used to help deploy systems with secure baselines.
- **Regularly audit security.** Systems should be periodically checked to ensure that they remain up to date. Tools like the **Microsoft Baseline Security Analyzer (MBSA)** can be used to perform compliance auditing.
- **Keep the system up to date.** As patches, hot fixes, and other updates are released, they need to be applied to systems that need the updates. Free tools such as Windows Server Update Services (WSUS) can be used for patch management.

When considering security, administrators constantly strive to find the right balance in the trade-offs between cost and usability. More secure environments have a higher cost and are less user-friendly. Less secure environments cost less and are more user-friendly.

An important concept of server security is the value of a baseline. In the context of server security, a baseline is a starting point for a server that locks it down as much as possible while also allowing it to operate. Instead of creating a separate baseline for every server, it's common for a company to create a single baseline for a group of similar servers and then apply this baseline equally to all of them.

As an example, imagine that a company is preparing to deploy 10 Web servers using Internet Information Services (IIS). Windows Server 2008 could be installed on this server, updates applied, IIS added, configuration changes made, and security settings implemented. Windows Deployment Services (WDS) could then be used to capture an image of this server and use the image as a baseline. Instead of building the other nine servers from scratch, the image could be deployed to these servers. All 10 servers would then start from a common secure state.

Baselines can also be implemented using other tools such as the Security Configuration Wizard and Group Policy, either in combination with imaging tools or separately. The value of the other tools is that compliance auditing can later be used to determine if the server has changed from the baseline.

The following sections cover these core principles. While all systems need to be hardened, the following sections focus on hardening a server using the available tools.

Reducing the Attack Surface

When hardening a system, you start by making sure that only the needed services and protocols are installed and enabled. Some services and protocols are essential, and must be installed and available to ensure that a system will run properly; other nonessential items should only be installed and available when needed.

As an example, the File Transport Protocol (FTP) can be used to allow users to upload and download files to a Web server. FTP has many security challenges; for instance, data is transported in the clear (unencrypted), making FTP susceptible to eavesdropping attacks, and anonymous logins can be enabled, allowing anyone to upload or download files. An unprotected server that has Internet access and runs the FTP service can easily be targeted; attackers can upload pirated software, music, and videos and advertise the FTP server as a source for the pirated media.

If FTP is not installed and enabled on a server, it is not susceptible to FTP attacks. If you do not need the FTP protocol on a server, you should not add it. Similarly, any other unneeded protocols or services should be removed or disabled.

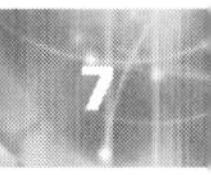

The challenge is identifying which services and protocols are needed and which ones are not. Thankfully, Windows Server 2008 was developed with a secure computing strategy, and Microsoft has adopted tools such as Server Manager and the Secure Configuration Wizard.

Secure Computing Strategy

Years ago, Microsoft adopted a secure development lifecycle strategy for its software known as **SD^3+C**. If you understand the basics of Microsoft's approach, it becomes easier to understand how other pieces of security are intertwined.

- **Secure by Design**. Security considerations are included when the application or operating system is first being designed; this element is an integral component of the design.
- **Secure by Default**. Security implementations start in a secure mode. As an example, an operating system starts with a firewall enabled. An administrator doesn't need to enable the firewall to add security, but he might need to disable the firewall to improve usability.
- **Secure in Deployment and Communications**. Systems are deployed in a secure manner using secure communications.

Administrators first saw SD^3+C when Windows XP SP2 was released. One big change with SP2 was that the Windows firewall was enabled by default. If a firewall exists, it is more secure when enabled by default; this strategy is consistent with the Secure by Default portion of SD^3+C. However, this strategy caused some usability problems when the firewall blocked traffic that was needed by some applications. When this problem occurred, administrators needed to make a conscious decision to weaken security by configuring the firewall so that the applications worked.

Before Windows XP SP2, administrators needed to take steps to enable the firewall. Because an enabled firewall could cause usability issues, it was easier to do nothing rather than enable the firewall.

The end result of SD^3+C in action is that systems start in a more secure state. However, you can't just enable a firewall and consider a system secure. Deploying and maintaining secure systems requires constant vigilance.

Server Core

Microsoft released Windows Server 2008 in different **Server Core** editions. Server Core includes only the most basic services and protocols needed for the system to operate and support different Windows Server 2008 roles. Server Core is such a basic implementation of reducing the attack surface that it doesn't even include a graphical user interface (GUI)—everything is done from the command line.

Many of the extra services and protocols that are needed for different roles and functions aren't included with Server Core. This approach makes it more secure because it is less susceptible to a wide variety of attacks.

Windows Server 2008 Server Core supports the following server roles:

- Active Directory Domain Services
- Active Directory Lightweight Directory Services
- DNS
- DHCP
- Web Server (IIS)
- Windows Media Server
- Hyper-V
- File Services
- Print Services

Windows Server 2008 R2 Server Core supports all of the same roles as Windows Server 2008 with the addition of Active Directory Certificate Services. A significant difference between Windows Server 2008 Server Core and Windows Server 2008 R2 Server Core is that the R2 edition includes the .NET Framework, which adds more capabilities.

Server Manager

The Server Manager is a valuable tool when adding roles and services. It's certainly helpful when the Add Roles and Add Features wizards are used, but these wizards also act as a security tool by helping you to add only the needed services and protocols.

Without the wizards in Server Manager, you'd have to know which protocols and services to add and enable. You might add unnecessary protocols and services, which could introduce unnecessary risks. Additionally, when you remove features and roles using Server Manager, the wizards know what should be removed; very little effort is required on your part.

Security Configuration Wizard

The Security Configuration Wizard (SCW) adds another layer of security for Windows Server 2008, and can be used to complement Server Manager. You can use SCW to create a security policy that can be applied to any system to reduce the attack surface. SCW uses roles to identify the services, features, and settings that are required on a system, and can remove or disable everything else.

SCW cannot be used to add roles and services. Instead, Server Manager is used to configure a server to perform specific roles; SCW can then be used to provide additional security for the installed roles.

When you run SCW, it creates a configuration database of all the possible server roles, client features, options, services, and Windows firewall settings. Figure 7-1 shows the SCW Viewer with the Security Configuration Database open, the Server Roles expanded, and the Active Directory Certificate Services – Certification Authority role selected.

You can see in the figure that the database includes details on the role, including the description, required services, required firewall rules, and the role's status on the server where SCW is run. Information in the database is compiled for a server, and then a security policy can be created to ensure that the required components are enabled for each installed role. Unnecessary components are not enabled.

The security policy created by SCW is saved in the form of an extensible markup language (XML) file. This file can be deployed to individual servers one at a time, or to multiple servers using Group Policy. Once created, the security policy can be used to perform the following tasks:

- Configure services
- Configure network security settings, including the firewall rules

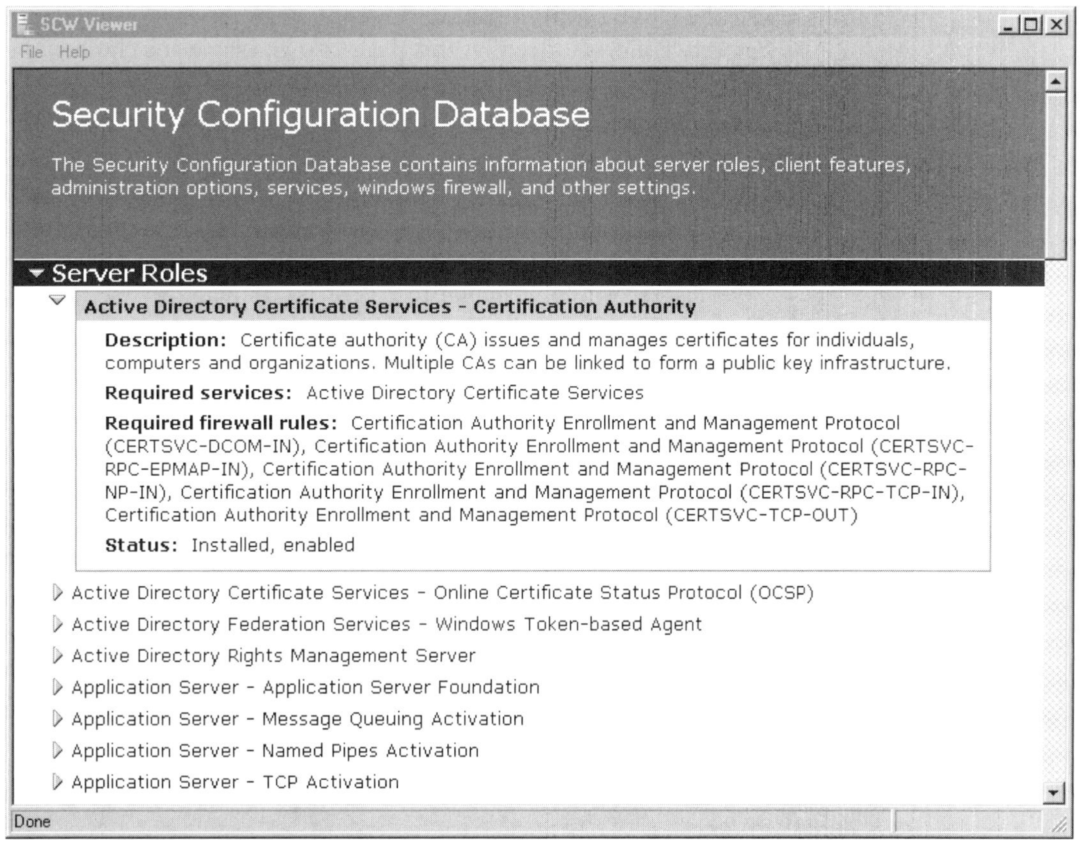

Figure 7-1 The Security Configuration Viewer displays components of the Security Configuration Database
Courtesy Course Technology/Cengage Learning

- Configure registry settings
- Configure an audit policy

SCW is installed by default on Windows Server 2008 and is available via the Administrative Tools menu. When you start SCW, you can create new security policies, edit and apply policies, or roll back a security policy that has been applied.

Activities in this chapter require several files that aren't included in Windows Server 2008. These files have been included on the CD for your convenience, in a folder named "Chapter 7 downloads." The activities include directions on how to download the files if the CD is misplaced.

Activity 7-1: Running SCW

Time Required: 45 minutes
Objective: Run the Security Configuration Wizard.

Description: You want to increase security for domain controllers in your organization. Your boss has asked you to run SCW and create a security policy for review. You will run SCW in this activity to create a policy, but you will not apply it. This activity should be run on DC1, which is used throughout the book.

1. Start **DC1** and log on with the domain **Administrator** account.
2. Start the **Security Configuration Wizard** via the **Administrative Tools** menu.
3. Review the information on the **Welcome** screen and click **Next**.

4. On the **Configuration Action** screen, accept the default setting of **Create a New Security Policy**. Notice that this page also gives you the choices of editing, applying, or rolling back security policies. Click **Next**.
5. Accept the default setting of **DC1** as the server and click **Next**.
6. When the **Processing Security Configuration Database** screen appears, SCW will scan the server and create a configuration database that includes detailed information on the installed roles and features. Click **View Configuration Database.** When prompted to allow an ActiveX control to run, click **Yes**. The SCW Viewer will start. Your display will look similar to Figure 7-2, though the Windows Firewall Rules will not be expanded.

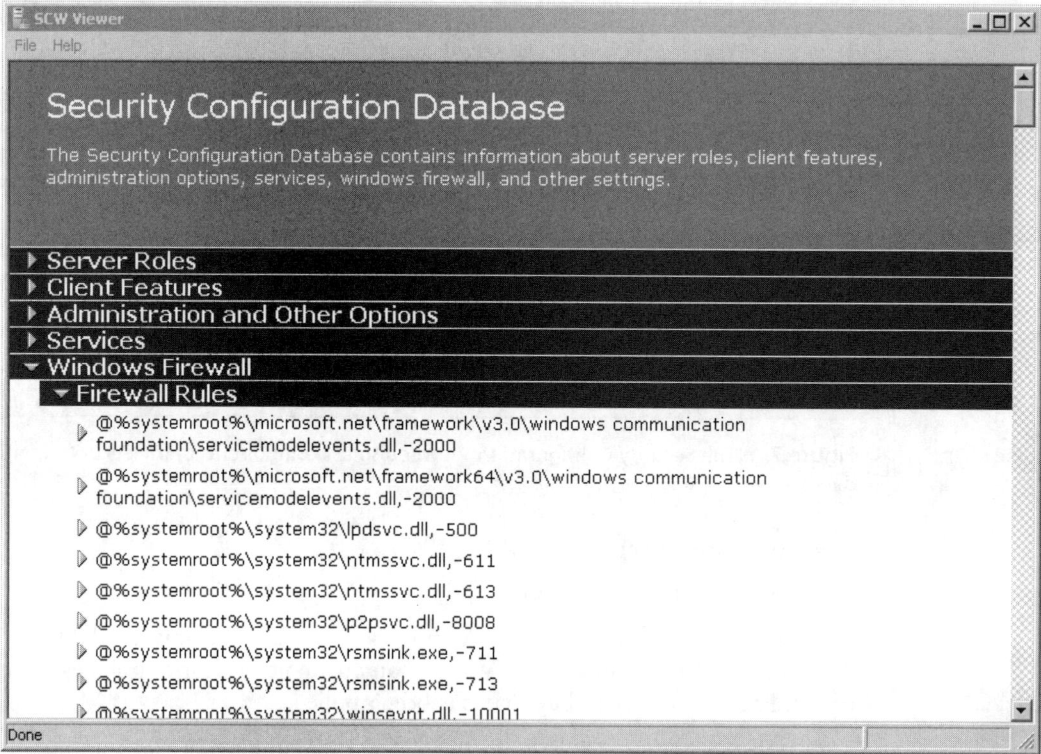

Figure 7-2 Viewing server role details in the Security Configuration Database

Courtesy Course Technology/Cengage Learning

7. Click **Server Roles.** Notice that it includes many more roles than the 13 that can be added to Windows Server 2008 using Server Manager. This list does not show all the roles installed on this server; it shows the roles that SCW can secure with a security policy.
8. Click **DNS Server** in the **Server Roles** list. Notice that the screen includes details on the DNS server and identifies the required services and required firewall rules. Feel free to select other server roles in the list and view the details.
9. Scroll down and click **Client Features.** Click **Background Intelligent Transfer Service (BITS)** and review the information in the **Required Services** section. Feel free to select other Client Features in the list and view the details.
10. Select **Administration and Other Options.** Select **.NET Framework 3.0** and view the details.
11. Select **Services.** Select **Active Directory Certificate Services** and view the details.

12. Select **Windows Firewall, Firewall Rules.** Select any of the firewall rules to view the details.

The point of reviewing these elements is to see the depth of information in this database. You probably could find these details separately by researching each role, service, or component, but SCW provides a compilation of exactly what you need for almost any Windows Server 2008 configuration. The wizard uses this database to create the security policy.

13. Close the SCW Viewer and return to the Security Configuration Wizard. Click **Next** on the Processing Security Configuration Database screen.
14. Click **Next** on the Role-Based Service Configuration screen.
15. Review the information on the Select Server Roles screen. Your display will look similar to Figure 7-3.

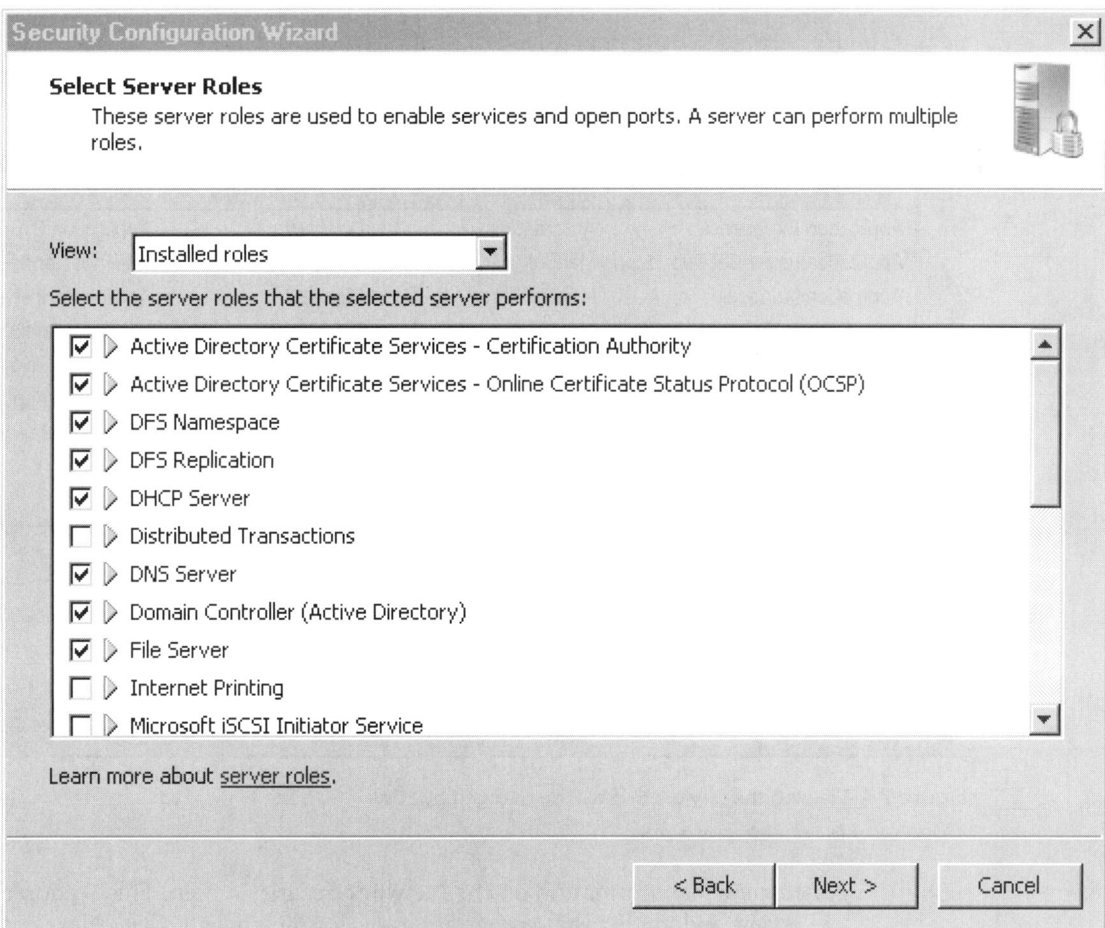

Figure 7-3 Identifying roles installed on a server

Courtesy Course Technology/Cengage Learning

When creating a policy for multiple servers, you can modify this screen to match the roles that will be installed on the servers. Accept the default settings and click **Next**.

16. Review the information on the **Select Client Features** screen. It shows the installed features, but you can modify the list to match the features that will be installed on a target server. Click **Next**.

17. Review the information on the **Select Administration and Other Options** screen. It shows the installed options, but you can modify the list to match the options that will be installed on a target server. Click **Next**.
18. Review the information on the **Select Additional Services** screen. Additional services can be selected from this screen depending on the needs for the target server. Click **Next.**
19. On the **Handling Unspecified Services** screen, leave the default selection of **Do Not Change the Startup Mode of the Service.** Click **Next.**
20. The **Confirm Service Changes** screen appears; it looks similar to Figure 7-4. Notice how many services will change to **Disabled** if this policy is applied. Click **Next.**

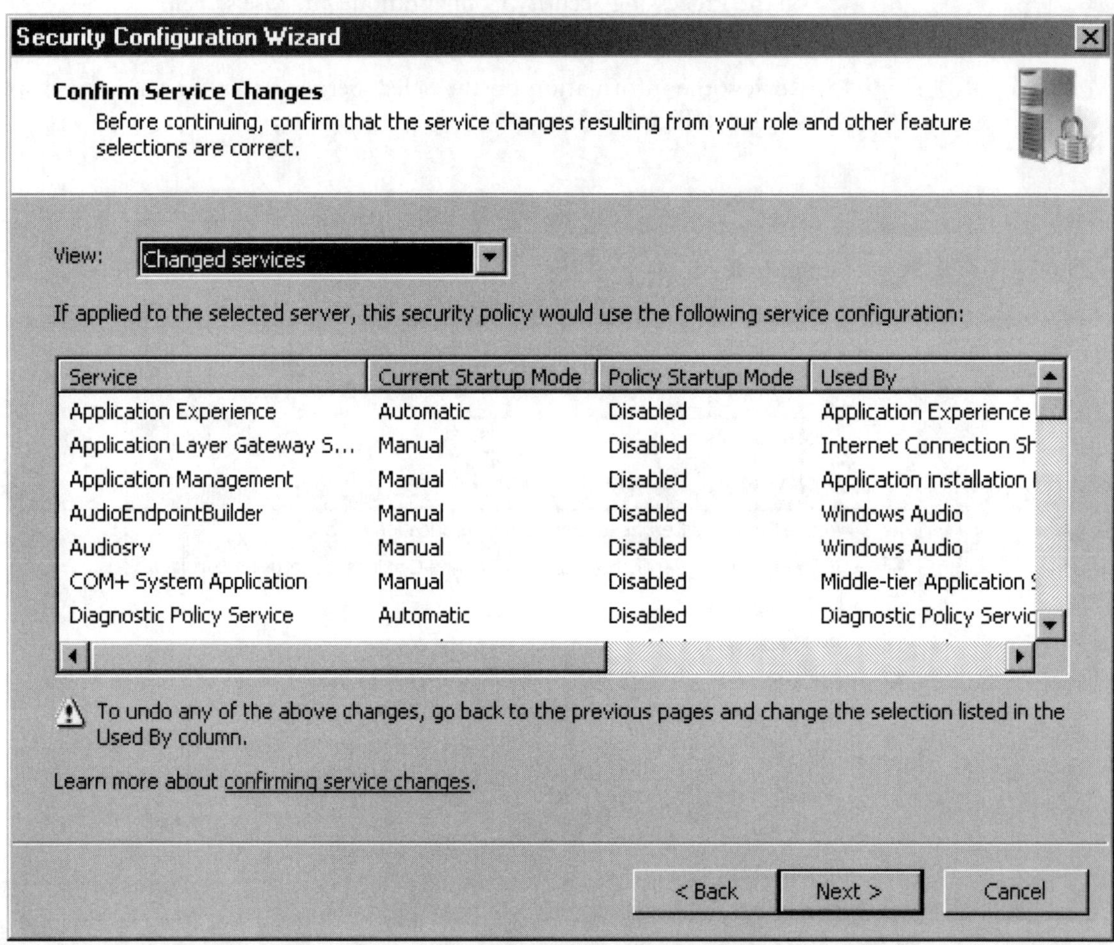

Figure 7-4 Viewing the services that will be changed by SCW

Courtesy Course Technology/Cengage Learning

21. Review the information on the **Network Security** screen. This section allows you to review and modify the settings and rules for the firewall. Click **Next**.
22. The **Network Security Rules** screen appears. It shows all the rules that are needed based on the configuration selected in the wizard so far. Notice how many rules are needed.
23. Select the **Active Directory Domain Controller** (**RPC**) rule and click **Edit**. Most information in the rule is dimmed and can't be modified, but you can click the **General**, **Programs and Services**, **Protocols and Ports**, and **Scope** tabs to view the details and get an idea of the complexity of the generated rules. After viewing the rules, click **Cancel**. Click **Next**.
24. Review the information on the **Registry Settings** screen. This section allows you to review and modify registry settings. Click **Next**.

25. Review the information on the **Require SMB Security Signatures** screen. Accept the default settings and click **Next.**
26. Review the information on the **Require LDAP Signing** screen. Accept the default settings and click **Next.**
27. Review the information on the **Outbound Authentication Methods** screen. Accept the default settings and click **Next.**
28. Review the information on the **Outbound Authentication using Domain Accounts** screen. Accept the default settings and click **Next.**
29. Review the information on the **Registry Settings Summary** screen. Accept the default settings and click **Next.**
30. The **Audit Policy** page begins the section to create the Audit Policy portion of the security policy. Review the information on this page and click **Next.**

If an audit policy is included with the security policy, it cannot be rolled back with SCW but must be undone manually.

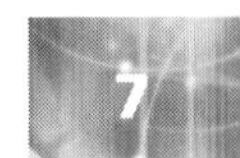

31. Review the information on the **System Audit Policy** page. Accept the default settings and click **Next.**
32. The **Audit Policy Summary** page appears; it looks similar to Figure 7-5. Accept the default settings and click **Next.**

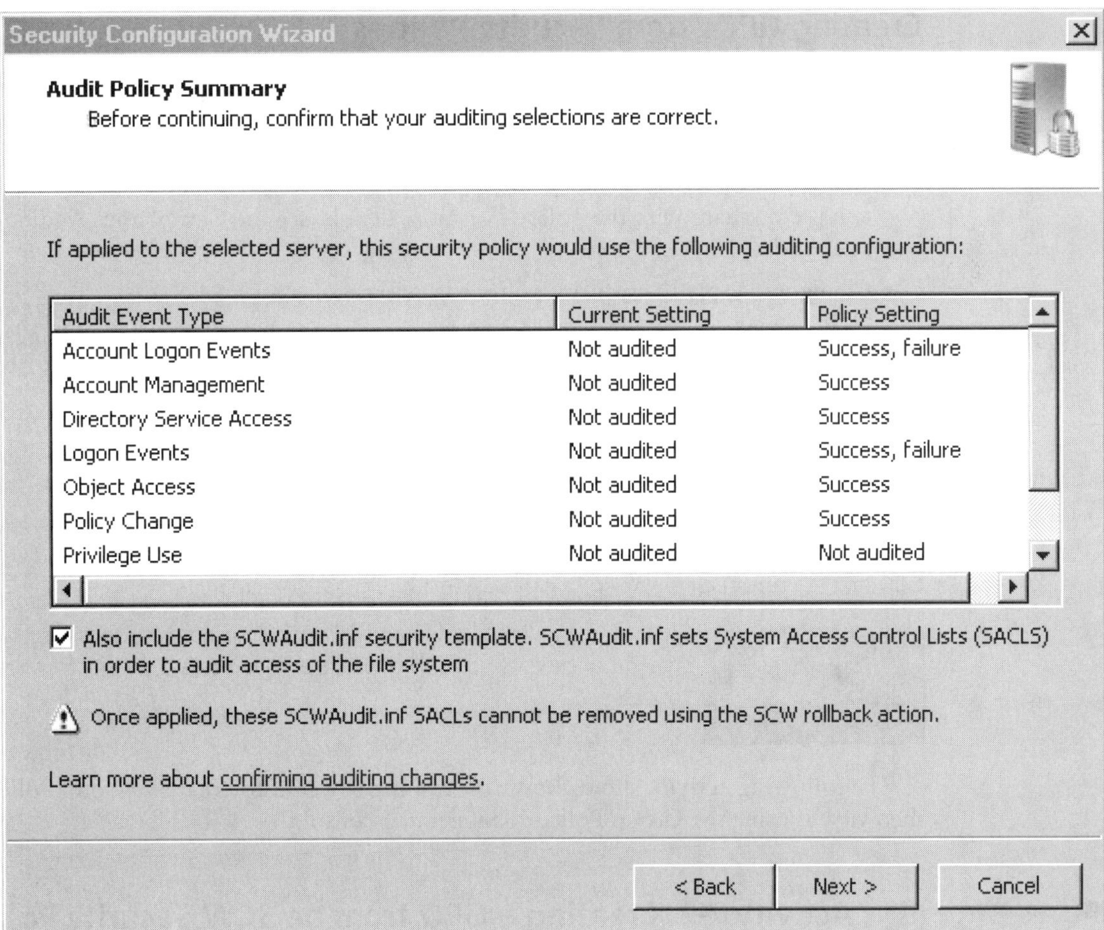

Figure 7-5 Reviewing the audit policy created by SCW

Courtesy Course Technology/Cengage Learning

33. On the **Save Security Policy** page, click **Next**.
34. Click **View Security Policy**. When prompted, click **Yes** to allow the ActiveX control. Click **Services** and browse through the different settings. Notice that the settings in this document indicate the actual settings if the policy is applied. Close the **SCW Viewer** to return to the **Security Configuration Wizard**.
35. Type **TestDC1** at the end of the Security Policy path so that it looks like **C:\Windows\security\msscw\Policies\TestDC1**. Click **Next**.
36. This policy can be applied now or later. Ensure that **Apply Later** is selected and click **Next**. Click **Finish**.

When changing security settings, you should test the changes in a non-production environment before actually deploying them. As security is increased, usability often decreases, and a secure server may no longer function as expected or desired.

37. Click **Start**, **Computer** to start **Windows Explorer**. Browse to **C:\Windows\security\msscw\Policies**. Double-click the **TestDC1.xml** file to open the policy file in Internet Explorer using the native XML format.
38. Close all open windows.

Once you have created the security policy file, you can apply it to any server by using the Security Configuration Wizard and choosing Apply an Existing Security Policy.

Creating GPOs from Security Policies

In addition to applying security policies to systems one at a time using the Security Configuration Wizard, you can create a Group Policy object (GPO) using **scwcmd**, the SCW command-line tool. Scwcmd includes support for the following commands:

- **Analyze.** Use this command to analyze a system against a policy and determine if the system is compliant with the policy. For more details, see the Compliance Auditing section later in this chapter.
- **Configure.** Apply the security policy to the system.
- **Register.** This command can be used to extend the SCW database by adding roles, tasks, services, and port definitions.
- **Rollback.** Roll back the settings of the last applied SCW security policy.
- **Transform.** Transform the security policy into a GPO.
- **View.** This command allows you to view the security policy XML file.

As an example, the Transform command takes the following format:

```
scwcmd Transform /p:PolicyFilePath /g:GPOName
```

As with most command-line tools, scwcmd is not case sensitive. A command can be entered as all uppercase, all lowercase, or any combination of case.

The following activity shows how you can use scwcmd to create a Group Policy object and then view it using the Group Policy Management console.

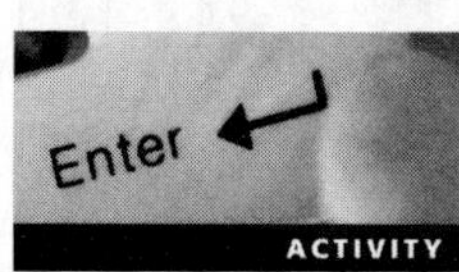

Activity 7-2: Creating a GPO from an SCW Security Policy

Time Required: 15 minutes
Objective: Create a GPO from an SCW security policy.

Description: You have created a security policy using SCW. You want to use Group Policy to apply this policy to several different computers. You first need to create the GPO from the security policy. This activity assumes that the previous activity was completed, and should be run on DC1.

1. Start **DC1** and log on with the domain **Administrator** account.
2. Start a command prompt by clicking **Start, Command Prompt.**
3. Enter the following command at the command prompt:

   ```
   scwcmd transform /p:C:\windows\security\msscw\Policies\
   TestDC1.xml /g:SCWTestDC1
   ```

   For clarification, this command has three spaces in it. One is between **scwcmd** and **transform.** The second space is between **transform** and **/p.** The last space is between **TestDC1.xml** and **/g.**

This is a long command, so typos are possible. If you get an error, you don't have to type the entire command again; instead, just press the up arrow to retrieve the last command. You can then edit the command using the left and right arrows to position your cursor.

4. Start the **Group Policy Management** console via the **Administrative Tools** menu.
5. Expand **Forest, Domains, Cengage.com,** and **Group Policy Objects.** Select the SCW-TestDC1 GPO that you just created. Select the **Settings** tab in the main window. Click **Show** next to **Security Settings.** Your display will look similar to Figure 7-6.

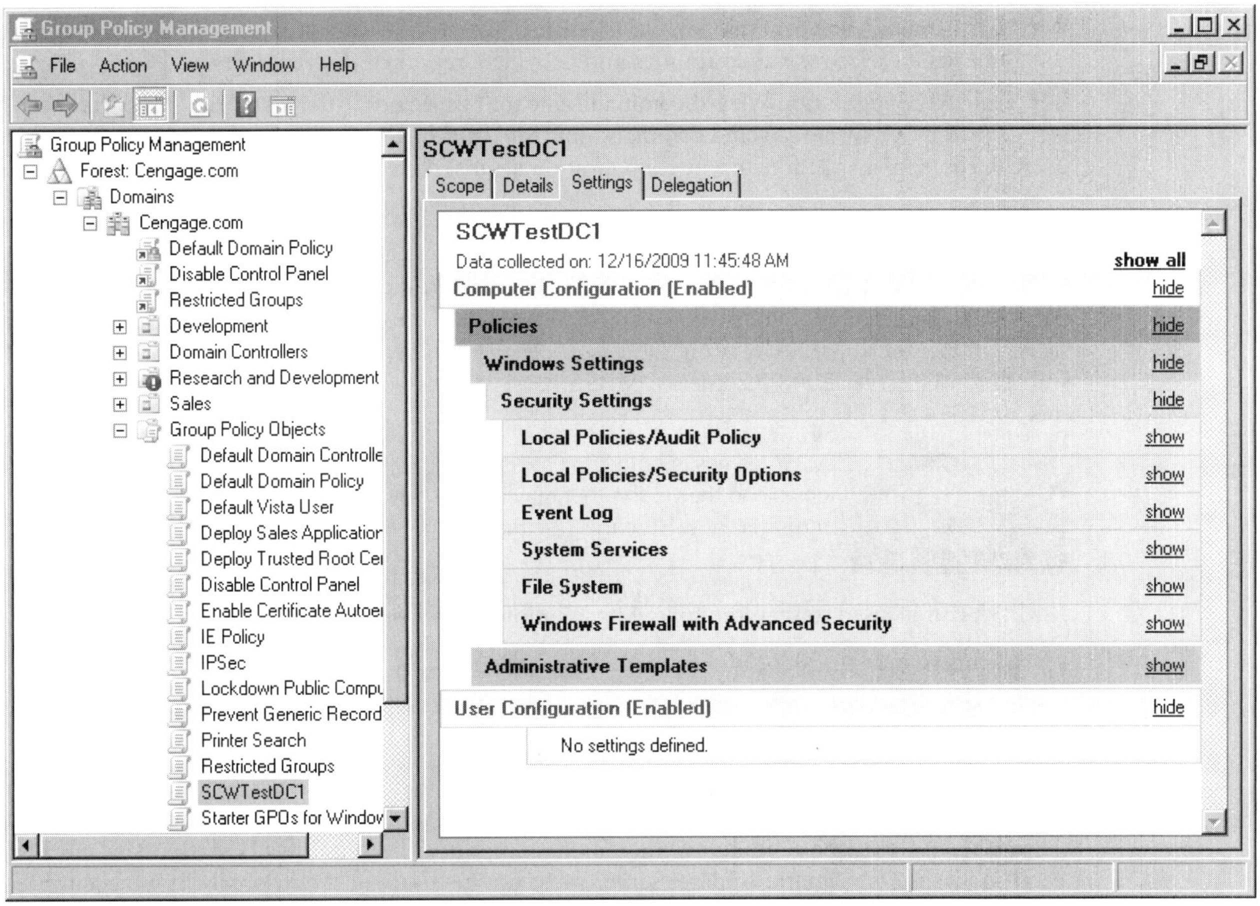

Figure 7-6 Viewing the GPO created from the SCW security policy

Courtesy Course Technology/Cengage Learning

Feel free to browse through the settings created in this GPO from the original SCW security policy. The GPO would take a long time to create from scratch, but SCW makes it relatively easy. The GPO can now be applied to a site, domain, or OU as needed.

6. Close all open windows.

Compliance Auditing

In addition to ensuring that systems start secure, you need to regularly check systems to ensure that they haven't been changed. This process is called **compliance auditing**. All too often, administrators make changes to configurations that inadvertently weaken security. You might take hours to design and create a sound security policy, only to have key settings undone by a well-intentioned but misinformed administrator.

Compliance auditing performs regular checks to see if systems still comply with predefined security settings. A compliance audit provides a report that can identify what configuration has changed and no longer matches the desired security setting.

Most IT organizations have change management and configuration management policies that prevent administrators from making changes without prior approval. If these processes are consistently used, compliance auditing can be done less often. However, if these processes are not in place, compliance auditing should be done much more often to catch the changes as soon as they occur.

You can use two primary tools for compliance auditing:

- **Microsoft Baseline Security Analyzer (MBSA).** The MBSA can scan one or more systems for a wide variety of vulnerabilities and provide a report of discrepancies.
- **Security Configuration Wizard command-line tool (scwcmd).** After a security policy has been created by SCW, the scwcmd command-line tool can use the policy as a security baseline. It can compare a system's current configuration against the baseline to identify discrepancies.

Using MBSA

MBSA is a free download. You can get it from Microsoft's download site (*www.microsoft.com/downloads*) by searching on "MBSA." MBSA version 2.1 supports Windows Vista and Windows Server 2008 clients. MBSA version 2.1.1 is a minor upgrade that adds support for Windows 7 and Windows Server 2008 R2 clients. MBSA 2.1.1 is backward compatible to all the same clients as MBSA 2.1.

MBSA comes in both x86 (32-bit) and x64 (64-bit) versions. You need to download the version that matches the server. If your server is hosted on Virtual PC, it will use the 32-bit version.

MBSA can be used to scan the following Windows systems:

- **Clients.** Windows 2000, Windows XP, Windows Vista, Windows 7
- **Servers.** Windows 2000 Server, Windows Server 2003, Windows Server 2008, Windows Server 2008 R2

Note that if MBSA is set up to scan systems in a production environment, the systems must be configured to allow the scans. The Server service, Remote Registry service, and File and Print Sharing service must be running on the remote computer. The Windows Update Agent must be installed and the Automatic Updates server must not be disabled. Additionally, if the client firewall is enabled, several ports need to be open to allow the scans.

The MBSA FAQ is a good resource to use if you have problems. You can view it at *http://technet.microsoft.com/cc184922.aspx*.

Figure 7-7 shows the MBSA opening screen. You can select several tasks from this screen, including:

- Scan a single computer
- Scan multiple computers
- View security reports (after you've performed at least one scan)

While the title bar shown in Figure 7-7 identifies the version as 2.1, the text on the page indicates that MBSA supports Windows 7 and Windows Server 2008 R2 clients. Therefore, you know it is actually version 2.1.1.

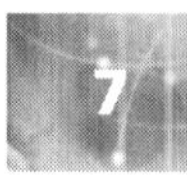

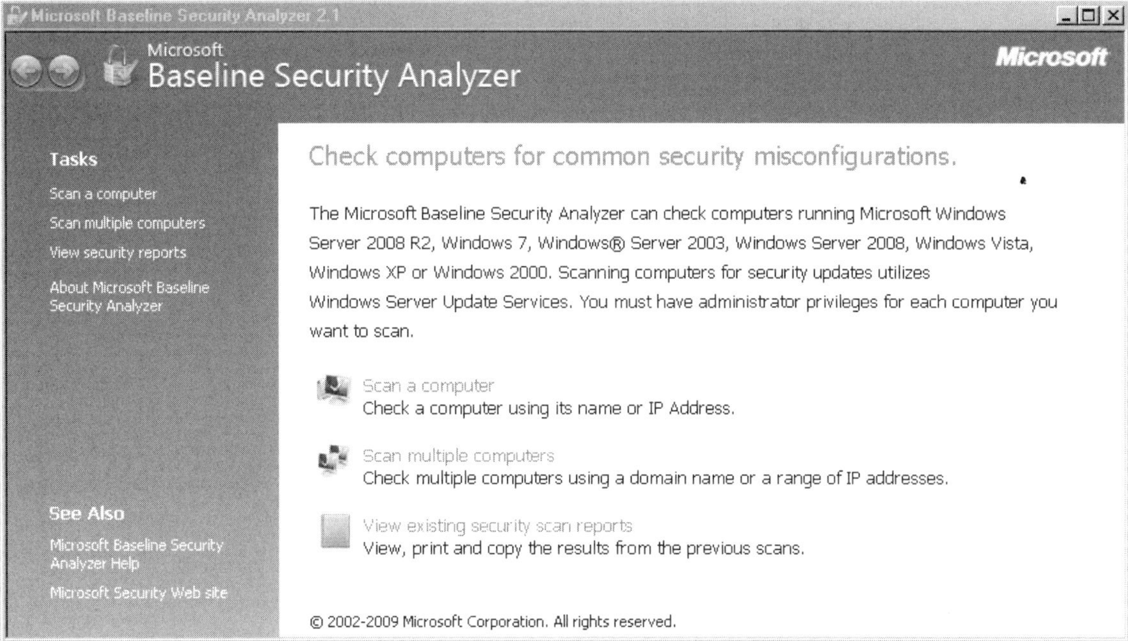

Figure 7-7 Starting MBSA

Courtesy Course Technology/Cengage Learning

If you click the link to scan a single computer, you'll see a screen similar to Figure 7-8. You can identify the computer by name or by IP address. If you choose to scan multiple computers, you can specify computers by the domain name or by a range of IP addresses. This screen also shows the checks that are performed by MBSA.

MBSA performs the following checks:

- **Windows administrative vulnerabilities.** These checks include possible security issues such as whether the Guest account is enabled, the file system isn't NTFS, or whether there are excessive members of the Administrators group.
- **Weak passwords.** This check identifies blank and weak passwords. Passwords should have at least eight characters and include three of the four character types (uppercase, lowercase, numbers, and special characters).
- **IIS administrative vulnerabilities.** If IIS version 5.0, 5.1, or 6.0 is installed, this check will scan for vulnerabilities with IIS. When the Web Server (IIS) role is added to Server 2008,

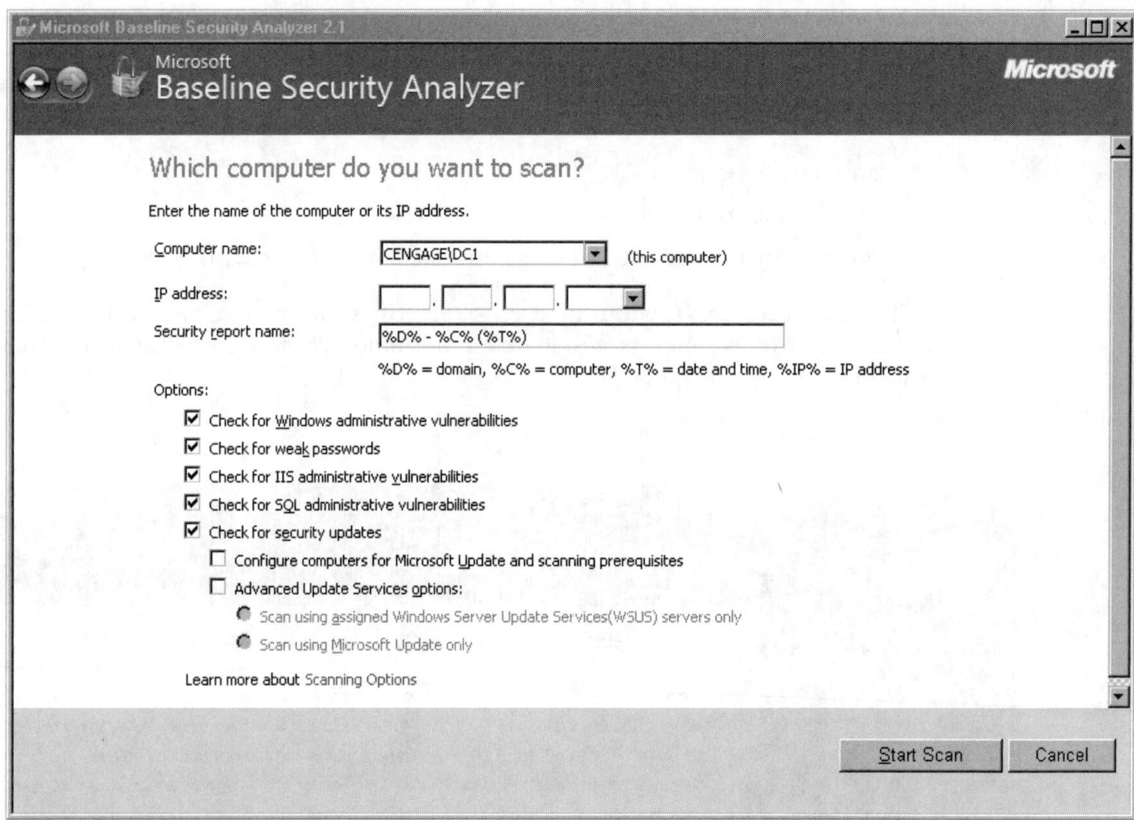

Figure 7-8 Preparing to scan a computer with MBSA

Courtesy Course Technology/Cengage Learning

IIS version 7 is installed; many of the vulnerability issues with earlier versions of IIS have been removed with IIS 7.

- **SQL administrative vulnerabilities.** If SQL Server or the Microsoft Data Engine (MSDE) is installed, this check will scan it for known security issues.
- **Security updates.** This check ensures that the system is current with updates. When this option is selected, MBSA will query Microsoft Update to retrieve a listing of updates.

After you run MBSA, it provides a report of any issues found, as shown in Figure 7-9. Most items in the report also include links such as "What was scanned" and "Result details." If an issue is reported, the listing will also include a link labeled "How to correct this."

For example, if the Password Expiration issue reports that some user accounts have non-expiring passwords, you can click "Result details" and retrieve a listing of such accounts. If you click "How to correct this," a screen will appear with information on the issue and how to resolve it.

When a scan is started and Security Updates is selected as one of the checks, MBSA will first download a catalog file from Microsoft's Web site to identify all of the current updates. It then checks the installed updates against this catalog file to see if the system is up to date. If it isn't, MBSA will list the missing updates. If it can't reach the Microsoft Web site to download the catalog file, it will return an error.

When MBSA is installed, the **MBSACLI** command-line utility is also installed. MBSACLI can be used to run MBSA from the command line. You can create scripts to automatically run

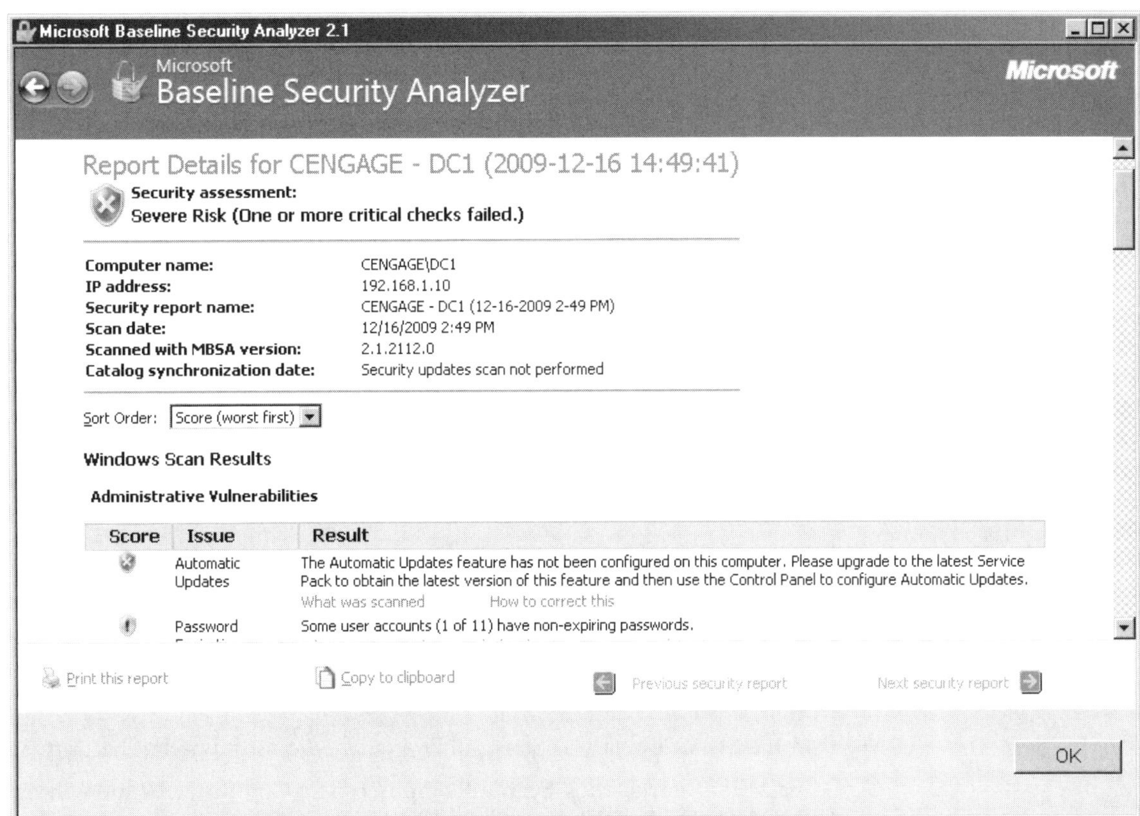

Figure 7-9 Viewing the MBSA report

Courtesy Course Technology/Cengage Learning

MBSACLI on a regular basis. Another significant feature of MBSACLI is that you can perform checks for systems that don't have Internet connectivity.

As an example, a secure network may be isolated from the Internet for security purposes. The first check by MBSA is to retrieve a file (wsusscn2.cab) from the Microsoft Update site that includes a listing of current updates. You can skip this step when using the MBSA GUI, but you'll also skip the check of clients for current updates, not just retrieval of the file. Instead, you can download the file on another system, copy it to the secure system, and then use the file to run MBSACLI from the command line. You'll also need the wuredist.cab file, as explained in Activity 7-4.

Earlier versions of MBSA used a file called wsusscan.cab, but that file has not been updated since March 2007 and is not compatible with MBSA 2.1. If you download the file for offline use, you must use the new wsusscn2.cab file.

The following two activities show how to install and run MBSA and MBSACLI. These activities require downloading files that take as much as 100 MB of disk space.

Activity 7-3: Installing and Running MBSA

Time Required: 20 minutes

Objective: Install and run MBSA.

Description: You want to begin compliance testing on systems in your domain. You have decided to check DC1 first. You need to download MBSA, install it on DC1, and then run it against DC1.

Before starting this activity, you should download the MBSA Windows Installer file from the *www.microsoft.com/downloads* site and copy it to the server. You should also download the wsusscn2.cab file from *http://go.microsoft.com/fwlink/?linkid=76054* and copy it to the server. If you're using virtual servers, you should download these files from the host system and then copy them to the virtual system. If you reconfigure the virtual machines for Internet access, you'll need to reconfigure them back to the lab configuration so that the activities work.

1. Start **DC1** and log on with the domain **Administrator** account.
2. If necessary, copy the MBSA Windows Installer file to your system. Double-click the file to start the installation.
3. Review the information on the **Welcome** screen and click **Next.**
4. Review the information on the **License Agreement** screen, select **I Accept the License Agreement,** and click **Next.**
5. Accept the default **Destination Folder** setting and click **Next.** Click **Install.** After the installation is complete, click **OK.**
6. Start the **MBSA** by clicking **Start, All Programs, Microsoft Baseline Security Analyzer 2.1.**
7. After MBSA starts, click **Scan a Computer.** The **Computer Name** will be entered as **CENGAGE\DC1.** Click **Start Scan.** The system will try to connect to the Internet; if Internet connectivity is not available, the scan will fail. MBSA needs the wsusscn2.cab and wuredist.cab files to continue. Click **Continue** to dismiss the report.

This step shows the result if a system doesn't have Internet connectivity and additional steps have not been taken. Activity 7-4 shows how to copy the two needed files to the correct location and successfully rerun this step when required.

8. Click **Scan a Computer** again. Deselect the check box to **Check for Security Updates,** which will prevent MBSA from downloading the cabinet files or from checking the system for updates. Click **Start Scan.**
9. When the scan is complete, review the **Scan Results** screen. Notice that critical issues are shown with a white X over a red shield.
10. Close all open windows.

Activity 7-4: Running MBSACLI

Time Required: 40 minutes

Objective: Run MBSACLI using offline cabinet files.

Description: You want to create a script to run MBSACLI so you can schedule compliance checking to occur on a regular basis. You also want the check to verify that the updates are current. This activity assumes that MBSA has been installed, and should be run on DC1.

Before starting this activity, you should download the wsusscn2.cab file and the wuredist.cab file from the following two locations, respectively: *http://go.microsoft.com/fwlink/?linkid=76054* and *http://go.microsoft.com/fwlink/?linkid=84399.* Both files should be copied to the server so they are available to copy to the correct path.

1. Start **DC1** and log on with the domain **Administrator** account.
2. Start **Windows Explorer** by clicking **Start, Computer**. Configure Windows Explorer to show Hidden Files by taking the following substeps:
   a. Select the **Organize** menu in **Windows Explorer** and click **Folder and Search Options.**
   b. Select the **View** tab. Click **Show Hidden Files and Folders.** Click **OK.**
3. Locate the **wsusscn2.cab** and **wuredist.cab** files you downloaded and copy them to the following folder: **C:\Users\Administrator\AppData\Local\Microsoft\MBSA\2.1.1\Cache.** This is where the files would be downloaded if the system had Internet access.
4. Open a command prompt by clicking **Start, Command Prompt.** The command prompt starts with a default path of **C:\Users\Administrator.** However, MBSACLI is located in the following folder: **C:\Program Files\Microsoft Baseline Security Analyzer 2.** Change the path by entering the following command:

```
cd C:\Program Files\Microsoft Baseline Security Analyzer 2\
```

5. Enter the following command to run MBSACLI on the local system:

```
mbsacli /target localhost
```

6. The scan will take several minutes to complete. When it does, start **MBSA** by clicking **Start, All Programs, Microsoft Baseline Security Analyzer 2.1.** Click **View Existing Security Scan Reports.** Your display will look similar to Figure 7-10, though you'll see only one report for 192.168.1.10 and one report for 127.0.0.1.

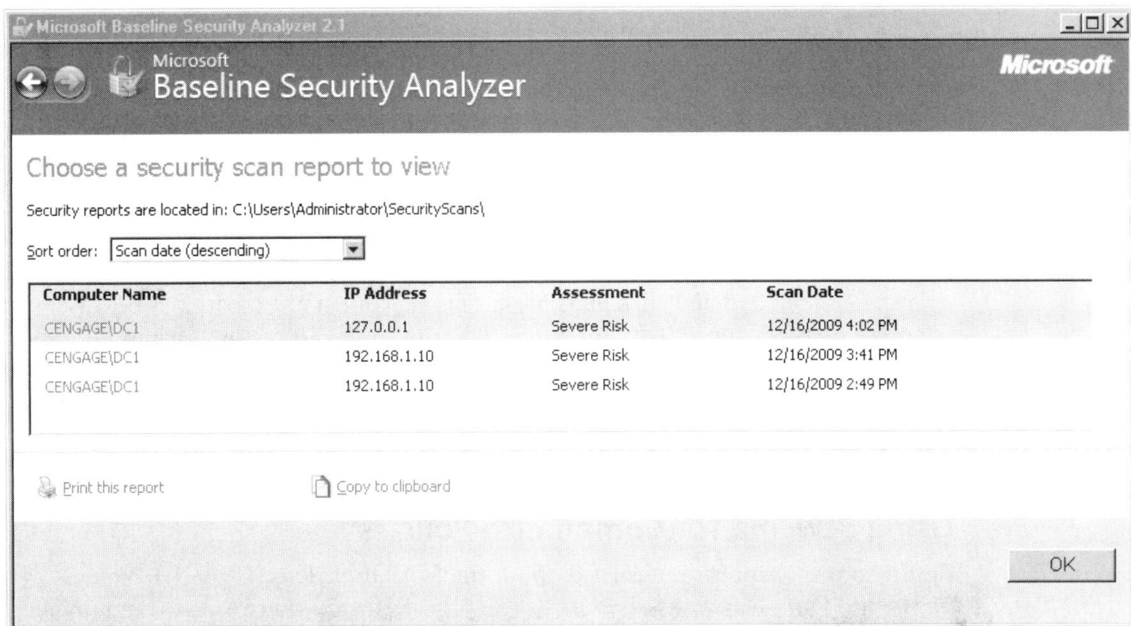

Figure 7-10 Viewing available reports in the MBSA report viewer

Courtesy Course Technology/Cengage Learning

The report that was executed against localhost in this activity was resolved to 127.0.0.1, but when the reports were executed against DC1, DC1 was resolved to its actual IP address of 192.168.1.10.

7. Select the report with an IP address of **127.0.0.1** and review it. The report includes details on updates because the wsusscn2.cab and wuredist.cab files were downloaded

and copied to the correct folder on your system. After you've reviewed the report, click **OK**.

8. Return to the command prompt and enter **Notepad** to start Notepad.
9. Enter the following two lines in Notepad. These are the same two commands you executed earlier.

```
cd C:\Program Files\Microsoft Baseline Security Analyzer 2\
mbsacli /target localhost
```

Command-line text can be copied. Use the mouse to highlight the text in the command line, and then press Enter to copy the text to the Clipboard. Move to Notepad and press Ctrl+V to paste the text. If this doesn't work, right-click the command prompt title bar and select Properties. Ensure that Quick Edit mode is enabled on the Options tab.

10. Click **File, Save.** Browse to the root of C: and create a folder named **Scripts.** Double-click the **Scripts** folder. Name the file **mbsascript.bat** and click **Save.**
11. Test your script by returning to the command prompt and entering the following command:

```
c:\scripts\mbsascript.bat
```

12. Start **Task Scheduler** via the **Administrative Tools** menu.
13. Right-click **Task Scheduler Library** and select **Create Basic Task.**
14. Name the task **MBSACLI** and click **Next.**
15. Select **Weekly** as the **Task Trigger** and click **Next.** Select **Saturday** and adjust the time if desired. Click **Next.**
16. On the **Action** screen, accept the default selection of **Start a Program.** Click **Next.** Click **Browse.** Browse to the **C:\Scripts** folder and select the **mbsascript.bat** file you created. Click **Open** and then **Next.** Click **Finish.**

    At this point, the script file is configured to run on a weekly basis on DC1 without any user interaction. You can modify the script file to scan other computers, such as all the computers in the domain or in an IP address range. After you set the schedule, you only need to check MBSA regularly and review the reports.
17. Return to **MBSA** and click **Scan a Computer.** Ensure that **Check for Security Updates** is selected and click **Start Scan.** This step failed in Activity 7-3 because you had no Internet connectivity, but MBSA will run successfully now because the two cabinet files (wsusscn2.cab and wuredist.cab) have been copied to the appropriate folder.
18. When the scan is complete, review the reports and click **OK.**
19. Close all open windows.

Using Scwcmd for Compliance Policies

Earlier in this chapter, you learned about the SCW tool. The SCW GUI version cannot be used to perform compliance auditing on a system; instead, you must use scwcmd (the command-line equivalent of SCW). Scwcmd includes the analyze command, which you can use to check a system and determine if it is compliant with a security file.

The value of any command-line tool is that it can be scripted. The script can be a simple batch file; once the batch file is created, it can be scheduled. A scheduled script provides automation and streamlines an administrator's job.

In this context, the security policy is viewed as the baseline, and is compared against the current configuration. If there is a difference, it is logged in the output file. By default, the scwcmd output file is named after the server. For example, if you run scwcmd on a server named DC1, the output file is DC1.xml.

You can perform the compliance audit with the following command:

```
scwcmd analyze /p:PolicyPathandName
```

If you did Activity 7-2 earlier in this chapter, you would have created an XML file named TestDC1.xml in the C:\Windows\security\msscw\policies folder. You could then run the following command to perform compliance auditing on the DC1 server, using that XML file as the security policy.

```
scwcmd analyze /p:C:\Windows\security\msscw\Policies\testdc1.xml
```

This command creates a results file named DC1.xml. You can view the file by typing DC1.xml and pressing Enter. The file will open in Internet Explorer.

Enabling Auditing

Auditing within Windows is used to identify when various events occur. Auditing can be used to track the actions of users and record the details of these actions in the Windows Security log. In general, auditing log entries record who performed an action, what action was performed, and when and where it was performed.

Both success and failure attempts can be recorded for these actions. For example, if you want a record for every time someone successfully deletes a user account, you would enable Success auditing for Delete User Objects. On the other hand, if you wanted to know when anyone tried unsuccessfully to delete a user account, you would enable Failure auditing for the event.

Figure 7-11 shows the Audit Policy settings for the Default Domain Controllers policy, which is applied to the Domain Controllers OU. All auditable events are listed. The Policy Setting column shows each of these categories as Not Defined, but this is misleading. Many of these settings have defaults, so if they are not configured with Group Policy, the default setting is used. For example, Audit directory service access is listed as Not Defined, but the default setting is to audit Success events.

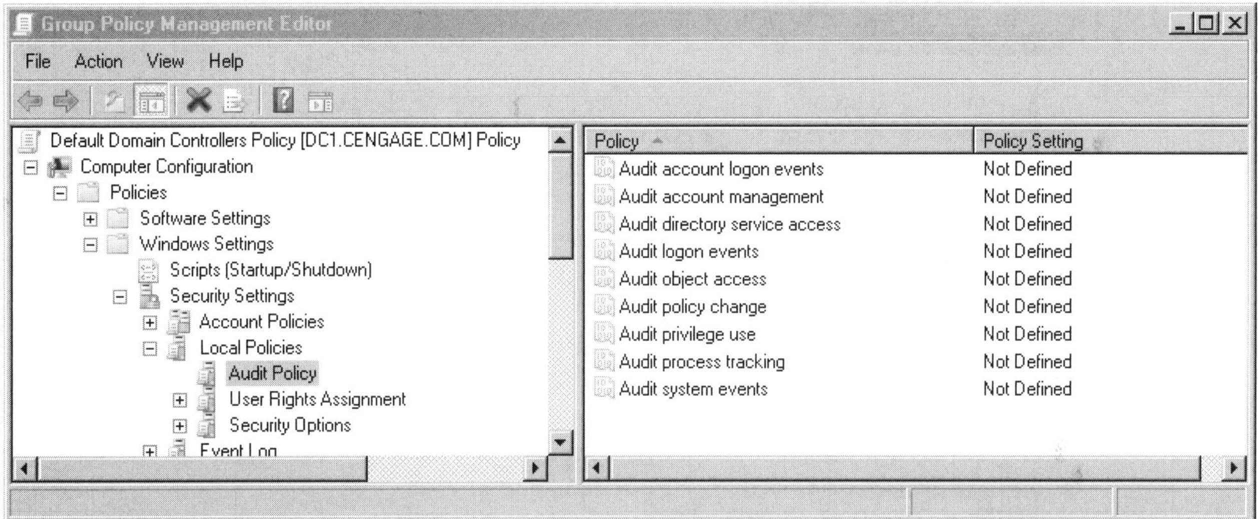

Figure 7-11 Viewing the Default Domain Controllers audit policy

Courtesy Course Technology/Cengage Learning

The Audit Policy settings are:

- **Audit account logon events.** Audits user logon events when a user is authenticated from a domain controller (not a local computer). The default setting is Success.
- **Audit account management.** Logs an event when a user account or group is added, deleted, or modified, or when a password is set or modified. The default setting is Success on domain controllers and no auditing on member servers.
- **Audit directory service access.** Allows auditing of Active Directory objects, although this setting does not automatically enable auditing of all Active Directory objects. When this setting is enabled and auditing of any individual Active Directory object is enabled, events will be logged. The default setting is Success on domain controllers and undefined on member servers.
- **Audit logon events.** Audits user logon events when a user is authenticated from a local computer (not a domain controller). The default setting is Success.
- **Audit object access.** Allows auditing of objects such as files, folders, and printers. This setting does not automatically enable auditing of all objects. When this setting is enabled and auditing of any individual object is enabled, events will be logged. The default setting is no auditing.
- **Audit policy change.** Audits any changes to user rights assignment policies, audit policies, or trust policies. The default setting is Success on domain controllers and no auditing on member servers.
- **Audit privilege use.** If enabled, logs events when a user exercises most user rights. Some commonly used rights, such as Back Up Files and Directories or Restore Files and Directories, are not logged by this setting to prevent generating too many events in the log. However, you can log these events by modifying the FullPrivilegeAuditing registry key. The default setting is no auditing.
- **Audit process tracking.** Logs tracking information events such as program activation and process exits. The default setting is no auditing.
- **Audit system events.** When enabled, logs entries generated by system events such as restarting and shutting down a computer, and modifying, clearing, or deleting the System or Security logs. The default setting is Success on domain controllers and no auditing on member servers.

Access logging must be configured in two places. For object access, the audit policy must be configured, and then auditing needs to be enabled on individual objects like files or folders. Similarly, directory service access auditing also needs to be enabled on Active Directory objects (such as OUs).

A significant addition to Windows Server 2008 is AD DS Auditing, which extends the details included in auditable events for directory service access. This advanced logging feature is referred to as a global audit policy, but it is not enabled by default. Basic directory service access auditing is enabled by default. When the global audit policy is enabled, AD DS Auditing will log additional details for the following subcategories:

- Directory service access
- Directory service changes
- Directory service replication
- Detailed directory service replication

Global auditing is enabled by selecting Audit Directory Service Access Success or Failure event auditing in the Default Domain Controllers policy.

Enabling directory service access auditing is a two-step process. First, the audit policy is enabled. Second, auditing must also be enabled for Active Directory objects. Consider Figure 7-12, which shows the various screens accessed through the Active Directory Users and Computers console to enable auditing for Active Directory objects. The dialog box on the right has auditing enabled for successful or failed attempts to Create User objects. Notice that other options (such as Delete User objects) are not selected, so these events will not be logged.

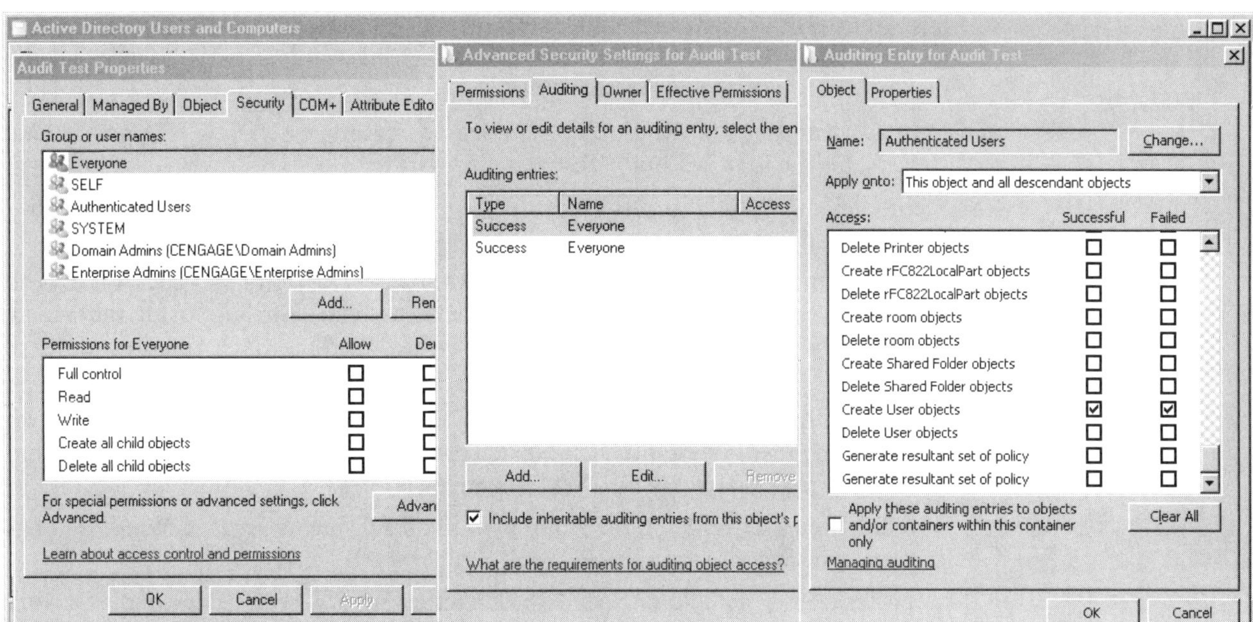

Figure 7-12 Enabling auditing

Courtesy Course Technology/Cengage Learning

If no changes are made to the audit policy in the Default Domain Controllers policy, and success and failure events are selected for the Create User objects option, basic logging will still occur when a user account is created. If the audit policy is changed to enable success and failure events, the advanced AD DS Auditing feature will be enabled, and more detailed entries will be logged in the Security log.

Changes made to directory service objects on any domain controller can be logged with either basic or advanced AD DS Auditing logging. With basic logging, the entries are minimal and don't provide many details. For example, if a user account is created, the basic event will indicate that An Operation Was Performed On An Object. If properties are changed on the account, an almost identical event is logged. However, when advanced AD DS Auditing is enabled, details of the additions and changes are logged. For example, if a user's name is changed, both the original name and the new name will be logged.

The following activity shows how basic auditing works, shows how advanced AD DS Auditing can be enabled, and shows the additional log entries that are provided with AD DS Auditing.

Activity 7-5: Enabling Directory Services Auditing

Time Required: 20 minutes

Objective: Enable auditing for Directory Services objects.

Description: You have been asked to increase the logging for Active Directory access. You need to enable advanced logging for directory service access and enable logging for the creation of user accounts with an OU. This activity should be run on DC1.

1. Start **DC1** and log on with the domain **Administrator** account.
2. Start the **Group Policy Management** console via the **Administrative Tools** menu.
3. Expand **Forest, Domains, Cengage.com,** and the **Domain Controllers** OU.
4. Right-click the **Default Domain Controllers Policy** and select **Edit.**
5. Browse to the **Computer Configuration, Policies, Windows Settings, Security Settings, Local Policies, Audit Policy** node. Notice that all of these settings are currently **Not Defined.** Leave this window open.

6. Start **Active Directory Users and Computers** via the **Administrative Tools** menu. Click the **View** menu and select **Advanced Features**, which will display the Security tab on the Property sheet.
7. Expand **Cengage.com**. Right-click **Cengage.com** and select **New, Organizational Unit.** Name the new OU **Audit Test** and click **OK.**
8. Right-click the **Audit Test** OU and select **Properties**. Select the **Security** tab and click the **Advanced** button.
9. Select the **Auditing** tab. Click **Add.** Enter **Authenticated Users** and click **OK**. Scroll down to **Create User Objects** and select the check boxes for **Successful** and **Failed.** Your display will look similar to Figure 7-12 shown earlier. Click **OK** three times to return to the main screen of **Active Directory Users and Computers.**
10. Right-click **Audit Test** and click **New User.** Type **Carl** in the **First Name** and **User Logon Name** text boxes and click **Next.** Type **P@ssw0rd** in the **Password** and **Confirm Password** text boxes. Click **Next,** then **Finish.**
11. Start the **Event Viewer** from the **Administrative Tools** menu. Expand **Windows Logs** and select the **Security** log.
12. In the Task Category column, locate the **Directory Service Access** entry in the **Security** log and double-click it. This entry will look similar to Figure 7-13. Remember that only the default auditing for directory service access is enabled at this point, so only minimal entries are logged.

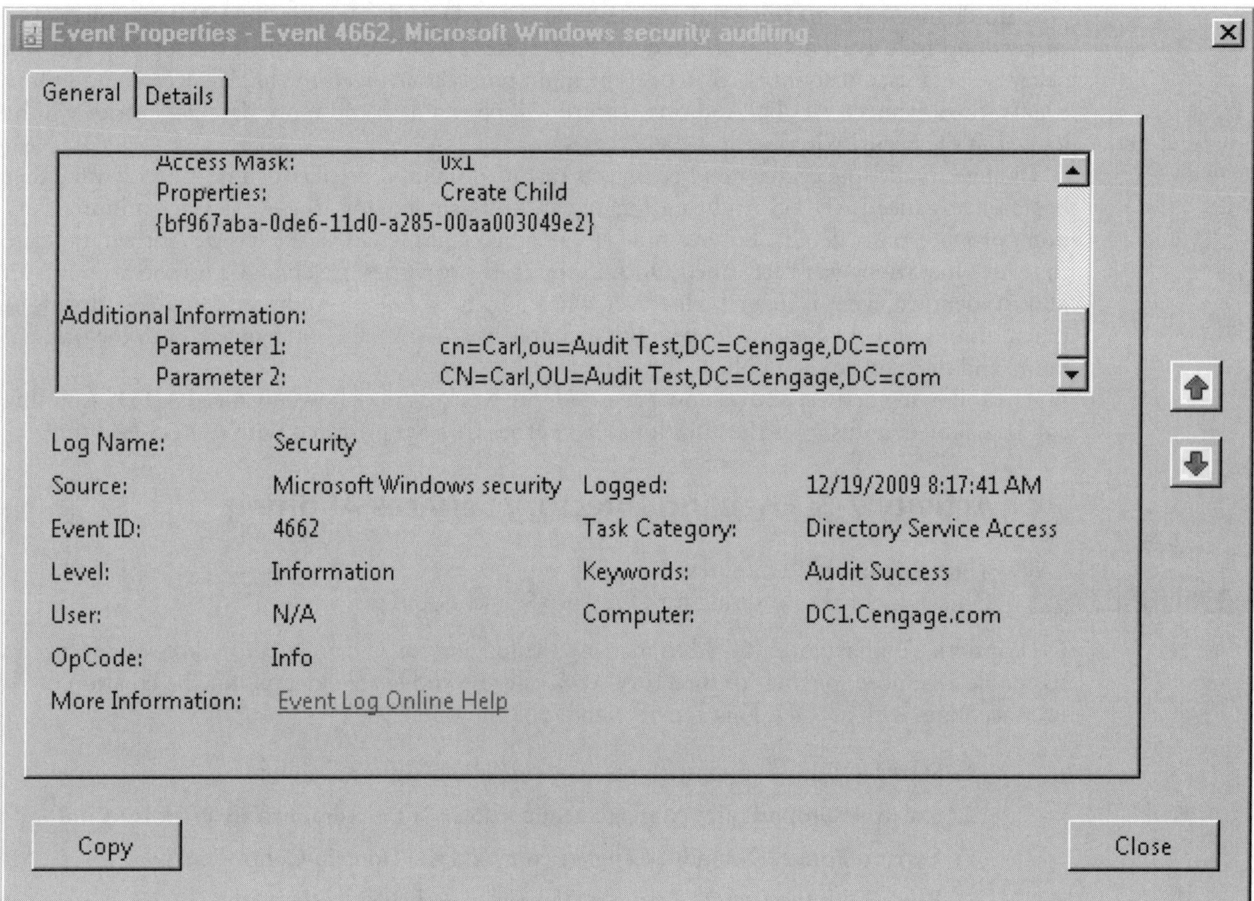

Figure 7-13 Viewing a basic directory service access auditing entry

Courtesy Course Technology/Cengage Learning

13. Return to the **Default Domain Controllers Policy** with the **Audit Policy** displayed. Double-click the **Audit Directory Service Access** setting. Select the check boxes to **Define These Policy Settings** and select **Success**. Click **OK**.
14. Open a command prompt by clicking **Start, Command Prompt**. Enter the following command:

    ```
    Gpupdate /force
    ```

    This will refresh the Group Policy settings for the system.
15. Return to **Active Directory Users and Computers**. Right-click **Audit Test** and click **New User**. Type **Sammy** in the **First Name** and **User Logon Name** text boxes and click **Next**. Type **P@ssw0rd** in the **Password** and **Confirm Password** text boxes. Click **Next**, then **Finish**.
16. Return to **Event Viewer**. Locate the **Directory Service Access** entry. You'll see several additional **User Account Management** log entries, as shown in Figure 7-14. Double-click any of these events to view the additional details.

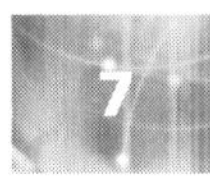

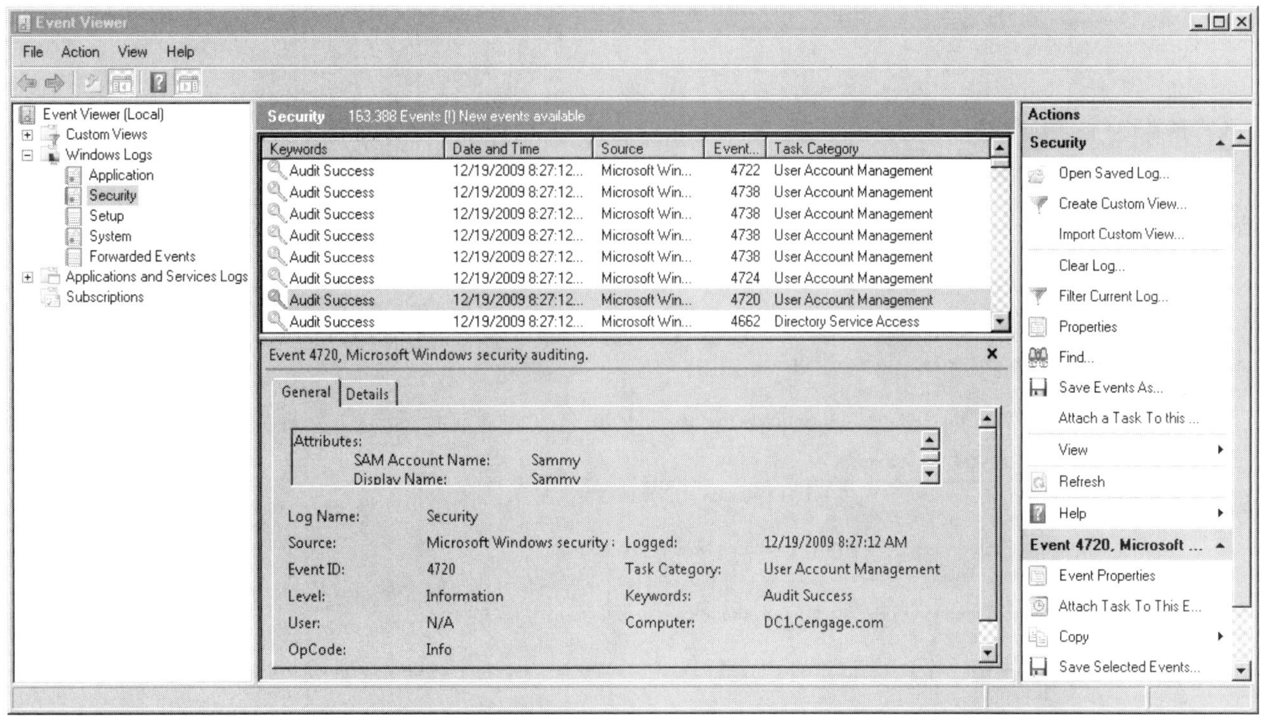

Figure 7-14 Viewing advanced directory service auditing events

Courtesy Course Technology/Cengage Learning

17. Close all open windows.

Keeping Systems Up to Date

Operating systems today can contain billions of lines of code. Despite extensive testing of any software product, bugs and vulnerabilities are eventually discovered. In a perfect world, every possible scenario would be tested and every defect discovered, but software is never perfect. Therefore, you must keep systems up to date.

No matter how secure a server is once you've applied a baseline with SCW or Group Policy, bugs and vulnerabilities will be discovered and a server will become less and less secure. The only way to keep a server secure is by keeping it patched. Microsoft regularly releases patches, hot fixes, and service packs; if they aren't regularly applied to systems, they soon become vulnerable again.

Windows Update, Microsoft Update, and Automatic Updates

Microsoft offers updates through two programs that are often considered the same; however, there are subtle differences between the two. The two programs are **Windows Update** and **Microsoft Update**; systems can be configured to retrieve automatic updates from both.

- **Windows Update.** This program provides updates for all supported versions of Windows operating systems.
- **Microsoft Update.** This program provides the same updates as Windows Update, but adds updates for Microsoft applications such as Office, Exchange Server, and SQL Server.

Figure 7-15 shows the Windows Update page, which is accessible from the Control Panel on Windows Server 2008. As configured, it will automatically download and install updates. The Windows Update client periodically checks for the updates and downloads them as needed. The time (3 a.m. in the figure) identifies when the updates are actually installed.

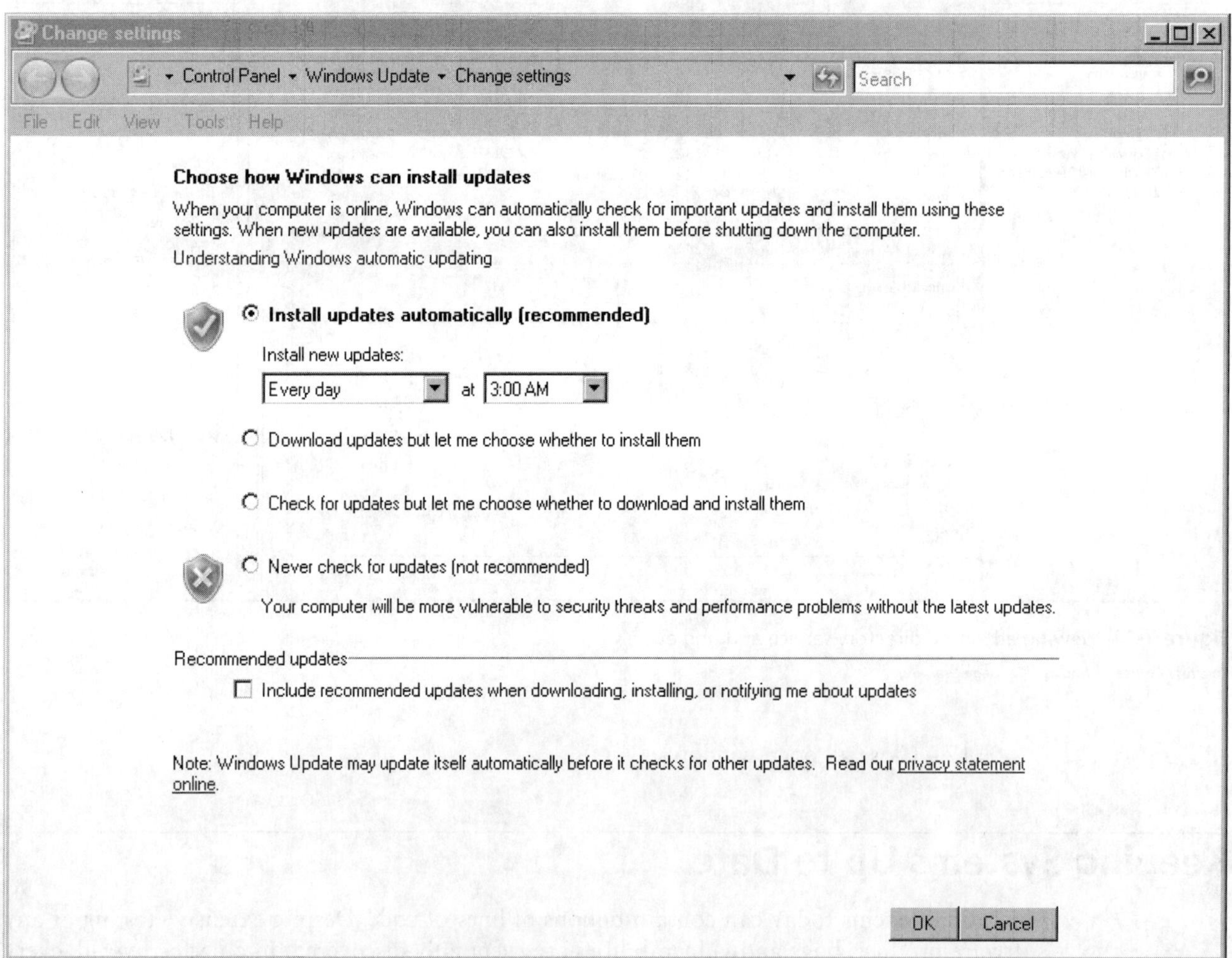

Figure 7-15 Enabling Windows Update in Windows Server 2008

Courtesy Course Technology/Cengage Learning

This page does not include Microsoft Update, which is used for applications. You can click the Get Updates for More Products link on the main Windows Update page to opt in for Microsoft Update.

In other operating systems, it's easier to opt in for Microsoft Update. For example, Figure 7-16 shows the Control Panel page for Windows 7. This figure helps clarify that Windows Update and Microsoft Update are separate entities.

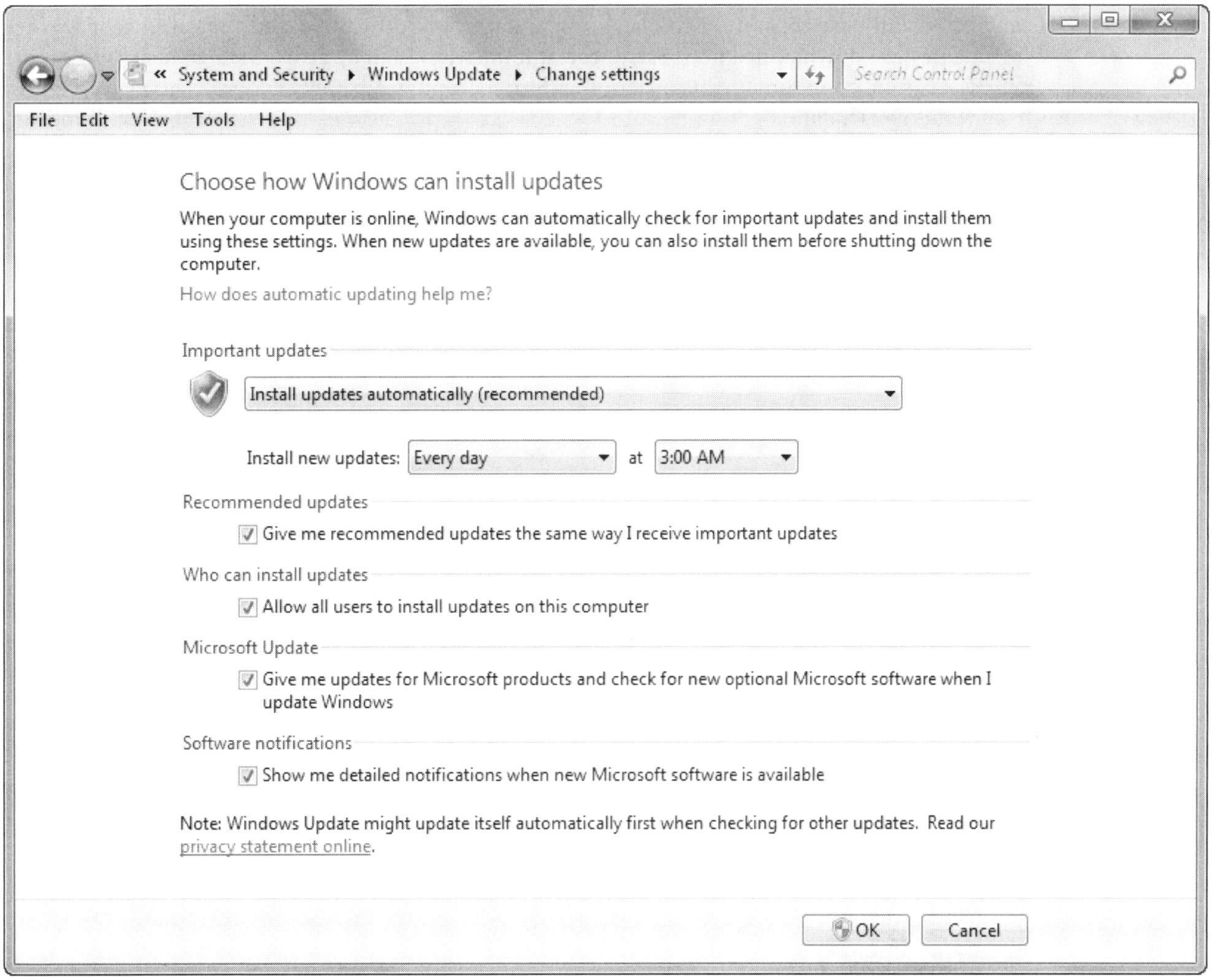

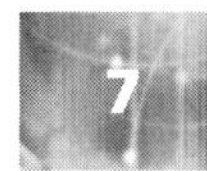

Figure 7-16 Enabling Windows Update and Microsoft Update in Windows 7

Courtesy Course Technology/Cengage Learning

It's common to configure clients within a domain to use Automatic Updates with Group Policy. You can direct the clients to get their updates from Microsoft (as shown in Figure 7-16) or from a WSUS server. An activity later in this chapter shows how a GPO is created to configure this option with WSUS.

Windows Server Update Services

Within a domain environment, **Windows Server Update Services (WSUS)** can be used as a central location to download and approve updates. Clients within the domain can download updates directly from the WSUS server instead of from the Windows Update site.

The 70-642 exam includes objectives on *configuring* WSUS. The 70-647 exam includes objectives on *designing* for software updates. This section isn't intended to teach you how to configure WSUS again; instead, it covers the important elements that should be included in the design. It does include activities to install WSUS and help remind you how it works.

Figure 7-17 shows a single WSUS server configured within the network. An administrator can periodically use this server to check for updates and download any that are needed. After the updates are downloaded and tested, the administrator can approve them. Clients within the network can be configured to receive only approved updates from the WSUS server (instead of from Windows Update).

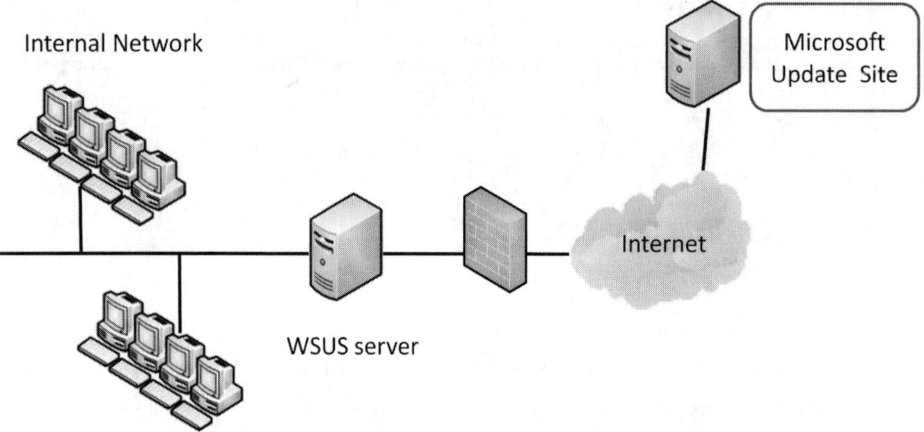

Figure 7-17 Using WSUS in a network
Courtesy Course Technology/Cengage Learning

The WSUS server is configured to periodically synchronize with the Microsoft Update site. Synchronization is commonly configured to occur on a schedule, although it can also be manually triggered. An administrator can then review the updates and approve only the updates that are needed. Unapproved updates are not deployed to any WSUS clients.

Updates should be tested before being approved. It's common to create a test computer group and approve updates for this group prior to approving the updates for production computers.

WSUS provides two primary benefits:

- **Reduced Internet bandwidth.** Internet bandwidth is only used once to download the update to the WSUS server. Each client receives the update from WSUS instead of the Windows Update site.
- **Administrative control.** Administrators can test and approve updates prior to deploying them. Because only approved updates are deployed, updates that have known issues can be held until the issues are resolved. Additionally, WSUS uses computer groups, so it's possible to deploy updates to specific groups of computers instead of all computers.

The current version of WSUS is 3.0. WSUS 3.0 SP1 was released for Windows Server 2008 and WSUS 3.0 SP2 adds support for Windows Server 2008 and Windows 7 clients. At this point, WSUS 3.0 SP2 is recommended because it includes backward compatibility to all the same clients, but adds capabilities for newer clients. Windows Server 2008 SP1 must be installed before you can install WSUS 3.0 SP2. You can download WSUS and access other WSUS resources from the WSUS home page at *http://technet.microsoft.com/wsus/*.

WSUS Capabilities

WSUS can be used to deploy updates for both the operating system and applications. It provides support for the following systems:

- **Clients.** Windows 2000 Workstation SP4, Windows XP, Windows Vista, and Windows 7.
- **Servers.** Windows Server 2000 SP4, Windows Server 2003 SP2 or later, Windows Small Business Server (2003, 2005, or 2008), Windows Server 2008 SP1, and Windows Server 2008 R2.

It's important to note what support is missing. In general, all operating systems since Windows 2000 SP4 are supported, but pre-Windows 2000 clients are not supported. If your organization still includes legacy clients, you either need to upgrade them or identify a different solution for keeping them up to date.

WSUS can also download Microsoft Update for applications and server products, including the following:

- **Microsoft Applications.** Microsoft Office, Microsoft Works, Microsoft Live, Silverlight, and more are supported.
- **Microsoft Server Products.** Microsoft Exchange, Microsoft SQL Server, Internet Security and Acceleration Server, Windows Small Business Server, and more are supported.

Figures 7-18 and 7-19 show the Products and Classifications property pages for WSUS options within the WSUS console. While the products supported by WSUS are self explanatory, the classifications aren't as clear. The various classifications are used for different purposes and have different risks.

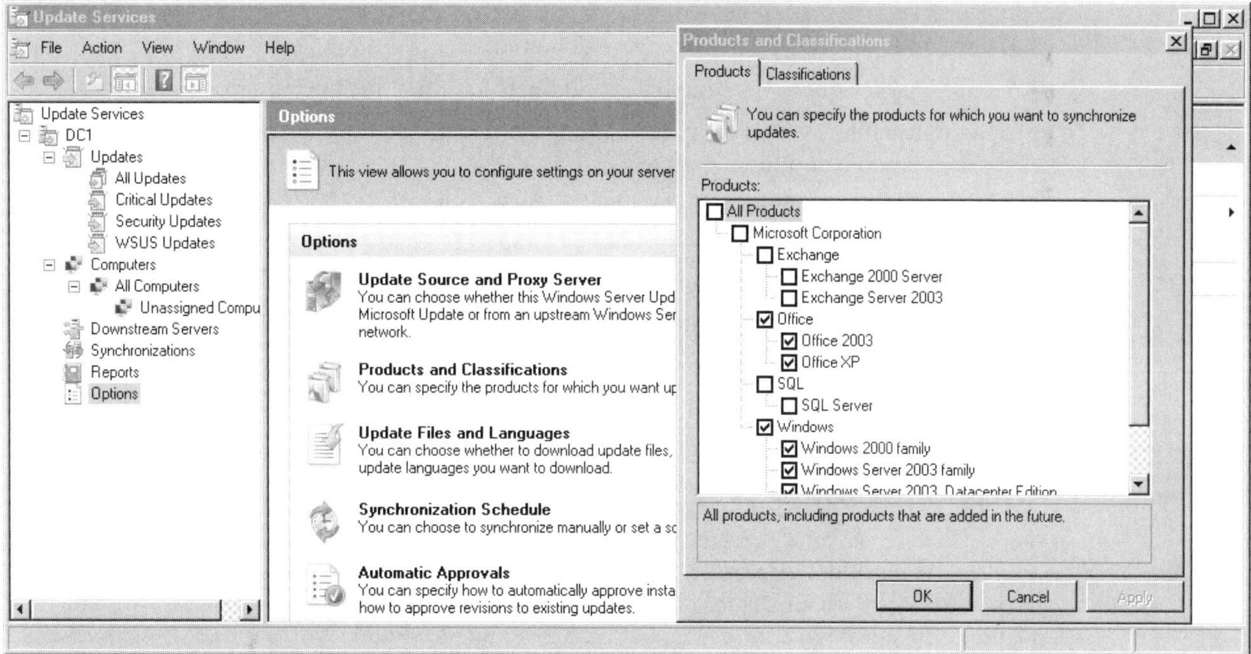

Figure 7-18 Viewing the WSUS products

Courtesy Course Technology/Cengage Learning

WSUS has the following classifications:

- **Updates.** Updates released to address bugs that are not critical or security-related.
- **Critical Updates.** Updates released for specific problems or to address bugs that are critical but not security-related.
- **Security Updates.** Updates released for specific security problems and security issues.

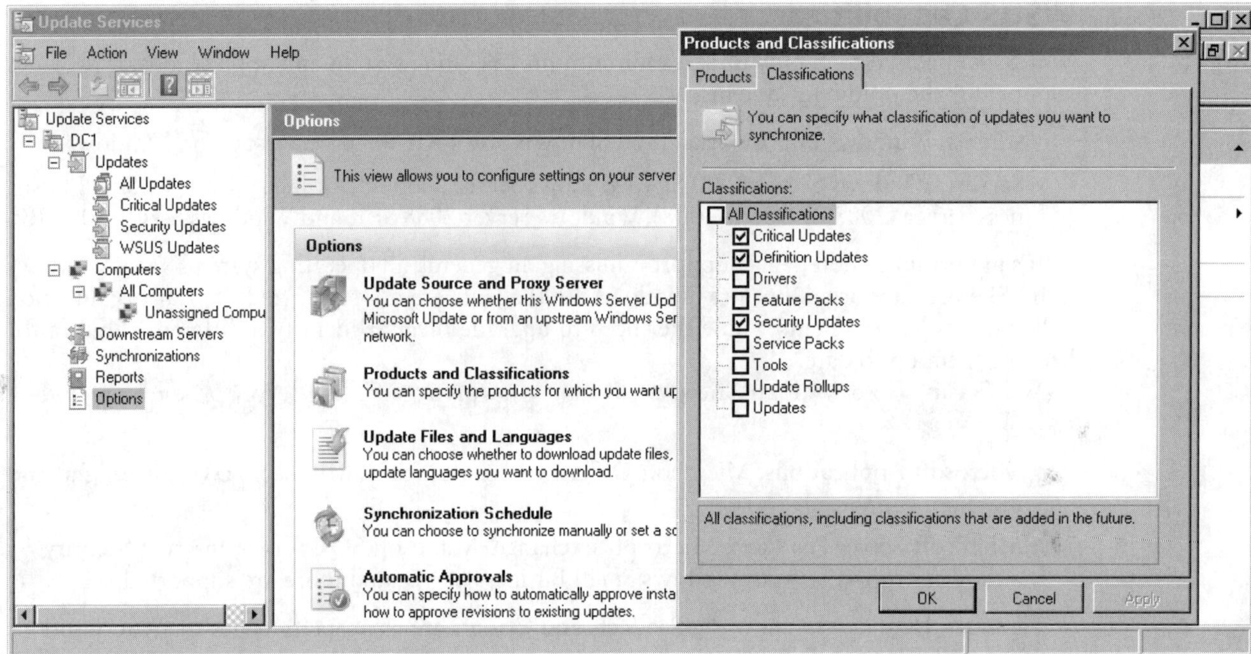

Figure 7-19 Viewing the WSUS classifications

Courtesy Course Technology/Cengage Learning

- **Definition Updates.** Updated malware definitions for Windows Defender.
- **Service Packs.** Collections of updates and fixes that often include additional features.
- **Update Rollups.** A group of updates used to target a specific area such as security, or a specific component or application.
- **Drivers.** Software components designed to support hardware. As drivers are tested by the Windows Hardware Quality Labs (WHQL), they are signed and made available.
- **Feature Packs.** Additional product functionality that wasn't included in the original release.
- **Tools.** Utilities or features that weren't included in the original release.

In general, newer updates have greater risks because they haven't been tested or deployed to as many clients. As updates are deployed, bugs or problems with the updates are discovered and corrected.

Reviewing WSUS Server Terminology

A single WSUS server can be created to download updates and deploy them to all the clients in your network, or you can design a more complex WSUS hierarchy with multiple WSUS servers. Before digging in too deep, it's important to understand some basic terminology with WSUS servers.

Figure 7-20 shows several servers that can be configured with WSUS. A WSUS server can be configured as an upstream server or a downstream server.

- **Upstream WSUS server.** The upstream server connects to the Microsoft Update site and downloads the updates.
- **Downstream WSUS server.** Downstream servers receive their updates from the upstream server.

Notice in the figure that WSUS1 is configured as an upstream server and is sending updates to downstream WSUS servers. WSUS2 is configured as an independent WSUS server; it's receiving the updates from Microsoft, but it is not sending the updates to any other WSUS servers. This setup can be useful if a WSUS server is in another physical location with its own Internet access.

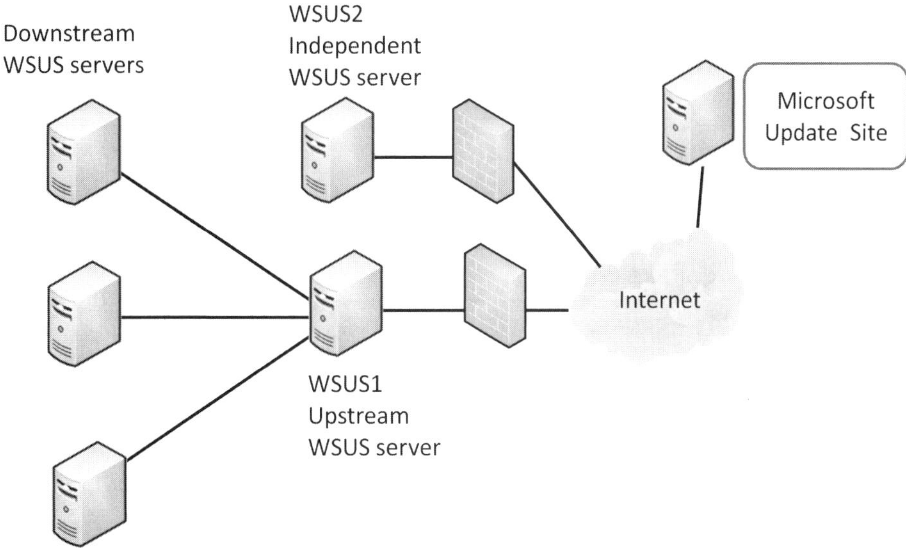

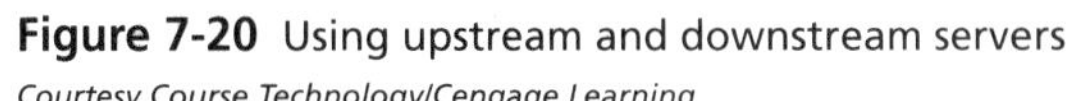
Figure 7-20 Using upstream and downstream servers
Courtesy Course Technology/Cengage Learning

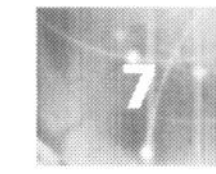

When upstream and downstream servers are used, you can configure how much control administrators of the downstream server have by setting the mode of the WSUS servers. WSUS supports two modes:

- **Autonomous mode.** When two WSUS servers are working as upstream/downstream servers in autonomous mode, the upstream server sends all the updates it receives to the downstream server. Administrators of the downstream server can approve updates independently of updates approved by the upstream server. The upstream server always operates in autonomous mode.
- **Replica mode.** When two WSUS servers are working as upstream/downstream servers, the downstream server can be configured to use replica mode. The upstream server sends approved updates and the approval status to downstream servers, and administrators of the downstream server cannot change the approval status. When using Replica mode, the downstream servers are commonly referred to as replica servers.

Using WSUS with Branch Offices

When your organization has branch offices, you can deploy more than one WSUS server. The primary reason to use multiple servers is to reduce the bandwidth used between the sites. Imagine a branch office with 100 clients. Without using WSUS, an update would have to be sent 100 times over the WAN link to reach each client. However, if a WSUS server were used, the update would be sent once from a WSUS server in the main office over the WAN link to a WSUS server in the branch office. The update would then be deployed to the clients in the branch office from the branch office WSUS server.

Once you decided to deploy a WSUS server to the branch office, you would then need to choose either centralized management or decentralized management. Your choice would affect the mode (autonomous or replica) the WSUS server used for operation.

Figure 7-21 shows an example of WSUS used with centralized management and replica servers. Imagine two physical locations with headquarters in Virginia Beach and a branch office in Norfolk. Administrators at the headquarters site want to control which updates are deployed in both offices, so WSUS2 is configured in replica mode.

Almost all of the administration occurs on WSUS1 at headquarters. Administrators review and approve the updates on the upstream server (WSUS1). When the downstream server at the branch office synchronizes with the upstream server, the approved updates are downloaded

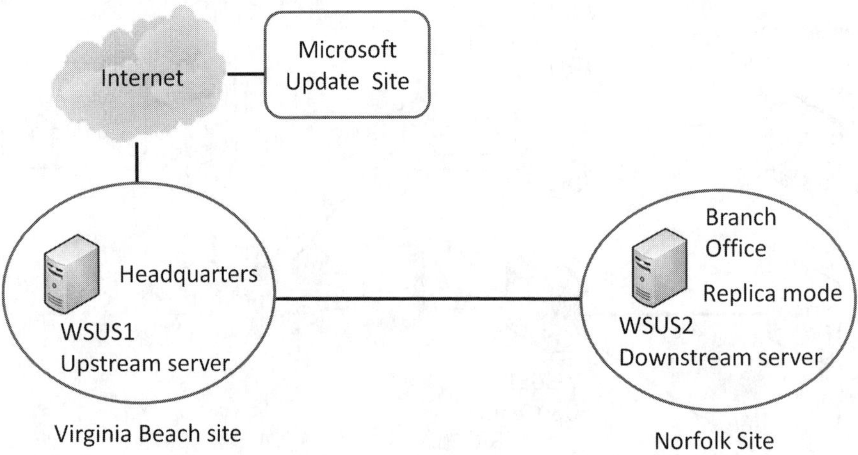

Figure 7-21 Using WSUS server for centralized management with branch offices
Courtesy Course Technology/Cengage Learning

with an approved status. Very little administration is required or even possible on the downstream replica server, although it does need to be checked to ensure that synchronization is occurring.

Figure 7-22 shows the WSUS configuration setting on the WSUS server at the branch office. The setting configures the branch office server as a replica server. You access this setting by selecting Update Source and Proxy Server from the Options menu of the Update Services window. The same replica setting would be unchecked on the upstream server so that it operates in autonomous mode.

Figure 7-23 shows an example of WSUS used with decentralized management. The difference between this figure and Figure 7-21 is that the server in the branch office is not configured as a replica server. It's still configured as a downstream server, but the check box that was selected in Figure 7-22 would not be selected. In this configuration, the downstream server is considered to be working in autonomous mode.

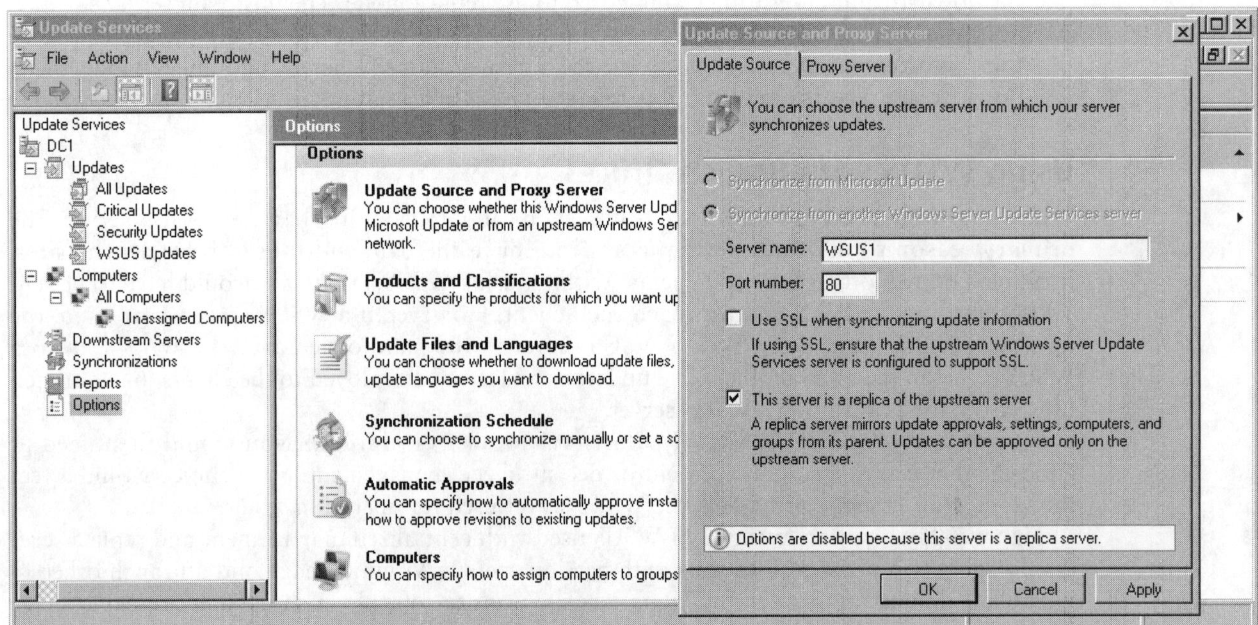

Figure 7-22 Configuring a replica WSUS server
Courtesy Course Technology/Cengage Learning

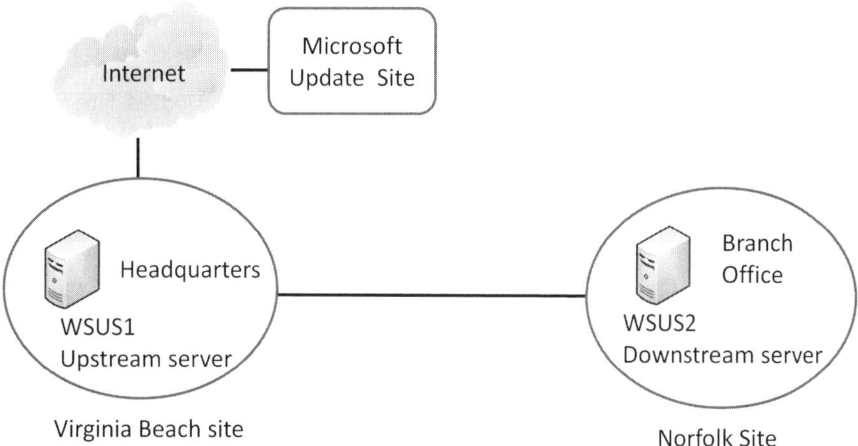

Figure 7-23 Configuring downstream WSUS servers in autonomous mode
Courtesy Course Technology/Cengage Learning

The downstream server will receive all updates received from the WSUS server at headquarters. However, administrators of the downstream server can approve updates independently of the upstream server.

It's also possible to configure WSUS servers at branch offices so that they work independently. Figure 7-24 shows how this could be done if the branch office had a suitable Internet connection. In this arrangement, each server would be configured to receive updates from the Microsoft Update site. Administrators at each site could make their own decisions on when to synchronize and what updates to approve.

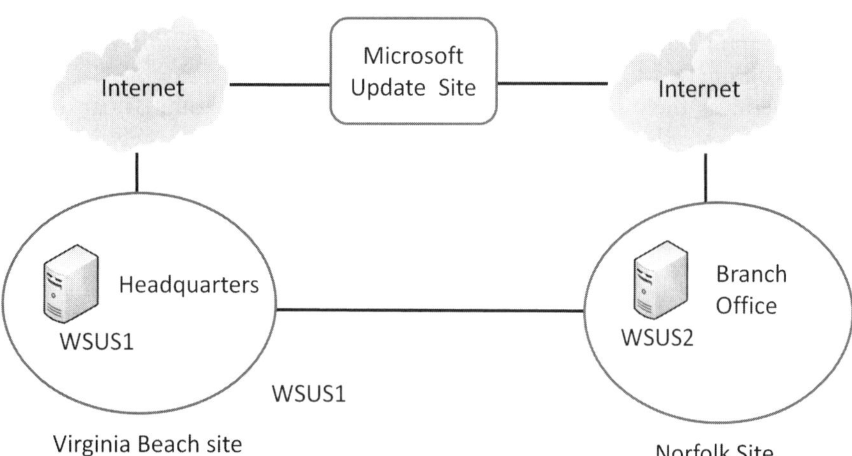

Figure 7-24 Configuring independent WSUS servers
Courtesy Course Technology/Cengage Learning

Using WSUS with Disconnected Networks

Many organizations host networks that are isolated from other networks for security reasons. For example, a network could have multiple connected computers that regularly share secret or proprietary data. The isolated network would not have connectivity with other networks and definitely would not have access to the Internet.

While such an arrangement certainly adds a lot of security to the network, keeping the systems updated can be a challenge if none of them can be connected to the Internet. Fortunately, WSUS includes the ability to export and import updates to and from media. Consider Figure 7-25.

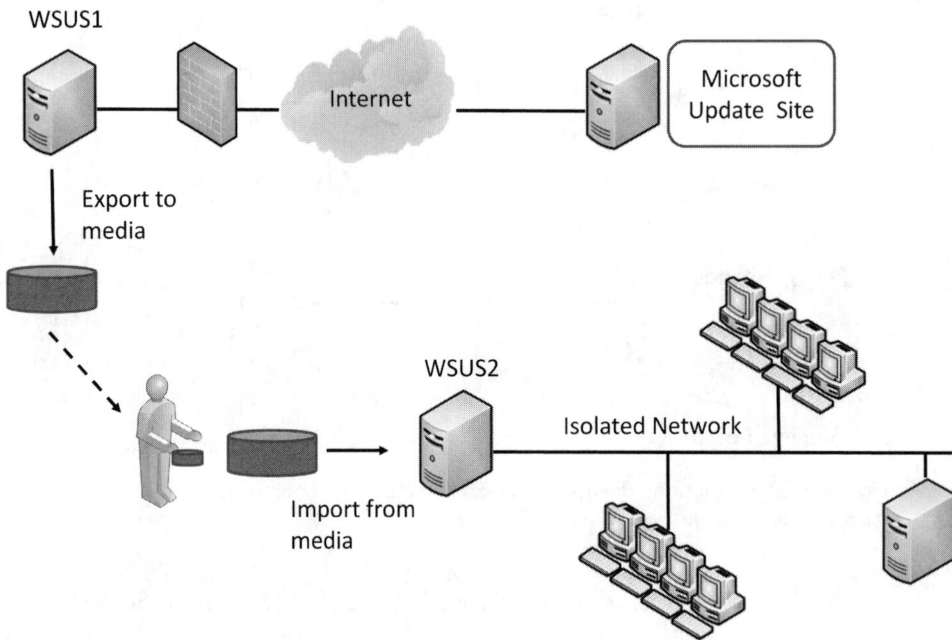

Figure 7-25 Distributing updates via media to isolated networks
Courtesy Course Technology/Cengage Learning

In the figure, WSUS1 has full connectivity to the Internet and is used to retrieve updates from the Microsoft Update site. Once the updates are retrieved, WSUS can be used to export the updates to media such as CDs, DVDs, or portable USB drives. Optical media such as CDs and DVDs are more secure because they only contain the data written to them, and the media are less likely to contain malware. The updates can be exported using traditional copy methods such as a backup program or XCopy from the command line.

This media is then carried to the isolated network by hand. It can be copied or restored onto WSUS 2 into the content folder that the WSUS server is configured to use—normally the C:\WSUS\WSUSContent folder. While WSUS2 will never be able to synchronize, the content in the WSUSContent folder will be up to date.

WSUS Requirements

When considering adding WSUS to your network, you should be aware of the basic requirements. The product is free, but it does require some configuration of the server. You have three primary concerns:

- **Hardware.** You'll need at least a 1 GHz CPU, though a processor of more than 2 GHz is recommended. At least 1 GB of RAM is required, though at least 4 GB is recommended on a 32-bit system. The network adapter should be at least 10 Mbps, though 1 Gbps is a better choice due to the amount of data that will be transferred. The hard disk needs to be formatted with NTFS; you should have at least 30 GB of storage space available for content.
- **Server roles.** The Web Server (IIS) role and the Application Server role both need to be added to support WSUS. Many specific role services also need to be added, as you will see in an activity later in this chapter.
- **Downloaded files.** Two files are needed: the Microsoft Report Viewer Redistributable 2008 file and the WSUS 3.0 SP2 file. Both are available from Microsoft's download site (*Microsoft.com/downloads*) by searching on "Microsoft Report Viewer Redistributable 2008" and "WSUS," respectively. Make sure you download the 32-bit (x86) or 64-bit (x64) version of WSUS 3.0 SP2 to match the architecture of the server.

Installing WSUS

Once you've ensured that your server has the minimum hardware and you've downloaded the files, you can begin the installation. Because of the interaction of the different components, it's best to start with a known state, add the prerequisites, and then install WSUS.

The following activities lead you through the process of installing WSUS in three steps.

1. **Return the server to a known state.** DC1 has had many different roles and services added. Activity 7-6 leads you through the process of returning it to a basic state. When you are finished, only Active Directory, DNS, and File Services will be installed.
2. **Install WSUS prerequisites.** The Web Server (IIS) and Application roles are added with the supporting role services. Additionally, the Microsoft Report Viewer Redistributable 2008 file is installed so that reports can be viewed within WSUS.
3. **Install WSUS.** The WSUS installation file is used to install WSUS. While WSUS needs to have Internet access to be fully functional, you can still install it and examine the console without having Internet access.

Activity 7-6: Reconfiguring DC1 to Host Only AD DS, DNS, and File Services

Time Required: 15 minutes
Objective: Restore DC1 to a known state of only AD DS and DNS.

Description: You have been using DC1 as a test environment and have added multiple roles and services to it. You want to add WSUS to this server, but want to ensure that everything except AD DS and DNS is removed first.

1. Start **DC1** and log on with the domain **Administrator** account.
2. Start the **Server Manager** console via the **Administrative Tools** menu.
3. Select **Roles** and click **Remove Roles**. Click **Next** on the **Before You Begin** page.
4. Deselect the check boxes for all roles except **Active Directory Domain Services, DNS Server**, and **File Services**. Click **Next**.

File Services is included because a share was added to DC1 previously. It's not necessary to remove the File Services role.

5. On the **Confirm Removal Selections** screen, click **Remove**.
6. When the removal process is complete, click **Close**. When prompted to restart the server, click **Yes**.
7. After **DC1** reboots, log on with the domain **Administrator** account. Server Manager will start automatically and resume the configuration. When the reconfiguration is complete, click **Close**.
8. Close all open windows.

Activity 7-7: Installing WSUS Prerequisites

Time Required: 20 minutes
Objective: Install the prerequisites needed for WSUS.

Description: You are planning to install WSUS. Prior to completing the installation, you need to add the IIS role and the Microsoft Report Viewer Redistributable 2008 SP1 file to the server. This activity should be run on DC1.

To download the Microsoft Report Viewer Redistributable 2008 SP1 file, go to *Microsoft.com/downloads*, search on "Microsoft Report Viewer Redistributable 2008," and select the file. If you are using a virtual PC, you should download the file from the host system and copy it to the virtual machine instead of reconfiguring the virtual system to have Internet access.

1. Start **DC1** and log on with the domain **Administrator** account.
2. Start **Server Manager** via the **Administrative Tools** menu.
3. Select **Roles**, and click **Add Roles**. Click **Next** on the **Before You Begin** screen.
4. Select the check box next to **Web Server (IIS)**. If a dialog box prompts you to add features, click the **Add Required Features** button. The Application role is also needed, but it is added automatically when additional role services are added for the Web Server (IIS) role. Click **Next**.
5. Review the information on the **Introduction to Web Server (IIS)** screen and click **Next**.
6. On the **Select Role Services** page, leave the default selections and ensure that the following additional role services are selected.
   a. Under **Common HTTP Features**, ensure that **Static Content** is selected.
   b. Under **Application Development**, select **ASP.NET**. When you are prompted to add more role services, click the **Add Required Role Services** button. Verify that **ISAPI Extensions** and **ISAPI Filters** have also been selected, as shown in Figure 7-26.
   c. Under **Security**, select **Windows Authentication**.
   d. Under **Management Tools**, select **IIS 6 Metabase Compatibility**.
   e. Click **Next**.
7. Review the selections on the **Confirm Installation Selections** screen and click **Install**.
8. After the installation is complete, click **Close**.
9. Copy the **Microsoft Report Viewer Redistributable 2008 SP1** file to **DC1**. This file is named **ReportViewer.exe**.
10. Start **Windows Explorer** and browse to the location of the **ReportViewer.exe** file. Double-click the **ReportViewer.exe** file to start the installation.
11. When the wizard opens, click **Next**.
12. Review the **License Terms**. Select the check box for **I Have Read and Accept the License Terms** and click **Install**.
13. When the installation is complete, click **Finish**.

Activity 7-8: Installing WSUS

Time Required: 30 minutes
Objective: Install WSUS.

Description: You have prepared a server for WSUS by installing prerequisites. You now need to install WSUS on the server. This activity should be run on DC1.

This activity requires the WSUS 30 SP2 file (WSUS30-KB972455-x86.exe or WSUS30-KB972455-x64.exe). You can download the file that matches your server's architecture (32-bit or 64-bit) from *Microsoft.com/downloads* by searching on "WSUS" and selecting the WSUS 3.0 SP2 link. If you are using a virtual PC, you should download the file from the host system and copy it to the virtual machine instead of reconfiguring the virtual system to have Internet access.

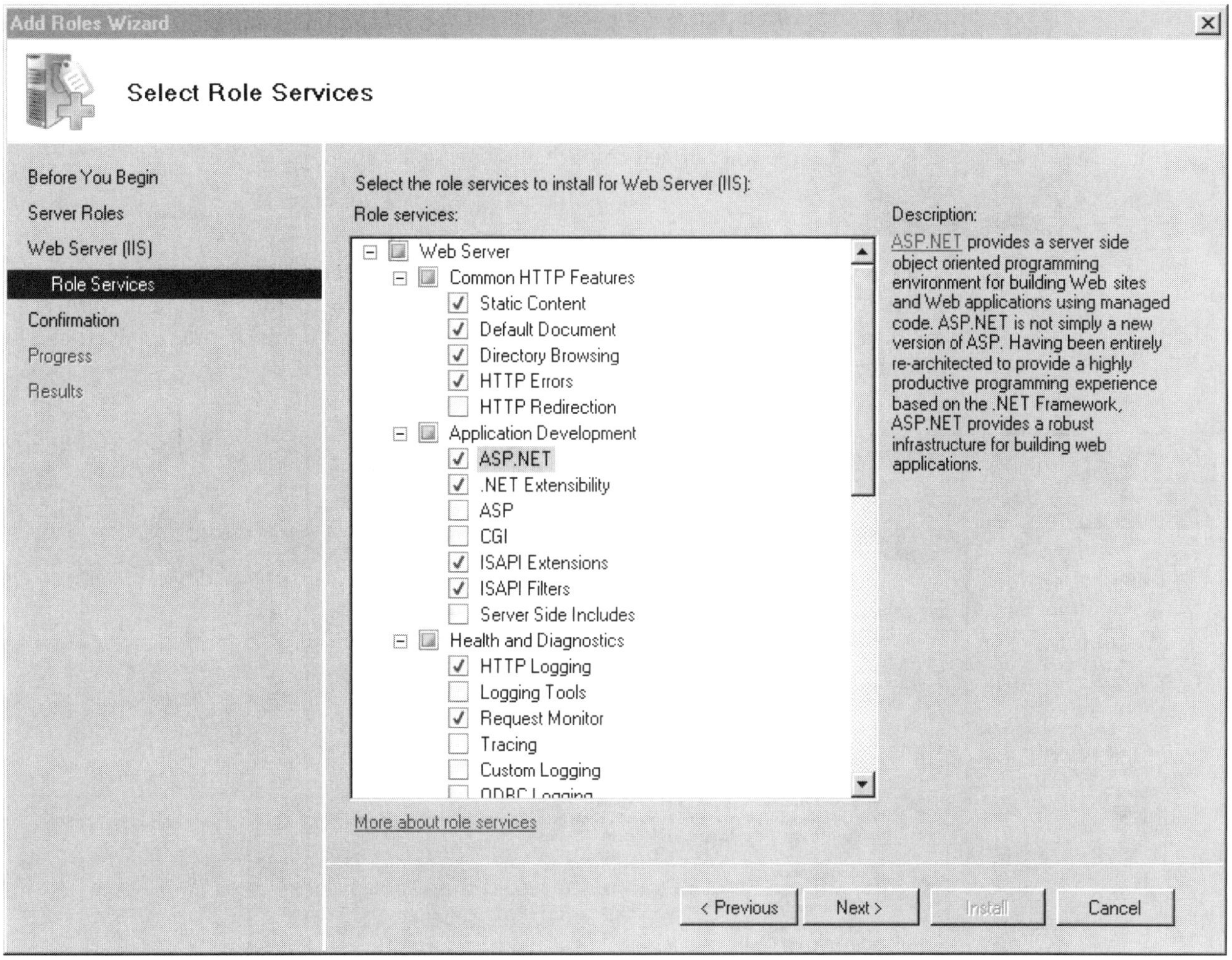

Figure 7-26 Selecting Application Development Role Services

Courtesy Course Technology/Cengage Learning

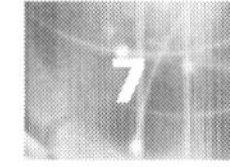

1. Start **DC1** and log on with the domain **Administrator** account.
2. Start **Windows Explorer** and browse to the location of the **WSUS30-KB972455-x86.exe** or **WSUS30-KB972455-x64.exe** file. Double-click the file to start the installation.
3. Review the information on the wizard's **Welcome** screen and click **Next**.
4. Accept the default selection of **Full Server Installation Including Administration Console** and click **Next**.
5. Review the **License Agreement**. Select **I Accept the Terms of the License Agreement** and click **Next**.
6. On the **Select Update Source** screen, accept the default path of **C:\WSUS**. WSUS content will be stored here. Click **Next**.
7. On the **Database Options** screen, accept the default option to **Use Windows Internal Database on This Computer** at **C:\WSUS**. Click **Next**.
8. On the **Web Site Selection** screen, accept the default option to **Use the Existing IIS Default Web Site (Recommended)**. Click **Next**.
9. Review your selections on the **Ready to Install** screen and click **Next**.

10. When the installation is complete, click **Finish**. The **Windows Server Update Services Configuration Wizard** will start. If you have Internet connectivity, you could complete the configuration. Click **Cancel**.

The goal of this activity isn't to completely configure WSUS, but to install it so you can view some of the configuration settings.

11. Start **WSUS** by clicking **Windows Server Update Services** via the **Administrative Tools** menu. Expand **DC1** and click **Options**. Your display will look similar to Figure 7-27. Feel free to look through the options and remind yourself what can be configured.

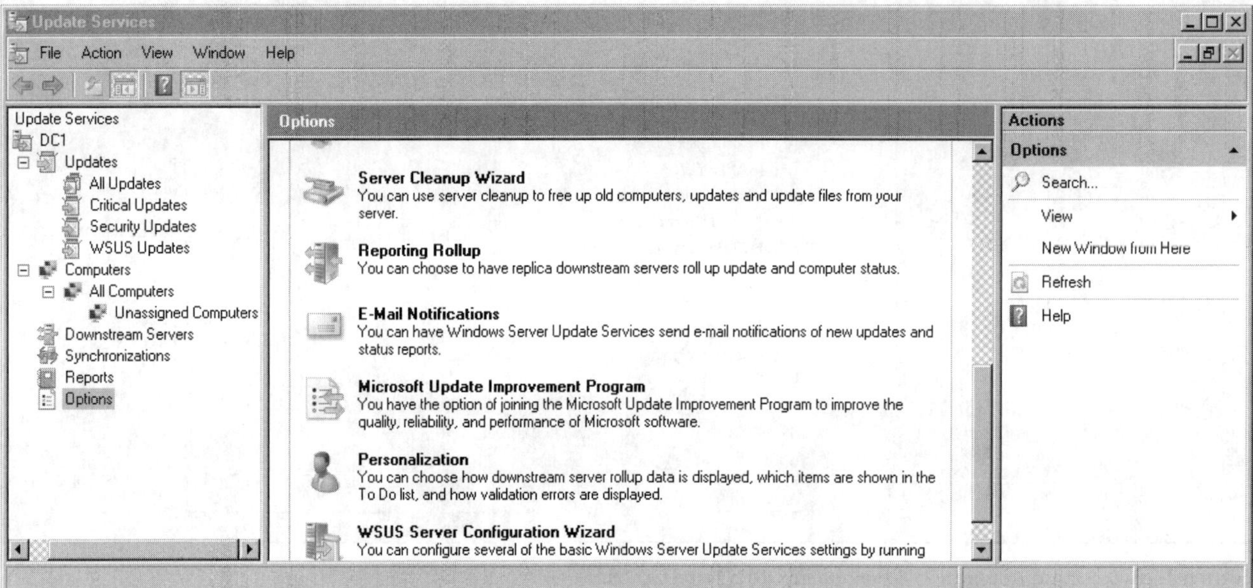

Figure 7-27 Viewing options in the WSUS console

Courtesy Course Technology/Cengage Learning

Configuring Clients to Use WSUS with Group Policy

Once the WSUS server is configured and in place, you want the clients to use it. You can create or modify a Group Policy object (GPO) to configure all the clients automatically. Two primary Group Policy settings need to be configured, and both are accessible in the Computer Configuration, Policies, Administrative Templates, Windows Components, Windows Updates Group Policy node:

- **Configure Automatic Updates.** This setting can be used with or without WSUS. It can be configured to ensure that clients automatically download and install updates on a regular basis. When configured without WSUS, clients will retrieve updates from the Microsoft Update site.
- **Configure the address of the WSUS server.** The URL of the WSUS server is added here, as shown in Figure 7-28.

The WSUS statistics server is a single WSUS server that collects information from all WSUS managed clients in the enterprise. If only one WSUS server is used, the statistics server has the same address as the WSUS server. If multiple WSUS servers are used, you can configure one statistics server that monitors the updates for all clients served by all the WSUS servers.

Specify intranet Microsoft update service location Properties

Setting | Explain | Comment

Specify intranet Microsoft update service location

Not Configured
Enabled
Disabled

Set the intranet update service for detecting updates:

http://DC1

Set the intranet statistics server:

http://DC1

(example: http://IntranetUpd01)

Supported on: At least Microsoft Windows 2000 Service Pack 3 or Mi...

Previous Setting | Next Setting

OK | Cancel | Apply

Figure 7-28 Configuring the address of the WSUS server for clients
Courtesy Course Technology/Cengage Learning

The following activity shows how to modify a GPO to automatically configure clients to use a WSUS server.

Activity 7-9: Using a GPO to Configure WSUS for Clients

Time Required: 10 minutes
Objective: Modify a GPO to configure clients to use a WSUS server.

Description: A WSUS server has been installed and configured in your network. You want all users in the domain to use the WSUS server, so you will modify the Default Domain policy. This activity should be run on DC1.

1. Start **DC1** and log on with the domain **Administrator** account.
2. Start the **Group Policy Management** console via the **Administrative Tools** menu.
3. Expand **Forest, Domains,** and **Cengage.com.**
4. Right-click the **Default Domain Policy** and select **Edit.**
5. Expand the **Computer Configuration, Policies, Administrative Templates, Windows Components, Windows Update** Group Policy nodes.

6. Double-click **Configure Automatic Updates**. Select **Enabled**. Your display will look similar to Figure 7-29. Click **Next Setting**.

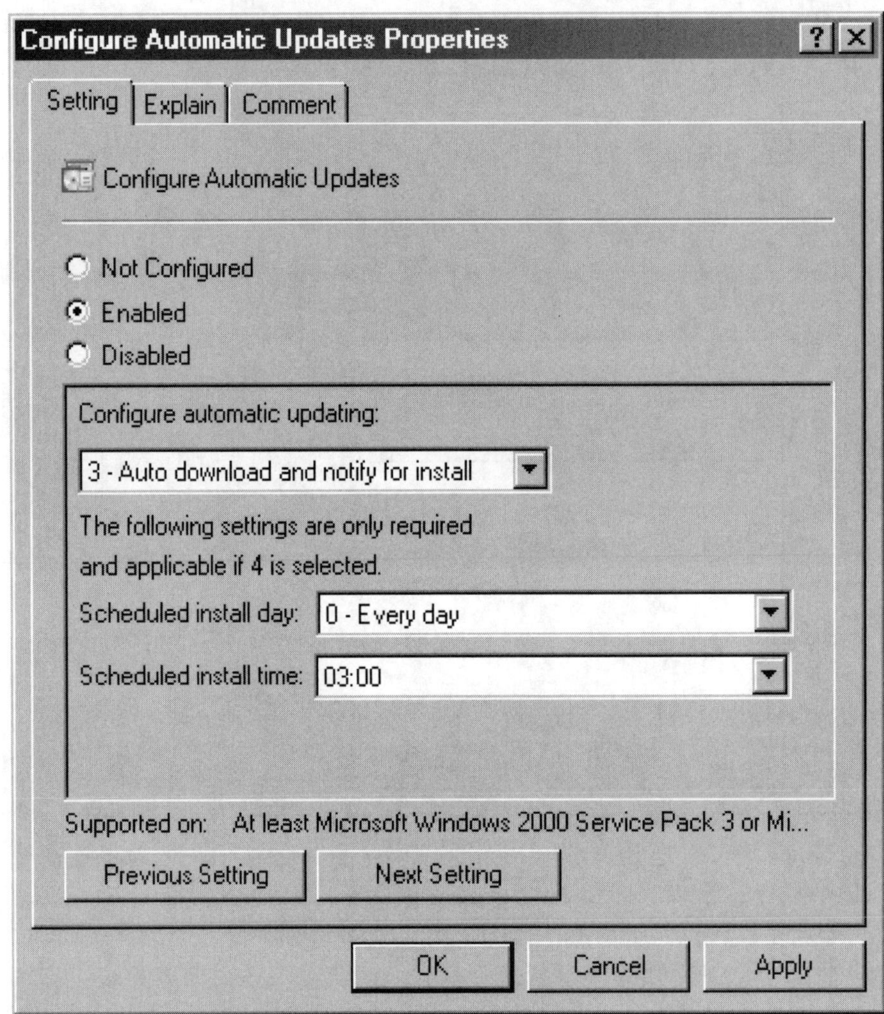

Figure 7-29 Configuring automatic updates for clients
Courtesy Course Technology/Cengage Learning

7. On the **Specify Intranet Microsoft Update Service Location** page, select **Enabled**. Enter **http://DC1** in both text boxes and click **OK**.
8. Close all open windows.

Perimeter Networks

Perimeter networks were mentioned in Chapter 5 within the context of configuring remote access solutions for networks. A **perimeter network** is a network added as a buffer between an internal protected network and an external unprotected network (such as the Internet). It is commonly referred to as a **demilitarized zone** (DMZ).

Figure 7-30 shows a perimeter network configured between a private network and the Internet with two firewalls. These three areas are also considered trust zones: trusted, semi-trusted, and untrusted. Servers hosted in the DMZ are Internet-facing servers such as a Web server, an FTP server, or an e-mail server.

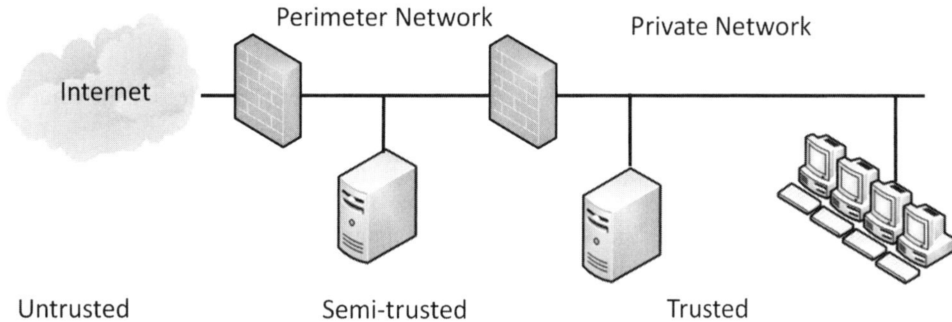

Figure 7-30 Perimeter network
Courtesy Course Technology/Cengage Learning

A perimeter network is commonly created with two firewalls, but it can also be created with a single firewall and three network interfaces. One interface connects to the Internet, one to the perimeter network, and one to the private network. While this arrangement is cheaper, the configuration is more complex.

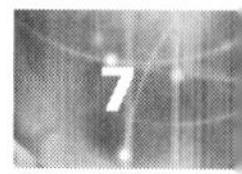

The trust zones are:

- **Trusted.** Connections on the internal network are from company-owned resources and employees are considered trusted.
- **Semi-trusted.** This zone will accept connections from the Internet from customers, remote employees, or trusted business partners.
- **Untrusted.** Connections from the Internet are considered a potential risk and are untrusted. The connections could be from customers, employees, and trusted business partners, but the connections could also be from attackers.

The perimeter network is sometimes referred to as the border, the edge, or the boundary within the terms "border security," "edge protection," and "boundary protection," respectively. Network traffic is highly controlled via firewall rules to restrict untrusted traffic from reaching the internal network.

Firewall Rules

Each firewall is configured with rules that allow or deny traffic based on different criteria. Basic firewall rules provide packet filtering based on IP addresses, ports, and protocols. More advanced firewall rules can provide filtering based on specific application commands or the state of the connection.

A firewall policy is created by designing and implementing different rules. These rules are often divided into different categories or rule sets:

- **Network rules.** These rules identify resources in one network that can communicate with resources in another network. For example, a Web server in the perimeter network may be authorized to access a SQL Server database server in the internal network, and a network rule can be created to authorize the access.
- **System policy rules.** These rules identify traffic and protocols that are allowed to and from the perimeter network. Traffic is often identified based on the port it uses. For example, HTTP traffic uses port 80 and HTTPS uses port 443.
- **Firewall publishing rules.** Publishing rules are commonly used to publish an Internet-facing server's connection information to the external firewall. When a publishing rule exists, the external firewall will forward requests from the Internet to the server hosting the service. For example, an HTTP or HTTPS publishing rule could be used to publish access to a Web server in the DMZ.

The following list is a small sampling of rules that may be created on a firewall. An actual firewall will use a much more extensive list, but this one gives you an idea of the different rules.

- Deny all traffic unless it's explicitly allowed by another rule. This is sometimes referred to as implicit deny.
- Block all incoming traffic that has an internal source IP address. Because the traffic is coming from the Internet, it should have a public IP address. If it has an internal source IP address, the traffic is trying to impersonate an internal host by spoofing the IP address. Such traffic should be blocked.
- Block all outgoing traffic that has a public source IP address. Because the traffic is coming from the internal network, the source IP address should be private. If the source IP address is public, the traffic is spoofed and should be blocked.
- Allow outgoing DNS traffic for name resolution and allow the return traffic.
- Allow outgoing HTTP and HTTPS traffic to Internet Web servers and allow the return traffic.
- If a Web server is in the DMZ, allow HTTP and HTTPS traffic to the Web server.
- Allow incoming and outgoing Simple Mail Transport Protocol (SMTP) traffic to and from an SMTP server.

When administering a firewall, you'll have a significant number of rules based on the requirements of the network. However, each additional rule adds an element of complexity to the firewall; also, by allowing additional traffic, the rule adds another potential risk. If you administer a firewall, you'll often want to minimize the number of rules in place, although it might put you at odds with network administrators who want to add rules to allow additional traffic. Firewall administrators constantly strive to find a suitable balance between security and usability.

Microsoft Firewall Products

Microsoft Internet Security and Acceleration Server (ISA Server) is a dedicated application that can be installed on a server to perform as a firewall. It provides filtering using basic packet filtering and more advanced stateful, application-layer filtering.

ISA Server has gone through several versions since 2000; ISA Server 2006 was issued as the last ISA Server version. Forefront Threat Management Gateway, the next generation of ISA Server, was released in 2009. Like Microsoft Exchange Server or Microsoft SQL Server, these server products are not free.

Chapter Summary

- Security is increased on a server by hardening the system. The key steps of hardening a system include reducing the attack surface, performing compliance auditing, and keeping the system up to date.
- The Security Configuration Wizard (SCW) is a built-in tool that can be used to create a security policy as an XML file based on roles of a server. This security policy can be applied to individual systems one by one or converted to a GPO and applied to many systems.
- Scwcmd is the command-line equivalent of SCW and can be used for compliance auditing. The scwcmd command can compare a system's current configuration with a security policy used as a baseline and report discrepancies. Scwcmd can also be used to create a GPO from the security policy.
- Compliance auditing is used to check systems to ensure that they comply with security policies or security requirements. Scwcmd and MBSA are two tools you can use to perform compliance audits.
- The Microsoft Baseline Security Analyzer (MBSA) is a compliance auditing tool that can be used to scan one or more systems for various vulnerabilities, including Windows administrative vulnerabilities, weak passwords, and current security updates.

- MBSACLI is the command-line equivalent of MBSA, and can be used to script and schedule regular compliance audits.
- Auditing can be enabled to log events in the Security log. The logged events are viewable in the Event Viewer. Basic directory service access logging is enabled by default, and events are logged when Active Directory objects are created and modified. Advanced directory service access logging can be enabled by modifying the Default Domain Controllers policy; this is also referred to as enabling the global audit policy.
- Windows Server Update Services (WSUS) can be used as a central location to download updates from the Microsoft Update site for an organization. Administrators can then identify the updates they want to approve, and these updates will be deployed to clients in the network.
- Multiple WSUS servers can be used in a network. A WSUS server can be configured as an upstream server to receive updates from the Microsoft Update site. Additional WSUS servers can be configured as downstream servers to receive their updates from the upstream server.

- Downstream servers can be configured either in autonomous mode or replica mode. In autonomous mode, administrators of the downstream server can approve updates separately from the updates approved at the upstream server. In replica mode, updates are received with an approved status and automatically deployed without administrative intervention.
- WSUS servers can be used in an isolated network without any Internet access. Content is exported or copied from a WSUS server that can synchronize with the Microsoft Update site, and then imported or copied to the WSUS server in the isolated network.
- A perimeter network is a network placed between a private internal network and public network such as the Internet. It is also referred to as a demilitarized zone (DMZ); normally it includes two firewalls. Each firewall includes a firewall policy that identifies what traffic is allowed and what traffic is blocked.

Key Terms

Autonomous mode A downstream server configured in autonomous mode that receives updates from an upstream server. Administrators of the downstream server can choose which updates to deploy.

Compliance auditing Checking systems to ensure that they comply with security policies or security requirements. Scwcmd and MBSA are two tools you can use to perform compliance audits.

Demilitarized zone (DMZ) A network placed between a private internal network and public network such as the Internet. A DMZ is typically created with two firewalls, and is sometimes referred to as a perimeter network.

Downstream WSUS server A server that receives updates from an upstream WSUS server. A downstream server can be configured either in autonomous mode or replica mode.

MBSACLI A command-line interface for MBSA that can be scripted and scheduled to run periodically.

Microsoft Baseline Security Analyzer (MBSA) A compliance auditing tool that can be used to scan one or more systems for several vulnerabilities, such as weak passwords or a system not being up to date.

Microsoft Update A program that provides all the same updates as Windows Update, but adds updates for Microsoft applications such as Office, Exchange, and SQL Server.

Perimeter network A network placed between a private internal network and public network such as the Internet. A perimeter network is typically created with two firewalls, and is sometimes referred to as a demilitarized zone (DMZ).

Replica mode A downstream server configured in replica mode receives pre-approved updates from an upstream server. Updates are automatically deployed without administrative intervention.

Scwcmd A command-line version of the Security Configuration Wizard (SCW). Scwcmd can be used to create a GPO from an SCW security policy. Scwcmd can also be used for compliance auditing.

SD³+C A secure computing strategy adopted by Microsoft that includes Secure by Design, Secure by Default, and Secure in Deployment and Communications.

Security Configuration Wizard (SCW) A security tool that can be used to create a security policy for one or more computers based on roles. The security policy is created as an XML file.

Server Core A minimal installation of Windows Server 2008 or Windows Server 2008 R2. Server Core only has a command-line interface; it does not have a traditional Windows graphical user interface.

Upstream WSUS server A server that connects to the Microsoft Update site and that can forward the updates to downstream WSUS servers. An upstream server is always configured in autonomous mode.

Windows Server Update Services (WSUS) Free Microsoft software that can be used by administrators as a central location to download, approve, and synchronize updates for clients within the network.

Windows Update A program that provides updates for Windows operating systems. It is different from Microsoft Update, which provides updates for Microsoft applications in addition to the operating system.

Review Questions

1. You administer several Windows Server 2008 servers used as Terminal Services servers that can be accessed from the Internet. You want to increase the security on each of these servers using the least administrative effort, and you want to ensure that all the settings on each server are applied identically. What should you use?

   a. MBSA

   b. SCW

   c. WSUS

   d. AD CS

2. A network was recently infected with malware that ultimately exploited a wide assortment of vulnerabilities that the company didn't even know existed. You're asked to help the company increase its security posture. You want to first perform basic compliance auditing to determine what issues exist, and create a security baseline to measure security compliance in the future. What tools would you use? (Choose two.)

   a. MBSA

   b. SCW

   c. WSUS

   d. ISA

3. Your single-domain forest includes more than 100 Windows XP, Windows Vista, and Windows 7 clients. You are asked to design a solution that will regularly check the client computers to ensure that they are secured from known vulnerabilities and are patched with security updates. What can you use to perform these checks? (Choose all that apply.)

   a. MBSA

   b. MBSACLI

   c. SCW

   d. WSUS

4. Your organization includes more than 500 Windows Vista and Windows 7 clients in a domain. Group Policy is used to manage the clients and WSUS is used to deploy updates

to the clients. You're asked to implement a compliance audit solution to regularly validate that clients are up to date and aren't susceptible to common security vulnerabilities, such as having the Guest account enabled or including accounts with passwords that don't expire. What would you do?

a. Regularly run MBSA against the clients.

b. Regularly run SCW against the clients.

c. Modify the Default Domain Controllers policy to include auditing.

d. Modify the Default Domain policy to include auditing.

5. You are the senior administrator for a single-domain forest. Seven other administrators also help to administer the domain. Recently, some suspicious changes have occurred to accounts in Active Directory, and you've been unable to determine who made the changes. You want to ensure that any future changes are logged with as much detail as possible. What should you do?

a. Enable object access auditing in the Default Domain policy.

b. Enable object access auditing in the Default Domain Controllers policy.

c. Enable MBSA auditing in the Default Domain policy.

d. Enable directory service access auditing in the Default Domain Controllers policy.

6. Your organization includes more than 5000 users and 10 domain controllers, and is managed by multiple administrators. Recently, a user account was deleted, but it couldn't be determined who deleted the account. You're asked to design a solution that will log details if an account is deleted from Active Directory again. What would you recommend?

a. Create a directory service audit policy in the Default Domain Controllers policy.

b. Create an object access audit policy in the Default Domain Controllers policy.

c. Create a script to run scwcmd on a weekly basis.

d. Create a script to run MBSACLI on a weekly basis.

7. You just installed Windows Server 2008 on a server and promoted it to a domain controller in a new forest. You started the Group Policy Management console to view the audit policy of the Default Domain Controllers Policy, as shown in Figure 7-31. If a change is made to a user account, will anything be logged about the change? If so, why?

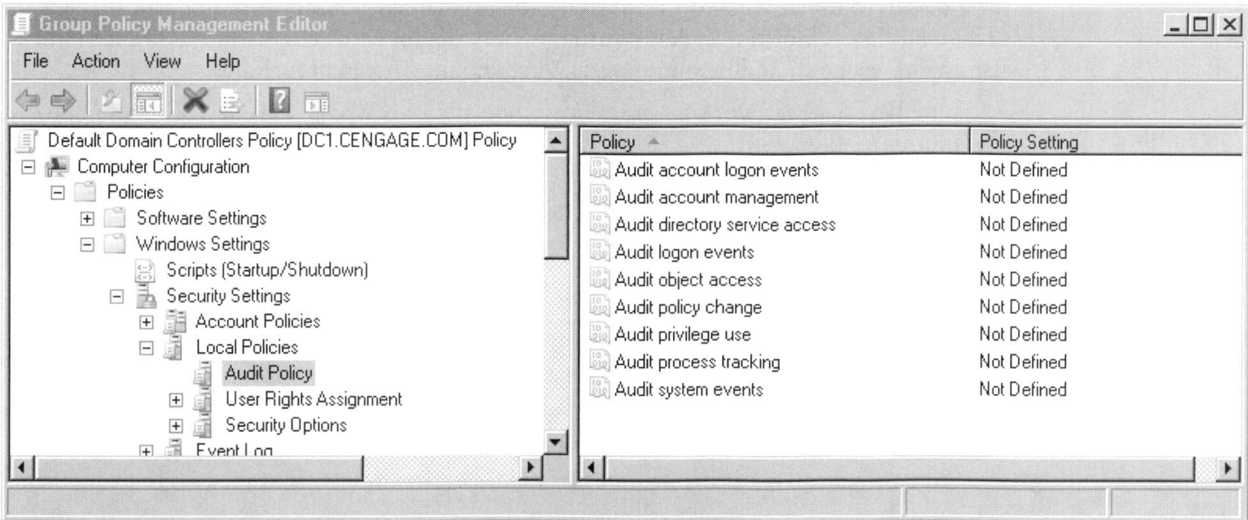

Figure 7-31 Viewing a default directory service access auditing entry

Courtesy Course Technology/Cengage Learning

a. Yes, because directory service access auditing is enabled by default.
b. No, because directory service access auditing is disabled by default.
c. No, because directory service access auditing is not defined.
d. It's not possible to tell because this is configured at the Default Domain policy.

8. You manage a small network with two servers. One of the servers is running SQL Server 2008 on Windows Server 2008. You need to ensure that the server is regularly updated with operating system updates and software updates for SQL Server 2008. Your solution should require the least administrative effort. What should you use?
   a. Microsoft Update
   b. Windows Update
   c. WSUS
   d. SCCM
9. Your organization includes a single domain of approximately 150 client computers. These computers include a wide assortment of Windows 2000 Workstation SP2, Windows XP SP1, Windows Vista SP1, and Windows 7 clients. You're asked to design a solution to use WSUS 3.0 to deploy updates to these clients. What should be included in the plan?
   a. The 150 computers need to be divided into groups of no more than 50 each.
   b. The plan must include at least two internal WSUS servers (at least one upstream server and at least one downstream server).
   c. Windows 2000 Workstation computers need to be upgraded to at least SP4.
   d. Windows 2000 Workstation computers need to be upgraded to at least SP4 and Windows XP clients need to be upgraded to at least SP2.
10. Your organization includes more than 500 clients configured in a single domain. You want to ensure that all the clients are kept current with Microsoft updates while minimizing bandwidth usage over the Internet. What should you use?
    a. MBSA
    b. SCW
    c. WSUS
    d. Configure clients to use Automatic Updates with Group Policy.
11. Your single-domain forest includes one main office and two branch offices. You are creating a design to use WSUS. You want to be able to manage and approve updates at the main office and have all of the updates automatically deployed to clients in the branch offices. Bandwidth usage should be minimized. What should your plan include?
    a. One WSUS server working in replica mode and two WSUS servers working in autonomous mode.
    b. One WSUS server working in autonomous mode and two WSUS servers working in replica mode.
    c. Three WSUS servers working in replica mode.
    d. Three WSUS servers working in autonomous mode.
12. Your single-domain forest includes one main office and two branch offices. You are creating a design to use WSUS. You want to be able to manage and approve updates at the main office, and all of the updates should be automatically deployed to clients in the branch offices. Bandwidth usage should be minimized. What should your plan include?
    a. An upstream server at the main office and downstream servers at the two branch offices.
    b. A downstream server at the main office and upstream servers at the two branch offices.
    c. Three downstream servers.
    d. Three upstream servers.

13. Your single-domain forest includes one main office and two branch offices. You are creating a design to use WSUS. You want each office to be able to manage and approve updates. Each branch office has Internet access through the main office. Bandwidth usage should be minimized. What should your plan include?
    a. One WSUS server working in replica mode and two WSUS servers working in autonomous mode.
    b. One WSUS server working in autonomous mode and two WSUS servers working in replica mode.
    c. Three WSUS servers working in replica mode.
    d. Three WSUS servers working in autonomous mode.
14. Your single-domain forest includes one main office and two branch offices. You are creating a design to use WSUS. You want each office to be able to manage and approve updates. Each branch office has independent Internet access. Bandwidth usage should be minimized, especially on the WAN link. What should your plan include?
    a. An upstream server at the main office and downstream servers at the two branch offices.
    b. A downstream server at the main office and upstream servers at the two branch offices.
    c. Three downstream WSUS servers.
    d. Three independent WSUS servers.

15. Your organization includes two networks. The primary network has Internet access, but company policy restricts an isolated network from having Internet access or connectivity with networks that have Internet access. You are creating a design to use WSUS for both networks. How should you configure WSUS?
    a. Configure the WSUS server in the isolated network in autonomous mode and synchronize with the Microsoft Update site.
    b. Export the content from the WSUS server with Internet access. Import the content to the isolated WSUS server.
    c. Import the content to the WSUS server with Internet access. Export the content from the isolated WSUS server.
    d. Configure the WSUS server in the isolated network as a replica and synchronize with the WSUS server in the primary network.
16. Your single-domain forest includes one main office and two branch offices configured as three sites. You are creating a design to use WSUS with a WSUS server placed in each site. You want users in each site to use the WSUS server in that site. How can you achieve this design with the least administrative effort?
    a. Create one GPO and link it to the domain.
    b. Create two GPOS. Link one GPO to the main office site and the other GPO to the other two sites.
    c. Configure three GPOs and link a GPO to each site.
    d. Configure the clients manually.
17. A new remote office location is being added to your single-domain forest. Your organization uses WSUS to deploy updates to clients from a WSUS server named WSUS1. A GPO is currently linked to the domain, directing all clients to use WSUS1. You're asked to design a method to ensure that clients in the remote office receive the same approved updates, using the minimum bandwidth and no additional administrative overhead. All clients in the new location will be in an OU. What should you do? (Choose two.)
    a. Add a WSUS server as a replica server in the new location.
    b. Add a WSUS server as an autonomous server in the new location.

c. Modify the existing GPO to include the new WSUS server.

d. Create a new GPO and link it to the OU for the new location.

18. Your organization currently has a single WSUS server at the main location. A GPO has been linked to the domain, directing all clients to use this WSUS server. The domain has other locations that access the Internet via the main location and use the same WSUS server for updates. Bandwidth between the main location and one of the remote locations is currently at peak capacity, and you're asked how the bandwidth load can be alleviated. What could be done without adding bandwidth capacity?

    a. Deploy an additional WSUS server at the remote location and allow it to get updates from the Microsoft Update site. Modify the existing GPO.

    b. Deploy an additional WSUS server at the remote location and allow it to get updates from the Microsoft Update site. Create an additional GPO.

    c. Deploy an additional WSUS server at the remote locations and configure it to get updates from the WSUS server at the main location. Modify the existing GPO.

    d. Deploy an additional WSUS server at the remote locations and configure it to get updates from the WSUS server at the main location. Create an additional GPO.

19. You are preparing to configure a Web server that will host a Web site for your company. Users will be able to access the Web site from the Internet; when purchasing products, they'll be able to use a secure HTTPS connection. You want to configure the infrastructure to host the Web server in a semi-trusted network. What would you use?

    a. Use ISA to create a perimeter network and host the Web server on the Internet.

    b. Use ISA to create a perimeter network and host the Web server in the perimeter network.

    c. Use ISA to create a perimeter network and host the Web server in the internal network.

    d. Use WSUS to create a perimeter network and host the Web server in the perimeter network.

20. Your company is hosting a Web server in the perimeter network. The Web server accepts secure connections using HTTPS and then authenticates clients. How can you configure the perimeter network to ensure that all connections to this Web server are encrypted and that no other traffic is allowed using port 443?

    a. Configure WSUS with an HTTPS publishing rule.

    b. Configure SCW to allow HTTPS traffic.

    c. Configure Microsoft ISA with a network policy rule to allow traffic on port 443.

    d. Configure Microsoft ISA with an HTTPS publishing rule.

Case Projects

Case Project 7-1: Creating a Security Baseline

Your organization includes several Web servers that have recently been attacked. You've discovered that unnecessary services and protocols are running on some of the servers. You want to secure them all using a security baseline. If possible, you also want to perform periodic checks on the servers to determine if the security baseline has been modified. What tool could you use and how would you use it? Explain your answer.

Case Project 7-2: Performing Compliance Auditing

You are an administrator for a domain that includes about 100 client computers. Computers are deployed with secure settings, but over time unauthorized changes have been made to these servers. Several security incidents have occurred in the past few months with different computers in the organization; these incidents could have been avoided if the original settings were used and the computers were kept up to date. You want to verify periodically that all clients are still running with basic security settings and are not vulnerable to known security issues. You want to automate the solution so that these checks are done regularly without additional administrative interaction. What should you do? Explain your answer.

Case Project 7-3: Updating Clients

You are planning to deploy WSUS in your single-domain forest. The domain includes three locations configured as three separate sites; one site is the headquarters location, and the other two sites are branch locations. You want all updates to be downloaded and approved by the WSUS server in the main office (WSUS1). The WSUS servers in the branch locations should receive the updates with an approved status. How should the WSUS servers be configured? Identify whether each WSUS server will be an upstream or downstream server, and identify the mode for each WSUS server.

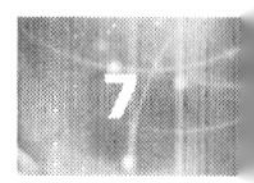

Case Project 7-4: Decentralizing an Update Plan

Your single-domain forest uses WSUS to deploy updates to clients. The company is planning to add a new branch office, and you're asked to design a plan to add a WSUS server for this remote location. The new WSUS server should receive updates from the WSUS server at the main location, and administrators in the remote location should be able to approve their own updates. Clients in the remote location should be configured to use this new WSUS server. How should the new WSUS server be configured to meet all of these requirements? Also, what mode should be used? Explain your answer.

chapter 8

Designing High Availability and Business Continuity

After reading this chapter and completing the exercises, you will be able to:

- Understand the differences between Network Load Balancing (NLB) clusters and failover clusters
- Design an NLB cluster
- Design a failover cluster
- Understand methods used to back up and restore Active Directory

Business continuity includes all the methods and technologies used to ensure that a business can continue to operate even after a failure occurs. Network Load Balancing clusters are commonly used to increase the scalability of an application and failover clusters are used to provide high availability. Backups ensure that data remains available after data loss; backing up domain controllers can protect against catastrophic data loss of Active Directory.

This chapter covers these key concepts of business continuity.

Load Balancing and Fault Tolerance

Load balancing and fault tolerance are two methods of ensuring that a service is available to users when they need it. Load balancing can be achieved at the server level using load-balancing clusters and fault tolerance can be achieved at the server level using failover clusters. Failover clusters are a primary method of achieving high availability at the server level.

There's a difference between fault tolerance at the disk level and at the server level. RAID disk subsystems can be used to provide fault tolerance at the disk level—if a disk drive fails, the disk subsystem will continue to operate. Failover clusters provide fault tolerance at the server level—if a server fails, the service will continue to be available.

In this context, a cluster is a group of servers that are configured together with similar goals. You will learn about two types of clusters in this chapter:

- **Load-balancing clusters.** Two or more servers are configured together and the load is balanced between the servers. As new clients connect, they are redirected to a server in the cluster to ensure that the load remains balanced. A primary goal of load balancing is to increase scalability for a service or application.
- **Failover clusters.** Two or more servers are configured together, with some servers designated as active nodes and others designated as inactive nodes. Active nodes provide services to clients and inactive nodes monitor the active nodes. If an active node fails, the inactive node can take over with little disruption to the clients. A primary goal of a failover cluster is high availability.

In Windows Server 2003, a failover cluster was known as a server cluster, which was sometimes confused with a Windows Server 2003 Network Load Balancing cluster. Windows Server 2008 uses the terms "failover clusters" and "Network Load Balancing clusters."

Two common goals of load balancing and failover clusters are scalability and high availability.

Scalability

Scalability refers to a service's ability to support more clients through the addition of resources such as more processing power or more servers. Applications that are scalable only require additional resources without changes to the application itself.

As an example, a Web server can easily serve Web pages to 1000 clients an hour, but if the client requests increase to 1000 per second, the same Web server can't keep up. However, if more resources are added, the same level of service can be provided to all the clients.

Scalability can be achieved by scaling up or scaling out.

- **Scale up.** Additional resources such as processing power and memory can be added to a server. Figure 8-1 shows an example of scaling up a server. The smaller server has less service capacity, and at some point the service is actually degraded when too many clients connect. The larger server has more hardware resources and can provide the same level of service to a larger number of clients. Of course, the service provided by the larger server will be degraded at some point; in Figure 8-1, this point is off the scale.

- **Scale out.** More servers are added, as shown in Figure 8-2. The load is balanced across each of the servers and progressively more clients can be added without degrading the service. Windows Server 2008 supports scaling out by using a Network Load Balancing (NLB) cluster.

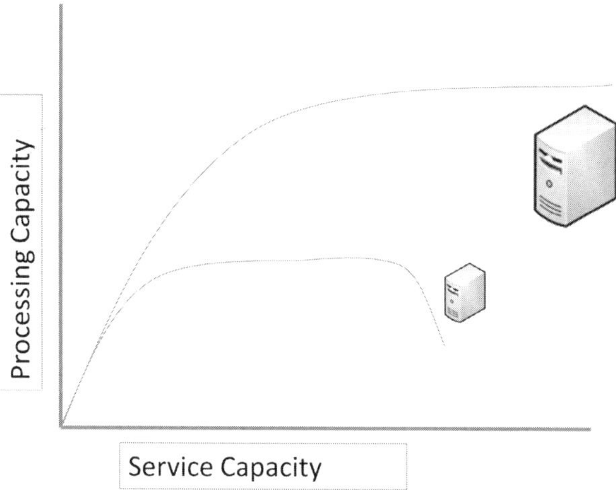

Figure 8-1 Scaling up by increasing hardware resources in a server

Courtesy Course Technology/Cengage Learning

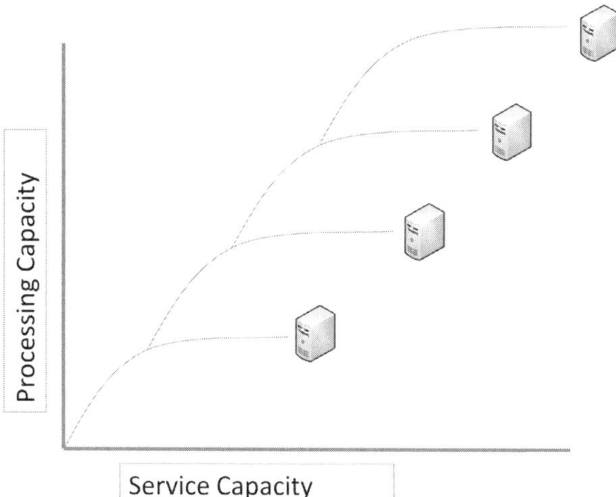

Figure 8-2 Scaling out by increasing the number of servers

Courtesy Course Technology/Cengage Learning

High Availability

High availability means that a service is available when it's needed. For example, a company may have a server running Microsoft SQL Server 2008 and hosting multiple databases. A high-availability solution ensures that the databases continue to operate even if a server fails or needs to be taken down for maintenance.

If an organization only needs a service during business hours, updates and maintenance can be done after hours or on weekends, with no loss of availability. However, for a server that's needed 24 hours a day, 365 days a year, a reboot at any time results in a loss of availability.

There are different levels of high availability. While 99 percent uptime sounds good, it is a little misleading. One percent downtime equates to more than 87 hours of downtime in a year. A high level of uptime is commonly referred to as "five nines," or 99.999 percent uptime. Table 8-1 shows different uptime percentages and their equivalent downtimes per year.

Table 8-1 Server availability percentages and times

Percentage	Total Possible Downtime per Year
99%	87 hours 36 minutes
99.9%	8 hours 46 minutes
99.99%	52 minutes 34 seconds
99.999%	5 minutes 15 seconds

Failover clusters are commonly used to achieve high availability. They are discussed in much more depth later in this chapter.

Network Load Balancing vs. Failover Clusters

NLB clusters and failover clusters have many distinct differences. Table 8-2 provides an introductory overview of some of these differences, and then the chapter explores the details of each.

Table 8-2 A comparison of NLB and failover clusters

	Network Load Balancing Cluster	Failover Cluster
Purpose	Balances load by balancing TCP/IP traffic across two or more nodes.	Provides redundancy and failover capability. If one node fails, another node takes over.
Resources	Each node has its own storage that is used independently. Storage is not shared.	Resources are shared. Nodes in the cluster share common storage and function together as a single logical unit.
Cost	Cheaper. Additional dedicated hardware is not required (other than the servers) and none of the hosts in the cluster are idle.	More expensive. Dedicated hardware is usually required and even the servers should have similar or matching hardware. One or more nodes in the cluster are typically inactive.
State	Applications are stateless. In other words, each client request can be treated independently and clients don't need to connect to the same server for subsequent connections.	Applications are stateful, and maintain a long-running, in-memory state of the client's session.
Example services and applications	Stateless Web servers, VPN servers, proxy servers, and firewalls.	Database servers, messaging servers, DHCP servers, file servers, and print servers.

It's also possible to combine an NLB cluster and a failover cluster in a comprehensive solution. You can't use both services on the same server, but within a network, you can use both services to provide different layers of support.

As an example, consider Figure 8-3. A company is hosting a Web server in the DMZ. To provide load balancing and increase scalability, the Web site is hosted on two servers in a two-node NLB cluster. The NLB cluster will dynamically balance the load between Web1 and Web2.

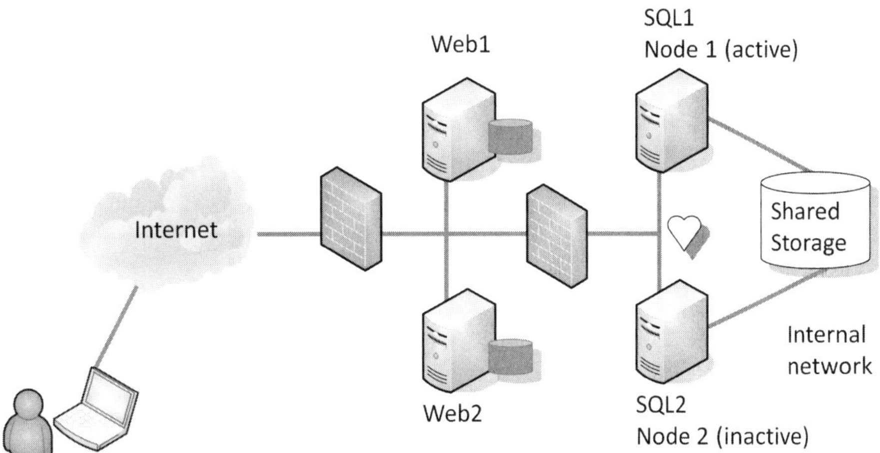

Figure 8-3 Using an NLB cluster and a failover cluster in a single solution

Courtesy Course Technology/Cengage Learning

The Web site is using Microsoft SQL Server 2008 as a back-end database. To provide high availability for the database, a two-node failover cluster is created using two servers (SQL1 and SQL2) with shared storage connected to both nodes. SQL1 starts as the active node servicing client requests. SQL2 is the inactive node, and only monitors the "heartbeat" of SQL1. If SQL1 fails, SQL2 can take over the load.

Network Load Balancing

The **Network Load Balancing (NLB)** feature of Windows Server 2008 can increase stability and provide scalability for applications and services. It is primarily recommended for Internet-facing or Internet-accessible servers such as Internet Information Services (IIS) Web servers, File Transfer Protocol (FTP) servers, firewalls, proxy servers, and VPN servers.

Each of these types of servers can be configured to operate as stateless servers. In other words, each server can be configured to operate independently of other servers in the cluster. Clients can connect to any server in the NLB cluster and receive the same level of service. Servers in an NLB cluster are referred to as hosts or nodes.

Consider Figure 8-4. Two Web servers are configured in an NLB cluster. Each server has identical content with independent storage. When clients connect, the NLB cluster service sends the clients to alternating hosts to ensure that each server is being used equally. Web1 would process the first request, Web2 would process the second request, the third request would go to Web1, and so on.

An NLB cluster also monitors hosts in the cluster and can dynamically add and remove hosts. Each host within the cluster exchanges heartbeat messages with other members in the cluster. When one of the hosts fails, the failure is sensed by the other hosts and the host is removed from the cluster.

Similarly, when a host is brought back online, it sends heartbeat messages and is converged or added to the cluster. The convergence of a new host takes only a few seconds after it is brought back online; as soon as the convergence is complete, the new host begins to service new client requests.

Network Load Balancing Manager

The primary tool you'll use to create and configure NLB clusters is the Network Load Balancing Manager. It is shown in Figure 8-5 with a two-node cluster.

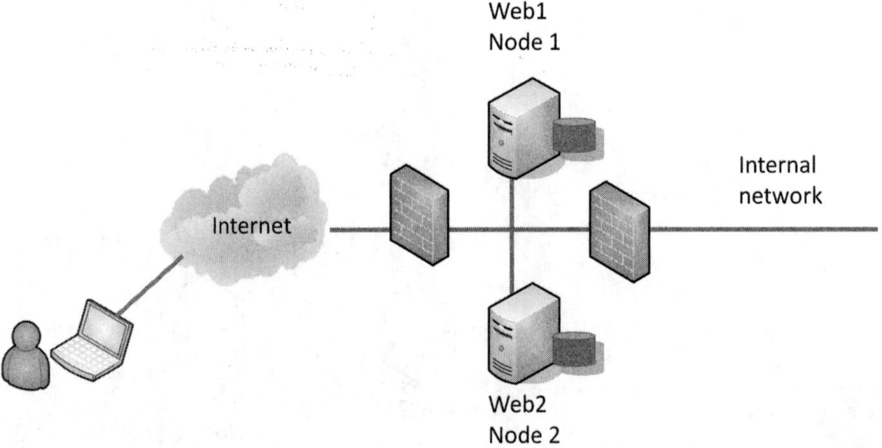

Figure 8-4 NLB cluster

Courtesy Course Technology/Cengage Learning

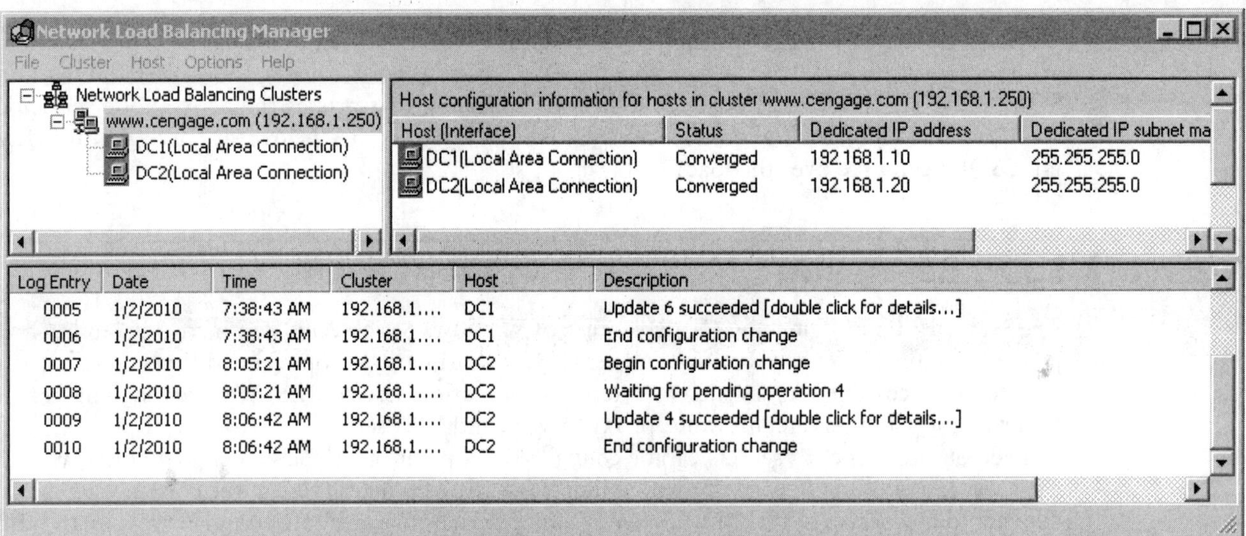

Figure 8-5 Cluster created in Network Load Balancing Manager

Courtesy Course Technology/Cengage Learning

The created cluster is named www.cengage.com and has its own IP address of 192.168.1.250; all hosts in the cluster can respond to this address. The two hosts (DC1 and DC2) are both added to the cluster, and each host has an individual IP address. A DNS entry is required to allow clients to resolve the name of the cluster (www.cengage.com) to the IP address of the cluster (192.168.1.250); the NLB cluster then directs the traffic to one of the hosts in the cluster.

If a host in the cluster fails, the status changes to Unreachable and clients are no longer directed to the failed host. If the failed host is brought back online, the status will change to Pending when it begins and then to Converged once it has been added to the NLB cluster.

Adding Network Load Balancing

All hosts within an NLB cluster must have the NLB feature installed. You can use Server Manager and the following steps to add this feature.

Activity 8-1: Adding the Network Load Balancing Feature

Time Required: 15 minutes
Objective: Add the NLB feature.

Description: You are planning to configure an NLB cluster with two servers. You first need to add the NLB feature to each server that will be in the NLB cluster. This activity should be run on DC1 and DC2, which are used throughout the book.

1. Start **DC1** and **DC2**. Log on to **DC1** with the domain **Administrator** account.
2. Start the **Server Manager** via the **Administrative Tools** menu.
3. Select **Features** and click **Add Features**. Select **Network Load Balancing**. Click **Next**.
4. On the **Confirm Installation Selections** page, click **Install**.
5. When the installation is complete, click **Close**.
6. Repeat these steps to add the NLB feature on **DC2**.

Creating an NLB Cluster

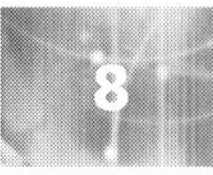

After adding the NLB feature to the hosts, you can use any of the hosts to create or manage the cluster using the Network Load Balancing Manager. When creating an NLB cluster, you need to identify parameters for the cluster and for the hosts in the cluster. You can also create or modify the IP traffic rules.

Figure 8-6 shows the cluster parameters screen for a new cluster being created in the Network Load Balancing Manager. Cluster parameters apply to the cluster as a whole and include the IP address, subnet mask, full Internet name, and network address. The full Internet name would also be added to DNS so that clients could resolve the name to the IP address.

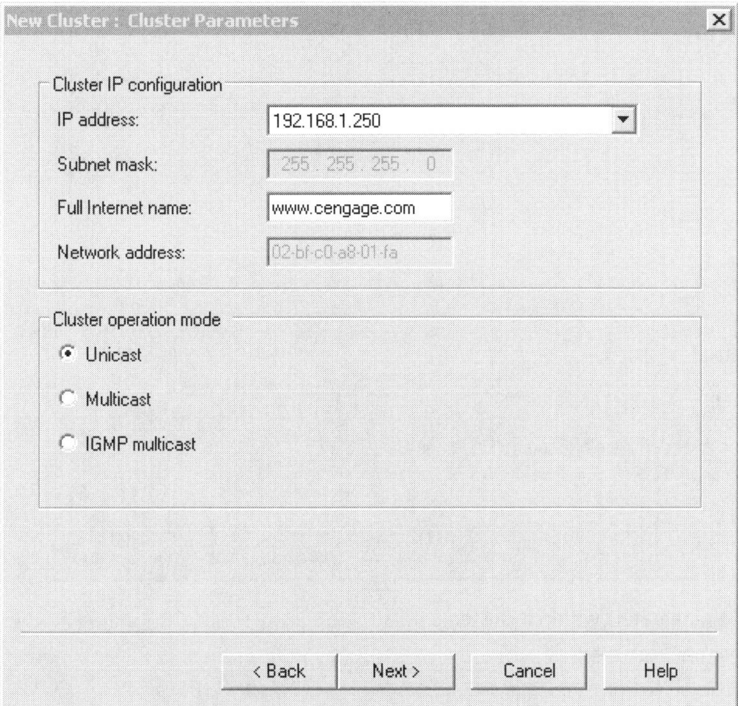

Figure 8-6 Cluster parameters for a new cluster

Courtesy Course Technology/Cengage Learning

The network address is also known as the physical address or media access control (MAC) address. The network address is normally assigned only to a single NIC and associated with the NIC's IP address, but in an NLB cluster it is assigned to the virtual IP address of the NLB cluster.

The cluster operation mode indicates whether the cluster will use unicast, multicast, or Internet Group Multicast (IGMP). Unicast is the most common mode used, and is recommended in Microsoft documentation. If traffic is reaching the NLB cluster from a switch, multicast or IGMP mode can be used to limit switch flooding.

Port rules are used to identify the traffic that will be balanced by the NLB cluster. By default, all IP traffic is load balanced and is identified with a filter that includes all cluster IP addresses and all TCP and UDP ports. It's also possible to create the cluster to balance only specific traffic, such as TCP port 80 for HTTP traffic or TCP port 443 for HTTPS traffic.

Figure 8-7 shows the parameters for a host within a cluster. The actual IP address and subnet mask of the host are added. Additionally, each host is identified with a priority, which is used as a unique identifier within the cluster. The host with the lowest priority number is considered the default host and is used for any traffic not identified by port rules for the cluster. The first host added to the cluster is assigned a default priority of 1, but this value can be changed.

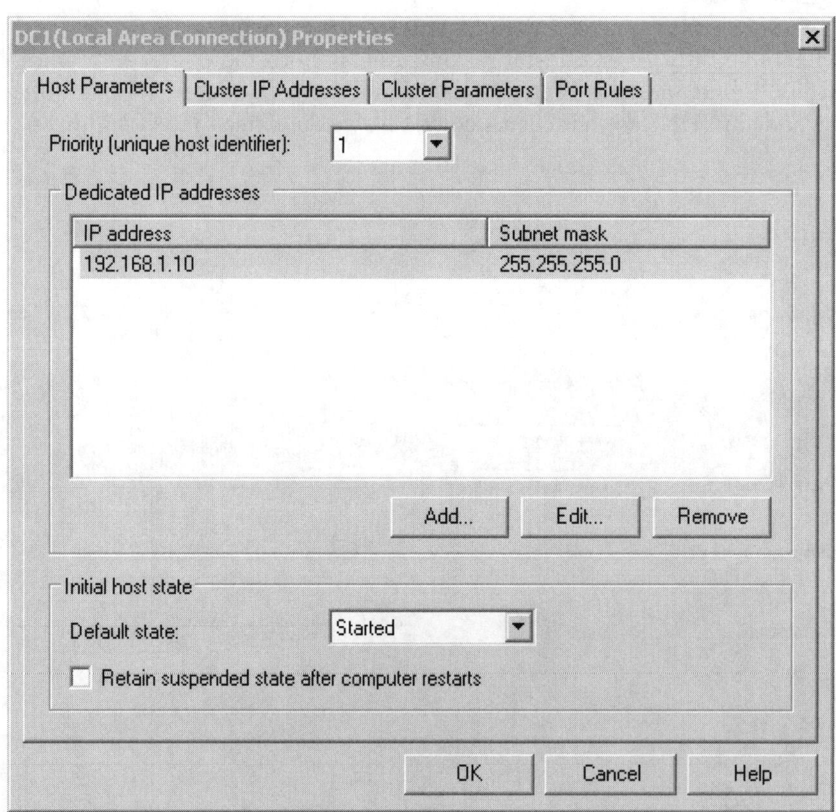

Figure 8-7 Host parameters within a cluster

Courtesy Course Technology/Cengage Learning

The following activity shows how to create and test an NLB cluster. It assumes that you completed the previous activity to add the NLB feature to DC1.

Activity 8-2: Creating a Network Load Balancing Cluster

Time Required: 20 minutes
Objective: Create and verify the operation of an NLB cluster.

Description: You have a Web site hosted on DC1 and have duplicated this Web site to DC2. You want both Web sites to be part of an NLB cluster, and clients should connect using the www.cengage.com address. After creating the cluster, you'll need to modify DNS so that www.cengage.com can resolve the IP address of the cluster. This activity should be run on DC1.

1. Start **DC1** and log on with the domain **Administrator** account.
2. Start the **Network Load Balancing Manager** via the **Administrative Tools** menu.
3. Select **New** from the **Cluster** menu.
4. Type **DC1** as the **Host** and click **Connect**. The service will connect to DC1 and the Interface name and Interface IP will appear, as shown in Figure 8-8. Click **Next.**

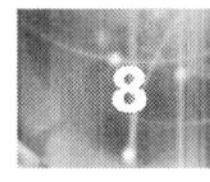

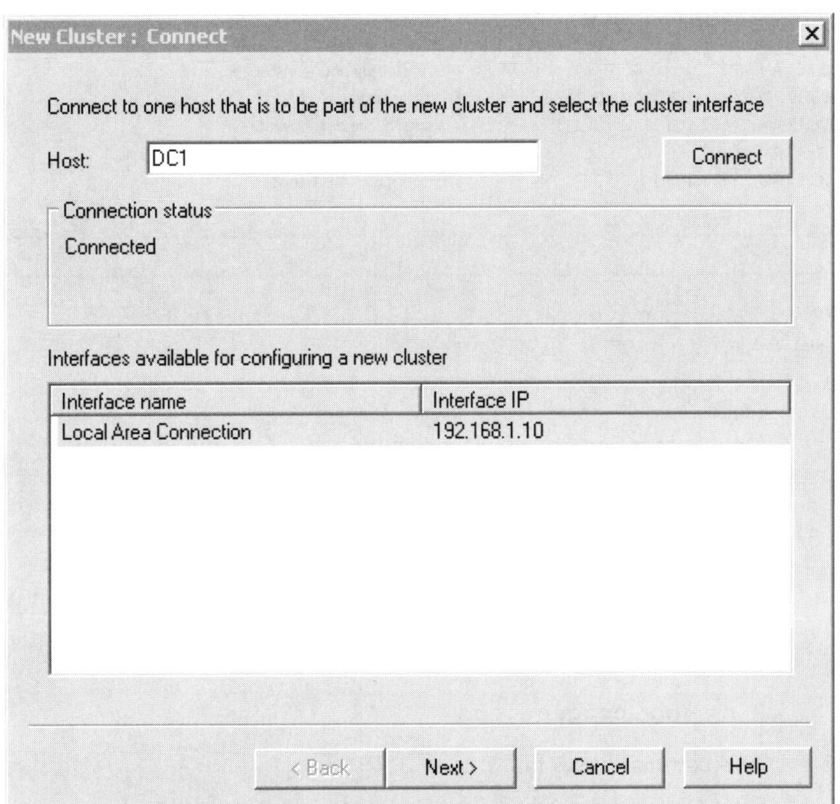

Figure 8-8 Connecting to DC1 as the first host in a cluster
Courtesy Course Technology/Cengage Learning

5. On the **New Cluster : Host Parameters** screen, verify that the **Priority** is set to **1**. Click **Next.**
6. On the **New Cluster : Cluster IP Addresses** screen, click **Add**. Enter an IP address of **192.168.1.250** with a subnet mask of **255.255.255.0**. This cluster IP address is shared by every member of the cluster. Click **OK**. Click **Next.**

7. The **New Cluster : Cluster Parameters** screen appears. Type **www.cengage.com** as the **Full Internet Name**. Accept the default **Cluster Operation Mode** of **Unicast** and click **Next**.
8. On the **New Cluster : Port Rules** screen, you can see the default port rule. This rule causes all traffic to be balanced against all the nodes in the cluster. Click **Finish**. The bottom pane of the Network Load Balancing Manager shows the progress of the cluster configuration. When it is complete, your display will look similar to Figure 8-9.

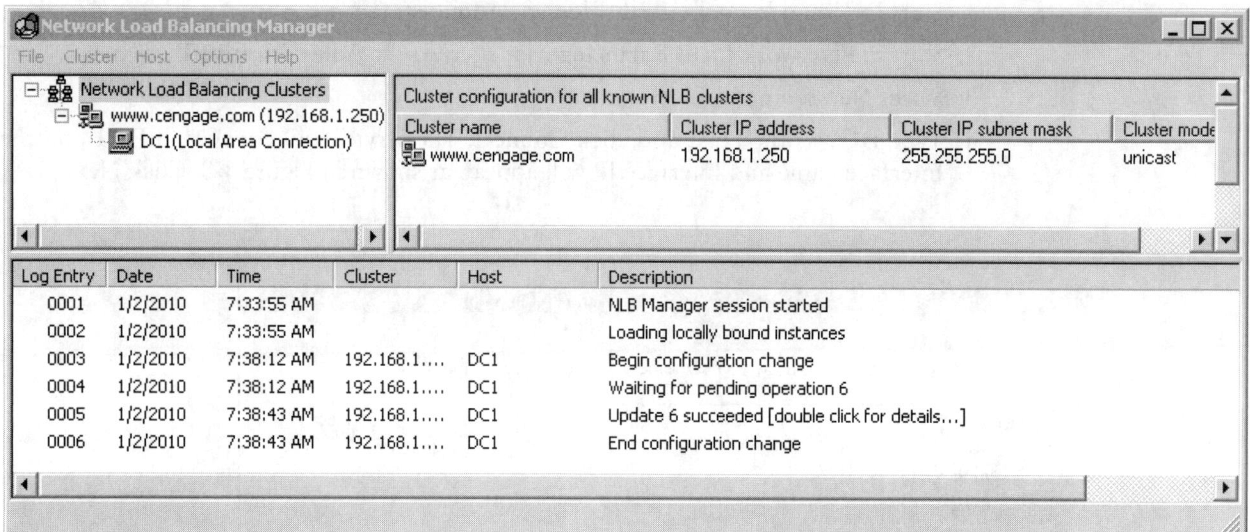

Figure 8-9 NLB cluster created

Courtesy Course Technology/Cengage Learning

9. Open a command prompt by clicking **Start, Command Prompt.**
10. Type the following command to ping the cluster:

```
Ping 192.168.1.250
```

You'll see four successful replies from the cluster, indicating that it is working.

11. Type the following command to verify that the cluster name cannot be resolved by DNS:

```
Ping www.cengage.com
```

This command will fail.

12. Start **DNS** via the **Administrative Tools** menu.
13. Expand **DC1, Forward Lookup Zones, Cengage.com.** Right-click **Cengage.com** and select **New Host (A or AAAA).**
14. Enter **www** as the **Name.** The **Fully Qualified Domain Name** will appear as **www.Cengage.com.** Enter an IP address of **192.168.1.250.** Click **Add Host.** A dialog box indicates that the host record was successfully created. Click **OK.** Click **Done.**
15. Return to the command prompt and enter the following two commands:

```
IPConfig /FlushDNS

Ping www.cengage.com
```

When the Ping command failed to resolve to an IP address in Step 11, a negative cache entry was added, indicating that the www.cengage.com name does not exist. The IPConfig /FlushDNS command removes this entry and forces ping to query DNS to resolve the name.

Notice that the ping successfully resolves to 192.168.1.250 and returns four echo replies.

16. Close all open windows.

Adding Hosts to an NLB Cluster

Once you've created an NLB cluster, you can add more hosts to the cluster. You must first add the feature to the server and then use the Network Load Balancing Manager to add the host. Hosts can be added using any server that has the Network Load Balancing Manager installed.

The following activity shows how to add DC2 to the NLB cluster created in the previous activity.

Activity 8-3: Adding a Host to an NLB Cluster

Time Required: 10 minutes
Objective: Add a host to an NLB cluster.

Description: You have created an NLB cluster for a Web site and have duplicated the contents of the Web site from DC1 to DC2. You now want to add DC2 to the NLB cluster. This activity should be run using DC1 and DC2.

1. Start **DC1** and **DC2**. Log on to **DC1** with the domain **Administrator** account.
2. Start the **Network Load Balancing Manager** via the **Administrative Tools** menu.
3. If necessary, expand **Network Load Balancing Clusters** and select **www.cengage.com**.
4. Right-click **www.cengage.com** and select **Add Host To Cluster**.
5. Type **DC2** as the host and click **Connect**. Click **Next**.
6. Review the information on the **Add Host to Cluster : Host Parameters** screen. Notice that the **Priority (unique host identifier)** is set to **2**, as shown in Figure 8-10. **DC1** was set to a priority of **1**. Click **Next**. Click **Finish**.

   After a moment, the configuration of **DC2** will be completed. The status of **DC2** will begin as **Pending** and then change to **Converged** after the configuration is complete.
7. Close all open windows.

Web Servers in an NLB Cluster

It's common to host multiple Web servers in an NLB cluster to support additional clients. Some companies have increased Web traffic during specific times, and add more servers to handle the traffic. They remove the servers when they're no longer needed. For example, the Christmas season generates increased Web traffic for e-commerce sites. Additional servers can easily be added to an NLB cluster during this time and then removed when no longer needed.

Remember, though, each Web server in the NLB cluster must be able to act independently. An important consideration is the use of certificates with NLB clusters. If a Web server must support HTTPS sessions, a certificate issued from a certification authority is needed. However, certificates are issued to a server, which represents a technical challenge when using NLB clusters.

When using NLB, you should obtain a certificate using the fully qualified domain name of the cluster as the common name in the certificate. For example, in the previous activities, the cluster was named www.cengage.com with two hosts of DC1 and DC2. A certificate would be issued

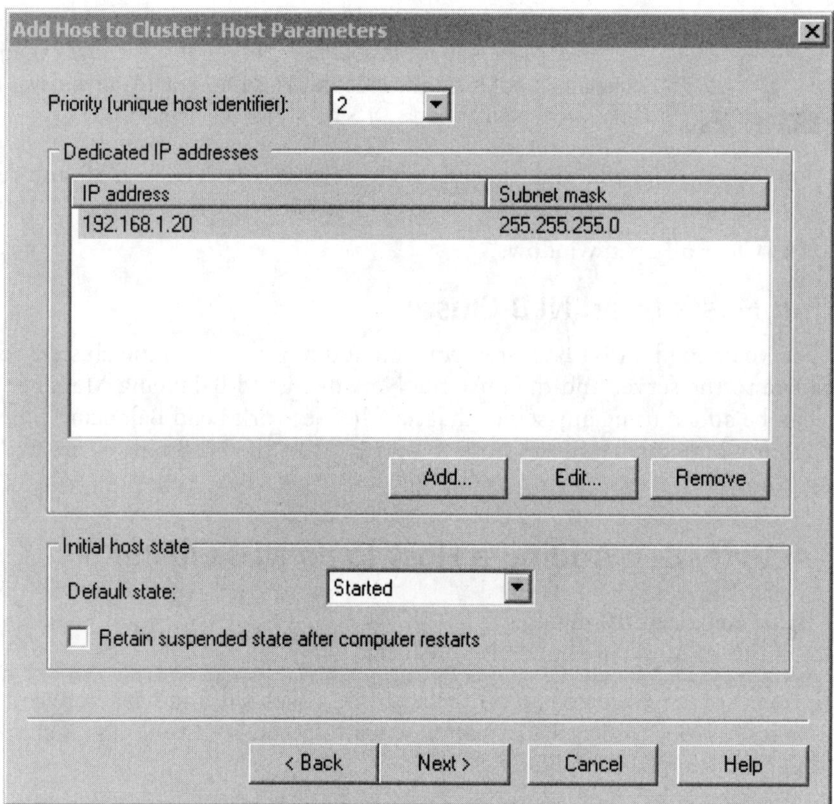

Figure 8-10 Verifying parameters of second host in NLB cluster

Courtesy Course Technology/Cengage Learning

with a common name of www.cengage.com and a copy of the same certificate would be used for both DC1 and DC2.

If a certificate is used for a cluster with any name other than the cluster name, the connection won't match the common name and the certificate won't be recognized as valid. Instead, it will result in an error for the clients.

Removing the NLB Cluster Service

NLB clusters can be removed without much effort. Because the NLB cluster feature can interfere with other components and services, you should remove it if it's not being used.

The following activity leads you through the process of removing the NLB cluster service from both DC1 and DC2.

Activity 8-4: Removing the NLB Cluster and the NLB Cluster Feature

Time Required: 20 minutes

Objective: Remove the NLB cluster and the NLB cluster feature.

Description: You no longer need the NLB cluster you created on DC1 and DC2. You want to remove the NLB cluster and the feature from both servers.

1. Start **DC1** and **DC2**. Log on to **DC1** with the domain **Administrator** account.
2. Start the **Network Load Balancing Manager** via the **Administrative Tools** menu. Expand the **www.cengage.com** cluster.
3. Right-click the **www.cengage.com** NLB cluster and select **Control Hosts, Drainstop** to stop all traffic to the cluster. Click **OK.**

4. Right-click the **www.cengage.com** NLB cluster and select **Delete Cluster**. Click **Yes** to confirm the deletion. After the cluster is removed, close the **Network Load Balancing Manager**.

This step might take a couple of minutes because the Network Load Balancing Manager removes both DC1 and DC2 from the cluster.

5. Start **Server Manager** from the **Administrative Tools** menu. Select **Features** and click **Remove Features**.
6. Deselect **Network Load Balancing** and click **Next**.
7. Click **Remove** to confirm that you want to remove **Network Load Balancing**. If prompted to restart the server, click **Restart Now**. If you are not prompted, restart the server anyway.
8. Log on to **DC2**. Start **Server Manager** from the **Administrative Tools** menu. Select **Features** and click **Remove Features**.
9. Deselect **Network Load Balancing** and click **Next**.
10. Click **Remove** to confirm that you want to remove Network Load Balancing. If prompted to restart the server, click **Restart Now**. If you are not prompted, restart the server anyway.
11. Log on to **DC1** with a domain **Administrator** account to allow the removal to be completed. After the system screen indicates that Network Load Balancing has been removed, click **Close**.
12. Log on to **DC2** with a domain **Administrator** account to allow the removal to be completed. After the system screen indicates that Network Load Balancing has been removed, click **Close**.

8

Failover Clusters

A **failover cluster** is a group of independent servers configured together to provide high availability of a service or application. Servers within a failover cluster are referred to as nodes; if one node fails, another node is able to take over the load.

Figure 8-11 shows a simple two-node failover cluster. One node (SQL1) is active and the other is inactive. All user requests are processed by the active node using the shared storage, which is also accessible to the inactive node.

The inactive node is connected directly to the active node and regularly monitors the heartbeat of the active node. If the active node fails, the inactive node can take over and provide the same level of service as the active node. Clients connect to the cluster, which presents itself to end users as a single server with a single name and IP address. Clients don't know whether they're connected to SQL1 or SQL2, and it doesn't matter—if a node fails, the cluster automatically switches to the other node and users experience the same level of service.

Windows Server 2008 Enterprise and Datacenter editions support as many as 16 nodes in a failover cluster. It is possible to host different services and applications on different nodes, but this can quickly become complex and reduce the reliability of the failover cluster. Most enterprises use a single two-node failover cluster for a specific service or application.

Two key terms related to failover clusters are failover and failback.

- **Failover.** When one node in a failover cluster fails, another instance will take over for the failed node.
- **Failback.** When a failed node comes back online, services that moved to another node in the cluster can be returned to the original node.

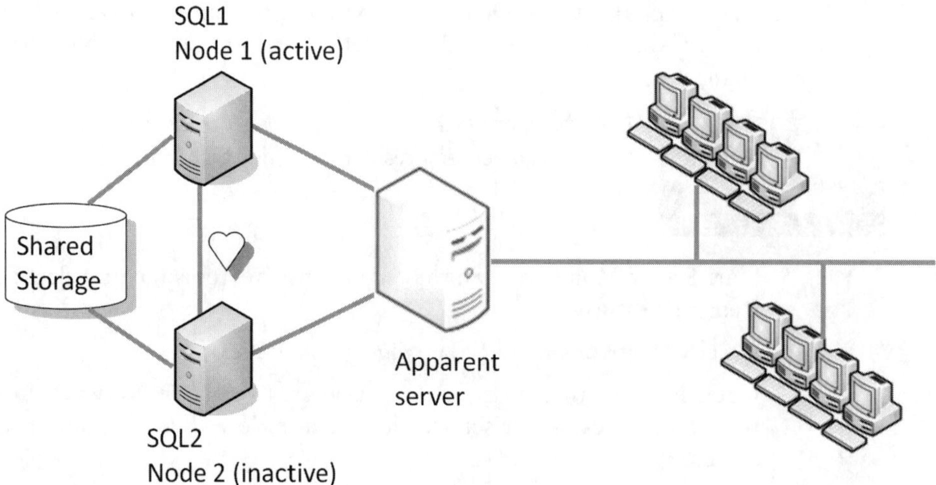

Figure 8-11 A two-node failover cluster

Courtesy Course Technology/Cengage Learning

An important point is that nodes in the cluster have access to shared storage. Storage can be in a serial attached SCSI (SAS) array or a storage area network (SAN), but the same data is available to every node in the cluster. Also, while the storage is shared among the nodes in the cluster, other systems do not have direct access to the storage. Storage solutions and connectivity to the storage are discussed later in this chapter.

Failover Cluster Requirements

The requirements to support failover clusters are much more stringent than those to support an NLB cluster. When a failover cluster is designed, the hardware is typically purchased specifically to support the failover cluster, which often results in a higher cost.

- **Operating system.** Your server must be running the Windows Server 2008 Enterprise, Datacenter, or Itanium Edition to support failover clustering. The Windows Server 2008 Standard and Web editions do not include the failover clustering feature.
- **Application.** The applications or services supported on the cluster must be *cluster aware*. Some applications like Microsoft Exchange Server and Microsoft SQL Server are cluster aware and can be hosted as nodes in a cluster. Others, like DFS Replication, are not cluster aware, which prevents DFS replicated folders from being hosted on a cluster's shared storage. A DFS namespace without DFS replicated data can be placed in a cluster.
- **Hardware.** Hardware used in a failover cluster is often more expensive. Whenever possible, servers in a failover cluster should be matched as closely as they can, and all hardware must be marked as "Certified for Windows Server 2008."
- **Shared storage.** Storage must be available to all nodes in the cluster. Because storage can be a single point of failure, it often includes internal redundancy, such as with RAID-5 or RAID-10.
- **Network adapters.** The nodes need connectivity to the network with at least one network adapter, and are often connected to other nodes in the cluster with a second network adapter.

Microsoft includes the Validate a Configuration wizard, which can validate hardware (servers, network and storage). An activity later in this chapter leads you through the steps to run this wizard.

Quorums

The **quorum model** has been changed in Windows Server 2008 and now combines nodes and shared disk resources to create a quorum. Each node and shared resource has a vote in the quorum, but the quorum can be established in different ways.

Generically, a **quorum** refers to the minimum number of members required to conduct business and make decisions. For example, an organization may require at least 51 percent of its members to be present for a meeting to create a quorum. Similarly, a failover cluster requires a majority of votes to continue operating the cluster after a failure. Nodes have a vote in the quorum, and disks or file shares can also have a vote in the quorum.

Four quorum models are available from the Failover Cluster Management console. Figure 8-12 shows the quorum model selection screen, which you can access by right-clicking the cluster and selecting More Actions, Configure Cluster Quorum Settings.

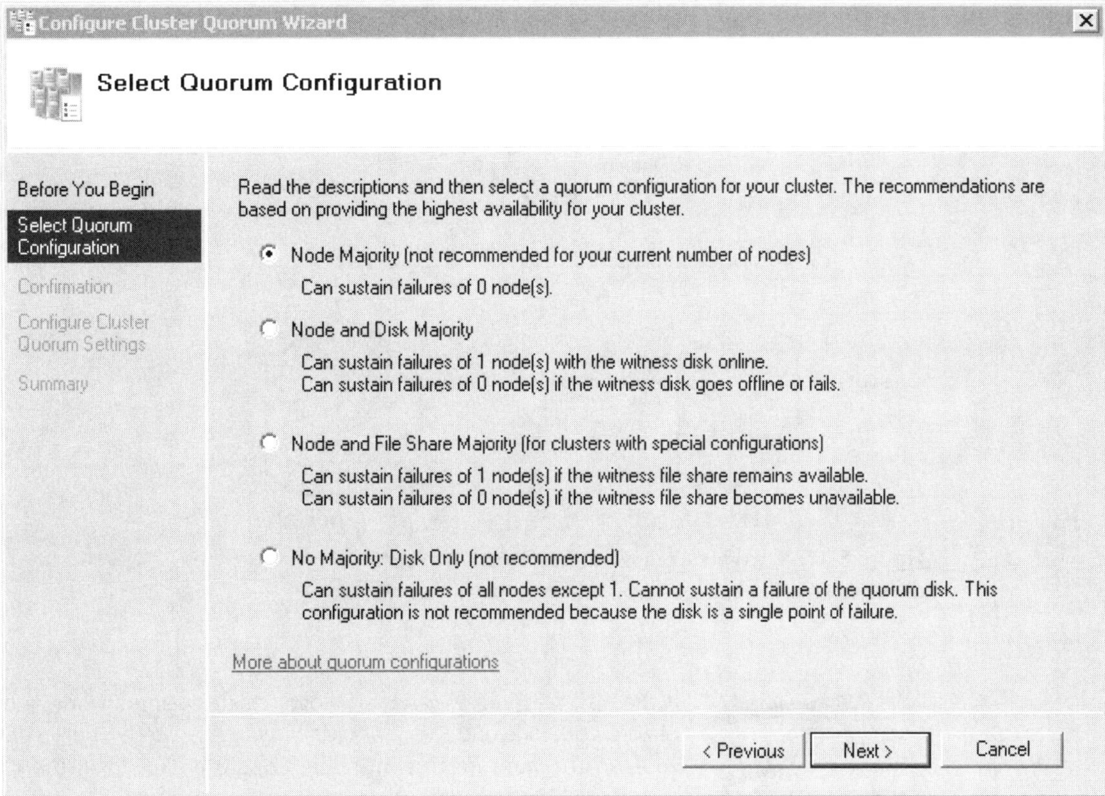

Figure 8-12 Selecting a quorum model

Courtesy Course Technology/Cengage Learning

Two of the models are the same as they were with Windows Server 2003 clusters, and two are new:

- **No Majority (Disk Only).** This model is the same as the Windows Server 2003 shared disk quorum. If the disk fails, the cluster fails.
- **Node Majority.** This model is the same as the Windows Server 2003 majority node set; it doesn't include the disk in the quorum. Clusters should have at least three nodes for this model. If one node of a two-node cluster failed, only one node (50 percent) would be up, which isn't enough for a quorum, so the cluster would fail. If one node of a three-node cluster failed, two nodes would be up and the cluster would continue to operate.
- **Node and Disk Majority.** Nodes and the disk are allowed to vote in the quorum. As long as a majority is available, the cluster will continue. For example, a two-node cluster has three votes; each node has a vote, as does the shared resource. Any one of the three can fail,

but the cluster will continue to operate. When using this model, the disk is referred to as a witness disk in the quorum.

- **Node and File Share Majority**. This model is similar to the Node and Disk Majority, except that the shared resource isn't actually a disk; it is a share accessible by nodes in the cluster. File shares are used as resources in multi-site cluster configurations, which are explored in greater depth later in this chapter. Each node and the file share have votes in the quorum.

As an example, Figure 8-13 shows a two-node failover cluster with a file share used as the shared resource. The shared resource could be stored either on a disk or a file share; it is called a witness in the quorum. Each node has a vote and the witness has a vote. If either node fails, the cluster can still operate because there are still two votes.

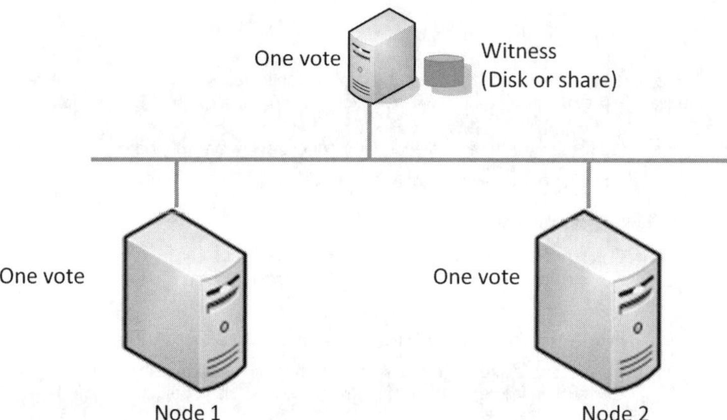

Figure 8-13 A two-node failover cluster with a witness

Courtesy Course Technology/Cengage Learning

If the disk fails in a two-node failover cluster using a Node and Disk Majority or Node and File Share Majority, the cluster will have enough votes in the quorum to continue to operate. However, the cluster will still fail because data stored on the disks is needed by the cluster nodes.

The choice of quorum model largely depends on the number of nodes in the cluster, as summarized in Table 8-3. If the cluster has an odd number of nodes, you would use the Node Majority quorum model. If the cluster has an even number of nodes, you would use either Node and File Share Majority (for multi-site failover clusters) or Node and Disk Majority.

Table 8-3 Quorum model recommendations

Description of Cluster	Quorum Model Recommendation
Odd number of nodes	Node Majority
Even number of nodes (in a single site)	Node and Disk Majority
Even number of nodes (in multiple sites)	Node and File Share Majority
Even number of nodes with no shared storage	Node and File Share Majority

Some applications also recommend specific quorum models. When adding applications (such as Microsoft SQL Server or Microsoft Exchange Server) to a failover cluster, you should refer to the documentation for the application.

Cluster Storage and Storage Solutions

Because failover clusters require dedicated storage, it becomes a significant concern. You should be aware of the different types of storage that are supported by Windows Server 2008 failover clusters and the different storage solutions used to host the disks.

The storage should be formatted as basic disks with NTFS. Windows Server 2008 failover clusters do not provide native support for dynamic disks.

Dynamic disks can be supported with third-party tools, but generally the extras you can get from dynamic disks are supported by GPT disks, so dynamic disks are not needed.

Two disk storage formats are supported by Windows Server 2008 failover clusters:

- **Master boot record** (**MBR**). This is traditional disk storage, but it has a 2 Terabyte (TB) maximum size, which can sometimes be a concern for failover clusters.
- **GUID Partition Table** (**GPT**). Newer Globally Unique Identifier (GUID) Partition Table disks are supported with Windows Server 2008 clusters. GPT disks support physical disks as large as 16 Exabyte (EB).

Disks for a failover cluster are hosted in a dedicated storage solution. This storage solution often includes built-in redundancy for each disk by using Redundant Array of Inexpensive Disks (RAID) such as RAID-5 or RAID-10.

RAID is also known as Redundant Array of Independent Disks.

Directly attached Small Computer System Interface (SCSI) disks were supported with previous versions of clustering, but they are not supported with Windows Server 2008 clustering. However, two types of common storage solutions are supported:

- A **serial attached SCSI** (**SAS**) array is a SCSI disk array connected to the servers using serial connections. This array can be used if the hosts in the cluster are physically close to each other.
- A **storage area network** (**SAN**) is a specialized network designed to host disks and make the disks appear to servers as though the disks are locally attached.

Logical Unit Numbers in Storage Arrays

Storage volumes within storage arrays are identified with logical unit numbers (LUNs). An important consideration when using LUNs with failover clusters is that they must be isolated from other servers. In other words, the LUNs used for shared storage in a failover cluster should only be available to servers in the cluster.

A LUN in a storage array is similar to a storage volume on a traditional server disk. Instead of identifying volumes with letters like C:, D:, and so on, LUNs are used to identify the separate volumes.

Because storage solutions often are used for much more than just failover clusters, you usually won't have a separate storage array dedicated to the failover cluster, but you will need to ensure that separate LUNs are dedicated for the cluster. Figure 8-14 shows one example of how a storage array could be configured for multiple clusters and servers in the organization. In the figure, LUN 1 is assigned to Cluster 1, LUN 2 is assigned to Cluster 2, and LUN 3 is being used by Server 5.

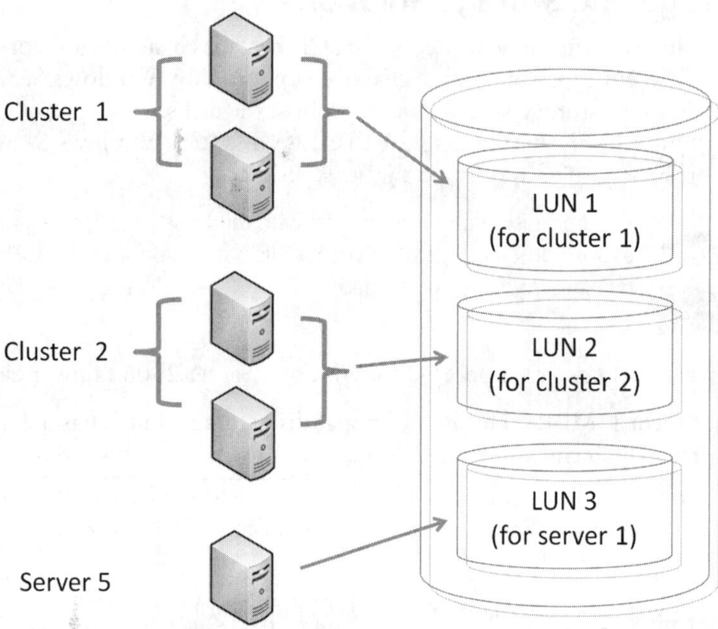

Figure 8-14 Assigning LUNs to failover clusters

Courtesy Course Technology/Cengage Learning

Multiple LUNs can be assigned to any cluster, depending on the needs of the applications and services within the cluster.

As another example, you can use Microsoft's Hyper-V virtualization technology to host several servers. Hyper-V allows you to consolidate multiple physical servers onto a single host server in a virtual environment. A drawback is that the host server becomes a single point of failure. To address this problem, a second identical server can be added and the virtual servers can be configured in three separate failover clusters.

Figure 8-15 shows how these servers could share the separate LUNs. Server1 and Server4 share LUN 1, Server2 and Server5 share LUN 2, and Server3 and Server6 share LUN 3. In other words, even though they are virtual servers, they are still configured with shared storage as if they were physical servers.

Cluster Connectivity to Storage Solutions

Connectivity to the storage disks is also a significant concern. The method of connecting to the storage solution can affect cost, performance, and fault tolerance.

The two primary types of supported connectivity are Fibre Channel (FC) and Internet Small Computer System Interface (iSCSI). Fibre Channel connections are dedicated connections and media, while iSCSI connections can use an existing network.

- **Fibre Channel** is the standard or traditional method used to connect to disk storage solutions. It can use either twisted-pair or fiber-optic media, but it more commonly uses fiber today. Only disk transfer traffic is transferred over the FC network. FC requires specialized hardware and can be expensive.
- **iSCSI** uses TCP/IP to transfer data. Because most networks already have a TCP/IP component, iSCSI can be implemented without extensive network modifications, and without

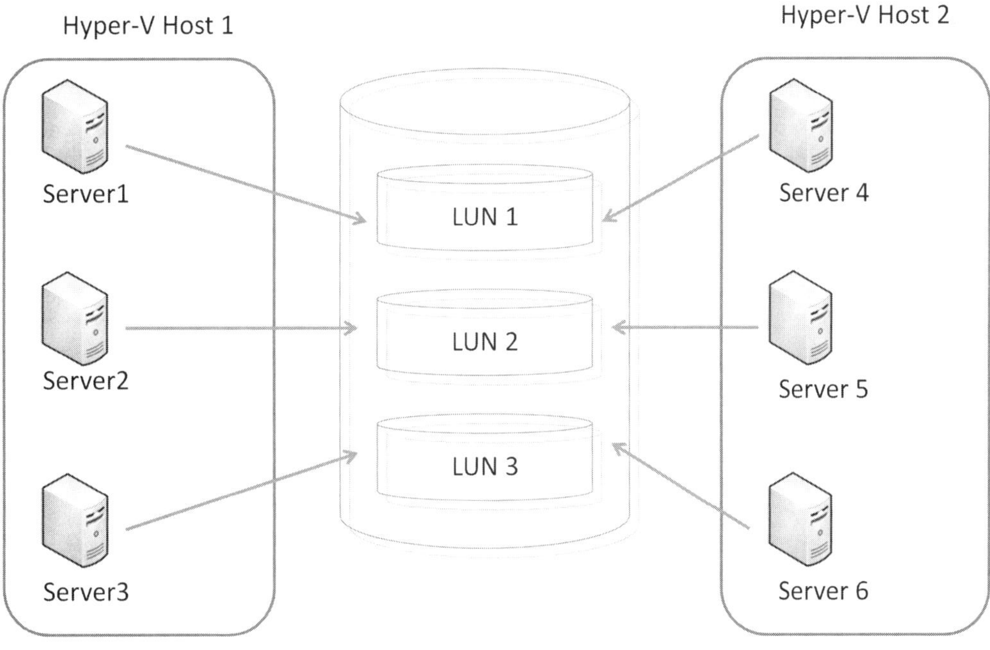

Figure 8-15 Assigning LUNs with Hyper-V

Courtesy Course Technology/Cengage Learning

purchasing additional dedicated hardware. This results in a lower initial cost, which is an overriding benefit of iSCSI. It can also be used to transmit data over long distances or across wide area networks (WANs).

Table 8-4 compares the characteristics of Fibre Channel and iSCSI.

Table 8-4 A comparison of Fibre Channel and iSCSI connectivity

	Fibre Channel	iSCSI
Hardware	Requires dedicated hardware.	Can use traditional network adapters and existing TCP/IP network infrastructure (if bandwidth is available).
Cost	More expensive than iSCSI because dedicated hardware is required.	Less expensive if existing hardware is used.
Performance	Generally the performance is better because dedicated hardware is used only for the disk access.	Performance is dependent on the network capabilities and usage. You can get high performance from a 10 Gbps LAN with current low utilization, but poor performance from a 100 Mbps LAN with current high utilization.
Network Adapters	Uses Multipath Input/Output (MPIO) for fault tolerance and load balancing.	Cannot use teamed network adapters. Can use multiple independent adapters.

Teamed network adapters are two or more network adapters using the same connection. They are sometimes used for fault tolerance in case one of the adapters fails, or for load balancing on multiple adapters.

Cluster-Aware Services and Applications

A **cluster-aware** service or application is designed to work with failover cluster components. It can easily communicate its status to the cluster so that the failover cluster knows when the service or application has failed, and when the cluster needs to fail over to another node. Some generic applications, scripts, and services can also work within a failover cluster, though the cluster may not be as reliable if a failure occurs.

Figure 8-16 shows the screen used to add services or applications. This screen provides a partial list of services or applications supported in failover clusters.

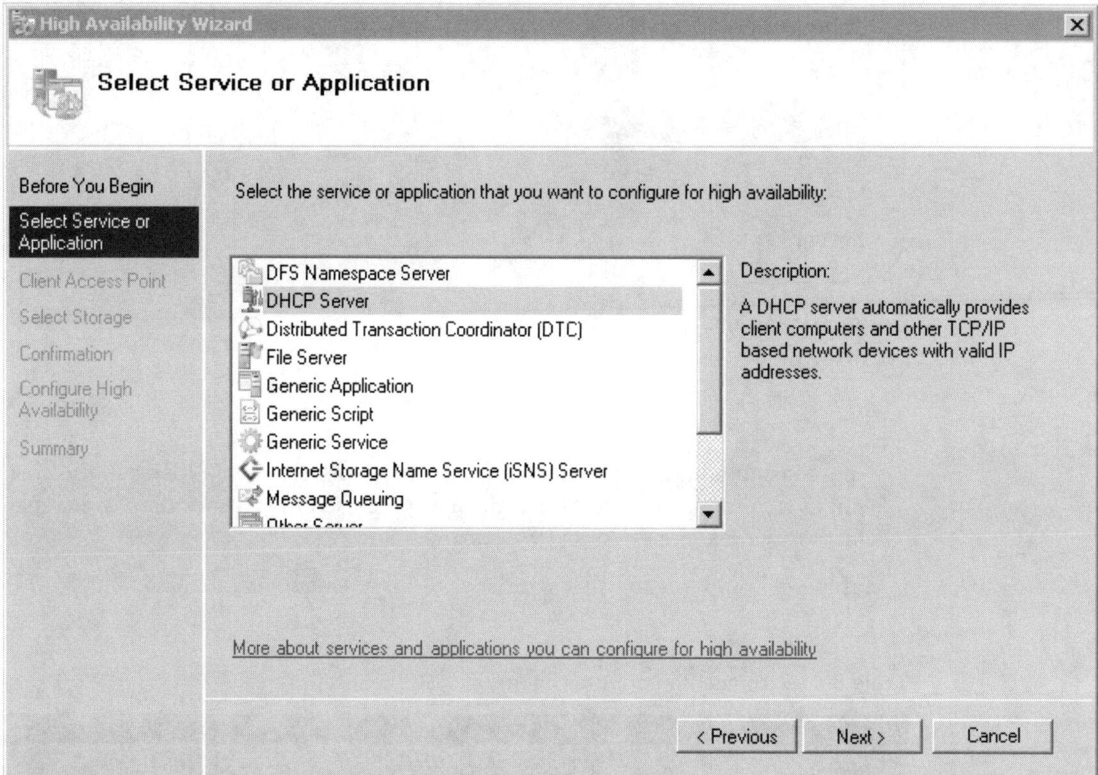

Figure 8-16 Selecting a service or application for a failover cluster

Courtesy Course Technology/Cengage Learning

Some common services and applications used with failover clusters are:

- **Application servers.** Microsoft SQL Server database servers and Microsoft Exchange Server messaging servers are two application servers that can be configured in a failover cluster.
- **DFS Namespace Server.** A Distributed File System (DFS) namespace provides a virtual view of shared folders on multiple servers. The DFS Namespace Server can be protected in a failover cluster. However, a DFS Replication server holds actual copies of the replicated data and cannot be protected by a failover cluster.
- **DHCP servers.** Dynamic Host Configuration Protocol (DHCP) servers issue TCP/IP lease information to clients and are cluster-aware.
- **File and print servers.** Both file and print servers can be used within clusters to increase the availability of file and print resources.

Failover Clusters for Multiple Sites

While it is most common to have failover clusters in the same physical location, it's also possible to have failover clusters with some nodes located in other sites. The benefit is that users can usually connect to the local server to get quick responses. However, if the local server fails, other nodes in other sites can still respond to user requests. Failover clusters are used and configured a little differently in multi-site configurations.

Figure 8-17 shows an example of a two-node, multi-site cluster configuration with both nodes configured as active and inactive nodes. SQL1 is configured as the active node for users in Virginia Beach and as inactive for users in Chesapeake in case SQL2 fails. SQL2 is configured as the active node for users in Chesapeake and as inactive for users in Virginia Beach in case SQL1 fails. When using a server as both an active and inactive node, the hardware must be robust enough to support both loads at the same time.

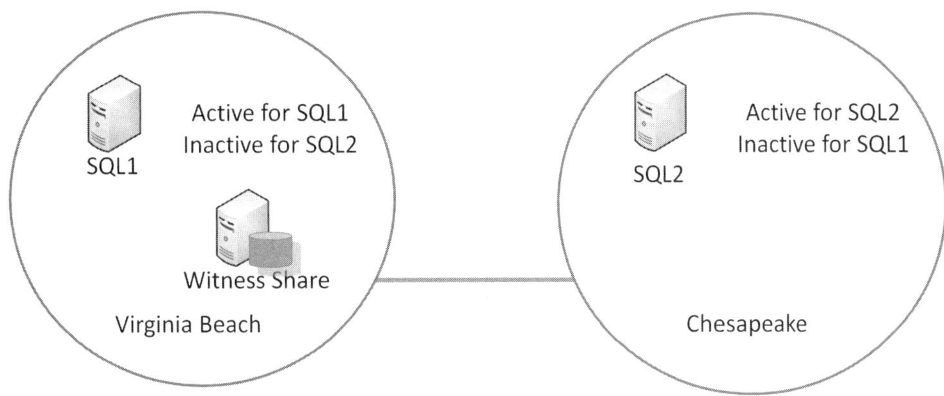

Figure 8-17 Multi-site failover cluster with a witness share

Courtesy Course Technology/Cengage Learning

Notice that the figure shows a witness share used for storage. Each node can access the data on the witness share over the WAN link. This witness share would have a vote in the quorum.

Instead of using a single share for storage, it's also possible to use replicated data. Each site would have a copy of the data stored locally. The witness share is still used to provide a vote for the quorum.

The Node and File Share Majority quorum model should be used in this two-node failover cluster so that the witness share has a vote. Using this model ensures that if either node fails, the other node can continue to operate. You should use the Node and File Share Majority quorum model in a multi-site cluster configuration any time you have an even number of nodes.

If you have three sites and three nodes in the multi-site cluster, you can use the Node Majority quorum model instead. If one of the nodes fails, two nodes will be up and able to vote, giving the cluster the majority needed for a quorum.

Adding the Failover Cluster Feature

The Failover Cluster Management console is used to validate the hardware configuration of nodes and to create and manage clusters. It was added as a feature in Windows Server 2008.

Figure 8-18 shows the Failover Cluster Management console. In addition to the tools used to create and manage clusters, it includes a wealth of links for help and additional documentation on clusters.

The following activity shows how to add the Failover Clustering feature.

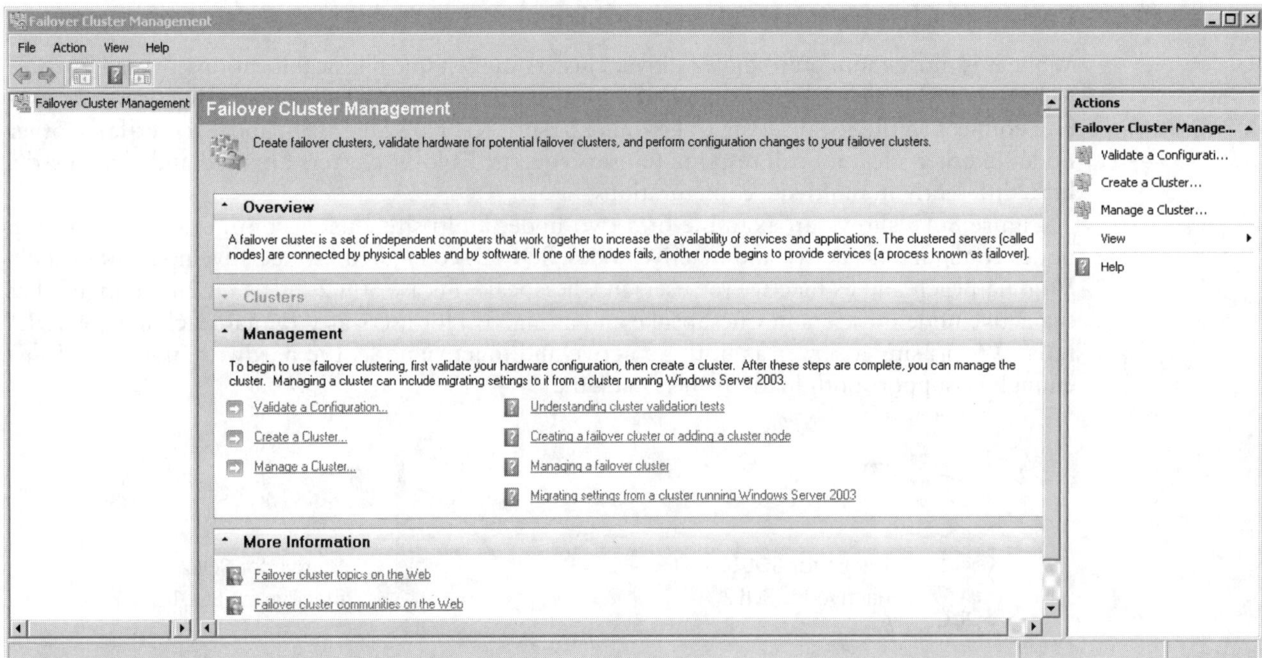

Figure 8-18 The Failover Cluster Management console

Courtesy Course Technology/Cengage Learning

Ensure that the Network Load Balancing feature was removed in Activity 8-4 before adding the Failover Clustering feature. While the wizard won't stop you from adding the Failover Clustering feature, errors can result and lock up the system.

Activity 8-5: Adding the Failover Clustering Feature

Time Required: 20 minutes
Objective: Add the Failover Clustering feature.

Description: You are considering creating a failover cluster with DC1 as one of the nodes. You first want to add the Failover Clustering feature so that you can run the Validate a Configuration wizard. This activity should be run using DC1 and DC2.

1. Start **DC1** and **DC2**. Log on to **DC1** using the domain **Administrator** account.
2. Start **Server Manager** via the **Administrative Tools** menu.
3. Select **Features** and click **Add Feature.**
4. On the **Select Features** page, select the **Failover Clustering** feature. Click **Next.**
5. Click **Install.**
6. When the installation is complete, click **Close.**
7. Repeat Steps 1 through 5 to add the Failover Clustering feature to **DC2.**

Running the Validate a Configuration Wizard

Once the Failover Clustering feature is added, you can run the Validate a Configuration wizard. This tool can be used to validate the hardware used in the failover cluster and the configuration of a cluster. Failover clusters can be very finicky; a primary reason they don't work as expected is hardware incompatibilities.

All tests must pass this wizard for Microsoft to provide formal support to the failover cluster configuration. The following activity shows how to run the wizard.

Activity 8-6: Validating Hardware

Time Required: 15 minutes
Objective: Run the Validate a Configuration Wizard.

Description: You are considering creating a failover cluster with DC1 as one of the nodes. You've added the Failover Clustering feature and now want to run the Validate a Configuration wizard. This activity should be run using DC1.

1. Start **DC1** and log on using the domain **Administrator** account.
2. Start **Failover Cluster Management** via the **Administrative Tools** menu.
3. Click the **Validate a Configuration** link in the **Management** section.
4. Review the information on the **Before You Begin** screen and click **Next**.
5. On the **Select Servers or a Cluster** screen, enter **DC1** and click **Add**. DC1 will be added as **DC1.Cengage.com**. Click **Next**.
6. Accept the default selection of **Run All Tests (Recommended)** on the **Testing Options** screen and click **Next**.
7. Review the information on the **Confirmation** screen and click **Next**.
8. When the wizard is complete, the **Summary** screen will appear and look similar to Figure 8-19. In the figure, the report has been scrolled down to the Storage section.

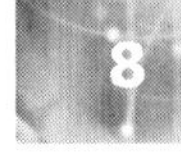

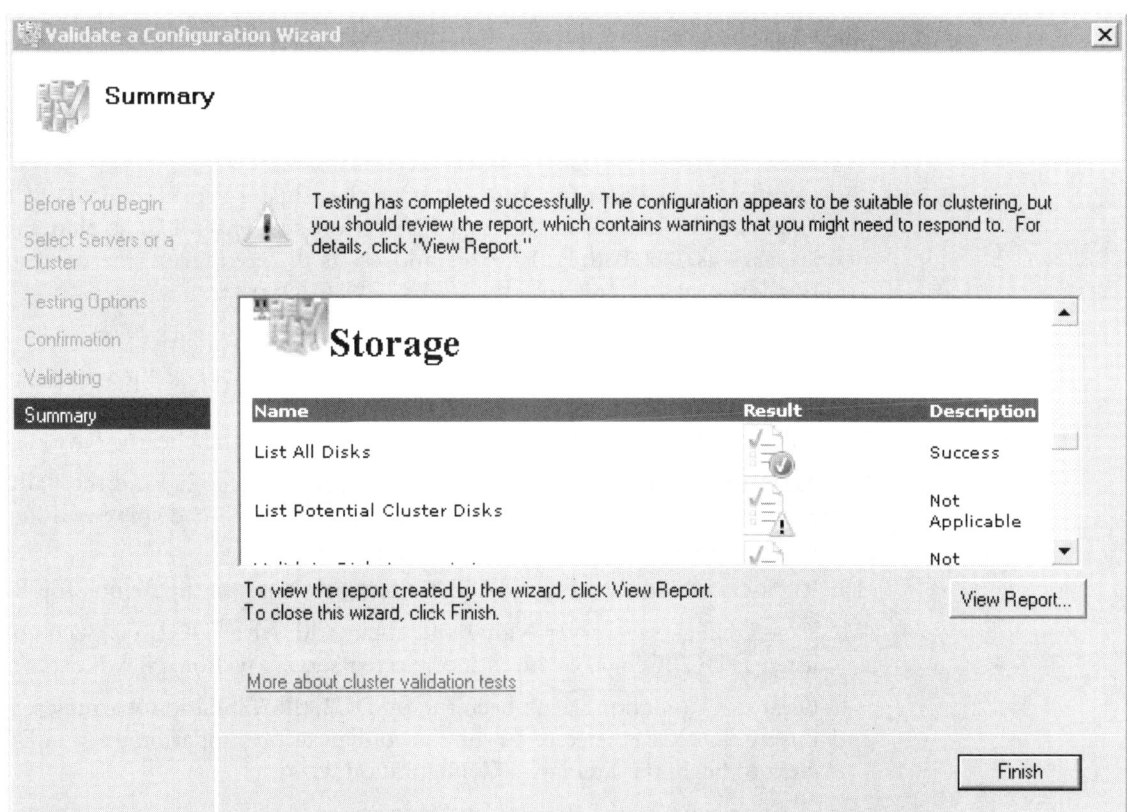

Figure 8-19 Viewing the result of the Validate a Configuration wizard

Courtesy Course Technology/Cengage Learning

Scroll through the summary to view the different warnings.

9. Click **View Report** to start **Internet Explorer** and view a detailed, dynamic HTML page. You can click any of the links to reveal more details. If desired, you can save the report by selecting **Save As** from the **Page** menu and clicking **Save**.
10. Return to the **Validate a Configuration Wizard** screen and click **Finish**.

Creating a Failover Cluster

The Failover Cluster Management console can be used to add a failover cluster. The following activity shows how to create a two-node failover cluster.

The following steps are not intended to create a fully functioning failover cluster. The hardware would be too expensive for a test environment. Instead, the goal is to familiarize users with some of the tools that can be used with failover clusters.

Activity 8-7: Creating a Failover Cluster

Time Required: 20 minutes
Objective: Create a failover cluster.

Description: You have installed the Failover Clustering feature on DC1 and DC2 and now need to create a failover cluster with these two servers as nodes.

1. Start **DC1** and **DC2** and log on to **DC1** using the domain **Administrator** account.
2. Start **Failover Cluster Management** via the **Administrative Tools** menu.
3. Click the **Create a Cluster** link in the **Management** section.
4. Review the information on the **Before You Begin** page and click **Next**.
5. On the **Select Servers** screen, type **DC1** and click **Add**. The server will be added as **DC1.Cengage.com**. Click **Next**.
6. On the **Access Point for Administering the Cluster** screen, enter **FailCluster** as the **Cluster** name. Click in the **Address** section and enter **110** so that the IP address appears as **192.168.1.110**. This address is different from the currently assigned IP address of 192.168.1.10 for DC1's NIC. Click **Next**.
7. Review the information on the **Confirmation** page and click **Next**.
8. Review the information on the **Summary** screen and click **View Report**. This report shows the detailed steps taken when the cluster was created. If desired, you can save the report by selecting **Save As** from the **Page** menu and clicking **Save**.
9. Return to the **Failover Cluster Management** console. Expand the **FailCluster.Cengage.com** cluster, expand **Nodes**, and select **DC1**. Your display will look similar to Figure 8-20.
10. Right-click **Nodes** and select **Add Node**. Click **Next** on the **Before You Begin** screen.
11. Type **DC2** as the **Server Name** and click **Add**. After **DC2** has been contacted and listed as **DC2.Cengage.com** in the **Selected Servers** section, click **Next**.
12. Because a validation hasn't been run on **DC2**, the **Validation Warning** screen appears. Ensure that **Yes** is selected to run the configuration validation tests on **DC2** and click **Next** to begin the **Validate a Configuration** wizard.
    a. Click **Next** on the **Before You Begin** screen.
    b. Ensure that **Run All Tests (Recommended)** is selected on the **Testing Options** screen and click **Next**.
    c. Review the information on the **Confirmation** screen and click **Next**.

d. When the wizard is complete, the **Summary** screen appears; it looks similar to Figure 8-21.

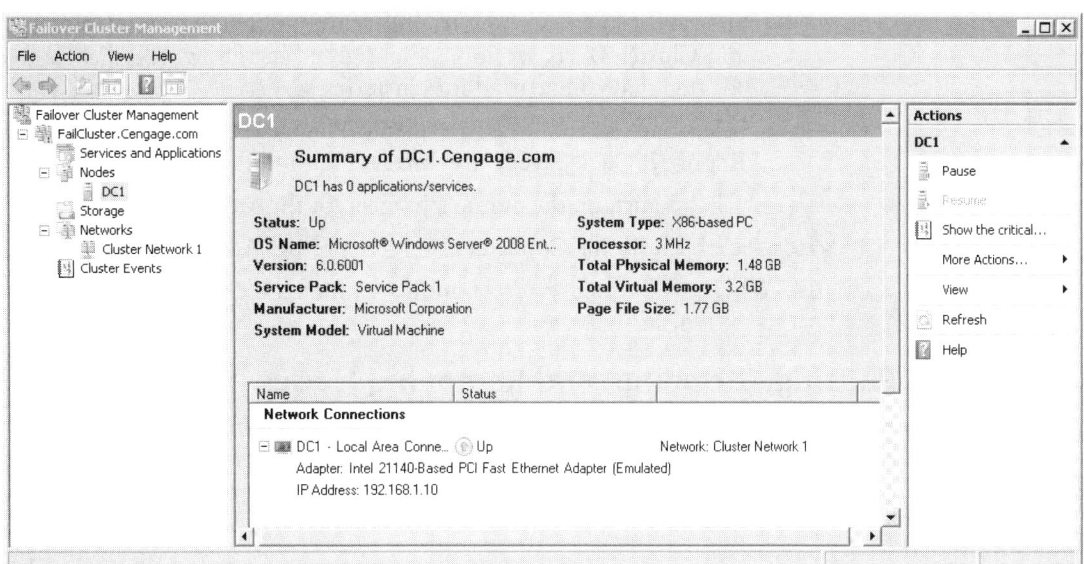

Figure 8-20 Using the Failover Cluster Management console to view the details of a node in a cluster

Courtesy Course Technology/Cengage Learning

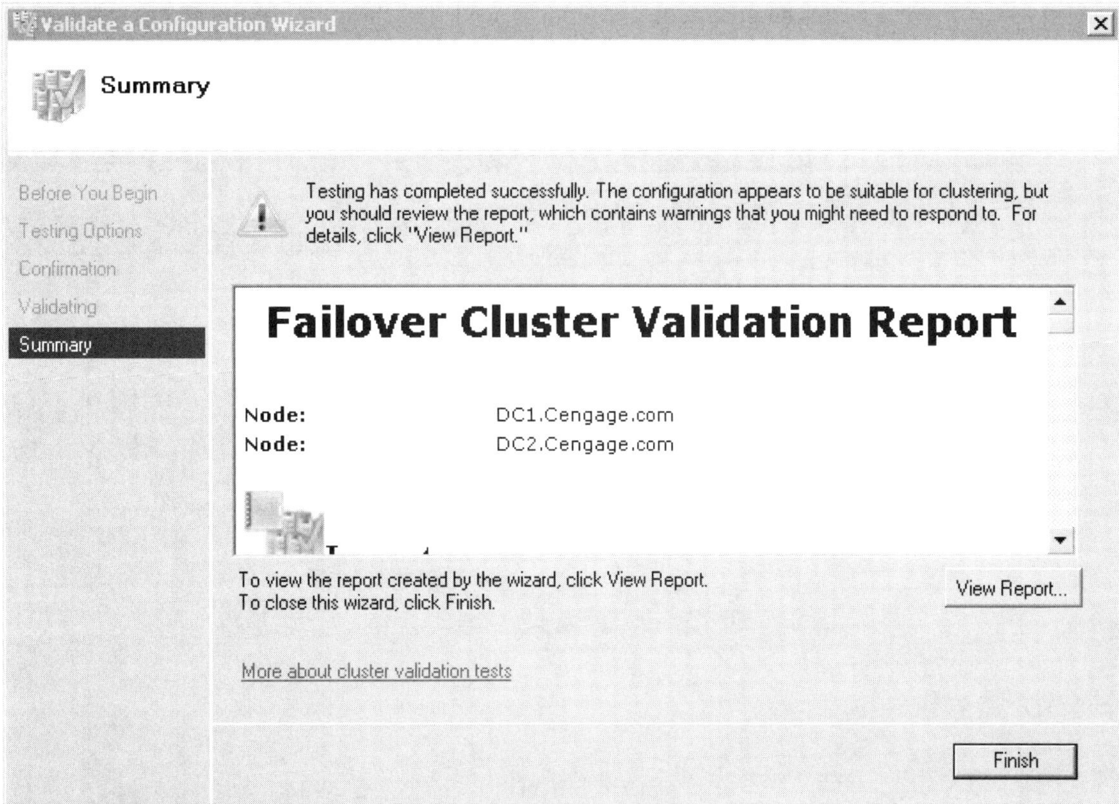

Figure 8-21 Viewing the result of the Validate a Configuration wizard

Courtesy Course Technology/Cengage Learning

Although the report indicates that the configuration is suitable for clustering, it doesn't have shared storage, so it won't be able to support a functioning failover cluster. Notice that this report shows the results from two nodes: DC1 and DC2.

e. Click **View Report**. Scroll through the report. You'll notice that several items in the report have a yellow triangle with an explanation mark in it. The **List Potential Cluster Disks** section is highlighted in yellow. It indicates that no disks were located that can be used for clustering.

f. Select **Save As** from the **Page** menu. Change the name to **Failover Cluster Validation Report 2**. Click **Save**. Close **Internet Explorer**.

g. Click **Finish** on the **Summary** screen of the **Validate a Configuration Wizard**.

13. Click **Next** on the **Confirmation** screen of the **Add Node Wizard**.

14. When the **Summary** screen indicates that the cluster node was successfully added, click **Finish**.

Pausing, Stopping, and Removing Nodes in a Cluster

It's sometimes necessary to pause, stop, or remove a node from a cluster. As a common example, when you need to perform maintenance on a node and then reboot it, the cluster service should be stopped. If the server is no longer needed in the failover cluster, the node should be evicted. The results of pausing, stopping, and evicting a node are:

- **Pause.** Existing users and resources stay online, but users or resources cannot be added. You can pause a node in preparation to stop a node without affecting connected clients. Connections can be monitored, and when the last connection is disconnected, the service can be stopped.
- **Stop.** This option stops the cluster service on the cluster node; it will no longer function in the cluster until the cluster service is restarted.
- **Evict.** When the node is no longer needed in the cluster, you can evict the node, as shown in Figure 8-22. In the Failover Cluster Management console, right-click the node and select More Actions, Evict.

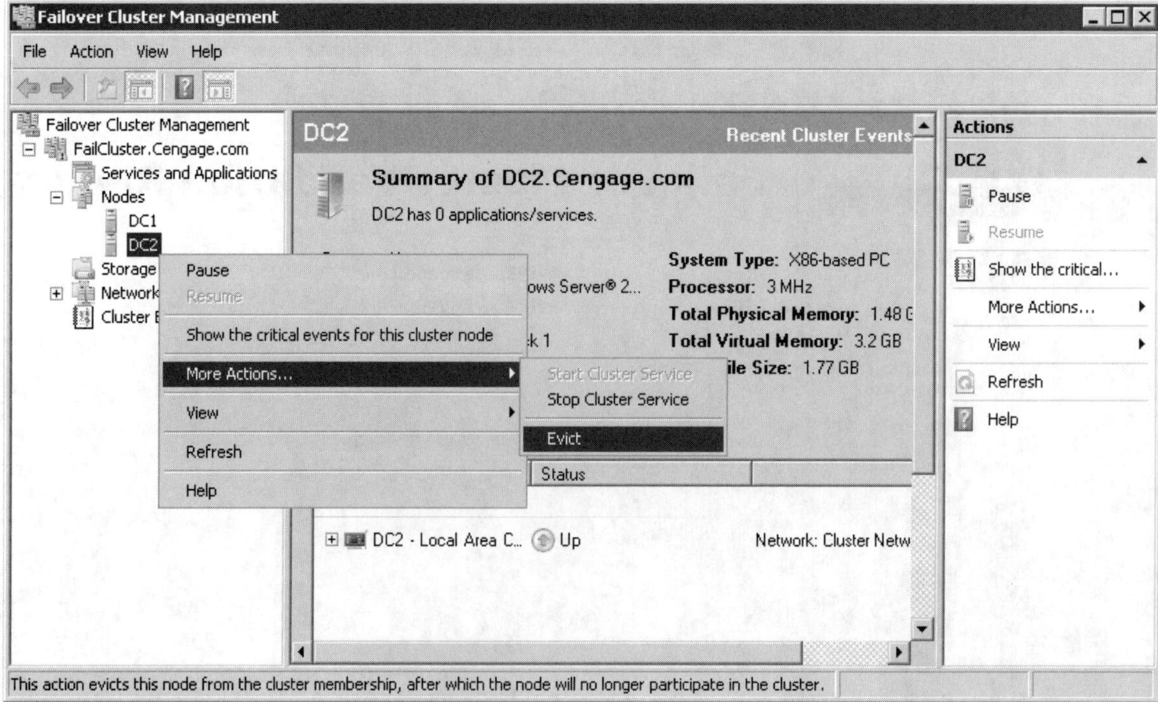

Figure 8-22 Evicting a node from a failover cluster

Courtesy Course Technology/Cengage Learning

Removing a Failover Cluster

If a failover cluster is no longer needed, you can remove it by destroying it in the Failover Cluster Management console. The Failover Clustering feature can interfere with other functions on the server, so it should also be removed if it is no longer needed. The following activity shows how you can destroy the failover cluster and remove the Failover Clustering feature.

Activity 8-8: Destroying a Failover Cluster and Removing the Failover Clustering Feature

Time Required: 20 minutes
Objective: Destroy a failover cluster and remove the Failover Clustering feature.

Description: A failover cluster that was created on DC1 and DC2 is no longer needed. You need to destroy the failover cluster and then remove the Failover Clustering feature from both nodes. This activity should be run using DC1 and DC2.

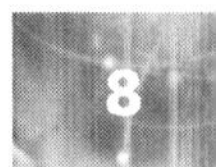

1. Start **DC1** and **DC2**. Log on to **DC1** with the domain **Administrator** account.
2. Start the **Failover Cluster Management** console via the **Administrative Tools** menu.
3. Right-click **FailCluster.Cengage.com** and select **More Actions, Destroy Cluster,** as shown in Figure 8-23. When prompted, click **Destroy Cluster FailCluster**. The cluster will be permanently removed. When the process is finished, close the Failover Cluster Management console.

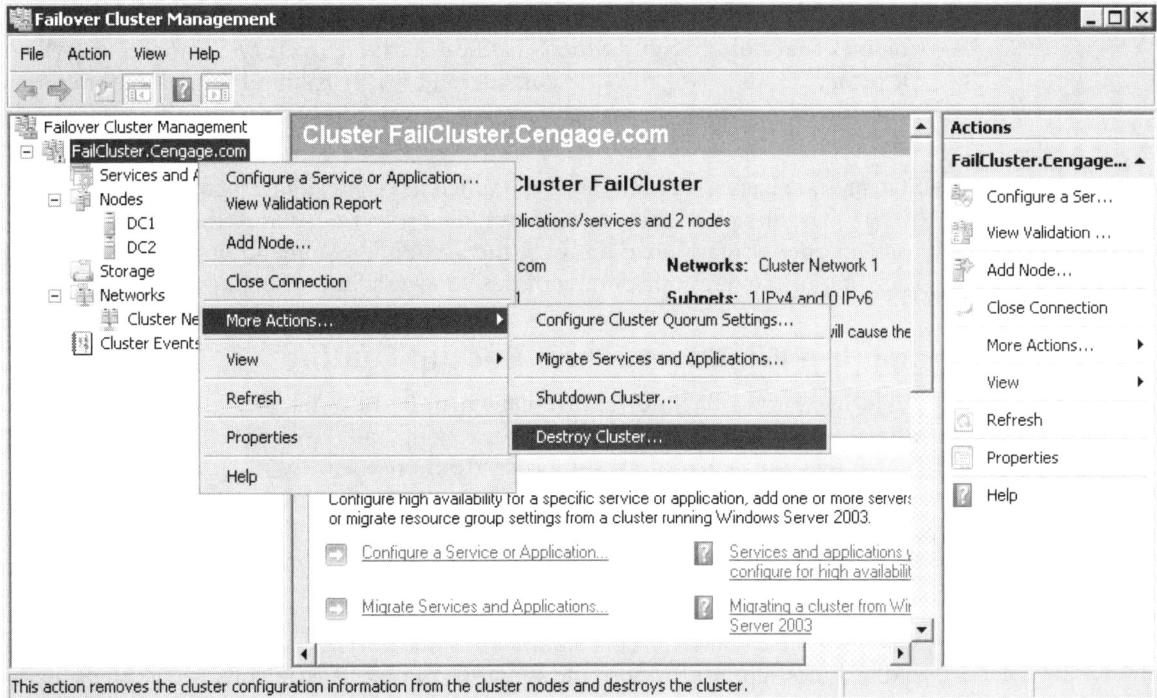

Figure 8-23 Destroying the failover cluster
Courtesy Course Technology/Cengage Learning

4. Start the **Server Manager** console via the **Administrative Tools** menu.
5. Select **Features** and click **Remove Features.**
6. Deselect **Failover Clustering.** When prompted, click **Yes** to continue. Click **Next.**

7. Click **Remove** on the **Confirm Removal Selections** screen. When the removal is complete, click **Close.** Click **Yes** to restart the server and finish the removal.
8. After the server reboots, log on using the domain **Administrator** account. When the removal is complete, click **Close.**
9. Log on to **DC2** with the domain **Administrator** account. If the **Failover Cluster Management** console is open, close it.
10. Complete steps 4 through 8 on **DC2.** The Failover Clustering feature may be removed from DC2 without requiring a reboot. If prompted, restart the server and log on to complete the removal.

Active Directory Backup and Restores

Windows Server 2008 includes a feature that can be used to back up and restore Active Directory. This feature includes several tools and wizards that can perform a single backup or schedule regular backups.

Windows Server Backup can also be used to back up files on Windows Server 2008 servers. However, the objectives for the 70-647 exam specifically mention directory service recovery as part of a business continuity plan, so recovery of Active Directory is the focus in this chapter.

Active Directory can be backed up using one of two methods:

- **Critical Volume backup.** Use the Windows Server Backup console or the Wbadmin command-line tool to back up the contents of all critical volumes. Volumes included as critical volumes are the system volume and the boot volume. Additionally, the volumes that hold SYSVOL, the NTDS.dit Active Directory database, and the Active Directory database log files are considered critical volumes on a domain controller. All of these elements are on the C: drive by default, but they can be moved to other drives.
- **System State backup.** System State data includes critical files such as the registry, boot and system files, files protected by Windows File Protection, and Active Directory files. You can back up only system state data using the Wbadmin command-line tool. However, you can't back up only system state data with the Windows Server Backup GUI.

Adding the Windows Server Backup Feature

The Windows Server Backup feature isn't installed by default. Many enterprises use more sophisticated third-party tools that make backing up and restoring Active Directory a little easier, so the Windows Server Backup feature isn't always needed.

Windows backup tools allow you to back up data to noncritical volumes on the same system, network shares, and writable CD or DVDs. Windows Server Backup doesn't include support for tape backups.

Two Windows Server Backup features can be added:

- **Windows Server Backup.** This feature adds the services used for backup and restore, and includes support for both the Windows Server Backup console and the Wbadmin command-line tool.
- **Command-line tools.** This feature includes support for doing backups with Windows PowerShell commands and scripts. Command-line tools are not needed for the Windows Server Backup console and the Wbadmin command-line tool to function.

Windows Server Backup must be included when the Windows Server Backup feature is added, so your only decision is whether to add the command-line tools. If you plan to automate backups using Windows PowerShell, you must add the command-line tools. However, you can also automate the backups using Wbadmin commands in batch files or the schedule feature within the Windows Server Backup GUI.

Activity 8-9: Adding the Windows Server Backup Feature

Time Required: 10 minutes
Objective: Add the Backup feature.

Description: You want to be able to back up Active Directory on a domain controller using Windows Server 2008 native tools, so you need to add the Windows Server Backup feature. This activity should be run on DC1.

1. Start **DC1** and log on with the domain **Administrator** account.
2. Start the **Server Manager** via the **Administrative Tools** menu.
3. Click **Features** and select **Add Features**.
4. Scroll down and expand the **Windows Server Backup Features** selection. Select **Windows Server Backup**, as shown in Figure 8-24. Click **Next**.

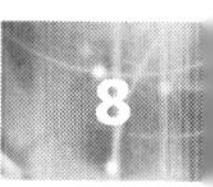

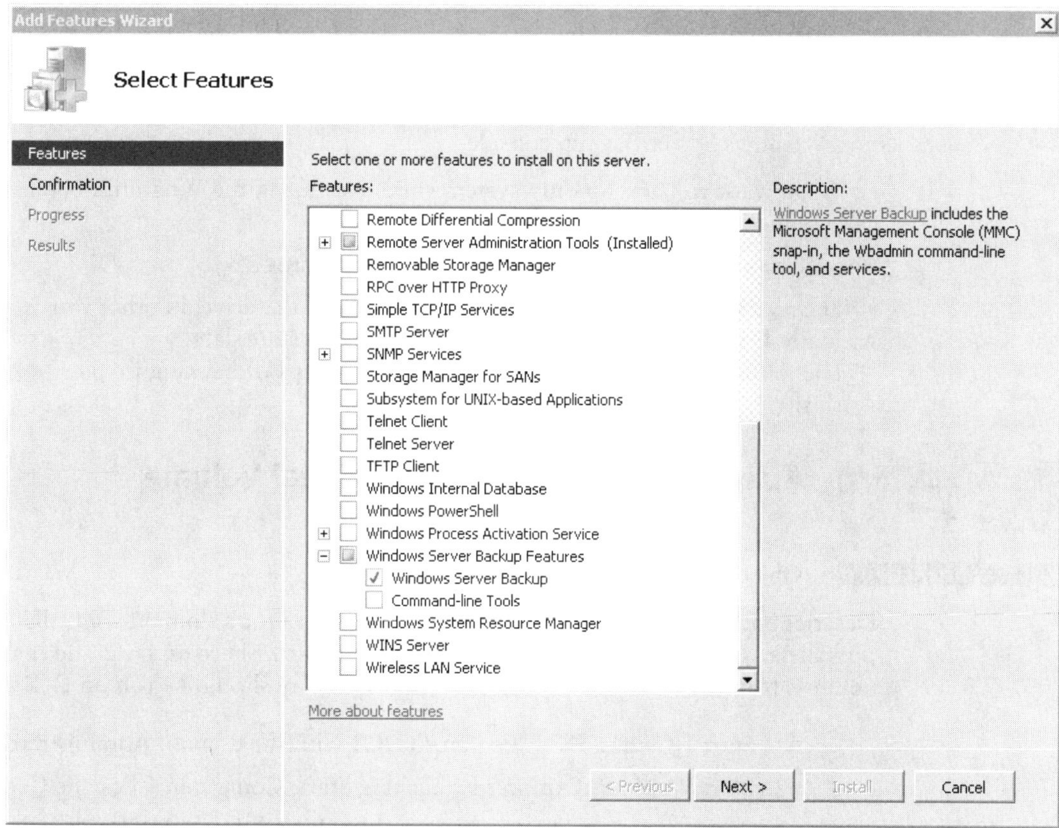

Figure 8-24 Adding the Backup feature
Courtesy Course Technology/Cengage Learning

5. Click **Install** on the **Confirm Installation Selection** screen.

Backing Up Active Directory

After the Windows Server Backup feature is installed, you can perform backups using either the Windows Server Backup graphical user interface (GUI) or the Wbadmin command-line tool. Both have their strengths.

- **Windows Server Backup console.** This console includes wizards that help you configure backups to occur once or on a schedule. The next activity shows you how to use the console to perform a backup. You can only back up Active Directory by performing a critical volume backup using the console. At a minimum, this requires you to back up the C: volume, but you may also have to back up other volumes if default configurations have been modified.
- **Wbadmin.** This command-line tool can be used to perform targeted backups and restores. For example, you can back up system state data without backing up all the data on all critical volumes.

In a critical volume backup, all of the data on the critical volumes is also backed up. Similarly, when a restore is done, all of the data is restored. You cannot restore only Active Directory or only system state data from a critical volume backup.

Be aware of the following limitations when using the native backup tools:

- You cannot back up data from a critical volume to the same critical volume. In other words, if you want to back up the C: drive on a domain controller, you cannot back it up to the C: drive. You can only back it up to another volume.
- You cannot back up only system state data using the Windows Server Backup console. If you want to back up only system state data, use the Wbadmin command.
- You cannot back up data to a network drive using the Wbadmin command. You can back up data to a network share using a Universal Naming Convention (UNC) path with the Windows Server Backup console.

If you want to back up only system state data using the Wbadmin command-line tool, you can use the following command:

```
Wbadmin start systemstatebackup -backuptarget:x:
```

The only variable in this command is the letter of the drive. In other words, you can replace x: with any available drive that doesn't include system state data.

The following activity leads you through the steps of backing up a critical volume to a network share.

Activity 8-10: Backing up a Critical Volume

Time Required: 30 minutes
Objective: Back up a critical volume.

Description: You need to back up the critical volumes for a domain controller to prepare for a possible loss of data. You first need to create a network share on DC2 and then back up critical volumes from DC1 to the network share. This activity should be run on DC1 and DC2.

1. Start **DC1** and **DC2.** Log on to **DC2** with the domain **Administrator** account.
2. Start **Windows Explorer** by clicking **Start, Computer.** Click the **C:** drive to select it.
3. Right-click **C:** and select **New, Folder.** Name the folder **ADBackup.**
4. Right-click the **ADBackup** folder and select **Share.** The **Administrator** is automatically added as an **Owner.** Click **Share.** Click **Done.**
5. Log on to **DC1** with the domain **Administrator** account.
6. Start the **Windows Server Backup** console via the **Administrative Tools** menu.
7. Click **Backup Once** in the right pane to start the **Backup Once Wizard.**
8. On the **Backup Options** screen, accept the default selection of **Different Options** and click **Next.**

9. Select **Full Server** (**Recommended**) as the type of configuration. Because the server has only a single drive (C:), there is no difference between the **Full Server** configuration and a **Custom** configuration. Click **Next**.
10. On the **Specify Destination Type** screen, select **Remote Shared Folder**. Click **Next**.
11. Enter **\\DC2\ADBackup** as the path to the remote shared folder at the top of the screen. Select **Inherit**. Your screen will look similar to Figure 8-25. Click **Next**.

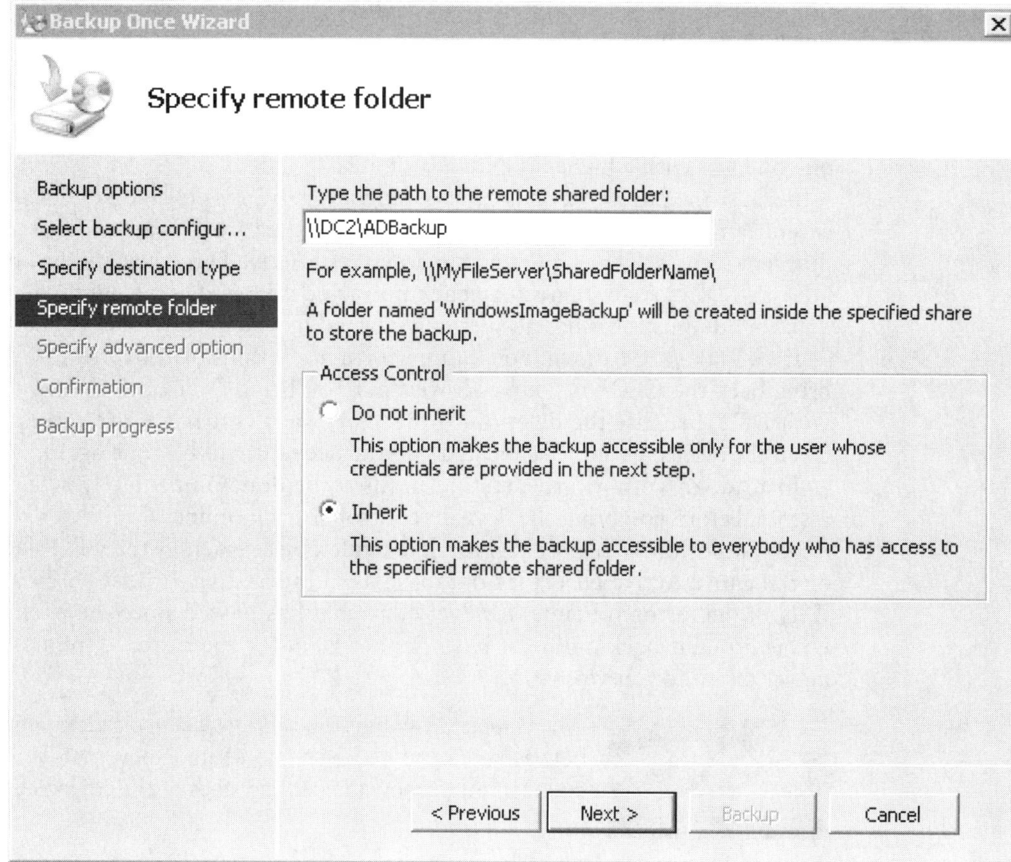

Figure 8-25 Designating the target location for the backup

Courtesy Course Technology/Cengage Learning

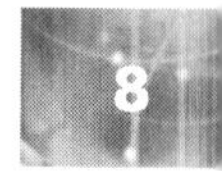

12. Accept the default setting of **VSS Copy Backup** (**Recommended**). Click **Next**.
13. Click **Backup** on the **Confirmation** screen. The backup will take 10 to 15 minutes.
14. When the backup is complete, click **Close**.

Restoring Active Directory

Active Directory can be restored as a **non-authoritative restore** or an **authoritative restore**. To fully understand the differences between the two, it helps to review how replication occurs between domain controllers.

During normal operation, any changes, modifications, and deletions that occur on one domain controller are replicated to all other domain controllers in the same site in approximately one minute. As an example, if a user account for Sally is added to DC1, the account will be replicated and appear on DC2.

The initial replication occurs within 15 seconds between replication partners. Secondary replication occurs within 3 seconds after receipt of the initial change, and all DCs are configured to receive the change with no more than 3 hops.

Active Directory uses Update Sequence Numbers (USNs) to identify the most current version of all objects. Newer changes to Active Directory have a higher USN and are considered the authoritative change.

Imagine that DC1 fails but you have a backup of Active Directory from last Saturday. Between Saturday and today, Sally changed her password. You can rebuild DC1 and then restore Active Directory, but there are two passwords for Sally's account: one on DC1 with a lower USN and one on DC2 with a higher USN.

Because the password on DC2 has a higher USN, it is considered the authoritative change and is replicated to DC1. This is a non-authoritative restore. For an authoritative restore, consider a different scenario. The CEO's account exists in Active Directory and has been replicated to both DC1 and DC2. Active Directory backups include the CEO's account, which is fortunate because a junior administrator has accidentally deleted it. You need to restore the account.

If you take DC1 down, you can perform a non-authoritative restore of Active Directory to bring back the CEO's account. However, if you bring DC1 back online, it will quickly replicate with DC2. Because the deletion of the CEO's account is a more recent change with a higher USN, the deletion will be replicated and the account will be gone again.

Instead, an authoritative restore needs to be done immediately after the non-authoritative restore, before you bring the domain controller back online.

An authoritative restore can mark a single object (such as the CEO's account), an entire OU, or the entire Active Directory database as authoritative. It does so by adding 100,000 to the USN of the restored item(s) for every day that has passed since the backup. When the restored DC is brought back online, it has a higher USN for the restored item(s) and is considered the newer or authoritative change.

When preparing for the 70-647 exam, it's important to know the difference between an authoritative and non-authoritative restore. However, it isn't as important to know the detailed steps of performing either restore.

You must take the following steps to perform a non-authoritative restore:

- **Reboot the server in Directory Services Restore Mode (DSRM).** This can be done by pressing F8 as the server starts, or by modifying the boot configuration data (bcd) store to reboot in safe mode using the `bcdedit /set safeboot dsrepair` command.
- **Log on to DSRM using the DSRM account.** This step is accessed as .\Administrator with the password that was entered when DCpromo was run on the system. (P@ssw0rd is used as the password in activities in this book.)
- **Restore Active Directory.** This step can be done with the Wbadmin command-line tool. You first need to get the version identifier of the backup using the `Wbadmin get versions -backuptarget:path` command, where *path* is the path to the backup (such as \\DC2\ADBackup). The version identifier looks like a timestamp with a date and 24-hour clock (such as 01/02/2010-16:05). You can then use the following command to restore Active Directory: `Wbadmin start systemstaterecovery -version:01/02/2010 -16:05`, where the version matches the actual version identifier.
- **After the restore completes, reboot the server.** If you modified the bcd store, you would use the following command to allow the system to boot normally: `bcdedit /deletevalue safeboot`.

Performing an Authoritative Restore

To perform an authoritative restore, you would follow the same steps you use for a non-authoritative restore. However, after restoring Active Directory and before rebooting the server, you would use the NTDSUtil command to restore the deleted objects authoritatively and update the USNs. NTDSUtil is a shell command-line tool that includes the authoritative restore commands. After the objects are marked for authoritative restore, you can reboot the server normally.

When the domain controller replicates with other domain controllers, the objects marked with NTDSUtil will be considered the authority and will be replicated to other domain controllers.

NTDSUtil was mentioned in Chapter 2 in the context of seizing FSMO roles. NTDSUtil is a rich command-line shell program that has many capabilities.

When performing an authoritative restore with NTDSUtil, you use the distinguished name (DN) of the object. DNs were covered in Chapter 4. As a reminder, the following DN uniquely identifies the user account named Darril in the Mgrs OU of the Wiley.com domain.

```
CN=Darril, OU=Mgrs, DC=Wiley, DC=com
```

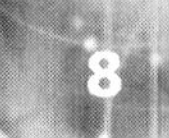

DNs can have the following components:

- **Common name (CN).** This is the name of the object. For example, if a user account was named Darril, the CN would be Darril and would be included in the DN as CN=Darril. CN is also used to identify the Users container and the Computers container. If the user account was in the Users container, the relevant portion of the DN would be CN=Darril, CN=Users.
- **Organizational Unit (OU).** If the user account is located in an OU, the OU is included in the DN. As an example, if the account is located in the Mgrs OU, the OU is identified as OU=Mgrs. When child OUs are included, the parent OU is first, followed by child OUs.
- **Domain component (DC).** The DC is used to identify the domain. Each element of the domain must be separated. In other words, a domain named Wiley.com is identified as DC=Wiley, DC=com. It will not work if you use DC=Wiley.com.

You would enter the following commands at the command prompt to authoritatively restore the Darril user account. This example assumes that the Darril user account exists in the backup that was just restored non-authoritatively.

1. Ntdsutil
2. Activate Instance ntds
3. Authoritative restore
4. Restore Object "CN=Darril, OU=Mgrs, DC=Wiley, DC=com"

You can walk through these commands by first executing the Net Stop NTDS command on a domain controller, which will stop the NTDS service and effectively stop Active Directory without stopping other services on the domain controller. While using the NTDSUtil command, you can enter ? at any prompt for help.

It's also possible to restore an entire OU using the Restore Subtree command instead of the Restore Object command. You would use the DN of the OU instead of the OU of any individual object.

Chapter Summary

- A Network Load Balancing (NLB) cluster includes two or more servers configured together. The load is automatically balanced among the different servers in the NLB cluster. A primary goal of load balancing is to increase scalability of a service or application in the cluster. NLB clusters are commonly used to increase the scalability of Internet-facing servers like Web servers.

- Scalability is the ability of a service or application to support additional clients at the same level of service by adding more resources. NLB clusters can be used to add more servers to increase the number of clients that can be served.
- NLB is added using the Network Load Balancing feature and is managed by the Network Load Balancing Manager.
- A failover cluster includes two or more servers configured together to provide high availability for a service or application. The servers are configured as nodes; some nodes are active and some are inactive. If an active node fails, an inactive node can become active to ensure that the service or application continues to run. Failover clusters are commonly used to provide fault tolerance for application servers like Microsoft SQL Server and Microsoft Exchange, but they can also be used for other services like DHCP.
- High availability ensures that a service or application is available when needed. Failover clusters can be used to increase the availability of a service or application even if a server fails.
- Failover clusters are often more expensive than NLB clusters due to the additional hardware costs.
- A quorum is used in a failover cluster to allow each node in the cluster to have a vote. Disks or file shares used to share data among the nodes can also be witnesses in the quorum. When a disk or file share is used as a witness, it also has a vote. As long as enough votes exist to make a majority, the cluster will continue to operate.
- Several quorum models exist: No Majority, Node Majority, Node and Disk Majority, and Node and File Share Majority. If a failover cluster has an odd number of nodes, the Node Majority quorum model is recommended. If a failover cluster has an even number of nodes, the Node and Disk Majority or the Node and File Share Majority model is recommended.
- Failover clusters commonly use either a serial attached SCSI (SAS) array or a storage area network (SAN). Direct attached SCSI storage will not work with Windows Server 2008 failover clusters. Storage needs to be shared between all nodes, but should not be accessible by any servers that are not in the failover cluster.
- Connectivity to shared storage is through Fibre Channel or iSCSI. Fibre Channel requires dedicated hardware, is more expensive, and can use either twisted-pair or fiber-optic cable for the connections. iSCSI can use the existing network infrastructure.
- Multi-site failover clusters can be used to reduce bandwidth usage over a WAN link and provide fault tolerance if a server fails. Nodes in the cluster would be placed in each physical location and a file share would be used by the nodes. The Node and File Share Majority quorum model would be used for multi-site failover clusters with an even number of nodes.
- Failover support is added using the Failover Clustering feature and is managed by the Failover Cluster Management console.
- Nodes are permanently removed from a cluster by evicting them. Clusters are permanently removed by destroying them.
- The Windows Backup feature includes tools to back up and restore Active Directory. When the feature is added, you can choose to add only Windows Server Backup, which includes the Windows Server Backup console and the Wbadmin command-line tool, or you can also add the command-line tools (which includes support for Windows PowerShell).
- Backups can be automated by using the Windows Server Backup console, by creating and scheduling batch files with Wbadmin, or by creating and scheduling scripts with Windows PowerShell.

- Active Directory can be restored non-authoritatively or authoritatively. A non-authoritative restore causes Active Directory to receive replicated updates from other domain controllers. An authoritative restore can be used to mark objects so that they are replicated to other domain controllers.

Key Terms

Authoritative restore Refers to Active Directory restore. After Active Directory is restored non-authoritatively, an authoritative restore can be done to mark specific objects as being authoritatively restored using NTDSUtil. After the domain controller is brought back online, these objects are replicated to other domain controllers.

Cluster-aware A characteristic of services and applications that makes them easy to add to a failover cluster. Cluster-aware services and applications can easily report their status to the failover cluster service, but non-cluster-aware services may not have this ability.

Failback Configuring a failover cluster so that when a failed node comes back online, the services or applications that it originally hosted can be returned to the node.

Failover Occurs when one node in a failover cluster fails and another node in the cluster takes over the load for the failed node. Failover is automatic in a failover cluster.

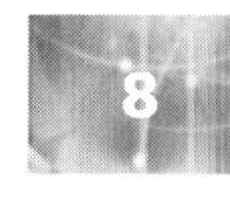

Failover cluster A Windows Server 2008 feature that can be used to provide high availability for applications and services. Two or more servers are used in a failover cluster; if one node fails, another node can pick up the load of the failed server.

Fibre Channel (FC) A standard method used by failover clusters to connect to disk storage solutions. FC can use either twisted-pair or fiber-optic media, but fiber is more commonly used. Only data transferred between the disk and the cluster node is transferred over the Fibre Channel.

High availability Ensuring that a service or application is available when it's needed. Failover clusters are commonly used to provide high availability for services or applications.

Internet Small Computer System Interface (iSCSI) An interface used to access disk storage solutions from failover cluster nodes. Data is transferred over TCP/IP networks, and existing networks can be used. iSCSI is a lower-cost alternative to Fibre Channel, which requires dedicated hardware. iSCSI can also be used to transmit data over long distances or across wide area networks (WANs).

Network Load Balancing (NLB) A Windows Server 2008 feature that can be used to increase the stability and scalability of applications and services. Two or more servers are used in an NLB cluster; as new users connect, they are directed to servers with the least number of current connections.

Non-authoritative restore Refers to Active Directory restore. After Active Directory is restored non-authoritatively, it is brought back online and receives updates from other domain controllers.

Quorum A majority used in failover clusters. Each node in a failover cluster has a vote in the quorum; the disk or file share can also have a vote. As long as a majority of votes exists, a quorum exists.

Quorum model The model used in a failover cluster to determine which elements have votes in the quorum. Four quorum models are available: No Majority, Node Majority, Node and Disk Majority, and Node and File Share Majority.

Scalability The ability of a service to support additional clients through the addition of resources such as more processing power or more servers. NLB clusters are used to scale applications out to additional servers.

Serial attached SCSI (SAS) A SCSI disk array connected to servers in a failover cluster using serial connections.

Storage area network (SAN) A specialized network designed to host disks in a failover cluster. The SAN makes the disks appear to servers as though the disks are locally attached, but they can be located elsewhere on the network.

Review Questions

1. Your company hosts a Web server in the DMZ. The volume of activity on the Web server has steadily increased; you're concerned that if its popularity continues to grow, it won't be able to handle the load. What can you do to ensure that the Web server can provide the same level of service to additional clients?
   a. Create an NLB cluster.
   b. Create a failover cluster.
   c. Configure the Web server with WSUS.
   d. Configure the DMZ with ISA.
2. Your company hosts a Microsoft SQL Server on its internal network. The SQL Server is used to host multiple databases accessed by Web servers in the DMZ. Recently, the SQL Server failed, which meant that no Web servers could access the database. You want to implement a solution to ensure that the databases will continue to be available even if a server fails, and without reconfiguring the Web servers. What should you do?
   a. Add another SQL Server.
   b. Add another SQL Server. Implement a two-node failover cluster.
   c. Add a single-node NLB cluster.
   d. Add another SQL Server. Implement two single-node clusters.
3. Your company is planning to host a Web site named *www.cengage.com*. Due to the expected volume, a two-host NLB cluster named www.cengage.com will be used. The two hosts are named Web1 and Web2. What should you do to ensure that the Web site can support HTTPS sessions?
   a. Purchase two certificates, one for each Web server, with common names of Web1 and Web2.
   b. Purchase one Web certificate with a common name of Web1 and copy it to both servers.
   c. Purchase one Web certificate with a common name of Web2 and copy it to both servers.
   d. Purchase one Web certificate with a common name of www.cengage.com and copy it to both servers.
4. Your organization hosts a Web site that queries Microsoft SQL Server as a database server. You're asked to design a high-availability plan that ensures databases served by Microsoft SQL Server will continue to operate even if a server fails. You want to ensure that the solution includes a witness disk. What should you use?
   a. An NLB cluster with a Node Majority quorum model.
   b. An NLB cluster with a Node and Disk Majority quorum model.
   c. A failover cluster with a Node Majority quorum model.
   d. A failover cluster with a Node and Disk Majority quorum model.
5. You are designing a two-node failover cluster for a DHCP server. You want to ensure that the cluster will continue to operate even if one of the servers fails. What quorum model should you use?
   a. No Majority (Disk Only)
   b. Node Majority
   c. Node and Disk Majority
   d. Node and File Share Majority

6. Your network includes a Microsoft SharePoint server named Web1 that hosts multiple Web sites on your internal network. The server uses a Microsoft SQL Server 2008 server for database access. The usage of Web1 and the back-end databases has become critical, and you're asked to design a fault-tolerant solution to ensure that the Web sites continue to operate if SQL Server fails. What should your design include?
   a. A failover cluster with shared storage.
   b. A failover cluster with at least three nodes.
   c. An NLB cluster with shared storage.
   d. An NLB cluster with at least three nodes.
7. Your single-domain forest includes an SQL Server 2008 server hosted on Windows Server 2008. You're asked to implement a fault-tolerant solution to ensure that the databases hosted on the SQL Server 2008 server will continue to be provided even if a server fails. Of the following solutions, which one would meet the goals? (Choose all that apply.)
   a. Create a failover cluster on the SQL Server.
   b. Add another SQL Server. Implement a two-node failover cluster using directly attached SCSI for shared storage.
   c. Add another SQL Server. Implement a two-node failover cluster using serial attached SCSI for shared storage.
   d. Add another SQL Server. Implement a two-node failover cluster using a storage area network for shared storage.

8. You are planning to implement a failover solution for Microsoft SQL Server. One of the disk storage solutions is advertised as using MPIO. What connectivity solution would be used with MPIO?
   a. GPT
   b. MBR
   c. Fibre Channel
   d. iSCSI
9. You are planning to implement a failover solution for Microsoft SQL Server 2008. One of the design requirements specifies that teamed network adapters must be used. What connectivity solution could be used?
   a. Fibre Channel
   b. iSCSI
   c. GPT
   d. MBR
10. You are reviewing a plan to implement a two-node failover cluster for an SQL Server 2008 database server. The failover cluster will use iSCSI for shared storage. You're asked to identify a solution to provide fault tolerance for the network adapters. What would you recommend?
    a. Use a Fibre Channel adapter for each connection.
    b. Use teamed network adapters for each connection.
    c. Use multiple network adapters for each connection.
    d. Use an NLB connection.
11. Your single-domain forest includes offices at two major locations configured as sites. SQL Server 2008 is hosted on identical servers using the same databases at both locations. You're asked to provide a fault-tolerant solution to ensure that users at both sites can access the

databases even if one of the database servers fails. Your solution should minimize costs. What would you suggest?

a. Deploy an additional server at each site and configure two two-node failover clusters.
b. Deploy an additional server at each site and configure a single four-node failover cluster.
c. Deploy an additional server at either site and configure a single three-node failover cluster.
d. Configure the two servers in a single two-node failover cluster.

12. Your single-domain forest includes offices at two major locations configured as sites. You are reviewing the design of a multi-site failover cluster that will host SQL Server 2008 at each of the sites. The failover cluster will use a witness share for shared storage. What quorum model should be used?

a. No Majority (Disk Only)
b. Node Majority
c. Node and Disk Majority
d. Node and File Share Majority

13. Your single-domain forest includes offices at three major locations configured as sites. You are reviewing the design of a multi-site failover cluster that will host SQL Server 2008 at each of the sites. The failover cluster will use a witness share for shared storage. What quorum model should be used?

a. No Majority (Disk Only)
b. Node Majority
c. Node and Disk Majority
d. Node and File Share Majority

14. Your single-domain forest includes offices at two locations configured as sites within the domain. Both locations have about 5,000 clients. Currently, one DHCP server is located at the main office and is used to serve both sites. However, the WAN traffic is becoming heavily used and needs to be minimized. You're asked to provide a solution that will minimize DHCP traffic over the WAN link and ensure that DHCP will continue to provide leases to clients, even if one of the DHCP servers fails. What should you suggest?

a. Add a DHCP server at the main office. Create a two-node failover cluster.
b. Add a DHCP server at the second location. Create a two-node failover cluster.
c. Add a DHCP server at the main office and two DHCP servers at the second location. Create a two-node failover cluster.
d. Add a DHCP server at the main office and two DHCP servers at the second location. Create a two-node failover cluster at each of the offices.

15. You are designing a consolidation of servers to Microsoft's Hyper-V virtual server. You plan to host four servers on one physical server. However, management is concerned that the single point of failure with the one server presents significant risk, and asks for an alternative. You propose adding another physical server and using four failover clusters to ensure high availability. An iSCSI array will be used for shared storage. How should the iSCSI array be configured?

a. Configure one LUN.
b. Configure two LUNs, one for each physical server.
c. Configure four LUNs, one shared by each virtual server.
d. Configure eight LUNs, one for each virtual server in both physical servers.

16. You manage a three-node failover cluster hosting SQL Server 2008. You need to perform maintenance on one of the nodes, which will require the node to be rebooted. What should you do?
    a. Pause the node.
    b. Stop the node.
    c. Evict the node.
    d. Remove the node.
17. You manage a three-node failover cluster hosting SQL Server 2008. It's been decided that only two nodes are needed, so you need to remove one of the nodes. What should you do?
    a. Pause the node.
    b. Stop the node.
    c. Evict the node.
    d. Delete the node.
18. You manage two domain controllers in a small enterprise. You perform manual backups of Active Directory once a week and want to automate the process so these backups are performed automatically without user intervention. How can this be accomplished? (Choose all that apply.)
    a. Schedule a backup with Windows Server Backup.
    b. Schedule a backup with NTBackup.
    c. Write a batch file using Wbadmin and schedule the batch file using Scheduled Tasks.
    d. Write a script using Windows PowerShell and schedule the script using Scheduled Tasks.
19. You manage two domain controllers (DC1 and DC2) in a small enterprise and regularly back up system state data. DC1 recently experienced a disk failure that corrupted Active Directory. While DC1 was down, several changes occurred on DC2. You want to restore Active Directory on DC1. What should you do?
    a. Perform an authoritative restore.
    b. Perform a non-authoritative restore.
    c. Perform a non-critical volume restore.
    d. Rebuild DC1 from scratch.
20. You manage two domain controllers (DC1 and DC2) in a small enterprise and regularly back up system state data. A junior administrator accidentally deleted a user account, and you need to restore it. What should you do?
    a. Perform an authoritative restore.
    b. Perform a non-authoritative restore.
    c. Perform a non-critical volume restore.
    d. Run a PowerShell script to back up Active Directory.

Case Projects

Case Project 8-1: Scaling a Web Site

Your company is hosting a Web server on a Windows Server 2008 server in the DMZ. The load on the Web server has steadily increased, and you are asked to design a plan to increase the number of users that the Web site can support by adding more servers. The additional servers need to support both HTTP and HTTPS. What should your design include?

Case Project 8-2: Fault Tolerance for SQL Server 2008

Your company hosts an SQL Server 2008 server as a back-end database server for a Web site. The Web site is hosted in an NLB cluster in the DMZ and the SQL Server 2008 server is hosted on a Windows Server 2008 server in the internal network. You're asked to provide a fault-tolerant solution for the SQL Server. What should you recommend? What should be purchased to support the recommendation? Explain your answer.

Case Project 8-3: Fault Tolerance for File Servers at Multiple Sites

Your organization includes two large locations configured as two separate sites. Currently a file server is accessed by users at both sites over the WAN link. You're asked to provide a fault-tolerant solution for the file server to ensure that the files will continue to be served even if the server fails. Your solution should minimize costs and minimize traffic over the WAN link. What solution and quorum model would you recommend? Explain your answer.

Case Project 8-4: Backing up Active Directory

Your single-domain forest includes two domain controllers. You're asked to design a plan to back up Active Directory by backing up system state data. You have limited funds, so you need to use native Windows tools. Also, the backups should occur regularly with only limited action by administrators. Your plan should include two possible methods to achieve the goal. What should you do?

chapter 9

Designing Supporting Services

After reading this chapter and completing the exercises, you will be able to:

- Understand the capabilities of the System Center suite of products
- Plan for data security, including the use of BitLocker Drive Encryption
- Design for data accessibility and redundancy using Distributed File System
- Design for data collaboration
- Understand the capabilities of additional Active Directory Roles

Windows Server 2008 can support several different services and applications to enhance operations within a domain. Some are included as roles or features with Windows Server 2008, others can be downloaded for free, and others are server products that can be purchased.

The System Center suite is a full range of server products you can buy to assist with the maintenance and administration of a network. BitLocker Drive Encryption can be used to encrypt entire hard drives of servers that don't have adequate security. The Distributed File System includes tools that can increase data accessibility and redundancy for users in a network, especially when users access data across a WAN. Windows SharePoint Services and Microsoft Office SharePoint Server are two valuable tools that can be used for data collaboration. Last, Active Directory includes several additional server roles that can meet specific needs.

All of these topics are covered in this chapter.

Understanding the System Center Suite

Microsoft System Center is a full range of supporting server products designed to enhance and automate the administration of large networks within an enterprise. The suite includes several server products whose names all begin with "Microsoft System Center." These products are useful and valuable, but they are add-on server products, which aren't free.

Because products in the System Center suite are add-ons to the operating system (and must be purchased separately), you aren't expected to know the intricate details of how the products work. However, you should know their capabilities so you can consider them in a design plan.

Some of the server products included in the System Center suite are:

- **Microsoft System Center Operations Manager.** SCOM is used to provide overall monitoring for a network. SCOM uses agents that are installed on servers or clients to watch for specific events and generate alerts to the server hosting SCOM. Administrators can monitor all of the key events on the SCOM server for the entire network. SCOM is explored in more depth later in this section.
- **Microsoft System Center Configuration Manager.** SCCM can be used to deploy full operating systems, applications, and updates to systems within the network. SCCM is explored in more depth later in this section. It combines and improves the capabilities of Windows Deployment Services (WDS) to deploy images, Windows Server Update Services (WSUS) to deploy updates, and Group Policy to deploy applications. SCCM can also query clients to determine whether updates have been deployed, using the same technology used by Microsoft Baseline Security Analyzer (MBSA).
- **Microsoft System Center Data Protection Manager.** SCDPM provides a centralized backup and recovery solution. It allows quick backups to disk, which can then be backed up to tape. SCDPM can be used to back up file servers, Microsoft SQL Server, Microsoft Exchange Server, Microsoft Office SharePoint Server, and more.
- **Microsoft System Center Essentials.** SCE can be used by smaller businesses of up to 500 clients and 30 servers to monitor servers, clients, applications, and hardware, similar to how SCOM is used in larger enterprises.
- **Microsoft System Center Virtual Machine Manager.** SCVMM is used for large-scale management of virtual servers using Hyper-V. It includes tools to easily migrate virtual servers from one physical server to another, and includes enhanced clustering capabilities.

The Microsoft SCVMM is explored further in Chapter 10.

System Center Operations Manager 2007

Microsoft System Center Operations Manager 2007 (SCOM) is an add-on server product that can be used to monitor servers and client computers in an enterprise. SCOM builds on the basic philosophy that an administrator wants to know about problems before they happen. By continuously monitoring systems in a network, SCOM can help track trends and identify problems before they become serious and affect the business.

Figure 9-1 provides an overview of how SCOM is used. Agents are installed on servers and client computers throughout the network. These SCOM agents monitor for activity such as specific logged events. When the events occur, an agent captures them and sends a report to SCOM. If Hyper-V is used for virtual servers, agents can be deployed on each virtual server as desired.

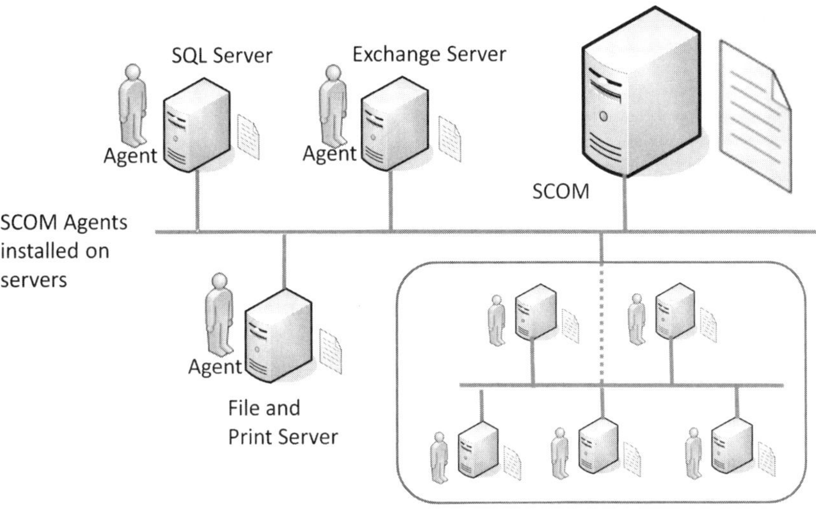

Figure 9-1 SCOM server and SCOM agents
Courtesy Course Technology/Cengage Learning

While the figure shows a single SQL Server and a single Exchange server, large enterprises could easily have hundreds of these servers. As an example, a large enterprise could have 100 SQL Servers that all require different levels of monitoring. An important element to monitor on an SQL Server is the state of the transaction log. If the transaction log is growing abnormally, the performance of the SQL Server could quickly degrade or the server could even shut down.

With SCOM, agents can watch for these specific events on all 100 SQL Servers; if any of the events occur on any of the servers, SCOM can immediately generate an alert that is sent to the SCOM server. With SCOM, administrators can use a single centralized server to monitor all servers in the organization. Additionally, the SCOM server can be configured to notify administrators when events occur.

SCOM also includes the Command Shell, which is a customized interface of Windows PowerShell. PowerShell can be used to create scripts that automate specific tasks required by administrators in a wide range of environments.

System Center Configuration Manager 2007

Microsoft System Center Configuration Manager 2007 (SCCM) is an add-on server product that can assess, deploy, and update large numbers of client computers or servers in an enterprise. SCCM is an update of Microsoft's System Management Server (SMS).

Figure 9-2 shows how SCCM is used in a network. It combines the strengths of several tools and can be used to deploy operating system images, software applications, and patches to servers and clients in a network.

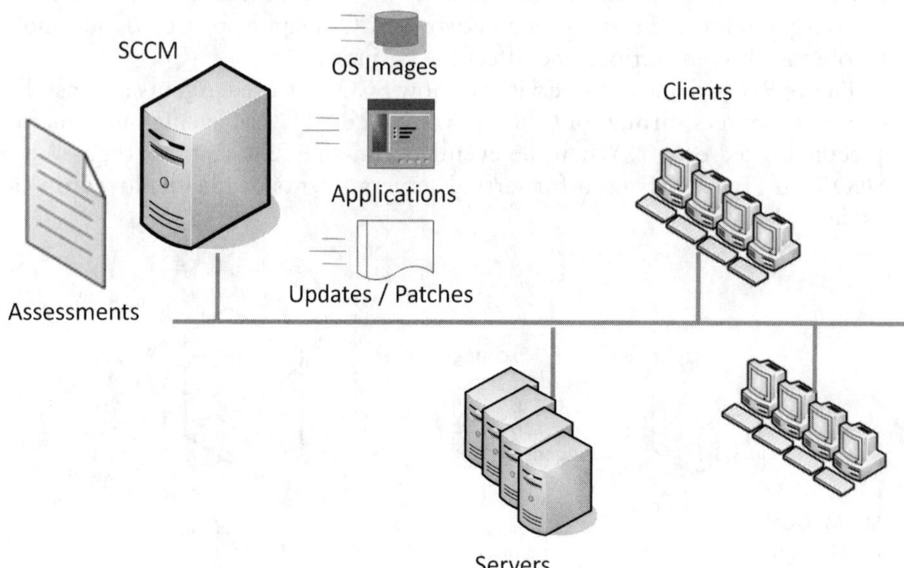

Figure 9-2 Using SCCM to deploy operating systems, applications, and updates
Courtesy Course Technology/Cengage Learning

SCCM provides multiple benefits for an organization:

- **Operating system deployment.** Entire operating systems can be deployed to computers. SCCM uses image-based deployments and can be used for zero-touch installations, where the installation is performed without the need for administrator interaction. Smaller enterprises can use Windows Deployment Services (WDS) to deploy operating systems, but WDS requires more administrator interaction. SCCM and WDS both allow the deployment of customized images that are completely configured. You can also use SCCM after the deployment to customize the installation by pushing out additional applications or updates as needed.
- **Software application distribution.** Applications can be deployed to clients with SCCM or Group Policy, but for large enterprises, Group Policy often doesn't provide enough control. As an example, SCCM allows you to schedule the installation of an application. This gives you the option of deploying the application over the network after normal business hours.
- **Patch management.** Patches and updates can be deployed to clients with SCCM. SCCM improves on the abilities of Windows Server Update Services (WSUS) to deploy updates, allowing SCCM to handle a much larger number of clients. With SCCM, updates can also be scheduled and more tools are available to target the clients.
- **Client assessments.** SCCM includes technology used in Microsoft Baseline Security Analyzer (MBSA) and WSUS to inspect and assess clients, ensuring that they are up to date and compliant with other security requirements in the network. SCCM can create reports of non-compliant computers so that administrators can easily identify clients that are having problems.
- **Remote control.** With SCCM, administrators and help desk support personnel can remote into systems to troubleshoot and resolve problems. Help desk professionals can use this feature to show a user how to resolve a problem, as with the Remote Assistance tool, but the user doesn't have to create a Remote Assistance request or approve the process. Administrators can also remote into systems to check their configuration.

- **Hardware and software inventory.** SCCM uses Windows Management Instrumentation (WMI), which can be used to query computers. Queries can identify computers on the network and the software installed on them.

In summary, SCCM provides administrators with a wealth of tools that can automate many tasks and improve the process where other automation already exists. In large organizations with thousands of clients, the tools work together to significantly reduce the total cost of ownership and to help ensure that the network is properly managed.

Designing for Data Security

As it becomes easier to house massive amounts of data, it becomes more important to ensure that the data is secure. Loss of data can cause several problems for a company:

- Loss of competitiveness if the data is proprietary financial or research data
- Loss of customer goodwill if a customer's personal information is lost
- Loss of valuable employees if internal data such as salary information is freely shared
- Loss of data needed for business continuity

While the term "data security" implies keeping data from being stolen, it also includes ensuring that data is not lost due to hardware failures. Chapter 8 covered failover clusters, which provide high availability for servers. Windows Backup can be used to back up data for smaller networks, and the Microsoft System Center Data Protection Manager can be used to back up data for larger networks.

Data security includes several elements:

- **Physical security.** Access to company property is protected using standard physical methods such as locked doors and cipher locks.
- **File system.** **New Technology File System** (**NTFS**) version 6.2 is standard on Windows Server 2008 server products. NTFS protects data with permissions and the Encrypting File System (EFS). It also increases stability for Windows systems through the use of transactional logs and continuous monitoring. The ChkDsk tool can be started manually to detect and repair disk problems. The new self-healing feature of NTFS performs like ChkDsk on the fly, allowing NTFS to automatically detect and repair file system problems without user intervention.
- **Data transferred over network.** Data can be protected by encryption when transferred over the network. IPSec is often used to protect data, and was discussed in Chapters 4 and 5.
- **Data storage.** Data stored on hard drives can be vulnerable if an attacker has unrestricted access to the server. Most servers are protected with strong physical security within a server room or data center, but at remote locations the physical security may not be as strong. Additional measures such as BitLocker Drive Encryption may be needed.

Using BitLocker Drive Encryption for Data Security

One thing to consider when planning for server security is the use of **BitLocker Drive Encryption** to protect the contents of disk drives. BitLocker can encrypt entire hard drives to protect them from offline attacks.

Within a domain, data on a hard drive is protected with permissions. Only authenticated users with the proper permissions can access these files or folders. However, these permissions don't protect the data from an offline attack.

As an example, an offline attack could occur if an intruder steals a server and has unrestricted access to the data. He could install the hard drive on a system where he has administrative permissions and take ownership of all the files. As the owner, he could then change all of the permissions.

BitLocker Drive Encryption provides full hard disk encryption. While this isn't needed in a server room with extensive physical security, it can be useful in remote offices with limited security. Chapter 2 covered the use of RODCs for remote offices; BitLocker can complement the security provided by an RODC.

BitLocker Drive Encryption prevents data from being copied. It provides an added layer of protection for servers without adequate physical security, such as those in remote offices.

BitLocker provides two primary benefits:

- **Prevents unauthorized access to data.** Attackers are unable to access data stored on the system when the hard drive is encrypted. Thus, the operating system drive and any data drives on the server are protected.
- **Verifies integrity of early boot components.** This allows BitLocker to detect whether the drive has been moved to another system. If the drive fails this check, the system is prevented from booting. This check only works if Trusted Platform Module 1.2 (or greater) is installed.

A **Trusted Platform Module (TPM)** is a microchip that is usually installed on the system motherboard. It provides the security-related functions for BitLocker, including the storage and encryption of different encryption keys.

BitLocker Drive Encryption Requirements

BitLocker Drive Encryption is not available by default on Windows Server 2008, but it can be added. When adding BitLocker, you should be aware of the following additional requirements:

- **Trusted Platform Module (TPM) version 1.2.** TPM is a hardware component built into the motherboard of the system. TPM is required for the system integrity check.
- **TPM-compatible BIOS.** TPM must be supported and enabled in the system BIOS to support the system integrity check.
- **Hard disk must be partitioned with at least two volumes.** The extra volume used for BitLocker must be formatted with NTFS and must be at least 1.5 GB.

BitLocker provides the best protection when TPM is available because it can perform the system integrity check, but BitLocker can still be used without TPM. In such cases, a USB flash drive is used with a startup key stored on the flash drive as a file. This flash drive must be inserted each time the system is started. BitLocker offers four possible modes:

- **BitLocker with a TPM.** This mode provides full support by encrypting entire hard drives and performing a system validation check.
- **BitLocker with TPM and a PIN.** This mode provides all the support of BitLocker with TPM and adds a layer of protection. When the server is booted, a user can enter a PIN to unlock the encrypted drive(s). If a user doesn't enter the correct PIN, the server will not boot.
- **BitLocker with TPM and a startup key.** When the server is started or rebooted, a USB startup key is inserted to work with the TPM and unlock the encrypted drive(s). However, the USB drive that holds the startup key must be removed after rebooting; otherwise, it provides no protection. If an attacker steals the server with the USB key inserted, he can easily boot the server and unlock the drive.
- **BitLocker with a startup key (but without TPM).** When the server is started or rebooted, a USB startup key is inserted to unlock the encrypted drive(s). This method does not perform a system integrity check because TPM is not present. The startup key must be removed after rebooting; otherwise, it provides no protection.

The following activity shows how the BitLocker feature can be added to a Windows Server 2008 server. Once added, the feature appears in the Control Panel.

Activity 9-1: Enabling the BitLocker Feature

Time Required: 20 minutes
Objective: Enable the BitLocker feature.

Description: You are preparing to deploy a server to a remote site and want to ensure that data on the hard drive is protected. You need to enable the BitLocker feature on the server. This lab should be completed on DC1.

1. Log on to **DC1** with an **Administrator** account and a password of **P@ssw0rd.**
2. Start the **Server Manager** via the **Administrative Tools** menu.
3. Select **Features** and click the **Add Features** link.
4. On the Select Features screen, select **BitLocker Drive Encryption**, as shown in Figure 9-3. Click **Next.** Click **Install.**

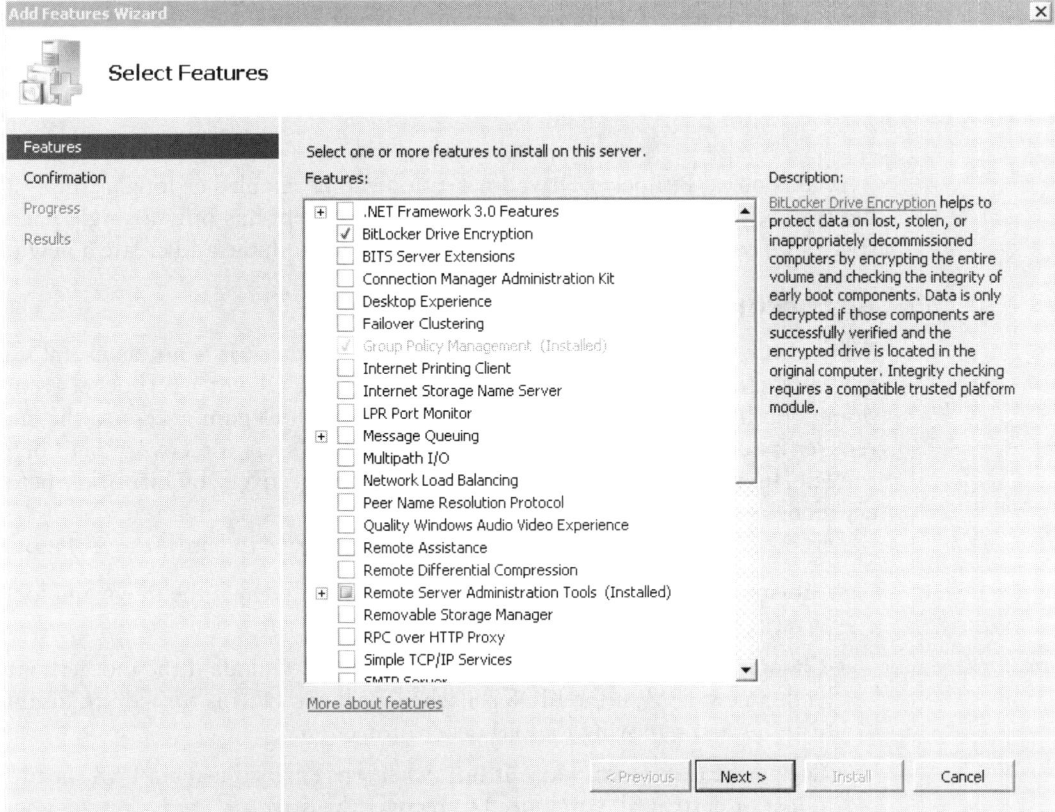

Figure 9-3 Enabling the BitLocker Drive Encryption feature

Courtesy Course Technology/Cengage Learning

5. When the installation is complete, review the results and click **Close.** You must reboot the server to complete the installation.
6. When prompted to restart the system, click **Yes** to reboot the server.
7. After the system restarts, log on using an **Administrator** account and a password of **P@ssw0rd.** The Installation Results screen appears, indicating that the installation succeeded. Click **Close.**

8. Open the **Control Panel** and click **Security**. If you don't see Security, select **Control Panel Home** to exit the Classic View, and then click **Security.** You'll see the BitLocker Drive Encryption selection, as shown in Figure 9-4.

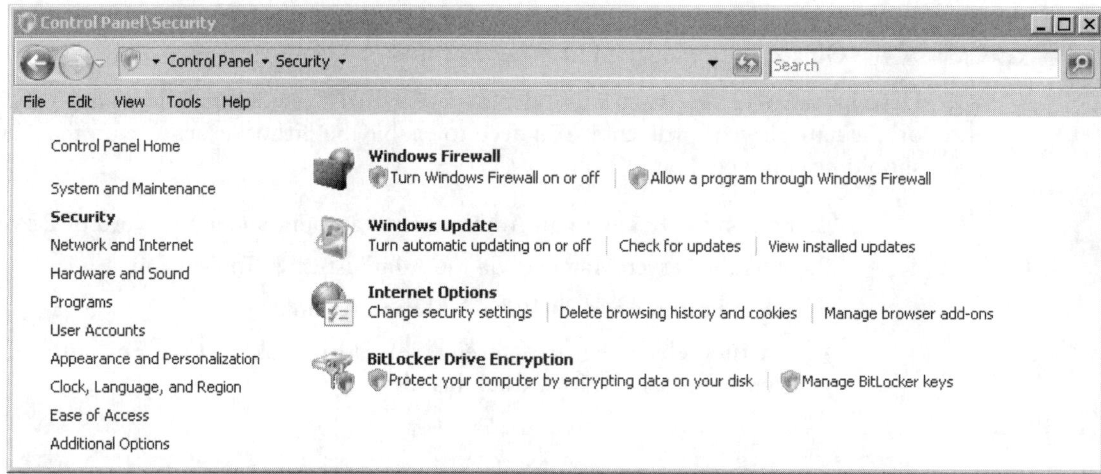

Figure 9-4 BitLocker Drive Encryption feature available in Control Panel

Courtesy Course Technology/Cengage Learning

At this point, BitLocker Drive Encryption can be enabled as long as the system has a separate blank disk partition of at least 1.5 GB. If the system has only a single partition with unused space, you can use Disk Management to shrink the volume and create a new partition.

BitLocker Drive Encryption Recovery

While BitLocker is valuable when it locks out attackers, it is not as useful if it locks out legitimate users. If BitLocker detects suspicious events, it will enter BitLocker recovery mode. At this point, you'll need to use your system recovery plan to gain access to the encrypted drive and recover its contents. If you haven't implemented a system recovery plan before this point, it's too late. In other words, you must plan for system recovery by BitLocker before it enters recovery mode.

Several events or actions can cause a BitLocker drive to enter recovery mode:

- **Moving the drive to a different system.** TPM will detect the move and lock the drive until it is recovered.
- **Changing the TPM.** The drive will enter recovery mode if the motherboard is replaced with a new TPM, if the BIOS is flashed, or if the TPM is turned off, disabled, or cleared without first removing the BitLocker protection.
- **Losing the USB startup key.** If BitLocker was enabled using a USB startup key and the key is lost or destroyed, you'll need to recover the drive.
- **Forgetting the PIN.** If BitLocker is enabled with a PIN and the PIN is no longer known, the data on the drive will remain locked until recovered.

While a locked drive presents an almost insurmountable challenge for an attacker, some relatively simple recovery processes are available if you have the recovery key. The recovery data can be stored in Active Directory Domain Services (AD DS), on a USB flash drive, or in a file; the data can also be printed. Recovery data is stored either as a recovery password or a recovery key.

Recovery data in AD DS is stored as a separate object with several properties used to identify the computer, the volume, and the recovery information. However, this object isn't available by default, and it isn't available on older domain controllers. The following requirements must be met to store the recovery data in AD DS:

- **All DCs must be running at least Windows Server 2003 SP1.** Otherwise, you'll need to upgrade the DCs first.
- **The schema must be extended.** A BitLockerTPMSchemaExtension.ldf file can be downloaded from Microsoft and applied to the schema. Once the schema has been extended, BitLocker information can be added. This step isn't required if the first DC in the domain was Windows Server 2008 or greater.
- **Modify domain permissions.** Microsoft provides the Add-TPMSelfWriteACE.vbs Visual Basic script, which can be used to create an Access Control Entry (ACE) to the top-level domain object.

Microsoft has published a document titled "Configure Active Directory to Back up Windows BitLocker Drive Encryption and Trusted Platform Module Recovery Information." The document takes you through the steps to make these changes if necessary. You can download the guide from *http://microsoft.com/downloads* by searching on the title or "BitLocker TPMSchemaExtension.ldf."

Once these requirements are met, you can use Group Policy to force the storage of BitLocker recovery data in AD DS. Figure 9-5 shows the Group Policy setting to Turn on TPM backup to Active Directory Domain Services. When enabled, you can select the Require TPM backup to AD DS setting.

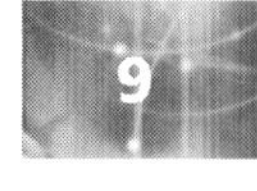

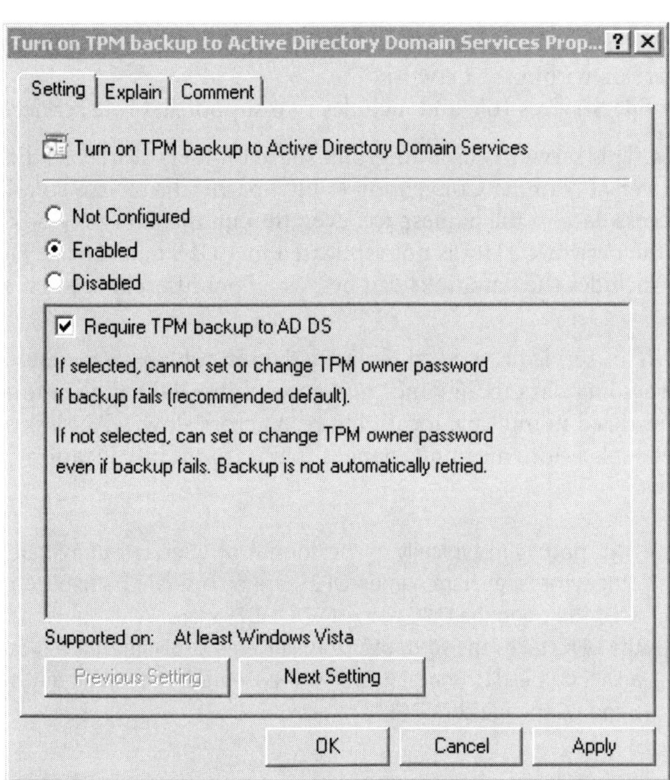

Figure 9-5 Using Group Policy to force BitLocker recovery information to be stored in Active Directory

Courtesy Course Technology/Cengage Learning

You can access this Group Policy setting from Computer Configuration, Policies, Administrative Templates, System, Trusted Platform Module Services. The following activity shows how to configure this setting for all users in the domain.

Activity 9-2: Storing BitLocker Recovery Information in AD DS

Time Required: 15 minutes
Objective: Configure a GPO to store BitLocker recovery information in AD DS.

Description: Some servers and desktop systems in your enterprise use BitLocker Drive Encryption. You need to ensure that BitLocker recovery data is stored in AD DS for any systems that use BitLocker Drive Encryption. This lab should be completed on DC1.

1. Log on to **DC1** with an **Administrator** account and a password of **P@ssw0rd.**
2. Start **Group Policy Management** via the **Administrative Tools** menu.
3. Right-click the **Default Domain Policy** and click **Edit.**
4. Browse to the **Computer Configuration, Policies, Administrative Templates, System, Trusted Platform Module Services** node.
5. Double-click **Turn on TPM backup to Active Directory Domain Services.** Select **Enabled.** Ensure that **Require TPM backup to AD DS** is selected. Click **OK.**
6. Close all open windows.

Designing for Data Accessibility and Redundancy with DFS

Microsoft's **Distributed File System (DFS)** in Windows Server 2008 is a set of technologies that can group folders from multiple servers into one path. DFS also can replicate the content of the folders to multiple servers within the network.

DFS is part of the File Services role and includes two supporting role services:

- **DFS namespaces.** This service is used to group shared folders stored on different servers into a single Universal Naming Convention (UNC) path. Clients can connect to a single UNC path to access data in the namespace, even though the data may be on multiple servers throughout the network. Data is not replicated in a **DFS namespace.** However, the namespace that includes the data links can be hosted on different servers, and these links are replicated.
- **DFS replication.** This service is used to replicate data in folders in the DFS namespace to other servers, providing data redundancy and accessibility. **DFS replication** can be used to keep data synchronized in multiple locations, even across slow WAN links. DFS replication uses multimaster replication, meaning changes that occur at any location can be replicated to other locations.

UNC paths are typically in the format of \\ServerName\ShareName. In other words, a share named DFSShare on a server named DC1 could be accessed using the UNC path of \\DC1\DFSShare. With domain-based DFS, the UNC takes the form of \\DomainName\DFSNamespace. For example, a DFS namespace named DFS in the Cengage.com domain is accessed using \\Cengage.com\DFS.

DFS Namespace

A DFS namespace is a group of folders from different servers that presents itself to clients as a single folder tree. From the client's perspective, the folders appear to be on a single server, so it's easy for clients to map to the drive. Even if the actual location of data changes within the namespace, the namespace can be modified without reconfiguring clients to point to the new location.

DFS namespaces can be configured as one of three types:

- **Stand-alone.** A stand-alone namespace would be created when the Windows Server 2008 server is not in a domain. The information on the namespace is stored on the server in cache and in the registry. Only one namespace server can be used to host a namespace.
- **Domain-based (Windows 2000).** If the domain functional level is not at least Windows Server 2008, you can create domain-based namespaces using Windows 2000 mode. The data for the namespace is stored in cache on the server and in Active Directory. Multiple namespace servers can be used to host the same namespace as long as they are all in the same domain.
- **Domain-based (Windows 2008).** If the domain functional level is at least Windows Server 2008, you can create domain-based namespaces using Windows Server 2008 mode. These are similar to the Windows 2000 namespace servers, but they increase the scalability of the namespace, allowing namespaces with more than 5,000 folders.

Consider Figure 9-6. A DFS namespace has been created on Server1 using the name of DFSShare. The Projects folder within DFSShare is located on Server2, the Graphics folder is located on Server3, and the Marketing folder is located on Server1 within the DFSShare folder. However, the clients only need to connect to DFSShare to access files and folders located on all three servers.

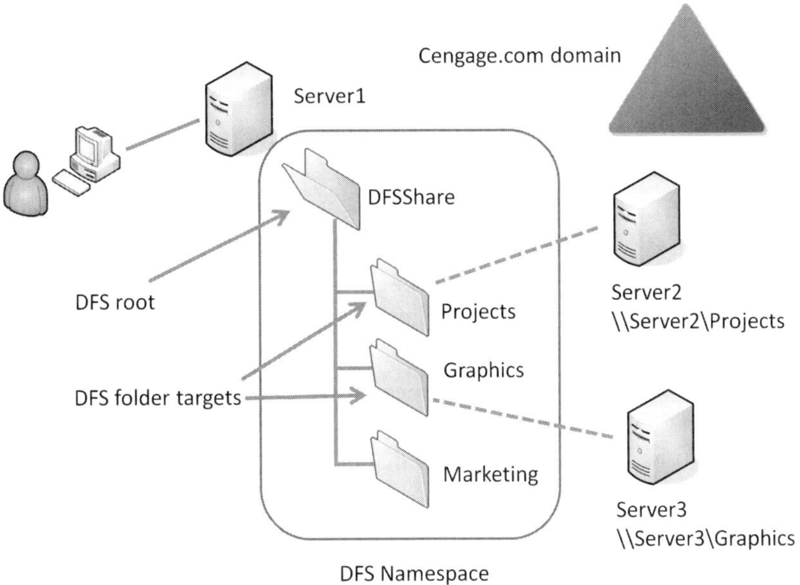

Figure 9-6 A DFS namespace
Courtesy Course Technology/Cengage Learning

The figure also identifies the DFS root and DFS folder targets:

- **DFS root.** The **DFS root** is the top-level folder for the DFS namespace. In the figure, the DFS root is the DFSShare folder. If it is created as a stand-alone DFS namespace, it is accessed using the conventional UNC path of \\Server1\DFSShare. However, it's more common to use domain-based DFS roots in a domain, so instead the path would be \\Cengage.com\DFSShare.
- **Folder targets.** Within the DFS root are two folders (Projects and Graphics) that are actually located on different servers. Clients could separately connect to the folders using UNC paths of \\Server2\Projects and \\Server3\Graphics. However, because these folder targets

are in the DFS root, they can also be accessed using \\Server1\DFSShare\Projects and \\Server1\DFSShare\Graphics. In other words, clients connect with Server1 and can access the data on different servers using the folder targets.

- **Folders**. Any folders that exist within the DFS root folder are shown and available in the DFS namespace.

Before you can add DFS namespaces, you must add the DFS role services, which are part of the File Services role. The following two activities show you how to add the DFS role services and create a DFS namespace.

Activity 9-3: Adding the DFS Role Services

Time Required: 20 minutes
Objective: Add DFS role services.

Description: You want to create a domain-based DFS namespace in your domain. It will host folders on both DC1 and DC2. You first need to add the DFS role services to DC1 and DC2.

1. Start **DC1** and **DC2**. Log on to **DC1** with an **Administrator** account and a password of **P@ssw0rd.**
2. Start the **Server Manager** via the **Administrative Tools** menu.
3. Click **Roles**. If the **File Services** role is not already installed on the server, use the following substeps to add it with the additional DFS role services. If it is installed, cancel the wizard and skip to Step 4.
   a. Select **Add Roles**. Review the information on the **Before You Begin** screen and click **Next.**
   b. Select **File Services** and click **Next**. Review the information on the **Introduction to File Services** screen and click **Next.**
   c. **File Server** is selected by default. Select **Distributed File System**; both **DFS Namespaces** and **DFS Replication** will also be selected, as shown in Figure 9-7. Click **Next.**
   d. The **Create a DFS Namespace** screen appears. Select **Create a Namespace Later Using the DFS Management Snap-in in Server Manager**. Click **Next.**
   e. Click **Install** on the **Confirm Installation Selections** screen. When the installation is complete, click **Close.**
4. If the **File Services** role is already installed, use the following substeps to add the DFS role services.
   a. Scroll down to **Role Services** below **File Services** and click **Add Role Services.**
   b. **File Server** will be selected and identified as **Installed**. Select **Distributed File System**; both **DFS Namespaces** and **DFS Replication** will also be selected. Click **Next.**
   c. The **Create a DFS Namespace** screen appears. Select **Create a Namespace Later Using the DFS Management Snap-in in Server Manager**. Click **Next.**
   d. Click **Install** on the **Confirm Installation Selections** screen. When the installation is complete, click **Close.**
5. Log on to **DC2** with an **Administrator** account and a password of **P@ssw0rd.**
6. Complete Steps 2 through 4 to add the **Distributed File System** role services to **DC2.**
7. Close all open windows.

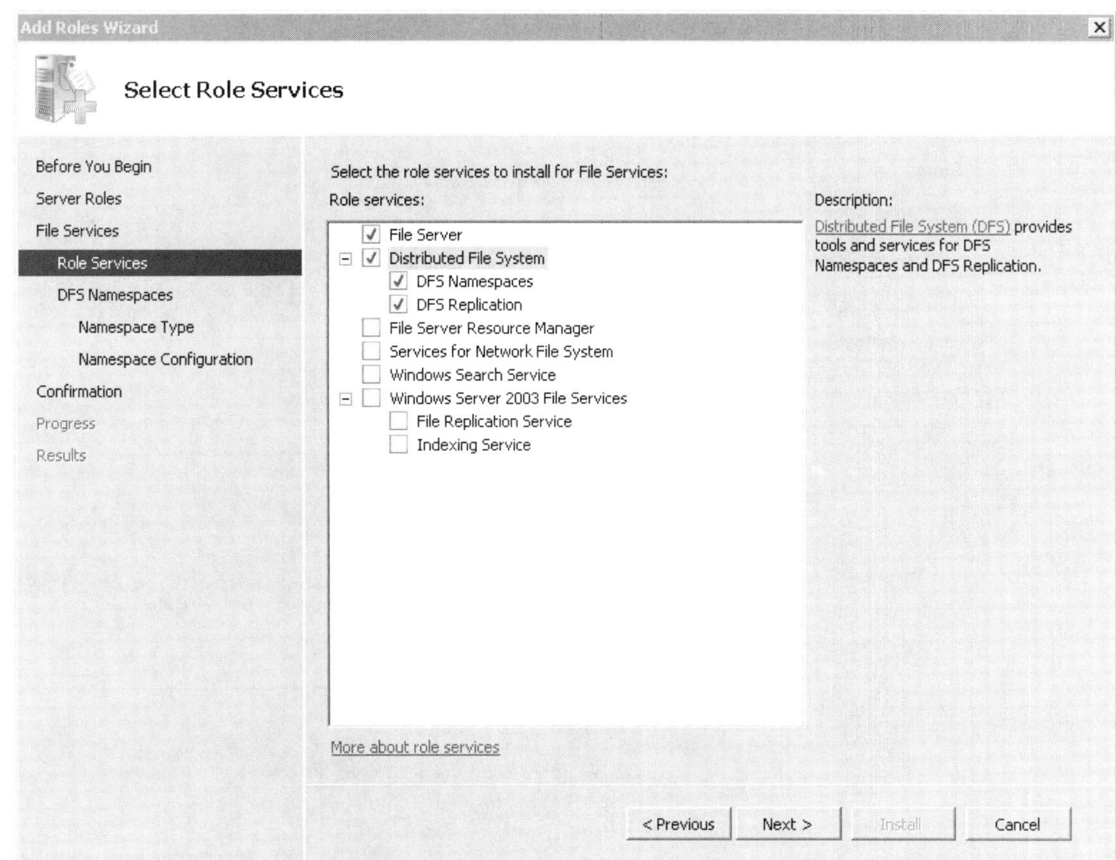

Figure 9-7 Selecting the DFS role services

Courtesy Course Technology/Cengage Learning

After the DFS role services have been added to the File Services role, you can use the DFS Management console to create a DFS namespace.

Activity 9-4: Creating a DFS Namespace

Time Required: 20 minutes
Objective: Create a DFS namespace.

Description: You have folders on DC1 and DC2 that you want to share in a single domain-based DFS namespace. You need to create a DFS namespace to unify the shared folders. This lab should be completed on DC1 and DC2.

1. Start **DC1** and **DC2**. Log on to **DC1** with an **Administrator** account and a password of **P@ssw0rd.**
2. Start the **DFS Management** console via the **Administrative Tools** menu.
3. Right-click **Namespaces** and select **New Namespace.**
4. Enter **DC1** as the name of the server on the **Namespace Server** screen. Click **Next.**
5. On the **Namespace Name and Settings** screen, enter **DFSNamespace** as the **Name.** Click **Next.**
6. On the **Namespace Type** screen, ensure that **Domain-based namespace** and **Enable Windows Server 2008 Mode** are both selected, as shown in Figure 9-8. Click **Next.**

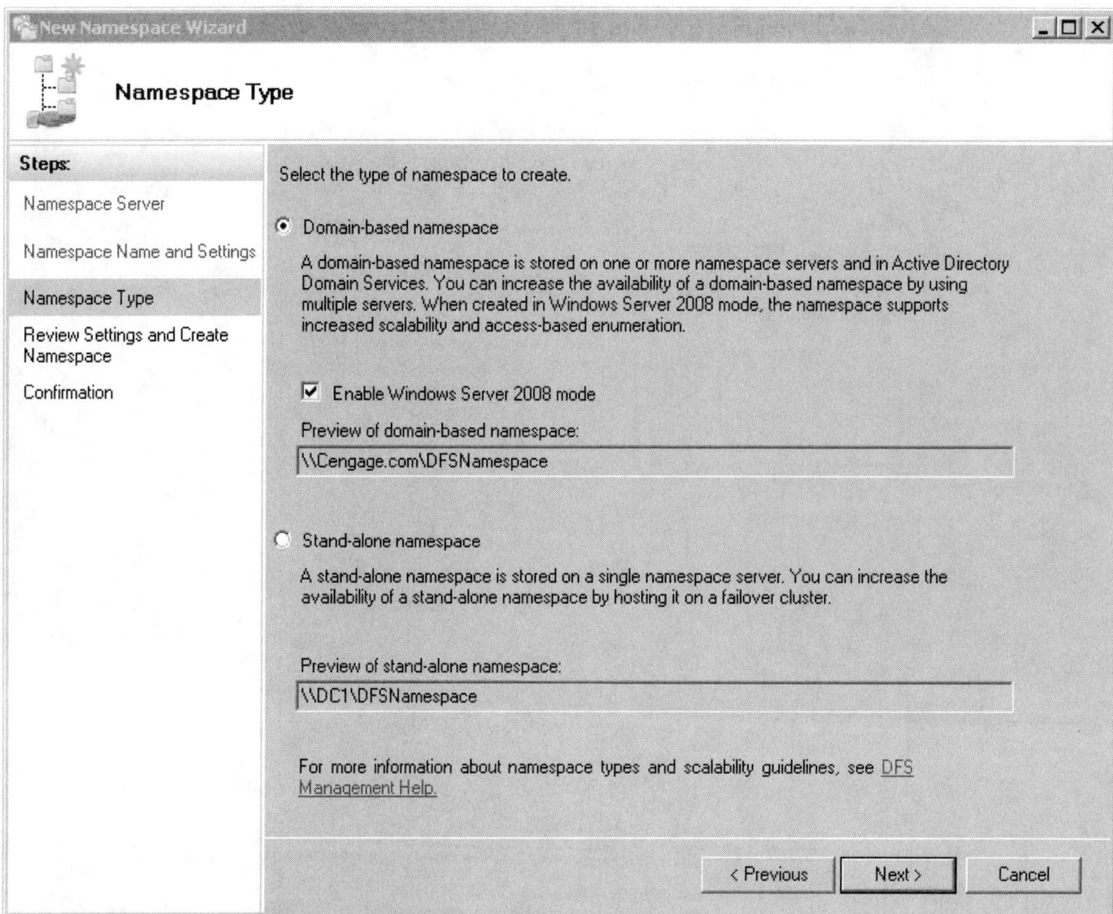

Figure 9-8 Creating a domain-based namespace with Windows Server 2008 Mode

Courtesy Course Technology/Cengage Learning

7. Review the information on the **Review Settings and Create Namespace** screen and click **Create**. After the namespace is created, click **Close**.
8. Start **Windows Explorer** and browse to **C:\DFSRoots**. This folder was created by the wizard; it includes the folder named **DFSNamespace**.
9. Double-click the **DFSNamespace** folder. Right-click within the folder and select **New, Folder**. Name the folder **DC1Folder**. You'll see later that this folder is automatically available under the DFSNamespace folder, just as any child folder is available if the parent folder is shared.
10. Browse to the root of **C:**. Right-click within the **C:** drive and select **New, Folder**. Name the folder **DC1Share**.
11. Right-click **DC1Share** and select **Share**. Select **Everyone** from the drop-down menu and click **Add**. Change the **Permission Level** to **Contributor**. Click **Share**. Click **Done** after the folder is shared. This shared folder will later be added to DFSNamespace. Even though it isn't a child folder under the DFSNamespace folder, it will act like a child folder when added to the DFS namespace.
12. Log on to **DC2** with an **Administrator** account and a password of **P@ssw0rd.**
13. Start **Windows Explorer**. Browse to the root of **C:** on **DC2**. Right-click within the **C:** drive and select **New, Folder**. Name the folder **DC2Share**.
14. Right-click **DC2Share** and select **Share**. Select **Everyone** from the drop-down menu and click **Add**. Change the **Permission Level** to **Contributor**. Click **Share**. Click **Done**

after the folder is shared. This shared folder will later be added to DFSNamespace. Even though it isn't even on the same server as the DFSNamespace folder, it will act like a child folder when added to the DFS namespace.

15. Return to the **DFS Management** console on **DC1** and expand **Namespaces**. Right-click **\\Cengage.com\DFSNamespace** and select **New Folder**. Type **ShareOnDC1** as the **Name.**
16. Click **Add** and then enter the UNC path of the share as **\\DC1\DC1Share**. Your display will look similar to Figure 9-9. Click **OK** twice.

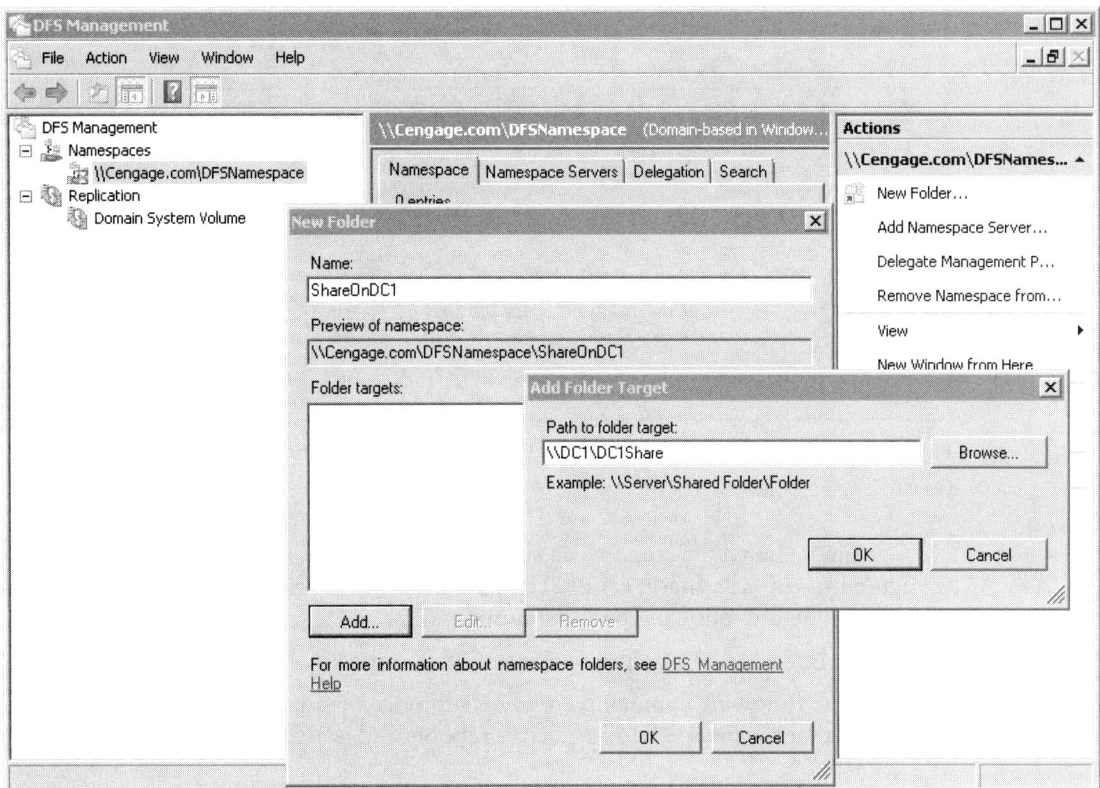

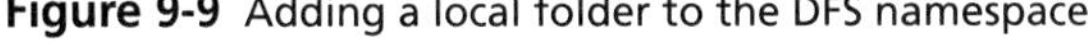

Figure 9-9 Adding a local folder to the DFS namespace

Courtesy Course Technology/Cengage Learning

17. Right-click **\\Cengage.com\DFSNamespace** and select **New Folder.** Type **ShareOnDC2** as the **Name**, click **Add**, and then click **Browse.**
18. Change the **Server** from **DC1** to **DC2** and click **Show Shared Folders** to view all the shared folders on **DC2**. Select **DC2Share** and click **OK**. Click **OK** two more times to return to the **DFS Management** console.
19. Click **Start**, type **\\Cengage.com\DFSNamespace** in the **Start Search** box, and press **Enter.** Your display will look similar to Figure 9-10. In the figure, the DFS Management console (top) shows what you've created, and Windows Explorer (bottom) shows what a user will see when connecting to the namespace using the UNC path.
20. Close all open windows on both **DC1** and **DC2.**

With the DFS namespace created, users can now access the namespace using \\Cengage.com\DFSNamespace. This can also be mapped to a drive, either for individual users or for a group of users with a script.

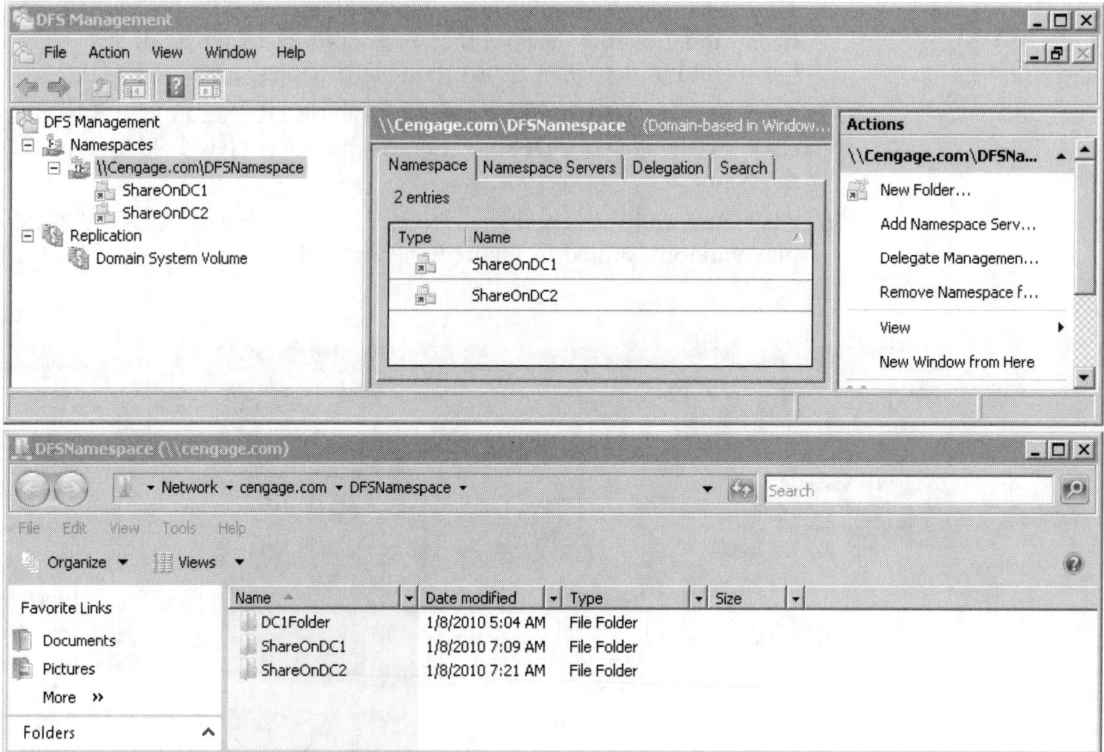

Figure 9-10 Viewing the namespace from the DFS Management console and Windows Explorer

Courtesy Course Technology/Cengage Learning

A simple batch file could use a single Net Use command and the batch file could then be configured to run as a logon script. The batch file could be created in Notepad, be named dfs.bat, and include the following one-line command:

```
Net Use P: \\Cengage.com\dfsnamespace
```

Or, the following command could be run once on a user's system. The /persistent : yes switch ensures that the mapped drive survives reboots and is available as long as the user doesn't remove the mapping.

```
Net Use P: \\Cengage.com\dfsnamespace /persistent : yes
```

The net use command, like most command-prompt commands, is not case sensitive.

DFS Replication

DFS replication can be used to copy and synchronize the content of DFS namespace folders from one DFS server to another. DFS replication provides redundancy for the data and can also be very useful when hosting data in different locations configured as Active Directory sites.

Because DFS replication is site-aware, users will be directed to a DFS server in their site when connecting to a domain-based DFS namespace. Additionally, if the content is replicated to a DFS server in the same site, the user doesn't need to wait for the data to traverse the slower WAN link.

When using DFS replication, three terms are important to understand:

- **Replication groups.** These groups of servers participate in DFS replication and hold copies of the data.

- **Members.** DFS servers identified in a DFS replication group are known as members. Members will house replicated data in replicated folders.
- **Replicated folders.** These folders are replicated to all members in the replication group.

As an example, consider Figure 9-11, which shows a main office and two remote sites configured as Active Directory sites. A server named FS1 is hosting a DFS namespace with two folders named Projects and Graphics. It could also host targeted folders from other servers in the site, but it hosts just the two folders to keep the example simple.

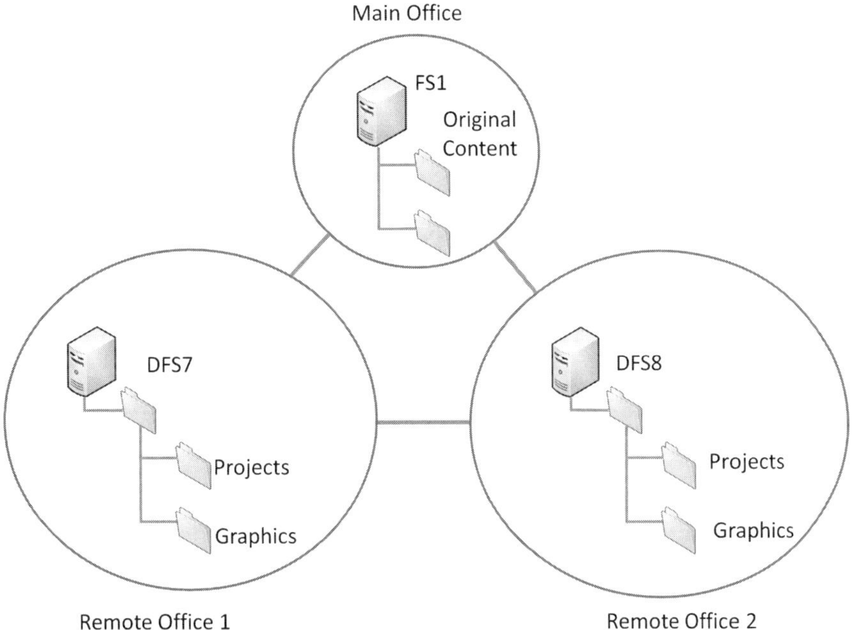

Figure 9-11 DFS replication
Courtesy Course Technology/Cengage Learning

A replication group can be created to include DFS7 and DFS8 as replication group members in the remote offices. The Projects and Graphics folders can be configured as replicated folders and the content will be replicated to DFS7 and DFS8 from FS1 in the main office. This configuration provides two significant benefits, especially if the WAN links are slow or unreliable:

- **Users access the data locally.** Because DFS is site-aware, users will access the data from the DFS server in their site instead of from a server in a different site. This improves the performance for site users and decreases the load on the WAN link.
- **Users continue to have access to the data even if the WAN links fail.** Because the data is housed on the local server, users can still access the replicated data even if the WAN link fails.

SYSVOL Replication

SYSVOL is a group of folders replicated to all domain controllers in the domain. It includes public files, system policies, logon scripts, and elements of Group Policy objects. Every domain controller hosts a shared copy of the SYSVOL folder, and its contents are replicated to all other domain controllers.

In Windows 2000 Server and Windows Server 2003, the SYSVOL folders were replicated using the File Replication Service (FRS). With FRS, every time a file was changed, the entire file was replicated to other domain controllers.

Microsoft introduced DFS replication in Windows Server 2003 R2, which significantly improves the performance of SYSVOL replication. Instead of replicating the entire file when it is changed, DFS replication can identify and replicate only the portion that has changed. For larger enterprises that have many domain controllers, this increased performance can reduce the bandwidth used for replication. This feature isn't as critical with smaller networks that use only two or three domain controllers.

If the domain is first created on a Windows Server 2008 server, DFS replication is automatically used for replication of the SYSVOL folder. However, if the domain started on an older operating system (such as Windows 2000 Server or Windows Server 2003) and domain controllers were later upgraded, FRS is used.

You can switch to DFS replication from FRS replication if desired. The steps are:

- **Upgrade all DCs to at least Windows Server 2008.** This must be done before the domain can be raised to Windows Server 2008.
- **Raise the domain functional level to at least Windows Server 2008.** Windows Server 2008 R2 would also work if all domain controllers were running it.
- **Migrate the SYSVOL folder from FRS replication to DFS replication.** This detailed process is documented at the following link if necessary: *http://go.microsoft.com/fwlink/?LinkID=119296.*

Designing for Data Collaboration

Most projects within organizations today require many users to work in collaboration to achieve their goals. The easier it is for a project team to work together, the better the chances for success.

Windows Server 2008 can be used to help an organization increase the collaborative efforts of workers. It includes the following tools to increase collaboration:

- **Windows SharePoint Services 3.0.** WSS 3.0 is a free product that can be downloaded and installed on Windows Server 2008. It allows employees and team members to easily share documents and coordinate activities. Activities later in this section lead you through the process of preparing Windows Server 2008 for WSS and installing WSS.
- **Microsoft Office SharePoint Server 2007.** MOSS is an advanced portal server product that can be purchased; it includes WSS as the foundation. It can do everything that WSS can do and adds a significant number of capabilities that are useful in an enterprise.
- **Services for Network File System.** These services can be added to Windows Server 2008 to allow interactivity with UNIX systems using the Network File System (NFS). An activity later in this section shows how to add these services.

Of the three tools, WSS 3.0 is clearly the one you should understand best when studying for the 70-647 exam. It is a free product (unlike MOSS) and it focuses on Microsoft technologies (unlike Services for Network File System).

Microsoft Windows SharePoint Services (WSS)

Windows SharePoint Services 3.0 can be installed on Windows Server 2008 to create and manage Web sites used for collaboration between employees or team members. A primary benefit of WSS is that it is free and can easily be installed on a Windows Server 2008 server. Once installed, it requires little configuration, which means users can quickly begin using it to collaborate on projects and share documents.

WSS has several tools that can be used for collaboration:

- **Document sharing.** Users can easily post and share documents via WSS Web sites. The full range of Microsoft Office documents (such as Microsoft Word and Microsoft Excel) can be shared on WSS, as well as other document types used in the organization.
- **Document version tracking.** Built-in tools can be used to track a document's history as it goes through different edits. Both minor and major document versions can be tracked.
- **Familiar Web interface.** Internet Explorer is used to access WSS Web sites, allowing users to quickly learn and use WSS.
- **Security controls.** These controls allow administrators to assign permissions based on roles such as managers or team members, and users can set permissions on individual documents if needed.

As an example, Figure 9-12 shows a user's view of the Create page on the WSS Web site. Users can create a wide variety of pages and items for their Web pages. This page shows the choices users have to share documents, calendars, lists, and more. Users can hover the mouse over a selection to get more information. In the figure, the mouse is hovering over Sites and Workspaces.

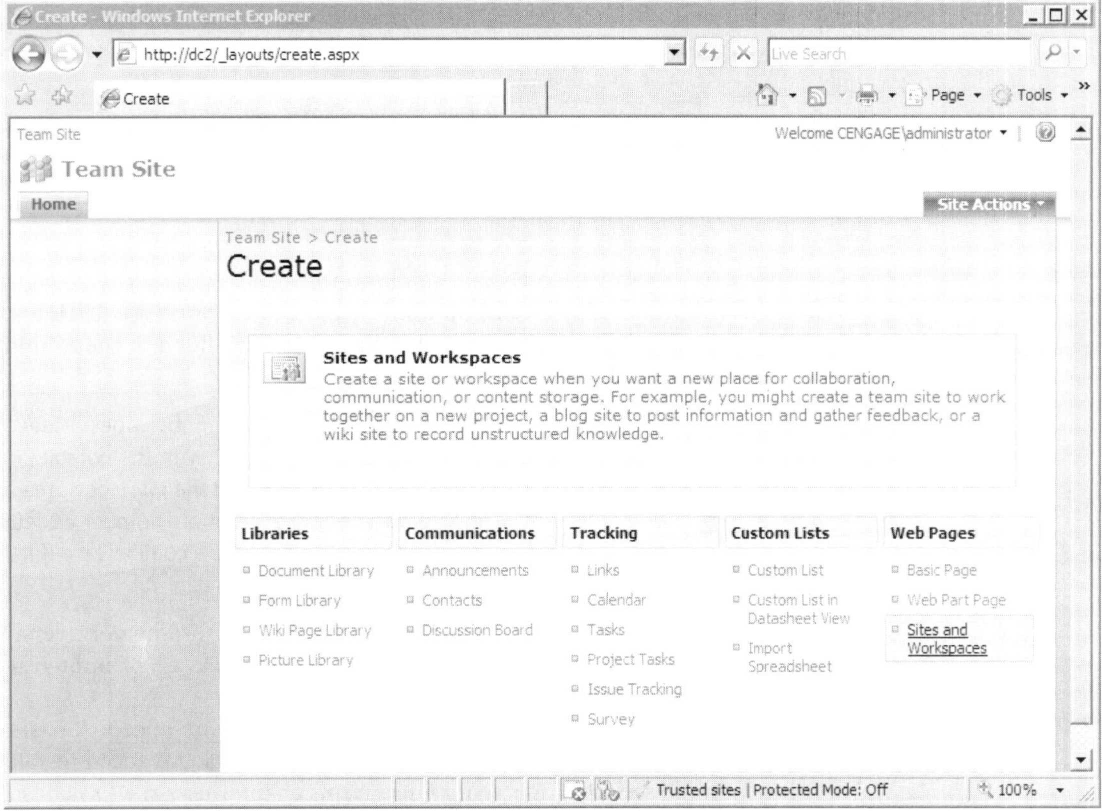

Figure 9-12 Using WSS to create libraries, communicate with others, track projects, create lists, and create Web sites and workspaces

Courtesy Course Technology/Cengage Learning

WSS can easily run on Windows Server 2008 with a little preparation. You should have at least a 2.5 GHz processor with at least 1 GB of RAM. If more users are needed, more hardware can be added to the server. WSS can also be configured to work with multiple servers in a Web farm.

If SQL Server is installed on the server before WSS is added, WSS will use SQL Server. Otherwise, it will install and use the Windows Internal Database.

WSS includes a Web interface that can be used to administer WSS. Figure 9-13 shows the interface with its three tabs: Home, Operations (selected in the figure), and Application Management. A random port number is assigned and used for the administration Web site. For example,

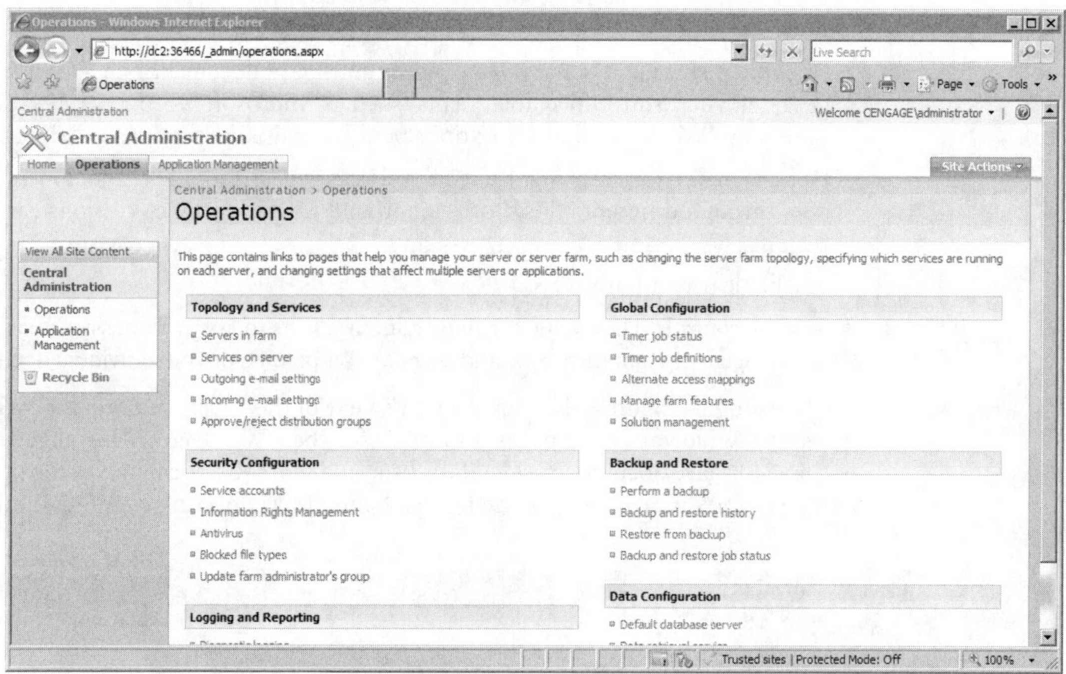

Figure 9-13 WSS Operations Management
Courtesy Course Technology/Cengage Learning

if WSS is added to a server named DC2, a random port of 36466 could be assigned and used as part of the URL as http://dc2:36466. You don't need to memorize this URL and port number because a link to the administration Web site is automatically added to the Administrative Tools menu when WSS is installed.

HTTP uses port 80 by default, so the port number doesn't need to be added to the URL. If you were accessing DC2 with the default port, you would use http://dc2. However, if you did add the HTTP port, the address would be similar to http://dc2:80, with the port number added at the end. Because the administration Web site uses a completely different port number for HTTP, it must be included in the URL.

Before installing WSS, you need to add the Microsoft .NET Framework version 3.0 feature. When this feature is added using Server Manager, you will also be prompted to add the Web Server (IIS) role, which is required for WSS.

When installing WSS 3.0, you have two choices: basic and advanced. A basic installation is used for a single stand-alone server with default settings. Use the advanced installation to create a Web farm of multiple servers. An activity later in this chapter uses the basic installation.

After WSS is installed, two items are added to the Administrative Tools menu:

- **SharePoint Products and Technologies Configuration Wizard.** This tool is run after the installation to configure WSS. It can also be run later if the configuration needs to be repaired.
- **SharePoint 3.0 Central Administration.** This option opens the Administration Web site for WSS and is the primary tool used to manage and administer WSS.

Activities 9-5, 9-6, and 9-7 lead you through the steps to install the prerequisites for WSS, install WSS, and access the WSS Administration console.

- **Activity 9-5: Add Microsoft .NET Framework version 3.0.** This activity will also add role services such as the Web Server (IIS) role and the Windows Process Activation Service.

- **Activity 9-6: Install and configure WSS 3.0.** This requires the WSS 3.0 file (SharePoint.exe) to be downloaded and copied to the server first. Go to Microsoft's download site (*www.microsoft.com/downloads*) and search on WSS 3.0.
- **Activity 9-7: Start and view the WSS Administration console.** No additional administration is needed right away, but this console can be used to change the configuration if desired.

When preparing for the 70-647 exam, you needn't learn the details of managing a WSS site, but you should know the capabilities so you can adequately consider them in the design. Likewise, the following activities won't make you an expert on WSS administration, but they allow you to explore WSS and learn some of its capabilities.

Activity 9-5: Adding the Microsoft .NET Framework 3.0 Feature

Time Required: 10 minutes
Objective: Add the Microsoft .NET Framework 3.0 feature.

Description: You want to install WSS 3.0 for evaluation purposes. To prepare the server, you must first install the Microsoft .NET Framework 3.0 feature. This lab should be completed on DC2 with DC1 running.

1. Start **DC1** and **DC2**. Log on to **DC2** with an **Administrator** account and a password of **P@ssw0rd**.
2. Start **Server Manager** via the **Administrative Tools** menu.
3. Select **Features** and select **Add Features**.
4. Select the check box next to **.NET Framework 3.0 Features**. A dialog box appears (see Figure 9-14) and prompts you to add role services and features. Click **Add Required Role Services**. Click **Next**.
5. Review the information on the **Introduction to Web Server (IIS)** screen and click **Next**.
6. Accept the default selections on the **Select Role Services** screen and click **Next**.
7. Click **Install** on the **Confirm Installation Selections** screen.
8. When the installation is complete, click **Close**.

Activity 9-6: Installing and Configuring WSS 3.0

Time Required: 30 minutes
Objective: Install WSS 3.0.

Description: You have installed the Microsoft .NET Framework 3.0 feature and you now need to install WSS 3.0. This activity assumes that Activity 9-5 has been completed. Activity 9-6 should be completed on DC2 with DC1 running.

WSS 3.0 with SP2 should be downloaded and copied to DC2 before you start this activity. The file is named SharePoint.exe; it can be obtained from Microsoft's download site (*www.microsoft.com/downloads*) by searching on "WSS 3.0." If you are using a virtual server, you should download WSS from the host and copy the file to the virtual server rather than reconfiguring the virtual server to have Internet access.

1. Start **DC1** and **DC2**. Log on to DC2 with an **Administrator** account and a password of **P@ssw0rd**.

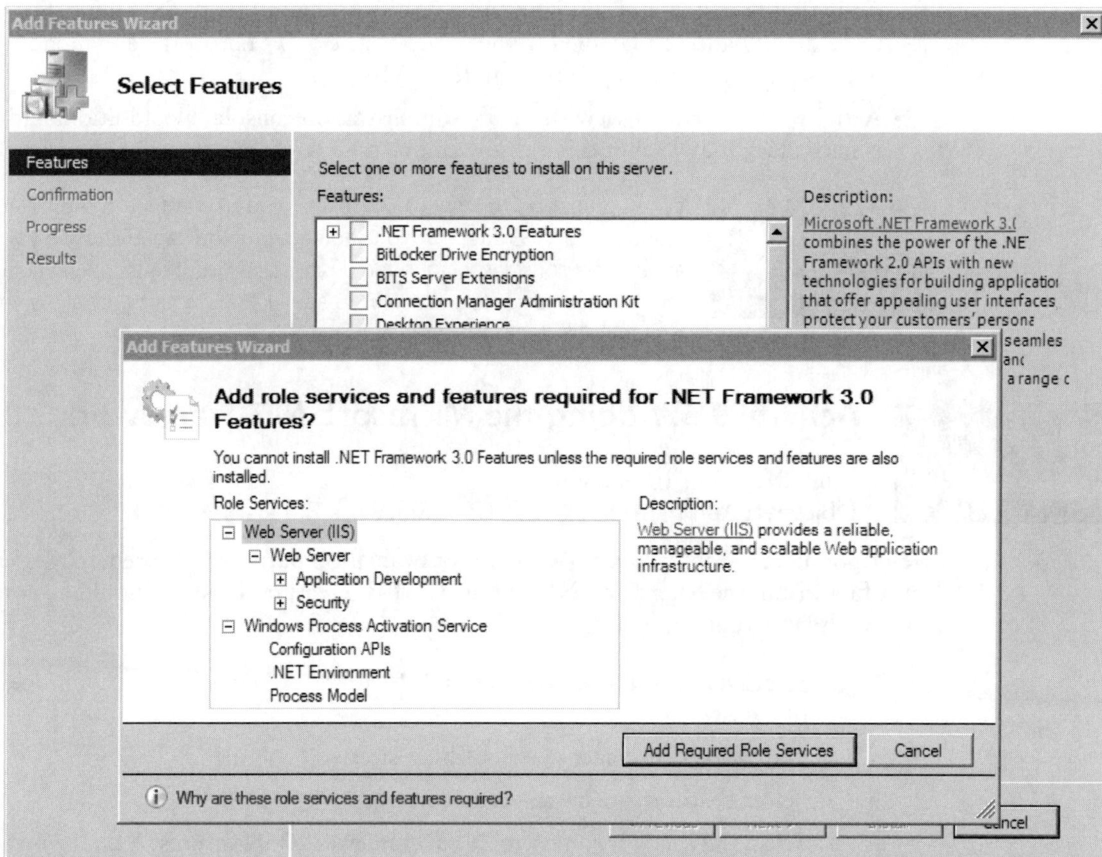

Figure 9-14 Adding role services for the .NET Framework 3.0 Features
Courtesy Course Technology/Cengage Learning

2. Start **Windows Explorer.** Browse to the location of the WSS 3.0 file that was downloaded. Double-click the **SharePoint.exe** file to start the installation.
3. Review the license agreement and select **I Accept the Terms of This Agreement.** Click **Continue.**
4. Click **Basic** to select the installation settings for a single stand-alone server. The installation will begin and take several minutes to complete.
5. After the installation is complete, ensure that **Run the SharePoint Products and Technologies Configuration Wizard** is checked and click **Close.**
6. Review the information on the **Welcome to SharePoint Products and Technologies** screen and click **Next.** A dialog box appears, as shown in Figure 9-15, prompting you to restart or reset several services. Click **Yes.**
7. The configuration wizard runs and reports its progress. When the configuration is complete, a **Configuration Successful** screen appears. Click **Finish.**
8. Internet Explorer opens with the address of **http://dc2**; you'll be prompted to provide credentials. Use **Cengage\Administrator** as the **User Name** and **P@ssw0rd** as the **Password.** Click **OK.**
9. **Internet Explorer** security prompts you to add the **http://dc2** Web site. Click **Add.** Click **Add** again to add the site to the list of **Trusted Sites** and click **Close.**
10. If prompted, select **Turn On Automatic Phishing Filter (Recommended).** Click **OK.** At this point, WSS is installed and users can access it to collaborate on different projects.

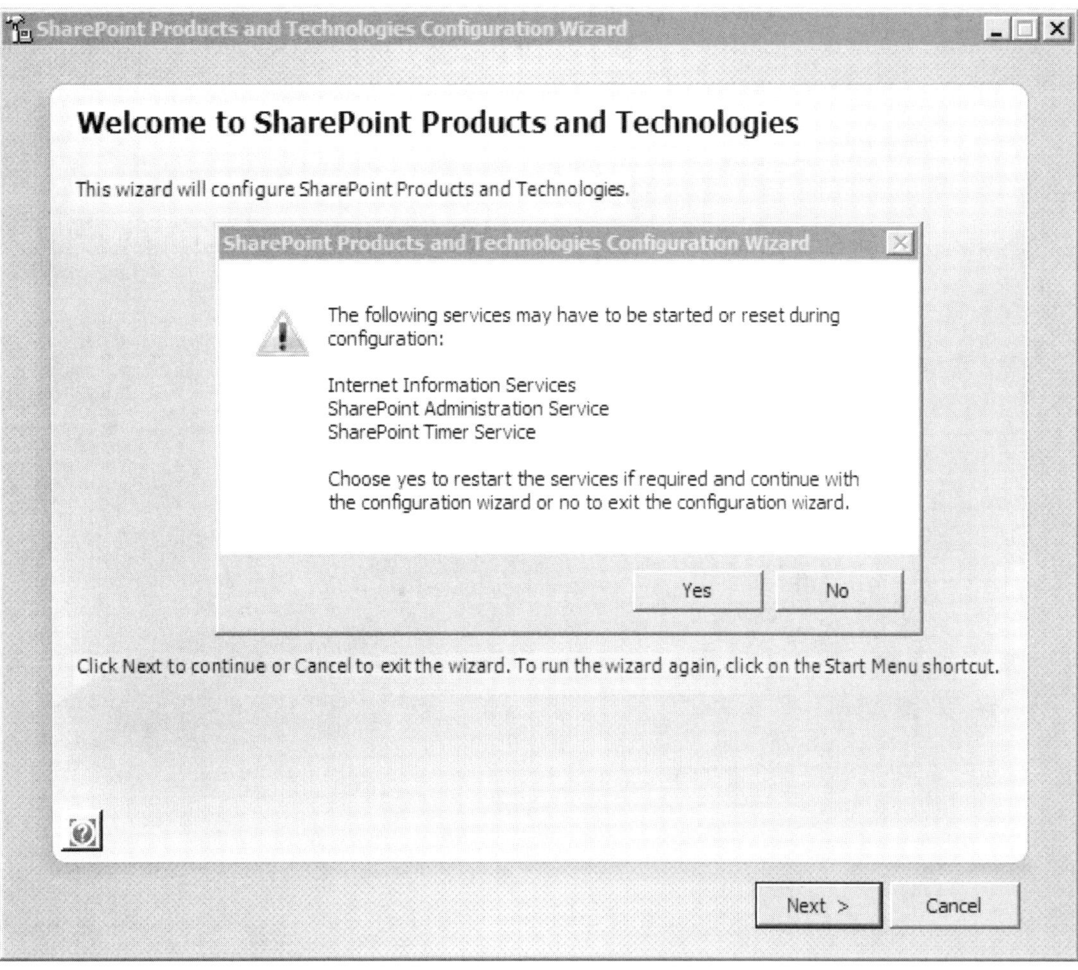

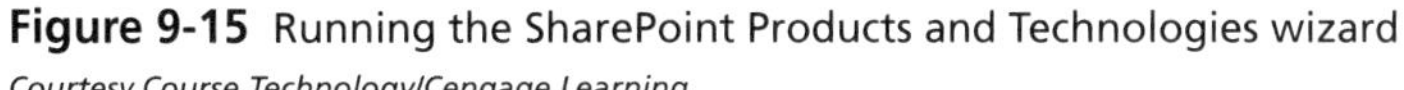

Figure 9-15 Running the SharePoint Products and Technologies wizard
Courtesy Course Technology/Cengage Learning

11. Click **Create** from the **Site Actions** menu in the upper-right corner. Notice that users can create a new site, edit pages here, and modify the site settings from this page. Feel free to look around, create a Web site, and edit some Web pages to see the capabilities of WSS.
12. Close all open windows.

Activity 9-7: Starting the WSS 3.0 Administration Console

Time Required: 10 minutes
Objective: Start SharePoint 3.0 Central Administration.

Description: After installing WSS 3.0, you want to familiarize yourself with the administration console. You will start the console and view the different capabilities. This activity assumes that Activity 9-6 was completed. Activity 9-7 should be completed on DC2 with DC1 running.

1. Start **DC1** and **DC2**. Log on to DC2 with an **Administrator** account and a password of **P@ssw0rd**.
2. Start **SharePoint 3.0 Central Administration** via the **Administrative Tools** menu.
3. When prompted for credentials, enter **Cengage\Administrator** as the **User Name**, and enter **P@ssw0rd** as the **Password**.

4. The **Central Administration** Web site appears, as shown in Figure 9-16. Notice that it starts with a task list of **Administrator Tasks**, which is a good starting point for new WSS administrators.

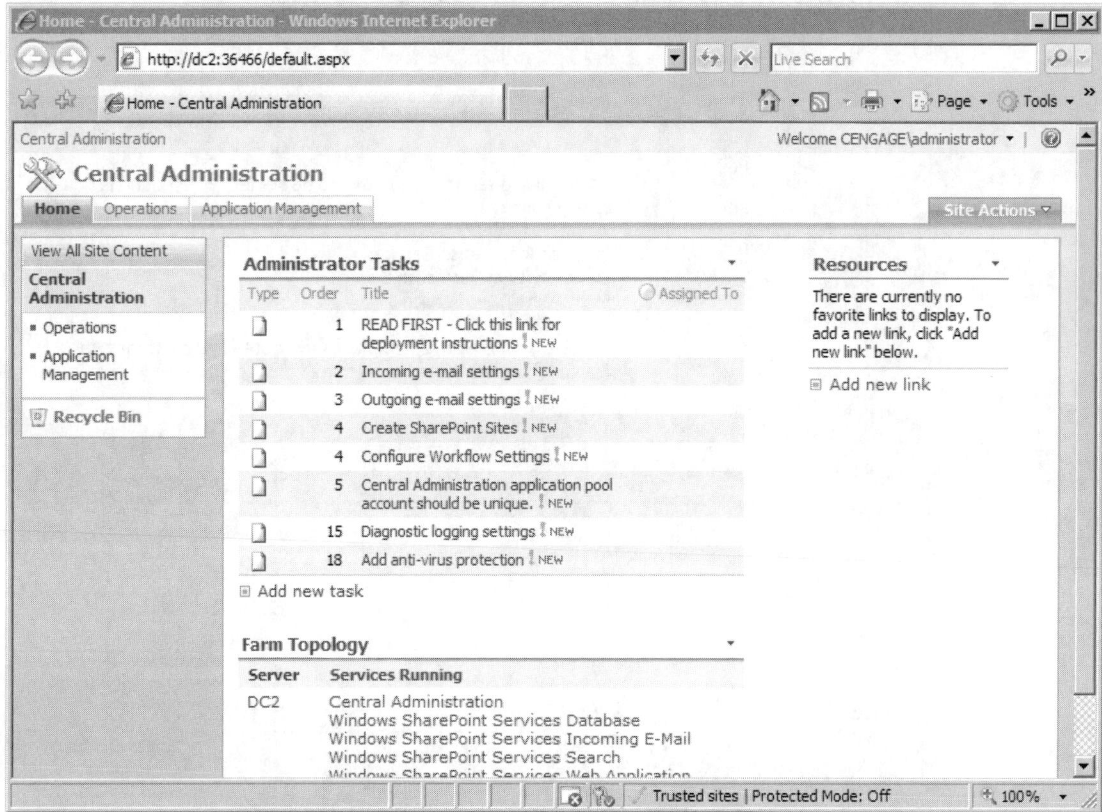

Figure 9-16 WSS Central Administration Web site
Courtesy Course Technology/Cengage Learning

5. Click the **Operations** tab and view the settings that can be managed here.
6. Click the **Application Management** tab and view the settings that can be managed here.
7. Close all open windows.

Microsoft Office SharePoint Server (MOSS)

Microsoft Office SharePoint Server 2007 (MOSS) is an advanced implementation of WSS. It includes two versions (Standard and Enterprise); both are server products that must be purchased. MOSS can scale to a much larger group of clients and includes many more features than WSS.

MOSS includes three key components:

- **WSS.** WSS was covered in the previous section. MOSS uses WSS as a foundation and significantly enhances the capabilities.
- **Office SharePoint Server 2007.** This group of server applications is designed to help end users and administrators create and manage Web portals used for collaboration.
- **Office SharePoint Designer 2007.** This group of tools can be used to customize MOSS sites. It includes many Web site application templates that can be used as is or modified to meet an organization's needs. The tools allow modifications without requiring users to write new code.

A common question is: What can MOSS do that WSS can't? Table 9-1 compares the products and lists some of the advanced features available with MOSS 2007.

Table 9-1 Comparison of WSS 3.0 and MOSS 2007

Feature	WSS 3.0	MOSS 2007
Integration with Microsoft Office Word 2007, PowerPoint 2007, Access 2007, and Excel 2007	Yes	Yes
Document sharing with document check out, and major and minor version numbering and tracking	Yes	Yes
E-mail, calendars, blogs, and wikis	Yes	Yes
Standard site templates	Yes	Yes
Advanced portal templates	No	Yes
Personalization by users including My Site and About Me	No	Yes
RSS feeds	No	Yes
User profiles	No	Yes
Content search	Limited	Yes
What You See Is What You Get (WYSIWYG) Web content editor	No	Yes

Both WSS 3.0 and MOSS 2007 can be scaled up and scaled out to increase the number of supported users. Scaling up means adding resources on a single server, such as additional processors or more RAM. Scaling out means adding more servers and often entails configuring the servers in a Web farm.

MOSS 2007 was heavily tested to determine its scalability and its ability to support a high-volume Web portal. The tests had positive results: MOSS 2007 could handle 400 concurrent users using an initial database of 10.5 million content items (such as documents), with 54,000 new content items added each day. The test simulated a real-world portal used for loan applications where documents are regularly posted, reviewed, and digitally signed. The conclusion of the study was that MOSS can successfully scale up and out to meet any Web portal needs.

You can access the full white paper that documents these tests at *http://go.microsoft.com/fwlink/?LinkId=120881*.

Services for Network File System

Services for Network File System gives UNIX client computers that do not support SMB communications access to files on a Windows Server 2008 server, and allows Windows Server 2008 servers to access data stored with the **Network File System (NFS)** on UNIX systems. The Services for Network File System role service is an additional option for the File Services role. UNIX systems use NFS to access files over a network, and this service allows the Windows Server 2008 server to interact with NFS.

After the service is added, you can access the Services for Network File System console via the Administrative Tools menu. Figure 9-17 shows the console. By default, both the Client for NFS and the Server for NFS components are started. If the server won't be used to access a UNIX server, the Client for NFS service should be stopped. Similarly, if UNIX clients won't be accessing the Windows Server 2008 server, the Server for NFS service should be stopped. If neither condition exists, Services for Network File System shouldn't be added.

Several command-line tools are also accessible after the role service is added. An understanding of UNIX commands is helpful in using these options, but basic help is available at the command line using the /? switch. These command-line tools include:

- **Mount.** Used to mount NFS shared network resources.
- **Umount.** Removes NFS-mounted drives.

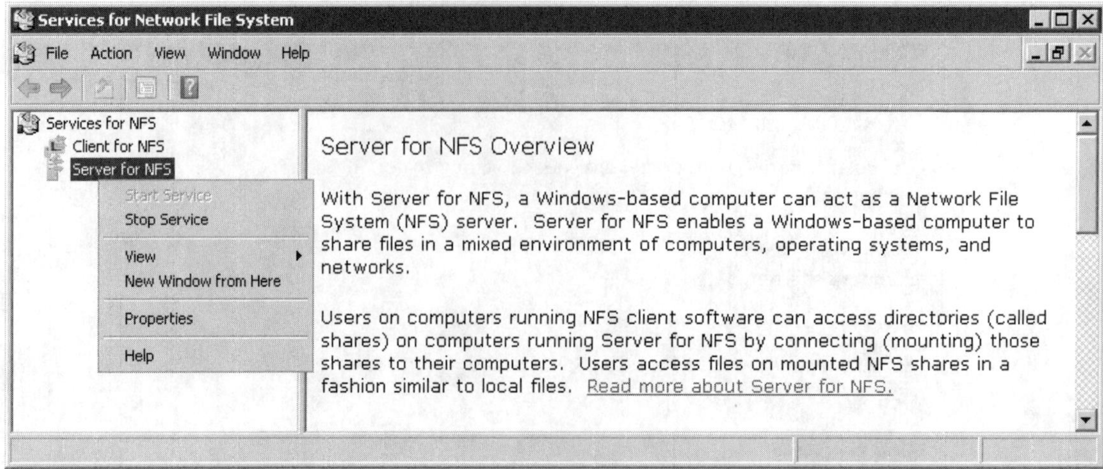

Figure 9-17 Services for Network File System console
Courtesy Course Technology/Cengage Learning

- **Showmount.** Provides a list of mounted file systems.
- **Nfsadmin.** Used to manage the Server for NFS and Client for NFS components.
- **Nfsshare.** Controls NFS shared resources.
- **Nfsstat.** Shows statistics for calls or requests to the Server for NFS component.

Support for UNIX was provided using Windows Services for UNIX in Windows Server versions before Windows Server 2003 R2.

By default, all UNIX users are granted the same level of access when using Services for NFS. However, you also can provide user-level security for UNIX users with Services for NFS. Two methods are used:

- **Implement user identifiers (UIDs) and group identifiers (GIDs).** Active Directory Domain Services is configured with UIDs and GIDs for the UNIX clients. Permissions can be assigned to the individual UIDs and GIDs. Third-party tools are available to make this process easier.
- **Implement User Name Mapping.** UNIX user accounts are associated with Windows User accounts in a user name mapping process. Permissions are assigned to the Windows User accounts and the UNIX users are granted access based on the mapped account.

The following activity shows how to add the Services for Network File System role service. After the service is added, the NFS command-line tools will also be available.

Activity 9-8: Adding Services for Network File System

Time Required: 10 minutes
Objective: Add Services for Network File System to add support for UNIX systems.

Description: You are preparing to add UNIX systems to your network and you want UNIX system users to be able to access data on your server. As a first step, you need to add the Services for Network File System role service. This lab should be completed on DC1.

1. Start **DC1** and log on with an **Administrator** account and a password of **P@ssw0rd.**
2. Start **Server Manager** via the **Administrative Tools** menu.
3. Expand **Roles** and select **File Services.** Scroll down to the **Role Services** section and select **Add Role Services.**

4. Select **Services for Network File System**, as shown in Figure 9-18. Click **Next**.

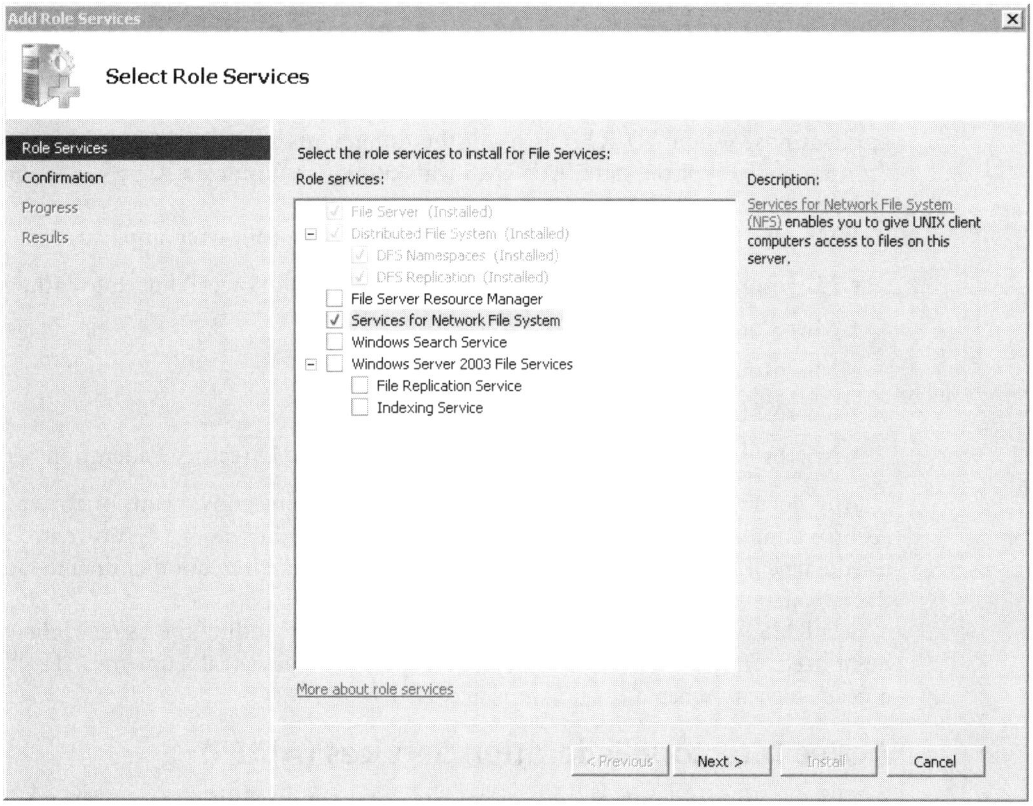

Figure 9-18 Adding Services for Network File System

Courtesy Course Technology/Cengage Learning

5. Click **Install**. When the installation is complete, click **Close**.

Designing for Additional Active Directory Services

When considering supporting services for an enterprise, you should be aware of the capabilities of additional Active Directory services. The primary service is Active Directory Domain Services (AD DS), which has been covered throughout the book. Chapter 6 covered Active Directory Certificate Services (AD CS).

You can add three other Active Directory server roles to Windows Server 2008:

- **Active Directory Rights Management Services (RMS)**. AD RMS can be used to protect documents after they have been sent to others. Protected documents are encrypted and AD RMS can restrict users from taking specific actions with the documents. For example, an e-mail document can be protected so that users can't forward it, print it, or paste it into another document.
- **Active Directory Federation Services (AD FS)**. AD FS provides a single sign-on capability for users in different security realms. It's commonly used to allow access to Web sites hosted by another organization without requiring users to log on again. AD FS uses federated trusts created between the two organizations. Tokens created when a user logs on are passed to federation servers in the organization and shared with federation servers in the trusted organization.
- **Active Directory Lightweight Directory Services (AD LDS)**. AD LDS can allow Active Directory-enabled applications to store and retrieve data in Active Directory using the

same resources as AD DS. AD LDS can be used with a domain hosted on a domain controller, or separate from a domain.

Active Directory Rights Management Services (AD RMS)

AD RMS is a role you can add to a Windows Server 2008 server. It can be used as a digital rights management (DRM) technology to protect access to documents created in various Microsoft applications. When AD RMS is used, the documents are encrypted and only certain users or groups can decrypt the data. AD RMS was known as Windows Rights Management Services in Windows Server 2003.

RMS can be used to protect documents through the following applications:

- Microsoft Office products (Microsoft Word, Excel, PowerPoint, InfoPath, Outlook)
- Microsoft Visio 2007
- Microsoft Project 2007
- Microsoft Office SharePoint Server 2007
- Microsoft Exchange Server 2007 and 2010 Active Directory Federation Services

Any document can be restricted so that users cannot copy, print, or forward sensitive data. As an example, sensitive data can be sent via e-mail and users can be prevented from forwarding the document to others, copying any portion of the e-mail into another document, or even printing the e-mail.

AD RMS works by encrypting a document and embedding the usage rights within the document itself. Only authorized users can decrypt and access the documents. AD DS is used to verify a user's identity when a document is accessed.

Active Directory Federation Services (AD FS)

AD FS is a Windows Server 2008 server role that can provide account verification for users outside an Active Directory forest, and even for users in a non-Microsoft environment. AD FS was first available in Windows Server 2003 R2.

AD FS is most commonly used to support single sign-on (SSO) with Web-based applications. SSO allows users to authenticate once and then use this single authentication for all access. As an example, users could log on once to a computer in their network, and later access a secure Web server hosted by another company without logging on again.

Consider Figure 9-19, which shows two separate domains that aren't part of the same forest. Domain B is hosting a SharePoint portal server that requires users to log on to access it. This

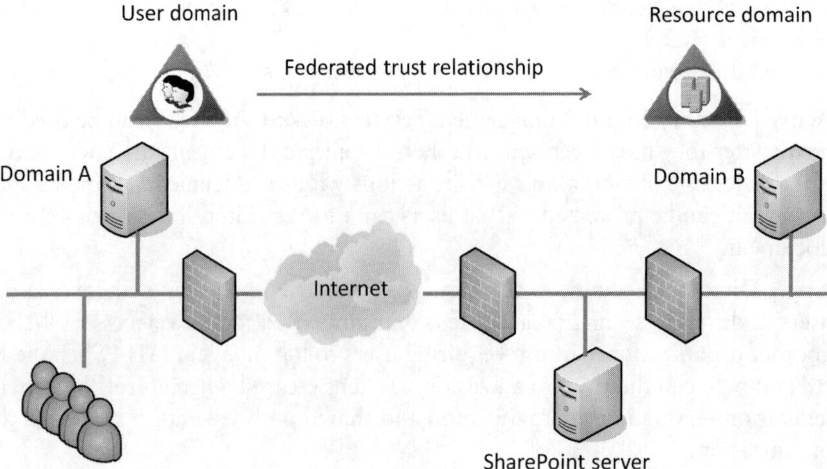

Figure 9-19 Federated trust used for single sign-on

Courtesy Course Technology/Cengage Learning

works well for users in Domain B using Windows Authentication—their user account in Domain B is presented to the SharePoint server, which is a member of Domain B. However, without a federated trust, users in Domain A need to provide credentials to access the SharePoint server.

When a federated trust is added, federation servers in Domain A pass tokens to federation servers in Domain B. These tokens are similar to the tokens created when a user logs on within a domain (as discussed in Chapter 2). The token is used by the federation server in the resource domain (which hosts the SharePoint server used as a resource) to validate that the user has already been authenticated in the user domain.

Because traffic typically goes over the Internet using Web-based protocols, traffic can be encrypted with either Secure Socket Layer (SSL) or Transport Layer Security (TLS). Hypertext Transfer Protocol over SSL (HTTPS) is commonly used to protect the data.

The implementation of AD FS is complex and detailed, but the result is that users in a separate forest can access the SharePoint server with SSO.

Active Directory Lightweight Directory Services (AD LDS)

AD LDS is an optional Active Directory service that can provide dedicated directory services for applications. AD LDS was known as Active Directory Application Mode (ADAM) in Windows Server 2003.

In AD DS, the NTDS.dit file holds all the objects for the domain, such as users, computers, groups, and so on. AD LDS provides the same services as AD DS, but instead of containing the Active Directory objects needed for a domain, AD LDS contains the objects needed by another directory-enabled application.

You can deploy an instance of AD LDS within or without a domain and domain controllers. AD LDS provides several benefits for Active Directory-enabled applications, including:

- **Multimaster replication.** Multiple servers can host AD LDS. Multimaster replication allows changes to be made to any server and then to be replicated and converged to all servers.
- **Support for applications using Active Directory Service Interface (ADSI) calls.** Developers can use familiar Application Programming Interfaces (APIs) to create AD LDS-capable applications.
- **Application directory partitions.** Separate partitions can be created if needed, similar to how Active Directory has different schema, domain, and configuration partitions.
- **Secure data transfer.** Replicated data is encrypted automatically using Lightweight Directory Access Protocol (LDAP) over SSL or TLS.

Chapter Summary

- The Microsoft System Center suite includes several server products that can enhance the administration and maintenance of a domain.
- Microsoft System Center Operations Manager (SCOM) is used to provide centralized monitoring of servers in enterprises. SCOM uses agents that are installed on systems in the network. The agents monitor for specific events and generate alerts that are sent back to the SCOM server.
- Microsoft System Center Configuration Manager (SCCM) can be used to deploy full operating systems as images, applications, and updates to client computers and servers in the network. SCCM improves on the capabilities of free products that perform these same tasks. For example, it improves the capabilities of Windows Deployment Services to deploy images of operating systems, Windows Server Update Services to deploy updates, and Group Policy to deploy applications.
- NTFS helps servers start with basic security. It allows files and folders to be protected using permissions and Encrypting File System (EFS). Additionally, NTFS version 6.2 (available with Server 2008) includes a self-healing feature that allows it to automatically detect and repair problems with disks.

- BitLocker Drive Encryption can be used to encrypt entire hard drives. If the hard drive is removed from the server and obtained by unauthorized users, data cannot be read. BitLocker Drive Encryption can be useful on servers at remote locations that don't have adequate physical security. Read-only domain controllers can be useful in the same situation. It would be common to use both BitLocker Drive Encryption and RODCs in remote offices to provide layered security, or security in depth.
- Trusted Platform Module (TPM) version 1.2 is required to fully support BitLocker Drive Encryption. The BIOS must be TPM-capable and the protected hard drive must be formatted as NTFS.
- BitLocker recovery data can be stored in Active Directory once specific requirements are met. All DCs must be running at least Windows Server 2003 SP1, the schema must be extended if the domain was created with domain controllers older than Windows Server 2008, and permissions need to be modified at the domain level of Active Directory.
- Microsoft's Distributed File System (DFS) provides a unified view of shared folders to users even if the shares are located on different services. DFS uses DFS namespaces and DFS replication.
- A DFS namespace is created to organize folders. It includes a DFS root as the top-level folder that users access, and includes target folders, which are links to shared folders on other servers.
- DFS replication is used to replicate data in DFS target folders from one server to another. It is commonly used to replicate data to servers in remote offices. This allows users in the remote sites to access the data even if the WAN link goes down. DFS replication also reduces the bandwidth consumed by users in remote offices.
- Windows SharePoint Services (WSS) 3.0 is a free product that can be downloaded and installed on Windows Server 2008 and used to host Web sites. It allows employees and team members to easily collaborate on projects by sharing documents and coordinating activities.
- Microsoft Office SharePoint Server 2007 (MOSS) is an advanced portal server product. It includes WSS as the foundation, so it has all of WSS' capabilities to increase collaboration efforts between employees and team members. MOSS also adds capabilities that are useful in larger enterprises.
- The Services for Network File System role service allows Windows Server 2008 servers and UNIX clients to interact with each other.
- Active Directory Rights Management Services (AD RMS) can be used to protect documents and e-mails so that users' actions with the documents can be restricted. Documents are encrypted and include information to identify what users can do with them. For example, users can be restricted from forwarding an e-mail, printing it, or copying data from it.
- Active Directory Federation Services (AD FS) can be used to provide single sign-on (SSO) capabilities to users in another forest using a federated trust. It is commonly used on Web sites to allow users in one organization to access data hosted by another organization.
- Active Directory Lightweight Directory Services (AD LDS) can be used to host Active Directory-enabled data using the same services as Active Directory Domain Services (AD DS). Data can be held in partitions just as AD DS data is held in different partitions.

Key Terms

Active Directory Federation Services (AD FS) AD FS can be used to provide single sign-on (SSO) capabilities to users in another forest using a federated trust. It is most commonly used to provide Web access for users in a partner's organization without requiring them to log on again.

Active Directory Lightweight Directory Services (AD LDS) AD LDS is used to host application partitions for Active Directory-enabled applications. It provides many of the same benefits of Active Directory as Active Directory Domain Services, but for separate applications.

Active Directory Rights Management Services (AD RMS) AD RMS can be used to protect documents and e-mails. When implemented, documents are encrypted and protected from certain user actions. For example, users can be prevented from printing, copying, or forwarding documents. Unauthorized users are unable to decrypt the documents.

BitLocker Drive Encryption A technology that allows entire hard drives to be encrypted. It can be used on RODCs to add a layer of security when physical security is limited.

DFS namespace A group of shared folders from different servers made available to clients using the Distributed File System (DFS). Clients connect to the DFS namespace and are directed to folder targets that are created under the DFS root.

DFS replication A tool used to replicate data contained in DFS namespaces. DFS replication is most valuable in a multiple-site configuration. Instead of users accessing data across the WAN link, the data can be replicated to a server in the local site. DFS replication can improve data accessibility and ensure that users have access to the data even if the WAN link fails.

DFS root The top-level folder in a DFS namespace. Users connect to the DFS root using a UNC path. The UNC path on a domain-based DFS root is in the format of \\domain\DFSRoot; the format in a stand-alone DFS root is \\ServerName\DFSRoot. Folder targets are created under the root, and point to shares on other servers in the network.

Distributed File System (DFS) A group of technologies used to group folders from different servers into a single UNC path. A DFS namespace includes a DFS root and folder targets that point to folders on other servers. DFS replication can be used to replicate the content of folders to different servers.

Microsoft Office SharePoint Server 2007 (MOSS) An add-on server product that increases the abilities of Windows SharePoint Services 3.0 (WSS). WSS is included as a basic foundation for MOSS. MOSS can host Web sites used for collaboration between employees and teams, as WSS does, but MOSS has additional capabilities. For example, its advanced portal templates are useful in an enterprise, and users can personalize their view of sites.

Microsoft System Center Configuration Manager 2007 (SCCM) A server add-on product that can be used to deploy operating systems, applications, and updates to systems within the network. It improves the capabilities of Windows Deployment Services to deploy operating system images, Group Policy to deploy applications, and Windows Server Update Services to deploy updates.

Microsoft System Center Operations Manager 2007 (SCOM) A server add-on product that can provide centralized monitoring for a network. SCOM uses agents installed on monitored servers that generate alerts captured by the SCOM server.

Network File System (NFS) A file system used by UNIX systems to access files over a network. NFS services can be installed on Windows Server 2008 servers to increase the interaction between Windows Server 2008 and UNIX-based systems.

New Technology File System (NTFS) A file system used by Windows operating systems. NTFS enhances security by allowing files and folders to be protected by permissions and encryption. NTFS version 6.2 (included with Windows Server 2008) includes a self-healing capability that can detect and repair disk problems.

Services for Network File System A File Services role service that can be added to a Windows Server 2008 server to increase the interaction with UNIX systems that use NFS.

SYSVOL A group of folders within each domain controller that includes public files, system policies, logon scripts, and portions of Group Policy objects. The SYSVOL folder was replicated between all domain controllers using File Replication Service (FRS) in previous versions of Windows, but DFS replication can be used to replicate SYSVOL in Windows Server 2008.

Trusted Platform Module (TPM) A microchip that is usually embedded in a motherboard and that provides security functions needed by BitLocker. TPM version 1.2 is required to fully support BitLocker.

Windows SharePoint Services 3.0 (WSS) A free service that can be downloaded and added to Windows Server 2008 to manage Web sites used for collaboration between employees and teams. WSS sites can be hosted on a single server running WSS or on multiple servers in a Web farm.

Review Questions

1. You are an administrator in a large enterprise that hosts 35 Microsoft SQL Servers. You're asked to design a plan to consolidate the monitoring of these servers so that server issues and problems can be identified as quickly as possible. What would you include in the plan?
   a. SCOM
   b. SCCM
   c. SCE
   d. SCVMM
2. You are an administrator in a large enterprise that hosts 35 Microsoft SQL Servers. You're asked to design a plan to consolidate the monitoring of these servers so that server issues and problems can be identified as quickly as possible. What should be installed on the servers to support the plan?
   a. DFS
   b. MOSS
   c. WSS
   d. Agents
3. You are an administrator in a large enterprise with approximately 5,000 users. The company is planning to purchase an application that needs to be deployed to about 2,000 of the client computers. What could be used to deploy the application?
   a. SCOM
   b. SCCM
   c. SCE
   d. SCVMM
4. You are an administrator in a large enterprise with approximately 10,000 clients. The organization is planning to upgrade approximately 6,000 Windows XP systems to Windows 7 and is looking for a way to automate the process. What could be used?
   a. WSS
   b. WSUS
   c. SCCM
   d. SCOM
5. You are an administrator in a large enterprise with approximately 8,000 clients in a single-domain forest. Clients are currently being updated and patched with Windows Server Update Services (WSUS). However, you'd like to have more control over when the approved updates are deployed and be able to schedule the deployments of updates. What tool could you use?
   a. SCOM
   b. SCCM
   c. MOSS
   d. SCVMM

6. You are an administrator for a small enterprise that includes five Windows Server 2003 servers. You are considering migrating the servers to Windows Server 2008 and you're creating a business case to justify the added cost. You want to add details on stability and protection of data. What Windows Server 2008 feature includes the ability to automatically detect and repair disk problems?
   a. Windows Server Backup
   b. IPSec
   c. NTFS
   d. Windows PowerShell
7. Your company recently purchased several new computers that include TPM modules. These computers will use BitLocker Drive Encryption. The domain functional level is currently set to Windows Server 2008 and the forest functional level is set to Windows Server 2003. You want to ensure that BitLocker recovery data is stored in AD DS. What needs to be done?
   a. Extend the schema, modify permissions at the domain level, and configure Group Policy.
   b. Extend the schema and configure Group Policy.
   c. Extend the schema, modify permissions at the domain controller OU level, and configure Active Directory using the BitLocker configuration wizard.
   d. Raise the forest functional level to Windows Server 2008.

8. Your domain includes domain controllers running Windows Server 2003 with no service packs and Windows Server 2008. The domain functional level is Windows Server 2003. Some users in the domain are using BitLocker Drive Encryption. You want to ensure that recovery data is stored in AD DS. What should you do?
   a. Raise the domain functional level to Windows Server 2008.
   b. Add SP1 to the Windows Server 2003 domain controllers.
   c. Ensure that GPO version 2.1 is being used.
   d. Ensure that TPM version 2.1 is being used.
9. You are an administrator for a single-domain forest in the forest functional level of Windows Server 2008. All clients are running Windows Vista or Windows 7. You want to ensure that if any users enable BitLocker Drive Encryption on their systems, they store recovery information in Active Directory Domain Services. What should you do?
   a. Write and publish a corporate policy.
   b. Ensure all systems have TPM 1.2.
   c. Configure a GPO to require BitLocker Backup to AD DS.
   d. Configure a GPO to require TPM 1.2.
10. You are designing a solution to protect data stored on servers with removable hard drives. You need to ensure that if the drives are stolen, users will not be able to access the data. Your solution also needs to ensure that human intervention is not required to restart or reboot the servers. What should you do?
    a. Implement BitLocker with or without TPM.
    b. Implement BitLocker with TPM 1.2.
    c. Implement BitLocker with TPM 1.1.
    d. Implement IPSec.
11. You are asked to increase the limited physical security of domain controllers located at remote offices. The remote offices have RODCs. You want to ensure that Active Directory

Domain Services data cannot be copied from any of the RODCs if they are stolen. What should be done?

a. Implement BitLocker Drive Encryption.
b. Protect the data with permissions.
c. Encrypt the data with EFS.
d. Implement a policy to encrypt the data when it's being transmitted.

12. Your organization includes a single-domain forest. The headquarters is configured as a single Active Directory site and three smaller locations are configured as Active Directory sites. Users in each site access the same sales and product data hosted on a server at headquarters, but connectivity between the sites is often very slow. You're asked to improve data accessibility for users in the smaller locations. What would you recommend?

    a. Create a failover cluster at the headquarters location.
    b. Implement a DFS namespace.
    c. Implement DFS replication.
    d. Host the data on a Microsoft SharePoint server.

13. You administer a single-domain forest using Windows Server 2003 and Windows Server 2008 domain controllers. Some domain controllers are in remote locations configured as sites. You are trying to reduce the bandwidth used on the WAN links, and you decide to implement DFS replication for the SYSVOL folder. What must be done before you can switch from FRS replication to DFS replication? (Choose all that apply.)

    a. Upgrade all DCs to Windows Server 2008.
    b. Raise the domain functional level to Windows Server 2008.
    c. Raise the forest functional level to Windows Server 2008.
    d. Move the SYSVOL folder to an NTFS drive.

14. You are preparing to replace a Windows Server 2003 file server with a Windows Server 2008 file server. The server hosts several shares that are accessed both by Windows clients and UNIX clients. You want to ensure that the UNIX clients can access the data on the new server. What should you do?

    a. Add the Windows Services for UNIX to the server.
    b. Add WSS to the server.
    c. Add MOSS to the server.
    d. Add the Services for Network File System role service.

15. You are an administrator for a single-domain forest with about 1,000 users. A Windows Server 2008 file server is used to share files among employees, but it isn't meeting users' needs. Users want to access documents using a Web browser and post them to be available to other users. You're asked to look into a solution that meets these requirements while minimizing costs. What do you suggest?

    a. DFS
    b. Services for Network File System
    c. WSS
    d. MOSS

16. You're an administrator for a company that is running Windows Server 2008 servers on the network. The company is considering using WSS as a collaboration tool, and you're asked to provide a list of benefits. Of the following, what are considered benefits of WSS? (Choose all that apply.)

    a. Available as a free download.
    b. Allows users to easily share documents (including Microsoft Office documents).

c. Allows permissions to be assigned at the document level.
d. Includes social networking Web Parts.

17. You are an administrator for a large enterprise that has about 10,000 users. Management is looking for a method to increase collaboration among users in the company. Users should be able to access Web sites using Internet Explorer and easily share documents with other users. Users should be able to personalize their views and add different Web Parts to their views, and the solution should store profile information for the users. What do you suggest?
    a. DFS
    b. Services for Network File System
    c. WSS
    d. MOSS
18. Your company is hosting several Web sites on the intranet using Microsoft Office SharePoint Server. Some of the documents are very sensitive, and permissions are used to ensure that specific users and groups have access to them. However, management also wants to protect these documents by preventing users from copying or printing them. What would you recommend to meet these needs?
    a. WSS
    b. AD RMS
    c. AD FS
    d. AD LDS
19. Your organization hosts a Web site on Microsoft Office SharePoint Server within the perimeter network. It is currently accessed by employees from the Internet and the intranet. The company recently entered into a partnership with another organization, and access to the Web site needs to be provided to users in that organization. The solution needs to support single sign-on. What would you recommend?
    a. WSS
    b. AD RMS
    c. AD FS
    d. AD LDS
20. You are an administrator of a single-domain forest named Cengage.com. Developers in your organization are creating an application and want it to be Active Directory-enabled, allowing them to host data used by their application in separate partitions. What would you recommend?
    a. WSS
    b. AD RMS
    c. AD FS
    d. AD LDS

Case Projects

Case Project 9-1: Deploying Applications

Your company has a single-domain forest of about 1,000 clients and 50 servers. The company is planning to purchase an application that needs to be installed on all 1,000 client computers. You're asked to identify two possible automated methods to install the application and provide comparisons between the two. What Microsoft technologies would you suggest? Explain your answer.

Case Project 9-2: Monitoring SQL Servers

Your organization has consolidated 15 SQL Servers onto three physical servers using Hyper-V technology. The three physical servers are named HV1, HV2, and HV3. The 15 SQL Servers are named SQL1 through SQL15. You're asked to identify a solution that can provide centralized monitoring of these 15 servers. Monitored events should be sent to the monitoring server almost as soon as they occur. What Microsoft solutions would you suggest? What should be installed on the servers to support your design? Explain your answer.

Case Project 9-3: Increasing Data Access for Sites

Your organization includes three locations configured as Active Directory sites. Users at each location regularly access data at other locations; however, the WAN links are slow and occasionally fail, and they cannot be upgraded at this time. You need to identify a solution that allows users to reliably access the data and reduce the load on the WAN links. What would you recommend, and how would this recommendation be implemented? Explain your answer.

Case Project 9-4: Data Collaboration

Your company has several teams involved in critical projects. Team members are often employees of different departments and sometimes work in different locations. The company wants to increase the ability of team members to collaborate on projects. Members should be able to access a Web site and view available documents for different projects. Some members should be able to view documents; other members should be able to edit and post the documents. The Web site needs to include a calendar that shows milestones and scheduled events. Additionally, team leaders want to post regular progress notes on the projects using a blog. What should be used? Explain your answer.

chapter 10

Designing Virtualization Strategies

After reading this chapter and completing the exercises, you will be able to:

- Plan for application virtualization
- Understand the capabilities of Microsoft Application Virtualization 4.5
- Design an operating system virtualization strategy
- Plan for server consolidation
- Identify virtualization management tools and capabilities

Virtualization is becoming much more popular as servers become more powerful and companies seek methods to trim costs. Virtualization can be applied to applications, desktops, and servers.

Application virtualization allows clients to run applications without installing them on their systems. Microsoft's Application Virtualization 4.5 (also known as App-V) can be used to stream virtual applications to clients, similar to how video can be streamed to clients over the Internet.

Desktop virtualization can be done using Microsoft Virtual PC or Windows Virtual PC. Windows Virtual PC (available on Windows 7) includes Windows XP Mode, which allows users to run virtual applications in the local virtual PC environment as if the application is installed on the Windows 7 system.

Server virtualization is accomplished in Windows Server 2008 with Hyper-V, which is available as a server role on 64-bit systems. A single physical server can host multiple virtual servers. When the virtual environment becomes larger and spans multiple virtual servers, management tools such as Microsoft System Center Virtual Machine Manager can assist with maintenance and administration.

All of these topics are covered in this chapter.

Application Virtualization

Application virtualization is the use of technologies that allow users to run applications on their computers without actually installing the applications first. Terminal Services can be used to host entire desktops or applications; the applications run on the server and only key clicks, mouse movements, and display changes are sent over the network. Terminal Services were covered in Chapter 5.

In this chapter, application virtualization focuses on streaming applications to the clients. The application runs on the client, not the server. However, the application isn't installed on the client; instead it is sent to the client in a stream of data needed to run the application.

Virtual application streaming works like video streaming. When you watch a video from the Internet, the entire video isn't downloaded before it starts. Instead, a portion of the video is sent to the computer and the computer starts to play it. As you watch the video, the remaining portion is sent in a steady stream to the computer.

Similarly, application streaming provides only a portion of the application needed by the user to begin working. As the user continues, additional data is streamed to the computer based on his actions and needs. There is a key difference, though. In video streaming, the entire video is eventually streamed to the client, but in application streaming, only the required elements are sent.

For example, an employee may be using Microsoft Word as a virtual application, but she might never use the thesaurus. In that case, there's no need to send it. Many elements are optional for an application, so an important part of application streaming is the server's ability to predict what the user needs.

Video streaming works in a sequential manner, but the virtual application stream varies based on user action. Virtual applications have to be prepared using a **virtual application sequencer** so that the **virtual application server** knows what data to stream to the client.

Consider Figure 10-1. A single server can be used to host and stream the virtual applications (V-apps). Users click a link to start the virtual application and the streaming server starts it, sending a stream of data blocks to the client. The client must have a service or application that can accept this stream and put them together to run the application.

As the user works with the application, additional blocks are sent to meet the user's needs. Virtual application streaming servers need to be powerful enough to host all of the clients because each user who connects and runs one or more virtual applications will consume resources on the server.

Citrix has been a powerful player in the field of application virtualization, and had a direct relationship with Microsoft that enabled companies to use Windows 2000 Server and Windows Server 2003 products with Citrix MetaFrame. The current server product offered by Citrix is XenApp. Microsoft has also had virtualization products of its own; the most recent is Microsoft Application Virtualization 4.5.

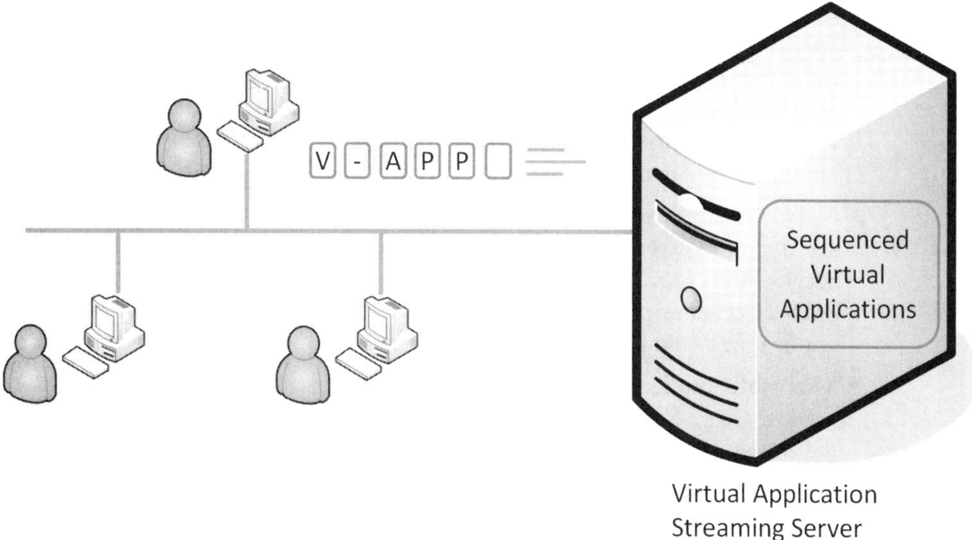

Figure 10-1 Application virtualization

Courtesy Course Technology/Cengage Learning

10

Microsoft Application Virtualization

Microsoft Application Virtualization 4.5 (App-V) is an additional method of application virtualization in an enterprise. It was formerly known as Microsoft SoftGrid; the SoftGrid terminology is still used in App-V.

When taking the 70-647 exam, you might be questioned about Microsoft SoftGrid or Microsoft Application Virtualization. Because Application Virtualization is an upgrade to SoftGrid, you should treat the topics as the same from a planning and design perspective.

App-V applications are designed to provide a seamless user experience. They appear to run on the user's computer rather than as a virtual application. The goal is to provide a simplified view to the user, reduce confusion, and improve the ultimate usability of the applications.

Application Virtualization 4.5 is available as part of the Microsoft Desktop Optimization Pack as an add-on subscription to Software Assurance customers. Enterprises that purchase operating system licenses for Microsoft products frequently subscribe to the Software Assurance program, so this product is available to them. With few exceptions, Application Virtualization 4.5 is only available to Software Assurance customers.

Microsoft Application Virtualization 4.5 Environment

The Application Virtualization 4.5 environment includes several elements that work together to allow clients to connect to the App-V server and run SoftGrid-enabled applications. These elements include:

- **SoftGrid-enabled application.** Any application that is configured to be served as a SoftGrid application using the SoftGrid Sequencer is referred to as a **SoftGrid-enabled application.**
- **SoftGrid Management Console.** This console is an MMC snap-in used to add, remove, manage, and administer virtual applications. It runs on the SoftGrid Application Server.
- **System Center Application Virtualization Streaming Server (or SoftGrid Application Server or App-V server).** A server used to stream SoftGrid-enabled applications when requested by clients. The server can interact with Active Directory to verify that requested applications are authorized for delivery to the requesting client.

- **Microsoft SoftGrid Application Virtualization for Desktops** (or **SoftGrid client**). This runs on the user's desktop to manage the virtual environment for SoftGrid-enabled applications. It accepts the streamed application and presents it to the user. User-specific settings are stored in the user's profile. Because the virtual application is managed in the SoftGrid client, the application can run in any operating system that will run the SoftGrid client, including all currently supported Microsoft desktop operating systems.
- **Microsoft Application Virtualization for Terminal Services.** This component can be used to set up and manage virtual applications that will be published and streamed to a Terminal Services desktop. User-specific settings for the virtual application are stored in the Terminal Services user profile instead of the client's user profile. This component can be useful if applications running on the client system are not compatible with the virtual application.
- **Microsoft Application Virtualization Sequencer (SoftGrid Sequencer).** A wizard-based tool used to create SoftGrid-enabled applications so that they can be streamed to clients from the App-V server.

SoftGrid-enabled applications can also be published in Citrix's XenApp server product, allowing the XenApp server to serve or stream the applications.

Figure 10-2 shows the different components included in an App-V deployment. Clients connect to the Microsoft System Center Application Virtualization Streaming Server (App-V server) to start the SoftGrid-enabled applications. Clients must be running Microsoft SoftGrid Application Virtualization for Desktops (also known as the SoftGrid client) to accept the streamed application and present it to the user. The App-V server uses Active Directory Domain Services for authentication and authorization and will serve the SoftGrid-enabled applications only to authorized clients.

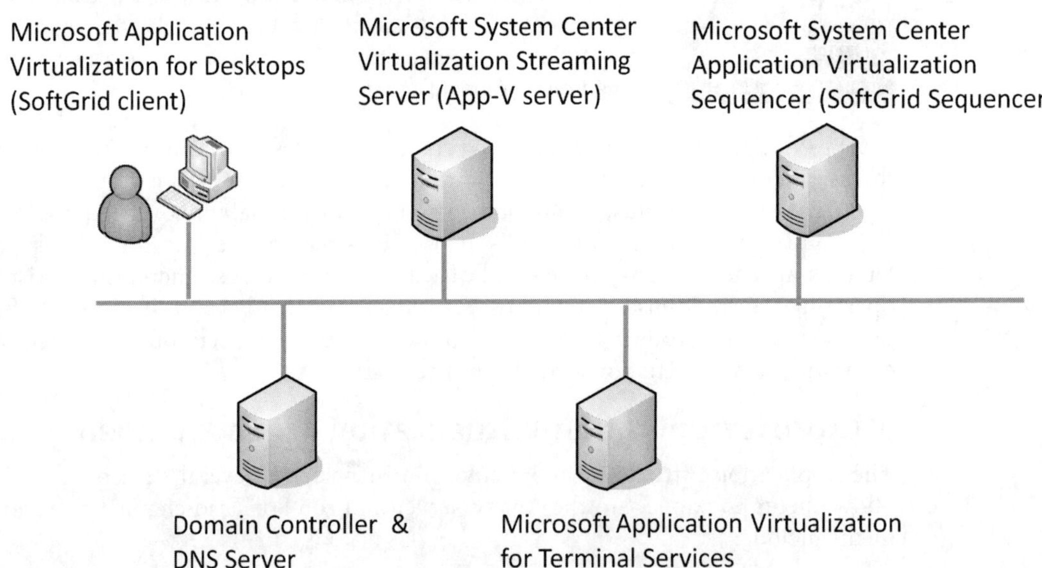

Figure 10-2 Microsoft Application Virtualization

Courtesy Course Technology/Cengage Learning

It's also possible to stream SoftGrid-enabled applications to a server hosting Microsoft Terminal Services. This topic is explained in more depth later in the chapter.

SoftGrid-enabled applications are created or sequenced on a server running the Microsoft Application Virtualization Sequencer. This can be the same server as the App-V server or another system.

Microsoft Application Virtualization includes two primary components:

- **Microsoft System Center Application Virtualization Management Server**. This component is used to manage and administer the server.
- **Microsoft System Center Application Virtualization Streaming Server**. This component runs or streams the applications for the clients.

SoftGrid Sequencer

Before any application can be streamed to clients, it must be sequenced. The **Microsoft Application Virtualization Sequencer** (also known as **SoftGrid Sequencer**) includes a wizard-based tool used to create SoftGrid-enabled applications. The application is formulated in a package of several files that can be published to the App-V server. The completed package includes:

- Microsoft Application Virtualization-enabled application file (.sft)
- One or more Open Software Description link files (.osd)
- One or more icon files (.ico)
- A manifest XML file (.xml)
- Microsoft Application Virtualization project (.sprj) file

Many SoftGrid recipes can be used to create SoftGrid-enabled applications. A recipe is a document that includes step-by-step instructions to create a SoftGrid-enabled application using the SoftGrid Sequencer. When a recipe exists, it should be used because it greatly simplifies the process.

Interacting with Terminal Services

It's also possible to stream virtual applications from an App-V server to a Terminal Services server. As a reminder, Terminal Services can be used to host entire desktop sessions or to host individual applications using TS RemoteApp.

One benefit of using Terminal Services is that the application runs on the Terminal Services server and can eliminate compatibility problems with applications running on the host system. As an example, if the settings of a virtual application interfere with the settings of another application, the virtual application can be run through Terminal Services. In such cases, the settings are stored on the Terminal Services server instead of the client system.

If SoftGrid-enabled applications are run on Terminal Services, the Microsoft Application Virtualization for Terminal Services component is added to the Terminal Services server. This component manages the connection between the Terminal Services server and the App-V server. Figure 10-3 shows how the virtual application is accessed by the client via a Terminal Services session.

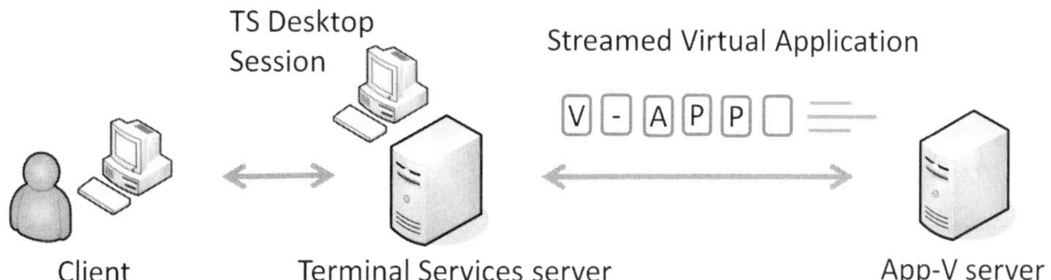

Figure 10-3 Client accessing SoftGrid-enabled application via Terminal Services

Courtesy Course Technology/Cengage Learning

The client connects to the Terminal Services server and establishes a desktop session on the server. The client then starts the virtual application from the Terminal Services desktop and the virtual application is streamed to the desktop session.

Because the virtual application is running on the Terminal Services desktop, all of the user profile settings are stored on the Terminal Services server. If the virtual application is streamed directly to the client, the profile settings would be stored on the client.

Using Virtual PCs for Applications

Microsoft Virtual PC and Windows Virtual PC are two similar virtual PC (VPC) environments that can be used for desktop virtualization; each can host complete operating systems. Desktop virtualization can allow users to run legacy applications in a virtual environment on a newer operating system.

You can run the Virtual PC applications on 64-bit hosts by installing the x64 versions. However, only 32-bit operating systems can be installed as VPC images. No current version of VPC supports 64-bit VPC images.

Due to security enhancements in Windows Vista and Windows 7, some applications that can run on Windows XP can't run on Windows Vista or Windows 7. If a company wants to upgrade clients for other benefits, but can't afford to lose access to a legacy application, VPC can be used as a solution.

Consider Figure 10-4. A client computer can be upgraded to Windows Vista or Windows 7 and then either Microsoft Virtual PC or Windows Virtual PC can be added. A VPC machine can be created on the upgraded host that runs Windows XP and the legacy application. When the user needs to run the older application, the VPC is started and the application is started from the VPC.

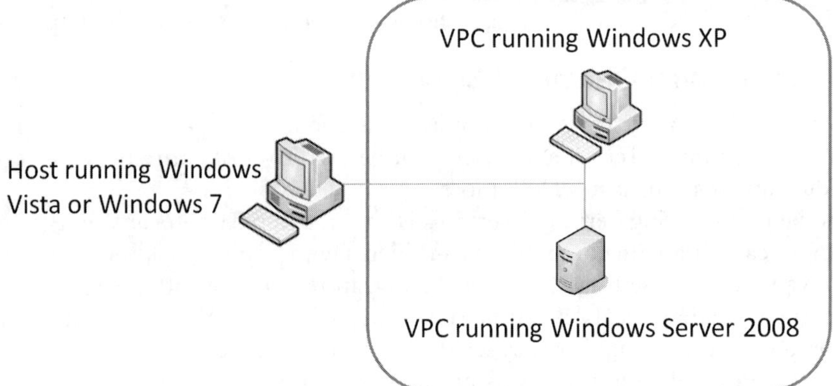

Figure 10-4 Virtual PC machines running within host operating system

Courtesy Course Technology/Cengage Learning

More operating systems can be added as additional VPC machines are networked together. You can configure them to have full connectivity on the network through the host, to have connectivity only to other VPCs running on the host PC and be isolated from the network, or to be completely isolated with no connectivity.

Appendix B includes more details on different virtual PC environments. Activities in this book and the companion lab manual were written so that they could easily be completed in a virtual environment.

It's common to use VPC machines in learning and test environments. They can also be used by administrators on the job. As an example, malicious software (malware) can be released on an isolated VPC machine to view its activity without risk to the host machine or network.

Microsoft Virtual PC

Microsoft Virtual PC has been available on Windows systems for several years; the current version is Microsoft Virtual PC 2007. It's available as a free download and is fully supported on Windows XP and Windows Vista systems.

Microsoft Virtual PC is not formally supported on Windows 7, although it can still be installed and will run many VPC images. Windows Virtual PC is recommended for Windows 7 instead.

After installing Microsoft Virtual PC, you can create and run VPC machines on the system. Microsoft Virtual PC can be used to install any current Microsoft 32-bit operating systems and some non-Microsoft operating systems.

Chapter 1 included activities to install Microsoft Virtual PC and add VPC machines running Windows Server 2008. You've probably been using Microsoft Virtual PC throughout this course. Instead of every student needing two servers, an individual system can be used to host the two servers. Additionally, you can download and install Microsoft Virtual PC for use on your home PC as an additional study tool outside the classroom.

Windows Virtual PC

Windows 7 includes support for the newer **Windows Virtual PC** product. It works like Microsoft Virtual PC, but it looks a little different and includes some significant additions.

Figure 10-5 shows the Windows Virtual PC interface with several VPC machines. The Windows Explorer taskbar includes links to view the settings of a VPC machine and to create additional virtual machines.

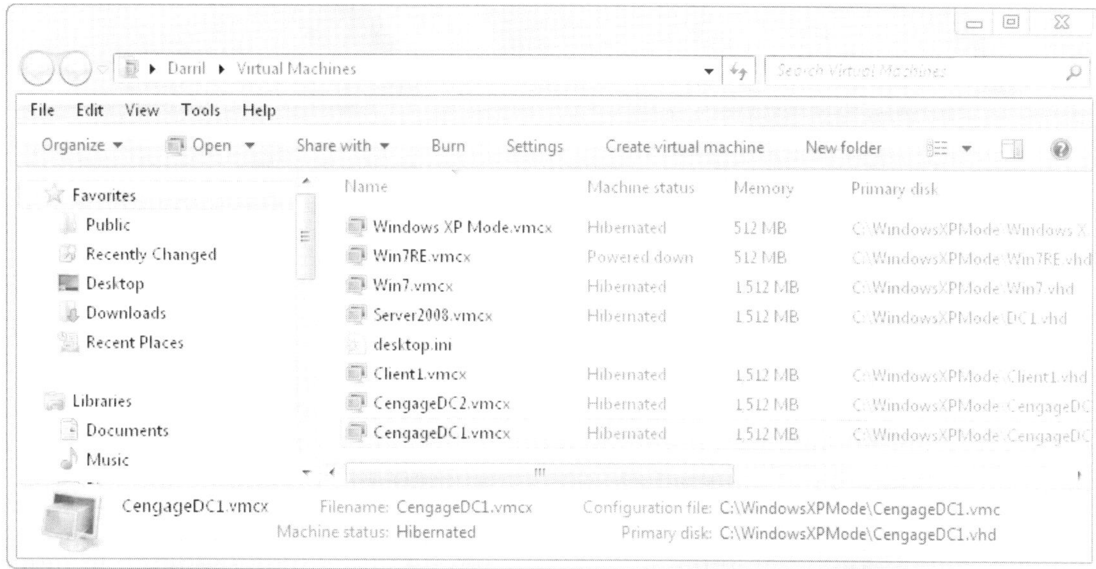

Figure 10-5 Windows Virtual PC with several VPC machines

Courtesy Course Technology/Cengage Learning

The most significant addition to Windows Virtual PC is Windows XP Mode, which supports brokered connections that allow users to access applications installed in the Windows XP Mode VPC without directly accessing the Windows XP VPC.

In other words, the user is not required to start the VPC, log on to the VPC, and then start the application from the VPC. Users can start virtual applications from the Start menu or from shortcuts on their desktop. From the user's perspective, there is little difference between an application installed normally on their system and a virtual application running through a brokered connection in Windows XP Mode.

To use Windows XP Mode, the system must support hardware-assisted virtualization. This is called Intel VT for Intel-based systems and AMD-V for AMD-based systems. In addition to ensuring that the processor is compatible, the BIOS also needs to be enabled for hardware-assisted virtualization.

Windows XP Mode can be downloaded for free and installed on Windows 7. It needs the following two components:

- **Windows XP Mode.** This component is available from Microsoft's download site (*www.microsoft.com/downloads*) by searching for "Windows XP Mode." It includes a fully functioning Windows XP image and is close to 500 MB.
- **Windows Virtual PC.** This component is downloaded as an update. It's labeled as KB 958559 and can be accessed from *http://support.microsoft.com/default.aspx/kb/958559*.

Once the two components are installed, you can install legacy applications on the Windows XP VPC image. This image can be used to automatically publish applications when you configure its VPC settings, as shown in Figure 10-6.

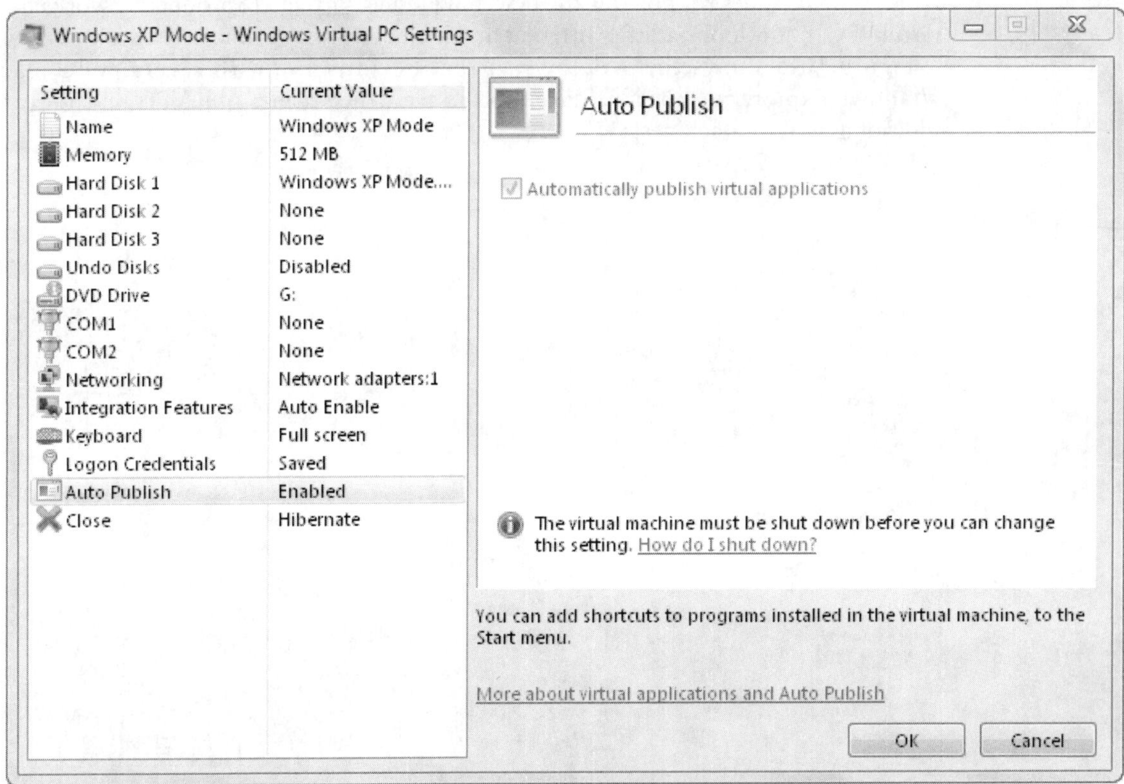

Figure 10-6 Windows XP Mode on Windows 7 configured to automatically publish applications

Courtesy Course Technology/Cengage Learning

While Auto Publish is primarily presented as a feature of Windows XP Mode, it can also be used to publish applications from a Windows 7 VPC to a Windows 7 host system.

When configured as shown in Figure 10-6, any shortcuts created in the C:\Documents and Settings\All Users\Start Menu path of the Windows XP Mode machine will automatically appear on the Windows 7 Start menu. Some applications add a shortcut to the Windows XP Start menu and automatically display it without additional steps. Some programs require a shortcut to be created and pasted to the All Users\Start Menu path.

Installing and Using Windows XP Mode

If your system is running Windows 7 and it supports hardware-assisted virtualization, you can run Activities 10-1 to 10-3 to see how a virtual application runs. If you don't have Windows 7 systems that support hardware-assisted virtualization, you can skip these activities.

You're not expected to know the details of configuring Windows Virtual PC when taking the 70-647 exam. However, if you can do these activities, it may help your overall understanding of application virtualization, especially because the App-V server product isn't available as a free download. The App-V server is covered later in this chapter.

The activities lead you through the following processes:

- Installing Windows Virtual PC on Windows 7 (Activity 10-1)
- Installing Windows XP Mode on Windows 7 (Activity 10-2)
- Publishing an application from Windows XP Mode to Windows 7 (Activity 10-3)

The activities in this chapter are optional. Although application and server virtualization are directly related to 70-647 exam objectives, not all student environments have the hardware and software resources to complete these activities.

Microsoft Virtual PC and Windows Virtual PC are not compatible with each other. If you're running Microsoft Virtual PC on your Windows 7 system, you need to remove it before Windows Virtual PC can be added.

Activity 10-1 (Optional): Installing Windows Virtual PC on Windows 7

Time Required: 10 minutes
Objective: Install Windows Virtual PC on a Windows 7 system.

Description: You want users to be able to run Windows XP Mode on their systems, so you first need to install the update to add Windows Virtual PC. This activity can only be run on a Windows 7 system.

Before starting this activity, you should download the Windows Virtual PC update from *http://support.microsoft.com/default.aspx/kb/958559*. The XP Mode site directs that this update should be installed after XP Mode, but the order isn't critical. You can install this update without XP Mode if you want.

1. Start Windows 7 and log on.
2. Start **Windows Explorer.** Browse to the location of the **KB 958559** file. Double-click it to start the installation.
3. When prompted to install the **Windows Software Update**, click **Yes.**
4. Review the license terms and click **I Accept.**
5. When the installation is complete, click **Restart Now.**
6. Log on to Windows 7. Start **Windows Virtual PC** by clicking **Start, All Programs, Windows Virtual PC, Windows Virtual PC.**

At this point, you can use Windows Virtual PC to create and run any virtual PC machines, just as you can with Microsoft Virtual PC. The two programs are slightly different, but help is readily available when you press the F1 key in Windows Virtual PC.

Activity 10-2 (Optional): Installing Windows XP Mode on Windows 7

Time Required: 20 minutes
Objective: Install Windows XP Mode on a Windows 7 system.

Description: You want users to be able to run virtual applications on their systems. You have installed Windows Virtual PC and now need to install Windows XP Mode. This activity can only be run on a Windows 7 system, and it assumes that the KB 958559 update has been installed.

Before starting this activity, you should download the Windows XP Mode file from *www.microsoft.com/downloads* by searching on "Windows XP Mode." Your system should have at least 1.6 GB of free disk space.

1. Start Windows 7 and log on.
2. Start **Windows Explorer**. Browse to the location of the downloaded **Windows XP Mode** file. Double-click it to start the installation.
3. If prompted by a **Security Warning** to confirm that you want to run the file, click **Run**.
4. Review the information on the **Welcome** screen and click **Next**.
5. Accept the default location of **C:\Program Files\Windows XP Mode** and click **Next**.
6. If prompted by **User Account Control** to continue, click **Yes**.
7. When the installation is complete, the **Setup Completed** screen appears. Ensure that **Launch Windows XP Mode** is checked and click **Finish**.
8. Review the **Windows XP Mode License Agreement**. Select **I Accept the License Terms** and click **Next**.
9. Accept the default installation folder location. The **User name** will be set as **XPMUser**. Enter **P@ssw0rd** in the **Password** and **Confirm password** boxes. Ensure that **Remember credentials (Recommended)** is selected. Your display will look similar to Figure 10-7. Click **Next**.

When Remember credentials is checked, users won't be prompted to enter credentials when a Windows XP Mode application is started.

10. Select **Help Protect My Computer by Turning Automatic Updates on Now**. Click **Next** and then click **Start Setup**.

After a few minutes, the installation and setup of Windows XP Mode will be completed and the desktop will appear.

Activity 10-3 (Optional): Publishing a Windows XP Mode Application

Time Required: 15 minutes
Objective: Publish a Windows XP Mode application.

Description: You have installed Windows Virtual PC and Windows XP Mode on your Windows 7 system. You now want to publish an application from Windows XP Mode so that it is available on the Windows 7 Start menu. To test the capability, you first want to publish Notepad from the Windows XP virtual machine. This activity can only be run on a Windows 7 system, and it assumes that Windows XP Mode and the KB 958559 update have been installed.

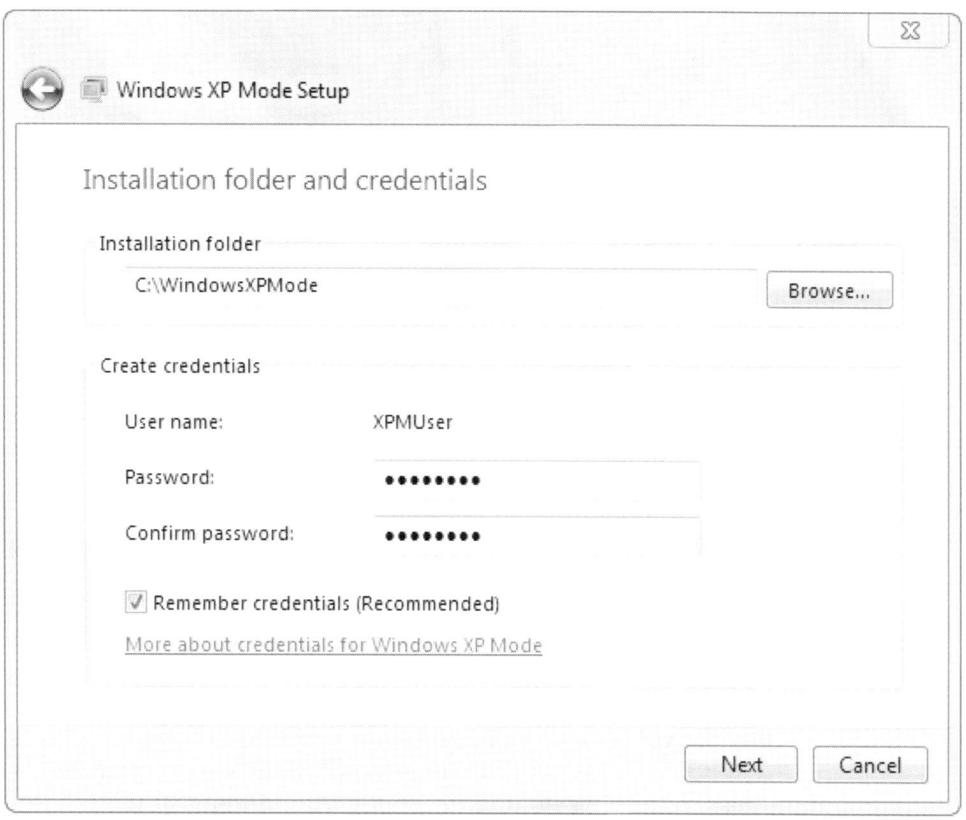

Figure 10-7 Configuring logon credentials for XP Mode
Courtesy Course Technology/Cengage Learning

10

1. If necessary, start Windows 7 and log on.
2. Click **Start, All Programs, Windows Virtual PC.** You'll see two applications in the Windows Virtual PC Start menu folder: **Windows Virtual PC** and **Windows XP Mode.** Select **Windows XP Mode.** When it starts, you'll automatically be logged on with the XPMUser account.
3. Right-click **Start** in the **Windows XP Mode** machine and select **Explore All Users** to start Windows Explorer in the following path: **C:\Documents and Settings\All Users\Start Menu.**
4. Right-click in an empty area of the **Start Menu** folder and select **New, Shortcut.**
5. In the **Create Shortcut** dialog box, click **Browse.**
6. Browse to **C:\Windows** and select **NOTEPAD.** Click **OK.** Click **Next.**
7. Type **XP Mode Notepad** as the name and click **Finish.** Close the Start Menu folder window.
8. From the Windows 7 **Start** menu, click **Start, All Programs, Windows Virtual PC.** Your display will look similar to Figure 10-8.

   You'll see that an additional folder named **Windows XP Mode Applications** has been created with the new shortcut. You can click this link or create a shortcut to use elsewhere.
9. Click **Windows XP Mode Applications.** Right-click **XP Mode Notepad** and select **Copy.**

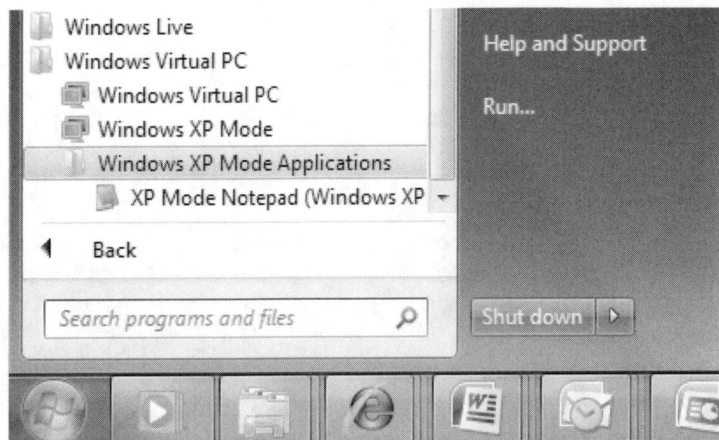

Figure 10-8 Viewing the shortcut for a published XP Mode application

Courtesy Course Technology/Cengage Learning

10. Click the **Show Desktop** link on the far right side of the Windows 7 taskbar. Right-click the desktop and select **Paste Shortcut.**
11. Double-click the shortcut to **XP Mode Notepad**. A dialog box appears, indicating that you must close the virtual machine before you can open a virtual application. Click **Continue**. The Windows XP Mode virtual machine closes and Notepad opens. A small window briefly appears, indicating that this is a Windows XP Mode application.
12. Click **Start, All Programs, Windows Virtual PC, Windows XP Mode.** You can see that the **Status** of the Windows XP Mode machine is set to **Running.** However, only the application (Notepad) is displayed from the Windows XP Mode virtual machine. Any applications installed on the Windows XP Mode system and published to the Windows 7 host will work the same way.

Figure 10-9 shows Windows XP Mode running and two instances of Notepad: one from Windows XP Mode and one from Windows 7. While there are some subtle differences between the two instances, most users will not be able to distinguish one from the other. From the user's perspective, Notepad is just another application running on the system.

These activities showed how a virtual application appears on Windows 7 using Windows XP Mode. Although there are many similarities in how virtual applications appear to users when Microsoft XP Mode or Microsoft Application Virtualization 4.5 is used, the underlying details of how the applications are served are much different.

Server Virtualization

Server virtualization is the use of technologies that allow a single physical server to host multiple virtual servers. Microsoft introduced **Hyper-V** as a server role that can be added in 64-bit versions of Windows Server 2008 Standard, Enterprise, and Datacenter editions to implement server virtualization. Hyper-V allows a single physical server to support multiple virtual machines. The virtual servers appear to be physical servers on the network; users can connect and use them as if they are physical servers.

Hyper-V can also be installed as a stand-alone product. In other words, you can download and install Hyper-V on a system without Windows Server 2008. It can then be managed remotely by installing the Hyper-V Manager on clients such as Windows Vista or Windows 7.

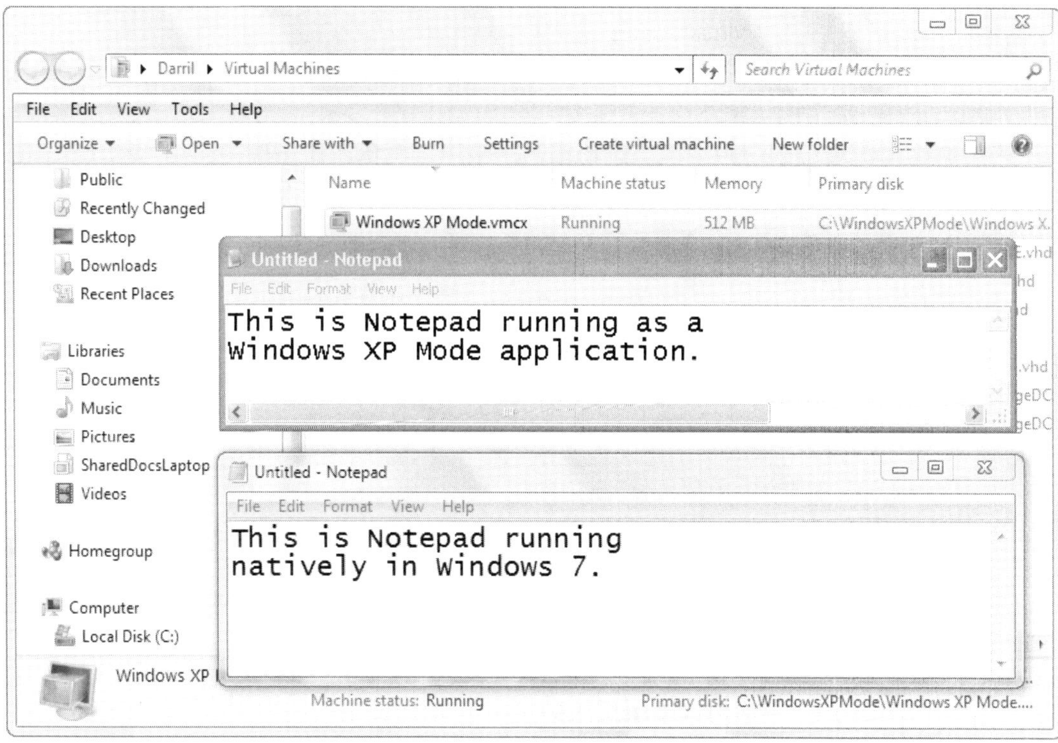

Figure 10-9 Windows Virtual PC with a published XP Mode application (Notepad) and a local instance of Notepad

Courtesy Course Technology/Cengage Learning

As an example, consider Figure 10-10. A single server named HV1 is hosting the Hyper-V role. Within the physical server, the five virtual servers (named SQL1 through SQL5) are running Microsoft SQL Server 2008 and are connected to each other via a virtual network. Also, each of the virtual servers can share the network adapter of the host system. The network diagram of these servers is also shown.

Server Consolidation

Server consolidation is the process of combining multiple physical servers onto a single virtual server. This process can be useful for companies that experience server sprawl, in which multiple physical servers are added for a specific purpose but are highly underutilized. These servers may run at only 5 to 10 percent of their capabilities.

These physical servers can instead be consolidated. Depending on the resources needed by the servers and their current capabilities, it's even possible for an existing server to host the others without having to purchase additional hardware.

Server consolidation can provide several benefits, including:

- **Lower hardware costs.** Although a single physical server may need to be beefed up to support multiple virtual servers, the overall cost is lower than purchasing several physical servers.
- **Less power used.** Each physical server draws power and requires air conditioning to keep it cool. When servers are consolidated, less power is required, resulting in lower facility costs.
- **Improved resource utilization.** Hardware resources (such as processor power, RAM, disk space, and networks) can easily be balanced between the virtual servers.
- **Improved uptime.** A single powerful server generally performs better than multiple servers. Additionally, Hyper-V virtual machines can be moved from one physical server to another much more easily than operations can be swapped between two physical servers.

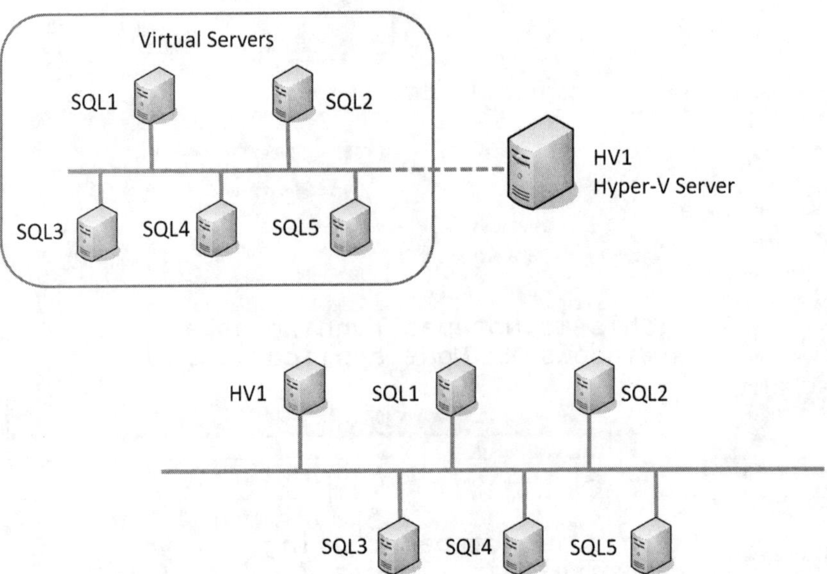

Figure 10-10 One physical server running Hyper-V and hosting five virtual servers

Courtesy Course Technology/Cengage Learning

Hyper-V Prerequisites

Before trying to add the Hyper-V role to a Windows Server 2008 server, you should ensure that the server meets the following hardware prerequisites:

- **x64 architecture.** The hardware must include an x64 processor and must be running a 64-bit version of the operating system.
- **Processor must include virtualization option.** Intel processors refer to this option as Intel VT and AMD processors call it AMD Virtualization (or AMD-V).
- **Hardware Data Execution Prevention (DEP).** The processors must support DEP and it must be enabled in the operating system, as shown in Figure 10-11. You can access this screen from the Advanced properties of the computer.

The following operating systems are supported as virtual servers using Hyper-V:

- Windows 2000 Server
- Windows Server 2003 and 2003 R2 servers
- Windows Server 2008 and 2008 R2 servers
- SUSE Linux Enterprise Server
- Windows 7
- Windows Vista
- Windows XP

Hyper-V and Server Licenses

Hyper-V is supported on Windows Server 2008 Standard, Enterprise, and Datacenter editions. Each of these versions also includes licenses for the virtual servers as follows:

- Windows Server 2008 Standard includes one additional license for a virtual server.
- Windows Server 2008 Enterprise includes four additional licenses for virtual servers.
- Windows Server 2008 Datacenter includes an unlimited number of licenses for virtual servers.

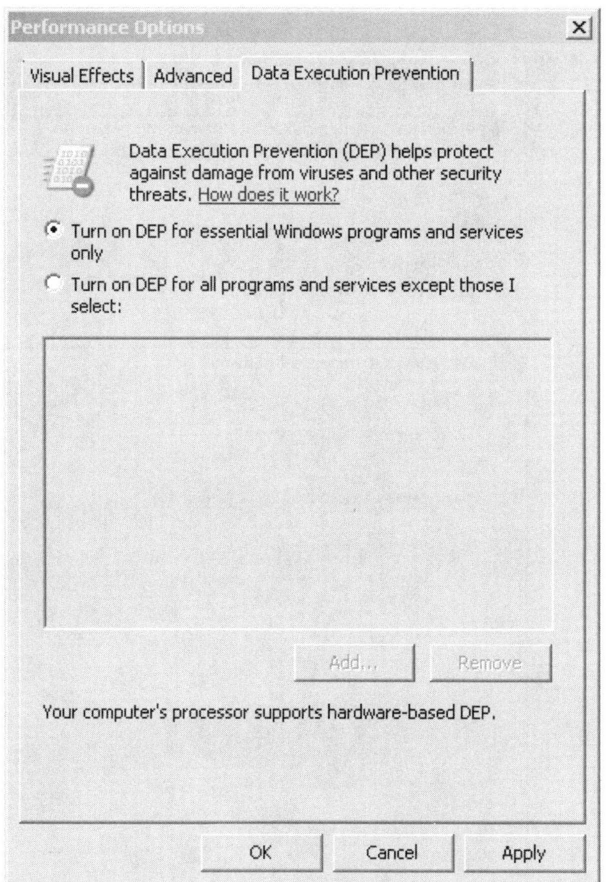

Figure 10-11 Enabling hardware Data Execution Prevention (DEP)

Courtesy Course Technology/Cengage Learning

As an example, a single server running Windows Server 2008 Enterprise Edition can run four Windows Server 2008 Enterprise virtual servers (for a total of five), which are all included in the initial cost of the single Windows Server 2008 Enterprise license.

Hyper-V Virtual Networks

The Hyper-V Manager includes the Virtual Network Manager, which can be used to create additional virtual networks or reconfigure the existing virtual network. Different virtual machines can be configured to use different virtual networks. This versatility allows you to create some virtual machines that have full connectivity on the network and some virtual machines that are completely isolated.

Figure 10-12 shows the Virtual Network Manager with an existing network selected.

The virtual networks can be configured to provide three different levels of connectivity with other computers:

- **External.** This setting allows the virtual machines to have full connectivity on the network using the selected network adapter.
- **Internal only.** This setting ensures that the virtual machines remain completely isolated. As an example, a virtual machine may be created to test malicious software (malware). The malware can be released and observed on the isolated machine without allowing it to infect other systems.
- **Private virtual machine network.** This setting connects virtual machines using this virtual network, but they will not have network connectivity with the host system or other systems on the network.

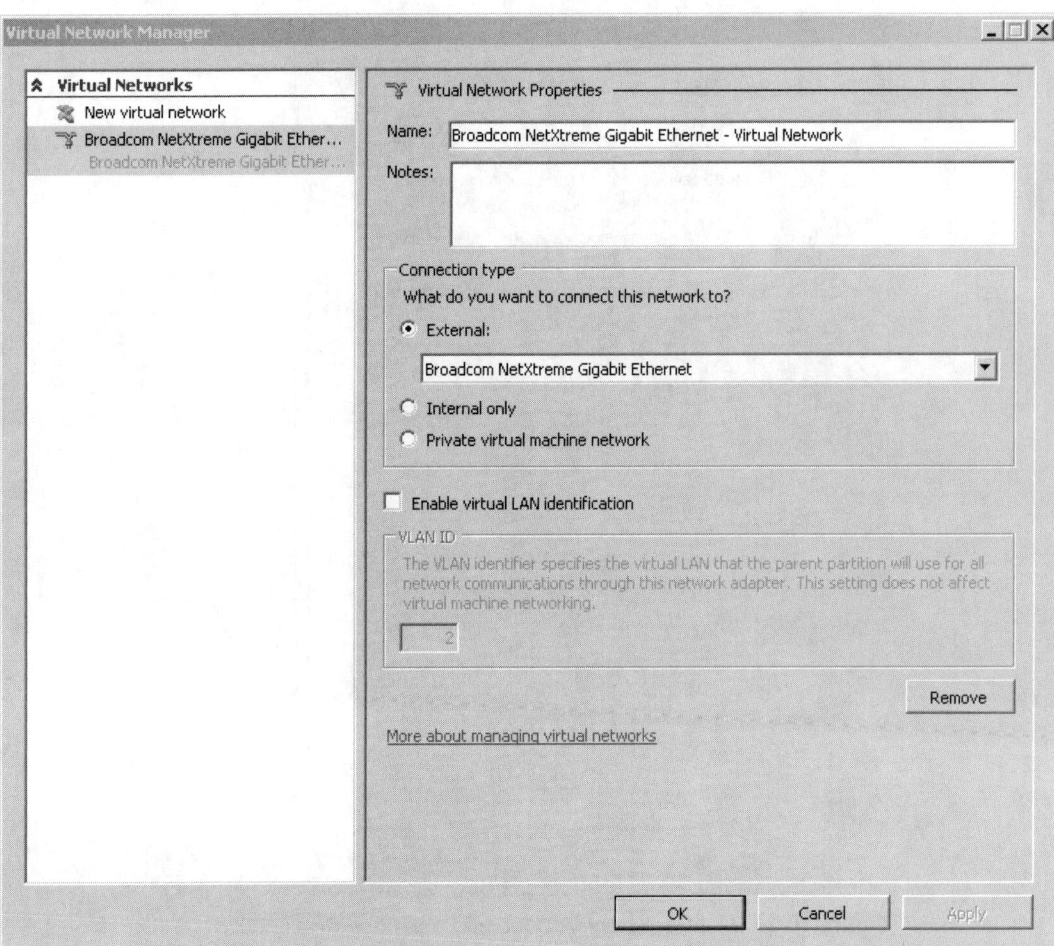

Figure 10-12 Hyper-V Virtual Network Manager

Courtesy Course Technology/Cengage Learning

Hyper-V Manager

The Hyper-V Manager is the primary tool used to manage virtual servers. It is installed when the Hyper-V role is added to a Windows Server 2008 server. It can be used to create virtual machines from scratch, import virtual machines over the network from another Hyper-V server, remove virtual servers, and modify the properties of an existing virtual server.

Figure 10-13 shows the Hyper-V Manager with three SQL Servers added and configured as SQL1, SQL2, and SQL3. In addition to managing the virtual machines, the Hyper-V Manager includes tools for editing and inspecting virtual disks used by virtual machines.

Virtual disks are configured as dynamically expanding disks. They only take as much space as needed; when more space is required, they expand to their maximum size, which is 127 GB by default. Once a disk dynamically expands, it won't shrink, even if it no longer needs the space. However, you can manually compact the disk if desired. You can also convert it to a fixed size rather than use a dynamically expanding disk.

Hyper-V cannot be added to a virtual server using Microsoft Virtual PC or Windows Virtual PC. Hyper-V can only be run on a 64-bit operating system and Virtual PC machines only support 32-bit operating systems. Also, Hyper-V needs direct access to the physical hardware, which isn't possible when it is installed as a virtual server.

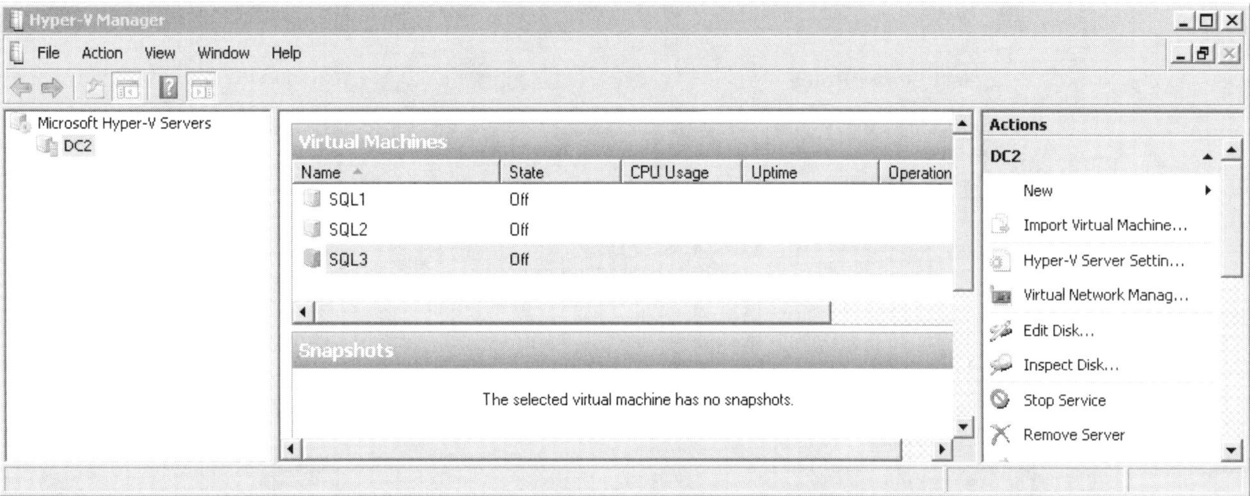

Figure 10-13 Hyper-V Manager hosting three virtual systems

Courtesy Course Technology/Cengage Learning

Activity 10-4 (Optional): Adding the Hyper-V Role

Time Required: 20 minutes
Objective: Use Server Manager to add Hyper-V.

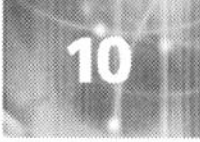

Description: You want to consolidate some physical servers onto virtual systems. You first need to add the Hyper-V role to Windows Server 2008. This activity can be run on any 64-bit server running Windows Server 2008. The server doesn't need to be a member of a domain.

1. Start the server and log on with an **Administrator** account.
2. Start **Server Manager** via the **Administrative Tools** menu.
3. Select **Roles** and click **Add Roles.**
4. Review the information on the **Before You Begin** page and click **Next.**
5. On the **Select Server Roles** screen, select **Hyper-V.** Your display will look similar to Figure 10-14. Click **Next.**
6. Review the information on the **Introduction to Hyper-V** screen and click **Next.**
7. On the **Create Virtual Networks** screen, ensure that at least one network adapter is selected, as shown in Figure 10-15. This network adapter will be shared by all of the virtual servers. Click **Next.**
8. On the **Confirm Installation Selections** screen, click **Install.**
9. When the installation is complete, click **Close.** When you're prompted to restart the server, click **Yes.**
10. After the server reboots, log on to the server with an **Administrator** account.
11. When the **Resume Configuration Wizard** finishes the installation, click **Close.**

Activity 10-5 (Optional): Creating a New Virtual Machine

Time Required: 15 minutes
Objective: Use Hyper-V Manager to create a new virtual machine.

Description: You have added the Hyper-V role and now want to add a new virtual machine. You will install the operating system for the virtual machine later. This activity can be run on any 64-bit server running Windows Server 2008, and it assumes that Activity 10-3 was completed on the server.

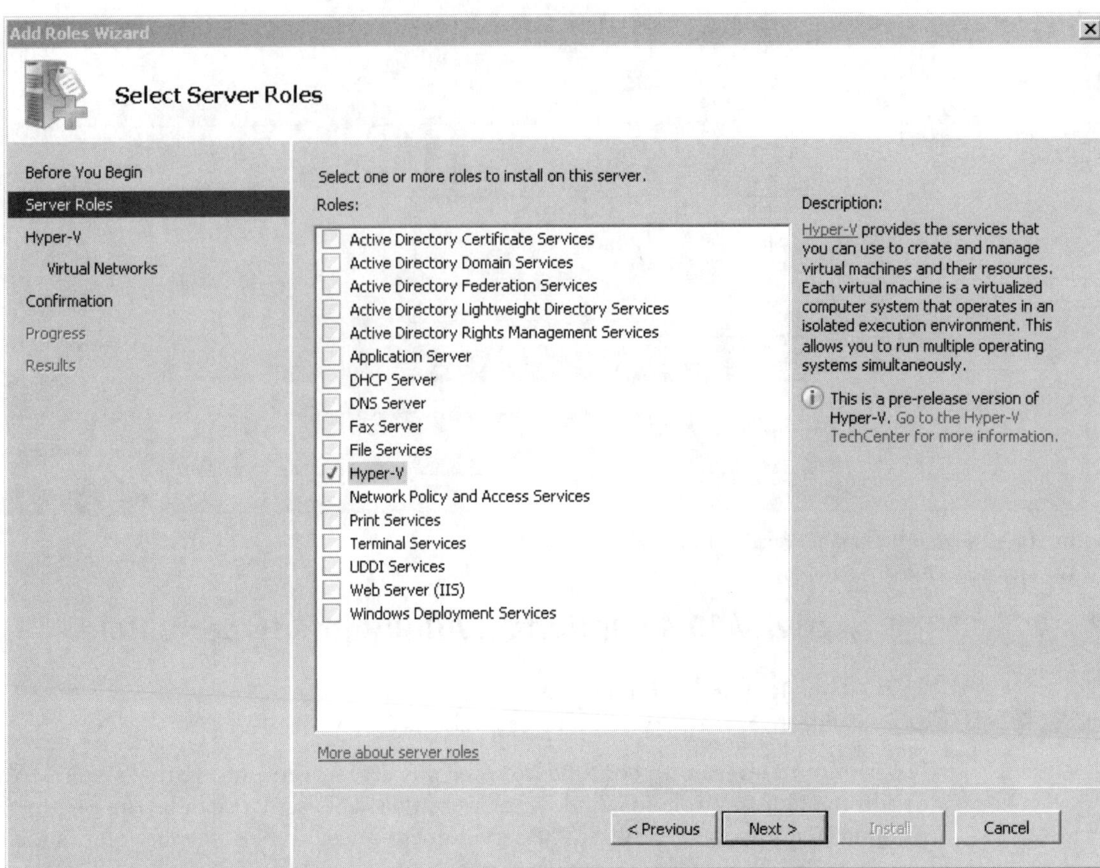

Figure 10-14 Adding the Hyper-V role

Courtesy Course Technology/Cengage Learning

1. Start the server and log on with an **Administrator** account.
2. Start **Hyper-V Manager** via the **Administrative Tools** menu.
3. If this is the first time you've started the Hyper-V Manager, review the license terms and select **I Have Read and Agree to this EULA**. Click **Accept**.
4. Right-click the server name and select **New, Virtual Machine** to start the **New Virtual Machine Wizard.**
5. Review the information on the **Before You Begin** screen and click **Next**.
6. On the **Specify Name and Location** screen, name the server **SQL1**. Click **Next.**
7. On the **Assign Memory** screen, change the **Memory** to **1512** MB and click **Next.**
8. On the **Configure Networking** screen, select the virtual network adapter created in the previous activity from the **Connection** drop-down box. Click **Next.**
9. The **Connect Virtual Hard Disk** screen appears. Ensure that **Create a virtual hard disk** is selected. Change the size of the disk to **40** GB. Your display will look similar to Figure 10-16. Notice that the hard disk is stored in the **Public** folder by default, allowing it to be easily accessible by other Hyper-V servers if necessary. Click **Next.**
10. On the **Installation Options** screen, ensure that **Install an Operating System Later** is selected and click **Next.**
11. Review the information on the **Summary** screen and click **Finish.**

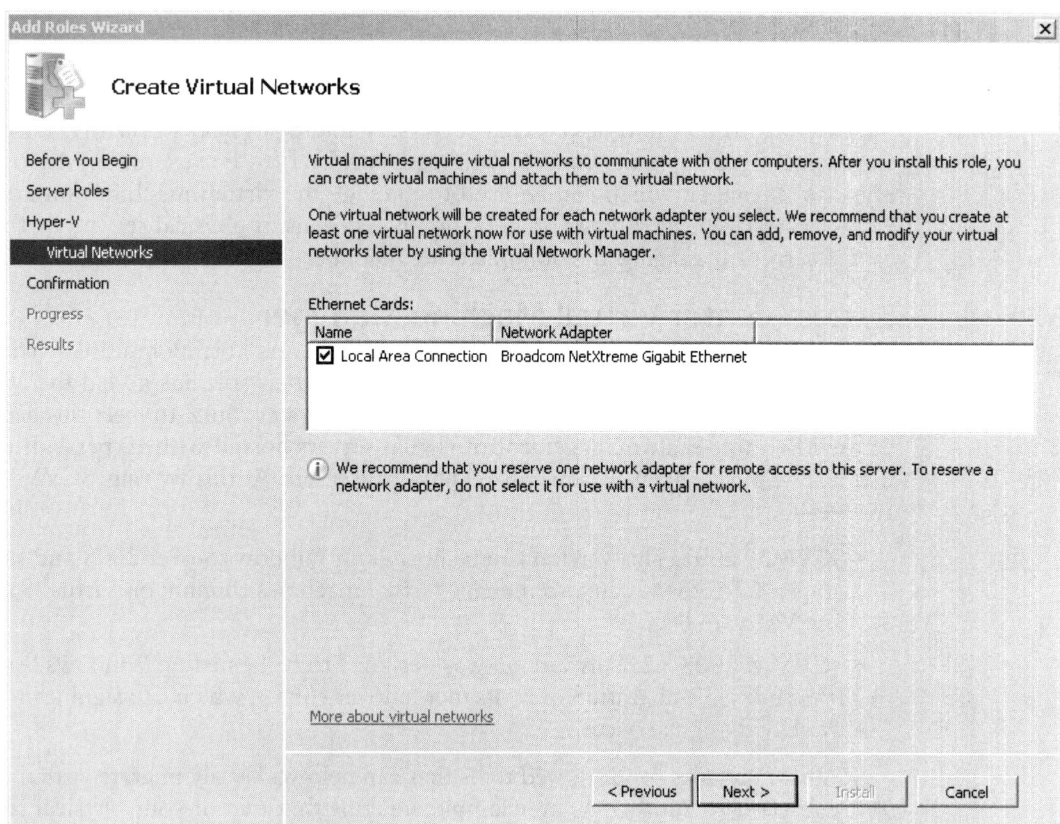

Figure 10-15 Selecting the shared network adapter

Courtesy Course Technology/Cengage Learning

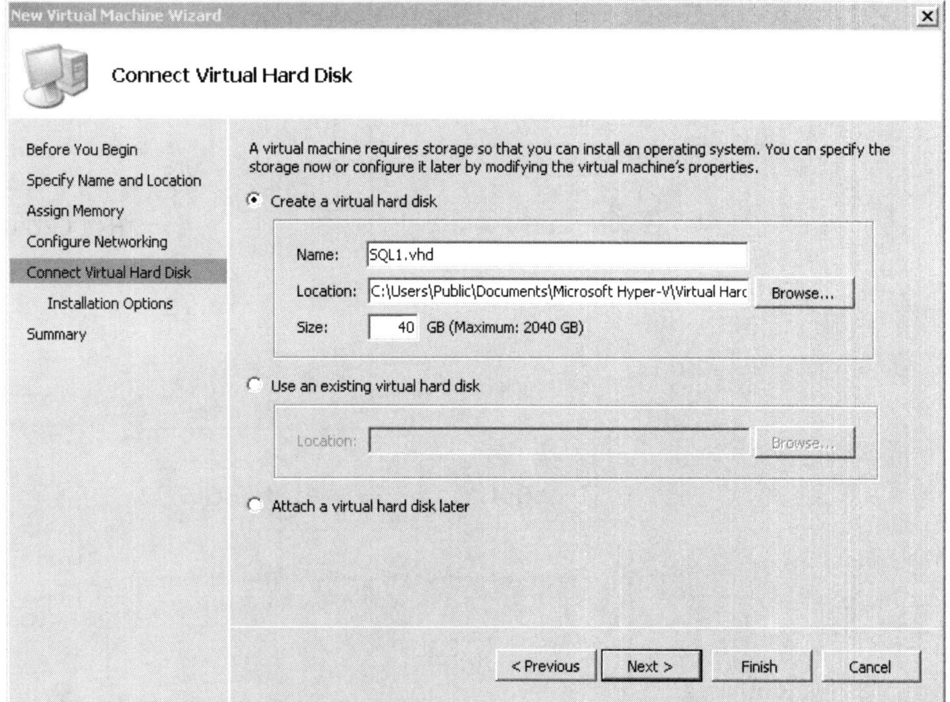

Figure 10-16 Configuring the virtual hard disk

Courtesy Course Technology/Cengage Learning

Virtualization Management

Virtualization management is the process of managing multiple virtual servers, usually when they are hosted on multiple physical servers. A single physical server that hosts virtual servers can be managed using the console on the physical server. For example, Microsoft includes the Hyper-V Manager, which can be used to manage the virtual machines on a Windows Server 2008 server. However, if your organization has dozens of physical servers that all host multiple virtual servers, managing and administering them becomes much more difficult.

System Center Virtual Machine Manager

When a company transitions to multiple physical servers hosting multiple virtual servers, a virtualization management solution is often needed. Microsoft has added the **Microsoft System Center Virtual Machine Manager (SCVMM)** to the System Suite to meet this need. SCVMM can be used for large-scale management of virtual servers hosted with Hyper-V. It includes wizards that can help consolidate underutilized physical servers. At this writing, SCVMM has two available versions:

- **SCVMM 2007.** This version can be hosted on Windows Server 2008 and supports Hyper-V. SCVMM can also manage virtual machines running on Virtual Server 2005 R2 and VMware ESX.
- **SCVMM 2008 R2.** This version was designed to be hosted on Windows Server 2008 R2. It includes live migration of hosts in a failover cluster, which can significantly improve the availability of a service.

SCVMM includes sophisticated tools that can help you easily migrate virtual servers from one physical server to another. As an example, imagine that two of your physical servers (HV1 and HV2) are hosting three SQL servers each, as shown in Figure 10-17. CPU usage of HV1 is extremely

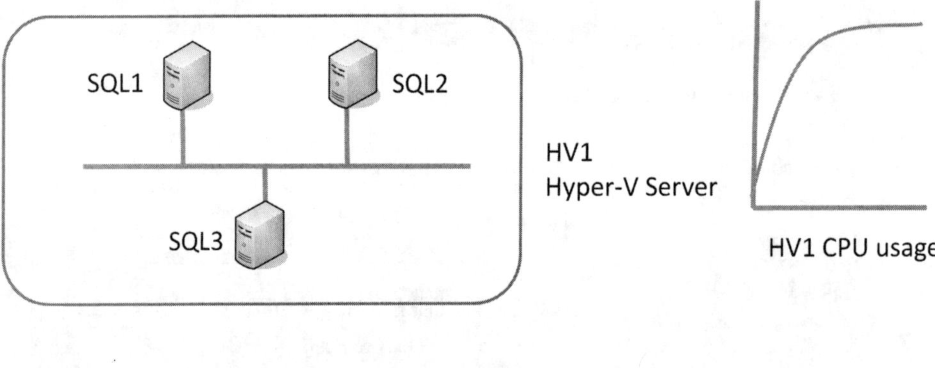

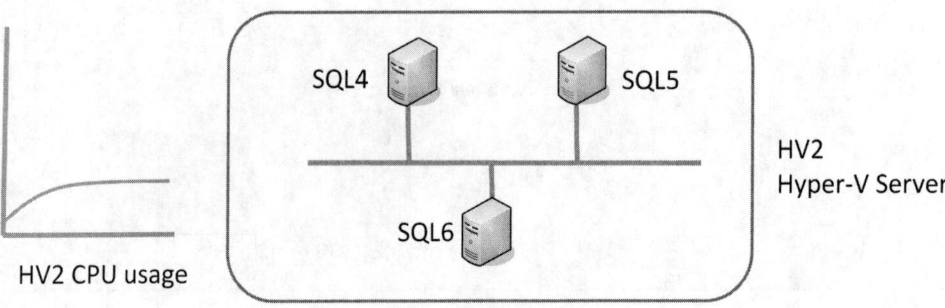

Figure 10-17 Hyper-V Manager hosting three virtual systems

Courtesy Course Technology/Cengage Learning

high and close to capacity because SQL1 and SQL2 are very busy. The other servers (including SQL4) aren't as busy and HV2's overall CPU usage is very low.

You can use SCVMM to migrate SQL2 to HV2 and then migrate SQL4 to HV1 to balance the load between the two Hyper-V servers.

SCVMM also includes wizards that help identify the best location of a physical server when it's migrated to a virtual server. Imagine that you have five physical servers (HV1 through HV5), each hosting virtual machines, and you're preparing to migrate another physical server to a virtual environment. To which server should you migrate it? The Virtual Machine Deployment wizard uses built-in calculations and user-selectable preferences to recommend the most suitable server to host the new virtual machine.

Chapter Summary

- Application virtualization allows users to run applications without installing them on their host system.
- One method of application virtualization is application streaming. The application is hosted on a streaming server; when started, the application is streamed to the client. As the client uses the application, additional portions are streamed and run on the client.
- Virtual applications must be prepared using a sequencer before they can be served from a virtual application server.
- Microsoft's Application Virtualization 4.5 (App-V) can be used to stream virtual applications to clients, similar to how video is streamed to clients over the Internet. App-V was formerly known as Microsoft SoftGrid, and some of the SoftGrid terminology is still used.
- SoftGrid-enabled applications are prepared using the Microsoft Application Virtualization Sequencer (SoftGrid Sequencer). Once prepared, they can be deployed to an App-V server and streamed to clients as virtual applications.
- Clients must be running Microsoft SoftGrid Application Virtualization for Desktops (SoftGrid client) to be able to run virtual applications streamed from an App-V server.
- Microsoft Virtual PC can be used for desktop virtualization. It runs as an application on a desktop system and can host one or more virtual desktops in a virtual environment. A user can upgrade to Windows Vista and then run legacy applications on the Microsoft Virtual PC desktop.
- Windows Virtual PC is an upgrade to Microsoft Virtual PC that runs on Windows 7. It can host one or more operating systems in a virtual environment just like Microsoft Virtual PC. Additionally, Windows XP Mode can be used to run applications on the virtual machine without requiring the user to start the virtual machine.
- Server virtualization is the use of technologies that allow a single physical server to host multiple virtual servers. Benefits include lower hardware costs, less money for facilities such as power and air conditioning, improved resource usage, and improved uptime.
- The Hyper-V role can be added to Windows Server 2008 so that a server can host multiple virtual servers. The hardware must be using x64 architecture and the processor must include the virtualization option.
- Microsoft System Center Virtual Machine Manager (SCVMM) is part of the System Center suite of server products. SCVMM includes tools and wizards that can assist with the maintenance and administration of large-scale virtual environments.

Key Terms

Application virtualization The use of technologies that allow users to run applications without installing them on the host operating system. Microsoft's Application Virtualization Streaming Server (App-V server) can be used to stream SoftGrid-enabled applications to users and provide application virtualization.

Hyper-V A server role that can be added to 64-bit versions of Windows Server 2008 to host virtual servers. Multiple virtual servers can be hosted on a single Windows Server 2008 server running Hyper-V.

Microsoft Application Virtualization 4.5 (App-V) A server product that can be used to serve SoftGrid-enabled applications. These applications have been prepared using the Microsoft Application Virtualization Sequencer (SoftGrid Sequencer) to be streamed from an application server to clients as virtual applications.

Microsoft Application Virtualization Sequencer (SoftGrid Sequencer) An application that prepares applications to be served from a virtual server. Once the application is prepared, it is referred to as a SoftGrid-enabled application; it can be deployed to an App-V server and streamed to clients that have Microsoft SoftGrid Application Virtualization for Desktops (SoftGrid client) installed.

Microsoft System Center Virtual Machine Manager (SCVMM) A server product in the Microsoft System Center suite. It can be purchased and used to manage large-scale deployments of virtual servers. It supports virtual servers hosted by Virtual Server 2005 R2, VMware ESX, and Hyper-V.

Microsoft Virtual PC An application that runs on a desktop system and can host one or more virtual desktops in a virtual environment. Microsoft Virtual PC can be used for testing, training, and running applications in a virtual environment if they will not run in the host environment.

Server consolidation The process of migrating physical servers to virtual servers to reduce the overall footprint of physical servers in the environment. The Hyper-V role can be added to Windows Server 2008 to support multiple virtual servers on a single physical server.

Server virtualization The use of technologies that allow a single physical server to host multiple virtual servers. Windows Server 2008 supports the Hyper-V role on 64-bit servers to implement server virtualization.

SoftGrid-enabled application An application prepared using the Microsoft Application Virtualization Sequencer (SoftGrid Sequencer) that can be deployed to a virtual application server. SoftGrid-enabled applications are streamed to the clients.

SoftGrid Sequencer The original name of the Microsoft Application Virtualization Sequencer; the name is still used in some documentation. It creates SoftGrid-enabled applications.

Virtual application sequencer An application that prepares an application to be served by a virtual application server. The application is sequenced into blocks that can be sent to the client without having to send the entire application.

Virtual application server A server that can stream virtual applications to clients so that the clients can run the virtual application without installing it. A server hosting Microsoft's Application Virtualization 4.5 (App-V) is an example of a virtual application server.

Virtual application streaming Sending a virtual application to a client in a stream of data blocks. This allows the client to run the virtual application without installing it. Applications must be sequenced before they can be served by a virtual application server.

Windows Virtual PC An upgrade to Microsoft Virtual PC that runs on Windows 7 and can host one or more operating systems in a virtual environment. Windows Virtual PC supports Windows XP Mode, which allows applications to run on the virtual machine without requiring the user to start it.

Review Questions

1. Your network includes the following servers:

   HV1 Server 2008 server hosting three virtual servers (DC1, DC2, and DC3)

   AppV1 Server 2008 server hosting System Center Application Virtualization Streaming Server

   DFS1 Server 2008 server hosting DFS

   TS1 Server 2008 server hosting Terminal Services

   Users of applications named Sales and Contacts are having compatibility problems when running both applications at the same time. Management decides to run the Sales application as a virtual application from the Terminal Services server. How should the application be configured?

   a. Configure the application to be streamed from HV1.
   b. Configure the application to be streamed from AppV1.
   c. Configure the application to be streamed from DFS1.
   d. Configure the application to be streamed from TS1.

2. Your network hosts a System Center Application Virtualization Streaming Server that hosts a virtual application named SalesApp. Windows Vista was recently installed on a client, but it cannot run SalesApp. What needs to be done so that the Windows Vista system can run the virtual application?

   a. SP2 needs to be added to Windows Vista.
   b. Install the SoftGrid Sequencer on the Windows Vista system.
   c. Install SalesApp on the Windows Vista system.
   d. Install the SoftGrid Application Virtualization for Desktops on the Windows Vista system.

3. Your network hosts a System Center Application Virtualization Streaming Server that is used to host virtual applications. The Sales department recently purchased a new application and wants to deliver it as a virtual application. What should be done before it is deployed to the server?

   a. Configure the application as a TS RemoteApp.
   b. Configure a package using the SoftGrid Sequencer.
   c. Configure it as an .msi file and deploy with Group Policy.
   d. Configure SCCM to deploy the application.

4. Your Windows Server 2008 network includes a mixture of Windows XP, Windows Vista, and Windows 7 clients. A line-of-business application is used by Windows XP clients but it cannot run on Windows 7. Management wants to be able to upgrade these clients to Windows 7 and allow all the users to keep running the application. Of the following choices, which will meet the needs?

   a. Configure the application to be streamed from an App-V server.
   b. Configure the application to be streamed from Windows Media Server.
   c. Configure the application to be streamed from an Application Virtualization Sequencer.
   d. Configure the application to be streamed from System Center Virtual Machine Manager.

5. You need to create a SoftGrid-enabled application for users in your network. What is the easiest way to do so?

   a. Use the System Center Application Virtualization Streaming Server.
   b. Use the SoftGrid Application Virtualization for Desktops.
   c. Use the SoftGrid Streamer.
   d. Use a recipe that's been created for SoftGrid Sequencer.

6. Your single-domain forest is currently at the Windows Server 2008 domain functional level. It includes a mixture of Windows XP and Windows Vista clients. The Windows XP clients run an application that is not compatible with Windows Vista, and a newer version is not available. You're asked to find a low-cost solution that allows all the clients to be upgraded to Windows Vista and retain the functionality of the older application. What would you suggest?
   a. Use Microsoft Virtual PC.
   b. Use a SoftGrid Sequencer.
   c. Use SoftGrid-enabled applications.
   d. Use Microsoft Application Virtualization (App-V).
7. Your Windows Server 2008 network includes a mixture of Windows XP, Windows Vista, and Windows 7 clients. A line-of-business application is used by Windows XP clients, but it won't run on Windows 7. Management wants these clients upgraded to Windows 7. Users should be able to start the applications from their Start menu and run them in a brokered connection. What would you suggest to meet this need?
   a. Use Microsoft Virtual PC.
   b. Use Windows Virtual PC.
   c. Use a SoftGrid Sequencer.
   d. Rewrite the LOB program as a SoftGrid application.
8. Your network includes 20 Windows XP clients that are running an application named SellNow. Management wants to upgrade the clients to Windows 7, but testing indicates that SellNow will not work in Windows 7. You need to identify a solution that allows the clients to be upgraded but still allows users to start the application from the Windows 7 Start menu. What would you suggest?
   a. Microsoft Virtual PC
   b. Windows XP Mode
   c. SoftGrid Streamer
   d. SoftGrid Sequencer
9. You are an administrator for a single-domain forest. Several users in the Accounting department use two computers. One runs Windows 7 and the other runs Windows 2000 to support a legacy accounting application that is not compatible with Windows 7. You'd like to eliminate the Windows XP computers while still allowing users to run the older accounting application. What can you do? (Choose all that apply.)
   a. Install Windows Virtual PC on Windows 7. Add a Windows XP VPC machine and install the legacy application on the Windows XP machine.
   b. Install Microsoft Virtual PC on Windows 7. Add a Windows XP VPC machine and install the legacy application on the Windows XP machine.
   c. Install Windows Virtual PC on Windows 7. Add a Windows XP VPC machine and install the legacy application on the Windows XP machine. Publish the application using Windows XP Mode.
   d. Install Microsoft SoftGrid Application Virtualization for Desktops. Stream the application from a Windows XP system.
10. Your network includes Windows 2000 Server, 2003, 2008, and SUSE Linux servers. You are considering adding a Windows Server 2008 Enterprise server to host virtual servers in your network. What types of servers can be hosted as virtual servers? (Choose all that apply.)
   a. Windows 2000 Server
   b. Windows Server 2003
   c. Windows Server 2008
   d. SUSE Linux

11. You are planning to purchase a Windows Server 2008 Enterprise server. It will host four virtual servers running Windows Server 2008. How many Windows Server 2008 server licenses are required?
    a. One
    b. Two
    c. Four
    d. Five
12. You are an administrator in a single-domain forest. You have four servers running Windows Server 2008 Standard Edition that were upgraded from Windows Server 2003 Standard Edition. Each server is running at approximately 5 percent utilization. Two of the servers have 32-bit hardware and two have 64-bit hardware. You need to consolidate them into a single server. What should you do? (Choose all that apply; each answer represents a partial solution.)
    a. Identify the server with the most powerful processor and most RAM. Install the Hyper-V role.
    b. Identify a 64-bit server with the most powerful processor and most RAM. Install the Hyper-V role.
    c. Purchase a new 64-bit server with processors that include virtualization capabilities. Install Windows Server 2008 Enterprise Edition and the Hyper-V role.
    d. Migrate the other servers to this server.
    e. Connect the physical servers to the Hyper-V virtual network.

13. Your organization is considering consolidating some physical servers to virtual servers. However, management is unconvinced of the benefits and asks for your input. Of the following, which are considered benefits of server virtualization? (Choose all that apply.)
    a. Lower hardware costs
    b. Lower facilities costs
    c. Improved resource utilization
    d. Decreased uptime
    e. Less bandwidth usage per physical server
14. Your organization includes 20 virtual machines hosted on several physical servers in a heterogeneous environment. Management is considering the purchase of System Center Virtual Machine Manager to help with the management of these servers. You are asked to provide your opinion. What benefits does System Center Virtual Machine Manage provide? (Choose all that apply.)
    a. Consolidation of servers
    b. Management of VMware ESX virtual machines
    c. Management of Virtual Server 2005 R2 virtual machines
    d. Management of Hyper-V virtual machines
    e. Movement of virtual servers between physical servers
15. Your organization includes 10 physical servers that host multiple virtual servers using a mixture of Hyper-V, VMware ESX, and Virtual Server 2005 R2. All of these physical servers are managed separately, but management wants them to be administered through a central console. What would you recommend?
    a. SCOM
    b. SCCM
    c. SCVMM
    d. Hyper-V Manager

Case Projects

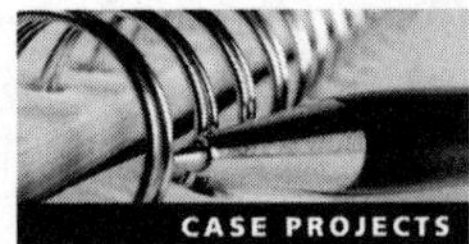

Case Project 10-1: Incompatible Applications

Your network includes 200 client computers in the Research department running Windows Vista. These users are running a scientific application named RnD. Users need an additional application for an important new project, but it is not compatible with the RnD application. What can be done to allow the users to run the application without having two computers? Explain your answer.

Case Project 10-2: Consolidating Clients

Five users in the HR department use two computers each. One computer runs Windows XP and supports a line-of-business application purchased by the company. The other computer runs Windows 7; users do all of their other work with this computer. Management wants to eliminate one of the computers and still retain all current usability. What can be done? Explain your answer.

Case Project 10-3: Server Consolidation

Your company recently completed an inventory and analysis of servers and discovered that four of them are highly underutilized. One server is running 32-bit Windows Server 2003, one is running 32-bit Windows Server 2008 Enterprise, one is running 64-bit Windows Server 2008 Standard, and one is running 64-bit Windows Server 2008 Enterprise. You're asked to develop a plan to consolidate the servers. What would you suggest and how could the plan be implemented? Explain your answer.

Case Project 10-4: Virtualization Management

Your company has 10 physical servers, each of which hosts an average of five virtual servers. Virtual servers are hosted on VMware and Hyper-V. Plans are in place to virtualize as many as 25 more servers this year. Management of these virtual servers has become more difficult and the company wants to ease the administrative burden. What Microsoft solution would you suggest and why?

Appendix A

MCITP 70-647 Exam Objectives

Table A-1 maps the MCITP Windows Server 2008 Enterprise Administrator (70-647) exam objectives to the corresponding chapter and section title where the objectives are covered in this book. After each objective, the percentage of the exam that includes the objective is shown in parentheses.

Table A-1 Objectives to chapter mapping

Domain objective	Chapter and section(s)
Planning network and application services (23 percent)	
Plan for name resolution and IP addressing.	Chapter 3, Improvements in Windows Server 2008 DNS, Name Resolution in a Domain, DNS Zones, Zone Files, and Zone Resource Records, Designing DNS Zones, Designing Zone Replication Scope
Design for network access.	Chapter 5, Network Access Protection
Plan for application delivery.	Chapter 5, Designing Remote Access Chapter 10, Application Virtualization, Microsoft Application Virtualization, Using Virtual PCs for Applications
Plan for Terminal Services.	Chapter 5, Designing Remote Access
Designing core identity and access management components (25 percent)	
Design Active Directory forests and domains.	Chapter 1, Basic Review of Active Directory Domain Services, Understanding Domain and Forest Functional Levels, Designing Active Directory Domains and Forests, Understanding Trusts, Using ADPrep, Migration Strategies
Design the Active Directory physical topology.	Chapter 2, Implementing Sites, Designing the Branch Office, Understanding Operations Master Roles Chapter 4, Group Policy Settings
Design the Active Directory administrative model.	Chapter 4, Designing Organizational Units Chapter 7, Compliance Auditing
Design the enterprise-level Group Policy strategy.	Chapter 4, Reviewing Group Policy Basics, Group Policy Settings, Manipulating GPO Deployments with Advanced Options, Fine-Grained Account Policies
Designing support identity and access management components (29 percent)	
Plan for domain or forest migration, upgrade, and restructuring.	Chapter 1, Designing Active Directory Domains and Forests, Understanding Trusts, Using ADPrep, Migration Strategies
Design the branch office deployment.	Chapter 2, Designing the Branch Office, Using RODCs
Design and implement public key infrastructure.	Chapter 6, An Overview of PKI and Certificates, Certificate Life Cycle Management, Types of Certification Authorities, Active Directory Certificate Services (AD CS), Implementing AD CS
Plan for interoperability.	Chapter 1, Understanding Trusts, Migration Strategies Chapter 9, Designing for Data Collaboration, Designing for Data Accessibility and Redundancy with DFS, Designing for Additional Active Directory Services

(continued)

Table A-1 *(continued)*

Domain objective	Chapter and section(s)
Designing for business continuity and data availability (23 percent)	
Plan for business continuity.	Chapter 8, Load Balancing and Fault Tolerance, Network Load Balancing, Failover Clusters, Active Directory Backup and Restores Chapter 2, Understanding Operations Master Roles
Design for software updates and compliance management.	Chapter 7, Hardening a System, Reducing the Attack Surface, Compliance Auditing, Keeping Systems Up to Date
Design the operating system virtualization strategy.	Chapter 10, Application Virtualization, Microsoft Application Virtualization, Using Virtual PCs for Applications, Server Virtualization, Virtualization Management
Design for data management and data access.	Chapter 7, Perimeter Networks Chapter 9, Understanding the System Center Suite, Designing for Data Security, Designing for Data Accessibility and Redundancy with DFS, Designing for Data Collaboration, Designing for Additional Active Directory Services

Appendix **B**

A Step-by-Step Guide to Using Server Virtualization Software

Virtualization enables a school or an individual student to get the most out of computer resources. Schools can use virtualization to turn a single server-grade computer into a virtual server that can host two, three, or more operating systems. For example, one computer can house three virtual servers running Windows Server 2008, which saves the school money and enables more students to work on their own operating systems.

Another feature of virtualization is that a school or student can turn a single PC into a virtual system on which to run another operating system—without having to alter the current operating system running on the PC. A single computer lab PC or a student's home PC can be turned into a host for Windows Server 2008. This is ideal, for example, when your textbook comes with an evaluation copy of Windows Server 2008. You can install virtualization software and then install Windows Server 2008 for completing hands-on projects and activities. You can use your originally installed operating system, such as Windows XP or Vista, and use Windows Server 2008 in a virtual "window" or "session," for example. After you have learned Windows Server 2008, you can simply remove the virtualization software and return to your original operating system.

This appendix is a step-by-step guide for converting a single computer into a virtual system that houses one or more virtual machines. The appendix focuses on three popular virtualization systems that are available for free:

- *Microsoft Virtual PC*—Intended for use with a workstation-grade PC to host another operating system, such as a Windows Server 2008 virtual machine
- *Microsoft Virtual Server*—Intended for use with a server-grade computer to host multiple virtual machines, including Windows Server 2008 and other operating systems
- *VMware Server*—Intended for use with server-grade computers to host multiple virtual machines, such as Windows Server 2008

For each of these virtualization systems, you will learn how to do the following:

- Obtain a free download version.
- Install it.
- Create a virtual machine.
- Install a guest operating system such as Windows Server 2008 in the virtual machine and then access that machine's operating system.
- Install ISO images.
- Configure virtual networking.
- Configure hardware components.

VMware Workstation 6 and Microsoft Hyper-V are also briefly described at the end of the appendix.

Microsoft Virtual PC

Microsoft Virtual PC can be installed in Microsoft Windows XP, Vista, and Windows Server 2003 operating systems. At this writing, it is not adapted to be installed in Windows Server 2008. Although Microsoft Virtual PC is intended to host workstation operating systems as virtual machines, you can also use it to create a Windows Server 2008 Standard Edition virtual machine. Microsoft Virtual PC is available from Microsoft as a free download. From an individual reader's perspective, it is ideal for running the Windows Server 2008 Standard Edition evaluation DVD (available at *www.microsoft.com*) on a Windows XP or Vista computer. It works equally well on Windows XP or Vista computers in a student computer lab.

Requirements for Microsoft Virtual PC

At this writing, Microsoft Virtual PC 2007 with Service Pack 1 (SP1) is the most recently available version. It can be loaded on the following operating system hosts:

- Windows XP Professional with SP2 or SP3
- Windows Server 2003 Edition SP2 (x86 or x64)
- Windows Vista Business Edition (x86 or x64 versions with or without SP1)
- Windows Vista Enterprise Edition (x86 or x64 versions with or without SP1)
- Windows Vista Ultimate Edition (x86 or x64 versions with or without SP1)

Microsoft Virtual PC 2007 SP1 has the following hardware requirements:

- *CPU*—Intel Celeron, Pentium II, Pentium III, Pentium 4, Core Duo, or Core 2 Duo CPU or AMD Athlon or Duron CPU (400 MHz or faster; x86 or x64).
- *RAM*—Enough RAM to meet at least the minimum requirements of the total number of operating systems you will be running. For example, if you are running Windows XP Professional (128 MB minimum) and want to load Windows Server 2008 (512 MB minimum) as a virtual machine, you'll need at least 640 MB to 1 GB of RAM. If Windows Vista is the host and you want to run a Windows Server 2008 Standard Edition virtual machine, you'll need at least 1 GB of RAM.
- *Disk space*—Enough disk storage for the operating systems you plan to run. For example, Windows XP requires at least 1.5 GB, Windows Vista requires at least 15 GB, and Windows Server 2008 requires at least 10 GB (although 15 GB to 20 GB is better for using different roles and services).

Virtual Machine Operating Systems Supported

After Virtual PC 2007 SP1 is loaded, you can run any of the following operating systems as virtual machines (guests) within it:

- Windows 98 and 98 SE
- Windows Me
- Windows 2000 Professional
- Windows XP Home or Professional with SP1, SP2, or SP3 (or no service pack)
- Windows Vista Business Edition (x86 or x64 versions with or without SP1)
- Windows Vista Enterprise Edition (x86 or x64 versions with or without SP1)
- Windows Vista Ultimate Edition (x86 or x64 versions with or without SP1)
- Windows Server 2008 Standard Edition
- OS/2 Warp

How to Download Microsoft Virtual PC

Microsoft Virtual PC can be downloaded from Microsoft's Web site for free. To download Virtual PC 2007 SP1, take the following steps. (Screen elements that you click are shown in bold.)

1. Log on to your computer.
2. Create a folder in which to download the setup.exe file for Microsoft Virtual PC (such as a temporary folder or a folder under your Program Files folder).

3. Open a Web browser such as Microsoft Internet Explorer.
4. Go to the URL **www.microsoft.com/downloads** or **www.microsoft.com/downloads/Search.aspx?displaylang=en** (for English).

Web links and specific instructions change periodically. You might need to search *www.microsoft.com* for the most current link if these links do not work.

5. Click the link for **Microsoft Virtual PC** in the Popular Downloads or Recommended Downloads section. (Also check the New Downloads section in case a new version is available.) If you do not see a link, click **Windows** under the Product Families heading. Click the **down arrow** in the Show downloads for: box, and click **Microsoft Virtual PC.** Click **Go.**
6. Click the link for **VPC 2007 SP1.**

To use Microsoft Virtual PC 2007 with Windows Server 2008 or Vista as the virtual machine (guest) operating system, you must use the download that contains SP1.

7. Click the **Download** button for the setup.exe file that is appropriate for your computer—32 BIT\setup.exe for an x86 computer or 64 BIT\setup.exe for an x64 computer.
8. Click the **Save** or **Save File** button.
9. Select the folder you created to save the setup.exe file.
10. Click **Save.**
11. Click **Close** in the Download complete box.
12. Close your Web browser.

How to Install Microsoft Virtual PC

Microsoft Virtual PC 2007 SP1 is easy to install. Take the following steps:

1. Browse to the folder in which you saved the setup.exe file for Microsoft Virtual PC.
2. Double-click **setup.exe.**
3. Click **Next** after the Microsoft Virtual PC 2007 SP1 Wizard starts (see Figure B-1).

Figure B-1 Microsoft Virtual PC 2007 SP1 Wizard

Courtesy Course Technology/Cengage Learning

4. Click the option button for **I accept the terms in the license agreement.** Click **Next.**
5. Enter your user name and organization name (if an organization name is appropriate). Notice that the product key should already be provided. Also, if you see the **Anyone who uses this computer (All Users)** option, leave it selected. Click **Next.**
6. Click **Install.** The installation takes a few minutes.
7. Click **Finish.**

Creating a Virtual Machine and Installing a Guest OS

After Microsoft Virtual PC 2007 SP1 is installed, the next step is to create a virtual machine in which to install a guest operating system.

Microsoft Virtual PC 2007 SP1 might not be compatible with hardware virtualization on some CPUs. If you experience a crash dump when configuring the virtual machine or loading the guest OS, first make sure that you enabled hardware virtualization in the preceding procedure. If this does not work, try disabling hardware virtualization in the BIOS and redo the preceding steps from the beginning.

The following steps help you set up the virtual machine with Windows Server 2008 Standard Edition as the guest operating system:

1. From the host operating system, such as Windows XP or Vista, click **Start.**
2. Point to **All Programs** and click **Microsoft Virtual PC.**
3. The New Virtual Machine Wizard opens (see Figure B-2). Click **Next.**

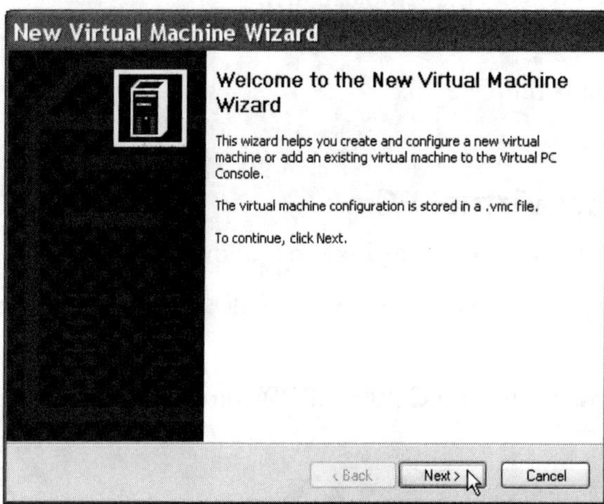

Figure B-2 New Virtual Machine Wizard

Courtesy Course Technology/Cengage Learning

4. Ensure that **Create a virtual machine** is selected and click **Next.**
5. Provide a name for the virtual machine, such as **Windows Server 2008.** Click **Next.**
6. Ensure that Windows Server 2008 is selected as the operating system to install and click **Next.**
7. Ensure that at least 512 MB to 1 GB of memory is allocated for the virtual machine. If necessary, click **Adjusting the RAM** and use the slider bar to allocate enough memory. Click **Next.**
8. Ensure that **A new virtual hard disk** is selected and click **Next.**
9. Make sure that the virtual hard disk is sized to meet your needs, or leave the default size selected. (You'll need 15 GB for Windows Server 2008 and might use at least 20 to 40 GB, for example.) Click **Next.**
10. Click **Finish.**

11. You should see the Virtual PC console open on the desktop. If it is not open, click **Start**, point to **All Programs**, and click **Microsoft Virtual PC**.
12. You can configure options by clicking the **File** menu and then clicking **Options**. Click each of the following options to see what they do and configure any options as necessary. When you finish, click **OK**.

    - *Restore at Start*—Pauses a running virtual machine when you exit the console and restores the virtual machine when you reopen the console.
    - *Performance*—Specifies how the CPU time is allocated to virtual machines and specifies what happens when a virtual PC is a process running in the background.
    - *Hardware virtualization*—Enables hardware virtualization if your CPU has this capability.
    - *Full-screen mode*—Enables the screen resolution to be made the same for the host and guest OSs (note the caution if this is enabled).
    - *Sound*—Configures virtual machine sound. Sound is muted by default. If you enable this option, the sounds from the host and guest OS can be difficult to differentiate.
    - *Messages*—Turns off error and informational messages from Virtual PC.
    - *Keyboard*—Specifies the host key for the guest operating system. The default host key is the right Alt key. When you press it, you can switch the mouse between the guest and host windows and execute guest key combinations, such as pressing Alt+Del to send the Ctrl+Alt+Del key combination to the guest OS for logging on.
    - *Mouse*—Specifies how the pointer is captured for use in the virtual machine window.
    - *Security*—Determines how to control access to Virtual PC functions.
    - *Language*—Specifies the language to use for Virtual PC.

13. Insert the Windows Server 2008 Standard Edition installation DVD.

At this point, you could install any of the supported guest operating systems. If you are installing a different operating system, you would insert the CD/DVD and complete Step 14. The subsequent steps would be unique to the operating system you are installing.

14. Click the **Start** button in the Virtual PC console window to open a second larger window called the Microsoft Virtual PC 2007 console window. Wait for a few minutes for the DVD to start loading. Click in the console window to enable the mouse to operate within the console. (If necessary, you can switch the mouse movement back so that it can traverse the entire screen by pressing the right Alt key, which is the "host" key.)

If you have problems moving the mouse in the active portion of the console window, close all console windows, go to Step 11, and start again. Also, some installations take longer in a virtual machine. Don't close the window or stop the installation prematurely, even if you seem to be stuck on a black screen for several minutes.

15. Select **English** or an appropriate option in the Language to install drop-down box. Select similar options in the Time and currency format box and the Keyboard or input method box. Click **Next**.
16. Click **Install now**.
17. Select **Windows Server 2008 Standard (Full Installation)** and click **Next**.
18. Read the license terms, click the box for **I accept the license terms**, and click **Next**.
19. Click **Custom (advanced)**.
20. The amount of unallocated disk space should be highlighted. You specified the disk space when you configured the virtual machine. Ensure that the amount is highlighted and click **Next**.

21. The installation of Windows Server 2008 begins. You'll see progress information about copying files, expanding files, installing features, installing updates, and completing installation. This part of the installation can take 30 minutes or longer.
22. The installation program restarts the operating system. You are asked to wait while Windows sets up your computer.
23. After the Install Windows window is displayed in the Completing installation phase, the system reboots again.
24. You'll be prompted to change your password before logging on the first time. Click **OK**. (You might have to click inside the active portion of the console window to make the mouse function within it).
25. Enter a new password for the Administrator account and then enter the same password again to confirm it. Click the **blue circle** with the white arrow inside it.

If you do not enter a strong password, you'll be informed that the system was unable to update the password. This means that your new password does not meet the length, complexity, or history requirements of the domain. Click OK and enter a different password that has more than seven characters and uses a mixture of letters, numbers, and characters such as &.

26. When informed that your password has been changed, click **OK**.
27. The Windows desktop opens and the Initial Configuration Tasks window is displayed.
28. You can configure Windows Server 2008 as you would in a nonvirtual environment.
29. When you close the Microsoft Virtual PC 2007 console window, you can either turn off the virtual machine or save its current state—in other words, keep the server in its current state without shutting it down. Unless you want to save its state, a good practice is to shut down the server prior to closing the window. When you shut down the server in this way, the Microsoft Virtual PC 2007 console window closes, but the Virtual PC 2007 console window remains open. To restart the virtual machine, open the Virtual PC console window, click **Start**, and wait for the system to boot in the Microsoft Virtual PC 2007 console window.

When you log on to Windows Server 2008 from the console window, the normal Ctrl+Alt+Del key sequence does not work. Instead, click the Action menu and press Ctrl+Alt+Del. Another alternative is to press and hold the right Alt key and press the Del key.

Installing an OS from an ISO Image

An ISO file is an optical disc (CD/DVD) image file that ends with the .iso file extension. An ISO file can be accessed in several ways, such as from a CD/DVD, a hard drive, or as a shared network file. When you download an operating system, such as an evaluation copy of a Windows operating system, you typically download an ISO file. When you use an ISO file to install a guest operating system into a virtual machine, the installation usually is faster. Microsoft Virtual PC enables you to install from an ISO file by using the following general steps:

1. Follow Steps 1 through 12 in the previous section, "Creating a Virtual Machine and Installing a Guest OS."
2. Click the **Start** button in the Virtual PC console window.
3. After the Microsoft Virtual PC 2007 window opens, press the **right Alt** key if necessary to access the menu at the top of the window.
4. Click the **CD** menu and click **Capture ISO Image.**
5. Navigate to the ISO file, click the file, and click the **Open** button.
6. You are returned to the Microsoft Virtual PC 2007 window. Restart the virtual machine.

Configuring Networking and Hardware Options

You can configure a range of networking and hardware options in Microsoft Virtual PC. For example, if the host computer has two or more NICs, you can specify which NIC to use for a virtual machine. In another example, you might need to create one or more additional virtual hard disks for a virtual machine.

Use these steps to configure networking and hardware options:

1. Open the Virtual PC console if necessary. Also, ensure that the virtual machine is turned off before you start.
2. Click the **Settings** button or click the **Action** menu and click **Settings** (see Figure B-3).

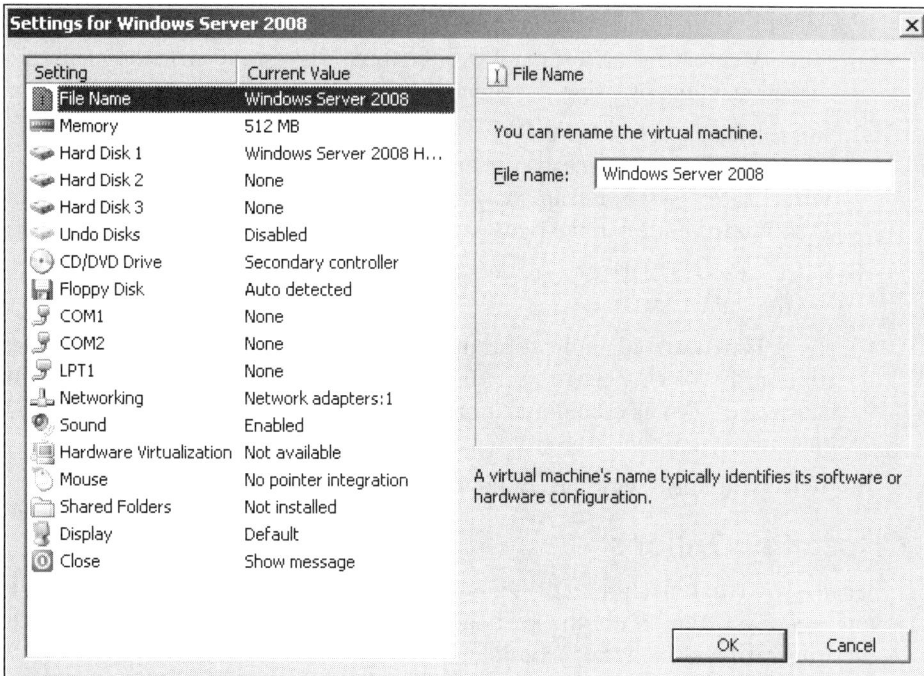

Figure B-3 Settings for a virtual machine

Courtesy Course Technology/Cengage Learning

3. Click **Networking** in the left pane. If your computer has multiple adapters, you can select the specific adapter(s) to associate with a virtual machine.
4. In the right pane, click the down arrow for the adapter that is selected by default. The following options are available:
   - *Not connected*—Select this option if the virtual machine will not access a network (including the Internet).
   - *Local*—If two or more virtual machines are set up, they can access each other; however, virtual machines cannot access the network.
   - *Network Interface Name*—The actual name of a NIC model, such as an Intel or Broadcom NIC, to which the virtual machine is directly connected for regular network and Internet access. With this selection, network configuration tasks that apply to other network computers also apply to the virtual machine. If a DHCP server is on the network or if the network uses a router with Network Address Translation (NAT), the virtual machine's network connection can be configured to use them. The same applies if a DNS server is set up.
   - *Shared Networking (NAT)*—Used to create a private Virtual PC network that has a virtual DHCP server and a virtual NAT-enabled router or firewall. The first virtual computer created typically acts as the DHCP server and provides NAT services. In this

arrangement, Microsoft Virtual PC performs as a virtual DHCP server, leasing IP addresses for virtual machines in the range of 192.168.131.1 to 192.168.131.253. Further, the virtual machines appear as computers within a private NAT-protected network. A connection to the Internet is shared among the virtual machines and is protected in a manner similar to a NAT-enabled router or firewall.

- *Loopback Adapter*—This option is available if the operating system is configured to have a Microsoft loopback adapter (configured as a network adapter, such as through the Add Hardware option in Control Panel). This option is used in two contexts: when no physical network connection is present but you want to simulate network connectivity between the host and all virtual machines, or when you create a network with many routers, firewalls, and virtual machines.

5. Make the appropriate networking selections.
6. Click **Memory** in the left pane. Notice that you can increase the memory allocation for the virtual machine by using the slider bar in the right pane.
7. In the left pane, click **Hard Disk 1** and notice that the right pane shows the path to the virtual hard disk file. Also, you can configure the Hard Disk 2 and Hard Disk 3 options for additional virtual hard disks. For example, you can click Hard Disk 2 in the left pane and click the Virtual Disk Wizard button in the right pane. (A virtual machine can have up to three hard disks.)
8. Click **CD/DVD Drive** in the left pane and notice that you can attach a CD or DVD drive via the right pane.
9. Click **Hardware Virtualization** in the left pane. Notice in the right pane that you can enable hardware virtualization if your computer supports it. You also can configure additional hardware, such as communication (COM) ports, a floppy disk, printer (LPT) ports, sound, the mouse, and the display.
10. When you finish with the configurations, click **OK**.

Host Key Options

Because a virtual machine represents an operating system running inside an operating system, you need to be able to use the keyboard so that your keystrokes communicate directly with the guest operating system. For example, pressing Ctrl+Alt+Del brings up the Windows Security window or a menu of options, depending on which version of Windows is the host operating system. It does not take you to a logon screen in the guest operating system.

Microsoft Virtual PC enables you to communicate with the guest operating system by using the host key, which is the right Alt key by default. Table B-1 lists important host key combinations you can use while accessing a virtual machine.

Table B-1 Host key options for Microsoft Virtual PC

Keyboard combination	Result
HostKey	Enables you to move the mouse outside the window area used by the guest OS (You can move the mouse back into the guest OS display and click when you want to work in the guest OS)
HostKey+Del	The virtual machine OS responds to this as Ctrl+Alt+Del
HostKey+P	Toggles the virtual machine between Pause and Resume
HostKey+R	Resets the virtual machine
HostKey+A	Selects all items in the active window of the guest OS
HostKey+C	Copies selected text and items in the active window of the guest OS
HostKey+V	Pastes text and items in the active window of the guest OS
HostKey+Enter	Switches between full screen and window modes
HostKey+DownArrow	Minimizes the virtual machine
HostKey+I	Enables you to install virtual machine additions

Microsoft Virtual Server

Microsoft Virtual Server 2005 is intended to host server operating systems as virtual machines. At this writing, Microsoft Virtual Server 2005 R2 SP1 is the most recent version. It supports hardware virtualization (integrated in the CPU), such as AMD CPUs equipped with AMD-V and Intel CPUs with Intel VT. Other new features include the following:

- The ability to be installed in x64 operating systems
- Support for Internet Small Computer System Interface (iSCSI), which is a technology used in Storage Area Networks (SANs)
- The ability to cluster virtual servers on a single computer
- Enhanced Active Directory support by publishing Virtual Server binding data through service connection points

Other features of Microsoft Virtual Server include the following:

- The ability of virtual disks to expand dynamically
- Support for most popular x86 operating systems
- The ability to mount a virtual disk on a different operating system
- Volume Shadow Copy Service (VSS) can be used for backups (used in newer versions of Windows operating systems, such as Windows Server 2008 and Vista)
- Virtual server management through Virtual Server Web console
- The use of scripting to control virtual machine setups
- The ability to resize memory access

Microsoft Virtual Server Guest Operating Systems Supported

Microsoft Virtual Server can house virtual machines for popular Windows and Linux server and workstation operating systems. The following operating systems can be guests:

- Windows Server 2008 Standard, Enterprise, Datacenter, and Web Server (x86 and x64)
- Windows Server 2003 Standard, Enterprise, Datacenter, and Web Server SP1 or SP2 (x86 or x64)
- Windows Server 2003 Standard, Enterprise, Datacenter, and Web Server R2 (x86 or x64)
- Windows Small Business Server 2003 (Standard and Premium Editions)
- Windows 2000 Server
- Windows XP Professional SP2
- Windows Vista Business, Ultimate, and Enterprise
- Red Hat Enterprise Linux versions 2.1 to 4.0
- SUSE Linux Enterprise Server 9.0
- SUSE Linux versions 9.2 to 10.0

Other operating systems can also run experimentally in Microsoft Virtual Server.

Microsoft Virtual Server Host Operating Systems Supported

Microsoft Virtual Server can be installed into the following Windows host operating systems:

- Windows Server 2008 Standard and Enterprise (x86 or x64)
- Windows Server 2003 Standard, Enterprise, and Web Server with SP1 or SP2 (x86 or x64)

- Windows Server 2003 Standard, Enterprise, and Web Server R2 (x86 or x64)
- Windows Small Business Server 2003 (Standard and Premium Editions, also R2 versions)
- Windows 2000 Server with SP3 or SP4
- Windows XP Professional (x86 and x64)
- Windows Vista Business, Ultimate, and Enterprise Editions

Requirements for Microsoft Virtual Server

Microsoft Virtual Server 2005 R2 with SP1 has the following hardware requirements:

- *CPU*—Intel Celeron, Pentium III, Pentium 4, Xeon, or AMD Opteron, Athlon, Athlon 64, Athlon X2, Duron, or Sempron (550 MHz or faster; x86 or x64).
- *RAM*—Enough RAM to match at least the minimum requirements of the total number of operating systems you will be running. For example, if you are running Windows XP Professional (256 MB minimum required for Virtual Server) and want to load Windows Server 2008 (512 MB minimum) as a virtual machine, you'll need at least 768 MB to 1 GB of RAM. If Windows Server 2003 R2 Standard Edition is the host and you want to run a Windows Server 2008 Enterprise Edition virtual machine, then you'll need at least 768 MB to 1 GB of RAM.
- *Disk space*—Enough disk storage for the operating systems you plan to run. For example, Windows Server 2003 R2 Standard Edition requires at least 3 GB, and Windows Server 2008 requires at least 10 GB (but 15 to 20 GB enables you to load more roles and services).

How to Download Microsoft Virtual Server

You can download Microsoft Virtual Server from Microsoft's Web site for free. To download Microsoft Virtual Server:

1. Log on to your computer.
2. Establish a folder in which to store the download (such as a temporary folder or a folder under your Program Files folder).
3. Start your Web browser, such as Internet Explorer.
4. Go to the URL **www.microsoft.com/downloads** or **www.microsoft.com/downloads/Search.aspx?displaylang=en** (for English).

Web links and specific instructions change periodically. You might need to search *www.microsoft.com* for the most current link if these links do not work.

5. Look for *Microsoft Virtual Server* in the Popular Downloads or Recommended Downloads sections. (You can also check the New Downloads section in case there is a new version.) If you find **Microsoft Virtual Server** in one of these sections, click its link. If you do not see a link, ensure that the search box near the top of the Web page is set to **Windows**. Enter **Virtual Server** in the blank box next to the Go button, and then click **Go**.
6. Click the link for **Virtual Server 2005 R2 SP1**.
7. Click the **Continue** button to register for the free download.
8. The information you provide next depends on whether you have signed up for Windows Live ID or if you have an MSN Hotmail, MSN Messenger, or Passport account. If you already have an account, provide your e-mail address and password for the Windows Live ID information, click **Sign in** to verify your information and answer any required questions, and click **Continue**. If you do not have an account or a Windows Live ID, follow the steps to sign up for a Windows Live ID.

9. Click the **Download** button for the setup.exe file that is appropriate for your computer, which is 32 BIT\setup.exe for an x86 computer or 64 BIT\setup.exe for an x64 computer.
10. Click the **Save** or **Save File** button.
11. Select the folder you created to save the setup.exe file.
12. Click **Save.**
13. Click **Close** in the Download complete box.
14. Close your Web browser.

How to Install Microsoft Virtual Server

Use the following general steps to install Microsoft Virtual Server into the host operating system:

1. Browse to the folder in which you saved the setup.exe file for Microsoft Virtual Server.
2. Double-click **setup.exe.**
3. Click **Install Microsoft Virtual Server 2008 R2 SP1** (see Figure B-4).

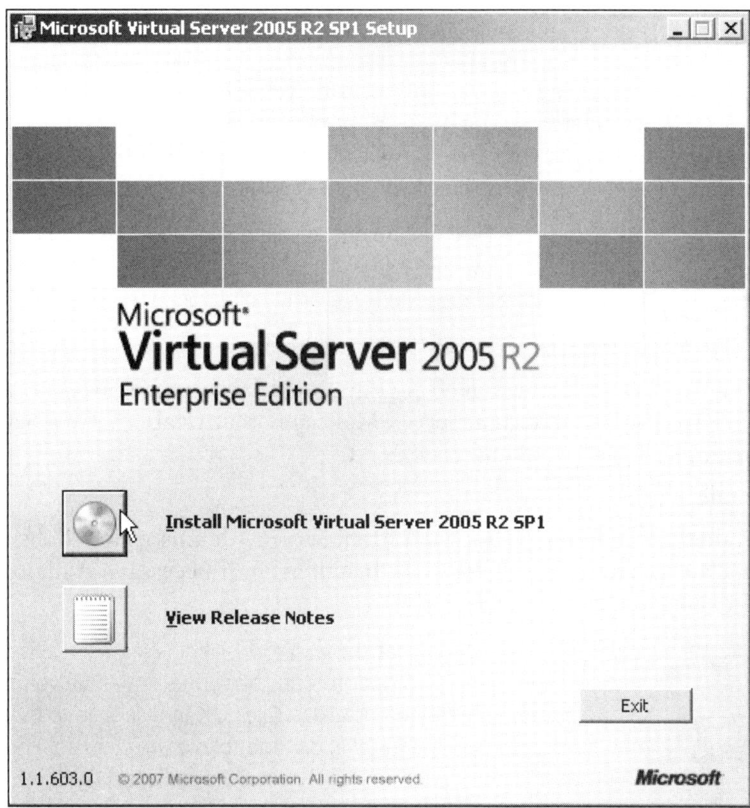

Figure B-4 Installing Microsoft Virtual Server 2008 R2 SP1
Courtesy Course Technology/Cengage Learning

4. Click **I accept the terms in the license agreement.** Click **Next.**
5. Enter your user name and organization name (if you represent an organization). Notice that the Product Key information is provided by default. Click **Next.**
6. Ensure that **Complete** is selected for the Setup Type, as shown in Figure B-5, and click **Next.**

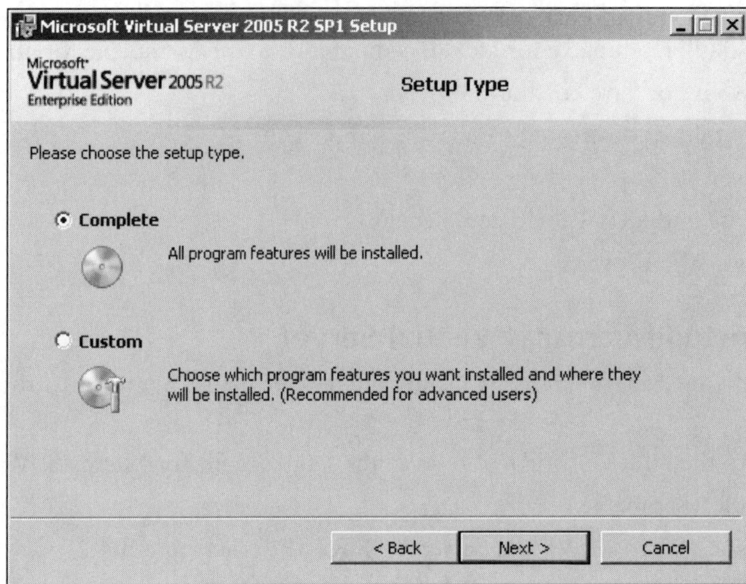

Figure B-5 Selecting the setup type

Courtesy Course Technology/Cengage Learning

7. Notice that the Virtual Server Administration Website will be added to Internet Information Services (IIS), and the default Website port is 1024. Further, if you see the option **Configure the Administration Website to always run as the authenticated user (Recommended for most users)**, ensure that it is selected. Click **Next**.

After you click Next, you might see a message that the installed version of IIS does not allow multiple websites. If so, the Virtual Server Administration Website will be added as a virtual directory under the default site.

8. If the Windows Firewall is enabled on your computer, you can have the setup process create firewall exceptions for Virtual Server. Make sure that **Enable Virtual Server exceptions in Windows Firewall** is selected and click **Next**.
9. Click **Install**.
10. If the required IIS components for the Virtual Server Administration Website are not already installed, click **Yes** to install them. Click **Install** again if necessary. A dialog box shows that the components are being installed.

If you see a message that the IIS World Wide Web service needs to be installed but there is no option to install it, the Virtual Server installation program probably cannot install IIS. Click OK in response to the message, click Cancel to stop the installation, and follow the steps for your host OS to install IIS. (You might need the host OS installation CD/DVD.) Start the Virtual Server installation again from Step 1.

11. A dialog box shows that Microsoft Virtual Server 2005 R2 SP1 is being installed.
12. Click **Finish** and close any open windows.

Creating a Virtual Machine and Installing a Guest OS

After Microsoft Virtual Server is installed, you can use the Virtual Server Administration Website tool to configure Microsoft Virtual Server, configure a virtual machine, and install a guest operating system. The following steps use Windows Server 2008 as the guest operating system:

1. Click **Start**, point to **All Programs**, and click **Microsoft Virtual Server**.
2. Click **Virtual Server Administration Website**.

3. Provide a user name and password (for an account that has administrator privileges) in the Connect to dialog box, and then click **OK**.
4. If you are using a recent version of the Windows Firewall, you might see the Internet Explorer box, which enables you to add the Web site to the list of trusted sites. (You probably will see this dialog box the first time you access the Virtual Server Administration Website tool.) Click the **Add** button. In the Trusted sites dialog box, click the **Add** button for the site you are adding and click **Close**. Also, if you see the Microsoft Phishing Filter dialog box, choose whether to turn on the Phishing Filter and click **OK**. (Turning the filter on is recommended.)
5. The Virtual Server Administration Website tool is displayed through Internet Explorer, as shown in Figure B-6. Notice that the left pane contains options to navigate, create, and add virtual machines, manage virtual disks, manage virtual networks, and manage the virtual server.

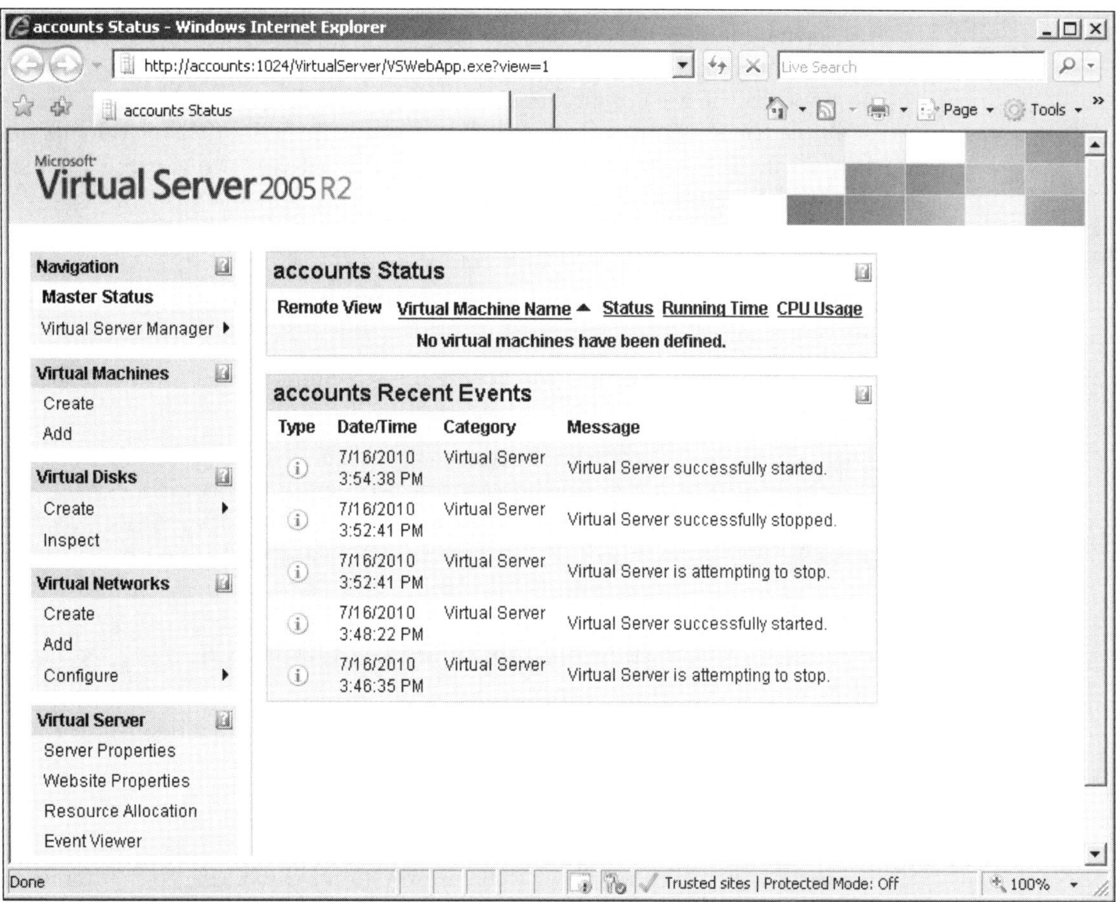

Figure B-6 Virtual Server Administration Website tool

Courtesy Course Technology/Cengage Learning

6. In the left pane under Virtual Machines, click **Create**.
7. Enter the name for the virtual machine and set the virtual machine memory. For Windows Server 2008, you should set at least 512 MB to 1024 MB. Also, choose to **Create a new virtual hard disk** with at least 15 GB (more is better) for Windows Server 2008. Finally, specify the virtual network adapter, such as an external network interface. Click **Create**.

The virtual network adapter options are Not connected, External Network, and Internal Network. The Not connected option (the default) does not provide any type of connection, so you can only access the virtual machine directly from the server. The External Network option allows users to connect to the virtual machine through the computer's network interface card. The Internal Network option allows a connection between virtual machines on the same computer.

8. If you see an option to turn on AutoComplete (to remember your entries used in Web forms), select **Yes** or **No**.
9. In the right pane, review the configuration information for your test server. You can use this pane to make changes. (See the following section, "Configuring Networking and Hardware Options," for more information.)
10. To allow access to a window in which to use the virtual server, click **Server Properties** under Virtual Server in the left pane.
11. In the right pane, click **Virtual Machine Remote Control** (**VMRC**) **Server**.
12. Ensure that the **VMRC server** is enabled and that the TCP/IP address of the host server is entered. (If you have trouble connecting after entering the TCP/IP address of the host server, try leaving the TCP/IP address setting at "All unassigned.") Also, ensure that Authentication is set to **Automatic**. Remove the check mark from the **Enable** box for **Disconnect idle connections** (so you are not disconnected during the OS installation). Check the **Enable** box for **Multiple VMRC connections** and check **Enable** for **SSL 3.0/TLS 1.0 encryption**. If necessary, set the SSL 3.0/TLS 1.0 certificate to **Keep** or **Request** (if Keep is disabled). Make sure that the host name matches the name of the computer you are using. Click **OK** in the lower-right corner of the window. (If you have problems using VMRC Server, you can return to this screen and adjust any parameters.)
13. In the left pane, point to **Configure** under Virtual Machines and click the name of the virtual machine you created.
14. Turn on the virtual machine by clicking the screen thumbnail for the virtual machine in the right pane.

You might see a message that you need to configure Internet Explorer security to proceed. Make the necessary security configurations. Also, if you see a message from Internet Explorer to install an add-on, click the message, click Install ActiveX Control, and follow the directions to continue.

15. Insert the Windows Server 2008 installation DVD.
16. If necessary, click the thumbnail again for the virtual machine. If you see a security message, click **Yes** to proceed.
17. Enter your user name and password (using an account with administrator privileges). Click **OK**.
18. If you see another security message, such as for NTLM Authentication, click **Yes** to proceed.
19. If necessary, scroll down to view the information for working in the Remote Control window. Notice the options to Pause, Save State, Turn Off, and Reset the virtual machine.
20. Scroll back to the top of the Remote Control window.
21. You should see an installation screen for Windows Server 2008. Move the mouse pointer into that screen area (the mouse becomes a small black dot). Click in the area until you see the normal arrow for your mouse. Notice that you can work only within the console for the virtual machine. Press the **right Alt** key (the default host key) to be able to use the mouse throughout the Remote Control window. Remember that you can always use the right Alt key to leave the console area as needed. (Also, to work inside the console again, click the mouse pointer inside the console.) In the upper-right corner of the Remote Control portion of the window, click the down arrow for **Remote Control**. Review the options on the menu, such as Special Keys and Connect To Server.

When you point to Special Keys, note that you can press the host key (the right Alt key) with the Del key to send the Ctrl+Alt+Del key sequence to the virtual machine. (This is important for logging on after you have installed Windows Server 2008.)

22. Move the mouse pointer back into the console area and click it so you can work in this area again.
23. Select **English** or an appropriate option in the Language to install drop-down box. Select similar options in the Time and currency format box and the Keyboard or input method box. Click **Next.**
24. Click **Install now.**

If your connection stops before the installation is finished, use the left arrow at the top of the window to return to the main Status window. Click the virtual machine thumbnail to open a new connection via the Remote Control window. Respond to any security messages, log on again, and respond to any additional security messages. The installation should still be running.

25. Select **Windows Server 2008 Enterprise (Full Installation).** (You can also select a different full installation edition, such as Standard Edition, if it is available.) Click **Next.**
26. Read the license terms, click the box for **I accept the license terms,** and click **Next.**
27. Click **Custom (advanced).**
28. The amount of unallocated disk space should be highlighted. You specified this disk space when you configured the virtual machine. Ensure that this amount is highlighted and click **Next.**
29. The installation of Windows Server 2008 begins. You'll see progress information about copying files, expanding files, installing features, installing updates, and completing installation. This process takes 30 minutes or more.
30. The installation program restarts the operating system. You'll be asked to wait while Windows sets up your computer.
31. After the Install Windows window is displayed in the Completing installation phase, the system reboots again.
32. You'll be prompted to change your password before logging on the first time. Click **OK.** (You might have to click inside the active portion of the console window to enable the mouse to work in it.)
33. Enter a new password for the Administrator account and then enter the same password again to confirm it. Click the **blue circle** with the white right-pointing arrow inside.

If you do not enter a strong password, you'll be told that the system was unable to update the password. This means that the new password does not meet the length, complexity, or history requirements of the domain. Click OK and enter a different password that is more than seven characters and uses a mixture of letters, numbers, and characters such as &.

34. When informed that your password has been changed, click **OK.**
35. The Windows desktop opens and the Initial Configuration Tasks window is displayed. From here you can start configuring Windows Server 2008.
36. You can close the Remote Control window (the Virtual Machine Remote Control Server) or the Status window (the Virtual Server Administration Website) at any time. The virtual machine continues running in the background. Also, you can return to the Administrator window by clicking the left-pointing arrow at the top of the Remote Control window.

You can shut down a server by first logging on through the Remote Control window. Also, you can use this window and the Status window to turn off a virtual machine (make sure you shut down the server first).

To access the documentation for Microsoft Virtual Server, click Start, point to All Programs, click Microsoft Virtual Server, and click Virtual Server Administrator's Guide.

Installing an OS from an ISO Image

If you have an ISO image file for the guest operating system, you can install it instead of performing a traditional installation through the installation DVD. Use the following general steps to install an ISO image file in a virtual machine within Microsoft Virtual Server:

1. Follow Steps 1 through 13 in the previous section, "Creating a Virtual Machine and Installing a Guest OS." The bottom portion of the right pane should show the configuration options for the virtual machine.
2. Click the link for **CD/DVD.**
3. Under Virtual CD/DVD Drive 1, click the option button for **Known image files**. Next, click the **down arrow** for **Known image files** and select the image file. If the ISO image file is not listed, enter the path to the ISO image file in the box for **Fully qualified path to file.**
4. Click **OK.** The display returns to the Master Status listing.

Configuring Networking and Hardware Options

The Microsoft Virtual Server Administration Web site allows you to configure virtual networks. For example, as you learned earlier, a connected network has two default virtual network options: external network and internal network. You can customize settings for both types of networks, such as settings for a virtual DHCP server. You can also create a new virtual network with properties you define.

A virtual network is used by virtual machines within a network and is independent of other virtual networks. Microsoft Virtual Server allows an unlimited number of virtual machines to be connected to a virtual network.

The Microsoft Virtual Server Administration Website also provides options to configure hardware settings, such as adding more memory for use by a virtual server. In the next sections, you learn how to configure virtual networking and to configure hardware for a virtual machine.

Configuring Virtual Networking

In the following steps, you examine how to configure virtual networking:

1. Open the Microsoft Virtual Server Administration Website tool if necessary. (Click **Start**, point to **All Programs**, click **Microsoft Virtual Server**, and click **Virtual Server Administration Website.**)
2. In the left pane under Navigation, click **Master Status** if necessary. Access any virtual servers that are running and shut them down. To do this, point to the server name (that has a right-pointing arrow) under Virtual Machine Name in the right pane, click **Turn Off**, and click **OK.** (You can configure virtual networking while virtual machines are running, but you should turn them off first.)
3. In the left pane under Virtual Networks, point to **Configure** and click **View All.**
4. In the right pane, point to **External Network** ***(NICname)*** and click **Edit Configuration.**
5. Review the information in the right pane.

6. In the right pane, click the link for **Network Settings**.
7. Review the properties information, including information about the NIC. Click **OK**.
8. In the right pane, click the link for **DHCP server**.
9. You can use the right pane to configure a virtual DHCP server that leases IP addresses through Microsoft Virtual Server (see Figure B-7). To enable the virtual DHCP server, check the **Enabled** box in the right pane. You can then configure the following:
   - *Network address*—Enter the network address for the virtual network.
   - *Network mask*—Enter the network mask.
   - *Starting IP address*—Enter the beginning address for the range (scope) of IP addresses that can be leased.
   - *Ending IP address*—Enter the ending address for the range of IP addresses that can be leased.
   - *Virtual DHCP server address*—Enter the IP address of the virtual DHCP server.

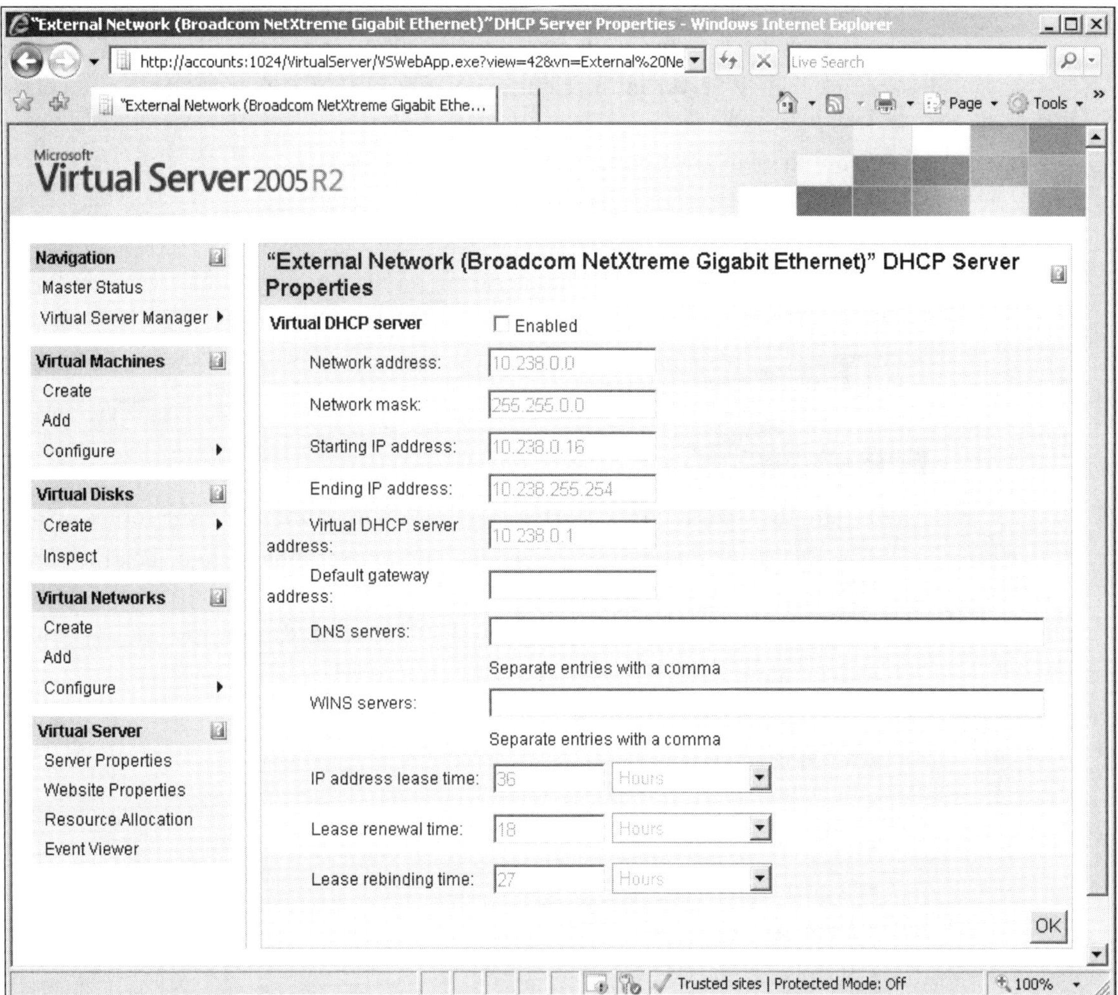

Figure B-7 Virtual DHCP server configuration options

Courtesy Course Technology/Cengage Learning

   - *Default gateway address*—Enter the IP address of a router that transports packets beyond the virtual network.
   - *DNS servers*—Enter the IP address of one or more existing DNS servers on the network.

- *WINS servers*—Enter the IP addresses of any Windows Internet Naming Service (WINS) servers (for converting NetBIOS computer names to IP addresses).
- *IP address lease time*—Enter the amount of time that an IP address can be leased. The time can be set in days, hours, minutes, or seconds. You would typically set this time for one or more days.
- *Lease renewal time*—Enter the amount of time in which the client can contact the virtual DHCP server to renew a lease. You can enter a time in days, hours, minutes, or seconds, but you must set a minimum of 30 seconds.
- *Lease rebinding time*—Enter the amount of time required to enable the client to contact another server to renew its lease when the main leasing server cannot be reached. You can enter a time in days, hours, minutes, or seconds, but you must set a minimum of 45 seconds.

10. In the left pane under Virtual Networks, point to **Configure** and click **Internal Network.**
11. Review the information in the right pane for the virtual network properties.
12. Click **Network Settings** in the right pane and review the information provided.
13. Click the **back arrow** at the top of the window.
14. Click **DHCP Server** in the right pane. Notice that you can enable and configure a virtual DHCP server.
15. Leave the window open for the next set of steps.

Configuring Hardware for a Virtual Machine

In addition to configuring a virtual network, you can configure hardware and other options for a virtual machine:

The virtual machine you select in the following steps should be turned off first.

1. Ensure that the Microsoft Virtual Server Administration Website tool is open.
2. In the left pane under Virtual Machines, point to **Configure** and click the name of the virtual server you have configured.
3. Scroll to the configuration section in the right pane. Review the options you can configure:
   - General properties
   - Virtual Machine Additions
   - Memory
   - Hard Disks
   - CD/DVD
   - SCSI adapters
   - Network adapters
   - Scripts
   - Floppy drive
   - COM ports
   - LPT ports
4. In the right pane, click **General properties.** If your computer supports hardware-assisted virtualization, you can enable it here. You can also specify a user account to run the virtual machine and specify what action to take when the Virtual Server stops. If you make changes, click **OK** in the lower-left side of the window.

5. Click the **back arrow** at the top of the window to return to the previous configuration display in the right pane.
6. In the right pane, click **Memory**. You can then change the amount of memory allocated to the virtual machine. If you make changes, click **OK**.
7. Click the **back arrow** at the top of the window.
8. In the right pane, click the link for **Hard disks**. The right pane shows the configuration of the virtual disk used by the virtual machine. If you select **Enable undo disks**, you can undo changes later on the virtual machine if necessary. You can also add a new virtual disk by clicking the Add disk button. If you make changes, click **OK** so they take effect.
9. Click the **back arrow**.
10. Click **CD/DVD** in the right pane. In the right pane, you can click the Remove option to remove a CD/DVD drive, and you can click the Add CD/DVD Drive button to add a new drive. If you make changes, click **OK**.
11. Click the **back arrow**.
12. Click the remaining Configuration options in the right pane to view what they cover. In particular, notice that you can add NICs by using the Network adapters option.
13. Close the Microsoft Virtual Server Administration Website tool when you finish (or restart your virtual server so it is in use).

Host Key Options

Microsoft Virtual Server designates the right Alt key as the default host key and offers host key options like those offered by Microsoft Virtual PC. Table B-2 lists important host key combinations you can use while accessing a virtual machine.

Table B-2 Host key options for Microsoft Virtual Server

Keyboard combination	Result
HostKey	Enables you to move the mouse outside the window area used by the guest OS (You can move the mouse back into the guest OS display and click when you want to work on the guest OS)
HostKey+Del	The virtual machine OS responds to this as Ctrl+Alt+Del
HostKey+C	Displays the Connect to server box for connecting to a specific virtual machine (or copies selected text)
HostKey+A	Toggles to the Administrator display window
HostKey+I	Shows the VMRC Connection Properties box with information about the connected virtual machine
HostKey+B	Provides information about the VMRC Client software
HostKey+V	Pastes text and items saved in the Clipboard into the active window of the guest OS
HostKey+H	Enables you to configure a different key as the host key

VMware Server

VMware Server enables you to set up virtual machines to run Windows or Linux operating systems. VMware Server version 2 is a significant update compared with previous 1.x versions. The new features of VMware Server 2 include:

- Ability to manage virtual machines from either the Web Access management interface or the non-Web-based VMware Remote Console
- Ability to configure different levels of permissions

- Ability to configure which operating systems will start when VMware is started
- Editors for hardware devices
- New support for Windows Vista, Windows Server 2008, Red Hat Enterprise 5.0, and Ubuntu Linux up through version 8.x.
- Ability to handle increased memory (up to 8 GB) and more NICs (up to 10) in the host machine
- Support for 64-bit guest operating systems on 64-bit (x64) host computers
- Hot-add capability for new SCSI and tape devices (without shutting down a virtual machine)
- Support for VSS for backups on Microsoft guest systems
- Ability to use Firefox 3 or Internet Explorer for the Web Access management interface
- Support for hardware virtualization, such as through AMD CPUs that have AMD-V capability and Intel CPUs with Intel VT
- Support for multiple monitors (to see different virtual machines on different displays)

VMware Server Guest Operating Systems Supported

VMware Server supports the following guest operating systems:

- Windows Server 2008 Standard, Enterprise, Datacenter, and Web Server (x86 or x64)
- Windows Server 2003 Standard, Enterprise, Datacenter, and Web Server with SP1 or SP2 (x86 or x64)
- Windows Server 2003 Standard, Enterprise, Datacenter, and Web Server R2 (x86 or x64)
- Windows Small Business Server 2003 (Standard and Premium Editions)
- Windows 2000 Server and Professional
- Windows XP Professional
- Windows Vista Business and Ultimate (x86 and x64)
- Red Hat Enterprise Linux Server and Desktop versions up through version 5 (x86 and x64)
- Ubuntu 6.x to 8.x
- SUSE Linux Enterprise Server up to 10.x (x86 and x64)
- SUSE Linux versions up to 10.x (x86 and x64)
- Novell NetWare
- Solaris

VMware Server Host Operating Systems Supported

VMware Server 2.x runs inside more types of host operating systems than Microsoft Virtual PC or Server because it can run on several Linux distributions. It also runs on x86 and x64 computers. The list of VMware host operating systems includes:

- Windows Server 2008 Standard, Enterprise, Datacenter, and Web Server (x86 or x64)
- Windows Server 2003 Standard, Enterprise, Datacenter, and Web Server with SP1 or SP2 (x86 or x64)
- Windows Server 2003 Standard, Enterprise, Datacenter, and Web Server R2 (x86 or x64)
- Windows Small Business Server 2003 (Standard and Premium Editions)
- Windows 2000 Server and Professional with SP3 or SP4
- Windows XP Professional and Home through the current service pack

- Windows Vista Business and Ultimate (x86 and x64)
- Red Hat Enterprise Linux Server and Desktop versions up through version 5 (x86 and x64)
- Ubuntu 6.x to 8.x
- SUSE Linux Enterprise Server up to 10.x (x86 and x64)
- SUSE Linux versions up to 10.x (x86 and x64)
- Mandrake Linux up to 10.x

VMware Server also can run on other Windows and Linux distributions, such as other Windows Vista editions or Fedora Linux, but they should be considered experimental because they might not be fully tested.

For Windows host operating systems, you must download the VMware Server version for Windows, which is in .exe format. For Linux host operating systems, you must download the VMware Server version for Linux, which is in .tar format.

Windows Server Core is not a supported host at this writing.

Requirements for VMware Server

VMware Server has the following hardware requirements:

- *CPU*—Any standard x86 or x64 computer, including the following processors: dual- or quad-core Intel Zeon, Intel Core 2, AMD Opteron or Athlon (733 MHz or faster)
- *RAM*—A minimum of 512 MB, but enough RAM to meet at least the minimum requirements for the total number of operating systems you'll be running (host and guest)
- *Disk space*—Enough disk storage for the operating systems you plan to run (host and guest)
- *Console Web Access*—Internet Explorer 6.0 or above (for Windows hosts) or Mozilla Firefox 2.0 or above (for Linux hosts)

VMware Server 2.x virtual machines can connect to hard drives, optical drives, and floppy drives. VMware 2.x also supports USB 2.x connections.

How to Download VMware Server

VMware Server can be downloaded from VMware's Web site at no cost. To download VMware Server:

1. Log on to your computer.
2. Establish a folder in which to store the download (such as a temporary folder or a folder under your Program Files folder).
3. Start your Web browser, such as Internet Explorer.
4. Go to the URL **www.VMware.com/products/server**.

Web links and specific instructions change periodically. You might need to search for the most current link at *www.VMware.com* if this link does not work.

5. Click **Download Now.**
6. Find the latest version of VMware Server (if multiple versions are listed) and click **Download** or **Download Now.**
7. If asked to provide registration information, complete the registration form.
8. Read the licensing information and click **Yes** or **Accept.**
9. Record the serial number for the Windows version. (You'll need this later when you install VMware Server.)
10. Click the link to download the Binary (.exe) file for VMware Server for Windows Operating Systems.
11. Click the **Save** button.
12. Select the folder you created to save the file.
13. Click **Save.**
14. Click **Close** in the Download Complete box.
15. Close your Web browser.

How to Install VMware Server

Use the following general steps to install VMware Server into the host operating system:

1. If possible, connect to the Internet so that updates can be installed automatically during the installation.
2. Browse to the folder in which you saved the install file for VMware Server.
3. Double-click **VMware-server-2.x.x-xxxxxx** (where 2.x.x-xxxxxx is the version of VMware Server).
4. You'll be informed that the system is preparing for the installation, and then you'll see the Windows Installer box.
5. When the Installation Wizard for VMware Server starts (see Figure B-8), click **Next.**

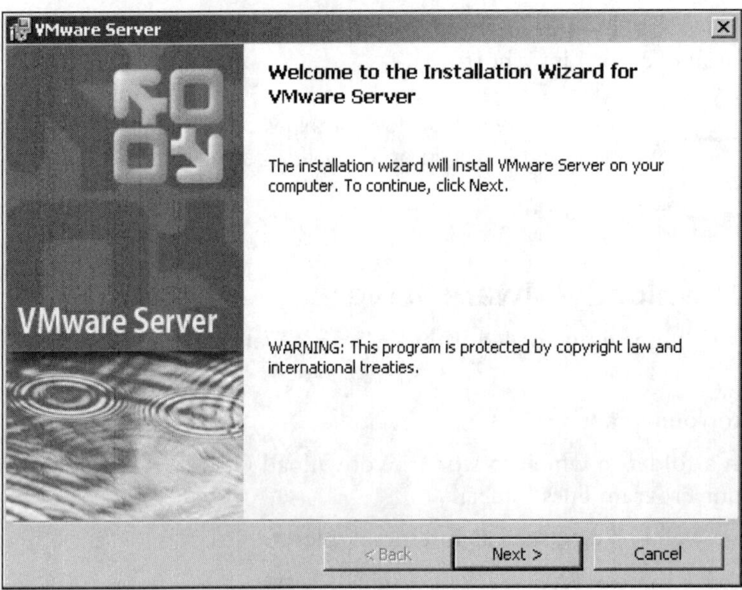

Figure B-8 VMware Server installation wizard

Courtesy Course Technology/Cengage Learning

6. Read the license agreement, click **Yes, I accept the terms in the license agreement,** and click **Next.**

7. Verify that the VMware server files will be written to the appropriate destination folder. (You can click the Change button to select a different destination.) Click **Next.**
8. Verify the fully qualified domain name for the host computer, and verify that the Server HTTP (port 8222) and Server HTTPS (port 8333) Ports are selected by default. Make any changes as needed, such as to the host and domain names. (Leave the default selections for the ports.) Click **Next.**
9. Ensure that the desired shortcuts are selected, as shown in Figure B-9. Click **Next.**

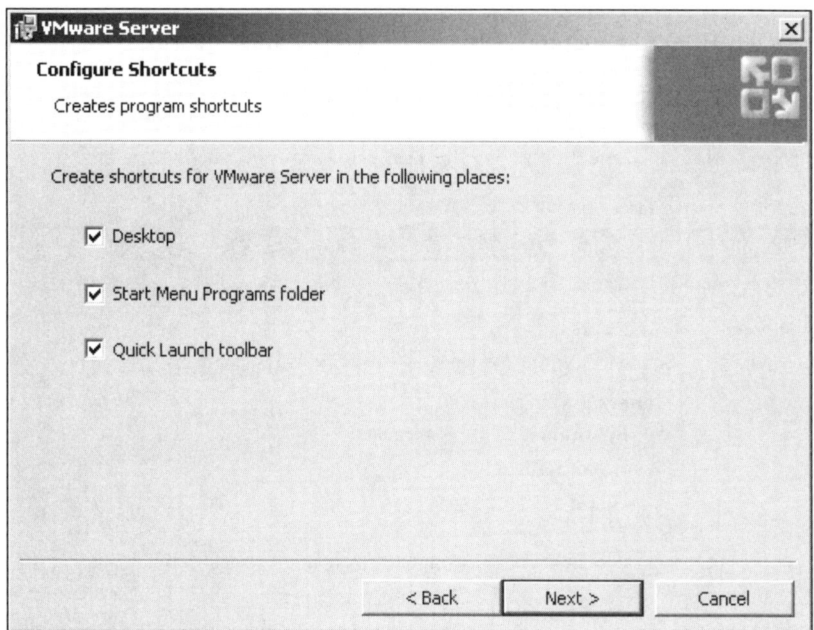

Figure B-9 Shortcut options

Courtesy Course Technology/Cengage Learning

10. Click **Install.**
11. You'll be informed that the installation might take several minutes.
12. If you see one or more boxes to install device software, click **Install.**
13. For the registration information, enter your name and school or company name, if appropriate. Next, enter the serial number you obtained when you downloaded the software. Click **Enter.**
14. Click **Finish.**
15. Ensure that all programs are closed and click **Yes** to restart the system.

Creating a Virtual Machine and Installing a Guest OS

Now that VMware Server is installed, the next step is to create a virtual machine and install the guest operating system. Here are the general steps using Windows Server 2008 as the guest:

The VMware Remote Console that you use in these steps requires that the VMware virtual server (host computer) can be resolved through Domain Name System (DNS). Before you start, make sure that your server can be resolved through DNS on your network (or that DNS is installed on the host). For example, there should be a host address (A) resource record in the DNS server for the host computer.

1. Double-click the **VMware Server Home Page** icon on the desktop or in the taskbar. (Alternatively, you can click **Start**, point to **All Programs**, click **VMware Server**, and click **VMware Server Home Page**.)

You might need to resolve security requirements for Internet Explorer, such as providing a digital certificate, answering whether to set up a phishing filter, and adding the site to make it a trusted site.

2. Log on using your host computer account name (or the administrator account) and provide the password. (Use the same account that you used to install VMware Server.)
3. The VMware Infrastructure Web Access window appears, as shown in Figure B-10.

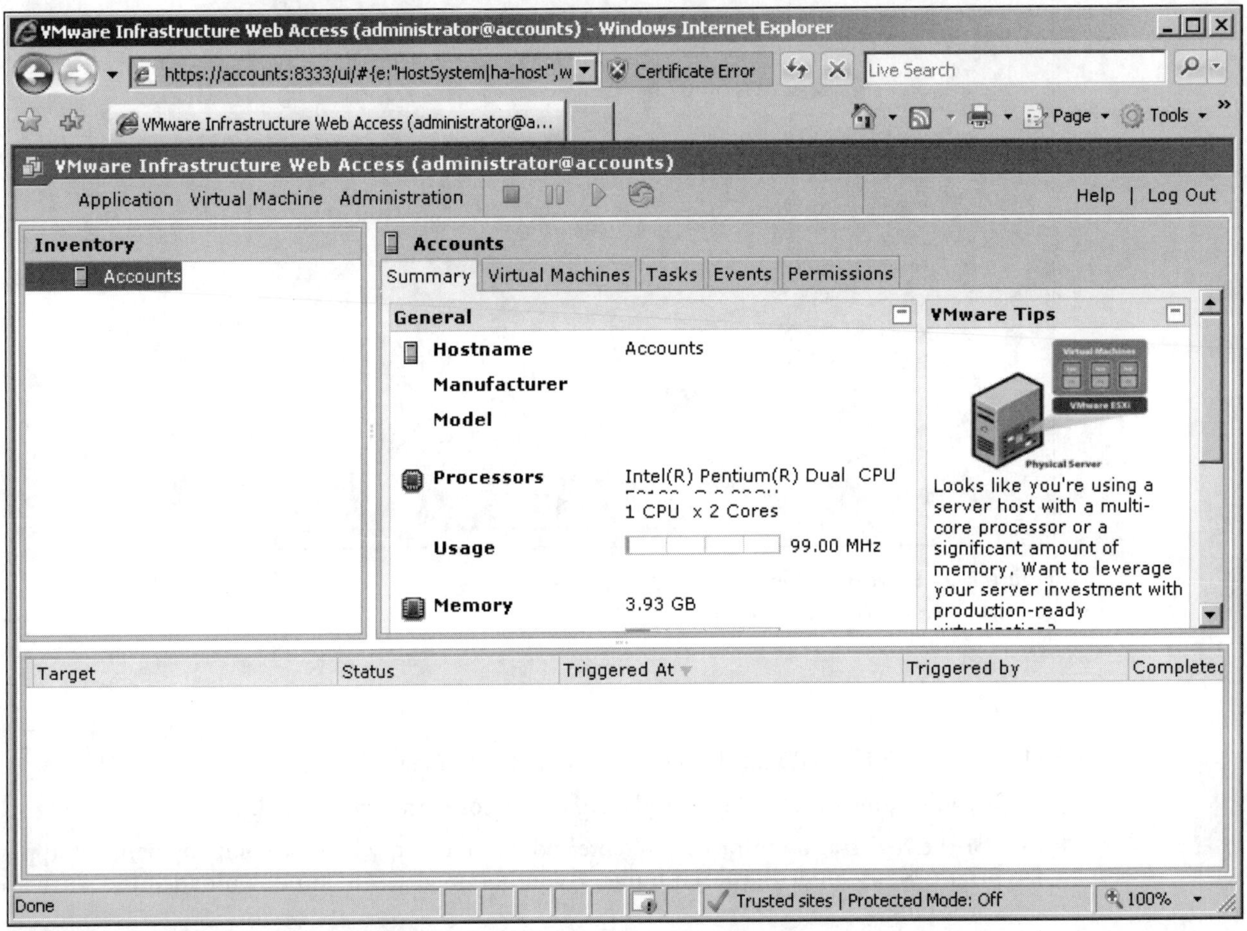

Figure B-10 VMware Infrastructure Web Access window

Courtesy Course Technology/Cengage Learning

Notice that a certificate error might be reported in Figure B-10 because this new site does not yet have a trusted certificate. If so, you might be able to import a certificate by clicking the Certificate Error box at the top of the window, clicking the link for View certificates, and clicking Install Certificate. Another option is to talk to your network administrator about importing a certificate.

4. Ensure that your virtual server computer is highlighted in the left pane.
5. Click the **Virtual Machines** tab.
6. In the right pane under the Commands heading, click **Create Virtual Machine**.

7. Enter the name for the virtual machine and click **Next**.
8. Ensure that **Windows operating system** is selected as the type of guest operating system, select the operating system (in the Version box), and click **Next**.
9. Set the memory size to **512 MB** or more. (1024 MB is the default setting when installing Windows Server 2008.) Also, if your system has a dual- or quad-core CPU or is an SMP system, you can select the number of processors to use. However, you should not reconfigure the number of processors after the virtual machine is set up. Click **Next**.
10. Select the virtual disk to use, such as by clicking **Create a New Virtual Disk** (a disk on the current computer). The other option is to Use an Existing Virtual Disk, which is a disk on a shared drive or a hard disk on a different computer. Enter the capacity for the virtual disk, such as **20 GB** (see Figure B-11). Adjust any parameters as needed:
    - *Location for the virtual disk file*—Allows you to select a file location other than the default path
    - *File Options*—Allocates disk space and lets you split the disk into two files
    - *Disk Mode*—Allows you to create independent disks that are not affected by snapshots
    - *Virtual Device Node*—Allows you to select the SCSI or IDE adapter and device
    - *Policies*—Allows you to optimize for safety or for performance

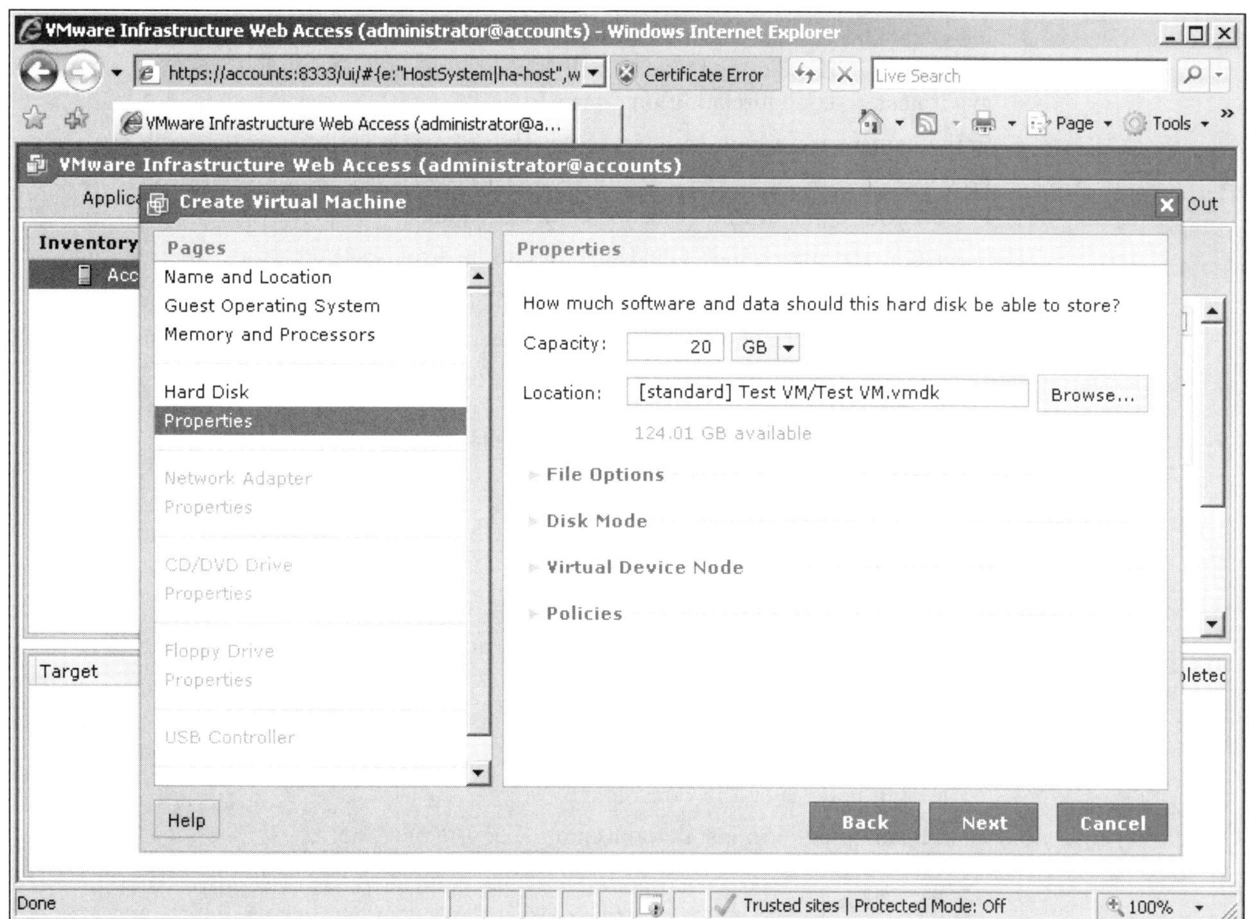

Figure B-11 Configuring virtual disk properties

Courtesy Course Technology/Cengage Learning

11. Click **Next**.

12. In the next window, you can add a network adapter for access over a network. Click **Add a Network Adapter.** If you do not want to use the default settings for Network Connection (Bridged) and for Connect at Power On (Yes), configure those settings. You can configure the following Network Connection parameters:
    - *Bridged*—This setting gives the virtual machine its own network identity (so that it is seen as a different computer than the host), which enables other computers on the network to communicate with it. The bridged setting also means that the virtual machine can access the Internet through the local network.
    - *HostOnly*—With this setting, only the host computer and other virtual machines on the same host can access the virtual machine, which means it is not accessible through the local network.
    - *NAT*—The virtual machine and host use the same IP and MAC addresses, which means that the virtual machine does not have its own identity on the local network. Choose this option if IP addresses are in short supply for the specific network or if an organization's network policy is to allow only one IP address for a specific computer.
13. Click **Next.**
14. You can configure whether to enable access to a CD/DVD drive or to use an ISO image for the installation of the operating system. For this sample set of steps, click **Use a Physical Drive.** Ensure that the correct CD/DVD drive is selected, such as drive E, and ensure that Connect at Power On is set to **Yes.** Click **Next.**
15. If your computer has a floppy drive, you can configure it to provide an image for the operating system. Select the appropriate configuration options. (To install Windows Server 2008, click **Don't Add a Floppy Drive.**) Click **Next** if necessary. Depending on your selection, you might need to configure additional properties.
16. In the next window, you can decide whether to add a USB controller, such as to access a flash drive. Make your selection and click **Next** if necessary.
17. Review your configuration selections and click **Finish.**
18. In the bottom pane, a Success message should be displayed under the Status column to show that you successfully created the virtual machine.

If you selected different configuration options and then clicked the Back button to return to the preceding steps, VMware Server might display an error message or the virtual machine might not be created. If so, start from scratch and avoid undoing selections you have made.

19. Insert the Windows Server 2008 installation DVD.
20. In the left pane, click the new virtual machine name under the host server name. (You might first have to expand the entries under the host server name.)
21. Ensure that the **Summary** tab is selected in the right pane.
22. In the right pane, scroll to the Hardware section. Click the **down arrow** within the icon in front of CD/DVD Drive 1 *(drivetype)* and click **Edit.**
23. Review the preselected parameters for the host media (CD/DVD drive), make any needed changes, and click **OK.**
24. In the right pane, click the **Console** tab.
25. Click **Install plug-in** to install the Remote Console plug-in.

If you see a window about the Information Bar, click Close. Also, if the plug-in is not successfully installed in Internet Explorer, you might see a message at the top of the window that you must click to continue. Click the message and click to install the elements required by Internet Explorer, such as the ActiveX Control. Next, click Install plug-in again, and click Install if necessary.

26. In the right pane, click **Powered off.** (This button functions like a switch to turn the virtual machine on or off.)
27. Click anywhere in the reduced console area of the right pane to start the console.
28. Select **English** or an appropriate option in the Language to install drop-down box. Select similar options in the Time and currency format box and the Keyboard or input method box. Click **Next.**
29. Click **Install now.**
30. Select **Windows Server 2008 Enterprise (Full Installation).** You can also select a different full installation edition, such as Standard Edition, if it is available. Click **Next.**
31. Read the license terms, click the box for **I accept the license terms**, and click **Next.**
32. Click **Custom (advanced).**
33. The amount of unallocated disk space should be highlighted. You specified the disk space when you configured the virtual machine. Ensure that the amount is highlighted and click **Next.**
34. The installation of Windows Server 2008 begins. You'll see progress information about copying files, expanding files, installing features, installing updates, and completing installation. This process takes 30 minutes or longer.
35. The installation program restarts the operating system. You'll be asked to wait while Windows sets up your computer.
36. After the Install Windows window is displayed in the Completing installation phase, the system reboots again.
37. You'll be prompted to change your password before logging on the first time. Click **OK.** (You might have to click inside the active portion of the console window to have the mouse function within it.)
38. Enter a new password for the Administrator account and then enter the same password again to confirm it. Click the **blue circle** with the white right-pointing arrow inside.

If you do not enter a strong password, you'll be informed that the system was unable to update the password. This means that the new password does not meet the length, complexity, or history requirements of the domain. Click **OK** and enter a different password that is more than seven characters and uses a mixture of letters, numbers, and characters such as &.

39. When informed that your password has been changed, click **OK.**
40. The Windows desktop opens and the Initial Configuration Tasks window is displayed. From here you can start configuring Windows Server 2008 or log out and use the Remote Control window later to access Windows Server 2008.
41. You can close the VMware Remote Console window at any time. The virtual machine keeps running.
42. Close the VMware Infrastructure Web Access window when you finish using it. The virtual machine will also continue running unless you shut it down in the VMware Remote Console window and turn it off in the VMware Infrastructure Web Access window.

If you need to access online help documentation from the VMware Infrastructure Web Access window, click the Help option near the upper-right corner.

Installing an OS from an ISO Image

VMware Server supports installing an operating system via an ISO image file. Use the following general steps for this type of installation:

1. Follow the steps to create a virtual machine.
2. In the left pane under Inventory in the VMware Infrastructure Web Access window, click the virtual server you created.
3. Click the **Summary** tab in the right pane.
4. Scroll down the right pane to view the Hardware section.
5. Click the **down arrow** for the **CD/DVD Drive 1** section and click **Edit.**
6. Under the Connection section, click the option button for **ISO Image.**
7. Enter the optical disk image path or use the **Browse** option to find and select it.
8. If necessary, select the appropriate device node in the Virtual Device Node section.
9. Click **OK.**
10. Click the **Console** tab.
11. Start the virtual machine if necessary.
12. Click inside the console and follow the instructions from the operating system.

Configuring Networking Options

As you learned earlier, the three network connection options are Bridged, HostOnly, and NAT. Each type of network has a default name:

- Bridged is called VMnet0.
- HostOnly is called VMnet1.
- NAT is called VMnet8.

You can configure virtual networking, including VMnet0, VMnet1, and VMnet8, using the Virtual Network Editor. For example, you can use the VMware internal DHCP server capability for HostOnly and NAT networks. Bridged networks use an external DHCP server, such as a Windows Server 2008 server configured for this service.

To explore the Virtual Network Editor:

1. Click **Start**, point to **All Programs**, click **VMware**, click **VMware Server**, and click **Manage Virtual Networks.**
2. The Virtual Network Editor appears. It has the following tabs (see Figure B-12):
   - *Summary*—Provides a summary of the virtual networks, including VMnet0, VMnet1, and VMnet8
   - *Automatic Bridging*—Controls bridging between the VMnet0 network and the network adapter
   - *Host Virtual Network Mapping*—Enables you to link virtual networks to physical network adapters and virtual network adapters, as well as configure subnet and DHCP properties
   - *Host Virtual Adapters*—Shows virtual adapter connections, virtual networks, and the status of the connections
   - *DHCP*—Enables you to configure DHCP for VMnet1 and VMnet8
   - *NAT*—Enables you to control the NAT service and configure NAT settings
3. Click each tab to view the options in it.
4. Click the **DHCP** tab again.

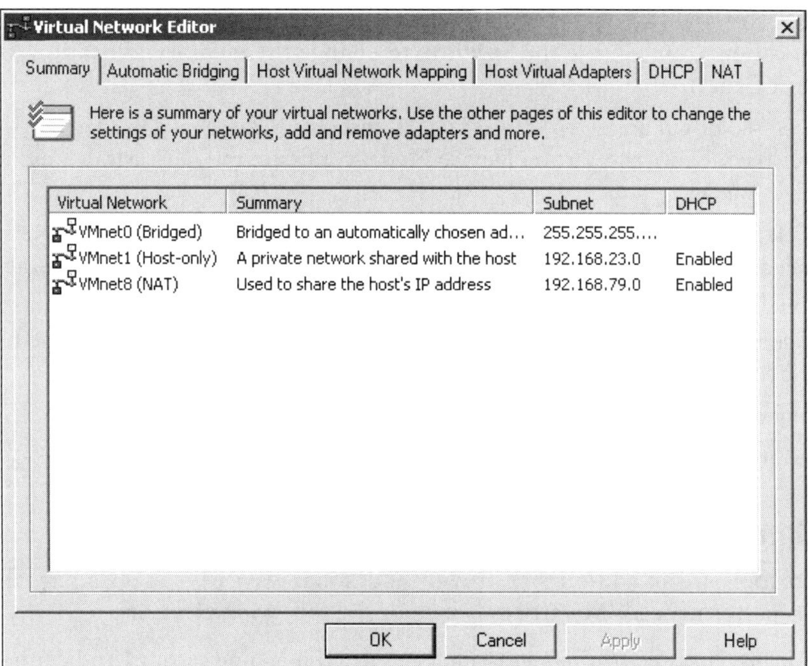

Figure B-12 Virtual Network Editor

Courtesy Course Technology/Cengage Learning

5. Click **VMnet1** and click **Properties.**
6. In the DHCP Settings box, notice that you can configure the range of IP addresses to use (Start and Stop IP addresses). You can also configure the lease duration parameters for clients. Click **Cancel.**
7. Notice that you can start, stop, and restart the DHCP service from the DHCP tab.
8. Click the **NAT** tab. You can use it to associate the NAT service with a virtual network or to start, stop, and restart the NAT service.
9. Close the Virtual Network Editor when you finish.

Configuring Hardware Options

After you set up a virtual machine, you might want to go back and configure hardware options. For example, you might change the network configuration and decide to switch from a Bridged network to a HostOnly network.

The following steps enable you to configure hardware:

1. Open the VMware Infrastructure Web Access window, such as by clicking the VMware Server Home Page icon on your desktop.
2. In the left pane under Inventory, expand your view to see the virtual machines under the host server, if necessary.
3. Under Inventory, click the virtual machine you want to configure.
4. To configure hardware, you first need to ensure that the virtual machine is turned off. Use the Console tab to shut down the OS. Also, click **Virtual Machine** in the button bar and click **Power Off.**
5. In the right pane, click the **Summary** tab.
6. Scroll down in the right pane to view the Hardware section.
7. Click the down arrow for **Processors** and click **Edit.** You'll see a note that advises against changing the number of virtual processors, if you have more than one processor. Click **Cancel.**

8. Click the down arrow for **Memory** and click **Edit**. Notice the recommended size for memory allocation. You can use the Size box to change the memory allocation (in multiples of 4). Click **Cancel**.
9. Click the down arrow for **Hard Disk 1** and click **Edit**. You can increase the virtual disk capacity, configure the Virtual Device Node, configure the Disk Mode, and configure Policies. Click **Cancel**.
10. Click **Network Adapter 1** and click **Edit**. You can change the type of Network Connection, such as from Bridged to HostOnly. Information about the connection status, MAC address, and virtual device is also displayed. Click **Cancel**.
11. Click the down arrow for **CD/DVD Drive 1** and click **Edit**. Review the properties you can set and the connection status information. Click **Cancel**.
12. Review information about any other hardware devices.
13. Restart the virtual machine when you finish.

Installing VMware Tools

VMware tools are an add-on that provide additional ways to manage a virtual machine and improve its performance. VMware tools include the following elements:

- *VMware Tools control panel* to change virtual machine settings and connect devices
- *VMware user processes* for Linux and Solaris guest operating systems
- *Device drivers* for enhanced video, audio, mouse, network, and SCSI disk performance
- *Tools service* options for messaging, mouse performance, screen resolution, and so on

When you install the VMware tools, the virtual machine must be started and you should be logged on to the guest operating system account from which you manage the virtual server software. The tools, including drivers, are installed into the guest operating system; you can access them from Control Panel in Windows Server 2008 and other Windows operating systems.

To install the VMware tools:

1. Open the VMware Infrastructure Web Access window.
2. Click a virtual machine under Inventory in the left pane.
3. Ensure that the guest operating system is running. Log on to the Administrator account or an account that has Administrator privileges.
4. In the VMware Infrastructure Web Access window, click **Install VMware Tools** in the Status column of the right pane for the virtual machine.
5. Click **Install**.
6. Open the virtual machine console by clicking the **Console** tab and clicking inside the console.
7. It might take several minutes for the AutoPlay box to appear in the guest operating system desktop within the console. Click the option to **Run setup.exe**.
8. The Windows Installer window reports that it is preparing to install. This process might take several minutes.
9. Click **Next** in the Welcome window (see Figure B-13).
10. Select the setup type from the following options:
    - *Typical*—Select this option if you plan to use only VMware Server.
    - *Complete*—Select this option if you plan to use VMware Server and other VMware products.
    - *Custom*—Select this option if you want to choose specific features to install.

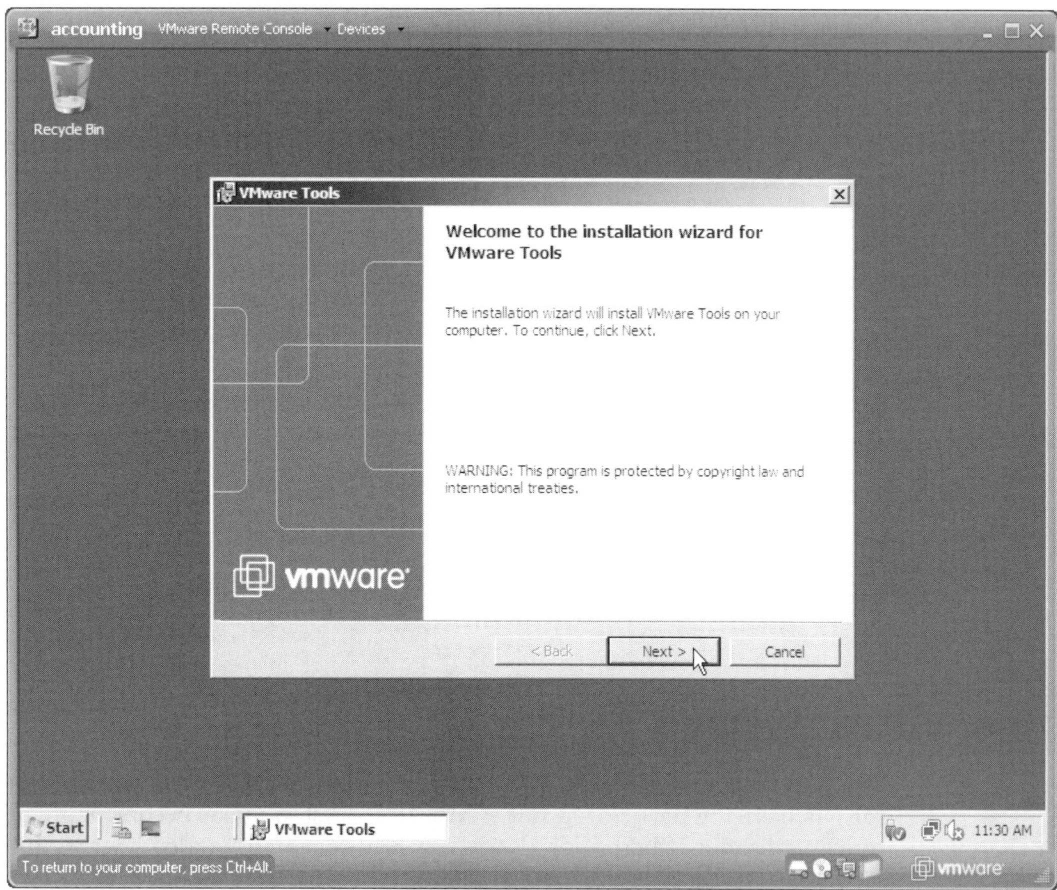

Figure B-13 Installation wizard for VMware Tools

Courtesy Course Technology/Cengage Learning

11. Click **Next**.
12. Click **Install**.
13. If you are informed that Windows can't verify the publisher of the driver software, click **Install this driver software anyway**. (You might see this message several times.)
14. If asked whether you want to install this device software, click **Always trust software from "VMware, Inc."** Click **Install**.
15. Click **Finish**.
16. Save any work on the virtual machine and click **Yes** to restart.
17. Log on again to the guest operating system in the console window.
18. In the guest operating system (Windows Server 2008), click **Start** and click **Control Panel**.
19. Click **Classic View** and click the new applet for **VMware Tools**. The VMware Tools Properties dialog box appears, as shown in Figure B-14.
20. Click each tab to see its options.
21. Click the **Help** button to learn more about VMware Tools.
22. Close the Help window when you finish.
23. Click **Cancel** to close the VMware Tools Properties dialog box.
24. A new icon is displayed in the guest operating system's taskbar in the tray near the clock. You can click this icon to open the VMware Tools Properties dialog box.
25. Close Control Panel in the guest operating system.

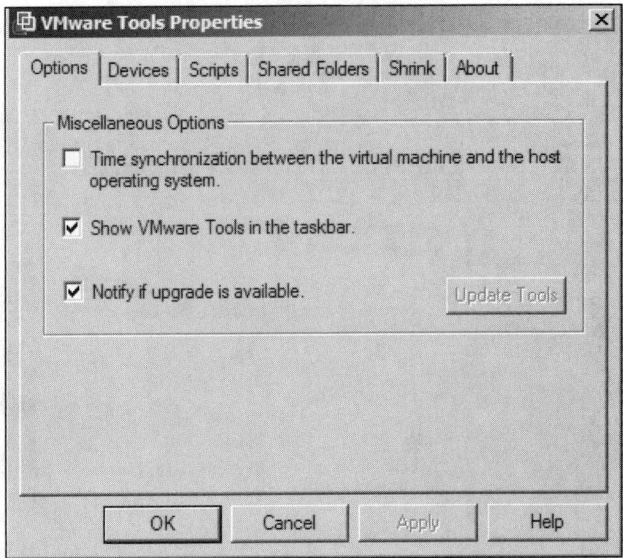

Figure B-14 VMware Tools Properties dialog box

Courtesy Course Technology/Cengage Learning

Other Virtual Systems

This appendix has focused on free virtualization systems, but other popular systems are available for purchase. On the desktop side, VMware Workstation has become more popular with desktop virtualization. Microsoft's Hyper-V system is new to Windows Server 2008. The following sections provide a brief overview of these systems, but they do not provide instructions for use.

VMware Workstation

VMware Workstation is popular among software developers and testers because it provides a safe environment in which to write and test development software before it is released to production. It is also used when one workstation-class computer needs to run multiple operating systems, including legacy operating systems. This option can be useful for running old software without having to convert it for a new operating system. It's also useful for learning a new operating system.

VMware Workstation 6.04 (or greater) supports Windows, Linux, and other operating systems as host and guest OSs. Newer operating systems supported as both hosts and guests include:

- Windows Server 2008 Standard, Enterprise, and Datacenter (x86 and x64)
- Windows Vista Home Basic, Home Premium, Enterprise, Business, and Ultimate (x86 and x64)
- Red Hat Enterprise Linux up to 4.6 (x86 and x64)
- Ubuntu Linux up to 7.10 (x86 and x64)
- SUSE Linux Enterprise Server 10 (x86 and x64)
- openSUSE Linux up to 10.3

VMware Workstation has several of the same new features as VMware Server:

- Handles increased memory (to 8 GB)
- Supports 64-bit guest operating systems on 64-bit host computers
- Supports hardware virtualization, such as through AMD CPUs that have AMD-V capability and Intel CPUs with Intel VT
- Supports USB 2.0 (including on Linux operating systems)
- Supports multiple monitors (to see different virtual machines on different displays)

As with VMware Server, you can configure hardware for the virtual machine, including multiple processors, memory, hard disks, USB access, and floppy disk access. You can also configure Bridged, HostOnly, and NAT virtual networks. A virtual DHCP server can be configured when you use HostOnly and NAT virtual networking. You can also set up a virtual machine through a wizard.

Also, like VMware Server you can install VMware tools that include specialized drivers, such as drivers for enhanced video and audio functions for the guest operating system. VMware Workstation offers a console display for accessing the guest operating system that resembles the VMware Server console.

VMware Workstation is specifically designed for workstation host machines and offers a wider range of host and guest operating system compatibility than Microsoft Virtual PC (at this writing). You can download a 30-day free evaluation version at *www.vmware.com/products/ws*.

Microsoft Hyper-V

Microsoft Hyper-V was released a few months after Windows Server 2008. Unlike other virtualization systems discussed in this appendix, Hyper-V is intended to run only on Windows Server 2008. It is loaded through the Windows Server 2008 Server Manager, like any other role in Windows Server 2008. In this regard, Windows Server 2008 offers perhaps the smoothest installation of any virtual system discussed in this appendix. Unlike the other systems in this appendix, Hyper-V only runs on x64 computers, which means the host systems include only the following:

- Windows Server 2008 Standard Edition x64
- Windows Server 2008 Enterprise Edition x64
- Windows Server 2008 Datacenter Edition x64

For an introduction to server virtualization and the features and requirements of Hyper-V, see Chapter 10.

You can purchase any of the Windows Server 2008 Standard, Enterprise, or Datacenter Editions with Hyper-V, or you can purchase Hyper-V separately. Its low cost, seamless installation, and integration with Windows Server 2008 are designed to make Hyper-V particularly appealing.

The guest operating systems that can be installed in Hyper-V include:

- Windows Server 2008 Standard, Enterprise, Datacenter, and Web Server (x86 or x64)
- Windows Server 2003 Standard, Enterprise, and Datacenter (x86 or x64)
- Windows Server 2003 Web Edition
- Windows 2000 Server and Advanced Server with SP4
- Windows Vista Business, Enterprise, and Ultimate (x86 and x64)
- Windows XP Professional with SP2 or SP3 (x86)
- Windows XP Professional with SP2 (x64)
- SUSE Linux Enterprise Server 10 with SP1 or SP2 (x86 or x64)

After Hyper-V is installed as a server role, you can open the Hyper-V Manager as a Microsoft Management Console (MMC) snap-in or from the Administrative Tools menu—both steps are familiar to Windows Server 2008 administrators. Use of Hyper-V Manager is relatively intuitive because it uses the same format as most Windows Server 2008 administrative tools. For example, to create a new virtual machine, you click the New option in the right pane of Hyper-V Manager and follow the steps in the New Virtual Machine Wizard.

To configure hardware and management settings for a virtual machine, click Settings under the machine name in the right pane of Hyper-V Manager. The Settings window (see Figure B-15) enables you to add hardware, configure hardware, and configure management capabilities.

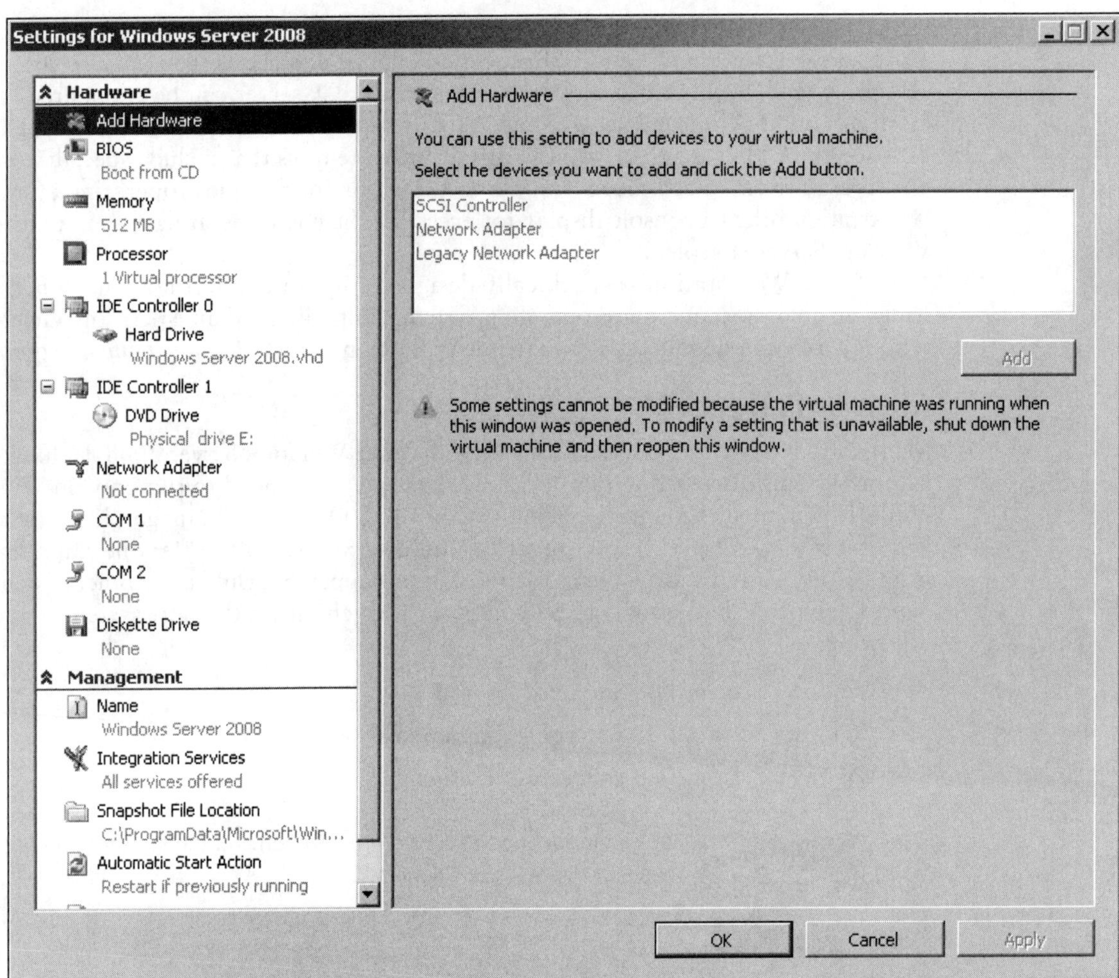

Figure B-15 Configuring settings for a virtual machine

Courtesy Course Technology/Cengage Learning

You can access the Virtual Network Manager from Hyper-V Manager to configure three types of virtual networks:

- *Private*—Offers communication only between virtual machines on the same virtual server
- *Internal*—Enables communication between virtual machines and the host virtual server
- *External*—Offers communication between virtual machines and the physical network (using a network adapter)

For an external virtual network, you can specify a virtual LAN identification number. This unique number is used for communication through the network adapter that distinguishes the virtual network from other networks.

The guest operating system appears in a console window, which includes an Action menu from which to send Ctrl+Alt+Del for logging on. You can also use the window to start, turn off, shut down, or pause a virtual machine. You also expand the console to fill the desktop display.

To start the console window, click its thumbnail. When the window opens, it displays a message about how to start the guest operating system.

At this writing, Hyper-V's range of guest and host operating systems is not as extensive as other virtualization systems. However, it is a good fit with Windows Server 2008 environments, and more guest operating systems probably will be added in the future. Hyper-V's installation and administration are consistent with those of other server roles.

Glossary

A and **AAAA record** An A record (also called a host record) is used to resolve a name to an IPv4 address. An AAAA record is used to resolve a name to an IPv6 address. A and AAAA records can be manually created or created with the dynamic updates process.

Active Directory Certificate Services (AD CS) Microsoft's implementation of a certification authority. AD CS can be used as an enterprise CA or a stand-alone CA. When used as an enterprise CA, it supports certificate templates, autoenrollment, and restricted enrollment agents.

Active Directory domain An administrative boundary that contains users, computers, and other objects. At least one or more domains are contained in a forest. The first domain in the forest is referred to as the root domain.

Active Directory Federation Services (AD FS) AD FS can be used to provide single sign-on (SSO) capabilities to users in another forest using a federated trust. It is most commonly used to provide Web access for users in a partner's organization without requiring them to log on again.

Active Directory forest A group of one or more domains organized in one or more trees. All domains in a forest share a common schema and a common global catalog.

Active Directory-integrated (ADI) zone This zone is hosted on a domain controller, and zone transfers are integrated into Active Directory replication. Unlike traditional DNS, which allow only one primary (or only one master), ADI zones use multiple primary ADI zones with the same multi-master model used on domain controllers.

Active Directory Lightweight Directory Services (AD LDS) AD LDS is used to host application partitions for Active Directory-enabled applications. It provides many of the same benefits of Active Directory as Active Directory Domain Services, but for separate applications.

Active Directory Migration Tool (ADMT) A free download available from Microsoft that can be used to migrate objects from a source domain to a target domain. ADMT v3.1 should be used for migrations involving Windows Server 2008.

Active Directory Rights Management Services (AD RMS) AD RMS can be used to protect documents and e-mails. When implemented, documents are encrypted and protected from certain user actions. For example, users can be prevented from printing, copying, or forwarding documents. Unauthorized users are unable to decrypt the documents.

Active Directory tree A group of one or more domains with a common namespace. A forest can have one or more trees.

ADPrep The Active Directory Preparation tool, which is used to prepare a forest and domains for Windows Server 2008 servers. It is run first with the /ForestPrep switch and then with the /DomainPrep switch. It can also be used with the /RODCPrep switch to allow the introduction of read-only domain controllers (RODCs).

Alias (CNAME) record An alias record is also known as a canonical name (or CNAME) record, and is created on DNS so that a server can be resolved to an IP address with more than a single name.

Allowed RODC Password Replication Group This Active Directory group identifies the only users or groups that can have passwords stored on RODCs. It does not have any members by default. This group applies to all RODCs.

Alternative UPN suffix A separate UPN suffix can be created using Active Directory Domains and Trusts. This alternative UPN suffix can then be used to assign different UPNs for users in the domain.

Application virtualization The use of technologies that allow users to run applications without installing them on the host operating system. Microsoft's Application Virtualization Streaming Server (App-V server) can be used to stream SoftGrid-enabled applications to users and provide application virtualization.

Authentication A process used to prove that entities and senders are who they claim to be. For example, users can provide a user name and password as authentication. Similarly, a digital signature is used to provide authentication and provide assurances that a user sent a message.

Authoritative restore Refers to Active Directory restore. After Active Directory is restored non-authoritatively, an authoritative restore can be done to mark specific objects as being authoritatively restored using NTDSUtil. After the domain controller is brought back online, these objects are replicated to other domain controllers.

Autoenrollment A process used on an enterprise CA that allows certificates to be enrolled automatically without user intervention. Only V2 and V3 certificate templates can be autoenrolled. A copy of a template is created, permissions (Read, Enroll, and Autoenroll) are assigned to the template, and a GPO is used to enable autoenrollment.

Autonomous mode A downstream server configured in autonomous mode that receives updates from an upstream server. Administrators of the downstream server can choose which updates to deploy.

Autonomy Provides independent but not exclusive control of a resource. A separate domain in a forest can provide service and data autonomy. A separate OU within a domain can provide data autonomy.

BitLocker Drive Encryption A technology that allows entire hard drives to be encrypted. It can be used on RODCs to add a layer of security when physical security is limited.

Block Inheritance A Group Policy option that can be applied to an OU. When enabled, GPO settings will not be inherited by any GPOs at higher levels unless a GPO has the Enforced GPO option enabled.

Bridgehead server The DC that is designated by the ISTG to connect to DCs in other sites and perform replication. Only one DC in a site is a bridgehead server at any time. If this DC fails, the ISTG will designate another DC in the list.

CA Web Enrollment A service added to AD CS that allows clients to use a Web interface to request and renew certificates, retrieve certificate revocation lists (CRLs), and enroll smart card certificates.

Certificate A digital file issued by a CA that holds identifying characteristics for a subject. Certificates include a public key, and can be used for identification, encryption, authentication, smart cards, and much more.

Certificate revocation list (CRL) A list of certificates that have been revoked by a CA prior to the expiration of the certificate. A certificate is revoked when the primary key is compromised. A certificate can also be revoked for other reasons—for example, if it is no longer needed.

Certificate templates Templates are only available in an enterprise CA and are used to create certificates instead of creating them from scratch. V2 templates and V3 templates can be autoenrolled. Windows XP cannot use V3 templates.

Certification authority (CA) An entity that issues certificates. A CA can be a company such as VeriSign or a software component such as Microsoft's Certification Authority.

Cluster-aware A characteristic of services and applications that makes them easy to add to a failover cluster. Cluster-aware services and applications can easily report their status to the failover cluster service, but non-cluster-aware services may not have this ability.

Compliance auditing Checking systems to ensure that they comply with security policies or security requirements. Scwcmd and MBSA are two tools you can use to perform compliance audits.

Default Domain Controllers policy A default Group Policy created when the domain is created. It applies to all objects in the domain controllers OU (which should be all the domain controllers in the domain as long as the domain controllers weren't moved).

Default Domain policy A default Group Policy created when the domain is created. It applies to all objects in the domain.

Delegation of Control Wizard A wizard used to delegate control and permissions in Active Directory Users and Computers. Permissions can be granted to groups at the domain and OU levels.

Demilitarized zone (DMZ) A network placed between a private internal network and public network such as the Internet. A DMZ is typically created with two firewalls, and is sometimes referred to as a perimeter network.

Denied RODC Password Replication Group This Active Directory group identifies the users or groups that cannot have passwords stored on RODCs. Several groups (such as Administrators, Account Operators, and others) are members of this group by default. This group applies to all RODCs.

DFS namespace A group of shared folders from different servers made available to clients using the Distributed File System (DFS). Clients connect to the DFS namespace and are directed to folder targets that are created under the DFS root.

DFS replication A tool used to replicate data contained in DFS namespaces. DFS replication is most valuable in a multiple-site configuration. Instead of users accessing data across the WAN link, the data can be replicated to a server in the local site. DFS replication can improve data accessibility and ensure that users have access to the data even if the WAN link fails.

DFS root The top-level folder in a DFS namespace. Users connect to the DFS root using a UNC path. The UNC path on a domain-based DFS root is in the format of \\domain\DFSRoot; the format in a standalone DFS root is \\ServerName\DFSRoot. Folder targets are created under the root, and point to shares on other servers in the network.

DHCP enforcement Using NAP to ensure that DHCP clients meet specific health requirements prior to being issued a DHCP lease. DHCP enforcement is considered the least secure method of NAP enforcement because it can be overridden by the client by manually assigning an IP address.

Digital signature A cryptographic component that provides authentication, integrity, and non-repudiation. When an e-mail is digitally signed, it is hashed, and the hash is encrypted with the sender's private key.

The receiver decrypts the encrypted hash with the sender's public key.

Distinguished name (DN) An LDAP name that uniquely identifies objects in Active Directory Domain Services (AD DS). A DN in an AD DS will typically have a domain component (DC), an OU component (OU), and a common name component (CN).

Distributed File System (DFS) A group of technologies used to group folders from different servers into a single UNC path. A DFS namespace includes a DFS root and folder targets that point to folders on other servers. DFS replication can be used to replicate the content of folders to different servers.

DNS zone A namespace where a DNS server can resolve names. Zone data is stored either in forward lookup zone files or reverse lookup zone files.

DomainDNSZones An application partition used in ADI zones that causes zone data to be replicated to all DNS servers in the domain. This partition is useful if you want to limit the replication of zone data between DNS servers in different domains.

Domain functional level The level of the domain that dictates what features are available within the domain. The domain functional level can be raised to a higher level after all domain controllers have been updated to that level. For example, if the domain functional level is Windows Server 2003, it can be raised to Windows Server 2008 after all domain controllers have been upgraded to Windows Server 2008.

Domain naming master One of the forest operations master roles. The DC hosting this role manages the addition and removal of domains and of application directory partitions. Only one domain naming master exists in a forest.

Downstream WSUS server A server that receives updates from an upstream WSUS server. A downstream server can be configured either in autonomous mode or replica mode.

DSMgmt A command-line tool that can be used to manage and administer Active Directory Domain Services. It can be used to enable the local Administrators role on an RODC.

Dynamic Update The process of allowing clients to automatically create or update their A record on DNS.

Enforced A Group Policy option that can be applied to a GPO. It will ensure that the GPO will be the winning GPO if any lower-level GPOs have conflicts. Additionally, it ensures that if an OU has the Block Inheritance policy set, the Enforced GPO will not be blocked.

Enterprise CA An enterprise certification authority is heavily integrated with Active Directory and automates many of the tasks for managing certificates in Active Directory. An enterprise CA would also be considered a private CA.

External trust A non-transitive trust created with a domain in a separate forest. The trust can be one-way or two-way, but an external trust is not transitive.

Failback Configuring a failover cluster so that when a failed node comes back online, the services or applications that it originally hosted can be returned to the node.

Failover Occurs when one node in a failover cluster fails and another node in the cluster takes over the load for the failed node. Failover is automatic in a failover cluster.

Failover cluster A Windows Server 2008 feature that can be used to provide high availability for applications and services. Two or more servers are used in a failover cluster; if one node fails, another node can pick up the load of the failed server.

Fibre Channel (FC) A standard method used by failover clusters to connect to disk storage solutions. FC can use either twisted-pair or fiber-optic media, but fiber is more commonly used. Only data transferred between the disk and the cluster node is transferred over the Fibre Channel.

ForestDNSZones An application partition used in ADI zones that causes zone data to be replicated to all DNS servers in the forest. This partition is useful if you want all DNS servers to be able to resolve host names for any domain in the forest.

Forest functional level The level of the forest that dictates what features are available in the forest. The forest functional level can be raised to a higher level after all domains in the forest have been raised. For example, if the forest functional level is Windows Server 2003, it can be raised to Windows Server 2008 after all domains in the forest have been raised to Windows Server 2008.

Forest trust A transitive trust created between two forests. Forest trusts are supported in Windows Server 2003 forest functional level.

Forest-wide authentication Used in a forest trust when the other forest is fully trusted. Forest-wide authentication allows all users in each forest to be granted access to any resources in the trusting forest.

Full mesh replication topology Each site can replicate with every other site. It is generally recommended when an organization has 10 or fewer sites.

Generic (non-site-specific) DNS records DNS records that can be used to locate domain controllers in any site. These records are created by default and are useful in a multi-site environment. If a DC fails in a site, generic (non-site-specific) records are used to allow clients to connect to any DC in the organization. In large organizations you can prevent these records from being created in specific sites using a GPO.

Global catalog A database of all objects in the entire forest, but with only a subset of the attributes of those objects. The global catalog is hosted on domain controllers called global catalog servers, and the global catalog is replicated to all global catalog servers in the forest.

GlobalNames zone (GNZ) This option can be used to resolve NetBIOS or single-label names. It's useful if an organization wants to completely eliminate WINS, such as when the organization migrates to IPv6.

GPO order of precedence The hierarchy of GPOs. GPOs are applied in the following order: site, domain, and OU. If there is a conflict, the settings that are applied last take precedence (unless the order is modified with the Enforced option or loopback processing).

Group Policy An administrative management tool that allows administrators to configure a setting once in a Group Policy object (GPO) and apply the policy to all users in a domain, in an organizational unit, or in a site. GPOs can be linked to a site, domain, or OU using the Group Policy Management Console (GPMC).

Group Policy Management console (GPMC) A management console used to manage Group Policy. You can create and link GPOs through the GPMC and manipulate different Group Policy settings.

Group Policy objects (GPOs) GPOs contain Group Policy settings and can be linked to sites, domains, and OUs.

Hash A number created by performing a hashing algorithm against a file or message. Hashes are used to provide integrity. No matter how many times the hash is calculated, it will result in the same number, unless the file or message has been changed. If the recalculated hash is different, the file or message is no longer the same—it has lost integrity.

Health Registration Authority (HRA) A service used in conjunction with a NAP solution to issue health certificates for clients. The HRA receives certificates from a certification authority (CA).

High availability Ensuring that a service or application is available when it's needed. Failover clusters are commonly used to provide high availability for services or applications.

Host name A computer or server name that can be up to 255 characters. Host names are resolved to IP addresses using DNS.

Hub and spoke replication topology A site design used when an organization has faster network connections between major hubs and slower network connections with outlying offices. When used, site link bridging is often disabled.

Hyper-V A server role that can be added to 64-bit versions of Windows Server 2008 to host virtual servers. Multiple virtual servers can be hosted on a single Windows Server 2008 server running Hyper-V.

Infrastructure master One of the domain operations master roles. The infrastructure master updates cross-domain group-to-user references. It ensures that changes made to object names from objects in another domain are accurately reflected in the group membership information. The infrastructure master should not be the global catalog server in a multidomain environment. Every domain in the forest holds one infrastructure master.

Install from media (IFM) An advanced option that can be used when promoting a server using DCpromo. It allows DCpromo to obtain the database information from a file instead of replicating it from another DC. It can be useful when promoting a server to a DC in a remote office without using a slow WAN link.

Internet Small Computer System Interface (iSCSI) An interface used to access disk storage solutions from failover cluster nodes. Data is transferred over TCP/IP networks, and existing networks can be used. iSCSI is a lower-cost alternative to Fibre Channel, which requires dedicated hardware. iSCSI can also be used to transmit data over long distances or across wide area networks (WANs).

Inter-Site Topology Generator (ISTG) The ISTG is responsible for managing different processes related to replication of data between sites. The ISTG designates the bridgehead server within the site.

IPSec enforcement Using NAP to ensure that clients are using IPSec. IPSec can provide secure end-to-end communication and prevent replay of data between clients.

IP site link The IP site link represents a WAN link. It uses a Remote Procedure Call (RPC) connection to establish a synchronous connection with a domain controller in the remote site. It requires firewalls between the sites to allow RCP traffic. It is also referred to as RPC over IP.

Isolation Provides independent and exclusive control of a resource. A separate forest is needed to provide isolation.

Layer 2 Tunneling Protocol (L2TP) A tunneling protocol used with VPN connections. L2TP uses IPSec to secure the connection. IPSec cannot pass through a connection using the network address translation (NAT) protocol.

Local Administrators role A role that can be enabled on an RODC in a remote site to grant local users rights and permissions to administer an RODC. It does not include any rights or permissions in the domain. It is enabled by adding a user account to the role. The DSMgmt tool can be used to add users to a role.

Loopback processing An advanced Group Policy setting. It makes Group Policy settings that apply to the computer take precedence over Group Policy settings that apply to the logged-on user.

MBSACLI A command-line interface for MBSA that can be scripted and scheduled to run periodically.

Microsoft Application Virtualization 4.5 (App-V) A server product that can be used to serve SoftGrid-enabled applications. These applications have been prepared using the Microsoft Application Virtualization Sequencer (SoftGrid Sequencer) to be streamed from an application server to clients as virtual applications.

Microsoft Application Virtualization Sequencer (SoftGrid Sequencer) An application that prepares applications to be served from a virtual server. Once the application is prepared, it is referred to as a SoftGrid-enabled application; it can be deployed to an App-V server and streamed to clients that have Microsoft SoftGrid Application Virtualization for Desktops (SoftGrid client) installed.

Microsoft Baseline Security Analyzer (MBSA) A compliance auditing tool that can be used to scan one or more systems for several vulnerabilities, such as weak passwords or a system not being up to date.

Microsoft Office SharePoint Server 2007 (MOSS) An add-on server product that increases the abilities of Windows SharePoint Services 3.0 (WSS). WSS is included as a basic foundation for MOSS. MOSS can host Web sites used for collaboration between employees and teams, as WSS does, but MOSS has additional capabilities. For example, its advanced portal templates are useful in an enterprise, and users can personalize their view of sites.

Microsoft System Center Configuration Manager 2007 (SCCM) A server add-on product that can be used to deploy operating systems, applications, and updates to systems within the network. It improves the capabilities of Windows Deployment Services to deploy operating system images, Group Policy to deploy applications, and Windows Server Update Services to deploy updates.

Microsoft System Center Operations Manager 2007 (SCOM) A server add-on product that can provide centralized monitoring for a network. SCOM uses agents installed on monitored servers that generate alerts captured by the SCOM server.

Microsoft System Center Virtual Machine Manager (SCVMM) A server product in the Microsoft System Center suite. It can be purchased and used to manage large-scale deployments of virtual servers. It supports virtual servers hosted by Virtual Server 2005 R2, VMware ESX, and Hyper-V.

Microsoft Update A program that provides all the same updates as Windows Update, but adds updates for Microsoft applications such as Office, Exchange, and SQL Server.

Microsoft Virtual PC An application that runs on a desktop system and can host one or more virtual desktops in a virtual environment. Microsoft Virtual PC can be used for testing, training, and running applications in a virtual environment if they will not run in the host environment.

MX records A mail exchanger record used to locate a mail server. In Microsoft networks, an MX record will point to a Microsoft Exchange server.

Name resolution The process of resolving a name to an IP address. DNS is used to resolve host names to IP addresses and WINS is used to resolve legacy NetBIOS names.

NetBIOS names A 16 byte name in which the first 15 characters are readable and the 16th is a hidden byte that identifies a service running on the system. NetBIOS names are traditionally resolved by WINS servers, but can be resolved by a GlobalNames zone. NetBIOS names are not supported in IPv6.

Network access policy A policy used on a remote access server to determine which users are granted access. Policies include conditions, permissions, constraints, and settings. A policy is used when the conditions are met. If conditions are not met for any policy, access is not granted.

Network Access Protection (NAP) A group of technologies used to ensure that clients are healthy before being granted full network access. Health is determined by a health policy that can be configured by the administrator.

Network Device Enrollment A service available on AD CS that allows certificates to be automatically enrolled for network devices such as routers.

Network File System (NFS) A file system used by UNIX systems to access files over a network. NFS services can be installed on Windows Server 2008 servers to increase the interaction between Windows Server 2008 and UNIX-based systems.

Network Load Balancing (NLB) A Windows Server 2008 feature that can be used to increase the stability and scalability of applications and services. Two or more servers are used in an NLB cluster; as new users connect, they are directed to servers with the least number of current connections.

Network Policy and Access Services A Windows Server 2008 role that includes the following services: Network Policy Server, Remote Access Service, Routing, Health Registration Authority, and Host Credential Authorization Protocol.

Network Policy Server (NPS) A server hosting the NPS service used to enforce policies for both remote access and Network Access Protection.

New Technology File System (NTFS) A file system used by Windows operating systems. NTFS enhances security by allowing files and folders to be protected by permissions and encryption. NTFS version 6.2 (included with Windows Server 2008) includes a self-healing capability that can detect and repair disk problems.

Non-authoritative restore Refers to Active Directory restore. After Active Directory is restored non-authoritatively, it is brought back online and receives updates from other domain controllers.

Non-repudiation A process that prevents a user from denying an action. Digital signatures provide assurances that a user sent a message, so that the user cannot believably deny sending the digitally signed message. Similarly, if a user is authenticated on a network and actions are logged by his user account, the user cannot believably deny that he performed the logged action.

NS record A name server (NS) record identifies a DNS server in a DNS zone. NS records can be created manually or automatically when DCpromo is run.

NTDSUtil A shell command-line tool used to manage and manipulate Active Directory Domain Services. It can be used to create the data used with the install from media (IFM) feature and seize operations master roles.

Online Responder A service added to AD CS to respond to Online Certificate Status Protocol (OCSP) queries, which can be used to determine the status of a certificate.

Operations master roles These five roles that can be held by DCs are also called flexible single master operations (FSMO) roles. The five roles are schema master, domain naming master, RID master, PDC emulator, and Infrastructure master.

Organizational unit (OU) A special container within Active Directory that allows Active Directory objects (such as users, computers, and groups) to be organized. Group Policy objects can be linked to an OU and administrative control can be delegated to an OU.

Password Replication Policy Every RODC has this policy, which defines what users or groups can have their passwords stored on the RODC. It doesn't have any members by default, but it would typically be populated with the users or groups of users working in the remote office hosting the RODC.

PDC emulator One of the domain operations master roles. The PDC emulator manages time synchronization and password changes in the domain. If an RODC is needed in the domain, the PDC emulator must be running on Windows Server 2008. Every domain in the forest holds one PDC emulator.

Perimeter network A network placed between a private internal network and public network such as the Internet. A perimeter network is typically created with two firewalls, and is sometimes referred to as a demilitarized zone (DMZ).

Pointer (PTR) records These records are used for reverse lookups providing IP address-to-name resolution. PTR records are only found in reverse lookup zones, and reverse lookup zones are optional.

Point-to-Point Tunneling Protocol (PPTP) A tunneling protocol used with VPN connections. PPTP uses Microsoft Point-to-Point Encryption (MPPE). It doesn't require a certification authority.

Preferred bridgehead server A manually designated bridgehead server. The ISTG will normally designate any DC as a bridgehead server, but when a preferred bridgehead server has been designated, the ISTG will only pick preferred bridgehead servers. If you designate one DC as a preferred bridgehead server, you should always designate at least one more.

Prestaged RODC A computer account created in Active Directory Users and Computers with information used by DCpromo. It allows DCpromo to be started by an administrator with elevated permissions and finished by an administrator with lesser permissions. The computer account is designated as an unoccupied RODC account.

Primary DNS zone A master copy of a zone hosted on a traditional (non-ADI) DNS server. With traditional DNS servers, the master copy of the zone is the only writable copy of the zone; only one server can host a primary zone for any namespace.

Private CA A private certification authority is internal to an organization. The root certificate is not published to users outside the organization.

Private key One of two keys in a matched public/private key pair used with asymmetric encryption.

When this key pair is used, one key encrypts the data and the other key decrypts the data. If a private key is compromised, the certificate that holds the matching public key is revoked and published in a CRL.

Public CA A public certification authority is used on the Internet. The public CA's root certificate is published to the Trusted Root Certification Authorities store for Internet users; certificates issued from a public CA are automatically trusted.

Public key One of two keys in a matched public/private key pair used with asymmetric encryption. When this key pair is used, one key encrypts the data and the other key decrypts the data. Public keys are embedded in a certificate and issued by a CA.

Public key infrastructure (PKI) A group of technologies used to create, issue, manage, store, and revoke certificates.

Quorum A majority used in failover clusters. Each node in a failover cluster has a vote in the quorum; the disk or file share can also have a vote. As long as a majority of votes exists, a quorum exists.

Quorum model The model used in a failover cluster to determine which elements have votes in the quorum. Four quorum models are available: No Majority, Node Majority, Node and Disk Majority, and Node and File Share Majority.

RADIUS proxy A server acting as a centralized routing point for multiple RADIUS servers. RADIUS clients contact the RADIUS proxy, which forwards the request to the appropriate RADIUS server.

Read-only domain controller (RODC) A DC that limits the passwords replicated to it (or cached on it). You can specify what passwords are cached on the DC. You can also enable the local Administrators role to allow users in a remote office to administer the RODC without having any rights or permissions in the domain.

redircmp A command-line tool that can be used to change the default location of newly created computers from the Computers container to a specified OU. This tool works when a computer account is created after the computer joins a domain.

redirusr A command-line tool that can be used to change the default location of newly created users from the Users container to a specified OU. This only works if the OU isn't specified when the account is created.

Remote access server A server used to provide access to the internal network from a remote location. A remote access server can support dial-up connections, VPN connections, or both.

Remote Authentication Dial-in User Service (RADIUS) A server used for centralized authentication and logging for multiple remote access servers. A Network Policy Server can be configured as a RADIUS server.

Replica mode A downstream server configured in replica mode receives pre-approved updates from an upstream server. Updates are automatically deployed without administrative intervention.

Replication The process of sending Active Directory additions, deletions, and modifications between DCs.

Restricted enrollment agents An available feature when AD CS is used as an enterprise CA. Restricted enrollment agents can allow a selected group of users permission to enroll specific certificate templates for specific users.

RID master One of the domain operations master roles. The RID master manages the pool of available RIDs and issues banks of RIDs to other domain controllers. RIDs are used to create SIDs, and the RID master ensures that all RIDs are unique within the domain, which ultimately ensures that all SIDs are unique in the domain. Every domain in the forest holds one RID master.

RODC filtered attribute set Any attributes added to this attribute set and marked as confidential will not be stored on the RODC.

Root CA The first certification authority in a CA hierarchy. The root CA issues certificates to subordinate CAs, which issue certificates to end users, or a root CA is used without subordinate CAs and thus issues certificates for end users. Every CA hierarchy must have a root CA.

RPC over IP site link Also known as an IP site link object. It's named IP in Active Directory Sites and Services, but is commonly referred to as RPC over IP in documentation.

Scalability The ability of a service to support additional clients through the addition of resources such as more processing power or more servers. NLB clusters are used to scale applications out to additional servers.

Schema A definition of objects and attributes in a forest. Each forest has only one schema and objects created in the forest must be defined by the schema. The schema can be modified (commonly called extending the schema) using a tool such as ADPrep.

Schema master One of the forest operations master roles. This is the only DC that has write permissions on the schema. When extending the schema, you must be able to reach the schema master. Only one schema master exists in a forest.

Scwcmd A command-line version of the Security Configuration Wizard (SCW). Scwcmd can be used to create a GPO from an SCW security policy. Scwcmd can also be used for compliance auditing.

SD^3+C A secure computing strategy adopted by Microsoft that includes Secure by Design, Secure by Default, and Secure in Deployment and Communications.

Secondary DNS zone A read-only copy of a zone used for fault tolerance and load balancing. A secondary zone can only be created if a primary zone exists. Changes are made to the primary zone (the master copy) and copied to the secondary zone using zone transfers.

Secure Dynamic Update Dynamic update with security. Only authenticated clients in the domain can create or update DNS records. Secure dynamic updates are only supported in ADI zones.

Secure Socket Tunneling Protocol (SSTP) A tunneling protocol used with VPN connections. It uses HTTP over SSL (HTTPS) connections on port 443. It provides a higher level of security than PPTP and is more flexible than L2TP/IPSec.

Security Configuration Wizard (SCW) A security tool that can be used to create a security policy for one or more computers based on roles. The security policy is created as an XML file.

Selective authentication Used in a forest trust when the other forest is not fully trusted. Selective authentication requires that users or groups be granted the Allowed to Authenticate permission on each server they will access.

Serial attached SCSI (SAS) A SCSI disk array connected to servers in a failover cluster using serial connections.

Server consolidation The process of migrating physical servers to virtual servers to reduce the overall footprint of physical servers in the environment. The Hyper-V role can be added to Windows Server 2008 to support multiple virtual servers on a single physical server.

Server Core A Windows Server 2008 edition that only includes the command prompt instead of the full graphical user interface. It enhances security by reducing the attack surface; only the most necessary services and protocols are installed.

Server virtualization The use of technologies that allow a single physical server to host multiple virtual servers. Windows Server 2008 supports the Hyper-V role on 64-bit servers to implement server virtualization.

Service location (SRV) records These DNS records are used to locate domain controllers in a domain. SRV records can be site specific (allowing site-aware applications to locate a DC in the site) and non-site-specific (allowing applications to locate any DC anywhere in the domain). SRV records are created automatically by the Netlogon service on the domain controller hosting DNS.

Services for Network File System A File Services role service that can be added to a Windows Server 2008 server to increase the interaction with UNIX systems that use NFS.

SID A security identifier used to uniquely identify objects in a domain and a forest.

SID filtering When enabled on a trust, prevents SID history from being used when a user accesses a resource. SID filtering is enabled by default when selective authentication is used and disabled by default when forest-wide authentication is used. SID filtering can be enabled and disabled with Netdom.

SID history An attribute in a user account that holds a listing of one or more SIDs assigned to a user. SID history allows users to access resources in the source domain without redoing the permissions in the source domain.

Simple Certificate Enrollment Protocol (SCEP) A protocol used with the Network Device Enrollment service to automatically issue certificates to network devices such as routers.

Site A group of well-connected hosts or subnets. Sites are typically connected to each other through slower wide area network (WAN) links.

Site-aware application An application or service that can determine what site it is in and optimize connections with other hosts in the same site.

Site link bridging A feature that allows site links to be transitive. In other words, if Site A can replicate with Site B and Site B can replicate with Site C, Site A can also replicate with Site C. Site link bridging is enabled by default, but is typically disabled in a hub and spoke topology to limit duplicated replication.

Site link object An Active Directory object that represents a wide area network (WAN) link used to connect two or more sites. Site link objects can be either IP (RPC over IP) or SMTP. Site link properties can be configured to control when replication occurs and to control the cost or priority of site links.

Site object An Active Directory object that represents a site. A site is a location that includes well-connected hosts or subnets. Site objects are commonly created in Active Directory to represent remote offices and branch offices.

SMTP site link object A site link object used to replicate configuration, schema, and application partitions using an asynchronous connection. It cannot be used to replicate data within the same domain.

SOA record The start of authority record used by DNS and other services, such as DHCP and the dynamic update process. It includes information about the zone, such as the primary server for the zone and information used by secondary zone DNS servers on zone transfer times.

SoftGrid-enabled application An application prepared using the Microsoft Application Virtualization Sequencer (SoftGrid Sequencer) that can be deployed to a virtual application server. SoftGrid-enabled applications are streamed to the clients.

SoftGrid Sequencer The original name of the Microsoft Application Virtualization Sequencer; the name is still used in some documentation. It creates SoftGrid-enabled applications.

Stand-alone CA A stand-alone certification authority can be a member of Active Directory and can have some information published through Active Directory, but it can also be completely separate from a domain and kept as an offline CA. A stand-alone CA could be a public CA or a private CA.

Storage area network (SAN) A specialized network designed to host disks in a failover cluster. The SAN makes the disks appear to servers as though the disks are locally attached, but they can be located elsewhere on the network.

Stub zone A mini-zone that only hosts information about another zone hosted on another DNS server. In Windows Server environments, a stub zone is used to hold information on delegated subdomains.

Subnet object An Active Directory object that represents a subnet in a site. Subnet objects are associated with site objects to help site-aware applications identify locations.

Subordinate CA A child CA in a CA hierarchy. A subordinate CA is issued a certificate from a root CA (or a higher-level subordinate CA). Subordinate CAs are used in larger organizations but are not required.

System Health Agent (SHA) An agent that runs on clients as part of the Network Access Protection Agent service. The SHA regularly validates the health of a client and reports this to the System Health Validator.

System Health Validator (SHV) SHVs receive reports of health from System Health Agents and create a Statement of Health (SoH). SoHs are combined to create a System Statement of Health (SSoH). NAP servers can read the SSoH and choose to restrict or grant access based on the client's health.

System Statement of Health (SSoH) A compilation of individual Statement of Health reports created by System Health Agents and System Health Validators. SSOHs are passed to NAP servers when they exist in a network.

SYSVOL A group of folders within each domain controller that includes public files, system policies, logon scripts, and portions of Group Policy objects. The SYSVOL folder was replicated between all domain controllers using File Replication Service (FRS) in previous versions of Windows, but DFS replication can be used to replicate SYSVOL in Windows Server 2008.

Terminal Services (TS) A group of technologies that allow clients to connect to a terminal server and run applications and/or full operating system desktops on the terminal server from the client computer.

Terminal Services connection authorization policy (TS CAP) A policy used with TS Gateway to specify which users or groups are authorized to connect.

Terminal Services farm A group of Terminal Services servers working together. The TS farm can be created to provide load balancing, fault tolerance, or both.

Terminal Services Gateway A TS service that can provide access to internal TS servers from the Internet. Clients connect to the TS Gateway server using HTTPS (on port 443), and the TS Gateway computer acts as a gateway to the internal TS server.

Terminal Services Licensing A TS service that runs on a server to manage TS client access licenses (TS CALs). TS CALs are purchased separately on a per-user or per-device basis.

Terminal Services RemoteApp An application that can be hosted on a TS server. When clients run the application, it appears to run on their system, but it is actually running in a session on the TS server.

Terminal Services resource authorization policy (TS RAP) A policy used with TS Gateway to specify which servers a client can connect with after being authorized by a TS CAP.

Terminal Services Session Broker A TS service that can provide load balancing support for multiple TS servers in a TS farm. TS Session Broker can also ensure that disconnected sessions are reconnected to the same server, and provide weighting to ensure that more powerful servers are used more often than less powerful servers.

Terminal Services Web Access A TS service that can allow clients to run TS RemoteApp programs from a Web browser. TS Web Access uses Internet Information Services (IIS).

Transitive trust A trust relationship that transits throughout a forest. If Domain A trusts Domain B, and Domain B trusts Domain C, then the transitive trust allows Domain A to trust Domain C.

Trust A relationship between two domains (or two forests) that allows users in one domain to access resources in the other domain. A trust can be one-way or two-way. A one-way trust allows users in a trusted domain to access resources in a trusting domain. Trusts are automatically created as transitive trusts within a forest, but they can also be created between domains outside of the forest or even other forests.

Trusted Platform Module (TPM) A microchip that is usually embedded in a motherboard and that provides security functions needed by BitLocker. TPM version 1.2 is required to fully support BitLocker.

Trusted Root Certification Authorities store The location on a computer where certificates for root CAs are stored. If a certificate for a root CA is stored here, all certificates issued by the root CA are trusted.

Universal Group Membership Caching An option that can optimize logon times for users within a site. The option is chosen instead of making the DC a global catalog server in a multi-domain environment to limit replication of the global catalog.

Upstream WSUS server A server that connects to the Microsoft Update site and that can forward the updates to downstream WSUS servers. An upstream server is always configured in autonomous mode.

Virtual application sequencer An application that prepares an application to be served by a virtual application server. The application is sequenced, or divided into blocks that can be sent to the client without having to send the entire application.

Virtual application server A server that can stream virtual applications to clients so that the clients can run the virtual application without installing it on the client. A server hosting Microsoft's Application Virtualization 4.5 (App-V) is an example of a virtual application server.

Virtual application streaming Sending a virtual application to a client in a stream of data blocks. This allows the client to run the virtual application without installing it on the client. Applications must be sequenced before they can be served by a virtual application server.

Virtual private network (VPN) A private connection created over a public network such as the Internet. VPNs are commonly used to allow clients to access a work network from a remote location.

VPN enforcement Using NAP to ensure that VPN clients meet specific health requirements prior to being granted full access to a network. This method of NAP enforcement is used with remote access solutions.

Windows Management Instrumentation (WMI) filtering A filtering tool that can be applied to GPOs. The tool makes the GPO apply only to computers that meet specific conditions. WMI filters use the WMI query language (WQL); only one WMI filter can be applied to a GPO.

Windows Server Update Services (WSUS) Free Microsoft software that can be used by administrators as a central location to download, approve, and synchronize updates for clients within the network.

Windows SharePoint Services 3.0 (WSS) A free service that can be downloaded and added to Windows Server 2008 to manage Web sites used for collaboration between employees and teams. WSS sites can be hosted on a single server running WSS or on multiple servers in a Web farm.

Windows Update A program that provides updates for Windows operating systems. It is different from Microsoft Update, which provides updates for Microsoft applications in addition to the operating system.

Windows Virtual PC An upgrade to Microsoft Virtual PC that runs on Windows 7 and can host one or more operating systems in a virtual environment. Windows Virtual PC supports Windows XP Mode, which allows applications to run on the virtual machine without requiring the user to start it.

Writable DC A normal DC. When discussing read-only DCs (RODCs) and normal DCs, normal DCs are referred to as writable DCs.

Index

802.1x
devices, 206
enforcement, 217–218, 235

A

A or AAAA record, 102–105, 133
Account lockout policies, 10, 178
Account policies, fine-grained. *see* Fine-grained account policies
Active Directory
backing up, 366–369
designing domains and forests, 13–16
domain, 15–16, 25, 37
forest, 25, 37
logical structure of, 13–16
read-only domain preparation, 26
restoring, 369–370
SRV records, 108–110
tree, 37
Active Directory Certificate Services (AD CS). *see also* Certification authority (CA)
certificate templates, 258–259
components of, 257
defined, 285
features of, 257
implementing, 257
installing certificate services, 259–262
issuing certificates, 269–272
managing, 260–261
Network Device Enrollment, 279–281
online responder service, 264–269
and PKI, 256–257
restricted enrollment agents, 281–283
revoking certificates, 269, 273–275
role services, 260, 263–264
Active Directory Domain Services (AD DS), 2–4
and DNS, 107–110
global catalog, 3–4
Group Policy, 4
migration strategies (*see* Migration strategies)
organizational unit, 4
recovery data and, 386–388
schema, 3
service autonomy and, 14
site, 4
tree, 2–3
trust relationships, 3, 17
Active Directory Federation Services (AD FS), 405, 406–407, 408
Active Directory Lightweight Directory Services (AD LDS), 405–406, 407, 409
Active Directory Migration Tool (ADMT)
defined, 37
installing, 32–33
as migration strategy, 26–27
running, 33–35
SID history, 27–28, 33
Active Directory Preparation (ADPrep), 3, 24–26, 37
Active Directory Rights Management Services (RMS), 405, 406, 409
Active Directory Sites and Services
site link objects, 52–54
subnet objects, 51–52
Active Directory-integrated (ADI) zones, 98, 101, 133
AD. *see* Active Directory
AD CS. *see* Active Directory Certificate Services (AD CS)
AD DS. *see* Active Directory Domain Services (AD DS)
AD FS. *see* Federation Services (AD FS)
AD LDS. *see* Lightweight Directory Services (AD LDS)
ADI zones, 98, 123–124
ADMT. *see* Active Directory Migration Tool (ADMT)
ADPrep, 3, 24–26, 37, 67
Alias records, 103, 133
Allowed RODC Password Replication Group, 88
Alternative UPN suffix, 30–32, 37
Application deployment, 164–166
Application streaming, 416
Application virtualization, 416, 436. *see also* Microsoft Application Virtualization
App-V server, 417
Assymetric encryption, 246–247
Auditing. *see* Compliance auditing
Auditor, 264
Authentication, 18–19, 247–250, 285
Authoritative restore, 369, 371, 373
Auto Publish, 422
Autoenrollment, 250–251, 277–279, 285
Automatic certificates, 277–279
Autonomous mode, 319, 320, 331
Autonomy, 13–14, 15, 37
Autoremediation, 209

B

Backup operator, 264
Baseline security, 292
BitLocker Drive Encryption
benefits of, 384
defined, 409
enabling, 385–386
objective, 383–384
recovery, 386–388
requirements for, 384
Trusted Platform Module and, 384
Block Inheritance, 171–172, 183
Bridgehead servers, 54–56, 88

C

CA. *see* Certification authority (CA)
CA administrator, 263
CA Web Enrollment, 260, 285
Caching-only DNS server, 102
Certificate manager, 263
Certificate revocation list (CRL), 251–252, 285
Certificate services
adding role, 261–262
administrative separation, 262–264
installing, 259–262
Certificates
automatic, 277–279
certificates snap-in, 250
defined, 244, 285
and EFS, 249
encryption, 246–247
enrollment, 250–251
installing services, 259–262
and life cycle management, 250–252
revoked, 251–252
and smart cards, 249–250
templates, 258–259, 285
validating, 252
Web enrollment, 251
and WinRM, 250
Certification authority (CA), 244
administrator, 263
defined, 285
issuing certificates, 269–272
revoking certificates, 269, 273–275
templates, 258–259
trusted certification, 245
types of, 253–256
Certification Authority Web Enrollment, 260, 285
Child domain, 2
Citrix, 416
Client assessments with SCCM, 382

Cluster-aware services, 358, 373
Command-line tools, 366
Compliance auditing
  and AD DS, 310–311
  defined, 331
  enabling Directory Services, 311–313
  enabling functionality, 309–311
  policy settings, 310
  primary tools, 302
  using MBSA, 302–305
Compliance policies with scwcmd, 308–309
Connection authorization policies, 230–232
Connection speed between sites, 46
Critical Volume backup, 366, 368–369
CRL, 251–252, 285

D

DA. *see* Domain controller
Data autonomy, 14
Data security, 383–384
DCpromo, 77–78, 80–81
Default Domain Controllers Group Policy object (GPO), 112, 155–156, 183
Default Domain policy, 155–156, 183
Delegated subdomain, 130–131
Delegation of Control Wizard
  defined, 143, 183
  for full control over OU, 146
  permissions to reset user passwords, 144–145
Demilitarized zone (DMZ), 194, 328–329, 331
Denied RODC Password Replication Group, 82, 88
Deploying applications, 164–166
Desktop virtualization, 416, 420
Device IDs, 161
Device manager, 160
DFS namespace. *see* Distributed File System (DFS)
DFS replication. *see* Distributed File System (DFS)
DFS root. *see* Distributed File System (DFS)
DHCP enforcement, 206, 217, 235
DHCP servers, 206, 215
Digital signatures, 247–249, 285
Directory Services Utilities tool, 86
Discretionary Access Control List (DALC), 27
Distinguished names (DN), 150, 183
Distributed File System (DFS)
  defined, 88, 409
  folder targets, 388–389
  namespaces, 388–389, 391–394, 409
  replication, 394–395, 409
  role of, 388
  role services, 390–391
  root, 388, 409
  for site-aware applications, 49–50
  SYSVOL replication, 395–396
DNS. *see* Domain name system (DNS)
DNS zones. *see* Domain name system (DNS)
Domain controller
  component of NAP, 206
  creating a replica controller, 69–71
  creating a single-domain forest, 69
  creating a virtual lab environment, 8
  critical volume backup for, 368–369
  global catalog, 62
  including DNS with, 61–62
  read-only, 61
  in a remote office, 60–61
  replication, 370
  transferring roles in, 67–68
  universal group membership caching, 62–64
  writable, 61
Domain functional levels, 9–11, 37
Domain name system (DNS)
  and Active Directory, 107–110
  configuring to support forest trust, 21–22
  delegated subdomain, 130–131
  and dynamic updates, 105–107
  files, 102
  improvements to, 98
  name resolution, 99–100
  primary zones, 114–116
  resource records, 102–105
  secondary zones, 119–123
  zone replication scope, 131–132
  zone transfers, 116–119
  zones, 61–62, 100–102, 127, 133
Domain naming master, 65, 88
Domain replication, 15
DomainDNSZones, 133
/DomainPrep, 24, 25, 67
Downstream WSUS server, 318–319, 331
DSMgmt.exe, 86, 88
Dynamic Update, 105–107, 133

E

Encrypting data, 246–247
Encrypting File System (EFS), 249
Enforced GPO, 172–173, 183
Enterprise CAs, 253, 255–256, 285
External trust, 17–18, 37

F

Failback, 351, 373
Failover clusters
  active node, 351
  adding feature, 359–360
  connectivity to storage solutions, 356–357
  creating, 362–364
  defined, 340, 351, 373
  failback, 351, 373
  inactive node, 351
  for multiple sites, 359
  NLB clusters vs., 342–343
  pausing, 364
  quorums, 352–354
  removing, 364, 365–366
  requirements, 352
  scalability, 340–341
  services and applications, 358
  stopping, 364
  storage solutions, 355
  two-node failover, 352, 354
Fault tolerance, 119, 340
Federation Services (AD FS), 405, 406–407, 408
FEK, 249
Fibre Channel, 356–357, 373
File Encryption Key (FEK), 249
File Transport Protocol (FTP), 293
Fine-grained account policies
  account lockout policy, 178
  creating, 179–182
  Kerberos policies, 179
  password policies, 178
  and password settings object, 179–182
  requirements, 179
Fine-grained password policies, 10
Firewall rules, 329–330
Flexible Single Master Operations (FSMO), 64
Forest discovery scope, 227
Forest functional levels, 9, 11–13, 37
Forest replication, 15
Forest trust
  configuring DNS, 21–22
  creating trusts between forests, 17–18
  creating with selective authentication, 19–21
  defined, 37
ForestDNSZones, defined, 133
/ForestPrep, 24, 25, 67
Forests
  in Active Directory, 2–3
  autonomy vs. isolation, 14

bandwidth requirements, 14–15
creating trusts between, 17–18
designing Active Directory, 13–16
granting access to users, 22–23
trust relationships within, 3
Forest-wide authentication, 18, 19, 37
Forward lookup zone files, 102
FTP, 293
Full mesh replication topology, 56–57, 88
Fully qualified domain name (FQDN), 99

G

Generic (non-site specific) DNS records, 111–113, 133
Global audit policies, 310–311
Global catalog (GC), 3–4, 37, 62, 66–67
GlobalNames zones (GNZ), 98, 102, 124–127, 133
Glue record, 129
Group Policy. *see also* Fine-grained account policies
default domain policy, 155–156
defined, 4, 37, 184
deploying applications, 380
and organizational units, 142–143
scope, 151–153
settings (*see* Group Policy settings)
site-linked GPOs, 151
and SRV records, 111
strategy using universal groups, 149–150
trusted root certificates, 275–277
Group Policy Management Console (GPMC), 4, 155–156, 184
Group Policy objects (GPOs)
administrative templates, 155
advanced options, 171–177
blocking inheritance, 171–172
defined, 184
to deploy an application, 165–166
enforced options, 172–173
filters, 173–176
to implement proxy server settings, 167–169
inheritance, 153–154
loopback processing, 177
naming structure, 152
order of precedence, 153–154, 183
at OU level, 152–153
preferences, 155
to restrict group membership, 162–164
security settings, 155
settings, 142, 154–155
software settings, 154
starter GPOs, 156–158
windows settings, 154
WMI filtering, 176–177
Group Policy settings
application deployment, 164–166
device installation, 159–161
group membership, 161
implementing restricted groups, 162–164
Internet Explorer proxy settings, 166–169
IPSec protocol, 170–171
printer location policies, 169
security policies, 300–302
security with, 292
with WSUS, 326–328
Group strategies, designing, 148–150
GUID Partition Table (GPT), 355

H

Hardening a system, 292. *see also* System security
Hash, 248, 285
Health Registration Authority (HRA), 196, 235
Health requirement servers, 206
High availability, 341–342, 373
Host Credential Authorization Protocol (HCAP), 196, 235
Host names, 99, 100, 133
HRA service, 206
Hub and spoke replication topology, 57–59, 88, 111
Hyper-V
adding role, 431
creating a new virtual machine, 431–433
defined, 426–427, 436
prerequisites, 428
and server licenses, 428–429
using Server Manager, 431
and virtual networks, 429
Hyper-V Manager, 430, 434–435

I

Infrastructure master, 65, 66–67, 88–89
Install from media option (IFM), 74–76, 89
Interforest migration, 27
Internet Explorer proxy settings, 166–169
Internet Protocol Security (IPSec), 170–171
Internet Small Computer System Interface (iSCSI), 356–357, 373
Inter-Site Topology Generator (ISTG), 55, 89
Intraforest migration, 27
IP site link, 53–54, 89
IPSec enforcement, 218, 236, 280
iSCSI, 356–357, 373
Isolation requirements, 13–14, 37

K

Kerberos policies, 179

L

Layer 2 Tunneling Protocol (L2TP), 195, 236
Life cycle management, 250–252
Lightweight Directory Access Protocol (LDAP) queries, 50–51
Lightweight Directory Services (AD LDS), 405–406, 407, 409
Load balancing. *see also* Network Load Balancing (NLB)
clusters, 340–343
on DNS servers, 119
high availability solution, 341–342
NLB clusters vs. failover clusters, 342–343
objective, 340
scalability, 340–341
Local administrators role, 85–87, 89
Logical unit numbers (LUN), 355–356
Logon optimization, 47
Logon process, 59–60
Loopback processing, 177, 178, 184

M

Mail exchange (MX) records, 103–105, 133
Master boot record (MBR), 355
MBSACLI command-line utility, 304–308, 331
Media access control (MAC) address, 346
Microsoft Application Virtualization
defined, 416, 436
for desktops, 418
environment, 417–419
sequencer, 418, 419
for terminal services, 418, 419
Microsoft Application Virtualization for Terminal Services, 418
Microsoft Application Virtualization Sequencer, 418–419, 436

Microsoft Baseline Security Analyzer (MBSA)
  and compliance auditing, 292, 302–305
  defined, 331
  installation, 305–306
Microsoft Internet Security and Acceleration Server, 330
Microsoft .NET Framework feature, 399
Microsoft Office SharePoint Server 2007 (MOSS), 396, 402–403, 409
Microsoft SoftGrid Application Virtualization for Desktops, 418
Microsoft System Center, 380–383
Microsoft System Center Configuration Manager 2007 (SCCM), 380–383, 409
Microsoft System Center Operations Manager 2007 (SCOM), 380–381, 409
Microsoft System Center Virtual Machine Manager (SCVMM), 380, 434–435, 436
Microsoft updates, 314–315, 331
Microsoft Virtual PC
  configuring, 6–8
  defined, 436
  for desktop virtualization, 420
  downloading, 5
  installing, 5–6
  use of, 420–421
Microsoft Windows SharePoint Services. *see* Windows SharePoint Services (WSS)
Migration strategies, 26–27
MX record, 103–105, 133

N

Name resolution, 99–100, 133
Name server (NS) record, 103, 133
Namespace, 50
NAP server, 206
NetBIOS names, 99, 100, 133
Netdom command, 29
netdom query fsmo, 25
Netdom query fsmo, 65
Netlogon process, 59–60
Network access policies
  conditions, 199
  configuration, 213–217
  constraints, 200
  day and time restrictions, 201
  defined, 236
  objective, 198–200
  permissions, 199
  settings, 200
  to support VPN users, 201–202
Network Access Protection (NAP)
  802.1x enforcement, 217–218
  access policies, 213–217
  adding NPS service, 207
  autoremediation, 209
  components of, 205–206
  defined, 236
  DHCP enforcement, 217
  goals of, 205
  health policy, 211–212
  HRA service, 206
  IPSec enforcement, 218
  NAP agents, 207
  NAP server, 206
  NPS servers, 206
  remediation server group, 212–213
  security of, 204–205
  System Health Agents (SHAs), 207
  System Health Validators (SHVs), 207–209
  VPN server, 206
Network access server, 194, 196
Network address, 346
Network Address Translation (NAT), 166
Network Device Enrollment, 279–281, 285
Network File System (NFS), 403–405, 409
Network Load Balancing (NLB), 343, 344–345, 373. *see also* Load balancing
Network Load Balancing clusters
  adding hosts, 349
  creating, 345–349
  failover clusters vs., 342–343
  removing, 350–351
  Web servers in, 349–350
Network Load Balancing Manager, 343–344
Network Policy and Access Services role, 196–198, 203, 236
Network Policy Server (NPS), 196, 236
Network rules, 329
New Technology File System (NTFS), 249, 409
Non-authoritative restore, 369, 370, 373
Non-repudiation
  defined, 285
  with digital signatures, 247
  with private keys, 246
Non-transitive trusts, 16–17
NPS servers, 206
NS record, 103, 133
NTDSUtil, 68, 89

O

One-way trust relationships, 16
Online Certificate Status Protocol (OCSP), 252
Online Responder service
  adding a certificate, 265–268
  configuring service, 269
  defined, 285
  objective, 264
Operating system deployment, 382
Operations master roles, 64–68, 71–73, 89
Organizational Units (OU)
  defined, 4, 37
  to delegate control, 143–144
  designing, 147
  and Group Policy, 142–143
  group strategies, 148–150
  user groups in, 150

P

Password policies, 10, 81–85, 178
Password Replication Policy, 82, 84, 89
Password settings object (PSO), 179–182
Patch management, 382
PDC emulator, 65, 89
Perimeter networks, 328–329, 331
Permissions, group, 149–150
Physical address, 346
Pointer (PTR) records, 103, 133
Point-to-Point Tunneling Protocol (PPTP), 195, 236
PowerShell, 76–77
Preferred bridgehead server, 55–56, 89
Prestaged RODC, 80–81, 89
Primary DNS zone, 101, 114–116, 123–124, 126, 133
Printer location policies, 169
Private certification authorities, 253–254, 285
Private keys, 246–249
Proxy server, 166–167
Proxy settings, 166–169
PTR records, 103, 133
Public certification authorities, 253–254, 285
Public key, 246, 286. *see also* Encrypting data
Public key infrastructure (PKI)
  and AD CS, 256–257
  and certificates, 244–250
  defined, 244, 286
  digital signatures, 247–249
  encryption, 246–247

private keys, 246–247
public keys, 246–247
root certification authority, 244
smart cards, 249–250
trusted certification authorities, 245
and WinRM, 250
Public keys
and digital signatures, 247–249
and encryption, 246–247

Q

Quorum, 353, 373
Quorum model, 352–354, 373

R

RADIUS proxy, 203–204, 236
RAID, 355
Read-only domain controller (RODC)
adding, 74
defined, 89
filtered attribute set, 83–85
installing, 74–76
local administrators role, 85–87
objectives of, 73–74
password replication policy, 81–83
prestaging, 80–81
running DCpromo, 77–80
server core and, 76–78
writable DC vs., 61
Redircmp, 150, 184
Redirusr, 150, 184
Redundant Array of Independent Disks, 355
Registration authority (RA), 280
Remediation server group, 212–213, 214
Remote access. *see also* Network Access Protection (NAP)
designing, 194–204
dial-up connection, 194
network access policies, 198–200
NPS console, 200
for perimeter networks, 328–329
RADIUS proxy, 203–204
with SCCM, 382
tunneling protocols, 194, 195–196
using RADIUS server, 202–203
VPN connection for, 194
Remote access server, 194–195, 236
Remote access service
installation, 197–198
on Windows Server 2008, 196
Remote Authentication Dial-in User Service (RADIUS), 196, 202–203, 236
Remote Desktop Connection (RDC), 219
Remote Desktop Users group, 224
Remote Procedure Call (RPC), 53. *see also* RPC over IP site link
RemoteApp, 218, 228–229
Replica mode, 319, 331
Replication
compressed, 47
controlling, 14–15
defined, 89
DFS, 50, 394–395
directed, 48
with hub and spoke sites, 57–59
optimization, 47–49
scheduled, 48
scope, 131–132
SYSVOL, 395–396
Restrict Group Membership settings, 161–164
Restricted enrollment agents, 281–283, 286
Reverse lookup zone files, 102
RID master, 65, 89
Rights Management Services (RMS), 405, 406, 409
RODC. *see* Read-only domain controller (RODC)
RODC filtered attribute set, 83–85, 89
RODC Password Replication Group, 81–85, 88–89
/RODCPrep, 24, 26, 67
Root CAs, 244, 253, 286
Root domain, 2
Routing service, 196
RPC over IP site link, 53–54, 90

S

Scalability, 340–341, 373
Schema, 3, 14, 37, 67
Schema master, 65, 90
Scwcmd, 300–302, 308–309, 332
SD^3+C, 293, 332
Secondary DNS zone, 101, 119–123, 133
Secure dynamic updates, 105–107, 134
Secure Socket Layer (SSL), 246
Secure Socket Tunneling Protocol (SSTP), 195, 236
Security. *see also* Data security; System security
digital signatures, 248–249
tunneling protocols, 194
USB flash drives, 159–160
Security Configuration Wizard (SCW)
defined, 332
and Group Policy object, 300–302
to harden the system, 292
objective, 294–295
running, 295–300
Security identifier (SID), 27–30, 37
Security policies
created by security configuration wizard, 294–295
and Group Policy object, 300–302
Selective authentication, 18–19, 23–24, 37
Serial attached SCSI (SAS), 355, 373
Server consolidation, 427, 436
Server core, 90, 293–294, 332
Server manager, 294
Server virtualization, 416, 426–427, 436
Service autonomy, 14
Service location (SRV) records
defined, 103, 134
generic records, 112–114
mnemonics, 112
non-site specific, 110–112
site specific, 108–110
Services for Network File System, 396, 403–405, 409
Session key, 246–247
SharePoint 3.0 Central Administration, 398
SharePoint Products and Technology Configuration Wizard, 398
SID. *see* Security identifier (SID)
SID filtering, 28–30, 37
SID history, 27–28, 37
Simple Certificate Enrollment Protocol (SCEP), 279–281, 286
Site link bridging, 57–59, 90
Site link objects, 46, 51–54, 90
Site-aware applications, 49–51, 90
Site-linked GPOs, 151
Sites
bridgehead servers, 54–56
creating, 51–52
defined, 4, 37, 90
designing a branch office, 59–64
full mesh replication topology, 56–57
and Group Policy objects, 142
hub and spoke topology, 57–59
logon optimization, 47
overview, 46
replication optimization, 47–49
site link benefits, 46
site links, 52–54
site-aware applications, 49–51
and subnets, 51–52
universal group membership caching, 62–64
Smart cards, 249–250
SMTP site link object, 53, 90

SOA records, 103, 116, 117, 127, 134
SoftGrid Application Server, 417
SoftGrid client, 418
SoftGrid Management Console, 417
SoftGrid Sequencer, 418, 419, 436
SoftGrid-enabled applications, 417–418, 436
Software application distribution, 382
Stand-alone CAs, 253, 255–256, 286
Standard secondary zones, 119–123
Start of authority (SOA) records, 103, 116, 117, 127
Starter GPOs, 156–158
Storage area network (SAN), 355–356, 373
Storage arrays, 355–356
Storage formats, 355
Storage solutions, 355–357
Stub zones, 102, 127–129, 134
Subnet object, 51–52, 90
Subordinate CAs, 253, 286
System Center Application Virtualization Streaming Server, 417
System Center Configuration Manager (SCCM), 380, 381–383, 409
System Center Data Protection Manager (SCDPM), 380
System Center Operations Manager (SCOM), 380, 381, 409
System Center Virtual Machine Manager (SCVMM), 380, 434–435, 436
System Health Agents (SHAs), 205, 207, 236
System Health Validators (SHVs), 205, 207–211, 236
System policy rules, 329
System security
  baseline, 292
  and File Transport Protocol, 293
  SD^3+C, 293
  security configuration wizard, 294–295
  server core, 293–294
  server manager, 294
System State backup, 366
System Statement of Health (SSoH), 205, 236
SYSVOL replication, 395–396, 409

T

Teamed network adapters, 357
Terminal servers
  adding roles, 220–223
  authorization policies, 230–232
  client access license, 226–228
  connection authorization, 230–232
  defined, 218
  DNS round robin, 232–233
  forest discovery scope, 227
  gateway, 220, 230–232
  licensing, 220, 226–228
  load balancing, 232–233
  Remote Desktop Connection (RDC), 219
  resource authorization, 230–232
  role services, 219–220
  server configuration, 223–225
  session broker, 220, 232–234
  terminal server service, 220
  Web Access, 220, 230
Terminal Services (TS)
  and application virtualization, 416
  defined, 236
  farm, 236
  gateway, 236
  licensing, 236
  and Microsoft Application Virtualization, 417–419
  RemoteApp, 218, 228–229, 237
  resource authorization policy, 237
  Web Access, 236
Terminal services connection authorization policy (TS CAP), 230, 236
Terminal Services resource authorization policy (TS RAP), 230
Topology
  full mesh replication, 56–57, 88
  hub and spoke replication, 57–59, 88, 111
Transitive trusts, 3, 16–17, 37
Transport Layer Security (TLS), 246
Trees in Active Directory, 2–3
Trust relationships
  authentication method, 18–19
  defined, 37
  external, 17–18
  within a forest, 3, 17–21
  non-transitive, 16–17
  one-way, 16
  transitive, 16–17
  two-way, 16
Trusted Platform Module, 384, 409
Trusted root certificates, 275–277
Trusted root certification authorities, 275, 286
TS CAP. *see* Terminal Services (TS)
TS RAP. *see* Terminal Services (TS)
TS RemoteApp, 218
Tunneling protocols, 194, 195–196
Two-way trust relationships, 16

U

Universal group membership, 59, 62–64, 148–150
Universal Group Membership Caching, 60, 62–64, 90
Update Sequence Numbers (USNs), 370
Updates. *see* Microsoft updates; Windows updates
UPN suffixes, 30–31
Upstream WSUS server, 318–319, 332
USB flash drives, 159–160
User Principal Name (UPN) suffixes, 30–31

V

Validate a Configuration wizard, 360–362
Video streaming, 416
Virtual application server, defined, 436
Virtual application streaming, 416, 436
Virtual Network Manager, 429
Virtual PC. *see* Microsoft Virtual PC
Virtual private network (VPN), 194, 237, 429. *see also* Terminal Services (TS)
Virtualization, 416
Virtualization management, 434–435
VPN. *see* Virtual private network (VPN)
VPN enforcement, 237
VPN server, 194–195, 206

W

Wbadmin command-line tool, 367–368
Web enrollment, 251
Windows Deployment Services (WDS), 380
Windows Internet Name Services (WINS) servers, 98
Windows Management Instrumentation (WMI) filtering, 176–177, 184
Windows Remote Management (WinRM), 250
Windows Security Health Validator, 208–209
Windows Server Backup, 366–368
Windows Server Update Services (WSUS)
  basic requirements, 322
  benefits, 316
  with branch offices, 319–321
  capabilities, 317